D0839812

Basic and Applied Memory Research
Practical Applications
Volume 2

Basic and Applied Memory Research
Practical Applications
Volume 2

Edited by

Douglas J. Herrmann
Indiana State University

Cathy McEvoy
University of South Florida

Christopher Hertzog
Georgia Institute of Technology

Paula Hertel
Trinity University

Marcia K. Johnson
Princeton University

LAWRENCE ERLBAUM ASSOCIATES, PUBLISHERS
1996   Mahwah, New Jersey

WINGATE UNIVERSITY LIBRARY

Copyright © 1996 by Lawrence Erlbaum Associates, Inc.
All rights reserved. No part of this book may be reproduced in
any form, by photostat, microfilm, retrieval system, or any other
means, without the prior written permission of the publisher.

Lawrence Erlbaum Associates, Inc., Publishers
10 Industrial Avenue
Mahwah, New Jersey 07430

| Cover design by Gail Silverman |

Library of Congress Cataloging-in-Publication Data

Basic and applied memory research / Douglas Herrmann . . . [et al.],
   editors.
      p.   cm.
   Includes bibliographical references and index.
   Contents: v. 1. Theory in context — v. 2. Practical applications.
   ISBN 0-8058-1542-2 (cloth : alk. paper). — ISBN 0-8058-1543-0
(pbk. : alk. paper)
   1. Memory. 2. Memory—Research. I. Herrmann, Douglas J.
BF371.B27 1996
153.1′2—dc20   95-40765
                                                     CIP

Books published by Lawrence Erlbaum Associates are printed on acid-free paper,
and their bindings are chosen for strength and durability.

Printed in the United States of America
10 9 8 7 6 5 4 3 2 1

Contents

Contributors

Chris A. Albright University of Oklahoma, Norman, OK

Dana Bain FAA Academy

Ami L. Barile University of Oklahoma, Norman, OK

David Baskind Bowling Green State University, Bowling Green, OH

Ivan Bendiksen Sandefjord, Norway

Miriam Schooler Bendiksen Sandefjord, Norway

Norman R. Brown University of Alberta, Edmonton, Alberta, Canada

Herman Buschke Albert Einstein College of Medicine, Bronx, NY

Erin R. Cashman Bureau of Labor Statistics, Washington, DC

John C. Cavanaugh University of Delaware, Newark, DE

Stephen I. Ceci Cornell University, Ithaca, NY

Frederick G. Conrad Bureau of Labor Statistics, Washington, DC

Cesare Cornoldi University of Padua, Padova, Italy

Graham Davies University of Leicester, Leicester, England

Rossana De Beni University of Padua, Padova, Italy

Stephen I. Deutsch Georgetown University School of Medicine, Washington, DC

Francis T. Durso University of Oklahoma, Norman, OK

Gilles O. Einstein Furman University, Greenville, SC

Amie Elliot Towson State University, Towson, MD

T. Daniel Fakouhi G.D. Searle, Skokie, IL

Mary Ann Foley Skidmore College, Saratoga Springs, NY

Morris Goldsmith University of Haifa, Haifa, Israel

Scott D. Gronlund University of Oklahoma, Norman, OK

Shahin Hashtroudi (deceased) George Washington University, Washington, DC

Helen Hembrooke Cornell University, Ithaca, NY

Douglas J. Herrmann National Center for Health Statistics, Hyattsville, MD

Robert L. Herting G.D. Searle, Skokie, IL

William Hirst New School for Social Research, New York, NY

D. Hommer NIH/NIAAA/LCS, Bethesda, MD

Margaret Jean Intons-Peterson Indiana University, Bloomington, IN

Timothy B. Jay North Adams State College, North Adams, MA

Jared B. Jobe National Center for Health Statistics, Hyattsville, MD

Amie Keller Towson State University, Towson, MD

Asher Koriat University of Haifa, Haifa, Israel

Annetta Kurvink University of Leicester, Leicester, England

Gail Kuslansky Albert Einstein College of Medicine, Bronx, NY

Von O. Leirer Decision Systems, Los Altos, CA

Stephan Lewandowsky University of Oklahoma, Norman, OK

Christopher B. Mayhorn University of Georgia, Athens, GA

David Manier New School for Social Research, New York, NY

Carol A. Manning FAA Civil Aeromedical Institute, Oklahoma City, OK

Andrew Mathews MRC Applied Psychology Unit, Cambridge, England

Andrew R. Mayes University of Sheffield, Sheffield, England

Mark A. McDaniel University of New Mexico, Albuquerque, NM

Cathy McEvoy University of South Florida, Tampa, FL

Elke van der Meer Humboldt-Universitat zu Berlin, Berlin, Germany

Rebecca Mitchell University of Leicester, Leicester, England

S. Molchan National Institute of Mental Health, Bethesda, MD

Daniel G. Morrow Decision Systems, Los Altos, CA

Paul A. Mullin Bureau of Labor Statistics, Washington, DC

Jeffrey S. Neuschatz State University of New York, Cortland, Cortland, NY

Rick Parenté Towson State University, Towson, MD

Denise C. Park University of Georgia, Athens, GA

David G. Payne State University of New York, Binghamton, Binghamton, NY

Elizabeth Pinner New School for Social Research, New York, NY

Dana J. Plude University of Maryland, College Park, MD

Michael Pressley State University of New York, Albany, Albany, NY

A. Raskin University of Maryland School of Medicine, Baltimore, MD

Hillary Horn Ratner Wayne State University, Detroit, MI

Lynne Reder Carnegie Mellon University, Pittsburgh, PA

Noelle Robertson University of Leicester, Leicester, England

J. K. Robinson State University of New York, Stony Brook, Stony Brook, NY

Robert S. Ryan University of Pittsburgh, Pittsburgh, PA

John M. Rybash Hamilton College, Clinton, NY

Theodore M. Schlechter U.S. Army Research Institute, Louisville, KY

Jonathan W. Schooler University of Pittsburgh, Pittsburgh, PA

Barbara L. Schwartz Georgetown University School of Medicine, Washington, DC

Lisa K. Schwartz University of Maryland, College Park, MD

Alan Searleman St. Lawrence University, Canton, NY

Jerome R. Sehulster University of Connecticut, Stamford, Stamford, CT

Martin Sliwinski Albert Einstein College of Medicine, Bronx, NY

Holly R. Straub University of South Dakota, Vermillion, SD

T. Sunderland National Institute of Mental Health, Bethesda, MD

Elizabeth Decker Tanke Decision Systems, Los Altos, CA

Michael P. Toglia State University of New York, Cortland, Cortland, NY

Todd R. Truitt University of Oklahoma, Norman, OK

Maxwell Twum Dalhousie University, Halifax, Nova Scotia, Canada

H. J. Weingartner Cognitive Neuroscience Section, Bethesda, MD

Michael J. Wenger State University of New York, Binghamton, Binghamton, NY

Gordon B. Willis National Center for Health Statistics, Hyattsville, MD

Preface

Cathy McEvoy
University of South Florida

Three International Conferences on Practical Aspects of Memory have been held over the past 15 years, with each conference attracting larger numbers of participants than the one before it. Research on practical applications of human memory is carried out in numerous settings around the world, and many of the researchers came together at the Practical Aspects of Memory Conferences to share their ever-increasing knowledge. In *Basic and Applied Memory Research: Practical Applications, Volume 2,* 33 of the researchers who were invited to speak at the Third Practical Aspects of Memory Conference present their own work and, in many cases, they include summaries of related new research described during the conference. These chapters cover numerous topics in which knowledge about human memory developed in the laboratory is applied in other settings, and knowledge gained in applied settings is used to modify and enhance basic memory theory. In other words, these chapters represent several examples of the convergence of basic and applied memory research, the theme of the Third Practical Aspects of Memory Conference.

In Part One, two chapters (Koriat & Goldsmith; Pressley) discuss issues of importance to researchers who engage in both basic and applied research. These authors discuss the commonalities between basic and applied research and the differences, and how researchers are able to navigate successfully in both worlds. This section, along with the introductory chapters of Volume 1, set the stage for the chapters that follow.

In Part Two, three chapters present new information relevant to currently popular and important issues of eyewitness memory. Davies and his colleagues present their research on memory for cars and the people driving them, testing the hypothesis that interest in the material influences memory for the material. Schooler and his colleagues discuss face memory, and their research on the effects of verbal rehearsal on face memory. Toglia and his colleagues present research on eyewitness memory abilities of young children.

Part Three includes three chapters on prospective memory, or remembering to do things in the future. Einstein and McDaniel discuss age-related differences in prospective memory, and differentiate between time-based versus event-based requirements for when in the future to perform a task. Park and Mayhorn discuss both memory and nonmemory variables that affect patients' adherence to medication schedules. Searleman presents research on personality characteristics that may affect performance in different prospective memory tasks.

Part Four includes a chapter by Payne and Wenger on the relationship between practice and improved learning, presenting new findings on a classic problem in memory research—how practice actually improves memory. In her chapter, van der Meer describes research on the relationship between memory and intelligence as demonstrated by analogical reasoning.

In Part Five, four research teams studying how people use memory in responding to surveys report on their work. Chapters by Willis and Conrad and Brown discuss the use of strategies by survey respondents. Mullin and his colleagues discuss their research on the effects of organizational structure within surveys on respondents' performance. Jobe and Herrmann describe various models of survey responding and discuss their implications for basic memory theory.

Part Six includes three chapters on metamemory, or beliefs about memory. Sehulster explores the relationship between individual differences in memory style and performance on an autobiographical memory task. Cavanaugh and Baskind take a lifespan perspective, and discuss the relations between memory beliefs, basic memory processes, and memory performance in children, adults, and older adults. Cornoldi and De Beni report research on memory beliefs and the use of mnemonic techniques in older adults.

In Part Seven, social and emotional variables that affect memory are the topic of four chapters. Foley and Ratner present research on how children remember group tasks, and the biases that enter into their remembering. Manier and his colleagues present their research on conversation as a social memory process. Mathews discusses the encoding of emotional information, particularly the selectivity of such encoding, and Jay presents his research on the long-term persistence of curse words in older adults' mental lexicons.

Part Eight includes five chapters on memory aids, from strategies to automation. In her chapter, Intons-Peterson describes a wide spectrum of memory aids, from internal strategies and environmental memory cues to the use of large reference sources as societal memories. Plude and Schwartz present a new use of compact disc-interactive technology—teaching older adults techniques for improving their memory performance. Leirer and his colleagues report on their research in developing automated voice message reminders for doctor's appointments, medication regimens, and so on. The chapter by Vortac and colleagues presents new data on training air traffic controllers in the use of upcoming computerized systems to track flight data. Schlechter discusses the use of computerized systems in the educational setting as an ecologically relevant venue for testing notions of human memory. Clearly, the computer is taking over many of the memory functions previously performed by humans, and the role of memory researchers in developing and testing these computerized "memories" is likely to increase greatly over the next few years.

In Part Nine, applications of memory research to clinical populations are discussed. Buschke and his colleagues present a new technique for detecting clinically relevant change in memory performance. Mayes presents the latest research on the specfic cognitive deficits that appear to underlie amnesia. Rybash presents a taxonomy of priming effects in aging and discusses the relationship between the memory impairment observed with older adults and that observed in clinical populations.

Part Ten includes four chapters on interventions for memory-impaired populations. Schwartz and her colleagues discuss the latest research on drugs directed at the NMDA receptor as a treatment for dementia. Weingartner and his colleagues discuss some of the theoretical and practical issues involved in the development and testing of memory-enhancing drugs. Parenté and his colleagues present three "curious" findings with head injury patients, and discuss the implications of those findings for treatment. Finally, Bendiksen and Bendiksen describe the approach they use to address memory problems in patients with toxic solvent injuries.

Thus, this volume contains 33 chapters that will take the reader into the classroom, the air-traffic control tower, the hospital, onto the witness stand, and into the survey booth along with the applied researchers who are bringing the science of the study of human memory to these and many other settings. The editors and authors of these volumes hope that they have whetted your appetite for research on the practical application of memory theory and memory phenomena. If so, we hope to see you at the Fourth Practical Aspects of Memory Conference.

Acknowledgments

We are grateful to our families and colleagues for their encouragement and support while working on this project. In addition, thanks are due to John Gustafson, Dean of the Social Sciences at the University of Maryland University College, and to Pat Perfetto, Director of the Conference Guest Services of the University of Maryland. We also are very appreciative of the many people who volunteered to serve on the conference staff.

Conference Staff

National Communications and Publicity: Jerry Sehulster

Washington/Maryland/Virginia Communications and Publicity: Mark Palmisano, George Spilich, Ron Okada, and Richard Roberts

Grant Preparation: Douglas J. Herrmann
  Framework: Christopher Hertzog
  Finances: Gordon Willis
  Proposal: Jared Jobe
  Administration: Jonathan Schooler and Mike Toglia

Receipt of Submissions and Organization of the Program:
  Paper Abstracts: David Payne
  Poster Abstracts: John Rybash

Program Abstracts: Fred Conrad
Program Preparation: Karen Whitaker

Conference Management: Ted Schlechter, Chair
  Lodging and Meals: Joan Sander
  Information Center: Paula Lipman and Susan Schechter

Entertainment: Mary Ann Guadagno, Paul Beatty, and Kate Palmisano

Conference Financial Accounts: Mike Toglia

Exhibits: Mike Sewall
  Memory Products and Services: Peggy Intons-Peterson
  Textbooks, Societies, and Organizations: John Schulman
  Societies: Dana Plude
  Companies: George Spilich

Society for Applied Research on Memory and Cognition: David Burrows and Ron Okada

Conference Text Editing: Cathy McEvoy, Paula Hertel, Christopher Hertzog, and Leslie Caplan

Editing Assistant: Abby Hisey

Conference Consultants:
  Michael Gruneberg   Peter Morris   Robert Sykes
  Jordan Grafman   Lennie Poon   Martin Conway
  Richard C. Atkinson   Douglas Raybeck

PART ONE

ON THE RELATIONSHIP BETWEEN BASIC AND PRACTICAL MEMORY RESEARCH

Memory as Something That Can Be Counted Versus Memory as Something That Can Be Counted On

Asher Koriat
Morris Goldsmith
University of Haifa

The study of everyday memory has come a long way since Neisser's provocative address at the first Practical Aspects of Memory (PAM) conference, as the volume and scope of the research presented at the third PAM conference clearly indicates. In what way, however, does this research really differ from the traditional, laboratory-based study of memory? Although the everyday-laboratory controversy has often been quite spirited (*American Psychologist*, January 1991), it is not completely clear what the commotion is all about (Tulving, 1991). Our reading of the various commentaries identified three distinct dimensions around which the controversy has generally revolved: *what* memory phenomena should be studied, *how* they should be studied, and *where*.

Concern with the "what" issue is reflected, for example, in the title of Neisser's (1978) leading paper, "Memory: What are the important questions." Thus, everyday memory research is often characterized in terms of its content: the focus on topics having "obvious relevance to daily life" (Klatzky, 1991). This concern is also implicit in discussions emphasizing the practical applications of everyday memory research (Gruneberg & Morris, 1992).

The "how" issue concerns the proper research methodology: Whereas proponents of the naturalistic study of memory have questioned the ecological validity of much laboratory experimentation (Conway, 1991), laboratory proponents have stressed the importance of experimental control and generalizability of results, which presumably can be better achieved under laboratory conditions (Banaji & Crowder, 1989).

3

The "where" or context-of-inquiry issue concerns the importance of studying memory in its natural contexts rather than under more artificial, laboratory conditions. Thus, many researchers have stressed the social–functional context of everyday memory (e.g., Bruce, 1989; Neisser, 1978, 1988a, 1991), pointing to findings in which "the real-life nature of the experience made a considerable difference to memory processing" (Gruneberg, Morris, & Sykes, 1991, p. 74; see also Ceci & Bronfenbrenner, 1991).

Importantly, although the three issues are correlated in the reality of memory research, they are not necessarily interdependent. What, then, might be their common denominator? A careful examination of the everyday memory literature reveals what seems to be a common theme, a particular way of thinking about memory—a different memory metaphor than that underlying the traditional study of memory. We suggest that this metaphor can account for some of the apparent correlation between the "what," "where," and "how" aspects in terms of a more fundamental distinction. It can also provide the metatheoretical foundation for distinguishing two essentially different approaches to memory assessment. In this chapter, we summarize the work we have done that attempts to delineate the two alternative metaphors, and that examines their implications for memory assessment and for the everyday-laboratory controversy (see Koriat & Goldsmith, 1994, in press-a, in press-b).

THE STOREHOUSE METAPHOR IN TRADITIONAL
MEMORY RESEARCH

Clearly, conceptual metaphors have had a pervasive influence on the study of memory (see Roediger, 1980). Prominent among these is the *storehouse metaphor*, which has dominated traditional memory research: "The conception of the mind as a mental space in which memories are stored and then retrieved by a search process has served as a general and powerful explanation of the phenomena of human memory. There is currently no other general conception of the mind or memory that rivals this view" (Roediger, 1980, p. 238). How is memory treated under this conception?

1. Memory is conceived as a storage place. Indeed, the list-learning paradigm, perhaps the hallmark of laboratory memory research (Neisser, 1991), essentially simulates the initial depositing and subsequent retrieval of memory items.

2. The contents of memory are assumed to consist of discrete, elementary units whose essential characteristic is their countability, allowing memory to be assessed in terms of the number of recovered elements.

3. Memory is assessed in an input-bound manner: One begins with the input and asks how much of it was recovered in the output. This implies a definition of forgetting in terms of item loss, that is, the proportion of input items that cannot be recollected.
4. The memory items are assumed to be interchangeable, that is, equivalent as far as memory performance is concerned. It makes no difference, for instance, whether *hat* was remembered and *gun* was forgotten, or vice versa. What matters is not what is remembered, but rather how much.

The storehouse conception, then, has engendered a *quantity-oriented* approach to memory (Schacter, 1989). This approach is reflected not only in the traditional experimental paradigms (e.g., list learning, paired associates), but also in the type of phenomena investigated (e.g., serial position, retention interval), and in the memory measures employed (e.g., percent recall, percent recognition). Thus, although perhaps no investigator today would explicitly subscribe to the strict storehouse conception, much memory research is still conducted as if we did.

THE CORRESPONDENCE METAPHOR
IN EVERYDAY MEMORY RESEARCH

Despite the productive role of the storehouse metaphor in guiding the study of memory, its shortcomings become readily apparent when considering many everyday memory situations. For instance, a courtroom witness may be asked to report what she can regarding the circumstances of a crime (Loftus, 1979), or a person may try to recount either an ordinary or a momentous, personally experienced event (Rubin, 1986; Winograd & Neisser, 1992). Such situations motivate a different way of thinking about memory, one where the basic criterion is not the quantity of items remaining in store, but rather the correspondence between what the person reports and what actually happened (see Ross, in press; Winograd, 1994). Indeed, many of the research reports and discussions appearing under the banner of everyday memory disclose a keen preoccupation with the reliability, accuracy, or faithfulness of memory that has no parallel in the traditional, quantity-oriented approach to memory. In order to capture the essential features of this alternative conception, we have explicated a *correspondence metaphor* of memory (Koriat & Goldsmith, 1994, in press-a) in terms of the following interrelated attributes:

1. Aboutness: Memory is considered to be *about* past events and states of affairs (Conway, 1991). Thus, memory reports are treated as descriptions,

consisting of propositional statements that have truth value, rather than as mere collections of recovered items.

2. Focus on accuracy: Interest lies primarily in the extent to which the memory report is reliable, trustworthy, or accurate, that is, the extent to which it accords with reality (or some other criterion; see Ross, in press). In a sense, the correspondence metaphor implies an evaluation of memory in terms of its goodness of fit with what actually happened (see later discussion).

3. Forgetting, then, is conceived as a loss of correspondence between the memory report and the actual event, that is, as a deviation from veridicality, rather than as a simple loss of items. Thus, in addition to a concern with information loss, this view (following Bartlett, 1932) leads to a focus on the many different types of qualitative memory distortions—simplification, fabrication, confabulation, and the like.

4. Content: Unlike in the quantity-oriented approach, in which interest focuses on *how much* is remembered, in the correspondence-oriented approach (and virtually all real-life memory situations) it may matter a great deal *what* is remembered and misremembered (Conway, 1991). In the courtroom, for instance, it might make a crucial difference whether the witness remembered that the assailant "carried a gun," but forgot that he "wore a hat," rather than vice versa.

5. Output-boundedness: The assessment of memory correspondence is inherently output bound. Unlike the storehouse approach, which leads one to begin with the input and ask how much of it is represented in the output, in a correspondence view of memory it is more natural to start with the output (e.g., an eyewitness report) and examine to what extent it accords with the input (e.g., a witnessed event). In general, accuracy can be measured only for what a person reports, not for what is omitted. Thus, whereas under the storehouse view subjects are held accountable primarily for what they fail to report, under the correspondence view subjects are accountable primarily for what they do report.

6. Memory as the perception of the past: The correspondence view of memory has much in common with the way we think about perception. In perception we are not concerned with how much of the impinging information is perceived, but rather, with the (output-bound) correspondence between what is perceived and what is out there. Similarly, memory may be conceived as the perception of past events, and the question then becomes to what extent is this perception dependable (cf. "memory psychophysics," Algom, 1992).

Collectively, these ingredients of the correspondence metaphor characterize an *accuracy-oriented* approach to memory. This way of treating memory is clearly seen in many areas of everyday memory, particularly in psycholegal and autobiographical memory research, in which the study of memory accuracy and distortion is given a high priority (see, e.g., Brewer, 1988; Loftus, 1979; Neisser, 1988a; Ross, in press; Winograd & Neisser, 1992). This treatment appears to derive from the function of memory in everyday life (Baddeley, 1988), where what is remembered is certainly no less important than how much, and where memory is naturally seen to afford a meaningful representation of past events and states (Conway, 1991). Hence, the dependability of memory, the extent to which it can be trusted for current actions and decisions, becomes primary. Furthermore, the correspondence metaphor seems better suited than the storehouse metaphor to capture the complexity of real life. Because real-life experiences generally consist of richly structured, meaningful scenes and events (Neisser, 1988b), memory for such experiences are subject to wholistic and relational changes that cannot be captured solely in terms of the loss of "items." Hence, one can understand the special interest in memory errors, particularly in the qualitative changes that occur over time (Bartlett, 1932). Such changes often reflect social, motivational, and functional biases that have become of special interest to everyday memory researchers (e.g., Loftus, 1982; Neisser, 1981, 1988a; Ross, 1989; Ross & Buehler, 1994).

In a word, then, whereas the storehouse metaphor treats memory as something that can be counted, the correspondence metaphor treats memory as something that can be counted on.

CORRESPONDENCE-ORIENTED MEMORY ASSESSMENT

Surprisingly, although many discussions of everyday memory phenomena imply a departure from the storehouse conception toward a correspondence view, the reality and potential impact of this metatheoretical shift have not been fully acknowledged, particularly with regard to memory assessment. In fact, it is not commonly realized that the correspondence view implies a very different approach to the evaluation of memory than the traditional, quantity-oriented approach. In this section we examine several different types of assessment procedures in an attempt to explicate further the correspondence metaphor and bring to the fore some of the distinctive features of correspondence-oriented memory assessment.

Let us first consider the *wholistic* approach to memory assessment, which attempts to measure the overall "goodness of fit" between the memory report and the stimulus information. What does the development of such a measure entail? As an illustrative example, consider Waterman and Gordon's (1984) attempt to measure the correspondence between a studied map and a remembered map. They had subjects draw the map of Israel from memory. The correspondence of each reproduction to the actual map was measured with respect to eight clearly identifiable geographic points, by first applying transformations to neutralize differences in rotation, translation, and scale, and then computing an overall "distortion index" in terms of the squared distances between corresponding points on the output map and the criterion map.

Clearly, this type of memory assessment is very different from the kind of storehouse-based "counting" procedures mentioned earlier, most prominently in its attempt to evaluate the overall correspondence between the memory report and the target stimulus. Such an evaluation must always specify which features of possible correspondence are relevant (e.g., relative distances) and which are to be ignored (e.g., scale and orientation). Also, in some cases the completeness of the report (e.g., extent of mapped area, number of landmarks) may be important, and the correspondence measure will need to be adapted to take this aspect into account (e.g., Hart, 1981), whereas in other cases the experimenter may be concerned only in evaluating the accuracy of the information contained in the output without regard to its completeness (e.g., the eight geographic points used by Waterman and Gordon were those that appeared in all of the subjects' maps). Thus, a major problem in applying wholistic correspondence measures is that the proper assessment criteria are neither standard nor readily apparent.

This problem becomes even more acute in evaluating the faithfulness of verbal reconstructions of real-life events. Such events can submit to a multitude of different descriptions, each of which may be "accurate" in some sense (Neisser, 1981, 1988b; Spence, 1982), or at some level of resolution or "grain" (Neisser, 1988a; Yaniv & Foster, 1990). Thus, in order to specify the relevant dimensions of correspondence or miscorrespondence, how they are to be measured and integrated, and at what level of resolution, the assessment model must incorporate functional assumptions regarding both the reasons for remembering and the particular circumstances of the memory report. In sum, unlike traditional quantity-based memory measures (e.g., percent correct on a recall task), which have been designed as all-purpose tools, measures of overall memory faithfulness may need to be domain specific, function specific, and theory specific.

Perhaps for this reason, wholistic assessment models are relatively rare in the literature, and have generally been confined to the domain of mental maps and spatial memory (although some efforts have been directed toward event memory as well; Neisser & Harsch, 1992). One option that circumvents the need for an assessment model is to rely on subjective global accuracy ratings. Indeed, a clever variation on this idea has been used to assess the faithfulness of memory for faces in terms of the proportion of correct target recognitions that could be achieved by independent judges on the basis of the subjects' memory reports alone (see Wells & Turtle, 1988).

A more common approach is to focus on a single attribute of (mis)correspondence, typically a continuous or ordered dimension (e.g., height, angle, speed, time). Thus, for example, a wealth of research on memory for visual form and spatial information has disclosed systematic memory biases for such attributes as closure and symmetry, orientation, angular and radial deviation, and so on (e.g., Goldmeier, 1982; Tversky & Schiano, 1989). In a similar vein, studies on the "psychophysics of memory" (see Algom, 1992, for a review) have examined how memory scale values map onto their physical referents, comparing the obtained functions to those found for perception of the same stimuli. Dimensional accuracy has been investigated for many other types of attributes as well, ranging from the date and time of past events (e.g., Baddeley, Lewis, & Ninno-Smith, 1978; Huttenlocher, Hedges, & Bradburn, 1990) to the subjects' own SAT scores (Bahrick, Hall, & Dunlosky, 1993).

It is important to note that dimensional accuracy assessment is actually quite foreign to the storehouse metaphor, and implies a correspondence metaphor instead. Unlike storehouse-inspired quantity measures that are typically based on the counting of dichotomously scored items, correspondence-based measures may be more graded in nature, tapping different degrees of deviation from veridicality.

QUANTITY VERSUS ACCURACY IN ITEM-BASED MEMORY ASSESSMENT

Despite their suitability for capturing many intrinsic aspects of memory correspondence, neither the wholistic nor the dimensional approaches just discussed yields a simple, all-purpose memory measure. Thus, most researchers interested in evaluating memory accuracy have opted to stay with the more traditional, item-based approach, segmenting both the input and the output into a set of discrete items or propositions. Typically, the reported answers are dichotomously scored as right or wrong (true or false), and are given equal weight in calculating the overall memory score. This approach allows memory accuracy to be measured using the same basic type of procedure traditionally used to measure memory quantity, but for this very reason, the differences between the two types of measures become dangerously subtle, and may in fact lead to apparent incongruities between empirical findings (see Koriat & Goldsmith, 1994, in press-a, in press-b).

To illustrate, consider an experiment reported by Neisser (1988a), examining memory for real-life events that took place during the course of a seminar that he taught. Memory was assessed using either a cued recall or a multiple-choice recognition procedure. Neisser found recall memory to be much more accurate than recognition memory, and pointed out that such a finding might come as a surprise to traditional memory researchers, who are accustomed to the general superiority of recognition memory found in laboratory studies.

Neisser's finding brings to the fore some of the potential sources of confusion in the interpretation of empirical results that cut across the everyday and laboratory research contexts. On the one hand, this finding may reflect the effects of *research context*, supporting the claim that memory behaves differently in real-life than in laboratory settings. On the other hand, however, it may also implicate the concern with two different *memory properties*, accuracy versus quantity: In Neisser's study, as in many naturalistic studies, the focus is on memory accuracy, in contrast to traditional memory research, which has focused almost invariably on memory quantity. Thus, Neisser's recall subjects were more accurate than the recognition subjects in the sense that what they reported was almost never wrong but, as Neisser also pointed out, they did not provide much information either. Neisser's finding could therefore reflect an interaction between memory property and *test format* (recall vs. recognition) that would be obtained, perhaps, regardless of the research context: Recognition yields better quantity performance than recall testing, but recall yields better accuracy. This hypothesized pattern (which we have called the "recall-recognition paradox"; Koriat & Goldsmith, 1994) is consistent with the established wisdom in eyewitness research, that directed-testing procedures such as recognition testing can have contaminating effects on memory (see, e.g., Boon & Davies, 1988; Hilgard & Loftus, 1979; Lipton, 1977; Loftus, 1979, 1982), and therefore that free-narrative modes of interrogation are preferable to directed-questioning modes in eliciting reliable—although less complete—information (see Hilgard & Loftus, 1979; Neisser, 1988a).

A further complication, however, stems from the common confounding between test format and *report option*, free versus forced reporting. This confounding is evident in the reality of both naturalistic and laboratory research: In naturalistic contexts, for instance, free-narrative reporting not only guards against "leading" or contaminating information (a test-format variable), it also allows the witness the freedom to choose what information to report, and at what level of generality. Directed questioning, on the other hand, often involves explicit or implicit demands that an answer be provided. Similarly, traditional item-based laboratory research almost invariably implements recognition testing as forced recognition in two distinct respects: Not only are subjects confined to the alternatives presented (test format), they are also forced to answer each and every item (report option). In contrast, recall testing typically allows subjects the freedom to decide both how and whether to report what they remember.

Report option is an important factor to consider not only because of its common confounding with test format, but also—and more important—because of its crucial role in the operational distinction between accuracy-based and quantity-based memory measures within the item-based framework. To clarify this point, let us first examine how these two types of measures are defined: As a measure of memory correspondence, accuracy is inherently output bound, reflecting the likelihood that each reported item of information is correct. Thus, it translates into the percentage of reported answers that are correct. Quantity-based measures, in contrast, are input bound, reflecting the likelihood that each input (stimulus) item is reproduced in the output. This, of course, translates into the percentage of studied items correctly reproduced. Thus, whereas the output-bound accuracy-based measures evaluate the dependability of the memory report, the input-bound quantity-based measures reflect the amount of input information recovered.

Despite their different definitions, however, the accuracy and quantity measures can be distinguished operationally only when subjects are given the option of free report. When a forced-report test is used, the input-bound quantity and the output-bound accuracy percentages are necessarily equivalent. For instance, if a subject answers correctly 60 out of 100 questions, we may conclude either that the likelihood that each item is remembered is .60 (quantity), or that the likelihood that each reported item is correct is .60 (accuracy). The difference between the two measures is entirely a matter of intention—whether the experimenter intends to measure quantity or accuracy. In contrast, assume that the same test is administered under free-report conditions, and that the subject feels confident enough to provide answers to 80 items, 60 of which turn out to be correct. In this case, the quantity score would again be .60 (60/100), but the accuracy score would now be .75 (60/80). Clearly, then, differences in report option can complicate the interpretation of empirical findings.

Overall, the preceding discussion implicates potential confusions between four basic factors: memory property, report option, test format, and context of inquiry. We conducted several experiments designed to disentangle these factors, and to demonstrate the utility of the distinction between the accuracy-oriented and quantity-oriented approaches to memory. In one experiment (Koriat & Goldsmith, 1994, Experiment 1), we had subjects answer 60 general-knowledge questions in a recall or a multiple-choice recognition format (all items required a one-word answer in order to equate the "grain" of the answers across the two test formats). In addition to the standard tests of free recall and forced-choice recognition, however, two relatively uncommon procedures were added: forced recall (requiring subjects to respond to all questions), and free recognition (permitting subjects to skip items). In this design, then, test format and report option were orthogonally manipulated. A payoff schedule provided all subjects with a common performance incentive, essentially rewarding them for each correct answer, but penalizing them by an equal amount for each incorrect answer. Performance was scored for both quantity (input-bound percent correct) and accuracy (output-bound percent correct). The results are presented in Table 1.1.

When comparing the standard memory measures, free recall and forced recognition, our results replicated the recall–recognition paradox: Recall was superior to recognition on the accuracy measure (*e* vs. *b*), but recognition

TABLE 1.1.
Memory Quantity and Memory Accuracy as a
Function of Test Format and Report Option

	Quantity		Accuracy	
	Recall	Recognition	Recall	Recognition
Free	(a) 47.8	(b) 61.5	(e) 76.6	(f) 76.9
Forced	(c) 47.6	(d) 67.0	(g) 47.6	(h) 67.0

Note. The quantity and accuracy scores are operationally equivalent under forced-report conditions. From Koriat and Goldsmith, 1994, Experiment 1.

was superior to recall on the quantity measure (*d* vs. *a*). However, examination of the remaining means indicates that although memory quantity performance does vary with test format, recognition better than recall (*b* vs. *a*, and *d* vs. *c*), it is report option that is critical for memory accuracy: The option of free report increased accuracy performance for both recall and recognition testing (*e* vs. *g*, and *f* vs. *h*). In fact, under free-report conditions (in which memory accuracy and quantity measures can be operationally distinguished), test format had no effect at all on memory accuracy: Given equal opportunity to screen their answers, the recall and recognition subjects achieved virtually identical accuracy scores (*e* vs. *f*)!

This same basic pattern was replicated in several further experiments, employing both list-learning (episodic) and general knowledge (semantic) memory tasks (Koriat & Goldsmith, 1994, in press-b). Because the superior accuracy of free recall over forced recognition characteristic of naturalistic research was obtained in these experiments within a typical laboratory setting, it would appear that at least some of the underlying dynamics are not uniquely tied to real-life contexts. The findings are also problematic for the general belief that recognition testing per se is inherently detrimental to memory accuracy. More generally, the results highlight the need to distinguish between the accuracy-oriented and quantity-oriented approaches to memory assessment even within the item-based framework, and underscore the crucial importance of subject control over memory reporting for output-bound memory accuracy performance.

THE STRATEGIC REGULATION OF MEMORY ACCURACY

The issue of subject control figures prominently both when comparing everyday and laboratory research in general, and when considering accuracy-oriented versus quantity-oriented memory assessment in particular. As alluded to earlier, the investigation of many real-life memory phenomena often calls for a compromise between the need for strict experimental control and the desire to remain true to the natural dynamics of the memory phenomena being investigated (Gruneberg & Morris, 1992). Hence, there is generally a greater willingness among students of real-life memory to allow subjects control over their memory reporting, as is seen, for instance, in the use of free-narrative and other open-ended questioning techniques that have little parallel in traditional memory research.

In addition, the effects of subject control appear to differ markedly for quantity-oriented and accuracy-oriented memory assessment. On the one hand, subjects do not seem to be able to increase their memory quantity performance when given incentives to do so (e.g., Nilsson, 1987), nor does encouraging or forcing subjects to produce more items generally improve their memory quantity performance much or at all beyond that obtained under standard instructions (e.g., Erdelyi, Finks, & Feigin-Pfau, 1989: Roediger & Payne, 1985). On the other hand, such results contrast sharply with our accuracy-based findings (Koriat & Goldsmith, 1994, in press-b): Not only can subjects improve their accuracy when given the option of free report, they can also increase their accuracy even further when given stronger incentives to be accurate. For example, in one experiment (Koriat & Goldsmith, 1994, Experiment 3), we used the same free report procedure described earlier, but this time subjects sacrificed all winnings if they volunteered even a single incorrect answer. Accuracy increased substantially compared to our earlier experiment, averaging over 90% for both recall and recognition (fully one fourth of the subjects were successful in achieving 100% accuracy!). This improvement, however, was attained at a cost in quantity performance (about a 25% reduction for both recall and recognition). Similar results were obtained using a 10:1 penalty-to-bonus payoff ratio (Koriat & Goldsmith, in press-b).

Thus, subject control over memory reporting should present a special challenge to researchers interested in memory accuracy. In recounting their experiences, people clearly can regulate their reporting in order to enhance its correspondence (among other goals; see Neisser, 1988a; Ross & Buehler, 1994): They may report only information about which they are confident, or adopt a level of generality at which they are not likely to be wrong (Neisser, 1988a; Yaniv & Foster, 1990). Two questions then emerge: How can subject regulation of memory correspondence be made amenable to experimental study, and how can "memory" be sensibly assessed given that memory performance is under the subject's control?

In our work, we tried to tackle these issues by focusing on one specific type of subject regulation—the tendency to withhold or volunteer particular items of information under conditions of free report option. As a framework for investigating such regulation, we proposed a model of monitoring and control processes that merges ideas from signal-detection theory with ideas from metamemory research (Koriat & Goldsmith, in press-b). We assume that people monitor the subjective likelihood that a candidate memory response is correct, and then set a control threshold on the monitoring output to determine whether to volunteer that response or not. The setting of the control threshold depends on the relative utility of providing complete versus accurate information. Several results supported the model: First, the tendency to report an answer was very strongly correlated with subjective confidence in the correctness of the answer (the intrasubject gamma correlation averaged .93 for recognition and .97 for recall!). Second, subjects given a high accuracy incentive (a 10:1 penalty-to-bonus ratio) adopted a stricter criterion than subjects given a more moderate incentive (a 1:1 ratio). Third, subjects were able to increase their memory accuracy at the expense of quantity performance by screening out low confidence answers. Importantly, however, the extent and even existence of the quantity–accuracy trade-off was shown to depend critically on both accuracy motivation and monitoring effectiveness: When monitoring is very effective (or when the incentive for accuracy is relatively low), accuracy may be improved significantly at little or no cost in quantity performance.

The second issue raised by subject control is how such control should affect our methods of assessing memory. The approach that we proposed (Koriat & Goldsmith, in press-b) allows the incorporation of metamemory processes into memory assessment by charting memory performance profiles that take retention, monitoring, and control into account. Thus, rather than seek a single point estimate of "true" memory, subjects' memory performance on a particular test is described in terms of a quantity-accuracy profile (QAP), which plots the quantity and accuracy performance that would ensue from the adoption of different control criteria. This method allows the ongoing regulation of memory performance to be treated as an integral aspect of memory functioning (cf. Nelson & Narens, 1990), while also permitting an evaluation of the specific contribution of metamemory processes to memory performance.

In sum, even within the somewhat restricted domain of item-based memory research, the focus on memory accuracy raises a new set of issues involving memory variables that have either been overlooked, or else treated quite differently in traditional, quantity-oriented memory research.

TOWARD A PSYCHOLOGY
OF MEMORY CORRESPONDENCE

In this chapter, we have argued that the study of everyday memory may harbor an implicit departure from the traditional storehouse approach to memory toward a correspondence-oriented approach. This divergence can be seen in the preference for complex stimulus materials having an internal structure, in the focus on the many qualitative ways in which memory can change over time, in allowing for the contribution of subject variables and subject control to memory performance, in the study of motivational and functional factors that may affect such contributions, and, of course, in the memory property of interest. Some of these biases are also becoming more apparent in mainstream, laboratory-based experimentation. Indeed, signs of a general shift toward a correspondence-oriented metatheory may be discerned in a wide variety of theoretical formulations, including the reconstructive, attributional, ecological, functional, nonmediational, procedural, and connectionist approaches to memory (see Koriat & Goldsmith, in press-a).

What are the implications of this analysis for the everyday-laboratory controversy? To the extent that the controversy reflects, at least in part, a difference in the underlying memory metaphor, then there really should be no reason for commotion. Metaphors are conceptual tools that respond to certain aspects of the phenomena of interest and guide the development of viable theories and research methods. Unlike the theories that they breed, however, metaphors are neither right nor wrong; their worth entirely depends on their productivity. Not only is there no real conflict between metaphors, but, in fact, it should be desirable to entertain a variety of different metaphors in order to capture the full richness of memory phenomena.

Clearly, the storehouse metaphor has many advantages that have made it immensely productive in generating memory research and theory. At the same time, however, we believe that the correspondence metaphor (perhaps in alliance with the emerging "brain" metaphor; see Rumelhart, 1989) has much to offer in capturing those aspects of memory functioning that lie outside the storehouse metaphor's "focus of convenience." Exploited to its fullest, the correspondence metaphor could engender a full-fledged psychology of memory correspondence to parallel the quantity-oriented tradition. For instance, the systematic development of wholistic correspondence measures might enable researchers to trace the course of forgetting over time in the sense of a reduction in the faithfulness of memory, to examine the effects of different factors on the rate of such forgetting, to study individual differences in memory accuracy, to explore the effectiveness of different questioning procedures and subject control in improving the faithfulness of memory reports, and so forth. This is the type of approach that would seem to follow most naturally from many discussions of everyday memory. Instead, however, there is often a tendency to force accuracy-oriented research into the storehouse mold (as, of course, we ourselves have done). Thus, many memory researchers today talk correspondence, but still practice storehouse (see Neisser, 1988b). This discrepancy may derive in part from the conceptual and technical difficulties inherent in correspondence-oriented memory assessment, but it may also reflect a desire to maintain continuity with the traditional laboratory approach (Klatzky, 1991; Winograd, 1988). We would advocate otherwise: Rather than seeking a compromise, we believe that the psychology of memory will be better served if the differences between the correspondence-oriented and quantity-oriented approaches are sharpened rather than reconciled, so that the most can be made of what each approach has to offer.

ACKNOWLEDGMENTS

This research was supported by grant No. 032-1106 (1990) from the Israel Foundations Trustees. It was conducted while Morris Goldsmith was supported by a National Science Foundation Graduate Fellowship, and completed while Asher Koriat was the Irv Acenberg visiting scientist at the Rotman Research Institute of Baycrest Centre, Toronto, Ontario, Canada. The work was carried out at the Institute of Information Processing and Decision Making, University of Haifa.

REFERENCES

Algom, D. (1992). Memory psychophysics: An examination of its perceptual and cognitive prospects. In D. Algom (Ed.), *Psychophysical approaches to cognition* (pp. 441–513). Amsterdam: Elsevier Science Publications.

American Psychologist. (1991). *46*(7).

Baddeley, A. D. (1988). But what the hell is it for? In M. Gruneberg, P. Morris, & R. Sykes (Eds.), *Practical aspects of memory: Current research and issues* (Vol. 1, pp. 3–18). Chichester, England: Wiley.

Baddeley, A. D., Lewis, V., & Ninno-Smith, I. (1978). When did you last . . . ? In M. Gruneberg, P. Morris, & R. Sykes (Eds.), *Practical aspects of memory* (pp. 77–83). London: Academic Press.

Bahrick, H. P., Hall, L. K., & Dunlosky, J. (1993). Reconstructive processing of memory content for high versus low test scores and grades. *Applied Cognitive Psychology, 7*, 1–10.

Banaji, M. R., & Crowder, R. G. (1989). The bankruptcy of everyday memory. *American Psychologist, 44*, 1185–1193.

Bartlett, F. C. (1932). *Remembering.* Cambridge, England: Cambridge University Press.

Boon, J. C. W., & Davies, G. (1988). Attitudinal influences on witness memory: Fact and fiction. In M. Gruneberg, P. Morris, & R. Sykes (Eds.), *Practical aspects of memory: Current research and issues* (Vol. 1, pp. 53–58). Chichester, England: Wiley.

Brewer, W. F. (1988). Memory for randomly sampled autobiographical events. In U. Neisser & E. Winograd (Eds.), *Remembering reconsidered: Ecological and traditional approaches to the study of memory* (pp. 21–90). Cambridge, England: Cambridge University Press.

Bruce, D. (1989). Functional explanations of memory. In L. W. Poon, D. C. Rubin, & B. E. Wilson (Eds.), *Everyday cognition in adulthood and late life* (pp. 44–58). Cambridge, England: Cambridge University Press.

Ceci, S. J., & Bronfenbrenner, U. (1991). On the demise of everyday memory: "The rumors of my death are much exaggerated" (Mark Twain). *American Psychologist, 46*, 27–32.

Conway M. A. (1991). In defense of everyday memory. *American Psychologist 46*, 19–27.

Erdelyi, M. H., Finks, J., & Feigin-Pfau, M. B. (1989). The effect of response bias on recall performance, with some observations on processing bias. *Journal of Experimental Psychology: General, 118*, 245–254.

Goldmeier, E. (1982). *The Memory Trace: Its formation and its fate*. Hillsdale, NJ: Lawrence Erlbaum Associates.

Gruneberg, M. M., & Morris, P. E. (1992). Applying memory research. In M. Gruneberg & P. Morris (Eds.), *Aspects of memory*, 2nd ed. (Vol. 1, pp. 1–17). London: Routledge.

Gruneberg, M. M., Morris, P. E., & Sykes, R. N. (1991). The obituary on everyday memory and its practical applications is premature. *American Psychologist, 46*, 74–76.

Hart, R. A. (1981). Children's spatial representation of the landscape: Lessons and questions from a field study. In L. S. Liben, A. H. Patterson, & N. Newcombe (Eds.), *Spatial representation and behavior across the life span* (pp. 195–233). New York: Academic Press.

Hilgard, E. R., & Loftus, E. F. (1979). Effective interrogation of the eyewitness. *The International Journal of Clinical and Experimental Hypnosis, 27*, 342–357.

Huttenlocher, J., Hedges, L. V., & Bradburn, N. M. (1990). Reports of elapsed time: Bounding and rounding processes in estimation. *Journal of Experimental Psychology: Learning, Memory, and Cognition, 16*, 196–213.

Klatzky, R. L. (1991). Let's be friends. *American Psychologist, 46*, 43–46.

Koriat, A., & Goldsmith, M. (1994). Memory in naturalistic and laboratory contexts: Distinguishing the accuracy-oriented and quantity-oriented approaches to memory assessment. *Journal of Experimental Psychology: General, 123*, 297–315.

Koriat, A., & Goldsmith, M. (in press-a). Memory metaphors and the real-life/laboratory controversy: Correspondence versus storehouse views of memory. *Behavioral and Brain Sciences*.

Koriat, A., & Goldsmith, M. (in press-b). Monitoring and control processes in the strategic regulation of memory accuracy. *Psychological Review*.

Lipton, J. P. (1977). On the psychology of eyewitness testimony. *Journal of Applied Psychology, 62*, 90–95.

Loftus, E. F. (1979). *Eyewitness testimony*. Cambridge MA: Harvard University Press.

Loftus, E. F. (1982). Memory and its distortions. In A. G. Kraut (Ed.), *G. Stanley Hall Lectures* (pp. 119–154). Washington DC: American Psychological Association.

Neisser, U. (1978). Memory: What are the important questions? In M. M. Gruneberg, P. Morris, & R. Sykes (Eds.), *Practical aspects of memory* (pp. 3–24). London: Academic Press.

Neisser, U. (1981). John Dean's memory: A case study. *Cognition, 9*, 1–22.

Neisser, U. (1988a). Time present and time past. In M. M. Gruneberg, P. Morris, & R. Sykes (Eds.), *Practical aspects of memory: Current research and issues* (Vol. 2, pp. 545–560). Chichester, England: Wiley.

Neisser, U. (1988b). What is ordinary memory the memory of? In U. Neisser & E. Winograd (Eds.), *Remembering reconsidered: Ecological and traditional approaches to the study of memory* (pp. 356–373). New York: Cambridge University Press.

Neisser, U. (1991). A case of misplaced nostalgia. *American Psychologist, 46*, 34–37.

Neisser, U., & Harsch, N. (1992). Phantom flashbulbs: False recollections of hearing the news about Challenger. In E. Winograd & U. Neisser (Eds.), *Affect and accuracy in recall: Studies of "flashbulb memories"* (pp. 9–31). New York: Cambridge University Press.

Nelson, T. O., & Narens, L. (1990). Metamemory: A theoretical framework and some new findings. In G. Bower (Ed.), *The psychology of learning and motivation* (pp. 125–173). San Diego, CA: Academic Press.

Nilsson, L.-G. (1987). Motivated memory: Dissociation between performance data and subjective reports. *Psychological Research, 49*, 183–188.

Roediger, H. L. (1980). Memory metaphors in cognitive psychology. *Memory & Cognition, 8*, 231–246.

Roediger, H. L., & Payne, D. G. (1985). Recall criterion does not affect recall level or hypermnesia: A puzzle for generate/recognize theories. *Memory & Cognition, 13*, 1–7.

Ross, M. (1989). Relation of implicit theories to the construction of personal histories. *Psychological Review, 96*, 341–357.

Ross, M. (in press). Validating memories. In N. L. Stein, P. A. Ornstein, B. Tversky, & C. Brainerd (Eds.), *Memory for everyday and emotional events*. Hillsdale, NJ: Lawrence Erlbaum Associates.

Ross, M., & Buehler, R. (1994). Creative remembering. In U. Neisser & R. Fivush (Eds.), *The remembering self: Construction and accuracy in the self-narrative* (pp. 205–235). New York: Cambridge University Press.

Rubin, D. C. (1986). *Autobiographical memory*. Cambridge, England: Cambridge University Press.

Rumelhart, D. E. (1989). The architecture of mind: A connectionist approach. In M. I. Posner (Ed.), *Foundations of cognitive science* (pp. 133–159). Cambridge, MA: MIT Press.

Schacter, D. (1989). Memory. In M. I. Posner (Ed.), *Foundations of cognitive science* (pp. 687–725). Cambridge, MA: MIT Press.

Spence, D. P. (1982). *Narrative truth and historical truth*. New York: Norton.

Tulving, E. (1991). Memory research is not a zero-sum game. *American Psychologist, 46*, 41–43.

Tversky, B., & Schiano, D. J. (1989). Perceptual and conceptual factors in distortions in memory for graphs and maps. *Journal of Experimental Psychology: General, 118*, 387–398.

Waterman, S., & Gordon, D. (1984). A quantitative-comparative approach to analysis of distortion in mental maps. *Professional Geographer, 36*, 326–337.

Wells, G. L., & Turtle, J. W. (1988). What is the best way to encode faces? In M. Gruneberg, P. Morris, & R. Sykes (Eds.), *Practical aspects of memory: Current research and issues* (Vol. 1, pp. 163–168). Chichester, England: Wiley.

Winograd, E. (1988). Continuities between ecological and laboratory approaches to memory. In U. Neisser & E. Winograd (Eds.), *Remembering reconsidered: Ecological and traditional approaches to the study of memory* (pp. 11–20). Cambridge, England: Cambridge University Press.

Winograd, E. (1994). The authenticity and utility of memories. In U. Neisser & R. Fivush (Eds.), *The remembering self: Construction and accuracy in the self-narrative* (pp. 243–251). New York: Cambridge University Press.

Winograd, E., & Neisser, U. (Eds.). (1992). *Affect and accuracy in recall: Studies of "flashbulb memories."* New York: Cambridge University Press.

Yaniv, I., & Foster, D. P. (1990). Judgment, graininess, and categories. In *Proceedings of the Twelfth Annual Cognitive Science Society* (pp. 130–140). Hillsdale, NJ: Lawrence Erlbaum Associates.

CHAPTER TWO

Personal Reflections on the Study of Practical Memory in the Mid-1990s: The Complete Cognitive Researcher

Michael Pressley
State University of New York, Albany

In my career, I have conducted basic, ecologically valid, and practical research on cognition (see Herrmann & Gruneberg, 1993, for a review of the distinctions among these types of research), with much of my work focused on cognitive strategies and development of their use through instruction. What is the difference between these three types of research in my case?

BASIC, ECOLOGICALLY VALID, AND PRACTICAL RESEARCH

My laboratory-based research typically has involved paradigms familiar to experimental psychologists (e.g., free recall of word lists, paired-associate learning, memory of isolated sentences) and carefully controlled experiments. The instructions to participants take a few minutes at most (e.g., construct interactive images involving paired items, say vocabulary words and their meanings over and over, imagine the meaning represented in sentences, etc.). Participation in this work was short term for subjects, and relatively short term for me. Even for the most ambitious of my basic research studies, conception of experiments to final writeup of the study, never required more than a couple of years.

The ecologically valid work has differed a little bit from the more basic research in that participants in the studies have been asked to learn the types of materials presented to students in school, such as new vocabulary and

19

prose. The instruction in these studies sometimes was more involved, but never greater than 20 or 30 minutes in duration. I believe that even the most complex of these efforts moved from the design scribblings on my blackboard to hard copy of a manuscript within 2 years, with none of these studies ever consuming even the majority of my time for more than a month or two.

My practical work is completely different from the basic and ecologically valid research. Consider the case of my most complete program of practical research in recent years, which was concerned with teaching of comprehension and memory strategies as part of reading instruction during the elementary school years:

1. Typically, the materials the students have studied have been part of an ongoing curriculum that participants were experiencing as part of actual schoolwork and, thus, much more connected with students' actual educational experiences than the materials in even the most realistic of my ecologically valid studies.

2. Although my basic and ecologically valid studies of strategy instruction were concerned with teaching of individual strategies, instruction of a repertoire of a few powerful strategies has been the concern in the practical studies. Why? Because when good teachers of strategies teach students to process text strategically, they typically instruct about a group of strategies, each of which is matched to some part of reading, with the package of strategies intended to increase comprehension and memory of text that is read. For example, students can be taught to predict what is coming up in text, relate new information in text to prior knowledge, construct images of meanings conveyed by text, seek clarification when confused, and summarize what has been read. Such a repertoire provides strategic options for use early in reading, during processing of the events and facts presented throughout the text, and at the conclusion of a passage. Students must be taught not only the individual strategies in the package but also how to self-regulate use of the repertoire of strategies. Much, much more complicated instruction is required to accomplish this than the most complex instruction in the basic and ecologically valid studies.

3. Such complicated instruction can be fit into school curricula, however, because of the long-term nature of instructional programs offered to children in school. In contrast to the brief instruction in the basic and ecologically valid studies, the practical memory instruction I have been studying is decidedly long term, involving from one to several years of teaching (see Pressley, El-Dinary, et al., 1992), consistent with the way much instruction is offered in school.

4. The time course of the practical cognitive research is longer than the time course for basic and ecologically valid research. I began thinking about practical reading strategies instruction in the late 1980s (e.g., Pressley, Good-

child, Fleet, Zajchowski, & Evans, 1989). What was transparent from these initial reflections was that in the late 1980s there was not even a good theory of in-school instruction of reading strategies. More positively, there did seem to be schools doing it well and, thus, I decided to study these settings in order to understand what realistic school-based strategies instruction should include (e.g., Pressley et al., 1991; Pressley, El-Dinary, et al., 1992). My initial idea was to figure out what strategies instruction was like in such schools, using observational methods, and then to design studies comparing realistic in-school strategies instruction with other types of instruction. It is now five years later, and although substantial descriptive work is completed and published, not even a single comparative experiment is yet in print, although one will be by the time this volume is published (Brown, Pressley, Van Meter, & Schuder, 1996). That such work demands more of a scientist is reflected by the fact that the Brown et al. (1996) study required more than a year to plan, a year to carry out, and a year and a half to analyze and write, with much of Rachel Brown's time consumed from the beginning to end of this project and a great deal of my own work week devoted to the study for months at a time.

My training and experiences in conducting basic and ecologically valid research did not prepare me for the challenge of studying practical comprehension and memory instruction. Just identifying the components of such instruction proved to be very challenging, requiring about a dozen qualitative studies of various sorts. Thus, during the last five years, for the first time ever, my colleagues and I generated ethnographies, case studies, discourse analyses, and both traditional and ethnographic interviews (Pressley et al., 1994; Pressley, El-Dinary, et al., 1992; Pressley, Schuder, SAIL Faculty and Administration, Bergman, & El-Dinary, 1992). The result of this work was a portrait of complex reading strategies instruction, differing in younger compared to older grade-school students, depending on the previous strategies instructional experiences of the teacher, and varying as a function of increasing student competency in carrying out strategies.

Complete description of the complex instructional model that emerged from this work is well beyond the scope of this chapter (see Pressley, El-Dinary, et al., 1992, for a summary; also Pressley et al., 1995). Suffice to point out here that in-school strategies instruction includes the following:

- Strategy instruction is a long-term affair, with effective strategies instructors offering it in their classroom throughout the school year; the ideal is for high-quality process teaching to occur across school years.
- Teachers explain and model effective comprehension strategies. Typically, a few, powerful strategies are emphasized.
- The teachers coach students to use strategies, on an as-needed basis, providing hints to students about potential strategic choices they might make.

There are many mini-lessons about when it is appropriate to use particular strategies.

• Both teachers and students model use of strategies for one another, thinking aloud as they read. Throughout instruction, the usefulness of strategies is emphasized, with students reminded frequently about the comprehension and memory gains that accompany strategy use. Information about when and where various strategies can be applied is commonly discussed. Teachers consistently model flexible use of strategies; students explain to one another how they use strategies to process text.

• The strategies are used as a vehicle for coordinating dialogue about text. Thus, a great deal of discussion of text content occurs as teachers interact with students, reacting to students' use of strategies and prompting additional strategic processing (see especially Gaskins, Anderson, Pressley, Cunicelli, & Satlow, 1993). In particular, when students relate text to their prior knowledge, construct summaries of text meaning, visualize relations covered in a text, and predict what might transpire in a story, they engage in personal interpretation of text, with these personal interpretations varying from child to child and reading group to reading group (Brown & Coy-Ogan, 1993).

After a great deal of descriptive work, my associates and I felt we finally understood reading strategies instruction in school well enough to conduct comparative studies at least approximating true experiments. When I began this venture to understand in-school strategies instruction, I never envisioned that these comparative studies would be so completely different from my previous controlled experiments. The complexity of in-school strategies instruction demanded very different tactics than had worked in my previous research:

1. In every basic and ecologically valid study of memory that I have conducted, participants were assigned randomly to conditions. That was not possible in the school-based comparative studies of strategies instruction. It takes a teacher 1–2 years to learn how to teach strategies, and once a teacher does so, there is commitment to the approach (El-Dinary, Pressley, & Schuder, 1992): Committed teachers will not give up a preferred teaching approach for the sake of a randomized experiment! Thus, our comparative studies of in-school reading strategies instruction are quasi-experiments, with great efforts made at the outset of the investigations to match the strategies instruction classes with control classes receiving conventional instruction.

2. In my basic research, I often had the luxury of conducting up to a half-dozen studies on a problem in a year, one following another, each informed by what was learned in the previous experiments; not so in my

practical work. Because it became apparent in the qualitative studies of in-school strategies instruction that such teaching is long term, only long-term comparative studies made sense. The comparative practical study that is completed took place over the course of a school year.

3. Many of my laboratory studies have involved a number of conditions; not so with Brown et al. (1996), which involved only two conditions, an intervention and a control condition. The expense and effort required to carry out even two-group practical studies (with only five classrooms per condition) stretched my personal and grant resources to the limit.

Has it paid off? To date, the answer is yes. In a study that is completed, Rachel Brown and I (Brown et al., 1996) succeeded in demonstrating that a year's worth of one type of strategies instruction substantially improved at-risk, second-grade children's comprehension and memory of what they read. By the end of the year, there were multiple effects of comprehension strategies instruction: (a) Students receiving strategies instruction remembered more from stories they covered during reading instruction than did students receiving conventional instruction over the same stories; (b) the memories of the students receiving strategies instruction included more sensible inferential interpretations of texts read in class than did the memory reports of students receiving conventional instruction; (c) when strategies instruction students thought aloud as they read a story on their own, their thinking about the text reflected use of more comprehension and word-attack strategies than did think-alouds generated by students receiving conventional instruction; and (d) although there were no differences at the beginning of the academic year between students who would receive strategies instruction and those who would receive conventional instruction on standardized measures of reading, by the end of the academic year, there were dramatic differences on both comprehension and word knowledge measures.

In short, the strategies instruction that my colleagues and I studied definitely improved the reading of at-risk second-grade students. One aspect of the standardized test performance data is especially important to highlight. Not only were the overall mean levels of performance higher for strategies instruction compared to conventional instruction students on the standardized measures, the variabilities in performance were much smaller for the strategies instruction students compared to the students receiving conventional instruction. Strategies instruction had an across-the-board positive impact on reading achievement, whereas the conventional instruction seemed to work for some of the at-risk second-grade students much better than it did for others. Needless to say, my confidence that comprehension strategies instruction makes sense for young children was bolstered substantially by the Brown et al. (1996) results. See Brown and Pressley (1994) for a more detailed, general summary of this study, although one short of the complete report in Brown et al. (1996).

The greatest lesson I have learned from my research experiences is that it is absolutely necessary to conduct diverse research in order to understand well such cognitive phenomena as strategy instruction. That is, basic, ecologically valid, and practical research efforts are all necessary in order to construct a sophisticated understanding of something like strategy instruction. For example, most of the strategies taught in the instructional packages we have encountered in school were first validated in laboratory studies. Thus, the imagery strategy so prominent in in-school strategies instructional packages of today can be traced back to research in the 1970s exploring whether imagery instructions affected memory of text, including work that I conducted (e.g., Pressley, 1976). That work, in turn, descended from even more basic research on imagery, such as the many studies of dual coding summarized by Paivio (1971). In addition, the direct explanation approach at the heart of the in-school instruction we have been studying recently owes much to many basic studies that demonstrated strategies can be taught using explanations and modeling (see Pressley, Heisel, McCormick, & Nakamura, 1982). There is no way that in-school strategies instruction would exist in anything like its current state without the previous basic research. Even so, there is no way that in-school strategies instruction could be understood based on the laboratory studies alone. Our qualitative research uncovered many instructional wrinkles never envisioned during the basic research (see Pressley, El-Dinary, et al., 1992). The consistent reaction from individuals experienced with reading strategies instruction to the instructional model emanating from this qualitative work has been nodding approval.

VALUE OF QUALITATIVE METHODS IN RESEARCH:
ADDITIONAL EXAMPLES

My work of the last 5 years has greatly increased my appreciation for a flexible repertoire of research approaches. Although cognitive research has traditionally relied on experimental methods—with internal validity valued more than other potential research virtues—true experimental techniques alone are not equal to the demands of practical studies. In particular, qualitative methods (e.g., Strauss & Corbin, 1990) permit development of theories of complex situations. For my colleagues and me, application of such methods has led to important new insights, even in an area such as strategies instruction, studied extensively in basic and ecologically valid laboratory research.

Qualitative methods lead to more complex models, models that can be evaluated in quantitative studies. Thus, once a number of qualitative studies of reading strategies instruction were completed, we knew which environmental variables should not be compromised for the sake of experimental control (i.e., teacher experience with strategies instruction in the case of reading strategies instruction). We also knew that students learn a repertoire of strategies slowly, so that studies comparing strategies instruction to alternatives must be conducted over a long period of time (i.e., at least a year for strategies instructional studies). We understood that well-controlled comparative studies of in-school strategies instruction would have to involve simple designs, because keeping track of strategies instruction in even a few classrooms is very labor intensive and expensive. The qualitative studies had prepared us to conduct realistic comparative studies.

If my colleagues and I were not convinced of the power of qualitative methods for theory generation after our experiences constructing a new model of effective reading strategies instruction, we became convinced during the conduct of other qualitative studies we have completed in the past 5 years. One was a protocol analysis of the strategies used by domain experts when they read text (e.g., Wyatt et al., 1993); another was an interview study of notetaking by university students (Van Meter, Yokoi, & Pressley, 1994). In both of these cases, application of qualitative methods resulted in much more complex theories than previous analyses of the same problems.

In the first case, when the qualitative analysis in Wyatt et al. (1993) is combined with other qualitative protocol analyses, the diverse responsive processes that are skilled reading can be detailed (Pressley & Afflerbach, 1995). These processes include the following:

- Overviewing before reading: determining what is there and deciding which parts of a text to process.
- Looking for important information in text and paying greater attention to it than other information.
- Attempting to relate important points in text to one another in order to understand the text as a whole.
- Activating and using prior knowledge to interpret text: generating hypotheses about what ideas will be encountered in the text.
- Relating text content to prior knowledge, especially as part of constructing interpretations of text.
- Reconsidering and/or revising hypotheses about the meaning of text based on text content.
- Reconsidering and/or revising prior knowledge based on text content.
- Adjusting reading speed and concentration depending on the perceived importance of text to reading goals.
- Attempting to infer information not explicitly stated in text when the information is critical to comprehension of the text.

- Changing reading strategies when comprehension is perceived not to be proceeding smoothly.

- Attempting to determine the meaning of words not understood or recognized, especially when a word seems critical to meaning construction.

- Using strategies to remember text: underlining, repetition, making notes, visualizing, summarizing, paraphrasing, self-questioning, and so on.

- Evaluating the qualities of text and the messages in it, with these evaluations in part affecting whether text has impact on reader's knowledge, attitudes, behavior, and so on.

- Reflecting on and processing text additionally after a part of text has been read or after a reading is completed: reviewing, questioning, summarizing, attempting to interpret, evaluating, considering alternative interpretations and possibly deciding between them, considering how to process the text additionally if there is a feeling it has not been understood as much as it needs to be understood, accepting one's understanding of the text, rejecting one's understanding of a text.

The second case is a new analysis of student notetaking, constructed from qualitative analyses of interviews with college students about the dynamics surrounding and the effects of notetaking. For two decades, the prevailing model of notetaking as studied by psychologists has focused only on encoding during notetaking and reviewing notes later. The students' theory of notetaking is much richer, including the following points (Van Meter et al., 1994):

- Students have a variety of goals that motivate taking of notes in class: increasing student attention to lecture; increasing student comprehension and memory of material presented in lecture; providing an opportunity to connect ideas, provide structure, and/or generate a holistic representation of lecture content; informing about content of exams; informing about solutions to practice problems; and providing information relevant to written assignments.

- Students believe that some content is more important to include in notes than other content, favoring such information as: lecture content redundant with text; material professor stressed; content on board/overheads; content cited on syllabus; definitions, main points, important concepts and ideas; and information not well understood or familiar.

- The preferred structure of notes varies from students to student, but commonly preferred approaches include the following: key terms, outline of some sort (e.g., flagging relationships between more and less important content), and personal shorthand. Notes vary in completeness from verbatim to paraphrased, with paraphrasing attractive because it demands less writing and can be a self-test of the understanding of content.

• There are a variety of contextual factors affecting notetaking, including the following: lecturer style (slow or fast, organized or disorganized, clear or vague); student knowledge and characteristics (prior knowledge of the content area of the class, know-how about notetaking, commitment to completeness in notetaking); type of content and course demands (e.g., verbatim with definitions, names, dates, examples; paraphrased if learning of principles is demanded in the course).

• How notes are used after class varies depending on situational factors, including these possibilities: occasionally class notes not used (e.g., notes are perceived as incomplete, material already known); notes are reviewed, rewritten with elaborations, or copied; used for homework assignments when lecture content is pertinent to it (e.g., worked examples); used proportionately more for exam preparation in easy-to-take-notes courses; combined with other sources of information (e.g., text, past exams, TA consultation, student discussions), especially in difficult-to-take-notes courses.

In short, just as my understanding of strategies instruction has increased through use of qualitative research on practical problems, so has my understanding of how good learners approach important tasks, such as learning from text and lectures. My success in creating new models of instruction, text processing, and notetaking with qualitative methods fuels my enthusiasm for their use in theory creation. When it comes to theory testing, however, there is still much to be said for hypothetico-deductive logic and methods emanating from it.

METHODOLOGICAL DESIDERATA
FOR THE CONDUCT OF PRACTICAL EXPERIMENTS
AND QUASI-EXPERIMENTS

Practical cognitive research has led to new conclusions regarding the design and conduct of intervention studies—that is, hypothetico-deductive evaluations of practical applications. Karen Harris and I (Pressley & Harris, 1994a, 1994b) recently initiated a special issue of *Educational Psychology Review* that was dedicated to commentary about increasing the quality of practical cognitive research in education. Earl Butterfield, Donald Deshler, Michael Kamil, Joel Levin, Barak Rosenshine, Timothy Shanahan, Jean Schumaker, and Joseph Torgesen, all of whom have conducted either outstanding ecologically valid and/or practical cognitive instructional research, also contributed to the issue.

A consensus in the issue was that educational intervention researchers needed to continue to attend to classic Campbell and Stanley (1966) concerns—that is, they need to design their studies to minimize alternative interpretations of intervention effects, such as history, maturation, or practice effects. The participants also agreed that comparisons with control conditions should be as free of confoundings as possible, with special attention to the elimination of confoundings that might account for any treatment effects observed. Beyond their commitment to conventional thinking about experimentation, however, the participants in the special issue also pointed out other important concerns in applied cognitive research, ones that do not come up with respect to basic research. These concerns include:

• Often a large number of control conditions are possible in practical studies, although the resources allocated to the study permit only one or two of them. At a minimum, practical researchers need to be aware of the alternative control conditions and construct a case in favor of the control conditions used in an investigation.

• Sometimes practical studies end up overcontrolled, in that the intervention of interest is compromised in some way for the sake of experimental control. At a minimum, practical researchers must reflect on whether the control they impose compromises treatments. Sometimes some aspects of control should be sacrificed in favor of a more valid intervention. There needs to be a balance between experimental control and practical validity.

• Often practical research involves comparisons between a researcher-preferred treatment and another treatment. It is important that there be intervention integrity (Harris, 1988) with respect to all of the treatments. This is challenging, because researchers are often not very familiar with comparison treatments, opening the possibility that an excellent version of the researcher-preferred intervention will be compared with inadequate operationalizations of alternative treatments. One possibility raised in the special issue was that researchers should consult with the developers of alternative treatments in designing a comparative study. Another recommendation was for careful monitoring of all treatments in a study by parties who do all that is possible to inform themselves about how the various treatments in the study can be operationalized well.

• Studies should be designed to map out the strengths and weaknesses of interventions. Is it possible that some interventions are better suited to some goals than others? That some interventions are more beneficial for some populations than for other populations? Practical researchers understand that practitioners need repertoires of interventions, for it is unlikely that any intervention will be universally effective.

• Studies must be designed so that they are sensitive to important effects of intervention, meaning effects that make noticeable, important differences to targeted populations. Studies need to be designed so that statistical significance and practical significance are in synchrony, so that there is sufficient power to detect important effects but not so much power that trivial effects are highlighted.

- Often practical studies need to tap both quantitative and qualitative effects, which is a challenge because many quantitatively oriented researchers are not skilled in qualitative analysis and many qualitative researchers lack quantitative skills. Good intervention research will never be paradigmatic, for the complexity of practical applications and the situations in which they are deployed are complex. Such complexity demands flexibility, especially with respect to what is measured.

- Intervention researchers recognize that their work benefits greatly from collaboration with practitioners. Practical research scientists must work collaboratively with nonresearchers, more so than basic researchers. Both knowledge of research and craft knowledge is essential to do practical research well.

- The writeups of practical studies need to be complete enough so that the intervention can be implemented elsewhere. This is often challenging in the case of complex interventions. It is also challenging because writeups need to represent acceptable variability in implementation, with the recognition that interventions are not straightjackets but rather frameworks, with individual intervenors constructing their own interpretation and version of the intervention. There is often a tension between the need for operational definitions of an intervention and the reality that interventions are constructed differently by different people and in different circumstances.

- There needs to be constant thinking about the relationship between theory and the application and about how the practical research can advance both theory and application.

In short, practical research is demanding in all of the ways that basic and ecologically valid research is demanding as well as in many other ways. The practical researcher must work closely with practitioners, respectfully embracing and adapting both quantitative and qualitative methods. Writeups must meet the needs of both the scientific and practice communities, being both theoretically rich and obviously practical. These are tall orders.

INTERACTIONS BETWEEN BASIC, ECOLOGICALLY VALID, AND PRACTICAL RESEARCH

Experiences during the last five years have substantially increased my understanding of how basic, ecologically valid, and practical research can interact. The practical studies I have conducted with colleagues have generated plenty of reason for additional laboratory research. For example, during the in-school reading instructional studies, my colleagues and I realized that imagery is taught so as to increase student interpretation of stories (i.e., rather than just memory of stories). We are beginning to reflect on potential basic evaluations that we might conduct examining the consequences of using images to code text content as exactly as possible to enhance memory versus in an interpretive fashion. Similarly, the Wyatt et al. (1993) qualitative analysis of expert reading identified personal evaluation of text content as a salient strategy, inspiring my colleagues and me to consider research on the consequences of teaching students to be very evaluative as they read. The Van Meter et al. (1993) qualitative evaluation of notetaking suggested that students take very different types of notes depending on the course demands (e.g., exact memory vs. paraphrased memory), causing us to consider how we might begin a program of basic research on notetaking as a function of the anticipated accountability standards.

The complete cognitive researcher is going to be moving back and forth continuously between basic, ecologically valid, and practical problems, with each new study potentially making obvious the need for additional basic, ecologically valid, and practical research. The complete cognitive researcher will use many different research tactics, recognizing that every method has strengths and shortcomings: The strengths of diverse methods are additive, and the weaknesses of different methods can cancel each other out when used in a multimethod program of research. The complete cognitive researcher is not a creature of habit but rather ever-creating basic and applied studies using complementary methods.

Finally, the complete cognitive researcher keeps cranking. As Herrmann and Gruneberg (1993) pointed out, applied studies often have limited generality. The same is true for basic and ecologically valid studies. The only way to have a generalizable cognitive theory is to study a cognitive phenomenon in many situations—many basic, many ecologically valid, and many applied circumstances. There is nothing like a lot of studies converging on the same and complementary conclusions to bolster confidence in a phenomenon.

So far, attempting to be a complete cognitive researcher has consumed half my career, with many more questions apparent at the start of the second half of my working years than were apparent when this adventure began. I expect to be very busy for the next 20 years, continuing to extend work that began for me in the middle 1970s. God willing, I am going to keep studying basic, ecologically valid, and practical memory research problems that ever-renew themselves and, in doing so, ever-renew me as a scientist. My lifelong self-improvement program is to continue to explore simultaneously both fundamental mechanisms of mind and interventions that can expand mind. In the middle 1990s, it is apparent to me that many others have the same self-improvement plan.

CONCLUDING COMMENTS:
BECOMING AN EXPERT PRACTICAL RESEARCHER

It is now well established that expertise takes a very long time to develop (see Chi, Glaser, & Farr, 1988). Still, many pursue their careers for years without becoming experts. Bereiter and Scardamalia (1993) recently offered an analysis about why some become experts and others simply competent. They contended that experts tackle ever-more challenging problems, ones that require that they continually problem solve and acquire new competencies and understandings to do so. As I read their book, I recognized that my career certainly has involved tackling of problems continually increasing in complexity. My reaction has been to acquire new competencies in order to tackle the new challenges, such as learning how to use qualitative methodologies in order to understand how strategies instruction is deployed in school. Old competencies have been sharpened as well, such as my movement from a traditional Campbell and Stanley (1966) perspective, which suffices for basic and ecologically valid research, to an understanding that controlled study of complex cognitive interventions demands much more: The practical cognitive researcher must understand his or her preferred interventions and those that compete with and complement it in order to construct fair comparisons between a preferred and a nonpreferred treatment. Practical experiments must map out the strengths and weaknesses of an intervention, as part of establishing its fit in a repertoire of practical techniques. If theoretical advancement is enough to justify basic research, it is not enough for practical research. The operations and measurements of practical experiments must permit theoretical and practical insights.

There are others whose work has evolved similarly, including contributors to this volume. They, too, are using methods new to them and adapting old methods to tackle challenging practical problems. Sadly, there are others who seem to treat practical problems like basic research efforts, applying only traditional methodologies, with their studies more resembling traditional experimental psychology than qualitatively different and richer work. My sense as I review the latter work is that often it compromises the practical intervention too much in order to study it in ways respected by basic researchers. That is not expertise in practical research: Expertise in practical research requires inventiveness in studying applications, determination to do such work so the application is compromised minimally in pursuit of information about it. Facility with Campbell and Stanley's (1966) criteria is not enough; what is needed is talent in constructing multiple-method evaluations that combine traditional and avant garde methods. Constructing such evaluations will require continuous creative problem solving by the scientist. As Bereiter and Scardamalia (1993) so capably pointed out, persistent reinvention of one's craft in this way is the route to expertise rather than routine competence. Routine competence suffices for paradigmatic research efforts and, thus, is enough for many areas of basic research. In an area such as practical applications, however, where there are no convincing paradigms, routine experimenter competence falls far short of what is needed.

REFERENCES

Bereiter, C., & Scardamalia, M. (1993). *Surpasssing ourselves: An inquiry into the nature and implications of expertise.* Chicago: Open Court.

Brown, R., & Coy-Ogan, L. (1993). The evolution of transactional strategies instruction in one teacher's classroom. *Elementary School Journal, 94,* 221–233.

Brown, R., & Pressley, M. (1994). Self-regulated reading and getting meaning from text: The transactional strategies instruction model and its ongoing validation. In D. Schunk & B. Zimmerman (Eds.), *Self-regulation of learning and performance: Issues and educational applications* (pp. 155–179). Hillsdale NJ: Lawrence Erlbaum Associates.

Brown, R., Pressley, M., Van Meter, P., & Schuder, T. (1996). A quasi-experimental validation of transactional strategies instruction with previously low-achieving grade-2 readers. *Journal of Educational Psychology, 88.*

Campbell, D. T., & Stanley, J. C. (1966). *Experimental and quasi-experimental designs for research.* Chicago: McNally.

Chi, M. T. H., Glaser, R., & Farr, M. J. (1988). *The nature of ~pertise.* Hillsdale, NJ: Lawrence Erlbaum Associates.

El-Dinary, P. B., Pressley, M., & Schuder, T. (1992). Becoming a strategies teacher: An observational and interview study of three teachers learning transactional strategies instruction. In C. Kinzer & D. Leu (Eds.), *Forty-first yearbook of the National Reading Conference* (pp. 453–462). Chicago: National Reading Conference.

Gaskins, I. W., Anderson, R. C., Pressley, M., Cunicelli, E. A., & Satlow, E. (1993). Six teachers' dialogue during cognitive process instruction. *Elementary School Journal, 93,* 277–304.

Harris, K. R. (1988). Learning disabilities research: The need, the integrity, and the challenge. *Journal of Learning Disabilities, 21,* 267–274.

Herrmann, D., & Gruneberg, M. (1993). The need to expand the horizons of the practical aspects of memory movement. *Applied Cognitive Psychology, 7,* 553–566.

Paivio, A. (1971). *Imagery and verbal processes.* New York: Holt, Rinehart, & Winston.

Pressley, G. M. (1976). Mental imagery helps eight-year-olds remember what they read. *Journal of Educational Psychology, 68,* 355–359.

Pressley, M., & Afflerbach, P. (1995). *Constructively responsive reading: Learning about reading through protocol analysis.* Hillsdale, NJ: Lawrence Erlbaum Associates.

Pressley, M., El-Dinary, P. B., Brown, R., Schuder, T., Bergman, J. L., York, M., Gaskins, I. W., & Faculties and Administration of Benchmark School and the Montgomery County MD SAIL/SIA Programs (1995). A transactional strategies instruction Christmas carol. In A. McKeough, J. Lupart, & A. Marini (Eds.), *Teaching for transfer: Fostering generalization in learning* (pp. 177–213). Hillsdale, NJ: Lawrence Erlbaum Associates.

Pressley, M., in long-term collaboration with El-Dinary, P., Brown, R., Schuder, T., Pioli, M., Gaskins, I., & Benchmark School Faculty. (1994). Transactional instruction of reading comprehension strategies. In J. Mangieri & C. C. Block (Eds.), *Creating powerful thinking in teachers and students: Diverse perspectives* (pp. 112–139). Fort Worth, TX: Harcourt Brace Jovanovich.

Pressley, M., El-Dinary, P. B., Gaskins, I., Schuder, T., Bergman, J. L., Almasi, J., & Brown, R. (1992). Beyond direct explanation: Transactional instruction of reading comprehension strategies. *Elementary School Journal, 92,* 513–556.

Pressley, M., Gaskins, I. W., Cunicelli, E. A., Burdick, N. J., Schaub-Matt, M., Lee, D. S., & Powell, N. (1991). Strategy instruction at Benchmark School: A faculty interview study. *Learning Disability Quarterly, 14,* 19–48.

Pressley, M., Goodchild, F., Fleet, J., Zajchowski, R., & Evans, E. D. (1989). The challenges of classroom strategy instruction. *Elementary School Journal, 89,* 301–342.

Pressley, M., & Harris, K. R. (1994a). Increasing the quality of educational intervention research. *Educational Psychology Review, 6,* 191–214.

Pressley, M., & Harris, K. R. (1994b). More about increasing the quality of educational intervention research. *Educational Psychology Review, 6,* 271–289.

Pressley, M., Heisel, B. E., McCormick, C. G., & Nakamura, G. V. (1982). Memory strategy instruction with children. In C. J. Brainerd & M. Pressley (Eds.), *Progress in cognitive development research, Vol. 2, Verbal processes in children* (pp. 125–159). New York: Springer-Verlag.

Pressley, M., Schuder, T., SAIL Faculty and Administration, Bergman, J. L., & El-Dinary, P. B. (1992). A researcher–educator collaborative interview study of transactional comprehension strategies instruction. *Journal of Educational Psychology, 84,* 231–246.

Strauss, A., & Corbin, J. (1990). *Basics of qualitative research: Grounded theory procedures and techniques.* Newbury Park, CA: Sage.

Van Meter, P., Yokoi, L., & Pressley, M. (1994). College students' theory of notetaking derived from their perceptions of notetaking. *Journal of Educational Psychology, 86,* 323–338.

Wyatt, D., Pressley, M., El-Dinary, P. B., Stein, S., Evans, P., & Brown, R. (1993). Comprehension strategies, worth and credibility monitoring, and evaluations: Cold and hot cognition when experts read professional articles that are important to them. *Learning and Individual Differences, 5,* 49–72.

PART TWO

EYEWITNESS MEMORY AND MEMORY FOR FACES

CHAPTER THREE

Memory for Cars and Their Drivers: A Test of the Interest Hypothesis

Graham Davies
Annetta Kurvink
Rebecca Mitchell
Noelle Robertson
University of Leicester, U.K.

Why study the development of memory for cars as opposed to butterflies or garden forks? Research on everyday memory is sometimes criticized for its atheoretical and, at best, problem-oriented approach (Banaji & Crowder, 1989), but I wish to argue in this chapter that memory for such ubiquitous objects is a neglected and important area of research with serious practical and theoretical implications. I first review the case for this before presenting the results of two recent studies that focus on these issues.

The practical dimensions of car memory is perhaps the more obvious. A survey of 1,000 parents conducted by the U.K. children's charity "Kidscape" revealed that parents' worst fear was abduction of their child; comfortably ahead of such well-researched areas as road accidents, drug abuse, and "video nasties." In all, 96% of parents (98% in the cities) mentioned kidnapping as their overriding fear (Fletcher, 1993). There is some solid evidence to buttress these concerns. According to Home Office figures the number of children abducted from the streets of British towns rose from 102 abduction offenses in 1985 to 337 in 1994: a 330% increase (Weale, 1995).

Children's and adult's ability to remember cars and car detail does not end with abduction. Car crime in general represents one of the most rapidly growing areas of criminality. This embraces not merely the more mundane theft of radios and other accessories but includes taking and driving away by juveniles ("joyriding"), the use of stolen vehicles to force entry into shops ("ramraiding"), and the stealing of cars to order for illicit export to Eastern Europe or the Far East. An international crime survey, coordinated by the

Dutch Ministry of Justice based on 50,000 interviews in 20 countries, named England and Wales as having at 3.3% the highest rate of car theft and at 8.7% the third highest rate of theft from cars (Travis, 1994). The British Police produce league tables of favorite villains' getaway vehicles, where GM's Vauxhall Marque is currently comfortably ahead of Ford and other competitors (Katz, 1993).

The ability of children and adults to report suspicious cars accurately is clearly of paramount importance to successful detection across a wide range of criminal activity. This has recently been recognized in the United Kingdom with the introduction of "Motorfit." This works along the same lines as the Identikit: Witnesses select the salient features of the vehicle they saw and these selections are then used as a heuristic to search for plausible models within a database. These are then displayed visually for the witness to attempt to make a correct identification (Grantham, 1992).

Turning to the theoretical value of such studies, memory for cars and their drivers provides an opportunity for studying the role of interest and expertise factors in memory. Recent approaches to memory theory have emphasized process factors as much as the hypothesized structural components of memory (Lockhart & Craik, 1990). Research in the levels of processing tradition (Craik & Lockhart, 1972; Jenkins, 1979) has highlighted the fact that a given stimulus may be recalled and recognized well or poorly depending on the amount of attention and processing the observer expends on it. Complementary to this approach is the growing literature on expertise that has drawn attention to the fact that experts are not necessarily distinguished by superior cognitive capacity so much as by the way in which they use their store of knowledge to attend to those aspects of a task that are informationally rich (Chi, Glaser, & Rees, 1982). In a real sense, knowledge drives perception: not merely what is encoded, but also in the enhanced motivation to encode. Expertise and interest go hand in hand (Ericcson & Pennington, 1993).

What is known about interest and expertise factors in eyewitness memory for cars? An obvious choice for experts might be police officers. Yuille (1984) compared the performance of university students and trainee and experienced police officers for a sequence of slides depicting a road accident. Police personnel were generally more accurate than the students in their description of the events and the vehicles involved and were more likely to report the licence plate correctly. However, there was no difference in the accuracy or completeness of reports between trainee and experienced officers, which led Yuille to speculate that motivational factors may have played a part in the results. Although older reviews of police/layperson memory tend to emphasize similarities rather than differences in overall performance (Clifford, 1976), Yuille's finding on license plates suggested that a more systematic study of car memory might well reveal other aspects of expertise.

FACES

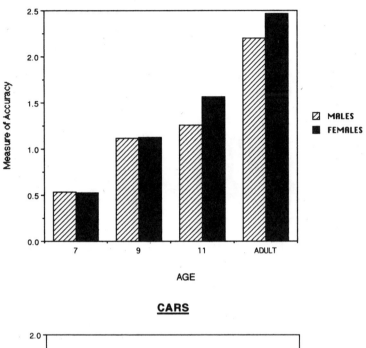

CARS

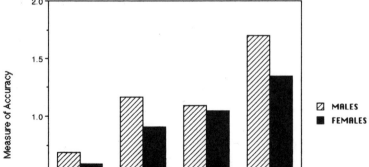

FIG. 3.1. Mean recognition accuracy (d') for faces and cars as a function of age and gender.

41

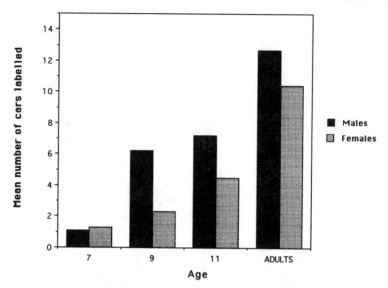

FIG. 3.2. Mean labeling accuracy for make or model of car in the test set as a function of age.

adulthood. However, this superior ability to label cars appropriately did not appear solely responsible for the generally higher recognition performance of males. Stimuli that can be labeled are generally better recognized than those that have no label or are not labeled consistently (Davies, 1972). In this study, a significant labeling effect occurred such that 82% of cars correctly labeled were also recognized, compared to 74% for unlabeled vehicles. However, this effect is relatively modest and there were very many more stimuli that were correctly recognized but not labeled by participants of both genders.

Taken together these findings suggest that, in general, males had somewhat more informationally rich and robust representations of cars to which to assimilate the test stimuli. Such representations frequently included the name as well as the appearance of the vehicle concerned. Such information enabled males to deal more effectively with transformations in orientation from study to test. Females generally exhibited greater prowess on faces where a richer encoding enabled them to cope more effectively with transformations of orientation. There is a direct parallel here to a study by Ellis and Deregowski (1981) on cross-racial recognition. Black adult males were superior to Whites at recognizing Black faces when pose was changed between study and test, whereas exactly the reverse was found when White faces were transformed in the same way. In the case of both gender and race, interest in and knowledge of physiognomic detail enabled persons of that group to deal more effectively with transformed stimuli.

A second recent study of face and car memory was reported by McKelvie, Standing, St. Jean, and Law (1993). Their first study compared recognition memory for line drawings of faces and cars by adult male and female subjects. Neither set of drawings represented particular people or makes of car, and both male and female faces were included in the target set. There was no significant gender by stimulus type interaction but gender of subject did interact significantly with gender of target face. Female faces were generally better recognized than male, the effect being disproportionate for women participants. Male participants, on the other hand, did proportionately better on the male faces than did the women.

A second experiment used actual photographs of cars in a recognition memory test, and performance on these was compared to that for a set of photographs of children's faces. On this occasion their results precisely replicated those of Davies and Robertson (1993): Women significantly outperformed men at recognizing the faces of children, whereas the position was reversed for cars. The effect for cars, although significant, was quite modest, which may reflect the less taxing demands of a recognition task where orientation did not change from study to test.

Both studies of car memory published to date have been unashamedly laboratory based, with no pretentions to ecological validity. As has been argued elsewhere (Davies, 1992), there is invariably a trade-off in eyewitness research between the demands of forensic realism on the one hand and rigorous precision and control on the other. Progress in understanding eyewitness behavior is likely to emerge not from an overrigid preoccupation with one approach or the other, but rather from attacking issues using more than one methodology and looking for similarities in outcome: what Ellsworth (1991) referred to as *convergent validity*.

In this spirit, Annetta Kurvink and I conducted a second study, again using adults and children as subjects, to explore the impact of gender on memory for faces and cars. On this occasion, however, we sought a more ecologically relevant scenario by using a videotape of a simulated child abduction. As a further concession to forensic reality, performance measures included verbal recall as well as visual identification of the relevant cars and faces. Once again, our hypothesis was that interest factors would promote differential retention for face and vehicle detail between males and females. In addition, we sought a measure of the expertise of the adults independent of gender in the form of a multiple-choice questionnaire concerning knowledge of motor vehicles and their characteristics.

The abduction scenario was specially videotaped for this study using trained actors and professional equipment. The film opens with an establishing shot of a school. A car containing a couple and their 8-year-old daughter drives up, and the mother and child emerge to hold a brief conversation before the mother returns to the car and is driven off. Subsequently, the child is seen playing outside the school before a second car containing another man and woman draws up. The woman ("the abductress") gets out of the car to ask the child for directions to a nearby street. She then encourages the child to enter the car and show them the way but then exhibits signs of panic. A policeman appears on the scene, whereupon the second couple drives off leaving the child talking to the police officer.

The study focused on memory for the mother, the abductress, and their respective cars. To ensure that any differences in retention could unequivocally be attributed to role, two versions of the film were made that were essentially identical except that actresses playing the mother and abductress exchanged roles, as did their associated cars. Careful editing ensured that both films were of the same length and offered similar exposure to both cars and actresses. The full length of both versions of the film was 5 minutes and 40 seconds, in which the actresses were glimpsed in longshot and close up for approximately 30 seconds and each car was seen from the front, side, and rear view for 45 seconds.

Three groups of subjects were involved in the study: two groups of children aged 8 and 10 years, respectively, and a group of students aged 18 through 25 years who formed an adult control group. A balanced design was employed such that half the subjects saw one version of the film whereas the remainder saw the other. Subsequently, all subjects attempted to provide verbal descriptions for the two cars and the appearance of the two female targets. Finally, all subjects attempted to select the vehicles and women involved from a series of photographic arrays. Each subject saw 4 arrays of 12 pictures, two for each of the cars and two for the abductress and the mother. Both target present and target absent arrays were used, such that for each subject two targets were always present and two absent, the precise combination being systematically varied between subjects. A total of 148 subjects took part in the study, ensuring representative results.

Overall, the results indicated a much less clear-cut picture of the impact of gender on memory for the cars and their drivers. Regarding identification, overall performance on both types of stimuli was generally poor. There were no differences in recognition due to the role (abductress/mother) associated with the stimulus concerned. Regarding the female actresses, subjects managed only 18% correct identification with the target present and rejected the array appropriately on 32% of occasions with the target absent. Regarding the cars, performance was rather better with the vehicle present (34%) and rather worse with the vehicle absent (23%). Such findings may be explainable in part by the relative difficulty of the tasks. The female actresses were encouraged in the interests of realism to alter their hairstyle from film to array, whereas the vehicles, although not identical, retained their same basic configuration.

As in the previous study, age had a major impact on performance on both tasks. Only 8 of the 100 children involved responded correctly to both identification arrays for the actresses involved, and 62 responded inappropriately on both arrays. For cars, the figures were marginally worse: Only 6 chose correctly on both arrays and 70 failed on both. Overall, however, the effects of age on performance were stronger for cars than for faces. Adults significantly outperformed children on both cars when the targets were present in the arrays and on one of the two cars when the target was absent. Although there was a general trend for adults to do better than children when recognizing the actresses, none of the comparisons were significant for both target present and absent arrays.

Given the modest recognition rates and the strong impact of age, the effects of gender were muted. Of the four possible comparisons by gender on identification of the cars, the difference in performance between males and females only reached significance on one: the larger of the two cars on the target present array. Of the same four comparisons for the actresses, there was little indication of any female superiority. The only significant effect was actually in the reverse direction: Males exceeded females at identifying one of the two actresses when she was present in the array.

Turning to the verbal descriptions of the cars and actresses, there was again no significant impact of the role associated with the target stimuli: It made no difference whether the abductress or mother and their respective cars were being described. Once again, as Fig. 3.3 demonstrates, there was a strong developmental trend for free recall of both classes of stimuli to improve with age. On average, adults recalled about three times as much correct information than did the 8-year-olds, and there was little difference in relative recall of cars and person detail.

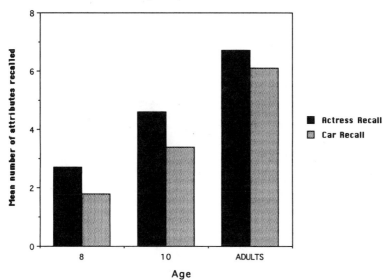

FIG. 3.3.　Mean verbal recall of vehicle and actress detail as a function of age.

For both children and adults three features were recalled disproportionately well (including by over 40% of the children): the style of the actresses' hair, general information regarding their clothing, and the color of the cars. Again, gender effects were present but not as emphatic as for the laboratory study-test procedure. Regarding relative performance on recall of the actresses and cars, a significant interaction was found such that males exceeded females in recall of car detail, and this was reversed for the actresses. As Fig. 3.4 demonstrates, the interaction is a modest one that was strongest for adult observers. Overall, females significantly outperformed males on recall of the appearance of the actresses involved but the reversed trend for males on vehicle detail did not reach statistical significance. For children, the tendency for girls to show superior recall to boys for the actress was particularly marked for clothing detail.

In addition to the gender data, questionnaire scores were also available for the adult subjects on their knowledge of cars and motoring. For an initial analysis, data were partitioned by gender and possession of a driver's license. Males outperformed females on the questionnaire and likewise those with a driving license produced higher scores than those without one. Scores on the car questionnaire were then correlated with memory performance for the cars seen in the film. For car identification, questionnaire score correlated +0.43 with accuracy, indicating that higher general knowledge about cars and motoring was associated with greater ability to identify the two target vehicles featured in the films. However, this effect only reached significance for identification: The correlation of questionnaire score with verbal recall fell short of significance (+0.21).

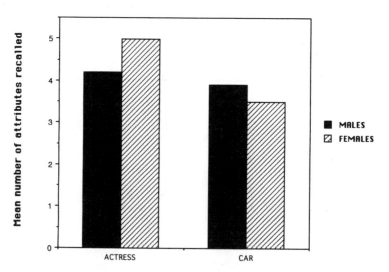

FIG. 3.4. Interaction of gender with stimulus type (actress/car) for correct recall scores.

In conclusion, the transmutation of the gender impact study from multiple slides to a videotaped incident (in Stern's, 1910, terms, from a picture test to an event test) resulted in a general attenuation of the effects of gender relative to age, the other principal factor. Some effects of gender, generally consistent with an interest hypothesis, were present, but the effects were stronger for recall than identification. Why should this be?

One major reason may be the specific targets employed in an incident study compared to the representative range of targets available in a study-test paradigm. As has been noted, the transformation of the actresses' appearance between film and array produced low overall identification scores. Although care was taken to choose cars that were high-volume best sellers in the United Kingdom (Austin Metro and Vauxhall Astra), individual familiarity with one or other of these vehicles would inevitably have played a role in determining results.

A next stage for this research will be a full-scale field test in which male and female subjects will interact live with a car and its driver and be subsequently assessed for their recall and recognition memory. Given the inevitable specificity of stimuli selected for such a study and the general tendency for a trade-off between increasing ecological realism and effect size (Davies, 1992), it seems possible that the impact of gender may be more muted than the video test.

Even if significant gender effects were reported in such a study, this would have interesting theoretical but minimal practical implications for the evaluation of testimony regarding vehicles and their drivers by the courts and the police. The effects of gender, where found, have always been modest. There have always been females whose scores have exceeded males' on cars, and likewise males who described their drivers more accurately than did females. What is more promising, both practically and theoretically, are the findings on the cars and motoring questionnaire reported for the video experiment. Unlike gender, questionnaire scores predicted car identification accuracy for adult subjects, although not amount of detail recalled. Questionnaire scores were certainly related to gender but there was significant overlap between the distribution of males and females. Future research would do well to deemphasize gender in favor of a more direct measure of interest reflected in questionnaire scores.

Finally, what practical implications can the results of existing research offer the police officer faced with conflicting testimony from different witnesses regarding the identity of a motor vehicle? It would be a travesty to imply that this research indicates that police officers should place greater weight on the testimony of a male rather than a female witness. Rather, the best course, on the basis of existing evidence, would be to explore witnesses' general knowledge of and interest in motor vehicles. Those who show the greatest prowess in this area, irrespective of age or gender, are most likely to be reliable witnesses to these details.

ACKNOWLEDGMENTS

We are grateful to the staff and students of Swallowdale School, Melton Mowbray, and Whitehills School, Northampton, for their participation in these studies. Thanks are also due to Rachel Harper, Ian Maclean, Ronit Marrs, and Sarah McClaren for assistance with Experiment 2.

REFERENCES

Banks, W. P. (1970). Signal detection theory and human memory. *Psychological Bulletin, 74,* 81–99.

Banaji, M. R., & Crowder, R. G. (1989). The bankruptcy of everyday memory. *American Psychologist, 44,* 1185–1193.

Chi, M. T. H., Glaser, R., & Rees, E. (1982). Expertise in problem solving. In R. J. Sternberg (Ed.), *Advances in the psychology of human intelligence* (Vol. 1, pp. 1–75). Hillsdale, NJ: Lawrence Erlbaum Associates.

Clifford, B. R. (1976). The police as eyewitnesses. *New Society, 36,* 176–177.

Craik, F. I. M., & Lockhart, R. S. (1972). Levels of processing: A framework for memory processing. *Journal of Verbal Learning and Verbal Behavior, 11,* 671–684.

Cross, J. F., Cross, J., & Daly, J. (1971). Sex, race, age and beauty as factors in the recognition of faces. *Perception and Psychophysics, 10,* 393–396.

Davies, G. M. (1972). Quantitative and qualitative changes in the retention of picture stimuli. *Journal of Experimental Child Psychology, 13,* 382–393.

Davies, G. M. (1992). Influencing public policy on eyewitnessing: Problems and possibilities. In F. Losel, D. Bender, & T. Bliesener (Eds.), *Psychology and law: International perspectives* (pp. 265–274). Berlin: De Gruyter.

Davies, G. M., & Robertson, N. (1993). Recognition memory for automobiles: A developmental study. *Bulletin of the Psychonomic Society, 31,* 103–106.

Ellis, H. D., & Deregowski, J. B. (1981). Within-race and between-race recognition of transformed and untransformed faces. *American Journal of Psychology, 94,* 27–35.

Ellsworth, P. C. (1991). To tell what we know or wait for Godot? *Law and Human Behavior, 15,* 77–90.

Ericcson, K. A., & Pennington, N. (1993). The structure of memory performance in experts: Implications for memory in everyday life. In G. M. Davies & R. H. Logie (Eds.), *Memory in everyday life* (pp. 241–272). Amsterdam: North Holland.

Fletcher, D. (1993, July 29). Worst fear of parents is child abduction. *Daily Telegraph,* p. 4.

Grantham, S. (1992). *Motorfit: The development of a system of vehicle identification for the police.* Unpublished master's thesis, University of Southampton, England.

Jenkins, J. J. (1979). Four parts to remember: A tetrahedral model of memory. In L. S. Cermak & F. I. M. Craik (Eds.), *Levels of processing in human memory* (pp. 429–446). Hillsdale, NJ: Lawrence Erlbaum Associates.

Katz, I. (1993, November 4). Big wheels of crime. *Guardian,* p. 10.

Lockhart, R. S., & Craik, F. I. M. (1990). Level of processing. A retrospective commentary on a framework for memory research. *Canadian Journal of Psychology, 44,* 87–112.

McKelvie, S. J. (1981). Sex differences in memory for faces. *Journal of Psychology, 107,* 109–125.

McKelvie, S. J., Standing, L., St. Jean, D., & Law, J. (1993). Gender differences in recognition memory for faces and cars: Evidence for the interest hypothesis. *Bulletin of the Psychonomic Society, 31,* 447–448.

Powers, P. A., Andriks, J. L., & Loftus, E. F. (1979). Eyewitness accounts of males and females. *Journal of Applied Psychology, 64,* 339–347.

Renninger, K. A. (1990). Children's play interests, representation and activity. In R. Fyvush & J. A. Hudson (Eds.), *Knowing and remembering in young children* (pp. 127–165). Cambridge, England: Cambridge University Press.

Renninger, K. A., & Wozniak, R. H. (1985). Effect of interest in attentional shift, recognition and recall in young children. *Developmental Psychology, 21,* 624–632.

Stern, L. W. (1910). Abstracts of lectures on the psychology of testimony and the study of individuality. *American Journal of Psychology, 21,* 270–282.

Travis, A. (1994, April 21). Vigilance fails to pay for English and Welsh. *Guardian,* p. 2.

Weale, S. (1995, August). Parent's protection dilemma. *Guardian,* p. 2.

Yuille, J. C. (1984). Research and teaching with the police: A Canadian example. *International Review of Applied Psychology, 33,* 5–24.

CHAPTER FOUR

The Costs and Benefits of Verbally Rehearsing Memory for Faces

Jonathan W. Schooler
Robert S. Ryan
University of Pittsburgh

Lynne Reder
Carnegie Mellon University

Witnesses of a crime are typically asked to describe the appearance of the perpetrator. Such descriptions can be of great help in assisting investigators. However, recent research suggests that one potential cost of describing a previously seen face is that, at least under some circumstances, verbalization can actually disrupt subsequent recognition performance. For example, in a study by Schooler and Engstler-Schooler (1990) subjects viewed a videotape of a bank robbery and then, after a brief delay, verbalization subjects were asked to describe the appearance of the bank robber in as much detail as possible, whereas control subjects engaged in an unrelated filler activity. All subjects were then given a recognition test that included photos of the target person and seven similar-appearing distractor photos. Compared to control subjects, verbalization subjects were significantly less accurate at recognizing the target face. In this chapter, we first review the evidence and current explanations for the disruptive effects of verbalizing previously seen faces (termed *verbal overshadowing*), and then describe some recent findings that reveal situations in which verbalization of faces can be helpful.

A BRIEF REVIEW OF VERBAL OVERSHADOWING

The basic finding that verbalizing a previously seen face can interfere with subsequent recognition performance has been replicated numerous times in the Schooler lab (Fallshore & Schooler, 1995; Ryan, 1992; Schooler &

Engstler-Schooler, 1990; Schooler, Ryan, & Reder, 1990) as well as in other labs (e.g., R. Chaffin, personal communication, 1990; Dodson, Johnson, & Schooler, in press; C. Kelley, personal communication, 1991; Read & Schooler, 1994; Westerman, 1991). The verbal overshadowing effect can be conceptualized within a more general framework that assumes that many activities involve a combination of both verbalizable and nonverbalizable task components. For example, as discussed in more detail later, face recognition can involve both an attention to verbalizable features (e.g., moles, shape of nose, size of ears, color of eyes, etc.) as well as difficult to articulate configural characteristics (e.g., the relationship between the features). From this perspective, a reasonable account of the effects of verbalization is that verbalization causes subjects to emphasize the reportable task components, thereby deemphasizing (overshadowing) the nonreportable components.

Consistent with the interpretation that verbalization shifts subjects' relative emphasis on verbalizable versus nonverbalizable components, verbalization has been shown to impair a variety of other activities for which successful performance is likely to require the substantial use of knowledge or processes that are difficult to articulate. They include: color memory (Schooler & Engstler-Schooler, 1990), insight problem solving (Schooler, Ohlsson, & Brooks, 1993), affective judgments (Schooler & Wilson, 1991; Wilson et al., 1993, Wilson & Schooler, 1991), implicit learning (Berry, 1984; Fallshore & Schooler, 1993), visual imagery (Brandimonte, Schooler, & Gabbino, 1995), recognizing deep structure analogies (Sieck, 1993), taste memory (Melcher, 1994; Melcher & Schooler, in press), map memory (Fiore, 1994; Fiore, Eisengart, & Schooler, 1993), and music memory (Houser, Fiore, & Schooler, 1995; Houser & Schooler, 1994). In contrast, verbalization has been shown to help or at least not impair performance when success can be effectively achieved by relying on readily reported knowledge. Such tasks include: memory for word lists (Darley & Glass, 1975), memory for a spoken statement (Schooler & Engstler-Schooler, 1990), analytic problem solving (Gagne & Smith, 1962; Schooler & Melcher, 1995; Schooler et al., 1993), and learning declarative knowledge (Chi, de Leeuw, Chiu, & LaVancher, 1994). The observation that verbalization disrupts a substantial variety of activities that depend on nonverbalizable information or processes while not disrupting more readily verbalized activities supports the notion that verbalization deemphasizes nonverbalizable task components.

In the domain of face recognition, additional research has been conducted in an effort to more precisely characterize the verbalizable and nonverbalizable task components that may be differentially affected by verbalization. Many conceptualizations of face recognition assume that it involves the consideration of two general types of information: featural information corresponding to the characteristics of individuals facial features and configural information corresponding to the relationship between those features (Carey

& Diamond, 1977; Diamond & Carey, 1986; Sergent, 1984; Tanaka, 1993; Wells & Hryciw, 1984). The featural aspects of faces are much easier to describe than are the configural components, which may account for why subjects who describe faces as they encode them are better able to identify the appropriate features with which to produce composite faces, whereas subjects who encode faces configurally by making personality judgments are better able to recognize the face (e.g., Wells & Hryciw, 1984). From the general characterization of verbal overshadowing outlined earlier, it follows that verbalization of the appearance of a previously seen face may cause subjects to focus on the featural aspects of a face while deemphasizing the configural aspects.

Fallshore and Schooler (1995) explored the relative effects of verbalization on the use of featural and configural information by examining the interaction between verbalization and other variables believed to influence the relative contribution these two types of facial information. Previous research has suggested that when the target face is of a different race than the subject (e.g., Rhodes, Tan, Brake, & Taylor, 1989) or when the recognition array is presented upside down (e.g., Bartlett & Searcy, 1993; Diamond & Carey, 1986; Young, Hellawell, & Hay, 1987), subjects rely more on featural information and less on the configural relationships between the features. If verbalization disrupts performance by reducing the use of nonreportable configural information, then the effects of verbalization should be maximized under conditions in which configural information is most likely to be used and minimized under conditions in which configural information is least likely to be used. Consistent with this prediction, Fallshore and Schooler observed that verbalization interfered with subjects' recognition of same-race faces when the recognition array was presented upright. However, verbalization did not impair recognition of other race faces, nor of same-race faces tested with inverted recognition arrays. A reasonable interpretation of these findings is that verbalization reduces subjects' use of configural information, and therefore its impact is minimized under situations in which configural information is less apt to be used.

Although consistent with the notion that verbalization deemphasizes configural information, it should be noted that Fallshore and Schooler's results are also consistent with the more general suggestion that verbalization may deemphasize visual information. From a dual code perspective (e.g., Pavio, 1986), the visual code is assumed to maintain a spatial analog and consequently should be expected to preserve configural information. In contrast, because the verbal code maintains propositions, it would be less likely to maintain difficult-to-describe configural information. Thus, the findings that verbalization may deemphasize the use of configural information are also consistent with the suggestion that verbalization deemphasizes visual information (e.g., Brandimonte et al., 1995; Schooler & Engstler-Schooler, 1990) and, more generally, with the suggestion that verbalization deemphasizes nonreportable information and processes (e.g., Schooler et al., 1993).

Additional research has sought to understand why subjects seem to favor the information associated with the verbalization activity. For example, one possibility involves the self-generated quality of the verbalizations. From the perspective of the generation effect (Slamecka & Graf, 1978), subjects might remember the information associated with their self-generated verbalization better than that associated with the merely presented visual stimuli. However, recent findings indicate that reading a verbal description of a face produces as great an impairment as self-generating a description (Dodson et al., in press). Another possibility is that subjects experience a source monitoring confusion in which they confuse what they said with what they saw. However, warning subjects about the possibility of such confusions fails to prevent the negative effects of verbalization (Dodson et al., in press).

The possibility that verbalization causes subjects to rely on the specific content of their descriptions is further discounted by the repeated failures to find any relationship between the content of subjects' descriptions and their recognition performance. For example, Schooler and Engstler-Schooler (1990) had independent raters code each description for the number of accurate and inaccurate features and found no relationship between the quality of subjects' descriptions and their recognition performance. Similarly, Schooler (1989) and Fallshore and Schooler (1995) gave the verbalization subjects' descriptions to yoked subject-judges who attempted to identify the target face solely on the basis of the descriptions. Although subject-judges' identification performance was above chance, there was no correspondence between the identification accuracy of subject-judges and the recognition accuracy of their yoked verbalization counterparts. Although it is possible that verbalization subjects were relying on idiosyncratic elements of their descriptions, uninterpretable to other subjects, the lack of a relationship between verbal descriptions and performance suggests that verbalization subjects were not simply relying on their verbal description but instead were engaging in a more general shift towards the type of information associated with verbal descriptions and away from the nonreportable information considered during encoding.

Additional evidence for the suggestion that verbalization may shift subjects' general focus away from the nonverbalizable information to which they attended during encoding is suggested by the finding that when subjects were asked to verbalize the appearance of one of two previously seen faces, impairment was observed for both the verbalized and the nonverbalized face (Dodson et al., in press). This generalized effect of verbalization suggests that it is not the specific content of subjects' verbalizations that is causing the interference but, instead, a more general disparity between the type of information emphasized during encoding versus verbalization.

In sum, although many questions remain to be answered, a reasonable account of the effects of verbalization is that it increases emphasis on verbalizable task components and decreases emphasis on nonverbalizable task components. In the context of face recognition, this shift may be associated with a deemphasis on configural information. This deemphasis of nonverbalizable components of face memory, typically attended to during encoding, results in a disparity between the type of information emphasized during encoding and that emphasized during test (cf. Morris, Bransford, & Franks, 1977; Tulving & Thomson, 1973).

THE BENEFICIAL EFFECTS
OF VERBAL REHEARSAL OF FACES

The suggestion that the effects of verbalization are due to the disparity between the nonreportable information typically emphasized during encoding and the verbalizable information emphasized at test raises the possibility that face verbalization need not necessarily be disruptive. Accordingly, although an emphasis on the difficult-to-articulate aspects of a face appears to be the default approach taken in encoding and recognition, it is, in principle, possible to focus on more verbalizable features of the face. For example, if one notices that a face has a distinguishing mole, this could be extremely useful for subsequent recognition. In short, although verbalization may disrupt the recognition of faces encoded under default conditions, if subjects encoded faces in a manner that was consistent with their later verbalization activity, their performance might not be impaired, and might even be facilitated if they were able to identify some critical discriminating feature.

According to this view, if subjects encoded a face with an awareness of the impending verbalization activity and the nature of the subsequent recognition array, then verbalization might not be as disruptive. Consistent with this prediction, we have observed on a number of occasions that the effects of verbalization are often reduced over repeated trials (e.g., Fallshore & Schooler, 1995; Houser et al., 1995; Melcher & Schooler, in press; Schooler, Ryan, & Reder, 1990). When subjects engage in repeated trials of the verbal overshadowing paradigm (i.e., encoding-verbalization-test), the negative effects of verbalization tend to attenuate. Although the precise reason for this trial effect is not known, if the disruptive effects of verbalization are the result of a disparity between the information considered at encoding, verbalization, and test, it stands to reason that over repeated trials subjects might learn to become more consistent in what they attend to.[1]

---

[1]There are, of course, other possible explanations for the reduced effect of verbalization over trials. For example, the verbalizations elicited on multiple trials may interfere with one another, thereby canceling out their impact. Subjects may also get fatigued in later trials (describing faces is rather difficult) and may consequently devote fewer resources to the verbal description, thereby reducing its impact.

The Effects of Re-Presenting the Face

The claim that verbalization effects are due to a disparity between the non-reportable information typically considered during encoding and the verbalizable information emphasized during verbalization suggests that these effects of verbalization should be eliminated if subjects are given the opportunity to see the face again after verbalization. Accordingly, if impairment is due to the inconsistency between the information emphasized under default encoding conditions and that emphasized during verbalization, then re-presenting the target face might enable subjects to recode the face in a manner that reduces this inconsistency and thereby eliminate the disruptive effects of verbalization. To address this issue, we examined the effects of re-presenting a target face after subjects had verbalized its appearance. Subjects viewed a target face, and then verbalization subjects were asked to describe it while control subjects engaged in an unrelated filler activity. After engaging in the control or verbalization activities, subjects assigned to the re-presentation condition were shown the target photo again. Finally, all subjects were given the recognition array that included a different photo of the target face and five similar distractors.

Based on the importance of the disparity of the information emphasized during encoding and verbalization, our prediction was that the disruptive effects of verbalization would be eliminated when the target face was re-presented following verbalization. As can be seen in Fig. 4.1, our prediction was generally observed, but with a twist. To our surprise, re-presentation not only eliminated the verbalization effect; it reversed it!

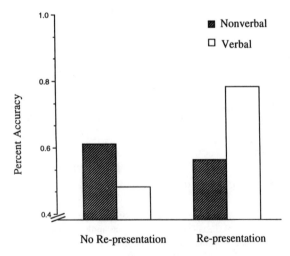

FIG. 4.1. The effects of verbalization and re-presentation on recognition accuracy.

Due to the somewhat surprising observation that re-presentation not only eliminated the negative effects of verbalization but actually reversed it, we replicated the procedure with a different set of faces, to ensure that the effect was both reliable and generalizable. To get a better understanding of the possible boundary conditions of this effect, we also added a third condition in which we re-represented the target face in an inverted position. Accordingly, if subjects extracted very simple featural information from the re-presented target face, then even inverted re-presentation could be of some value. If re-presentation refreshed subjects' configural memory or facilitated a more sophisticated analysis of individual features, then only the upright re-presentation should be of value. As can be seen in Fig. 4.2, the beneficial effects of re-presentation combined with verbalization were clearly replicated in the upright condition; however, there was no similar benefit for re-presentation of the inverted face.

The observation that re-presentation and verbalization reliably interacted in the manner that they did provides an important constraint on how we interpret the effects of re-presentation. Had re-presentation merely attenuated the verbal overshadowing effect, then the effects of re-presentation could have been attributed to a refreshing of the configural information, thereby reducing the disparity between the information emphasized during encoding and verbalization. Had re-presentation affected performance in both the verbalization and no-verbalization condition, then the effects of re-presentation could have been attributed simply to rehearsal. However, the fact that re-presentation improved performance only when subjects previously verbalized the face suggests that verbalization was responsible for causing subjects to extract new information from the face during re-presentation.

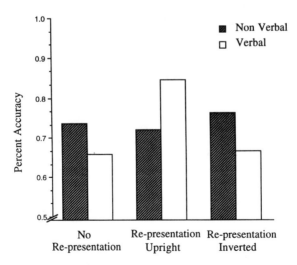

FIG. 4.2. A replication of the re-presentation study with the addition of an inverted re-presentation condition.

The impact of previously attempting to verbalize a face on subjects' subsequent ability to benefit from seeing it again is reminiscent of the beneficial effects of working on a problem without immediately being given its solution. When subjects are required to solve problems on their own, they often show better learning than when they are given the solutions simultaneously with the problems (Charney & Reder, 1986). Moreover, even when subjects work on problems that they are unlikely to solve on their own, they still benefit from working on the problems before being given the solutions (Needham & Begg, 1991). This benefit of working on a problem prior to receiving a solution has been attributed to subjects' hypothesized increased ability to appreciate the gaps in their knowledge. Accordingly, subjects who are given a solution without working on a problem fail to recognize which aspects of the solution are particularly helpful. A similar account may explain why verbalization enables subjects to benefit from re-presentation. Subjects who view re-presented faces following verbalization may be able to appreciate the aspects of the face that they failed to generate or generated inaccurately during verbalization, and thus may be better prepared to fill in or correct their memories.

This account leaves open the question of what type of information subjects used to repair their memories. The finding that subjects did not benefit from re-presentation of the face when it was inverted argues against the notion that verbalization subjects are benefiting from the very basic featural information that is extractable from inverted faces (e.g., moles, scars). The question remains: What exactly were subjects extracting from the upright faces that was unavailable from the inverted faces? It seems likely that re-presentation of the upright face may have refreshed subjects' memory for the nonreportable aspects of the face that they had deemphasized as a consequence of verbalization. Nevertheless, a "refreshing" explanation does not explain why verbalization not only eliminated the verbal overshadowing effect but actually reversed it. Although we can only speculate at this time, it seems likely that the unique benefit of verbalization plus upright re-presentation results from a combination of both refreshing the visual/configural memory and increasing subjects' ability to inspect the features for subtle qualities that may not have been available to subjects in the inverted condition. Although speculative, such an interpretation would also be consistent with Tanaka's (1993) finding that subjects' sensitivity to subtle featural differences is reduced when the configural properties of a face are disrupted. In short, when verbalization is followed by re-presentation, subjects may be in a position to optimally apply all of the facial information potentially at their disposal. On the one hand, reviewing the face in its entirety may have refreshed subjects' memories for the otherwise de-emphasized nonreportable aspects of the face. On the other hand, verbalizing the face at length may have prepared subjects to carefully inspect the re-presented face to determine which aspects they remembered correctly and which they had wrong.

Although this account must still be considered somewhat speculative at this time, the general finding that re-presentation of the target face can reverse the negative effects of verbalization does offer some rather straightforward insights into the nature of the effects of verbalization. First, the fact that reencoding the face following verbalization eliminates the verbal overshadowing effect further supports the suggestion that the disruptive effects of verbalization are due to the inconsistency between the information emphasized under standard encoding conditions and the information emphasized following verbalization. Second, the fact that verbalization is actually helpful when combined with re-presentation of the face supports the claim that consideration of verbalizable aspects of a face can be helpful, particularly when it is done in such a way as to not be inconsistent with the manner in which the face was encoded.

The Relationship Between Verbalization and Interference

In the standard verbal overshadowing paradigm, subjects view a single face, verbalize it or not, and then are tested. However, real-world settings may not be as tightly controlled; subjects may see many faces at the time of the witnessed event, or they may be exposed to multiple mug shots after the event. Although a few studies have found that the deleterious effects of verbalization can persist for some time after subjects viewed and verbalized the face (2 days in the case of Schooler & Engstler-Schooler, 1990; 2 weeks in the case of Read & Schooler, 1994), it is still possible that the effects of verbalization would be quite different if subjects were exposed to multiple faces at the time of encoding. For example, Deffenbacher, Carr, and Leu (1981) found that exposure to multiple faces near the time of encoding of a target face produced a significant degree of interference, even though subjects were generally resistant to additional forgetting when tested 2 weeks later. This finding is also consistent with other demonstrations that the interference associated with seeing multiple faces primarily occurs from exposure to faces presented under comparable encoding conditions (e.g., Davies, Sheperd, & Ellis, 1979). Thus, although verbalization effects have been shown to be relatively unaffected by delay, it is an open question as to whether verbalization interacts with the effects of interference associated with encountering multiple faces within the context of the encoding situation.

In fact, there is some reason to believe that verbalization might help to insulate subjects against the interfering effects of seeing multiple faces. For example, Deffenbacher et al. (1981) also observed that, relative to faces, words were less susceptible to interference resulting from encountering intervening stimuli between encoding and test. Thus, another potentially useful characteristic of face verbalization is that it may provide semantic tags that may help subjects keep track of the target face when they are exposed to multiple faces prior to being tested.

To address the relationship between verbalization and interference, Ryan and Schooler (1994) conducted a face verbalization experiment in which the recognition test was introduced after subjects had viewed (and verbalized if assigned to the verbal condition) four faces. In this experiment subjects viewed a face, verbalized it or not, and then repeated this procedure for the remaining three faces. Subjects were then given a series of four recognition tests presented in an order corresponding to that in which the target faces originally appeared. The order of faces was counterbalanced so that each face appeared equally often in each position.

The results are presented in Fig. 4.3. As can be seen, control subjects' performance declined substantially for faces that were presented and tested later in the procedure (i.e., comparing performance on Face 1 to Face 4). This result suggests the possible impact of both proactive interference (the encoding of faces occurring later in the sequences may have been impaired by prior exposure to earlier faces) and retroactive interference (the retrieval of faces that were tested in later trials may have been impaired by the prior exposure to earlier recognition tests). What is particularly striking about these data, however, is the fact that subjects who engaged in verbalization showed markedly less interference than control subjects.

Although it is not possible at present to determine precisely why verbalization reduces the interfering effects of exposure to multiple faces, it seems likely to do with the differential susceptibility of words and visual stimuli to interference. As mentioned, Deffenbacher et al. (1981) observed that faces

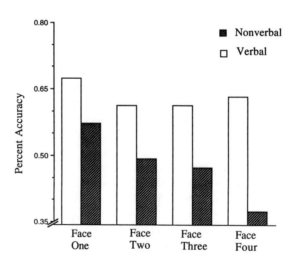

FIG. 4.3. The effects of verbalization and interference from the presentation of interpolated faces.

(and landscapes) were more susceptible than words (nouns) to retroactive interference. Deffenbacher et al. speculated that this difference might be due to the relative role of phonological and semantic encoding mechanisms for visual and verbal stimuli. They suggested: "Interference is not initially observed for the nouns, however, because the phonological and semantic encoding mechanisms are much more successful with them than the landscapes and faces, activating already learned well established codes that could possibly serve as pegs on which to hang episodic information" (Deffenbacher et al., 1981, p. 304).

It may be that the verbalization of a face helps to associate it with a semantic code that provides a tag which enables subjects to differentiate it from other faces to which they have been exposed. In short, verbalizing faces may cause them to be treated more like words; on the one hand, this may disrupt the consideration of the unique configural properties of faces, but on the other hand, this may enable faces to be better tagged and therefore to withstand the interference associated with exposure to multiple faces.

CONCLUSIONS, CAVEATS, AND IMPLICATIONS

In sum, there appear to be both costs and benefits to verbal rehearsal of faces. On the down side, verbalization can deemphasize critical nonreportable task components associated with a variety of nonverbal activities. In the domain of face recognition, verbalization of faces appears to result in a deemphasis at the time of recognition of the configural information typically involved in the encoding of upright same-race faces. This disparity between the nonreportable configural information emphasized during encoding and the more readily verbalized information emphasized at test can result in reduced performance of subjects who attempt to verbalize a previously seen face.

On the positive side, when the disparity between the information attended to during encoding and postencoding verbalization is reduced through re-presentation, the negative effects of verbalization are not only reduced but actually reversed. This combination of verbalization and re-presentation may improve subjects' performance both by eliminating the inconsistency between encoding and postencoding activities and by highlighting differences between subjects' verbalized memories and the target, thereby providing subjects with an opportunity to fill in and correct their memories. Another positive effect of verbalization is to insulate subjects against the disruptive effects of interference, perhaps by providing semantic tags that enable them to better differentiate the faces.

The potential for practical applications of this research is quite substantial. First, it seems clear that we must not assume that asking witnesses to describe the appearance of the perpetrator has no consequence on the witnesses' memory. Instead, it appears that verbalization may have both costs and benefits, depending on a variety of factors. With respect to the findings reported here, the observation that subjects benefit from verbalization when seeing a face re-presented raises the possibility that it may be helpful if, during a crime, witnesses verbalize the perpetrator's appearance to them-selves and then recheck the face to see how their verbalization fits. (Of course, it is not clear how often witnesses would have the presence of mind to be able to engage in such complex processing activity!) There may also be some practical significance to the finding that verbalization may offer insulation against interference. Specifically, verbalization may help to protect subjects against the interference that can result from exposure to multiple mug shots (e.g., Davies et al., 1979).

Although this line of research has potentially important practical impli-cations, some caveats should be considered before direct applications are contemplated. Most important, it should be noted that, although the negative effects of verbalization on face recognition have been replicated many times in various labs, they are not always observed (e.g., S. Lindsay, personal communication, 1990; Lovett, Small, & Engstrom, 1992; Yu & Geiselman, 1993). It is not entirely clear why these differential effects of verbalization are sometimes observed; many possible factors may be involved. For ex-ample, in the studies reviewed here it has been seen that the presence of verbalization effects depends on the degree to which subjects spontaneously rely on nonreportable face components (e.g., configural) at encoding, the degree to which subsequent recognition considerations are shifted away from what was emphasized during encoding, and whether interference is encountered. It is possible that some of the failures to find disruptive effects of verbalization may have been the result of variations in these variables.

There also may be important population variables at play. It seems quite possible that subjects vary in the degree to which they spontaneously focus on nonreportable face components during encoding, which may mediate whether or not they are subsequently impaired by verbalization. Consistent with this view, Ryan and Schooler (1995) found that verbalization impaired the performance of subjects who scored above the median on various visual memory tasks (e.g., embedded figures, general face recognition tasks), but not subjects who scored below the median on these tasks. It is also possible that subjects may differ in their ability to apply verbal processes to faces, and this difference may also mediate the impact of verbalization. For example, Ryan and Schooler also observed that subjects with above-average GPAs (and presumably higher verbal abilities) showed less impact of verbalization than subjects with below-average GPAs. Additional evidence for the importance of verbal ability comes from research in a very different domain: verbalization and expertise in wine. Melcher and Schooler (in press) observed that verbali-zation impaired the wine recognition performance of nonexpert wine drinkers but not wine professionals. Wine professionals also showed markedly greater verbal wine knowledge, which suggests that their relative resistance to verbal overshadowing was due to their superior wine vocabulary.[2]

There appear to be quite a few variables that can influence how verbalization influences performances. The complexity of factors involved in mediating verbal overshadowing effects constrains our ability to offer hard and fast advice about how this research should be applied in real-world contexts that typically involve many uncontrolled variables. Thus, more research will be needed before we can move this research endeavor from the potentially applicable to the truly applied (cf. Herrmann, in press). Nevertheless, we are well on the way toward an understanding of the general principles involved in determining when verbalization is likely to be harmful, helpful, or of no consequence.

ACKNOWLEDGMENTS

The research reported in this chapter was supported by a grant to the first author from the National Institute of Mental Health and by grant BNS-8908030 to the third author from the National Science Foundation. We thank Stephen Fiore for helpful comments on earlier drafts of this chapter.

REFERENCES

Bartlett, J. C., & Searcy, J. (1993). Inversion and configuration of faces. *Cognitive Psychology, 25,* 281–316.

Berry, D. C. (1984). *Implicit and explicit knowledge in the control of complex systems.* Unpublished doctoral dissertation, University of Oxford, United Kingdom.

Brandimonte, M. A., Schooler, J. W., & Gabbino, P. (1995). *Preventing verbal overshadowing through visual retrieval cues.* Manuscript submitted for publication.

Carey, S., & Diamond, R. (1977). From piecemeal to configurational representation of faces. *Science, 195,* 312–314.

Charney, D. H., & Reder, L. M. (1986). Designing tutorials for computer users: Effects of the form and spacing of practice on skill learning. *Human Computer Interaction, 2,* 297–317.

---

[2]Interestingly, wine novices (individuals who drank wine less than once a month) also showed no effect of verbalization. Comparison of the effects of verbalization on the performance of wine novices and nonprofessional wine drinkers thus replicates, in principle, Fallshore and Schooler's (1994) finding that verbalization impairs face recognition exclusively within domains where subjects possess a substantial degree of perceptual expertise (i.e., verbalization disrupts memory for same-race but not other-race faces). This interaction is also consistent with Ryan and Schooler's (1995) finding that verbalization impaired subjects with high perceptual abilities but not low perceptual abilities. Presumably in all three cases this interaction occurs because the effects of verbalization are limited to those domains in which subjects' perceptual memories exceed what they are able to verbalize about their memories.

Chi, M. T. H., de Leeuw, N., Chiu, M., & LaVancher, C. (1994). Eliciting self-explanations improves understanding. *Cognitive Science, 18*, 439–477.

Darley, C. F., & Glass, A. L. (1975). Effects of rehearsal and serial list position on recall. *Journal of Experimental Psychology: Human Learning and Memory, 104*, 453–458.

Davies, G., Shepherd, J., & Ellis, H. (1979). Effects of interpolated mugshot exposure on accuracy of eyewitness identification. *Journal of Applied Psychology, 64*, 96–101.

Deffenbacher, K. A., Carr, T. H., & Leu, J. R. (1981). Memory for words, pictures, and faces: Retroactive interference, forgetting, and reminiscence. *Journal of Experimental Psychology: Human Learning and Memory, 7*, 299–305.

Diamond, R., & Carey, S. (1986). Why faces are and are not special: An effect of expertise. *Journal of Experimental Psychology: General, 115*, 107–117.

Dodson, C. S., Johnson, M. K., & Schooler, J. W. (in press). Can subjects escape the verbal overshadowing effect? *Memory and Cognition.*

Fallshore, M., & Schooler, J. W. (1993). Post-encoding verbalization impairs transfer on artificial grammar tasks. In *Fifteenth Annual Meeting of the Cognitive Science Society* (pp. 412–416). Boulder, CO: Cognitive Science Society.

Fallshore, M., & Schooler, J. W. (1995). The verbal vulnerability of perceptual expertise. *Journal of Experimental Psychology: Learning, Memory, and Cognition, 21*, 1608–1623.

Fiore, S. M. (1994). *Verbal overshadowing of macro-spatial memory.* Unpublished masters thesis, University of Pittsburgh.

Gagne, R. H., & Smith, E. C. (1962). A study of the effects of verbalization on problem solving. *Journal of Experimental Psychology, 63*, 12–18.

Herrmann, D. J. (in press). Applied cognitive psychology vs. applicable cognitive psychology: Review of *Cognitive Psychology Applied* (edited by Chizuko Izawa). *Applied Cognitive Psychology,*

Houser, T., & Schooler, J. W. (1994). [Verbal overshadowing and music memory]. Unpublished data.

Lovett, S. B., Small, M. Y., & Engstrom, S. A. (1992, November). *The verbal overshadowing effect: Now you see it, now you don't.* Paper presented at the Annual Meeting of Psychonomic Society, St. Louis, MO.

Melcher, J. M. (1994). *Speaking of wine: Differential effects of verbalization on wine recognition across various levels of expertise.* Unpublished masters thesis, University of Pittsburgh.

Melcher, J., & Schooler, J. W. (in press). The misremembrance of wines past: Verbal and perceptual expertise differentially mediate verbal overshadowing of taste. *The Journal of Memory and Language.*

Morris, C. D., Bransford, J. D., & Franks, J. J. (1977). Levels of processing versus transfer appropriate processing. *Journal of Verbal Learning and Verbal Behavior, 16*, 519–533.

Needham, D. R., & Begg, I. M. (1991). Problem-oriented training promotes spontaneous analogical transfer: Memory-oriented training promotes memory for training. *Memory & Cognition, 19*, 543–557.

Pavio, A. (1986). *Mental representations: A dual coding approach.* New York: Oxford University Press.

Read, J. D., & Schooler, J. W. (1994, August). *Verbalization decrements in long-term person identification.* Paper presented at the Third Practical Aspects of Memory Conference, College Park, MD.

Rhodes, G., Tan S., Brake, S., & Taylor, K. (1989). Expertise and configural coding in face recognition. *British Journal of Psychology, 80*, 313–331.

Ryan, R. S. (1992). *Does transfer appropriate processing mediate the verbal overshadowing effect?* Unpublished masters thesis, University of Pittsburgh.

Ryan, R. S, & Schooler, J. W. (1994). *Verbalization can reduce interference.* Unpublished manuscript, University of Pittsburgh.

Ryan, R. S., & Schooler, J. W. (1995, June). *Describing a face impairs the face recognition of holistic processors more than analytic processors.* Poster presented at the annual meeting of the American Psychological Society, New York.

Schooler, J. W. (1989, November). *Verbalization can overshadow the non-verbal components of visual memories.* Paper presented at the Annual Meeting of the Psychonomic Society, Atlanta, GA.

Schooler, J. W., & Engstler-Schooler, T. Y. (1990). Verbal overshadowing of visual memories: Some things are better left unsaid. *Cognitive Psychology, 17,* 36–71.

Schooler, J. W., & Melcher, J. (1995). The ineffability of insight. In S. M. Smith, T. B. Ward, & R. A. Finke (Eds.), *Creative cognition approach* (pp. 97–133). Cambridge, MA: MIT Press.

Schooler, J. W., Ohlsson, S., & Brooks, K. (1993). Thoughts beyond words: When language overshadows insight. *Journal of Experimental Psychology: General, 122,* 166–183.

Schooler, J. W., Ryan, R., & Reder, L. M. (1990, July). *Better the second time around: Re-presentation reverses verbalization's impairment of face recognition.* Paper presented at The International Conference on Memory, Lancaster, United Kingdom.

Schooler, J. W., & Wilson, T. W. (1991). When words hurt: The disruptive effects of verbally analyzing reasons. In M. Lynn & J. M. Jackson (Eds.), *Annual Convention of the American Psychological Association* (p. 29). San Francisco: American Psychological Association.

Sergent, J. (1984). An investigation into component and configural processes underlying face preception. *British Journal of Psychology, 75,* 221–242.

Sieck, W. (1993). *Verbal overshadowing effects on the judgement of analogy.* Unpublished honors thesis, University of Pittsburgh.

Slamecka, N. J., & Graf, P. (1978). The generation effect: Delineation of a phenomenon. *Journal of Experimental Psychology: Human Learning and Memory, 4,* 592–604.

Tanaka, J. W. (1993). Parts and wholes in face recognition. *Quarterly Journal of Experimental Psychology: Human Experimental Psychology, 46A,* 225–245.

Tulving, E., & Thompson, D. M. (1973). Encoding specificity and retrieval processes in episodic memory. *Psychological Review, 80,* 352–373.

Wells, G. L., & Hryciw, B. (1984). Memory for faces: Encoding and retrieval operations. *Memory & Cognition, 12,* 338–344.

Westerman, D. L. (1991, April). *The effects of verbalization on face and car recognition.* Paper presented at the North East Ohio Undergraduate Psychology Conference.

Wilson, T. D., Lisle, D. J., Schooler, J. W., Hodges, S. D., Klaaren, K. J., & Lafleur, S. J. (1993). Introspecting about reasons can reduce post-choice satisfaction. *Personality and Social Psychology Bulletin, 19,* 331–339.

Wilson, T. D., & Schooler, J. W. (1991). Thinking too much: Introspection can reduce the quality of preferences and decisions. *Journal of Personality and Social Psychology, 60,* 181–192.

Young, A. W., Hellawell, D., & Hay, D. C. (1987). Configurational information in face perception. *Perception, 16,* 747–759.

Yu, C. J., & Geiselman, R. E. (1993). Effects of constructing indenti-kit composites on photospread identification performance. *Criminal Justice and Behavior, 20,* 280–292.

CHAPTER FIVE

Children's Memory Following Misleading Postevent Information: A Contextual Approach

Michael P. Toglia
Jeffery S. Neuschatz
State University of New York, Cortland

Helene Hembrooke
Stephen J. Ceci
Cornell University

Within the last 20 years, psychologists studying eyewitness memory have begun to investigate the factors and conditions that may influence memory impairment (cf. Belli & Loftus, in press; Ceci & Bruck, 1993). This research has fueled a controversy over the fate of original memory traces after a witness has been exposed to postevent information, especially when it is misleading. Sometimes the misinformation effect is observed, which refers to the inaccurate reporting of original information after exposure to biased or misleading information.

Loftus and her associates (Greene, Flynn, & Loftus, 1982; Loftus & Palmer, 1974) repeatedly demonstrated a misinformation effect. The procedure that has been most frequently employed, the standard or original procedure, involves three phases. In the first phase subjects witness an event, which may be staged or presented via a film or slide sequence. For example, Loftus, Miller, and Burns (1978) asked subjects to watch a film of an accident in which a car runs a stop sign. During the second phase the subjects in the control condition are exposed to neutral information about a critical item. In this type of design (between-subjects) the subjects do not serve as their own controls. In contrast, subjects in the misled condition receive misleading or biased information about critical items. Loftus et al. (1978) told these subjects that the driver had passed through a yield sign. Stage three occurs at some later time when subjects in both conditions are asked, in the form of a forced-choice recognition test, to decide whether the initial sequence of events contained the misleading or original information (i.e., stop sign

67

vs. yield sign in the present example). Researchers who have employed this design have found the misinformation effect with adults (Loftus, Miller, & Burns, 1978) and with children (Ceci, Ross, & Toglia, 1987; Toglia, Ross, Ceci, & Hembrooke, 1992).

McCloskey and Zaragoza (1985) suggested that the misinformation effect reported with the standard test may be an artifact of demand characteristics inherent in the procedure rather than impairment due to exposure of postevent information. Specifically, they argued that the subjects in the misled condition who forget the original information but remember the postevent information will be systematically wrong on the final recognition test and perform at a level less than chance (50%). Thus, McCloskey and Zaragoza expected worse performance in the misled condition as long as some subjects remembered only the postevent information.

In an attempt to provide a more valid measure of memory impairment, McCloskey and Zaragoza (1985) argued for the use of a different method of testing. This method, referred to as the *modified test*, requires subjects to choose between the original and novel information on the final recognition test. For example, subjects may witness a hammer in the original event and subsequently be misled that the tool was actually a wrench. However, on the recognition test during the final phase subjects are asked if a hammer (original) or a screwdriver (novel) appeared in the original event. In contrast, subjects in the standard procedure must choose between the original (hammer) and misleading postevent information (wrench). McCloskey and Zaragoza argued that this modified procedure eliminates the response bias inherent in the standard procedure because subjects in both conditions will operate at the same level of recognition accuracy if there is no memory impairment.

In a series of six experiments with adults, McCloskey and Zaragoza reported no memory impairment with the modified procedure. This null result was also reported by other researchers who employed the modified test with adults (Bonto & Payne, 1991) and children (Zaragoza, 1987, 1991). McCloskey and Zaragoza suggested that the postevent misinformation has no impairing effect on either the storage or retrieval of the original information.

McCloskey and Zaragoza's argument is tenuous considering that memory impairment has been found by some researchers who have employed a between-subjects manipulation of the control and misled factor with the modified procedure (Ceci et al., 1987; Toglia et al., 1992). However, in studies where this variable was within subjects, typically no misinformation effect has been reported (McCloskey & Zaragoza, 1985; Toglia, Hembrooke, Ceci, & Ross, 1994; Zaragoza, 1987, 1991; Zaragoza, Dahlgren, & Muench, 1992). In the context of between-subjects designs there is a subset of information (i.e., critical items) about which subjects receive either misleading information or neutral information. Thus, memory for control items cannot be influenced by misinformation, because none was presented. Alternatively, in within-subjects designs subjects receive both misleading and neutral information. This raises the possibility that misinformation may influence memory for control items because neutral references to them occur in conjunction with misleading references to other items. In this vein, Toglia (1991) suggested that in within-subjects designs misinformation not only has a specific effect on the intended (i.e., misled) items but also has a general unintended influence on control/unbiased items. This general effect may lower the recognition performance on unbiased items. Thus, due to contextual factors there may be a "spreading effect" of misleading postevent information. However, there have been some exceptions (i.e., Belli, Windschilt, McCarthy, & Winfrey, 1992).

Because the design issue has been only addressed across experiments, there is a need to empirically investigate in a single study the extent to which between- versus within-subjects designs impact performance on modified tests. As just noted, Ceci et al. (1987) and Toglia et al. (1992) employed between-subjects designs with the modified procedure, and found that subjects in the misled condition performed significantly worse on the recognition test than did the control subjects. Zaragoza et al. (1992) attempted to replicate the findings of Ceci et al. but found no misinformation effect. However, their study could not be considered a replication on several accounts, especially because Zaragoza and her colleagues employed a within-subjects design. It is plausible that the inconsistent results are due to the differences in methodology. However, it may also be that the modified test is a more sensitive measure of memory impairment in the context of a between-subjects design rather than within-subjects design because only in this latter design is obtaining a pure estimate of control performance threatened (i.e., by the presence of misinformation).

Thus, one purpose of the present investigation was to examine the extent of memory impairment when a between- compared to a within-subjects design was employed. Age (4-year-olds vs. 8-year-olds) was another major factor that was considered. The choice of these ages was based on the results of studies that have developmentally charted the influence of misleading postevent information on the memory of children of varying ages (cf. Ceci et al., 1987). Specifically, older children have been shown to be more adultlike in their susceptibly to suggestion, whereas preschoolers have been found to be disproportionately vulnerable to the effects of misinformation.

It was expected that subjects who were exposed to neutral information about critical items would perform more accurately than subjects who received misleading information, with the difference more pronounced for preschoolers because they should be more easily misled due to an underdeveloped ability to monitor their memories. It was predicted that this would be the case regardless of design type (between vs. within subjects). It was also predicted that when the biased/unbiased variable was between subjects a greater misinformation effect would be observed than when it was a within-subjects factor. This prediction follows from the "spreading effect" notion, because if control performance is reduced in a within-subjects design it is more likely that there would be a concomitant reduction in the control/misled difference (Toglia, 1991).

In light of this argument one might expect memory impairment should be more easily detectable in a between-subjects design because the control performance level should be higher. In fact, Payne, Toglia, and Anastasi (1994) and Toglia, Payne, and Anastasi (1991) suggested that control recognition performance was related to the occurrence of the misinformation effect. Specifically, Payne et al. noted that when a control group's recognition performance level is near the extremes (i.e., above 90% or near chance, 50%), little if any memory impairment should be observed. Their meta-analysis of studies with the modified procedure generally confirmed this expectation and revealed that in those studies reporting a significant misinformation effect the control group's recognition accuracy was greater (81.8%) than in those studies for which there was no evidence of a misinformation effect (73.6%). In light of this finding, it was also expected that memory impairment would be more likely if the control performance level was relatively high (80%–85% accuracy) but below ceiling.

EXPERIMENT 1

In both this investigation and the subsequent experiment the modified testing procedure was employed. The manipulation of the control-misled factor was between subjects in Experiment 1.

Method

Subjects.   A total of 61 children participated in the study. There were 29 preschoolers (average age 3 years, 11 months) and 32 second graders (average age 7 years, 11 months). All the subjects were selected from preschools and elementary schools in central New York. Before participating, written informed consent from the parents or legal guardians of all the children was obtained.

Design.   The experiment conformed to a 2 × 2 between-subjects design. The independent variables were age (preschoolers and second graders), and critical items that served as either control events (unbiased) or misled events (biased). The dependent measure was the percentage of correct identifications on a two-alternative forced-choice modified recognition test.

Materials and Procedure.   All subjects heard a story about a little girl name Loren, which was Lindsay, Gonzales, and Eso's (1995) adaptation of the original version introduced by Ceci et al. (1987). The story was accompanied by 10 pictures that illustrated the main events of the story. On the first meeting a female experimenter read a story to the children about Loren's first day of school while showing the 10 illustrations. The story includes Loren eating breakfast (e.g., eggs) and feeding her pet (e.g., cat) before leaving for school. These were two of the three critical items in the episode. It took approximately 3 minutes to present the entire story to groups of about five children of the same age. The subjects were then randomly assigned to a critical item (control, misled) condition.

The second experimental session occurred one day after the presentation of the story. A male experimenter conducted a brief interview about the story with each subject individually. The interview contained information concerning the critical items that varied depending on the subject's condition (control or misled). Subjects who were in the control condition were exposed to neutral information about the three critical items. These children were asked if they remembered various details about the Loren story interspersed with statements indicating that she ate breakfast and fed her pet. In contrast, subjects in the misled condition were exposed, via the interspersed comments, to misinformation about the critical items. The experimenter mentioned, for example, that Loren ate her French toast and fed her dog.

The test was administered two days after the presentation of the misleading or neutral information. A third experimenter, another female whom the children had not seen before, conducted the two-alternative forced-choice recognition test during individual sessions. On each test trial the children were instructed to select the picture that they saw during the original presentation of the story. One of the pictures in any given trial was the item as pictured in the original story, whereas the other picture was exactly the same as viewed in the story with the exception that the critical item was replaced with a novel item (i.e., one picture of her eating eggs and one picture of her eating pancakes). Note that the misled item in our example, French toast, is not an option on the modified test. For any given critical item (e.g., breakfast food) there were three versions (eggs, pancakes, and French toast) that each served as control, misled, and novel items approximately equally often to achieve near counterbalancing. The order and the position of the correct item (left or right) was also counterbalanced.

Results and Discussion

A 2 × 2 analysis of variance (ANOVA) was computed on the mean percent correct recognition scores for the two age groups by critical item conditions (control, misled). This analysis revealed a significant main effect for age, as the 8-year-old subjects demonstrated considerably superior correct recognition performance ($M = 93$) compared to the their 4-year-old counterparts ($M = 62$). There was no main effect for critical item condition nor an interaction, which was contrary to the expectation that only the preschoolers would suffer memory impairment.

An item analysis conducted on the recognition data revealed no evidence of a misinformation effect (greater control vs. misled recognition accuracy), which was consistent with the analysis treating subjects as a random factor. Importantly, there was no indication of any item effects. In other words, no item was correctly or incorrectly identified more often than the other items. The analysis did reveal an age effect, because the preschoolers were much less accurate in identifying each critical item than were the second graders.

The findings of better recognition performance for older subjects compared to younger subjects has been consistently reported in the literature (e.g., Ceci et al., 1987; Toglia et al., 1992; cf. Ceci & Bruck, 1993, for a further review). A reduced or absent misinformation effect for children 8 years old and older has been frequently observed (Ceci et al., 1987; Zaragoza, 1987), as was the case in the present study.

However, the failure of the misleading information to affect the 4-year-old children's recognition accuracy in a between-subjects design was unexpected. This finding was particularly surprising given that Ceci et al. (1987) and Toglia et al. (1992) both reported memory impairment for children of the same age range as the preschoolers in the present study. A closer examination of these data suggested that the misinformation effect may have been masked by the extremely low control performance level ($M = 56$). In both the Ceci et al. and Toglia et al. studies the control group's level of accuracy in recognition was much higher ($M = 84$ and $M = 79$, respectively) than in the present experiment.

The lack of a misinformation effect at near chance or near ceiling levels of performance in control conditions is, however, what would be predicted by the control level hypothesis (Toglia et al., 1991; Toglia, Payne, Anastasi, & Neuschatz, 1994). Toglia, Payne, et al. (1994) indicated that memory impairment is most likely to occur when the control recognition level is relatively high but below ceiling. According to this hypothesis a misinformation effect would not be expected when the control performance is near floor, as it was for the preschoolers in the present study. Toglia et al. also suggested that control recognition accuracy above ceiling (90%) masks the detection of any misinformation effect. The control recognition accuracy for the older subjects (93%) was quite good and there was no evidence of a misinformation effect. Thus, the data from both age groups were congruous with the control level of performance hypothesis.

EXPERIMENT 2

Experiment 2 was designed to investigate the occurrence of memory impairment when the control/misled factor was varied within subjects. As was the case in Experiment 1, the modified recognition testing procedure was employed.

Method

Subjects. There was a total of 45 subjects who served in the second study: 19 preschoolers (average age 4 years, 1 month) and 36 second graders (average age 7 years, 10 months), attending the same school as in Experiment 1.

Design. The study conformed to a 2 × 2 mixed design. The between-subjects variable was age, and the within-subjects variable was critical item in which some served as control (unbiased) events and others as misled (biased) events. The dependent measure was the percentage of correct identifications on the forced-choice modified recognition test.

Materials and Procedure. The materials employed in Experiment 2 were the same as those in Experiment 1. The children were presented with the same story and procedurally the second experiment was very similar to Experiment 1. In Phase 2 the subjects individually received information about four critical items (in Experiment 1 it was three items). The subjects were exposed to neutral information about two items and misleading information about the other two critical items. These items were counterbalanced such that each item was neutral and misled equally often. The final forced-recognition test was the same as it was in Experiment 1, with the exception that subjects were required to make identifications of items about which they received neutral and misled information.

Results and Discussion

Mean percent correct recognition performance was analyzed with a 2 × 2 mixed-factor ANOVA, because in Experiment 2 critical item (control, misled) was a within-subjects variable. The results of this analysis once again revealed a significant main effect for age such that the older subjects were considerably more accurate in their recognition judgments ($M = 90$) than the younger children ($M = 66$). There was no evidence of a main effect of critical item condition as control performance ($M = 80$) was only slightly higher than misled performance ($M = 76$). For preschoolers the corresponding means were $M = 65$ and $M = 67$, whereas for second graders the control and misled averages were $M = 96$ and $M = 84$. Although there appears to be an interaction, it only approached significance. That is, although the preschoolers did not differ on control and misled items, surprisingly, a follow-up test revealed a misinformation effect for 8-year-old subjects. Specifically, the older subjects had superior recognition accuracy on control items ($M = 96$) than they did on items for which they were misled ($M = 84$). An item analysis was consistent with these findings.

A null misinformation effect for the preschoolers in a within-subjects design is in line with several studies (Toglia, Hembrooke, et al., 1994; Zaragoza, 1987, 1991; Zaragoza et al., 1992). Note that the control level hypothesis (Toglia, Payne, et al., 1994) predicts little or no misinformation effect in this experiment because the control performance ($M = 66$) was relatively low for the 4-year-old subjects. Toglia, Payne, et al. suggested that control performance levels between 80%–85% correct were optimal for the detection of memory impairment. When control performance is below this level (as it was for the preschoolers) it is more difficult to detect a misinformation effect because the original memory trace is weak, and therefore already substantially impaired due to factors other than misleading information.

It is not clear why there was relatively lower recognition performance for the second graders when they were exposed to misleading as opposed to neutral information. This finding is inconsistent with most of the literature, as well as in opposition to the expectations of the control level hypothesis. That is, second graders in this study were misled even when control performance was at ceiling. Even though there was evidence of memory impairment, practically speaking it is important to note that misled performance was still very high ($M = 84$). Furthermore, recognition accuracy for second graders on misled items was still superior to the performance of the preschoolers on misled items.

GENERAL DISCUSSION

Taken together, the experiments reported in this chapter clearly demonstrated that 8-year-old children are likely to be more accurate witnesses than are 4-year-old children. The older children were substantially better at providing correct responses for both control and misled items. It is also evident from the results that misleading postevent information had no impairing effect on the younger children's recognition memory. Similarly, the 8-year-old subjects in Experiment 1 (between-subjects study) were not influenced by the exposure to misleading postevent information. However, in Experiment 2 (within-subjects study) they did show a misinformation effect.

The lack of memory impairment for second graders and preschoolers requires separate explanations. The older subjects demonstrated recognition accuracy levels above ceiling that, as described earlier, should prevent or disguise any impact of postevent information. This is in fact what happened in Experiment 1 and parallels results with subjects of a similar age range in between-subjects designs (Ceci et al., 1987; Toglia et al., 1992). The fact that the second graders were somewhat swayed by misleading information with control performance level at ceiling in the second study was not predicted but is not anomalous. For example, Lindsay et al. (1995) and Delamothe and Taplin (1992) both observed control accuracy levels above 90%, yet misinformation significantly impaired memory for children as old as 10. It is important to emphasize that in these studies control performance was at ceiling as in Experiment 2. Thus, for our subjects, the presence of misinformation did not produce any negative "spreading effect" to control items. This finding suggests an important forensic implication that merits further study; namely, that if misleading questions creep into an interview they need not taint other aspects of an interrogation.

In contrast, the performance levels for the preschoolers were very different. Their recognition accuracy was near chance levels for all conditions. Thus, the younger subjects experienced difficulty remembering any information regardless of whether it was misleading or neutral, prohibiting any detection of memory impairment. Perhaps the young age and the lack of cognitive sophistication of the preschoolers may have contributed to their poor control recognition performance. However, this argument is weak because Ceci et al. (1987) demonstrated considerably higher than chance control performance levels on the modified test with 3- and 4-year-olds.

When the results for control and misled items are analyzed separately for both experiments combined (i.e., design was treated as a between-subjects factor) the highly similar pattern of results across experiments is evident, but a different picture of memory impairment emerges. The older subjects had superior recognition accuracy for both control and misled ($M = 94$ and $M = 88$, respectively) items than did the preschoolers ($M = 62$ and $M = 67$, respectively) across both Experiments 1 and 2. These results seem to indicate the older subjects were more resistant to misleading information than the younger subjects. This interpretation is consistent with Ceci et al. (1987) and Toglia et al. (1992), who both reported that 8-year-old subjects were less susceptible to suggestion than were 4-year-old subjects.

It is important to note that it is difficult to ascertain to what degree the findings presented in this chapter extend to memory of children who are actual witnesses to or victims of a crime. The laboratory situation is relatively benign compared to real-life events, which are frequently accompanied by emotional overtones. Even though field and laboratory studies tend to produce congruent findings, it would be prudent to interpret the present results based on a story event cautiously because of concerns with external validity.

REFERENCES

Belli, R. F., & Loftus, E. F. (in press). The pliability of autobiographical memory: Misinformation and the false memory problem. In D. C. Rubin (Ed.), *Constructing our past: An overview of autobiographical memory.* New York: Cambridge University Press.

Belli, R. F., Windschilt, P., McCarthy, T., & Winfrey, S. (1992). Detecting memory impairment with a modified test procedure: Manipulating retention interval with centrally presented event items. *Journal of Experimental Psychology: Learning, Memory, and Cognition, 18,* 356–367.

Bonto, M. A., & Payne, D. G. (1991). Role of environmental context in eyewitness memory. *American Journal of Psychology, 104,* 117–134.

Ceci, S. J., & Bruck, M. (1993). Suggestibility of the child witness: A historical review and synthesis. *Psychological Bulletin, 113,* 403–439.

Ceci, S. J., Ross, D. F., & Toglia, M. P. (1987). Suggestibility of children's memory: Psycholegal implications. *Journal of Experimental Psychology: General, 117,* 38–49.

Delamothe, K., & Taplin, E. (1992, November). *The effect of suggestibility on children's recognition memory.* Paper presented at the annual meeting of the Psychonomic Society, St. Louis, MO.

Greene, E. D., Flynn, M. S., & Loftus, E. F. (1982). Inducing resistance to misleading information. *Journal of Verbal learning and Verbal Behavior, 21,* 513–529.

Lindsay, D. S., Gonzales, V., & Eso, K. (1995). Aware and unaware uses of memories of postevent suggestions. In M. S. Zaragoza, J. R. Graham, G. C. N. Hall, R. Hirschman, & Y. S. Ben-Porath (Eds.), *Memory and testimony in the child witness* (pp. 86–108). Thousand Oaks, CA: Sage.

Loftus, E. F., Miller, D. G., & Burns, H. J. (1978). Semantic integration of verbal information into visual memory. *Journal of Experimental Psychology: Human Learning and Memory, 4,* 19–31.

Loftus, E. F., & Palmer, J. C. (1974). Reconstruction of an automobile deconstruction: An example of the interaction between language and memory. *Journal of Verbal Learning and Verbal Behavior, 13,* 585–589.

McCloskey, M., & Zaragoza, M. S. (1985). Misleading postevent information and memory for events: Arguments and evidence against memory impairment hypotheses. *Journal of Experimental Psychology: General, 114,* 1–16.

Payne, D. G., Toglia, M. P., & Anastasi, J. S. (1994). Recognition performance level and the magnitude of the misinformation effect in eyewitness memory. *Psychonomic Bulletin & Review, 1,* 376–382.

Toglia, M. P. (1991). Memory impairment—It is more common than you think. In J. L. Doris (Ed.), *The suggestibility of children's recollections* (pp. 40–46). Washington, DC: American Psychological Association.

Toglia, M. P., Hembrooke, H., Ceci, S. J., & Ross, D. F. (1994). Children's resistance to misleading postevent information: When does it occur? *Current Psychology, 13,* 21–26.

Toglia, M. P., Payne, D. G., & Anastasi, J. S. (1991, November). *Recognition level and the misinformation effect: A meta-analysis and empirical investigation.* Paper presented at the annual meeting of the Psychonomic Society, San Francisco.

Toglia, M. P., Payne, D. G., Anastasi, J. S., & Neuschatz, J. S. (1994). *Recognition accuracy and memory impairment: A meta-analysis.* Paper presented at the biennial meeting of the American Psychology-Law Society, Santa Fe, NM.

Toglia, M. P., Ross, D. F., Ceci, S. J., & Hembrooke, H. (1992). The suggestibility of children's memory: A social-psychological and cognitive interpretation. In M. L. Howe, C. J. Brainerd, & V. F. Reyna (Eds.), *Development of long-term retention* (pp. 217–241). New York: Springer-Verlag.

Zaragoza, M. (1987). Memory, suggestibility and eyewitness testimony in children and adults. In S. J. Ceci, M. P. Toglia, & D. F. Ross (Eds.), *Children's eyewitness memory* (pp. 53–78). New York: Springer-Verlag.

Zaragoza, M. (1991). Preschool children's susceptibility to memory impairment. In J. L. Doris (Ed.), *The suggestibility of children's recollections* (pp. 27–39). Washington, DC: American Psychological Association.

Zaragoza, M., Dahlgren, D., & Muench, J. (1992). The role of memory impairment in children's suggestibility. In M. L. Howe, C. J. Brainerd, & V. F. Reyna (Eds.), *Development of long-term retention* (pp. 184–216). New York: Springer-Verlag.

PART THREE

REMEMBERING TO
DO THINGS

CHAPTER SIX

Remembering to Do Things: Remembering a Forgotten Topic

Gilles O. Einstein
Furman University

Mark A. McDaniel
University of New Mexico

It has been more than 10 years since Harris (1984) wrote his influential review paper on prospective memory titled "Remembering to Do Things: A Forgotten Topic." In the introduction to his paper, Harris pointed out that prospective memory has received virtually no attention by memory researchers, and thus he used the word *forgotten* in the sense that it was an "ignored" topic. Indeed, the earliest experimental study that Harris could find was conducted in 1940, and few of the cited papers were published in main memory journals. It some ways, however, prospective memory was also a "forgotten" topic as pioneers of the field of psychology such as James, Freud, and Lewin spoke in interesting ways of remembering intentions. For example, Freud characterized prospective memories as ones that reside at an unconscious level until they suddenly "pop" into awareness. Lewin was interested in, among other things, the tension produced by these "unfinished" memories and how these unfinished or intended actions come to mind (for further information see Goschke & Kuhl, 1996; Mantyla, 1996).

An examination of Harris' classic chapter reveals that in 1984 there were only hints of laboratory paradigms for studying prospective memory, few theoretical views, and little connection between the prospective and retrospective memory literatures. As might be expected in the early stages of research on a topic, the chapter mainly consisted of descriptions of different kinds of prospective memory situations and conceptual classifications of different kinds of prospective memory tasks (with the exception of a compelling theory by Harris & Wilkins, 1982). In fact, Harris concluded the chapter by saying, "If the account seems to be like a list, it is because the studies have been performed in the absence of encompassing theory and the researchers have performed their investigations for various, sometimes applied reasons, with little knowledge of each other's work" (pp. 89–90).

Although today's journals are not saturated with papers on prospective memory, there seems to be heightened recent interest in the topic. This probably stems from the fact that issues related to prospective memory are relevant to current topics and interests in retrospective memory—perhaps giving psychologists a new tool or approach for studying some of these topics. For example, a good deal of prospective memory seems to occur spontaneously and without consciously controlled retrieval processes, and this view of prospective memory fits nicely with current interest in nonconscious, automatic memory processes (e.g., Jacoby & Kelley, 1991). Prospective memory also appears to be a fruitful area for examining and exploring theories of aging (e.g., Einstein & McDaniel, 1990). Processes that are thought to be important components of prospective memory such as self-initiated retrieval, reality monitoring, and output monitoring (see Maylor, in press-a) are thought to be especially susceptible to the effects of aging. Prospective memory is also an interesting area from the cognitive neuropsychological perspective, because it seems that prospective memory functioning should be related to the integrity of the frontal lobes.

Finally, prospective memory is a good example of a kind of memory task that occurs often in the real world, and hence research on this topic fits nicely with increased interest in everyday memory and the applications of memory research. Good prospective memory, for instance, is of utmost importance for air traffic controllers, who often must wait for traffic to clear before they can execute an instruction to reroute a plane (Vortac, Edwards, & Manning, 1995). Recent research by Park (1992) on medication adherence and Camp, Foss, Stevens, and O'Hanlon (1996) on effective strategies for improving prospective memory in persons with Alzheimer's disease have clearly shown that prospective memory research has implications for addressing real-world memory problems. In summary, then, there are many reasons to remember this forgotten topic.

The increased recent interest in prospective memory is starting to have an effect. There are a growing number of prospective memory papers appearing in major journals and a growing number of techniques for examining prospective memory (see Kvavilashvili & Ellis, in press), and these are allowing a good deal of cross fertilization to take place. Broad conceptual frameworks (Ellis, 1996) as well as specific theoretical positions (Cohen & O'Reilly, 1996; Einstein & McDaniel, 1996; Goschke & Kuhl, 1993, 1996; Mantyla, 1993) are being developed and these are helping to define the important questions and motivate programmatic research. Thus, we anticipate substantial progress in our understanding of prospective memory over the next 10 years.

In the memory literature, prospective memory typically has been contrasted with retrospective memory, and as such prospective memory tends to be treated as a single kind of memory task. Our general aim in this chapter is to review our recent research suggesting that it would be a mistake to take a unitary view of prospective memory. Following a conceptual analysis of the special retrieval characteristics of prospective memory in general, we focus on what we see as an important distinction between event-based and time-based prospective memory tasks (these are described in a subsequent section). Next, we present some empirical evidence supporting this distinction. We close this chapter by suggesting a cognitive intervention strategy for improving prospective memory on time-based tasks.

PROSPECTIVE MEMORY
AND SPONTANEOUS RETRIEVAL

Our initial interest in prospective memory centered around what seemed to us to be special retrieval requirements for this kind of memory task. An intriguing characteristic of most prospective memory tasks (i.e., at least tasks in which we do not use special external cues like alarms to remind us that we are supposed to do something) is that they require us to "remember to remember." That is, unlike most laboratory tests of retrospective memory (e.g., recognition, cued recall, free recall) in which there is some kind of external cue that prompts or initiates a directed search of memory (e.g., an experimenter tells you to begin to recall), prospective remembering requires that the prospective memory interrupt our train of thought, ongoing activities, and routine reactions to events. For example, remembering to give a message to a friend requires that we notice our friend as a cue for a message (without an external prompt to do so) and not just as someone with whom to have a conversation, or remembering to turn off the garden sprinkler in an hour requires that we recognize the passage of an hour as a cue for an action. Often, prospective memories seem introspectively to pop into memory and appear there spontaneously without direct attempts to interrogate memory. Using Ste-Marie and Jacoby's (1993) terminology, prospective memories typically involve spontaneous remembering whereas most laboratory retrospective memory tasks seem to rely on directed remembering.

In addition to conceptualizing prospective memory tasks as high in spontaneous remembering, Craik's (1986) analysis led us to view prospective memory tasks as high in self-initiated retrieval (i.e., tasks that provide subjects with little external support for cueing retrieval), perhaps even more so than retrospective memory tasks that are high in self-initiated retrieval (e.g., free recall). Again, this is because prospective memory tasks require that we "remember to remember" on our own. This self-initiated component seemed to us to be basic to prospective memory tasks, and we initially examined this idea by testing younger and older subjects on a laboratory-based test of prospective memory. The rationale for varying age followed directly from Craik's (1986) theory that aging disrupts self-initiated retrieval processes and, thus, we expected to see especially large age-related deficits on a prospective memory task.

Our paradigm required subjects to remember to perform an action in the future while they were busily involved in an ongoing activity, and this seemed to us to capture the features of at least some real-life prospective memory situations. Specifically, we (Einstein & McDaniel, 1990) involved younger and older subjects in a short-term memory task, where on each trial subjects were presented with a set of up to nine words and then asked to recall those words. The prospective memory task was embedded within this task, as we asked subjects to press a designated key on the computer keyboard whenever a particular word occurred (we called this the *target item*). Three of these target items occurred across the 42 trials. To our surprise, we found no age differences on this prospective memory task. Several aspects of this research are worth noting. First, although others have found age differences in prospective memory (Maylor, 1996), this has been a very reliable result in our laboratory as we have failed to find age differences with this experimental procedure in three separate experiments. Second, our failure to find age differences in prospective memory contrasted with our finding of reliable age differences on free recall and recognition tests. Third, our failure to find age differences was not the result of using an insensitive laboratory procedure for measuring prospective memory, because prospective memory performance did vary as a function of other manipulated variables (such as the availability of external aids and the nature of the target event).

EVENT-BASED AND TIME-BASED PROSPECTIVE MEMORY

Until this point, our assumption was that all prospective memory tasks shared the common feature of being high in self-initiated retrieval and, thus, that all should show large age-related deficits. To paraphrase Gertrude Stein and to slightly alter her meaning, our initial thinking was that "a prospective memory task is a prospective memory task is a prospective memory task." On reflection, it seemed more reasonable to assume instead that prospective memory tasks, like retrospective memory tasks, vary in the degree to which they require self-initiated retrieval. In particular, some prospective memory tasks require that an action be performed when an external cue occurs (e.g., remembering to give a message to a friend or remembering to take a pill with dinner), and we have labeled these *event-based prospective memory tasks* (Einstein & McDaniel, 1990; in press; Einstein, McDaniel, Richardson, Guynn, & Cunfer, 1995; McDaniel & Einstein, 1992). Other prospective memory tasks require that an action be performed at a certain time or after a specified period of time has elapsed (e.g., remembering to turn off the garden sprinkler in 10 minutes or remembering to go to a meeting at 10:00 A.M.). These two different kinds of prospective memory tasks seem to differ in their retrieval dynamics, with event-based tasks providing subjects with external cues or triggers and therefore being relatively low in self-initiated retrieval. Time-based prospective memory tasks, by comparison, would seem to be relatively high in self-initiated retrieval. It should be noted that although these two tasks seem to differ in the degree of self-initiated retrieval that they require, both kinds of tasks seem to involve spontaneous remembering. That is, in prospective memory tasks that do not involve the use of external aids for cueing a search of memory (like alarms), the occurrence of an event or a time must spontaneously activate the prospective memory.

To the extent that time-based tasks are high in self-initiated retrieval and to the extent that aging disrupts self-initiated retrieval processes, time-based tasks should be more likely to produce age differences. We recently tested this possibility (Einstein et al., 1995, Experiment 1) by comparing the performance of younger and older subjects on a time-based prospective memory task. In this experiment, subjects were presented with a long list of words (one at a time in the center of a computer screen) and told that they would occasionally be stopped and asked to recall the last 10 items that had been presented. In addition, they were told that we had an interest in their ability to remember to do something in the future and that they should try to press a key on the keyboard at 10 minutes and again at 20 minutes (for previous use of time-based tasks, see Ceci & Bronfenbrenner, 1985; Harris & Wilkins, 1982). Subjects were told that they could keep track of time by monitoring a large digital clock that displayed elapsed time. The clock was located behind subjects and this enabled us to record when they monitored the time. In sharp contrast to our previous results with an event-based task, we found that younger subjects were more likely to be on time (i.e., respond within 1 minute of the target time) than were older subjects. Moreover, these age differences were associated with more frequent monitoring of the clock (for younger subjects), and consistent with Harris and Wilkins' (1982) results, monitoring of the clock was highly related to on-time prospective memory responses. Our interpretation of these results is that appropriate monitoring of the clock is essential for good time-based prospective memory performance, and monitoring is a process that is high in self-initiated retrieval (i.e., there are no external cues to prompt remembering). Thus, the poorer performance on a time-based task by older subjects, who are thought to have particular difficulty with self-initiated retrieval, is understandable.

In a recent experiment, conducted by Sarah Richardson at Furman University (Einstein et al., 1995, Experiment 3), we collected additional support for the conclusion that there are fundamental differences between time-based and event-based tasks, with time-based tasks being especially difficult for older subjects. One problem with our prior research is that the evaluation of age effects on time-based and event-based prospective memory tasks involves cross-experimental comparisons. Another problem is that subjects had to look over their shoulders in order to monitor the time. It is possible that this response was more physically inconvenient and demanding for older subjects, and this (rather than problems with self-initiated retrieval) could explain why older subjects monitored the clock less often than did younger subjects. To address these limitations, Richardson varied the type of prospective memory task (event based, time based) as well as age (younger, older) in one experiment. (She also included two middle-age control groups; these are not discussed here except to point out that their results were very similar to those of the younger groups.) Furthermore, care was taken to ensure that the two tasks were comparable (e.g., there were six target events, and these occurred at about the same time in both tasks). Also, the monitoring response was changed so as to not pose physical challenges for any age group (subjects pressed a designated key on the keyboard to display the elapsed time).

The younger (mean age = 20.2) and older subjects (mean age = 66.3) in this experiment were presented with an ongoing question-answering task in which they received a long set of questions testing general knowledge, problem-solving skills, and knowledge of trivia. Subjects in the time-based condition were told to remember to press the designated key on the keyboard every 5 minutes. They were told to try to be on time and that they could keep track of the time by pressing a designated key on the keyboard. Subjects in the event-based condition were asked to press a designated key on the keyboard whenever they encountered a question about a president. There were six questions in which the word *president* occurred and, in order to make this comparable to the time-based task, these questions were programmed to occur approximately every 5 minutes.

Our measure of prospective memory for both conditions was the proportion of times (out of six) that subjects remembered to press the designated key when a target event or target time occurred. In the event-based condition, subjects quickly responded to the occurrence of a target event or not at all. In the time-based condition, we counted a response as on time if it was early by as much as 15 seconds or if it occurred within 60 seconds following the occurrence of the target time. (We counted early responses because it seems that some subjects monitored the clock prior to the target time and then "guessed" the occurrence of the target time, and occasionally this resulted in a response that was a few seconds early.) The analysis of these scores indicated significantly higher performance on the event-based task (mean = .90) than on the time-based task (mean = .62). This result makes sense from our analysis that event-based tasks contain external cues that can support or trigger remembering. Most important, there was a reliable interaction between the age and type of prospective memory task variables. Younger subjects (mean = .72) were more likely than older subjects (mean = .45) to remember to perform an action on time in the time-based condition. In contrast, younger (mean = .93) and older (mean = .86) subjects did not differ in the event-based condition.

To explore the nature of the age differences on the time-based task, we analyzed the number of times subjects monitored the clock as a function of 1-minute periods preceding a target time. Both age groups tended to monitor the clock more often as the target time approached, with greatest monitoring of the clock occurring in the 1-minute period immediately preceding a target time. However, as indicated by a reliable interaction between age and periods, this pattern was particularly pronounced for younger subjects, such that they monitored the clock about three times as often as did older subjects during the last or critical 1-minute period. That monitoring frequency was critical for good prospective memory was suggested by correlational analyses that revealed high positive relationships between the frequency of monitoring and the proportion of on-time responses (for both age groups). Monitoring frequency during the last 1-minute period was especially predictive of on-time responses. Our results suggest that good time-based prospective memory depends on self-initiated thoughts about the prospective memory task (i.e., monitoring the time), and it seems that these kinds of thoughts occur less often in older subjects.

SOME PRELIMINARY IDEAS ABOUT THE ROLE OF TIME PERCEPTION ON TIME-BASED PROSPECTIVE MEMORY

As mentioned earlier, prospective remembering on event-based tasks seems to be cue driven, and there is ample evidence that characteristics of the cue (such as its distinctiveness and familiarity) affect performance (McDaniel & Einstein, 1993). An interesting question concerns what causes us to think about the prospective memory task in the absence of specific triggers or cues—such as on a time-based task. One possibility is that there are indeed external cues, albeit more subtle ones, operating in time-based tasks. For example, in our experiment items in the question-answering task (perhaps some referred to time) and typing on the keyboard (a response that is similar to the prospective memory response) could have reminded subjects of the prospective memory task and cued them to monitor the clock. Some evidence for this kind of reminding comes from Harris and Wilkins' (1982) subjects who reported that certain events in the movie they were watching (e.g., the visual presence of a clock) triggered thoughts of the prospective memory task. By this view, the poorer performance of older subjects on a time-based task could be the result of decreased sensitivity to incidental details that could potentially cue reminding on a prospective memory task. In the same vein, younger subjects may do a better job of planning or anticipating the retrieval context (i.e., creating associations between the questions answering task and the prospective memory task) such that the question-answering task was more likely to remind subjects of the prospective memory task.

Another possibility is that monitoring of the clock and thinking about the prospective memory task is accomplished through processes that rely on the ability to accurately perceive time. Accurate time perception would have direct implications for monitoring if, for example, we "set" an internal timer to initiate monitoring at certain intervals or if we periodically conduct a subjective evaluation of the amount of time elapsed in order to determine whether or not it is necessary to monitor or check a clock.

Recently, Craik and Hay (1994) presented data suggesting that aging disrupts time perception. Younger and older subjects in their experiment performed a visual information-processing task and were asked either to estimate the amount of time that had elapsed or to signal the experimenter when a specified amount of time had elapsed. Both procedures yielded the result that older subjects underestimated time more so than did younger subjects (e.g., older subjects were more likely to perceive a 100-second elapsed interval as having taken 60 seconds). In other words, for older subjects objective time passed by more quickly than subjective time, and this pattern of results has the potential to explain the age-related decrements on a time-based prospective memory task.

It is interesting to consider the mechanisms by which subjects judge time, and how aging affects these mechanisms. One basis for judging time may be an internal biological clock that may function like an internal pacemaker or timer (Coren, Ward, & Enns, 1994). Data showing that variables that affect our physiology (e.g., illness, temperature, stimulants, and depressants) also affect time perception (Coren et al., 1994) are consistent with this theory of time perception. One interpretation, then, of age differences in time perception is that aging "slows down" the biological clock, causing objective time to proceed more quickly than perceived time.

A very different basis for judging time involves using a cognitive clock. Rather than consulting a timer, perhaps we estimate elapsed time on the basis of the events that have occurred over a period of time. This view predicts that the number and nature of the intervening activities should influence the passage of time (see Boltz, 1994, for evidence of this sort). For instance, we (and our students also) understand that the perceived duration of time depends on the nature of our activities. One implication of this perspective is that the perception of time should be closely connected to memory for those events. Interestingly, in many situations that involve judging time we have no external cues to remind us of the activities that occurred. Thus, like time-based prospective memory tasks, time perception may be an activity that is high in self-initiated retrieval and therefore an activity that is especially difficult for older subjects. The specific prediction is that subjects who have difficulty with self-initiated retrieval should underestimate time (i.e., because they cannot remember the intervening events, they estimate a shorter amount of time to have passed than objectively occurred). Such a finding would be consistent with Craik and Hay's (1994) time perception results as well as our results with a time-based prospective memory task.

A recent experiment by Julie Holliday (at Furman University) provides some support for the view that subjects use a cognitive clock to estimate time. In this study, we asked 10 younger and 11 older subjects to perform simple math problems on a sheet of paper and at the same time to estimate the duration of three different time intervals (15, 30, and 60 seconds). Subjects were told to work as quickly as possible on the math problems, and during this task they were interrupted three times and asked to estimate how long they had been working on the problems since the last interruption. (On the first trial, they were asked to estimate the time that had passed since the start of the task.) The critical difference between this study and that of Craik and Hay (1994) is that a record of the intervening events was available to subjects on their worksheet (i.e., the problems that had been solved over the interval). Thus, in our study, subjects had external cues to remind them of what had occurred over the interval. If subjects were using a biological clock to judge time, then the availability of retrieval cues should have no effect and, like Craik and Hay, we should find that older subjects underestimated the time intervals more so than younger subjects. On the other hand, if subjects were using a cognitive clock and were estimating time on the basis of their memory of the elapsed time, then the availability of cues should reduce the degree of underestimation that was observed by Craik and Hay, and this should be particularly so for older subjects.

Our results were consistent with this latter expectation. On average, younger subjects estimated the 15-, 30-, and 60-second periods as taking 18.5, 28.0, and 48.5 seconds, respectively. Thus, younger subjects tended to be accurate although they underestimated the 60-second interval. Contrary to Craik and Hay's results, our older subjects overestimated time, in some cases estimating twice as much time to have passed as did younger subjects. Their estimates for the 15-, 30-, and 60-second periods were 36.8, 60.0, and 86.8 seconds. These differences between younger and older subjects were highly reliable ($p < .01$). Thus, the availability of external cues (for the events that have passed) seems to change the pattern of time perception results for older subjects. In fact, with cues older subjects appear to overestimate time, possibly because they have difficulties remembering the number of interruptions that have occurred and/or exactly where the last interruption took place.

Obviously, these interpretations should be accepted with caution. There were many differences between our procedures and those of Craik and Hay (1994) other than the availability of external cues, and further research is needed to isolate the cause of the different patterns of time estimations for younger and older subjects. Very little research has examined the effects of aging on time perception, and our results suggest that memory problems that tend to occur with old age may have important implications for time perception and possibly also for time-based prospective memory performance. We turn now to other data suggesting basic differences between time-based and event-based prospective memory tasks.

THE NEUROPSYCHOLOGY OF PROSPECTIVE MEMORY

Given the interest in cognitive neuropsychology in the contemporary literature, a natural avenue for extending current prospective memory research is to investigate the neuropsychological basis of prospective memory. Aside from the inherent interest in this topic, a neuropsychological approach may prove to be invaluable for legislating some fundamental issues in prospective memory. For example, central to the concerns of this chapter is the issue of whether or not different processes underlie time-based and event-based prospective memory. Although age-related decrements obtain with time-based but not with event-based prospective memory, it remains unclear if this age-based dissociation implies that time-based and event-based prospective memory encompass fundamentally different subprocesses. It could be, for example, that the different age-related effects are due to variations in difficulty across the two types of tasks (cf. Einstein, Holland, McDaniel, & Guynn, 1992). Neuropsychological study of time-based and event-based prospective memory could help illuminate the degree to which those two types of prospective memory tasks are mediated by different processes. In this section, we present a preliminary study that illustrates this approach.

There are at least two theoretical positions that can be developed regarding the neuropsychological systems that subserve time- and event-based prospective memory. One popular assumption is that prospective memory is a frontally mediated process. This notion is based on the observation that the frontal system is important for processes that seem to be intimately involved in prospective memory such as strategic planning, monitoring of plans, and execution of plans. On this view, event-based and time-based prospective memory should both decline with disruption in frontal functioning. A second approach would be to suggest that time-based prospective memory is primarily frontal, whereas event-based prospective memory is subserved by some other system—perhaps medial–temporal. The basis for this suggestion rests on the notion that the frontal lobes appear to be especially vulnerable to the aging process (Moscovitch & Winocur, 1992), and the finding that the time-based task is the prospective memory situation that displays the aging deficits. Furthermore, as described earlier in the chapter, successful time-based prospective memory is dependent on strategic and planful monitoring of a clock—putative frontal processes. In contrast, event-based prospective memory tasks seem to be more cue based—more like cued recall or recognition, processes typically thought to be subserved by medial–temporal cortical structures (Moscovitch & Winocur, 1992).

To explore these possibilities, we (McDaniel, Glisky, Routhieaux, & Remers, 1994) tested older adults (average age of 73) who varied in terms of their frontal lobe functioning. From approximately 50 older adults we gathered scores on five measures that are typically used to assess frontal lobe functioning [Wisconsin Card Sorting Task, verbal fluency, arithmetic from the WAIS-R, and digits backwards and mental control from the Weschler Memory Scale (Revised)]. From the group of 50, we selected 32 subjects, 16 of whom scored below the mean on a composite of the five measures (mean z-score = −.61) and 16 of whom scored above the mean (mean z-score = .52). These two groups were essentially equivalent on other subject characteristics (e.g., mean age was 72.8 and 73.8, mean years of education were 14.8 and 16.4, and mean score on the Mini-Mental State Exam was 28.3 and 28.9, for low and high frontal subjects, respectively). Subjects were given both event-based and time-based prospective memory tasks, and the experiment was modeled after the questioning-answering task used by Richardson. For the time-based prospective memory task, subjects were asked to press a key on the keyboard (F8) every 5 minutes. For the event-based task, subjects were asked to press a key every time they saw a question that contained a particular word (such as *president*). The main differences between this experiment and the Richardson experiment were that the task was longer, and there were eight trials for each type of task.

The proportions of successful prospective memory responses were analyzed as a function of type of prospective memory task and frontal status. Similar to the Richardson's study, a successful response (for both types of prospective memory tasks) was defined as any response made within a minute of the target event or time. Low-frontal subjects performed significantly worse on event-based prospective memory than did high-frontal subjects (means = .48 and .77, respectively). In contrast, there was a small and nonsignificant difference between the groups on time-based prospective memory (means = .35 and .43 for low- and high-frontal subjects, respectively). It is not the case that the low-frontal subjects were simply worse on the more difficult task, because in line with other findings in our laboratory (described earlier in this chapter), performance was significantly worse on time-based prospective memory than on event-based prospective memory.

Perhaps it is the case that the composite measure used to segregate subjects did not, in fact, produce groups representative of high- and low-frontal functioning. This appears not to have happened; the low frontals performed less well on a source-memory test but not on an item-memory test than did the high frontals.

How then might we interpret the present results? They are not consistent with either of the two frameworks presented at the outset. A very tentative possibility might be based on the suggestion that orbitofrontal structures may be heavily involved in planning. On the other hand, dorsolateral frontal structures are typically viewed as being involved in monitoring external events (e.g., responsible for recency and source judgements). Given that time-based prospective memory seems to require more self-generated planning—one has to plan to check the clock and self-initiate the checking behaviors—perhaps time-based prospective memory could be an orbitofrontal process. For execution of an event-based prospective memory, some have suggested that at some level the system is set to monitor for the environmental event that signals the appropriateness of the intended action (cf. Shallice & Burgess, 1991). Thus, event-based prospective memory may require more involvement of the dorsolateral frontal system.

This view is clearly quite speculative and bears more direct testing. Generally, however, this work demonstrates the potential fruitfulness of exploring the neuropsychology of prospective memory. The results support the value of dividing prospective memory into event- and time-based prospective memory, and further delineates a subgroup of older adults (based on neuropsychological assessment) for which certain classes of prospective memory tasks may be problematic.

EPILOGUE

Perhaps the main reason that our research is of interest to a volume devoted to the practical aspects of memory is that we are studying a kind of memory that exists in the real world and has heretofore received very little attention. Our bias has been to study it in the laboratory, where greater control over variables is possible. By involving subjects in an engaging ongoing task and asking them to perform an action in the future, we think that we have captured a basic component of real-world prospective memory tasks in the laboratory. Moreover, we (McDaniel & Einstein, 1992) have shown that performance on this kind of laboratory task is correlated with performance on a more natural task.

Our results strongly suggest that there are basic differences between time-based and event-based prospective memory tasks. We found no age differences on an event-based task, whereas we found age differences on a time-based task. Moreover, our preliminary neuropsychological work showed that frontal lobe functioning (as assessed by neuropsychological testing) was associated with performance on an event-based but not time-based task. Although both kinds of tasks seem to rely on spontaneous remembering processes, they seem to differ in the extent to which they are cued by external events. In an event-based task, there is an external cue that is associated with the to-be-remembered action (remembering to give a message is potentially cued by the event of encountering the person for whom the message is intended). Accordingly, we assume that an event-based prospective memory task provides the rememberer with a good deal of environmental support. This is not the case with a time-based task, where the passage of time or the occurrence of a particular time is what determines whether or not it is appropriate to perform an action. Our analysis is that this kind of task is more dependent on self-initiated retrieval, because it requires subjects to be sensitive to less direct or more peripheral cues and/or to monitor the time at appropriate intervals. Indeed, there are some intriguing suggestions that performance on this type of task may be related to the ability to perceive time.

The availability of external cues in event-based prospective memory tasks generally suggests that memory performance should be higher on event-based tasks relative to time-based tasks, and this has practical applications. (Although this should usually be the case, it is possible to imagine situations in which the prospective memory cue for an event-based task occurs rapidly, is disguised in some fashion, or not noticed for some reason and therefore could produce poorer prospective memory performance.) Specifically, it seems that one reasonable way to improve prospective memory is to recon-ceptualize a time-based prospective memory task into an event-based one. For example, if our task is to take a pill at 7:00 P.M. (a time-based task), there should be advantages to connecting this action with a salient external cue that occurs around that time. For instance, we could reconceptualize the task as taking a pill with dinner or taking the pill while watching the evening news (an event-based task). That this kind of strategy should im-prove prospective memory is suggested not only by our results, but more directly by Maylor's (1990) data collected in a natural setting. She showed that subjects who use this conversion kind of strategy were more likely to remember to telephone the experimenter on time than subjects who did not. It should be noted, however, that Maylor did not directly vary this instruction, and it is possible that subjects who used this kind of strategy were more capable in other ways as well. We think Maylor's naturalistic research and our laboratory research complement each other and together provide more compelling evidence for the mnemonic benefits of this kind of prospective memory strategy than either research result alone.

In closing, we acknowledge that a potential problem in conducting labo-ratory research is that one can distort the nature of the laboratory task so that it does not reflect the important components of that process in the real world. We have engaged in certain biases in designing our laboratory procedures, and we recognize that our tasks capture only some characteristics of real-world prospective memory tasks. For example, in general our tasks involve very little planning and are not integrated into one's life space and habitual activities. In principle, however, we believe that the present limitations in prospective memory research do not signal an inescapable problem with using laboratory approaches to studying prospective memory, but rather they underscore the nascent character of prospective memory research. In the future, we need to be especially creative in designing laboratory tasks that capture more characteristics of real-world prospective memory tasks.

ACKNOWLEDGMENT

The writing of this chapter was supported by National Institute on Aging Grant No. AG08436 to the authors.

REFERENCES

Boltz, M. G. (1994). Changes in internal tempo and effects on the learning and remembering of event durations. *Journal of Experimental Psychology: Learning, Memory, and Cognition, 20*, 1154–1171.

Camp, C. J., Foss, J. W., Stevens, A. B., & O'Hanlon, A. M. (1996). Improving prospective memory performance in persons with Alzheimer's disease. In M. Brandimonte, G. O. Einstein, & M. A. McDaniel (Eds.), *Prospective memory: Theory and applications* (pp. 351–368). Mahwah, NJ: Lawrence Erlbaum Associates.

Ceci, S. J., & Bronfenbrenner, U. (1985). "Don't forget to take the cupcakes out of the oven": Prospective memory, strategic time-monitoring, and context. *Child Development, 56*, 152–164.

Cohen, J. D., & O'Reilly, R. C. (1996). A preliminary theory of the interactions between prefrontal cortex and hippocampus that contribute to planning and prospective memory. In M. Brandimonte, G. O. Einstein, & M. A. McDaniel (Eds.), *Prospective memory: Theory and applications* (pp. 267–295). Mahwah, NJ: Lawrence Erlbaum Associates.

Coren, S., Ward, L. M., & Enns, J. T. (1994). *Sensation and perception* (4th ed.). Orlando, FL: Harcourt Brace.

Craik, F. I. M. (1986). A functional account of age differences in memory. In F. Klix & H. Hagendorf (Eds.), *Human memory and cognitive capabilities: Mechanisms and performances* (pp. 409–422). North Holland, Amsterdam: Elsevier.

Craik, F. I. M., & Hay, J. F. (1994, April). *The effects of aging and task demands on subjective time judgments.* Paper presented at the 1994 meeting of the Cognitive Aging Conference, Atlanta, GA.

Einstein, G. O., Holland, L. J., McDaniel, M. A., & Guynn, M. J. (1992). Age related deficits in prospective memory: The influence of task complexity. *Psychology and Aging, 7*, 471–478.

Einstein, G. O., & McDaniel, M. A. (1990). Normal aging and prospective memory. *Journal of Experimental Psychology: Learning, Memory, and Cognition, 16*, 717–726.

Einstein, G. O., & McDaniel, M. A. (1996). Retrieval processes in prospective memory: Theoretical approaches and some new empirical findings. In M. Brandimonte, G. O. Einstein, & M. A. McDaniel (Eds.), *Prospective memory: Theory and applications* (pp. 115–141). Mahwah, NJ: Lawrence Erlbaum Associates.

Einstein, G. O., McDaniel, M. A., Richardson, S. L., Guynn, M. J., & Cunfer, A. R. (1995). Aging and prospective memory: Examining the influences of self-initiated retrieval. *Journal of Experimental Psychology: Learning, Memory, and Cognition, 21*, 996–1007.

Ellis, J. A. (1996). Prospective memory or the realization of delayed intentions: A conceptual framework for research. In M. Brandimonte, G. O. Einstein, & M. A. McDaniel (Eds.), *Prospective memory: Theory and applications* (pp. 1–22). Mahwah, NJ: Lawrence Erlbaum Associates.

Goschke, T., & Kuhl, J. (1993). Representation of intentions: Persisting activation in memory. *Journal of Experimental Psychology: Learning, Memory, and Cognition, 19*, 1211–1226.

Goschke, T., & Kuhl, J. (1996). Remembering what to do: Explicit and implicit memory for intentions. In M. Brandimonte, G. O. Einstein, & M. A. McDaniel (Eds.), *Prospective memory: Theory and applications* (pp. 53–91). Mahwah, NJ: Lawrence Erlbaum Associates.

Harris, J. E. (1984). Remembering to do things: A forgotten topic. In J. E. Harris & P. E. Morris (Eds.), *Everyday memory, actions, and absent-mindedness* (pp. 71–92). New York: Academic Press.

Harris, J. E., & Wilkins, A. J. (1982). Remembering to do things: A theoretical framework and an illustrative experiment. *Human Learning, 1*, 123–136.

Jacoby, L. L., & Kelley, C. (1991). Unconscious influences of memory: Dissociations and automaticity. In A. D. Milner & M. D. Rugg (Eds.), *The neuropsychology of consciousness* (pp. 201–233). Boston: Academic Press.

Kvavilashvili, L., & Ellis, J. (1996). Varieties of intention: Some classifications and distinctions. In M. Brandimonte, G. O. Einstein, & M. A. McDaniel (Eds.), *Prospective memory: Theory and applications* (pp. 23–51). Mahwah, NJ: Lawrence Erlbaum Associates.

Mantyla, T. (1993). Priming effects in prospective memory. *Memory, 1*, 203–218.

Mantyla, T. (1996). Activating actions and interrupting intentions: Mechanisms of retrieval sensitization in prospective memory. In M. Brandimonte, G. O. Einstein, & M. A. McDaniel (Eds.), *Prospective memory: Theory and applications* (pp. 93–113). Mahwah, NJ: Lawrence Erlbaum Associates.

Maylor, E. A. (1990). Age and prospective memory. *The Quarterly Journal of Experimental Psychology, 42A*, 471–493.

Maylor, E. A. (1996). Does prospective memory decline with age? In M. Brandimonte, G. O. Einstein, & M. A. McDaniel (Eds.), *Prospective memory: Theory and applications* (pp. 173–197). Mahwah, NJ: Lawrence Erlbaum Associates.

Maylor, E. A. (in press). Age-related impairment in an event-based prospective memory task. *Psychology and Aging.*

McDaniel, M. A., & Einstein, G. O. (1992). Aging and prospective memory: Basic findings and practical applications. In T. E. Scruggs & M. A. Mastropieri (Eds.), *Advances in learning and behavioral disabilities* (Vol. 8, pp. 87–105). Greenwich, CT: JAI Press.

McDaniel, M. A., & Einstein, G. O. (1993). The importance of cue familiarity and cue distinctiveness in prospective memory. *Memory, 1*, 23–41.

McDaniel, M. A., Glisky, E. L., Routhieaux, B. C., & Remers, L. A. (1994, April). *The role of frontal lobe functioning in temporally-based and cue-based prospective remembering in older adults.* Paper presented at the Cognitive Aging Conference, Atlanta, GA.

Moscovitch, M., & Winocur, G. (1992). The neuropsychology of memory and aging. In F. I. M. Craik & T. A. Salthouse (Eds.), *The handbook of aging and cognition* (pp. 315–372). Hillsdale, NJ: Lawrence Erlbaum Associates.

Park, D. C. (1992). Applied cognitive aging research. In F. I. M. Craik & T. A. Salthouse (Eds.), *The handbook of aging and cognition* (pp. 51–110). Hillsdale, NJ: Lawrence Erlbaum Associates.

Shallice, T., & Burgess, P. W. (1991). Deficits in strategy application following frontal lobe damage in man. *Brain, 114,* 727–741.

Ste-Marie, D. M., & Jacoby, L. L. (1993). Spontaneous versus directed recognition: The relativity of automaticity. *Journal of Experimental Psychology: Learning, Memory, and Cognition, 19,* 777–788.

Vortac, O. U., Edwards, M. B., & Manning, C. A. (1995). *Functions of external cues in prospective memory.* Unpublished manuscript.

CHAPTER SEVEN

Remembering to Take Medications: The Importance of Nonmemory Variables

Denise C. Park
Christopher B. Mayhorn
The University of Georgia

An everyday behavior that is frequently cited as an example of a practical memory problem is remembering to take medication correctly (Wilkins & Baddeley, 1988). The term *medication adherence* is typically used to describe accurate use of medication, that is, taking the appropriate number of doses at the right time in the amount prescribed by a physician (Park, 1992). Despite the interest taken by memory researchers in medication adherence, the majority of literature on the topic reflects a biomedical and psychosocial framework, with relatively little attention explicitly paid to the cognitive aspects of the behavior. Within the biomedical domain, the relationship of variables such as illness severity, nature of symptoms, side effects associated with medications, number of pills prescribed, and demographic variables to medication adherence have been examined (Hulka, 1979; Rowe, Ahronheim, & Lawton, 1992). An even broader range of psychosocial variables have been hypothesized to affect adherence (Park, 1994), including the role of patient beliefs about illness and medications (Becker, 1989), the effects of social support (Ferguson & Bole, 1979), doctor–patient relationships (Geertsen, Gray, & Ward, 1973), and coping style (Folkman, Bernstein, & Lazarus, 1987). Within the cognitive domain, Park and Kidder (in press) reviewed and analyzed the cognitive components of medication adherence in detail, particularly the relationship of working memory and long-term memory variables to the prospective aspects of medication adherence.

The fact that such a broad range of perspectives that span so many areas of psychology as well as medicine have been used to study medication adherence points to the complexity of the behavior. It is important for memory researchers to recognize that a practical memory behavior such as medication adherence is embedded in a complex context that extends well beyond variables typically studied within a cognitive framework. Keeping these points in mind, the goal of this chapter is to provide an overview of how belief systems and the psychosocial environment associated with illness may interact with and moderate the role of memory variables in the study of medication adherence. This is followed by a discussion of how age variables impact on each domain and the relationship of age to nonadherence. The hope is that this approach will result in a more integrated, comprehensive approach to the important research problem of how beliefs, illness, and cognitive function interact to affect the way adults use their medications. Additionally, the approach taken here may provide a prototype for cognitive researchers to consider and analyze the complexity of other practical memory problems in their research paradigms. There needs to be more emphasis within the domain of practical memory on recognizing and studying non-memory variables in conjunction with the more traditional cognitive variables in order to gain a complete understanding of the behavior in question, a point elaborated by Hertzog and Dunlosky (in press).

THE ILLNESS REPRESENTATION

In order to assess the effects of cognitive variables on medication adherence such as regimen complexity, working memory function, and cognitive supports, it is essential first to determine an individual's intentions to adhere to the medication. Leventhal and Cameron (1987) provided a framework for understanding medication adherence that addresses the role of intentions. They proposed that medication adherence should be conceptualized as a self-regulatory behavior employed by the individual to manage his or her illness. They suggested that the individual has an evolving cognitive representation or belief system about his or her illness. Leventhal, Leventhal, and Schaefer (1992) suggested that dimensions that are particularly salient with respect to an illness representation include the disease label, perception of the time course of the disorder, causes of the illness, seriousness, and controllability. There are a range of questionnaire instruments available to measure these perceptions of illness (see review by Park, 1994). It is easy to see how an illness representation could drive adherence behavior. An individual with hypertension might correctly believe that the disorder is serious, highly controllable with medication, and has a long-term disease course. Such an individual would likely be more adherent than an individual who concludes that because they are asymptomatic, this disorder is not a problem. In the former case, nonadherence could very well be driven by cognitive variables.

That is, such an individual has an illness representation congruent with adherence, but doesn't understand when to take the medication or can't remember to do so. In the second case, the nonadherence would be driven by the illness representation, not by cognitive failure, so that studying the role of memory strategies and cues as the basis for nonadherence in this case would not make sense.

In addition to measuring illness beliefs, it may also be important to measure beliefs about specific medications. For example, an individual who recovers from a strep infection within 48 hours of beginning the medication may, because he or she feels better, elect to discontinue the medication. The individual perceives that there is no illness and that the medication itself serves no purpose. Again, the failure to adhere in this instance would not be a result of an inability to comprehend instructions or of prospective failure, but rather would relate to the individual's representation that he or she is not ill and no longer needs the medication. Similarly, individuals who receive a medication that doesn't have a therapeutic effect for several weeks (common with rheumatoid arthritis, depression, and other disorders) might conclude that, because they continue to be symptomatic, the medication is useless and thus discontinue it. These examples illustrate why it is important when studying medication adherence within a practical memory framework to measure not only an illness representation, but a medication representation. It is important to ascertain that an individual's illness and medication representation is consistent with medication adherence before attempting to determine, for example, the role of forgetting and memory aids in medication adherence.

Another important point for the memory researcher in the Leventhal and Cameron (1987) model is the dynamic nature of the illness representation that may change over the time course of the disease. An individual's illness representation is shaped and modified by feedback, so that an individual's perceptions about a medication will be modified based on experience. Thus, if an individual believes that sustained usage of a medication has resulted in undesirable side effects, the individual may experience a lowered desire to adhere. He or she may consciously attempt to get by with lesser amounts of medication, even though the individual believes the medication to be effective, in an effort to modify the side effects. It can be important to measure changes in illness representations, particularly as it relates to beliefs about medication, in attempting to understand the role of cognition in medication adherence.

Finally, it is important to mention that to the extent that an individual has multiple disorders, they will have multiple illness representations (Park & Kidder, in press). The individual with diabetes and hay fever likely has very different cognitions attached to these two disorders. The existence of multiple illness representations suggests that medication adherence may not be a global behavior and that individuals who are highly adherent with respect to one medication may not be particularly adherent on another. This within-subject variability in adherence with respect to different medications has been documented and termed *selective nonadherence* (Park, Morrell, Lautenschlager, & Firth, 1993; Park, Willis, Morrow, Diehl, & Gaines, 1994). It is important to recognize that adherence behaviors may be medication and/or illness specific within an individual, and that measurement of adherence behaviors of a single medication may not provide a good estimate of overall adherence behavior with respect to an entire regimen.

MOTIVATION TO TAKE MEDICATIONS

As part of an illness representation, it is important to assess how seriously ill an individual perceives himself- or herself to be, how much the disorder interferes with everyday life, as well as how useful medications are perceived to be in controlling the disorder. Individuals who have an illness representation that suggests they perceive their disorder to interfere substantially with everyday life but that they believe medications are very effective in controlling the disorder could be characterized as being highly motivated to adhere. There is clear evidence from the memory literature that the perceived importance of remembering a prospective event actually contributes to the probability that the task will be performed. Meacham and Kushner (1980), for example, found that college students reported forgetting to perform more tasks that they rated as unimportant compared to important tasks. Similarly, Meacham and Singer (1977) reported that when students received an incentive for remembering to mail a series of postcards, remembering to do so was facilitated.

It seems likely that a prospective task that is important is more likely to be performed, because musings about it are more likely to enter working memory and the individual will then enter what Harris and Wilkins (1982) called the Test–Wait; Test–Exit (TWTE) cycle of prospective memory. That is, when thoughts about a prospective task become activated in working memory, an individual will test or check whether it is time to perform the task (e.g., take medication for the illness about which they are seriously concerned), and either execute the task (and thus complete the TWTE cycle) or determine that one must wait and plan to reenter the TWTE cycle in the future because it is not the right time to perform the prospective task.

At present, there is not a substantial literature relating motivational factors associated with illness to adherence. A high perceived severity of illness might cause a high level of motivation with respect to illness behaviors and could affect adherence in several ways. First, the recognition that one has a serious illness would make it likely that one would have an illness representation consonant with a strong intention to adhere. As Meacham and Singer (1977) demonstrated, a strong incentive to perform a prospective act enhances the probability the act will be performed. Second, a perception of a serious illness would also likely be a constant source of anxiety and concern to an individual, resulting in frequent musing about the illness. The considerable musing or anxiety about the illness could serve as cues or reminders for adherence. Finally, as Park and Kidder (in press) noted, many serious illnesses result in pain, discomfort, and other physiological cues. The physiological cues themselves could act as contextual reminders to enter Harris and Wilkins' TWTE sequence, resulting in a high rate of adherence. Thus, motivational issues as they relate to adherence are complex. A high level of anxiety or a high degree of salience of the illness could not only result in a motivated illness representation with respect to adherence, but may actually serve as a cognitive prosthesis to aid remembering to perform actions associated with mitigating the illness.

The literature on illness severity and adherence is not entirely supportive of this perspective, however. Hulka (1979) reported that disease severity did not appear to be related to adherence measures for diabetics, and a similar finding was reported by Ferguson and Bole (1979) and Lee and Tan (1979) for arthritics. Such findings are counterintuitive to a self-regulatory model of adherence as well as the view of symptoms as contextual cues for prospective remembering. What is lacking, however, from these studies is a measure of patient beliefs about the severity of their illness and their perceptions that medications would effectively mitigate troubling symptoms or effect a cure. Objective measures of illness severity may not predict adherence because motivational effects will occur only if the patient perceives him- or herself to be ill. Moreover, perceived severity likely interacts with perceived efficacy of a medication. Both high perceived illness severity and medication efficacy would predict a high level of motivation, which would mediate good adherence. Finally, no studies have addressed the amount of time patients spend thinking about their illness, or whether internal cues such as pain serve as reminders to take medication.

Although there is no direct evidence on motivation and activation of musing about illness with respect to adherence, there is some limited evidence on adherence to treatment regimens in cancer patients, individuals who likely are strongly motivated regarding their illness, given its serious nature. It is likely that patients with cancer perceive themselves to be seriously ill, muse about their illness, and recognize that adherence with a chemotherapy regimen is an important treatment available to them. The data generally suggest that adherence to chemotherapy is quite high, at least for women with breast cancer, with observed rates of appointment keeping ranging from 92% (Taylor, Lichtman, & Wood, 1984) to 100% (Carey et al., 1979). Berger, Braverman, Sohn, and Morrow (1988) reported a similar finding for women of low socioeconomic status, although length of treatment did predict declining adherence rates.

There is one disturbing finding on this topic, however. Lebovits et al. (1990) studied adherence in breast cancer patients to self-administered chemotherapy. Nonadherence rates in this situation were estimated to be 43%, although the researchers relied on verbal reports of nonadherence as estimates. Demographic variables such as income and treatment setting predicted nonadherence. The framework proposed in this chapter would suggest that these variables might be markers for different illness representations or that the poor adherence could be a result of cognitive variables, such as not comprehending the regimen or forgetting to take the medications at the appointed time. It seems likely that when failures occur in a situation where the individual is highly motivated, they may be due to cognition. The role of side effects experienced from the therapy also needs to be taken into account, as this likely is a very important factor in understanding adherence to a chemotherapy regimen. Given the lower cost associated with self-administration of chemotherapy combined with the potential of chemotherapy to extend life, it is of critical importance to better understand the factors that place individuals at risk of nonadherence in a situation where motivation levels and perceived efficacy should be very high. The present discussion provides few answers but does clarify the complexity of the issues, particularly the entwinement of motivational factors with memory factors in understanding adherence to medications and treatments.

ADHERENCE AND THE EXTERNAL ENVIRONMENT

Thus far we have focused on the role of internal factors such as belief systems, illness cues, and anxiety about illness as variables that are related to medication adherence. Let us now direct attention to external contextual factors that can play an important role in adherence behaviors. The two of most interest are social support and personal engagement. Most cognitive psychologists would not view social support as an important aspect of cognitive functioning in everyday life. Nevertheless, research participants who come to our laboratory consistently report to us that one way that they manage their medication schedule is that their spouses remind them when it is time to take medication. This is a good informal example of collaborative cognition, with social support playing the role of a cognitive prosthesis for the taking of medication. This aspect of medication adherence has not received much investigation in the literature, although Schwartz, Wand, Zeitz, and Goss (1962) reported that more medication errors were made by elderly individuals who were living alone, and Doherty, Schrott, Metcalf, and Iasiello-Vailas (1983) found that spousal support was an important aspect of adherence in men following coronary episodes. Formal studies of the role of social support, or lack of it, as an important factor in medication adherence are needed.

Another aspect of the external environment that may play an important role in medication adherence, especially the prospective aspect of it, is the degree to which an individual is personally engaged by his or her daily environment. Let us take, for example, a trial lawyer who has a demanding job that is highly deadline oriented, and who is also a single parent of two children. It is likely that the lawyer's day is not characterized by much of a repetitive routine and that she is continually responding to both expected and unexpected external contextual demands from both the professional and domestic domains. Due to this extremely high degree of contextual engagement, the trial lawyer almost certainly has little working memory available for off-goalpath thoughts and internal musings that might lead to a review of prospective plans. Such an individual would seem to be at much greater risk generally for nonadherence compared to a retired trial lawyer who enjoyed reading and gardening as primary hobbies. This lawyer would have more time to muse and review plans, frequently entering the TWTE sequence proposed by Harris and Wilkins (1982), unlike the more contextually engaged lawyer described earlier. This would result in much better prospective memory and thus adherence.

There is support in the literature for the notion that engagement affects performance on a prospective memory task. Brandimonte and Passolunghi (1994), for example, found that prospective memory was worse during a delay when it was filled with a demanding task compared to an undemanding task. At present, we have developed a questionnaire to determine how contextually engaged or busy individuals are, and in our research will determine if this scale is related to medication adherence behaviors as hypothesized here.

AGING AND MEDICATION ADHERENCE

Although a number of authors have suggested that older adults are more nonadherent than are young adults (Bergman & Wiholm, 1981; Lamy, 1984; Lamy & Kitner, 1971), others have suggested that nonadherence is a bigger problem for the middle aged (Davis, 1966). Leventhal et al. (1992) presented evidence that older adults are, in fact, more adherent than are young adults to most treatments and medications, data that are consonant with findings in our own laboratory. Why would differences in nonadherence rates be expected as a function of age? Older adults may differ from young adults in the manner in which they represent illness, in the likelihood that they live alone, in contextual engagement, as well as in cognitive function. To the extent that these are important components of adherence, we may see differences between young and old in rates of adherence.

Leventhal et al. (1992) considered the possibility that older adults represent illness differently than do young adults. They noted that older adults are less likely to drop out of treatment for hypertension, experience fewer symptoms from chemotherapy, and report less distress associated with specific illnesses when compared to younger adults. They find no evidence of enhanced feelings of vulnerability on the part of older adults. Leventhal, Leventhal, Schaefer, and Easterling (1993), however, found that older adults were more likely to seek treatment more quickly than were younger adults for comparable symptoms. Leventhal et al. (1993) suggested that older adults have an efficient, energy-conserving strategy for coping with worrisome symptoms that minimizes both objective and emotional distress, and that they differ primarily from young in self-regulatory strategies rather than in illness representation. There is little evidence that any aspect of the older adults' illness representation is consistent with a representation that would be characterized by a high rate of nonadherence. Indeed, the Leventhal et al. (1992) perspective as well as data they presented would seem to suggest higher levels of adherence for older adults. Data from our own laboratory generally support this perspective. We found in two different studies (Park, Morrell, Frieske, & Kincaid, 1992; Park et al., 1993) that young-old adults (those roughly between 60 and 75) were the most adherent group of patients of all ages, but also that the oldest-old were the least adherent. In Park et al. (1993), we reported the middle aged to be moderately nonadherent—making more errors than the young-old but fewer than the old-old. We ascribe the high rates of nonadherence in the old-old to cognitive difficulties with the retrospective aspects (working and long-term memory) of memory, such as what time of day medications should be taken and what dosage has been prescribed by the physician, rather than to difficulties in illness representation. Generally, the data available suggest that the illness representation held by older adults should drive higher rather than lower rates of adherence.

With respect to social support and aging, although there is evidence to suggest that perceived level of social support does not decline with age (Antonucci, 1990), there is clear evidence that, with age, the number of individuals living alone increases, particularly for women. Although 23% of Americans live alone, 40% of these households consist of individuals aged 65 or older (Sussman, 1985). The high proportion of older adult women in nursing homes is, to some extent, a result of the limited social support available to very elderly women in our society. Thus, to the extent that the presence of other individuals in the household plays an important role in adherence, reminding the individual to take medications, increased age would be a risk factor for nonadherence. The Park et al. (1992, 1993) findings that the very old are most nonadherent is consonant with a social support hypothesis. With respect to social and professional engagement, it seems likely that older persons, as a group, are much more likely to be out of the work force, to have minimal child-rearing duties, and, in general, have more leisure time available to them. As discussed earlier, this leisure time may provide them with more opportunity to focus on prospective plans and thus should be associated with higher rates of adherence relative to a middle-aged group.

To summarize, there is little evidence to suggest that older adults have fundamentally different illness representations than do young adults, but they may adopt strategies designed to minimize distress associated with illness, and they likely have more leisure time. These are factors predictive of adherence and data collected in our lab and reported by Leventhal et al. (1993) suggest that young-old adults do indeed have high levels of adherence. The picture is different for very old adults—adults who are more likely to live alone and who may be experiencing significant declines in cognitive function. These adults appear to be the most nonadherent of any group we have studied. This finding suggests decreased levels of cognitive function that is frequently invoked as a cause may be the underlying basis of nonadherence in the very old. We turn now to a discussion of evidence that older adults' adherence behavior is affected by decreased cognitive function relative to young adults.

Age-Related Cognitive Variables in Medication Adherence

Park (1992) and Park and Kidder (in press) discussed the role of age-related changes in cognitive function and its relationship to medication adherence. Park (1992) theorized that important cognitive aspects of medication adherence include comprehension of instructions; integration of information across medications (a working memory function) to develop a daily plan; long-term memory (or preparation of a written record) of the plan; and, finally, remembering to take the medication (a prospective task). Morrell, Park, and Poon (1989) provided evidence that older adults do have more difficulty comprehending and remembering instructions than young adults, suggesting that the memory and comprehension components could impact negatively on adherence in older adults. Working memory and long-term memory decline is well documented in older adults (Salthouse, 1991; Salthouse & Babcock, 1991), although these memory deficits have not been directly linked to medication adherence. We have collected some data that suggests that this is a viable hypothesis, however. Using medication monitors to record medication usage, we found the oldest-old to be most nonadherent. Adherence was significantly better, however, for oldest-old subjects who received organizational charts and medication organizers that provided a daily plan, hour by hour, for taking medications (Park et al., 1992). These aids were designed to support comprehension, working memory, and long-term memory. These findings suggest that cognitive decline in the retrospective aspects of memory (working memory and long-term memory) is a likely source of nonadherence in the very old. It seems likely that the young-old adults have self-regulatory strategies congruent with adherence as well as adequate cognitive function to perform the medication adherence task.

There is a growing body of literature on aids that can be used to support the retrospective aspects of adherence. Morrow, Leirer, Altieri, and Tanke (1991) and Morrow, Leirer, and Andrassy (1993) reported that memory for medication information is better when the information is presented so that it is compatible with older adults' mental model for taking medications. Morrell, Park, and Poon (1990) reported that pictorial labels facilitated memory of medication information for young but not old adults. The failure to find facilitation for the elderly may have been due to the novelty of the manipulation and more work is needed in this area before it is concluded that pictorial information is not an effective modality for presenting medication information for older adults. In general, it seems clear that the retrospective memory component of medication adherence is impaired with age, a point elaborated on by Park and Kidder (in press).

The practical memory literature has tended to define medication adherence as a primarily prospective task, but it is possible that the effects of age are primarily working through poor comprehension and declines in retrospective memory. An older adult taking medication at the wrong time or omitting it completely may not represent prospective failure, but rather represent a poor understanding of or memory for their medication regimen.

Less is actually known about the prospective aspect of medication adherence than the retrospective aspect. Einstein and McDaniel (1990) distinguished between event-based (respond when a certain cue occurs) and time-based (respond at a particular time) prospective memories. They reported age differences only for time-based tasks, although we have observed reliable age differences for event-based tasks when the frequency of cue presentation varied (Park, Hertzog, Morrell, Kidder, & Mayhorn, 1994). Time-based tasks require the subject to consistently monitor when a response is to be made and require substantial self-initiated responding, whereas event-based tasks are contextually supported: Some external event or cue serves as a reminder that a prospective response is to be made. Medication adherence would appear to be a time-based task. Missing a medication could be viewed as a failure to enter the TWTE cycle for prospective memory described by Harris and Wilkins (1982).

However, there is some evidence that the inability to determine if one already performed the prospective act of taking the medication may contribute to nonadherence. Essentially, this aspect of adherence is a reality-monitoring task in which the individual must decide if he or she actually took the medication or merely thought about it. In other words, the individual must decide whether he or she entered the TWTE cycle but decided to take the medication later, or whether the act was actually completed. In a study relevant to this issue, Morse, Simon, and Balson (1993) had health practitioners take three placebos four times a day in an effort to educate them about the issues facing patients taking azidothymidine therapy for human immunodeficiency virus. The health care professionals reported striking problems with reality monitoring. Morse et al. (1993) stated that "the participants reported difficulties remembering whether they had even taken their pills. . . . Although the staff wanted to participate and be compliant, they reported that often, irrespective of efforts to concentrate, they just could not pull from memory a sense of verification that pills had been taken appropriately" (p. 695). The reality-monitoring aspect of adherence is likely most problematic when the context is invariant for taking medication across days. For example, determining whether one took the medication with juice at this breakfast or yesterday's breakfast could become confusing, very much like it is hard to remember exactly where one's car is parked in the lot on any particular day if you always park in the same lot. The work of Hashstroudi, Johnson, and Chrosniak (1990) and of Cohen and Faulkner (1989) suggested that older adults are less effective at reality monitoring in the laboratory than are young adults, so it appears that this aspect of cognition could contribute to nonadherence in the elderly. The reality-monitoring aspect of prospective memory in general and adherence in particular has received little attention and may be fertile grounds for future research.

NEW DIRECTIONS FOR MEDICATION ADHERENCE RESEARCH

It should be clear from the present discussion that medication adherence is a complex cognitive behavior that is embedded in a rich framework of beliefs as well as a social context. Traditional experimental paradigms used to study memory and cognition are likely to miss important factors that contribute to nonadherence, resulting in an inaccurate and in adequate characterization of the psychological dimensions that underlie the behavior. The approach that we have taken in our laboratory has been an individual difference approach that integrates the psychosocial, biomedical, and cognitive approaches to the problem. Our research team includes social psychologist Howard Leventhal; individual difference and cognitive expert Chris Hertzog; two physicians, Elaine Leventhal and Daniel Birchmore; as well as Roger Morrell, a specialist in applied cognitive aging research.

Because of the theoretical importance of illness representation to patterns of adherence, we elected to study adherence within two specific disorders: rheumatoid arthritis and osteoarthritis. These two disorders share some similar symptoms, but the meaning of adherence is very different for each illness. For rheumatoid arthritis, adhering to medication prevents the progression of a serious, systemic, disabling disorder, whereas for osteoarthritis, medications are used solely to control the pain associated with this localized disorder. Medication cannot prevent deterioration of individual joints in osteoarthritis. The self-regulatory model would predict somewhat different models of adherence for these two disorders, assuming that individuals have illness representations consonant with adherence. The use of an individual difference approach combined with structural equation modeling techniques allows us to evaluate the different relationships of multiple constructs to adherence behaviors for each of these disorders. We can simultaneously evaluate the roles of both psychosocial and cognitive variables in predicting adherence behaviors.

The basic paradigm involves collecting a detailed battery of information over two relatively lengthy testing sessions, followed by a one-month monitoring period of adherence, using electronic devices that record date and time information each time an individual removes the lid from his or her medication bottles. The testing battery consists of psychosocial measures that include an assessment of illness representation, medication representation, social support, personal engagement, depression, anxiety, well being, coping strategies for illness, self-efficacy, and bodily awareness and preoccupation. Biomedical and demographic variables measured include illness severity, number of medications, overall health, functional mobility and capabilities, and perceptions. The cognitive battery includes measures of working memory, long-term memory, prospective memory, reasoning vocabulary, and metamemory. Our hypothesis is that adherence behaviors will be mediated by cognitive variables for very old adults, but that psychosocial variables will be more important for younger adults. We expected that the effects of biomedical variables will be mediated through belief systems. We are testing approximately 500 arthritis patients and will have sufficient power to develop separate models for osteoarthritis and rheumatoid arthritis patients, allowing us to gain an understanding of how different factors may be more or less important in predicting adherence for disorders where the objective importance of adherence differs.

Preliminary data (Park, Morrell, et al., 1994) indicate that for an elderly sample of 21 young-old (aged 60 to 74, $M = 68.56$) and 19 old-old (aged 75 and older, $M = 78.02$) osteoarthritis patients, medication representation controlled a substantial amount of variance in adherence behaviors, and that in this relatively small sample, cognitive variables contributed little. In fact, the only cognitive variable significant in any regression equation was metamemory, specifically a subscale that measured the use of external memory aids. Thus, in this sample, it appears that beliefs about medication control substantial amounts of variance. We were able to account for 56% of the variance in a regression equation by including only four factors from the many that were measured. The four factors were beliefs that one should take less of a medication, age, general anxiety, and bodily awareness. These factors provided strong support for a socialpsychological interpretation of adherence behavior. The finding that metamemory was the only cognitive variable that influenced variance in adherence is an interesting one. It suggests that when cognitive resources are limited, then individuals, in a sense, attempt to self-regulate by adopting and using external aids to support memory rather than risking poor performance on a task as important to overall function as medication adherence. These results, although preliminary, nicely illustrate why it is important to attempt to understand the cognitive components of adherence within the network of specific beliefs about illness and medications as well as against the background of more general predispositions like anxiety. We continue to believe that cognitive variables do exert a role on medication adherence, but that we were unable to capture this role with this relatively small, select sample. We expect a more complete picture will become available as the data come in from the larger samples we are presently collecting.

CONCLUSION

The present discussion represents an attempt to systematically understand the many factors that may affect the prototypical everyday memory behavior of medication adherence. In addition to providing an integrative theoretical framework across several subareas of psychology within which to conduct research on medication adherence, we hope that the ideas presented in this chapter will stimulate thinking about other aspects of everyday cognitive function. It seems essential that we understand the interplay of both psychosocial and cognitive variables to understand every day cognitive behaviors like way finding, financial decision making, medical choices, and use of technology. The somewhat startling findings from our laboratory that cognitive variables had almost no effect on a behavior that has typically been considered to be within the purview of everyday cognition should give us pause. We now have methodologies and analytic tools in the form of individual differences techniques and structural equation modeling procedures to investigate complex hypotheses and evaluate the relative contributions of different theoretical constructs simultaneously. These powerful techniques are ideally suited to investigating issues of everyday memory function and should be used to help us gain a richer and more complete understanding of the interplay between the individual's cognitive processes and the context in which these processes occur.

ACKNOWLEDGMENTS

Preparation of this chapter was supported by grants to the first author from the National Institute on Aging (R01 AG09868 and R01 AG060625), as well as through the Southeastern Center for Applied Cognitive Aging Research, an Edward R. Roybal Center for Research on Applied Gerontology funded by the National Institute on Aging (P50 AG11715).

REFERENCES

Antonucci, T. C. (1990). Social supports and social relationships. In R. H. Binstock & L. K. George (Eds.), *Handbook of aging and the social sciences*, 3rd ed. (pp. 205–226). San Diego, CA: Academic Press.

Becker, L. A. (1989). Family systems and compliance with medical regimen. In C. N. Ramsey, Jr. (Ed.), *Family systems in medicine*. New York: Guilford.

Berger, D., Braverman, A., Sohn, C. K., & Morrow, M. (1988). Patient compliance with aggressive multimodal therapy in locally advanced breast cancer. *Cancer, 61,* 1453–1456.

Bergman, U., & Wiholm, B. (1981). Patient medication on admission to medical clinic. *European Journal of Clinical Pharmacology, 20,* 85.

Brandimonte, M. A., & Passolunghi, M. A. (1994). The effect of cue-familiarity, cue-distinctiveness, and retention interval on prospective remembering. *Quarterly Journal of Experimental Psychology, 47A*(3), 565–587.

Carey, R. E., Sohier, W. D., Kaufman, S., Weitzman, S. A., Kelley, R. M., Lew, R. A., & Halpern, E. (1979). Five-drug adjuvant chemotherapy for breast cancer. *Cancer, 44,* 35–41.

Cohen, G., & Faulkner, D. (1989). Age differences in source forgetting: Effects on reality monitoring and on eyewitness testimony. *Psychology and Aging, 4,* 10–17.

Davis, M. (1966). Variations in patients' compliance with doctors' orders: Analysis of congruence between survey responses and results of empirical investigations. *Journal of Medical Education, 41,* 1037–1048.

Doherty, W. J., Schrott, H. B., Metcalf, L., & Iasiello-Vailas, L. (1983). The effects of spouse support and health beliefs on medication adherence. *Journal of Family Practice, 17,* 837–841.

Einstein, G. O., & McDaniel, M. A. (1990). Normal aging and prospective memory. *Journal of Experimental Psychology: Learning, Memory, and Cognition, 16,* 717–726.

Ferguson, K., & Bole, G. G. (1979). Family support, health benefits, and therapeutic compliance in patients with rheumatoid arthritis. *Patient Counseling and Health Education, 1,* 101–105.

Folkman, S., Bernstein, L., & Lazarus, R. S. (1987). Stress processes and the misuse of drugs in older adults. *Psychology and Aging, 2,* 366–374.

Geertsen, H. R., Gray, R. M., & Ward, J. R. (1973). Patient non-compliance within the context of seeking medical are for arthritis. *Journal of Chronic Diseases, 26,* 689–698.

Harris, J. E., & Wilkins, A. J. (1982). Remembering to do things: A theoretical framework and an illustrative experiment. *Human Learning, 1,* 123–136.

Hashtroudi, S., Johnson, M. K., & Chrosniak, L. D. (1990). Aging and qualitative characteristics of memories for perceived and imagined complex events. *Psychology and Aging, 5,* 119–126.

Hertzog, C., & Dunlosky, J. (in press). The aging of practical memory: An overview. In D. J. Herrmann, C. McEvoy, C. Hertzog, P. Hertel, & M. Johnson (Eds.), *Basic and applied memory research: Theory in context*. Hillsdale, NJ: Lawrence Erlbaum Associates.

Hulka, B. S. (1979). Patient–clinician interactions and compliance. In R. B. Haynes, D. W. Taylor, & D. L. Sackett (Eds.), *Compliance in health care* (pp. 63–77). Baltimore: Johns Hopkins University Press.

Lamy, P. (1984). Hazards of drug use in the elderly: Commonsense measures to reduce them. *Postgraduate Medicine, 76,* 50–61.

Lamy, P., & Kitner, M. (1971). Drugs and the geriatric patient. *Journal of the American Geriatrics Society, 19,* 23–33.

Lebovits, A. H., Strain, J. J., Schleifer, S. J., Tanaka, J. S., Bhardwaj, S., & Messe, M. R. (1990). Patient noncompliance with self-administered chemotherapy. *Cancer, 65*, 17–22.

Lee, P., & Tan, L. J. P. (1979). Drug compliance in outpatients with rheumatoid arthritis. *Australian and New Zealand Journal of Medicine, 89*, 165–167.

Leventhal, H., & Cameron, L. (1987). Behavioral theories and the problem of compliance. *Patient Education and Counseling, 10*, 117–138.

Leventhal, H., Leventhal, E. A., & Schaefer, P. M. (1992). Vigilant coping and health behavior. In M. G. Ory, R. P. Abeles, & P. D. Lipman (Eds.), *Aging, health, and behavior* (pp. 109–140). Newbury Park, CA: Sage.

Leventhal, E. A., Leventhal, H., Schaefer, P. M., & Easterling, D. (1993). Conservation of energy, uncertainty reduction, and swift utilization of medical care among the elderly. *Journal of Gerontology: Psychological Sciences, 48*, 78–86.

Meacham, J. A., & Kushner, S. (1980). Anxiety, prospective memory, and performance of planned actions. *Journal of General Psychology, 103*, 203–209.

Meacham, J. A., & Singer, J. (1977). Incentive effects in prospective remembering. *Journal of Psychology, 97*, 191–197.

Morrell, R. W., Park, D. C., & Poon, L. W. (1989). Effects of the quality of instructions on memory and comprehension of prescription information in young and old adults. *The Gerontologist, 29*, 345–353.

Morrell, R. W., Park, D. C., & Poon, L. W. (1990). Effects of labeling techniques on memory and comprehension of prescription information in young and old adults. *Journal of Gerontology: Psychological Sciences, 45*, 166–172.

Morrow, D., Leirer, V., Altieri, P., & Tanke, E. (1991). Elders' schema for taking medication: Implications for instruction design. *Journal of Gerontology: Psychological Sciences, 46*, 378–385.

Morrow, D., Leirer, V., & Andrassy, J. (1993). Designing medication instructions for older adults. *Proceedings of the 37th Annual Meeting of the Human Factors and Ergonomics Society, 1*, 197–201.

Morse, E. V., Simon, P. M., & Balson, P. M. (1993). Using experiental training to enhance health professionals' awareness of patient compliance issues. *Academic Medicine, 68*, 693–697.

Park, D. C. (1992). Applied cognitive aging research. In F. I. M. Craik & T. A. Salthouse (Eds.), *Handbook of cognition and aging* (pp. 449–493). Hillsdale, NJ: Lawrence Erlbaum Associates.

Park, D. C. (1994). Self-regulation and control of rheumatic disorders. In S. Maes, H. Leventhal, & M. Johnston (Eds.), *International handbook of health psychology* (pp. 189–217). New York: Wiley.

Park, D. C., Hertzog, C., Morrell, R. W., Kidder, D. P., & Mayhorn, C. B. (1994, August). *Event-based and time-based prospective memory: Effects of age and frequency of prospective tasks.* Paper presented at the Third Practical Aspects of Memory Conference, College Park, MD.

Park, D. C., & Kidder, D. P. (in press). Prospective memory and medication adherence. In M. Brandimonte, G. Einstein, & M. McDaniel (Eds.), *Prospective memory: Theory and applications* (pp. 369–390). Hillsdale, NJ: Lawrence Erlbaum Associates.

Park, D. C., Morrell, R. W., Frieske, D., & Kincaid, D. (1992). Medication adherence behaviors in older adults: Effects of external cognitive supports. *Psychology and Aging, 7*, 252–256.

Park, D. C., Morrell, R. W., Hertzog, C., Leventhal, H., Birchmore, D., & Kidder, D. P. (1994, July). *Psychosocial and cognitive predictors of medication adherence in elderly osteoarthritis patients.* Paper presented at the meeting of the Third International Congress of Behavioral Medicine, Amsterdam, The Netherlands.

Park, D. C., Morrell, R. W., Lautenschlager, G., & Firth, M. (1993, March). *Electronic monitoring of medication adherence hypertensives: Nonadherence is predicted by advanced age.* Paper presented at the meeting of the Society of Behavioral Medicine, San Francisco, CA.

Park, D. C., Willis, S. L., Morrow, D., Diehl, M., & Gaines, C. L. (1994). Cognitive function and medication usage in older adults. *Journal of Applied Gerontology, 13*, 39–57.

Rowe, J. W., Ahronheim, J. C., & Lawton, M. P. (Eds.). (1992). *Annual review of gerontology and geriatrics* (Vol. 12). New York: Springer.

Salthouse, T. A. (1991). *Theoretical perspectives on cognitive aging.* Hillsdale, NJ: Lawrence Erlbaum Associates.

Salthouse, T. A., & Babcock, R. L. (1991). Decomposing adult age differences in working memory. *Developmental Psychology, 27*, 763–776.

Schwartz, D., Wand, M., Zeitz, L., & Goss, M. E. (1962). Medication errors made by elderly chronically ill patients. *American Journal of Public Health, 52*, 2018–2029.

Sussman, M. D. (1985). The family life of old people. In R. H. Binstock & E. Shanas (Eds.), *Handbook of aging and the social sciences*, 2nd ed. (pp. 415–449). New York: Van Nostrand Reinhold.

Taylor, S. E., Lichtman, R. R., & Wood, J. V. (1984). Compliance with chemotherapy among breast cancer patients. *Health Psychology, 3*, 553–562.

Wilkins, A. J., & Baddeley, A. D. (1988). Remembering to recall in everyday life: An approach to absentmindedness. In M. M. Gruneberg, P. E. Morris, & R. N. Sykes (Eds.), *Practical aspects of memory* (pp. 27–34). New York: Academic Press.

CHAPTER EIGHT

Personality Variables and Prospective Memory Performance

Alan Searleman
St. Lawrence University

When a person remembers the words to a favorite song, who won Wimbledon two years ago, or how many feet there are in a mile, he or she is demonstrating proficiencey in using retrospective memory. However, there is another type of memory that has been studied a great deal less but that is also of great value to us in our daily lives. This other type of memory is called *prospective* memory and it involves the ability to remember to carry out future tasks. Examples of everyday tasks that require good prospective memory skills abound, such as remembering to pick up the kids from daycare, to keep an appointment with your stock broker, or to send birthday cards (in a timely fashion!) to your siblings. Several studies have indicated that there does not appear to be a positive correlation between the two types of memory tasks (Einstein & McDaniel, 1990; Kvavilashvili, 1987; Maylor, 1990; Meacham & Leiman, 1975/1982), and, in fact, one study actually found a negative relationship between a retrospective and a prospective memory task (Wilkins & Baddeley, 1978).

Whether or not a particular act of future remembering successfully occurs critically depends on the type of prospective memory task the person has to perform. For instance, Meacham and Kushner (1980) found that a task of an interpersonal nature (e.g., remembering to honor an appointment) is more likely to be remembered than is a task that is only of personal importance (e.g., remembering to take your umbrella to work). This makes sense, because there are dire social consequences to pay if a person repeatedly fails to honor commitments that affect others. This person's behavior will

111

provoke anger and resentment and soon the person will be considered unreliable. Searleman and Herrmann (1994) suggested a number of other task-related factors that undoubtedly influence the likelihood that a prospective memory task will be successfully completed. These include whether there are ample external cues present, whether the task is self-imposed or imposed by others, if exact timing is required, if the task is of sufficient importance, and if the task involves only a single act or a whole series of interrelated acts.

Meacham and Leiman (1975/1982) also made a useful distinction between what they called *habitual* and *episodic* prospective memory tasks. An habitual task is one in which a person engages in the task on a regular basis, such as routinely brushing your teeth each night before going to sleep, whereas in contrast an episodic task is performed rarely (calling the dentist to schedule an appointment to have your teeth cleaned) or only once (calling the dentist to schedule surgery to remove your erupting back molars). People generally forget to do episodic tasks more often than habitual ones.

More recently, Einstein and McDaniel (1990, 1991, chap. 6, this volume) suggested another dichotomous way in which many prospective memory tasks can be viewed. They referred to these two types of tasks as *event-based* and *time-based*. Event-based tasks involve situations in which the future action should occur only when some external event happens or is present. An example would be remembering to tell your mail carriers that you will be on vacation for the next two weeks and to please hold your mail at the post office until you return. Seeing the person deliver the mail acts as an external cue to remind you of what you intended to say to him or her. A time-based prospective task does not involve the appearance of any specific external cue to act as a reminder (such as seeing the mail carrier). Instead, the person must remember using his or her own initiative to perform the task either at a certain time (getting a haircut at 3:15 P.M.) or after a certain amount of time has elapsed ("I'll meet you at the store in 30 minutes"). With regard to these two types of prospective tasks, there is evidence to indicate that people are more likely to remember to perform event-based tasks (Einstein & McDaniel, 1991).

From everyday experience we know that people vary tremendously in their ability to successfully carry out many types of prospective memory tasks—some are astonishingly proficient at such tasks, whereas others are absolutely terrible at them. We were interested in determining if some personality factors could account for some of this variability in performance. There are dozens of personality factors that we could have measured. We decided to limit our investigation to four personality factors that we thought might logically be related to performance on prospective memory tasks. We chose to measure the Type A/B behavior pattern, obsessive-compulsiveness, self-actualization, and self-monitoring behavior.

The Type A behavior pattern was first described as a set of behaviors that were related to the development of coronary heart disease (Friedman & Rosenman, 1959). People with a Type A personality profile are said to exhibit, among other traits, a strong sense of time urgency, an intense need to complete tasks, and a preoccupation with meeting deadlines. In contrast, people with Type B behavior patterns are much less driven than are their Type A counterparts. These individuals are considerably less concerned with completing tasks on time and meeting deadlines in general. Based on these general characteristics, we predicted that people with Type A profiles would perform better at prospective memory tasks than would people with Type B profiles.

A person who has an obsessive-compulsive personality can be characterized as being very persistent, thorough, self-willed, and overly conscientious (Fischer & Juni, 1982). These individuals have a strong tendency to do things in their own way and resist interference from others. Given the high degree of perseverance, thoroughness, and conscientiousness that people with an obsessive-compulsive personality exhibit, it could be expected that these people would also do well on tasks involving prospective memory.

People who are considered to be high in self-actualization are often described as being reliable, capable, conscientious, dedicated, and worry free (Jones & Crandall, 1986; Shostrom, 1964). They can perform at peak levels and are inner directed, meaning that they are guided more by inner motives and principles than by outside influences or opinions. The qualities of conscientiousness and dependability suggest that people with high levels of self-actualization may do well on prospective memory tests.

Finally, Snyder (1974) described the person who is high in self-monitoring as being very concerned with issues relating to socially appropriate behavior. The high self-monitor will regulate his or her actions based on the actions of others, whereas the low self-monitor is much less attentive or caring about the actions of others and is less likely to be concerned with the social appropriateness of his or her own behavior. Because of the social, interpersonal nature of many prospective memory tasks (Meacham, 1988; Meacham & Kushner, 1980; Searleman & Herrmann, 1994), people who are high self-monitors may outperform those who are low self-monitors on such tasks.

STUDY 1

In our first study we measured a group of 60 college students on these four personality dimensions and compared the results with performance on two unobtrusive prospective memory tasks (Searleman & Gaydusek, 1989). We used the Jenkins Activity Scale Form T (JAS; Krantz, Glass, & Snyder, 1974) to assess the Type A/B behavior pattern. This questionnaire is specifically intended to measure this behavior pattern in college-age people. To measure obsessive-compulsiveness the Kline Ai3 Anality Scale (Kline, 1968) was administered. The short form of the Personality Orientation Inventory (POI) as revised by Jones and Crandall (1986) was used to assess self-actualization. Finally, to get a measure of self-monitoring tendencies, the Self-Monitoring Scale (Snyder, 1974) was given to each subject. Each of the four scales are questionnaires and higher scores are equated with having more of the personality construct being measured. Thus, for instance, a higher score on the JAS reflects a higher degree of Type A behavior.

Potential subjects were sought from Introductory Psychology classes and were asked to participate (for course credit) in a study investigating the "Likes and Dislikes of College Students." Each subject was tested individually in a small research room. When each subject arrived for the study, he or she was given a packet containing the four tests used to measure the personality traits mentioned earlier. The experimenter then sat down at a desk with her back to the subject.

The first unobtrusive prospective memory task was of an interpersonal nature, but it held no personal importance for the subject. Approximately 1 minute after each subject had started to fill out the first of the four personality questionnaires, the experimenter turned to the subject and asked if he or she could remind her to make a telephone call in "a few minutes." The time of the request was surreptitiously noted by the experimenter who then turned around to work at her desk. If the subject remembered to remind her about the telephone call, she again noted the time on a digital clock. The subject was then told to continue working on the questionnaires and the experimenter left the room for approximately 3 minutes, ostensibly to make the telephone call. When the experimenter returned she went back to work at her desk. If the subject failed to remember to remind the experimenter to make her telephone call, the experimenter never mentioned the fact and did not leave the room.

When the subject indicated that he or she had completed all four personality questionnaires (which took approximately 25 minutes), the experimenter indicated that there was just one more short survey to fill out. The subject was then handed a 4 × 6 index card that required the subject to return to his or her dormitory room or apartment and to count the number of certain objects found there. It was emphasized that the subject would not receive credit for being in the study unless the card was fully completed and returned. The last question on the card required the subject to indicate the date and time the card was returned. The subject was also encouraged (both by the experimenter verbally and by what was written on the card) to return it as soon as possible by sliding it under the door of the research room. This was the second unobtrusive prospective memory task. It was a task that could be considered noninterpersonal in nature, because the subjects were instructed to simply slide the card under a door when completed.

In addition, unlike the other prospective memory task (reminding the experimenter to make a telephone call), this task did have personal importance for the subject.

In regard to the first prospective memory task, 46 out of the 60 subjects remembered to remind the experimenter to make the telephone call. Subjects who did not remind were assigned a score of 1 and subjects who did a score of 2. These scores were then correlated with the data obtained from each of the four personality tests. (All correlational values reported throughout this paper are significant at or below the .05 level.) It was found that only the subjects who scored higher on the JAS (indicative of having more of the Type A behavior pattern) were more likely to have remembered to remind the experimenter to make the call [$r(58) = .28$].

For the 46 subjects who did remember to remind about the call, it took them an average of 9.76 minutes ($SD = 5.04$ minutes). Correlations were computed comparing the scores on each of the personality tests and the time taken to remind the experimenter. There was only one significant correlation—the higher that subjects scored on the POI (reflecting higher levels of self-actualization), the faster they tended to remind about the telephone call [$r(44) = -.35$]. To provide some mean values for the self-actualization measure, the amount of time taken to remind the experimenter was compared for subjects who scored either within the top or bottom quartiles on the POI. The top-quartile subjects responded significantly faster ($M = 7.53$ minutes, $SD = 3.43$ minutes) than did the bottom-quartile subjects [$M = 13.54$ minutes, $SD = 4.01$ minutes, $t(22) = 2.84$, $p < .01$].

The second prospective memory task concerned returning the card to the research room as fast as possible. Only 4 out of the 60 subjects failed to return it, which is not surprising because it was made very clear to the subjects that credit for participating in the study would be granted only if the completed card was returned. The average time it took to return the card was 82.35 hours ($SD = 95.97$ hours). The scores on each of the four personality tests were correlated with the number of hours each of the 56 subjects took to return the card. Only for the subjects who scored higher on the JAS was there a significant correlation [$r(54) = -.29$], reflecting the fact that subjects with higher levels of Type A behavior were more likely to return the cards faster. Instead of using the top and bottom quartiles to provide mean values, the JAS has suggested cutoffs for distinguishing those with a clear Type A behavior pattern from those with a clear Type B profile. Subjects who scored 9 or above on the JAS were classified as being Type A, whereas those scoring 6 or below were classified as Type B. Using these cutoffs, it was found that Type As returned the card significantly faster ($M = 38.45$ hours, $SD = 32.13$ hours) than did their Type B counterparts [$M = 102.53$ hours, $SD = 98.25$ hours, $t(33) = 2.61$, $p < .05$].

STUDY 2

Before discussing the significance of these results, I would like to briefly describe the relevant findings of another study (Searleman & Groth, 1991). One part of this other study further examined the relationship between the two personality variables of Type A/B behavior pattern and self-actualization with performance on two new prospective memory tasks. In the first of these two tasks, the experimenter asked each subject a series of oral questions concerning the popular media. For example, they were asked several questions about their television viewing habits, to which radio shows they listened, and the type of magazines they read regularly. At the beginning of the survey, the experimenter asked each subject to please remember to report the name of his or her favorite current television show immediately after answering the last question on the survey. The subjects were told not to tell their favorite show immediately, because it might bias their answers on the survey. We considered this to be an interpersonal prospective memory task that was not personally important for the subject. Upon completion of the oral media survey, whether or not the subject remembered to tell his or her favorite television show, all the subjects were given the JAS and POI questionnaires to complete.

For the second prospective memory task, subjects had to keep track of both the number of hours of television they watched and the number of magazines they read during the next seven days. Each subject was given a response sheet to record the data. They were then asked to call the experimenter one week later and leave a message describing their data on the experimenter's answering machine. We considered leaving a message on an answering machine to be a noninterpersonal prospective memory task and that this task would not be of personal importance to the subjects because they were explicitly told that they would get credit for participation even if they did not make the telephone call.

Overall, 49 out of the 80 college students who took part in the study remembered to tell the experimenter their favorite television show. Most relevant to the present discussion, significantly more people with Type A personalities (75%, 24 out of 32) remembered than did people with Type B personalities (43%, 13 out of 30, X^2 (1, $N = 62$) = 6.45, $p < .05$). However, in terms of the self-actualization measure, no significant difference was seen in the number of people who remembered to report their favorite television show. Of those who scored in the top quartile on the POI, 60% (12 out of 20) remembered, compared with 55% (11 out of 20) for those scoring in the bottom quartile.

Only 54 out of the 80 subjects left a message reporting their data one week later for the experimenter. On this prospective memory task, neither personality factor was significantly related to performance. For instance, 62%

(20 out of 32) of the people with Type A personalities remembered to call, but so did 63% (19 out of 30) of the people with Type B personality profiles. Similarly, 65% (13 out of 20) of those in the top quartile on the POI scale called one week later, whereas 60% (12 out of 20) of the people scoring in the bottom quartile called in their information.

DISCUSSION

The results of the first study (Searleman & Gaydusek, 1989) indicated that subjects with a Type A personality were both more likely to remind an experimenter to make a telephone call and more likely to return a card faster than were individuals with a Type B behavior pattern. Only the first of these two prospective memory tasks was interpersonal in nature, and only the second was personally important to the subject. With regard to the other three personality variables, only the self-actualization factor was significantly related to either prospective memory task. Of the people who remembered to remind the experimenter to make the phone call, those with high levels of self-actualization took significantly less time than did those who scored low in self-actualization.

In the second study (Searleman & Groth, 1991), only the two personality factors that were significantly related to prospective memory performance in the first study were further examined. It was observed that people with Type A personalities were significantly more likely to remember to tell the experimenter their favorite television show at the end of the oral media survey. This is an interpersonal task with little personal importance for the subjects. In the second prospective task, the subjects were asked to call back one week later and leave a message on an answering machine. Performance on this task, which was neither interpersonal in nature nor personally important to the subjects, was unrelated to either personality dimension.

Overall, the pattern of results from these two studies suggest that if a prospective memory task is interpersonal in nature (e.g., reminding the experimenter to make a telephone call or telling the experimenter your favorite television show), people with Type A personalities are more likely to remember the task than are their Type B counterparts. Moreover, if the task is not interpersonal in nature (e.g., returning a card under a door) but is of personal importance to the subjects, then Type A individuals will perform the task better than will Type B people. However, if a prospective memory task is neither of an interpersonal nature nor of personal importance to the subjects (e.g., 1 week later leaving a message on a machine), then Type A individuals are no more likely than Type B people to complete the task.

These results could have important practical implications. For example, if the findings from these studies can be replicated with people living in nursing homes or with elderly people, then by determining Type A/B behavior patterns it may be possible to predict which individuals will need more help in remembering to take medications, keep doctor's appointments, and so forth. This could be especially helpful to staff members in institutions that have a high ratio of clients/patients to caregivers. Parole officers and social workers could also benefit from knowing in advance which clients may need extra help in carrying out certain requirements, such as remembering to regularly report to counseling sessions. The present results suggest that to increase the likelihood that prospective memory tasks will be successfully completed, the tasks should be structured to be interpersonal in nature and so that they have clear personal relevance for the people expected to perform them; this is especially true for individuals with Type A personalities.

REFERENCES

Einstein, G. O., & McDaniel, M. A. (1990). Normal aging and prospective memory. *Journal of Experimental Psychology: Learning, Memory, and Cognition, 16,* 717–726.

Einstein, G. O., & McDaniel, M. A. (1991, November). *Aging and time versus event-based prospective memory.* Paper presented at the Annual Meeting of the Psychonomic Society, San Franciso, CA.

Fischer, R. E., & Juni, S. (1982). The anal personality: Self-disclosure, negativism, self-esteem, and superego severity. *Journal of Personality Assessment, 46,* 50–58.

Friedman, M., & Rosenman, R. H. (1959). Association of specific overt behavior pattern with blood and cardiovascular findings. *Journal of the American Medical Association, 169,* 1286–1296.

Jones, A., & Crandall, R. (1986). Validation of a short index of self actualization. *Personality and Social Psychology Bulletin, 12,* 63–73.

Kline, P. (1968). Obsessional traits, obsessional symptoms, and anal eroticism. *Journal of Medical Psychology, 41,* 299–305.

Krantz, D. S., Glass, D. C., & Snyder, M. L. (1974). Helplessness, stress level, and the coronary prone behavior pattern. *Journal of Experimental Social Psychology, 10,* 284–300.

Kvavilashvili, L. (1987). Remembering intention as a distinct form of memory. *British Journal of Psychology, 78,* 507–518.

Maylor, E. A. (1990). Age and prospective memory. *The Quarterly Journal of Experimental Psychology, 42,* 471–493.

Meacham, J. A. (1988). Interpersonal relations and prospective remembering. In M. M. Gruneberg, P. E. Morris, & R. N. Sykes (Eds.), *Practical aspects of memory: Current research and issues* (Vol. 2, pp. 354–359). Chichester, England: Wiley.

Meacham, J. A., & Kushner, S. (1980). Anxiety, prospective remembering, and performance of planned actions. *Journal of General Psychology, 103,* 203–209.

Meacham, J. A., & Leiman, B. (1975/1982). *Remembering to perform future actions* (Paper presented at the Annual meeting of the American Psychological Association, Chicago, September 1975). In U. Neisser (Ed.), *Memory observed: Remembering in natural contexts* (pp. 327–336). San Francisco, CA: Freeman.

Searleman, A., & Gaydusek, K. A. (1989, November). *Relationship between prospective memory ability and selective personality variables.* Paper presented at the Annual meeting of the Psychonomic Society, Atlanta, GA.

Searleman, A., & Groth, K. A. (1991). *Variables affecting prospective memory: Commitment, external reminders, and personality factors.* Unpublished manuscript.

Searleman, A., & Herrmann, D. (1994). *Memory from a broader perspective.* New York: McGraw-Hill.

Shostrom, D. L. (1964). An inventory for the measurement of self-actualization. *Educational and Psychological Measurement, 24,* 207–218.

Snyder, M. (1974). Self-monitoring of expressive behavior. *Journal of Personality and Social Psychology, 30,* 526–537.

Wilkins, A. J., & Baddeley, A. D. (1978). Remembering to recall in everyday life: An approach to absentmindedness. In M. M. Gruneberg, P. E. Morris, & R. N. Sykes (Eds.), *Practical aspects of memory* (pp. 27–34). London: Academic Press.

PART FOUR

LEARNING AND INTELLIGENCE

CHAPTER NINE

Practice Effects in Memory: Data, Theory, and Unanswered Questions

David G. Payne
Binghamton University

Michael J. Wenger
Indiana University

This chapter is concerned with the manner in which practicing memory tasks influences subsequent acquisition and retention. This is admittedly a very broad topic, and most if not all of the sessions at the Third Practical Aspects of Memory Conference had something to say about memory practice effects. What differentiates our review is that we are interested in the effects of memory practice per se, rather than more specific topics such as strategy use or the effectiveness of classical mnemonics. Here we review work from three domains: skilled memory, the effects of encoding and retrieval practice, and some recent developments concerning implicit memory and implicit learning (see Schacter, 1987; Seger, 1994, for reviews).

EXTENDED MEMORY PRACTICE: THE DEVELOPMENT OF SKILLED MEMORY

Subjects in expert memory studies have devoted hundreds of hours to the memory tasks of interest, either as a result of participating in a laboratory study (e.g., Ericsson, Chase, & Faloon, 1980; Wenger & Payne, 1993, 1995) or through repeatedly performing the memory task in their everyday activities (e.g., Deakin & Allard, 1991; Ericsson & Polson, 1988a, 1988b; Stevens, 1993). Knowledge obtained from these individuals is certainly relevant to our understanding of memory practice effects, and hence in this section we will overview important and representative work examining expert memory performance.

Chase and Ericsson (1981, 1982) reported a series of investigations of how performance changes in a digit span task when subjects are given extensive practice with the task. Chase and Ericsson followed the performance of two individuals, SF and DD. SF was eventually able to serially recall more than 80 digits presented at a 1-second rate (Chase & Ericsson, 1981, 1982), whereas DD eventually achieved serial recall of more than 100 digits (Staszewski, 1993). We recently extended this empirical work by showing that undergraduates given weekly practice at memorizing lists of words presented once in a random order can achieve perfect serial recall of up to 80 words within less than 15 weeks of practice (Wenger & Payne, 1993, 1995). These are impressive levels of performance and they suggest that expert (or skilled) levels of memory performance can be achieved by seemingly average individuals without explicit instruction on mnemonic techniques.

Chase and Ericsson developed Skilled Memory Theory based on data from the digit span task, verbal protocols, and other tasks designed to probe SF's and DD's developing skills. There are three central principles to this theory: mnemonic encoding, structured retrieval, and speed-up. The mnemonic encoding principle holds that high levels of serial recall are supported by encoding activities that rely on existing knowledge to organize and make meaningful the target items. SF and DD were both long-distance runners with extensive knowledge of running statistics (e.g., record times for specific distances), and they used this knowledge to meaningfully organize the random strings of digits they studied. For example, if presented with the digit string 349, SF or DD could encode the digits as a single item (a near-record mile time) rather than three unrelated digits. After SF discovered that running times (and later, ages and other associates for strings of digits) could be used to make the presented digits more meaningful, his performance became systematically dependent on the presence of strings of digits that could be meaningfully coded according to his mnemonic strategy. The importance of mnemonic encoding was demonstrated in two experiments conducted by Chase and Ericsson. First, when SF was provided with lists of digits that could not possibly be coded as running times, his performance dropped to near baseline levels. Second, when the lists were composed of digit strings all of which could be coded as running times, SF's performance improved by 27%.

The second principle of Skilled Memory Theory is the structured retrieval principle, which holds that memory experts develop abstract and reusable organizational structures (referred to as *retrieval structures*) that are derived from the mnemonic encoding system. According to the theory, these structures function to guide recall. Evidence to support the concept of retrieval structures comes from parallels between the dynamics of encoding and retrieval, such as high correlations between interitem pause times in self-paced study and retrieval (Staszewski, 1993; Wenger & Payne, 1993, 1995), and agreement between the details of the logical structure of the mnemonic encoding system and pauses in verbal recall (Chase & Ericsson, 1981).

Finally, the speed-up principle holds that both encoding and retrieval processes get faster with increasing amounts of practice. Chase and Ericsson (1981) documented the speed-up at encoding and retrieval for SF in a number of ways. For example, they noted that in self-paced study sessions SF's study time per item dropped significantly from Day 69 to Day 200 (see Chase & Ericsson, 1981, Figure 5.15, p. 181). We recently replicated this speed-up at encoding in our extended practice study using random word lists (Wenger & Payne, 1993, 1995). It appears that the generalized increase in the fluency with which subjects can encode information is observed with a range of materials and encoding strategies.

Skilled Memory Theory has been applied to a number of studies of the acquisition and use of memory skill and it has proven to be a valuable conceptual framework. Some of the topics that have been examined using this framework include the expert memory of figure skaters (Deakin & Allard, 1991), waiters memory for meal orders (Ericsson & Polson, 1988a, 1988b; Stevens, 1993), the development of proficiency in tasks such as mental calculation (Staszewski, 1988), memorizing random word lists (Wenger & Payne, 1993, 1995), and playing blindfold chess (Ericsson & Staszewski, 1989). Collectively, these studies indicate that Skilled Memory Theory can be applied to a broad range of topics, including the acquisition of skill within a laboratory context and the assessment of skill developed outside of the laboratory. We will consider one of these studies in detail.

Ericsson and Polson (1988a, 1988b) studied the performance of a waiter (JC) who showed exceptional memory for patrons' meal orders. JC's encoding strategies were based on his knowledge of the regularities within each category of food items on the menu and were bolstered by use of common mnemonic strategies, such as interactive imagery. JC would organize the orders from a table of patrons as a matrix in which the rows were categories of menu items (e.g., entrees, salad dressing, starch) and the columns were the orders of individual patrons. He would then generate an interactive image involving elements of each order and the face of the customer. Within each menu item category, JC had developed a specific encoding scheme, based on the characteristics and range of possible items within each category. For example, he encoded salad dressings according to the first letter of the choice, starches as serial patterns (given that there were only three possible starches), and meat temperatures as spatial patterns (given that temperatures could be represented graphically on an ordinal scale).

Ericsson and Polson (1988a, 1988b) also provided data relevant to JC's use of organized, reusable structures for recall across lists of items. Ericsson and Polson contrasted JC with naive subjects in terms of the degree to which recall of orders was organized by category of menu items. Although the naive subjects used serial recall strategy (recalling ordered items in the sequence in which they were presented) for 96% of all items, JC used the categorical strategy (as discussed in the previous section) for 96% and 100% of all items in two separate tests. Ericsson and Polson also documented impressive speed-up in encoding for JC. Across the one year of experimental involvement, JC reduced his study times for tables of five patrons from approximately 80 seconds to approximately 40 seconds, while reducing his study times for tables of eight patrons from approximately 160 seconds to approximately 90 seconds.

Finally, it is important to note that JC's mnemonic performance was clearly dependent on his background knowledge of the menu items—a long-term memory phenomenon. However, JC could also use this background knowledge when presented with novel tasks that fit into this knowledge structure: When he was given lists of items unrelated to dinner orders (e.g., flower names) that could be structured in ways similar to restaurant orders (e.g., five flower names that could be organized similarly to the five salad dressings used in the restaurant), JC showed a high degree of positive transfer relative to novice subjects. However, when JC was presented with items that could not be organized along the lines of the meal orders, his memory performance was rather undistinguished.

Summary

Skilled Memory Theory can be usefully applied to organize the findings from studies of expert memory in a wide range of domains. The principles of mnemonic encoding, structured retrieval, and speed-up appear to describe acquisition and skilled performance in each of these areas. There is little strong evidence for a broadly generalized improvement in memory performance as a function of practice, and there is actually rather convincing evidence that memory practice is highly dependent on the types of materials and training procedures used to acquire the expert levels of memory performance. Finally, there is considerable evidence from the work reviewed here and in other studies (e.g., Ceci, DeSimone, & Johnson, 1992; Thompson et al., 1991) that extensive practice does not alter the functional characteristics of short-term (or working) memory, but rather it increases the efficiency with which the memorists are able to encode information into, and retrieve information from, long-term memory.

ITEM-SPECIFIC PRACTICE EFFECTS

Encoding Variables

Nearly a century ago, Jost (1897; cited in Hintzman, 1974) inferred from Ebbinghaus' (1885/1964) data that learning is improved if practice is spread out in time rather than massed together. In the time since this initial observation there have been hundreds of studies (see Bruce & Bahrick, 1992) examining the spacing effect and the distribution of practice. Although these studies generally supported the conclusion that spaced practice produced better memory than massed practice, there is no single theoretical account that can handle all of the data on spacing effects, and basic research on the spacing effect continues today (e.g., Challis, 1993; Kahana & Greene, 1994; Toppino, 1993). It is interesting to note that, despite the strong empirical support for the utility of the spacing effect, to date there has been little application of this finding (see Dempster, 1988). We turn our attention now to illustrative investigations of the spacing effect.

Zechmeister and Shaughnessy (1980) examined the spacing effect in free recall as well as subjects' metacognitive assessments of the benefits of spacing. They presented subjects with common nouns to study. Some of the items appeared only once whereas others were repeated, either massed together or spaced throughout the list. For some of the list items subjects were asked to estimate the likelihood that they would be able to recall the items when tested later. For the repeated items these ratings were always made after the second presentation of the item. After list presentation subjects were asked to recall all of the items and, not surprisingly, recall was better for the repeated items than the once presented items. Furthermore, the typical spacing effect was obtained in that the spaced items were more likely to be recalled than were the massed items. Interestingly, subjects' estimates of how likely they would be to recall the repeated items was exactly opposite to the actual recall probabilities, that is, the subjects rated the massed items as more likely to be recalled than the spaced items. These self-report data suggest that subjects believe that rehearsing/studying items in a massed fashion is an effective way to commit information to memory.

A study by Modigliani and Hedges (1987) suggests that the belief in the advantage of massed over spaced practice is also reflected in the manner in which subjects rehearse items. Modigliani and Hedges presented subjects with lists of 20 words and required some of the subjects to rehearse the items aloud during list presentation. These overt rehearsals were tape recorded and later analyzed to examine the types of rehearsal patterns observed and how these rehearsal patterns related to recall levels. For present purposes the data of interest concern the proportion of items that were rehearsed in a distributed manner. Modigliani and Hedges defined a rehearsal set as the items that were overtly rehearsed between successive presentations of study items. Items can be divided into those items that are rehearsed for one or more rehearsal sets and then never rehearsed again; these items are called *immediate and consecutive rehearsal items*. In contrast, other items may be rehearsed for one or more rehearsal sets, dropped from rehearsal, and then returned to the rehearsal set later on; these items are referred to as *distributed rehearsal items*. Modigliani and Hedges' data indicate that of all of the items that were rehearsed at least once following its presentation, 65.1% and 74.5% were rehearsed in the immediate and consecutive rehearsal manner in Experiments 1 and 2, respectively. These data indicate that when subjects are given free rein over how they rehearse, they do so in a manner analogous to massed presentation. Modigliani and Hedges also found that, as would be expected based on the literature on distributed practice, items were much more likely to be recalled when they had been rehearsed in the distributed manner than the immediate and consecutive manner. These results also have implications for the value of retrieval efforts, and we return to this issue later in the chapter.

Finally, note that the tendency to think that massed presentations are effective may account for the fact that most people report that when they are given new information to learn (e.g., telephone numbers, people's names), they go about attempting to memorize this information by repeating it silently to themselves; in other words, they use massed practice. Because this seems to be a rather general tendency that people have it is worth reminding the reader that spacing *can* improve memory. So remember: Spacing improves memory.

Spacing has also been studied using list-learning tasks that more closely approximate real-world tasks. For example, Dempster (1987) examined whether spaced or massed presentations were more effective in a vocabulary-learning task. Subjects were presented with unfamiliar words and their meanings in either a massed or a spaced condition (Experiments 3 & 4). Memory for the meanings was tested by presenting the vocabulary words and asking the subjects to provide the meaning. In two experiments, the spaced presentations yielded a significant improvement in performance relative to the massed condition. Furthermore, the size of the improvement was considerable, ranging from 23% to 102% across the various conditions.

The spacing effect has also been demonstrated with units larger than words or word meanings. For example, when sentences are presented for study multiple times, there is also a spacing effect (e.g., Rothkopf & Coke, 1963). One important boundary condition for producing the spacing effect with sentences is that the repetitions must be identical. Dellarosa and Bourne (1985) found that the spacing effect was either attenuated or eliminated completely when the second presentation of the sentence was changed by varying either the surface structure of the sentence or the person speaking the sentence. Similar results were obtained by Glover and Corkill (1987) using paragraphs. It thus seems that, at least for sentences and paragraphs, the manner in which the items are re-presented plays a major role in determining the presence or absence of the spacing effect.

The spacing principle is known to apply over longer intervals as well. Bloom and Shuell (1981) compared memory of French vocabulary items studied using either spaced practice (three 10-minute sessions, completed on

3 successive days) or massed practice (all three sessions completed within a single 30-minute session). When memory was assessed on a delayed recall test, the spaced condition showed a sizable (35%) advantage over the massed practice condition; similar results were reported by Dempster (1987). Glenberg and Lehman (1980) demonstrated that spacing repetitions in list learning over 1 day or 1 week can improve performance dramatically. Taken together, the results of these studies indicate that learning and retention of single words, as well as foreign vocabulary items, are aided by spacing the practice sessions.

Spaced practice has also been shown to improve retention of text, lecture, and other educational materials. Reder and Anderson (1982) had subjects read information derived from introductory texts in several fields (e.g., ecology, photography) under either a massed or distributed (i.e., spaced) presentation format. They found that spacing produced a significant improvement in subjects' retention of the main points of the passages. Di Vesta and Smith (1979) examined students' retention of the main points of a lecture. Within the lecture, there were discussion periods that were either interspersed throughout the lecture period (spaced practice) or massed at either the beginning or end of the lecture. Here again, spacing facilitated retention of the main points. Smith and Rothkopf (1984) also examined the effects of spacing materials in an educational setting. In this case, the "materials" consisted of four lectures on statistics that were presented either all on the same day or spaced across 4 days. Note that in this study, the target knowledge was not simply information repeated verbatim in the four lectures but rather each lecture involved separate and presumably different presentations. Nonetheless, the topics of the lectures were similar, and this provided some overlap. Smith and Rothkopf reported significantly better recall with the spaced lectures than with the massed lectures. [Note that this result appears to be somewhat at odds with the findings of Dellarosa and Bourne (1985) and Glover and Corkill (1987), who found that varying the surface form of sentences or paragraphs reduced or eliminated the spacing effect. There are many differences in the materials and procedures used in these studies, and it is impossible at this point to identify the factor(s) responsible for producing the observed results.] In another study, Rea and Modigliani (1985) compared students' memory of spelling lists and multiplication facts learned under either massed or distributed practice. When performance was assessed on a delayed recall test, there was a clear advantage for spaced practice.

Finally, it appears that the spacing effect reflects a fairly general memory process. There are two lines of evidence that support this claim. First, when memory is assessed with a free recall measure, the spacing effect is unaffected by whether learning is intentional or unintentional (e.g., Greene, 1989). Second, Cornell (1980) reported evidence of a spacing effect in recognition memory in infants 5 to 6 months of age. This finding suggests that the spacing effect reflects a basic aspect of the human memory system, that is, one that is not necessarily dependent on subjects employing strategic encoding processes. Furthermore, Kausler, Wiley, and Phillips (1990) demonstrated that spacing effects can be obtained with both young and older adults, further attesting to the generality of spaced repetition as a potent means for improving memory.

Summary

Duke, Haley, and Berquist (1991) argued that, as a group, encoding processes may be the single most important means by which to improve memory. Taken together, the studies reviewed in this section are consistent with the suggestion of Duke et al. in the sense that these studies demonstrate clearly that practice in encoding material can be greatly improved by spacing the practice sessions. The spacing effect has been obtained with a wide range of learners, materials, encoding conditions, retention intervals, and memory tasks. It is thus safe to conclude that spacing represents a very potent encoding variable that could potentially be used to improve memory performance. Note, however, that even relatively sophisticated subjects (i.e., college students) do not spontaneously employ distributed practice. (Remember: Spacing improves memory.) One question that remains unanswered is whether subjects would employ spacing as a general strategy if they were given training in the use of this strategy. If so, this would speak to the general issue of the specificity of memory skills.

Retrieval Variables

Item-specific improvement in memory performance has also been demonstrated in investigations of the effects of repeated retrieval practice. In an influential study, Erdelyi and Becker (1974) reported that memory for pictorial information improves across repeated tests, whereas memory for verbal materials remains constant. Erdelyi and Becker coined the term *hypermnesia* to refer to the increase in net recall levels they obtained with the pictorial items. Subsequent research on the hypermnesia phenomenon has delineated several factors that contribute to the observed improvement in net recall levels across repeated tests (see Payne, 1987, for a review).

Roediger and Payne (1982) demonstrated that hypermnesia was not attributable to changes in the memory trace that occurred over time (e.g., consolidation), but rather hypermnesia depended on repeated testing. They compared the recall performance of groups that had had the same length retention interval but a different number of prior tests and found that performance levels varied directly with the number of prior tests, suggesting that the process of administering repeated tests somehow facilitated subsequent performance. They also found that the rate of recalling items increases with increasing test experience, suggesting that the act of recalling items increases the accessibility of these items.

Further investigations of hypermnesia have indicated that the phenomenon is both robust and explicable in terms of the processes operating at the time of retrieval. These studies have demonstrated that: (a) the gain in items recalled across the repeated tests is attributable to additional time to retrieve target items (Payne, 1986; Roediger, Payne, Gillespie, & Lean, 1982; Roediger & Thorpe, 1978); (b) the hypermnesic effect for verbal items is obtained with both free and cued recall tests but not recognition tests (Otani & Whiteman, 1994; Payne, Hembrooke, & Anastasi, 1993; Payne & Roediger, 1987; however, see Erdelyi & Stein, 1981); and (c) the improvement in net recall of verbal items across successive tests does not appear to be due to subjects adopting a more lenient response criterion, because the hypermnesic effect is obtained even when response criterion is held constant by forcing subjects to produce the same number of items on each test (e.g., Erdelyi & Becker, 1974; Otani & Whiteman, 1994).

The results of these studies indicate that practice in retrieving items confers a direct benefit on later recall of these items. There is also evidence that there is an indirect benefit of retrieval practice for nonrecalled items in the sense that the speed-up of retrieval of recalled items allows subjects to spend more time searching memory for unrecalled target items. There is, however, some evidence which suggests that the benefits of retrieval are specific to the target items and do not generalize to other items. For example, Roediger et al. (1982, Experiment 3) asked subjects to recall items from common categories on three successive trials. Subjects who recalled items from the same category showed significant improvements across trials, whereas subjects who recalled items from different categories showed no improvement across trials. Herrmann, Buschke, and Gall (1987) replicated and extended this basic pattern of results by providing subjects with much more retrieval practice than did Roediger et al. In the Herrmann et al. study, up to 42 different categories (Experiment 3) were used to examine whether there would be an improvement that would generalize across items.

One other line of research that has examined the effects of various types of retrieval processes is the work by Geiselman, Fisher, MacKinnon, and Holland (1985), who investigated the "cognitive interview" as a means to improve eyewitness memory. This approach involves instructing an eyewitness to attempt to recall information using a variety of retrieval strategies, including varying the order in which the event is recalled and attempting to reinstate the emotional context surrounding the event. The cognitive interview has proven to be a useful technique for improving subjects' memory performance (for a review, see Geiselman & Fisher, in press). One question that has not yet been adequately addressed in this line of research is the extent to which practice in using the retrieval strategies acquired in the cognitive interview will enhance memory performance when the person is not explicitly instructed to use the strategy.

Summary

The work on retrieval practice indicates that such practice produces sizable improvements in subjects' ability to recall the practiced items. There is relatively little evidence to suggest that retrieval practice generalizes to new items or across tasks, with the possible exception being a speed-up in retrieval. However, recall that the research on expert memory indicates that the advantages of extensive practice tend to be limited to certain classes of materials, a pattern that would suggest that any generalized improvement in performance as a function of practice is more the exception than the rule.

Combined Encoding and Retrieval Practice: Expanding Rehearsal

It appears that spacing of practice (both encoding and retrieval) enhances memory performance. (Remember: Spacing improves memory.) Landauer and Bjork (1978) combined spaced encoding and retrieval practice in a simple yet effective memory improvement technique. Landauer and Bjork were interested in the types of real-world situations in which an item is presented once, and the learner must decide how to rehearse that item in order to remember it (e.g., remember the name of a newly introduced stranger). Landauer and Bjork noted that people's tendency to try to remember a person's name by rehearsing it over and over in succession is equivalent to massed practice which, based on the spacing effect research, can be assumed to be a less-than-optimal procedure.

Landauer and Bjork (1978) demonstrated that a procedure they called *expanding rehearsal* produced the best retention. With this procedure, initial recall attempts occur soon after the items have been presented in order to ensure that the learner can retrieve them. However, retrieving the item serves as a re-presentation of the item, and in order for these re-presentations to be maximally effective, they should be spaced in time. Thus, with the expanding rehearsal procedure, after the initial short retention interval, the time between successive retrieval attempts is increased. Landauer and Bjork reported that in a laboratory study with college students, the expanding rehearsal procedure produced very good memory performance.

Following Landauer and Bjork's report there have been several additional demonstrations that attest to the effectiveness and generality of the expanding rehearsal procedure. Camp and McKitrick (1992) reported considerable success using a modified version of the expanding rehearsal procedure to train face–name and object–location associations in demented patients.

Schacter, Rick, and Stamp (1985) also reported success with the technique using a clinical subject sample.

Finally, the expanding rehearsal procedure even works for memory researchers. Linton (1988) used the procedure in her single-subject study (Linton was the subject) of the acquisition of common and scientific names for flowers and was able to learn to identify over 1,600 varieties. In an informal test of this procedure, the first author of this chapter recently used the procedure to learn the names of members of a sports team he had joined. After meeting the team members and getting a list of members names, the group began to practice their tennis skills. Names were tested initially after each game, then at the end of the first set, the end of the match, and so on. Although the results were not as impressive as Linton's (there were only 24 people involved) it was nonetheless rewarding to see that the procedure worked and the author was able to learn all 24 names (with the correct faces!) after a relatively short time period.

PRACTICE EFFECTS CAPTURED BY IMPLICIT MEMORY AND IMPLICIT LEARNING TASKS

In the past decade there has been a tremendous increase in interest in the phenomena of implicit memory and implicit learning (for reviews, see Reber, 1993; Schacter, 1987). Glisky and Schacter (1987, 1988, 1989) reported a series of studies in which they successfully taught computer terms, computer programming concepts, and a data entry task to amnesic patients. Glisky and Schacter noted that although amnesics are severely impaired relative to normal control subjects in terms of their ability to perform explicit tasks such as free recall or recognition, there is often no difference between these groups on implicit memory tasks such as stem completion. That is, if amnesics and normals are given letter-fragment cues (e.g., given *cha* and asked to write down the first word that comes to mind, the amnesics are as likely as normal subjects to produce a response that corresponds to a recently presented item, e.g., *chair*). This preserved priming in amnesics was exploited by Glisky and Schacter in a teaching technique they referred to as the *method of vanishing cues*. In this procedure, subjects are exposed to a series of novel items (e.g., computer programming terms) and asked to use these in a structured learning environment. Subjects are required to use these terms in a programming task and are initially cued with as many letters of the target words as necessary to elicit a correct response. Across the training sessions letters are gradually withdrawn until the patients are eventually using the terms in the context of the programming task in the absence of any letter cues. This procedure has proven to be remarkably effective; although the amnesic subjects took longer to learn the terms than the normal controls, the amnesics showed retention of their acquired knowledge and skills over intervals of up to 9 months (Glisky & Schacter, 1987). Furthermore, one of the amnesic subjects in this research was able to master a rather demanding real-world data entry task.

One additional aspect of the method of vanishing cues that warrants mention is the fact that the procedures used by Glisky and Schacter share some parallels with the expanding rehearsal procedure developed by Landauer and Bjork (1978). In the method of vanishing cues the subjects are given multiple opportunities to recall the target information and as the amount of information they are learning increases the intervals between successive retrievals increases. Also, the procedure of presenting fewer and fewer letters as retrieval cues requires subjects to retrieve the item with decreasing dependence on external retrieval information. These aspects of training are consistent with the expanding rehearsal procedure. Additional research is needed to examine the relative contributions of the various components of the training procedure.

There is also a large literature on implicit learning (for reviews, see Reber, 1993; Seger, 1994). Reber (1993) defined implicit learning as "the acquisition of knowledge that takes place largely independently of conscious attempts to learn and largely in the absence of explicit knowledge of what is acquired" (p. 3). Research by Reber, Broadbent (e.g., Broadbent, Fitzgerald, & Broadbent, 1986), and others has documented that this type of learning can be observed in a variety of tasks, including some that are reasonable analogs of real-world tasks of interest. For example, Broadbent et al. (1986) asked subjects to control the production of a hypothetical manufacturing plant by controlling parameters of the system (e.g., input of raw materials). Results indicated that subjects could perform the task quite well (i.e., they were able to control the system so as to maximize the likelihood of a desired outcome), and that the subjects were unable to provide a verbal description of how they were performing the task or what the underlying functional relations were among the variables in the simulated task. Note that if one were to focus on explicit memory measures as a means to assess what was acquired in these tasks one would come to the incorrect conclusion that subjects had not learned. We would argue that, just as Glisky and Schacter were able to utilize implicit memory to train their subjects, there is a tremendous potential for using implicit learning techniques in real world domains. This is, of course, speculation, and additional research is needed to examine the validity of these claims. (And remember: Spacing improves memory.)

Although there are a number of important empirical and theoretical issues being debated within the domains of both implicit memory and implicit learning, it is clear that there is a great deal of learning and retention that takes place on a regular basis that is not readily available to introspection. Furthermore, the work of Glisky and Schacter indicates that taking these "nonconscious" forms of memory into account may provide a valuable means for aiding the memory remediation of memory-damaged individuals.

REFERENCES

Bloom, K. C., & Shuell, T. J. (1981). Effects of massed and distributed practice on the learning and retention of second-language vocabulary. *Journal of Educational Research, 74,* 245–248.

Broadbent, D. E., Fitzgerald, P., & Broadbent, M. H. P. (1986). Implicit and explicit knowledge in the control of complex systems. *British Journal of Psychology, 77,* 33–50.

Bruce, D., & Bahrick, H. P. (1992). Perceptions of past research. *American Psychologist, 47,* 319–328.

Camp, C. J., & McKitrick, L. A. (1992). Memory interventions in Alzeheimer's-type dementia populations: Methodological and theoretical issues. In R. L. West and J. D. Sinnott (Eds.), *Everyday memory and aging: Current research and methodology* (pp. 155–172). New York: Springer-Verlag.

Ceci, S. J., DeSimone, M., & Johnson, S. (1992). Memory in context: A case study of "Bubbles P.," a gifted but uneven memorizer. In D. Herrmann, H. Weingartner, A. Searleman, & C. McEvoy (Eds.), *Memory improvement: Implications for memory theory* (pp. 169–186). New York: Springer-Verlag.

Challis, B. H. (1993). Spacing effects on cued-memory tests depend on level of processing. *Journal of Experimental Psychology: Learning, Memory, and Cognition, 19,* 389–396.

Chase, W. G., & Ericsson, K. A. (1981). Skilled memory. In J. R. Anderson (Ed.), *Cognitive skills and their acquisition* (pp. 141–189). Hillsdale, NJ: Lawrence Erlbaum Associates.

Chase, W. G., & Ericsson, K. A. (1982). Skill and working memory. In G. Bower (Ed.), *The psychology of learning and motivation* (Vol. 16, pp. 1–58). San Diego, CA: Academic Press.

Cornell, E. H. (1980). Distributed study facilitates infants' delayed recognition memory. *Memory & Cognition, 8,* 539–542.

Deakin, S. M., & Allard, F. (1991). Skilled memory in expert figure skaters. *Memory & Cognition, 19,* 79–86.

Dellarosa, D., & Bourne, L. E. (1985). Surface form and the spacing effect. In R. L. Solso (Ed.), *Theories in cognitive psychology: The Loyola Symposium* (pp. 123–144). Hillsdale, NJ: Lawrence Erlbaum Associates.

Dempster, F. N. (1987). Effects of variable encoding and the spaced presentations on vocabulary learning. *Journal of Educational Psychology, 79,* 162–170.

Dempster, F. N. (1988). The spacing effect: A case study in the failure to apply the results of psychological research. *American Psychologist, 43,* 627–634.

Di Vesta, F. J., & Smith, P. A. (1979). The pausing principle: Increasing the efficiency of memory for ongoing events. *Contemporary Educational Psychology, 4,* 288–296.

Duke, L. W., Haley, W. E., & Berquist, T. F. (1991). Cognitive–behavioral interventions for age-related memory impairment. In P. A. Wisocki (Ed.), *Handbook of clinical behavior therapy with the elderly client* (pp. 245–272). New York: Plenum.

Ebbinghaus, H. (1964). *Memory: A contribution to experimental psychology* (H. A. Ruger & C. E. Bussenius, Trans.). New York: Dover. (Original work published 1885)

Erdelyi, M. H., & Becker, J. (1974). Hypermnesia for pictures: Incremental memory for pictures but not words in multiple recall trials. *Cognitive Psychology, 6,* 159–171.

Erdelyi, M. H., & Stein, J. B. (1981). Recognition hypermnesia: The growth of recognition memory (d') over time with repeated testing. *Cognition, 9,* 23–33.

Ericsson, K. A., Chase, W., & Faloon, S. (1980). Acquisition of a memory skill. *Science, 208,* 1181–1182.

Ericsson, K. A., & Polson, P. G. (1988a). A cognitive analysis of exceptional memory for restaurant orders. In M. T. H. Chi, R. Glaser, & M. J. Farr (Eds.), *The nature of expertise* (pp. 23–70). Hillsdale, NJ: Lawrence Erlbaum Associates.

Ericsson, K. A., & Polson, P. G. (1988b). An experimental analysis of a memory skill. *Journal of Experimental Psychology: Learning, Memory, and Cognition, 14,* 305–316.

Ericsson, K. A., & Staszewski, J. J. (1989). Skilled memory and expertise: Mechanisms of exceptional performance. In D. Klahr & K. Kotovsky (Eds.), *Complex information processing: The impact of Herbert A. Simon* (pp. 235–267). Hillsdale, NJ: Lawrence Erlbaum Associates.

Geiselman, R. E., & Fisher, R. P. (in press). Ten years of cognitive interviewing. In D. G. Payne & F. G. Conrad (Eds.), *Intersections in basic and applied memory research.* Hillsdale, NJ: Lawrence Erlbaum Associates.

Geiselman, R. E., Fisher, R. P, MacKinnon, D. P., & Holland, H. L. (1985). Eyewitness enhancement in the police interview: Cognitive retrieval mnemonics versus hypnosis. *Journal of Applied Psychology, 70,* 401–412.

Glenberg, A. L., & Lehman, T. S. (1980). Spacing over 1 week. *Memory & Cognition, 8,* 528–538.

Glisky, E. L., & Schacter, D. L. (1987). Acquisition of domain-specific knowledge in organic amnesia: Training for computer-related work. *Neuropsychologia, 25,* 893–906.

Glisky, E. L., & Schacter, D. L. (1988). Long-term retention of computer learning by patients with memory disorders. *Neuropsychologia, 26,* 173–178.

Glisky, E. L., & Schacter, D. L. (1989). Extending the limits of complex learning in organic amnesia: Computer training in a vocational domain. *Neuropsychologia, 27,* 107–120.

Glover, J. A., & Corkill, A. K. (1987). Influence of paraphrased repetitions on the spacing effect. *Journal of Educational Psychology, 79,* 198–199.

Greene, R. L. (1989). Spacing effects in memory: Evidence for a two-process account. *Journal of Experimental Psychology: Learning, Memory, and Cognition, 15,* 371–377.

Herrmann, D. J., Buschke, H., & Gall, M. B. (1987). Improving retrieval. *Applied Cognitive Psychology, 1,* 27–33.

Hintzman, D. L. (1974). Theoretical implications of the spacing effect. In R. L. Solso (Ed.), *Theories of cognitive psychology: The Loyola symposium* (pp. 77–97). Potomac, MD: Lawrence Erlbaum Associates.

Jost, A. (1987). Die assoziationstestigkeit in ihrer Abhangigkeit der Verteilung der Wiederholungen. *Z Psychology, 14,* 436–472.

Kahana, M. J., & Greene, R. L. (1993). Effects of spacing on memory for homogeneous lists. *Journal of Experimental Psychology: Learning, Memory, and Cognition, 19,* 159–162.

Kausler, D. H., Wiley, J. G., & Phillips, P. L. (1990). Adult age differences in memory for massed and distributed repeated practice. *Psychology and Aging, 5,* 530–534.

Landauer, T. K., & Bjork, R. A. (1978). Optimal rehearsal patterns and name learning. In M. M. Gruneberg, P. E. Morris, & R. N. Sykes (Eds.), *Practical aspects of memory* (pp. 625–632). London: Academic Press.

Linton, M. (1988). The maintenance of knowledge: Some long-term specific and generic changes. In In M. M. Gruneberg. P. E. Morris, & R. N. Sykes (Eds.), *Practical aspects of memory: Current research and issues* (Vol. 1, pp. 378–384). New York: Wiley.

Modigliani, V., & Hedges, D. G. (1987). Distributed rehearsals and the primacy effect in single-trial free recall. *Journal of Experimental Psychology: Learning, Memory, and Cognition, 13,* 426–436.

Otani, H., & Whiteman, H. L. (1994). Cued recall hypermnesia is not an artifact of response bias. *American Journal of Psychology, 107,* 401–421.

Payne, D. G. (1986). Hypermnesia for pictures and words: Testing the recall level hypothesis. *Journal of Experimental Psychology: Learning, Memory, and Cognition, 12,* 16–29.

Payne, D. G. (1987). Hypermnesia and reminiscence in recall: A historical and empirical review. *Psychological Bulletin, 101,* 5–27.

Payne, D. G., Hembrooke, H. A., & Anastasi, J. S. (1993). Hypermnesia in free recall and cued recall. *Memory & Cognition, 21,* 48–62.

Payne, D. G., & Roediger, H. L. (1987). Hypermnesia occurs in recall but not in recognition. *The American Journal of Psychology, 100,* 145–165.

Rea, C. P., & Modigliani, V. (1985). The effect of expanded vs. massed practice on the retention of multiplication facts and spelling lists. *Human Learning: Journal of Practical Research and Applications, 4,* 11–18.

Reber, A. S. (1993). *Implicit learning and tacit knowledge: An essay on the cognitive unconscious.* New York: Oxford University Press.

Reder, L. M., & Anderson, J. R. (1982). Effects of spacing and embellishment for the main points of a text. *Memory & Cognition, 10,* 97–102.

Roediger, H. L., & Payne, D. G. (1982). Hypermnesia: The role of repeated testing. *Journal of Experimental Psychology: Learning, Memory, and Cognition, 8,* 66–72.

Roediger, H. L., Payne, D. G., Gillespie, G. L., & Lean, D. S. (1982). Hypermnesia as determined by level of recall. *Journal of Verbal Learning and Verbal Behavior, 21,* 635–655.

Roediger, H. L., & Thorpe, L. A. (1978). The role of recall time in producing hypermnesia. *Memory & Cognition, 6,* 296–305.

Rothkopf, E. Z., & Coke, E. U. (1963). Repetition interval and rehearsal method in learning equivalences from written sentences. *Journal of Verbal Learning and Verbal Behavior, 2,* 406–416.

Schacter, D. L. (1987). Implicit memory: History and current status. *Journal of Experimental Psychology: Learning, Memory, and Cognition, 13,* 501–518.

Schacter, D. L., Rick, S. A., & Stamp, M. S. (1985). Remediation of memory disorders: Experimental evaluation of the spaced retrieval technique. *Journal of Clinical and Experimental Neuropsychology 7,* 19–26.

Seger, C. A. (1994). Implicit learning. *Psychological Bulletin, 115,* 163–196.

Smith, S. M., & Rothkopf, E. Z. (1984). Contextual enhancement and distribution of practice in the classroom. *Cognition and Instruction, 1,* 341–358.

Staszewski, J. J. (1988). Skilled memory and expert mental calculation. In M. T. H. Chi, R. Glaser, & M. J. Farr (Eds.), *The nature of expertise* (pp. 71–128). Hillsdale, NJ: Lawrence Erlbaum Associates.

Staszewski, J. J. (1993). *Skilled memory: Evidence for its generality.* Paper presented at the 1993 Annual Meeting of the American Psychological Society, Chicago, IL.

Stevens, J. (1993). An observational study of skilled memory in waitresses. *Applied Cognitive Psychology, 7,* 205–217.

Thompson, C. P., Cowan, T., Frieman, J., Mahadevan, R. S., Vogl, R. J., & Frieman, J. (1991). Rajan: A study of a memorist. *Journal of Memory and Language, 30,* 702–724.

Toppino, T. C. (1993). The spacing effect in preschool children's free recall of pictures and words. *Bulletin of the Psychonomic Society, 31,* 27–30.

Wenger, M. J., & Payne, D. G. (1993). *Extending the study of skilled memory: Evidence for retrieval structures and contextual encoding in expertise developed with limited practice.* Paper presented at the Annual Meeting of the Midwestern Psychological Association, Chicago, IL.

Wenger, M. J., & Payne, D. G. (1995). On the acquisition of mnemonic skill: Application of skilled memory theory. *Journal of Experimental Psychology: Applied, 1,* 194–215.

Zechmeister, E. B., & Shaughnessy, J. J. (1980). When you know that you know and when you think that you know but you don't. *Bulletin of the Psychonomic Society, 15,* 41–44.

CHAPTER TEN

Memory and Analogical Reasoning

Elke van der Meer
Humboldt University, Berlin, Germany

The organism is constantly exposed to a large amount of information. But its information processing capacity is restricted. Based on need and depending on the task to be performed, only a small amount of relevant information is selected for conscious processing, a procedure referred to as the *selective and optimizing function of the human brain.* This is quite unique: No technical or other system has reached a comparable level.

By contrast, thinking as expressed, for example, in problem solving and especially in reasoning is considered to create an extension of available information by means of internal cognitive processes. Fig. 10.1 illustrates these aspects by making use of the compartment model suggested by Klix (1984, 1992).

The model describes aspects of the acquisition and representation of knowledge in long-term memory (LTM). Concepts and the relations between them are considered to be basic components of knowledge. Information from the environment is mediated by sensory systems. LTM is divided into two parts: The quasi-stationary part comprises concepts, stored relations between them, and attached wordmarks, that is, the "open" mental lexicon. The procedural part comprises procedures of different types (e.g. comparison, concatenation, reduction, transformation, etc.) that process information from the environment as well as from the quasi-stationary part of LTM. They take place within a functional unit, the so-called operational compartment. The operational compartment (working memory, short-term memory) initiates and controls a variety of detection techniques and problem-solving

139

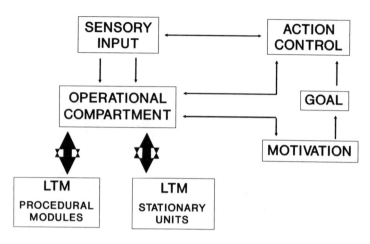

FIG. 10.1. Compartment model.

processes, which are also determined by the motivational background and individual goals of a person. The capacity of the operational compartment depends, within certain limits, on demand. Accordingly, modular cognitive subsystems functioning at different levels of efficiency are assumed. Their interaction causes knowledge structures to be flexible and provides thinking or reasoning processes of different quality and efficiency.

ANALOGICAL REASONING

Reasoning as expressed in a variety of inferences is an indicator of human intelligence. Depending on classification criteria, different taxonomies of inferences have been established (cf. Guthke & Beyer, 1992). Analogical reasoning plays a crucial role in these taxonomies. At least two aspects must be discussed in this context.

First, analogical reasoning is classified in different ways. Some researchers claim that analogizing is a special type of inductive inference (cf. Holland, Holyoak, Nisbett, & Thagard, 1986; Plötzner & Spada, 1994; Sternberg, 1977; Waldmann & Weinert, 1990). Others assume that analogical reasoning represents a distinguishable class of inferences (cf. Klix, 1992). I am inclined to support the latter assumption (van der Meer, 1994). An analogy consists of four terms: A, A', B, B' (e.g., geometrical figures, pictures, numbers, concepts expressed in words of natural language, etc.). A and A' form the base or source domain (familiar domain), B and B' the image or target domain (unfamiliar domain). The analogy condition is satisfied if the relations between A–A' and B–B' are at least partially identical. Instead of generalizing a number of individual perceptions or experiences, as is the case in inductive reasoning, analogical reasoning requires a similarity decision between two pairs of structures, or the generation of similarity between these pairs of structures. This process refers to the identification of at least partially identical relations in both analogy domains or the mapping of critical relations from the base domain onto the target domain (or vice versa). The transfer of relations to structures B–B' [which can be characterized by completely different properties compared with A–A', and which may be similar to A–A' only with regard to the critical relation(s)] will generate new information. This is why analogical reasoning is considered to be a separate class of inferencing.

Second, analogizing plays a fundamental role in the mental sphere of human beings. The history of science demonstrates that many discoveries and inventions have been due to analogical reasoning. Think of the measurement of the height of pyramids by Thales of Miletus (cf. Klix, 1993b). Analogical reasoning can thus be regarded as a mechanism of using knowledge available to master new or only partly known aspects of reality. This is due to cognitive components that reduce the amount of information offered to what is actually necessary to make a decision.

Empirical evidence indicates that analogical reasoning is based on several processing steps. Kedar-Cabelli (1988), for example, assumed the following elementary processing components to be relevant for analogy detection: (a) retrieval of the base domain from LTM, (b) selective elaboration of the base domain (accentuation of elements of structures within the base domain, comparison and identification of relations, selection of relevant relations), (c) mapping of relevant relations from the base domain into the target domain, (d) justification (verification of mapping), and (e) learning by analogy (representation of the modified target domain in LTM).

There are various hypotheses and quite a few findings concerning the question of the relevant elementary components of analogical reasoning (e.g., is it necessary to assume a verification component?) and discussing the way these components are processed (processing order, parallel vs. sequential processing of components) (cf. Gentner, 1983, 1989; Holyoak & Thagard, 1990; Keane, 1990). A multitude of different processing algorithms rather than a single algorithmic structure of processing have been found. These algorithms vary in efficiency, depending on specific demand and the structures of base and target domains.

However, our knowledge about mechanisms underlying analogy construction is restricted. Relatively little is known about the process of finding an analog base domain suitable for structuring and modifying the target domain (cf. Bachmann, 1994). It must be taken into account in this context that similarity is regarded as a heterogeneous phenomenon consisting of a number of different aspects (Klix, 1993a).

MEMORY-BASED DIFFERENCES
IN ANALOGICAL REASONING

Considering the quality and efficiency of analogical reasoning processes, the influence of the quasi-stationary and the procedural parts of LTM is assumed to be of major importance (cf. Fig. 10.1). Procedures of different types (e.g., inhibition, accentuation, comparison, mapping, etc.) are applied to knowledge (memory) and to information perceived. They integrate new information into previously existing knowledge. In doing so procedures transform, modifying the new information as well as the knowledge structures.

The Procedural Approach: Experiment I

In order to find out the way in which the procedural part of LTM determines the process and the result of analogical reasoning we carried out various investigations. In the following we discuss in more detail only one aspect: the memory-based structuring of perception by inhibiting or accentuating certain elements.

Method. We analyzed the way in which subjects with different levels of expertise in mathematics identified geometric analogies (Klix, 1992; Offenhaus, 1984; van der Meer, 1994). The analogy terms consisted of chessboard patterns of differing complexity. Between these analogy terms one of the following relation types could appear: mirroring along the vertical, the horizontal, or the diagonal lines (Fig. 10.2).

In accordance with Sternberg (1977) the method of analogy detection on the basis of graded preinformation was used. By means of this method it is possible to analyze in more detail the components of the reasoning process. Before subjects were asked to detect the analogy they were given different kinds of preinformation [a fixation point, the first term, the first term pair (base domain), or the first three analogy terms]. Subjects were instructed to look at the preinformation as briefly as possible. Then the complete analogy was given (50% positive examples, 50% negative examples). Subjects had to check as soon as they could, but possibly without mistakes, whether or not each complete item met the analogy condition. The time required for both preinformation and analogy detection as well as the error rate were measured.

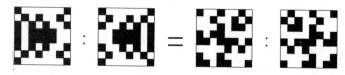

FIG. 10.2. Example for an analogy item. The analogy condition is satisfied: The relation between base and target domains (mirroring along the vertical line) is identical.

We tested two groups of subjects: First, a control group consisting of undergraduate students of psychology in their first semester, who had passed the high school leaving examination with excellent results (n = 15; mean age: 20.1 years); second, an experimental group consisting of pupils attending, for a few weeks, a specialist course of mathematics at Humboldt University (n = 15; mean age: 16.5 years). In addition to a high level of general intelligence, these pupils had proved to be particularly gifted at mathematics.

Results. The mean error rates did not differ between the two groups of subjects. A two-way between/within ANOVA compared encoding times for preinformation between groups of subjects and levels of preinformation. It revealed significant main effects of groups of subjects, of levels of preinformation and a significant interaction. Members of the experimental group encoded preinformation significantly faster as compared with the control group. A two-way between/within ANOVA compared time required for analogy detection between groups of subjects and analogy items depending on levels of preinformation. It revealed a significant main effect of levels of preinformation and a significant interaction of the two factors. Members of the experimental group detected analogies significantly faster as compared with the control group if no specific preinformation was given (see Klix, 1992; Offenhaus, 1984; van der Meer, 1994). By means of a detailed analysis we showed that these results are not due to elementary processes of different speeds. The better performance of the experimental group was rather caused by a specific mental representation of analogy terms and by specific strategies used for solving analogies (see Klix, 1992; van der Meer, 1994).

Next we discuss the role of mental representations in analog inferences in more detail. We argued that analogical reasoning is based on cognitive components that are involved in intelligence performance. One of these components is responsible for structuring perception based on a selection of the relevant information: Properties of analogy terms of relevance for the detection of relations between analogy terms (i.e., rotation-sensitive properties) have to be accentuated, and irrelevant properties have to be inhibited. This process of selection results in a type of mental representation of analogy terms that, in its most efficient version, only consists of relation-specific properties. In line with these assumptions we found that the experimental and the control groups have shown considerable differences in their mental representation of analogy terms: First, the experimental group had shorter times for encoding and processing preinformation 1 (only the first term of analogy is given) compared with the control group. In addition, it was less influenced by the variation in the complexity of analogy terms (cf. Fig. 10.3).

Second, by means of a special drawing assignment we have further differentiated these results: After solving 30 complete analogy tasks, subjects were given the analogy terms of a different complexity in an isolated way. Subjects were instructed to look at each term as long as deemed necessary in

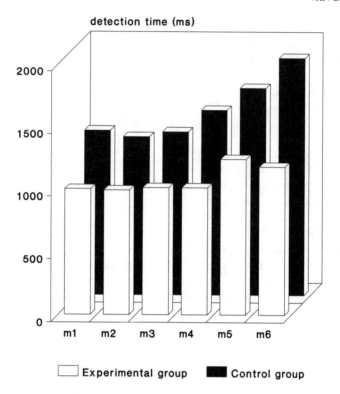

FIG. 10.3. Detection time for preinformation 1 (first term of analogy) depending on the complexity of analogy terms. (m_1, m_2, m_3: low complexity; m_4, m_5, m_6: high complexity).

order to be able to reproduce the properties relevant to identifying the respective analogy term. After that they were asked to draw these properties in empty frames.

The data illustrate the following: First, the experimental group had significantly lower inspection times as compared with the control group. Second, the drawings indicated that this was the result of different encoding formats of the two groups of subjects (Fig. 10.4).

The drawings of mathematically gifted subjects consisted—as compared with the control group—of significantly fewer partial figures (2.25 vs. 4.02), fewer total figure elements (9.30 vs. 17.50), and a significantly higher number of relation-specific elements (85.40% vs. 69.30%). In addition, the experimental group showed a greater interpersonal variation of the mental representation of the analogy terms than did the control group (cf. van der Meer, 1994).

These findings support the assumption that the mental representation of analogy items differs between the experimental and control groups qualitatively and quantitatively: Mathematically gifted subjects show a less complex

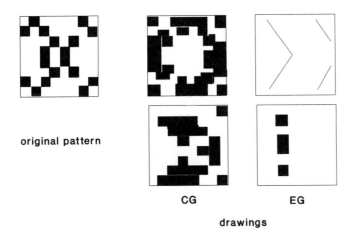

original pattern

CG   EG

drawings

FIG. 10.4. Mental representation of relevant properties of analogy terms as indicated in drawings of subjects (EG: experimental group; CG: control group).

and a more relation-specific mental representation, that is, a more efficient selection of relevant properties as compared with the control group. This stronger redundancy reduction facilitates the subsequent identification and mapping of relations, which, in turn, is reflected in shorter analogy detection times of mathematically gifted subjects. The comparison with the control group reflects this fact. Moreover, detailed analysis and simulation experiments indicate that mathematically gifted subjects prefer more effective strategies consisting of fewer processing steps (see Klix, 1992).

The first experiment indicates one of the memory-based sources of the better reasoning performance of mathematically gifted subjects: It consists in their higher flexibility as to the multiple classification of the analogy terms based on the accentuation of relevant properties on the one hand and the inhibition of irrelevant ones on the other. The selection of relevant information (rotation-sensitive representation of terms) is controlled by knowledge structures. This corresponds with findings made when experts and novices in chess, in physics, and in many other knowledge domains were compared in specific experiments (cf. Kluwe, 1990).

The Quasi-Stationary Approach: Experiment II

Another source of quantitative and qualitative differences in analogical reasoning is the quasi-stationary part of LTM. We analyzed this factor by means of semantic analogy tasks (Becker, van der Meer, & Meißner, 1983; van der Meer, 1994).

Method. The first three analogy terms were given. Subjects were asked to find out or to generate in their memories the missing fourth term of analogy. Examples include:

brush : paint :: knife : ? (instrument)
bird : nest :: cow : ? (location)
fish : animal :: doll : ? (sub-superconcept)
heat : cold :: giant : ? (antonym)

Between the structures of base and target domains there could exist either event relations (location, instrument, finality) or feature-dependent relations (coordination, sub-superconcept relation, antonymy, comparative relation). We know from a variety of experiments that event relations (at a medium level of abstraction) are stored stationarily in LTM. They can be activated automatically. By contrast, feature-dependent relations are not stored stationarily. They have to be generated by means of algorithmiclike procedures based on comparative processes operating on concept features (Klix, 1992; Klix, van der Meer, Preuß, & Wolf, 1987). The generation procedure involves decision modules of different types and can be optimized according to need.

We have analyzed the way in which different groups of second graders coped with semantic analogies based on different relation types as mentioned earlier. We compared three groups of subjects: intellectually normal subjects (IQ = 99; mean age: 7.9 years), mentally retarded subjects (IQ = 79; mean age: 8.4 years), and dyslexic subjects (IQ = 93, mean age: 9.4 years).

Results. Fig. 10.5 illustrates the mean error rate in solving analogies based on event relations and feature-dependent relations, respectively. As indicated by the analogy experiment, the mentally retarded subjects differed significantly from intellectually normal subjects in their failure to produce analogies based on event relations and on feature-dependent relations. The deficit of dyslexic subjects was restricted to feature-dependent, that is, procedural based, knowledge.

What about the reasons for this difference? The deficit of mentally retarded subjects seems to be due to a lower degree of differentiation of conceptual structures in LTM. This was indicated by the results of a controlled association test (performed with the same subjects several weeks after the main analogy experiment) that required the identification of essential components of concepts used in the analogy test (van der Meer, 1990). In this task, there was a population specific difference in the degree to which subjects mentioned features as essential components of concepts: Dyslexic subjects mentioned significantly more features per concept and mentally retarded subjects significantly fewer features per concept than intellectually normal subjects (cf. van der Meer, 1994).

These results support the notion that the deficit of mentally retarded subjects in solving semantic analogies is based on a reduced knowledge base. The deficit of dyslexic subjects seems to be due to other reasons. They

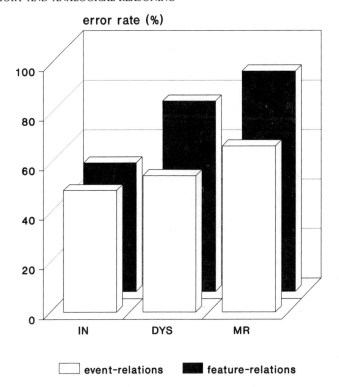

FIG. 10.5. Mean error rate of intellectually normal (IN), mentally retarded (MR), and dyslexic (DYS) subjects in solving semantic analogies based on event relations and on feature-dependent relations.

have an extended knowledge base: The relevant features are stored in LTM and can be activated. However, dyslexic subjects seem to be hampered in identifying and isolating relevant features. The growing complexity of the database used requires the procedures necessary for detecting or generating relations to involve more complex and less specific feature sets. As a result, the identification and mapping of relations are more difficult, which, in turn probably leads to higher error rates in analogical reasoning.

Of course, the performance differences between our populations could be also attributable to some further factors: First, feature-dependent relations are generated by algorithmiclike procedures. In addition to the identification and accentuation of relevant features, these procedures consist of further steps (e.g., comparison of features, relation identification, mappings, etc.). If we assume that these operations are also hampered or if the algorithmiclike procedures run incorrectly, then feature-dependent relations cannot be generated and analogies cannot be constructed. Second, the ability to execute a strategy does not guarantee its actual application. This phenomenon emphasizes the importance of considering the impact of meta-mnemonic knowledge on cognitive performance (Naus & Ornstein, 1983; Waldmann & Weinert, 1990).

In conclusion, the results of our second experiment show the influence of the conceptual knowledge base on the quality of analogical reasoning. They also indicate the close interaction between the conceptual and the procedural knowledge base.

FINAL REMARKS

Are the empirical data presented of any use when one attempts to investigate or correct a problem in the real world (Herrmann & Gruneberg, 1993)? Besides its diagnostic value (e.g., in intelligence tests), analogical reasoning is considered to be essential for the development of intelligent technical systems (Plötzner & Spada, 1994) and for enhancing the everyday intelligence of human beings.

Learning by analogies is crucial in knowledge acquisition (Forbus & Gentner, 1986; Klix, 1993b). Our scientific knowledge of analogical reasoning concerns some points of relevance and utility to optimizing the process of knowledge acquisition in the real world:

1. The efficiency of analogical reasoning depends, to a large extent, on the mental representation of problems. This representation should contain all relevant elements and should be of task-depending minimal complexity. The identification of relevant elements is the starting point for relation identification and mapping or projection. This process can be stimulated by instruction. If subjects are instructed to look for relations between features of analogy terms rather than for features alone, their performance in analogical reasoning increases significantly (see Becker et al., 1983).

2. Of course, efficient and creative analogical reasoning is not based on some identified relation. Therefore, information received by perception or from LTM must be compared, combined, and arranged in a new way, for example, by means of changing the representation format or level, a process referred to as *flexible structuring of information.* It has proved to be of high relevance to efficient and creative reasoning. This process can also be stimulated by instruction and training (Klix, 1993b; van der Meer, 1994).

3. In general, analogical reasoning is considered to be a powerful mechanism of human intelligence and an efficient method of acquiring complex knowledge. However, there are also findings suggesting that remembering details or facts does not seem to be facilitated by analogical reasoning (Mayer, 1989).

REFERENCES

Bachmann, T. (1994). *Aspekte der Analogiebildung* [Mechanisms of analogy construction]. Diplomarbeit, Humboldt-Universität zu Berlin (unpublished).

Becker, R., van der Meer, E., & Meißner, R. (1983). Zu Denken und Sprache bei geschädigten und nichtgeschädigten Schülern—dargestellt am Beispiel semantischer Analogieanforderungen [Reasoning and language processing: A diagnostic approach]. *Die Sonderschule, 3,* 155–161.

Forbus, K. D., & Gentner, D. (1986). Learning physical domains: Toward a theoretical framework. In R. S. Michalski, J. G. Carbonell, & T. M. Mitchell (Eds.), *Machine learning. An artificial intelligence approach* (Vol. 2, pp. 311–348). Los Altos, CA: Kaufmann.

Gentner, D. (1983). Structure-mapping: A theoretical framework for analogy. *Cognitive Science, 7,* 155–170.

Gentner, D. (1989). The mechanisms of analogical reasoning. In S. Vosniadou & A. Ortony (Eds.), *Similarity and analogical reasoning* (pp. 199–241). Cambridge, England: Cambridge University Press.

Guthke, T., & Beyer, R. (1992). Inferenzen beim Satz- und Textverstehen [Inferences in sentence and text processing]. *Zeitschrift für Psychologie, 200,* 321–344.

Herrmann, D., & Gruneberg, M. (1993). The need to expand the horizons of the practical aspects of memory movement. *Applied Cognitive Psychology, 7,* 553–565.

Holland, J. H., Holyoak, K. J., Nisbett, R. E., & Thagard, P. R. (1986). *Induction: Processes on inference, learning, and discovery.* Cambridge, MA: MIT Press.

Holyoak, K. J., & Thagard, P. R. (1990). A constraint-satisfaction approach to analogue retrieval and mapping. In K. J. Gilhooly, M. T. G. Keane, R. H. Logie, & G. Erdos (Eds.), *Lines of thinking: Reflections on the psychology of thought* (Vol. 1, pp. 205–220). Chichester, England: Wiley.

Keane, M. T. G. (1990). Incremental analogizing: Theory and model. In K. J. Gilhooly, M. T. G. Keane, R. H. Logie, & G. Erdos (Eds.), *Lines of thinking: Reflections on the psychology of thought* (Vol. 1, pp. 221–235). Chichester, England: Wiley.

Kedar-Cabelli, S. (1988). Analogy—from a unified perspective. In D. H. Helman (Ed.), *Analogical reasoning* (pp. 65–103). Dordrecht, The Netherlands: Kluwer.

Klix, F. (1984). Denken und Gedächtnis—über Wechselwirkungen kognitiver Kompartments bei der Erzeugung geistiger Leistungen [Thinking and memory: Interactions among cognitive compartments in cognitive performance]. *Zeitschrift für Psychologie, 192,* 213–244.

Klix, F. (1992). *Die Natur des Verstandes* [The nature of mind]. Göttingen, Germany: Hogrefe.

Klix, F. (1993a). Analytische Betrachtungen über Struktur und Funktion von Inferenzen [An analysis of structure and function of inferences]. *Zeitschrift für Psychologie, 201,* 393–414.

Klix, F. (1993b). *Erwachendes Denken* [Awakening thoughts]. Heidelberg: Spektrum.

Klix, F., van der Meer, E., Preuß, M., & Wolf, M. (1987). Über Prozeß- und Strukturkomponenten der Wissensrepräsentation beim Menschen [Procedural and structural components of knowledge representation]. *Zeitschrift für Psychologie, 195,* 39–61.

Kluwe, R. H. (1990). Gedächtnis und Wissen [Memory and knowledge]. In H. Spada (Hrsg.), *Lehrbuch Allgemeine Psychologie* (pp. 115–188). Bern: Huber.

Mayer, R. E. (1989). Models for understanding. *Review of Educational Research, 59,* 43–64.

Naus, M. J., & Ornstein, P. A. (1983). Development of memory strategies: Analysis, questions, and issues. In M. T. H. Chi (Ed.), *Trends in memory development research* (Vol. 9, pp. 1–30). Basel: Karger.

Offenhaus, B. (1984). *Analyse des analogen Schlußprozesses unter differentiellem Aspekt* [Differences in analogical reasoning]. Unpublished doctoral dissertation, Humboldt-Universität zu Berlin.

Plötzner, R., & Spada, H. (1994). Wissenserwerb: Funktionsprinzipien von Lernprozessen [Knowledge acquisition: Some underlying learning mechanisms]. In D. Dörner & E. van der Meer (Hrsg.), *Gedächtnis: Probleme—Trends—Perspektiven* (pp. 381–412). Göttingen, Germany: Hogrefe.

Sternberg, R. J. (1977). Component processes in analogical reasoning. *Psychological Review, 84,* 353–378.

van der Meer, E. (1990). Dynamics of knowledge structures: Some underlying strategies. In W. Schneider & F. E. Weinert (Eds.), *Interactions among aptitudes, strategies, and knowledge in cognitive performance* (pp. 134–146). New York: Springer.

van der Meer, E. (1994). Gedächtnis und Inferenzen [Memory and inferences]. In D. Dörner & E. van der Meer (Eds.), *Gedächtnis. Probleme—Trends—Perspektiven* (pp. 341–380). Göttingen, Germany: Hogrefe.

Waldmann, M., & Weinert, F. E. (1990). *Intelligenz und Denken* [Intelligence and thinking]. Göttingen, Germany: Hogrefe.

PART FIVE

MEMORY AND SURVEYS

CHAPTER ELEVEN

The Use of Strategic Processes by Survey Respondents

Gordon B. Willis
National Center for Health Statistics
Centers for Disease Control and Prevention

A key issue in the field of applied cognitive psychology is the extent to which individuals use strategies in completing various cognitive tasks. In general, mental tasks can be considered to be either strategy free or strategy intensive (Campione, Brown, & Bryant, 1985). From the point of view of those who strive to improve human performance on cognitive tasks, a focus on these as either strategy free or strategy intensive gives rise to fundamentally different intervention approaches. This chapter details the application of these approaches to the area of survey methodology, which endeavors to lead respondents to provide accurate information on survey questionnaires. Answering survey questions is assumed here to be heavily cognitively based, as proposed by many authors (Cannell, Miller, & Oksenberg, 1981; Hippler, Schwarz, & Sudman, 1987; Jabine, Straf, Tanur, & Tourangeau, 1984; Moss & Goldstein, 1979). I consider the task of answering these questions to be either strategy free or strategy intensive, and discuss the ramifications of each viewpoint, for the purposes of actively taking steps to improve respondent performance.

THE STRATEGY-FREE VIEW OF SURVEY RESPONDING

One view of a survey question such as: "How many times have you been to the dentist in the past two years?" would be to consider this as requiring simply what Reder (1987) labeled *direct retrieval* of information, without

153

any significant reliance on strategy. In the most simple case, the requested memory is read directly from long-term storage, and performance variation is observed across individuals because they differ in their ability (or willingness) to complete this process.

Under the strategy-free viewpoint, approaches to maximizing performance are relatively straightforward (whether or not these are actually successful). The survey taker strives to simplify the task to the greatest degree possible, so that the majority of respondents will be able to respond correctly. Approaches that might be taken here include: the use of simple phrasing that is easy to comprehend (Royston, 1989), the shortening of the reference period (e.g., one month instead of 12 months), or the use of direct retrieval cues that may trigger memory (Lessler, Tourangeau, & Salter, 1989). Such approaches are common in the survey research literature (see Jobe & Mingay, 1991, for a review of this research), and represent the dominant trend in the development of questionnaire design methods, beginning with the classic text by Payne (1951). That is, there is little emphasis on the qualitative manner in which different individuals approach the task of answering survey questions; questionnaire designers are encouraged mainly to follow rules, such as "use simple wording," which maximize the number of veridical responses produced.

THE STRATEGY-INTENSIVE VIEW
OF SURVEY RESPONDING

Recent studies contained in the survey research literature have departed from the traditional approach just outlined, by emphasizing the importance of respondent strategies as underlying the survey response process. For example, using the dental visit question posed earlier, one strategy, as described by Burton and Blair (1991), might be to try to enumerate each episode of visiting the dentist, whereas another is to use estimation, according to a "baseline rule with adjustment" (e.g., "I go two times a year for checkups, and generally one other time to have cavities filled, so I'll say six times in the past two years"). For current purposes, I define a *strategy* as an active process that is under the executive control of the survey respondent. That is, respondents may choose to make use of strategies under a variety of circumstances, but strategy use is not automatically elicited under any set of conditions that are introduced by the survey administrator. For example, the provision of retrieval cues is viewed as triggering strategy use to the extent that the respondent selects a strategy that makes use of these cues. However, if the effect of cue presentation is simply to elicit memories, without any mediation by the respondent, then this process is not viewed as strategic in nature. A key distinction is made, therefore, between the cognitive processes that the survey administrator intends the respondent to use, and those that he or she actually invokes.

I have discussed briefly the basic ways in which the strategy-free viewpoint leads the survey administrator to attempt to obtain better-quality data. Clearly, the adoption of the strategy-intensive view imposes a very different approach; specifically, it advocates the examination of respondents' spontaneous strategic processes, as well as the use, by survey administrators, of interventions that attempt to direct respondents to use optimal strategies. I propose that, in order that this orientation actually lead to interventions that improve respondent performance, several underlying conditions must hold. Because these conditions are not often explicitly recognized by survey researchers, I consider them in turn, along with the support for each from the research literature.

RESPONDENT RELIANCE ON STRATEGIC PROCESSES

Clearly, in order that a focus on respondent cognitive strategies be worthwhile, the first condition that must hold is that such strategies are actually selected, in the course of answering survey questions. If responses to survey questions are invariably based on a direct retrieval mechanism, the strategy-intensive viewpoint is of little utility. A review of this issue is fairly complex, because in application to the area of survey responding, the term *strategy* refers to a wide range of possible behaviors. Strategy use has been studied mainly with respect to the retrieval of autobiographical information from memory (Jobe, Tourangeau, & Smith, 1993, review this literature). However, there may be a number of strategies involved in the overall survey response process that have not been previously well described, or even recognized as strategies that underlie survey responding.

To facilitate a review of the evidence for strategy use in answering of survey questions, I first classify and consider separately the types of strategies that have been either detected, or else proposed to operate, in the course of the survey response process. I rely on the model proposed by Willis, Royston, and Bercini (1991), which incorporates encoding, retrieval, decision, and response subprocesses, and that modifies the basic scheme presented by Tourangeau (1984). The Willis et al. model proposes that the respondent's answer to a survey question may not be automatic, and that the retrieval subprocess in particular is highly strategic in nature. To extend this idea further, each subprocess described in the model may have associated with it a number of strategies that the survey respondent will invoke as needed. A discussion of the use of strategy for each subprocess, along with relevant research findings, is presented next.

Encoding Strategies

It has long been argued that encoding of many types of verbal stimuli is not an automatic process, and that there may be a set of directive, higher-order processes that influence information encoding (see Morris, 1978, for a discussion of constructive processes in encoding). In particular, we often do not simply process a question as a simple request, but first attempt to determine the intention of the requestor of the information. For example, interpretation of the question "Where is Bob?" will vary, depending on whether one is present at a meeting that Bob is supposed to be attending, or reviewing a floor plan in order to assign office space.

In application to survey methodology, the relevant issue is the extent to which survey respondents apply strategies that strive to interpret the intentions of the survey designer. Although the nature of survey question encoding is not well understood, several researchers have suggested that respondents do take strides to determine the intended meaning of a survey question, especially when that meaning is vague or is open to multiple interpretations. Evidence for this is generally qualitative, and often undocumented, including cases in which informal pretesting has produced comments by respondents such as: "If you mean X, I would say one thing, but if you mean Y, I'd say something else." Clearly, respondents are well aware that implicit behavioral requirements differ from those of a naturalistic conversation, and attempt to interpret questions in terms of the inferred purpose of both the individual question and the survey in general (Cannell et al., 1981). Although these factors have been recognized in the survey methodology literature, there has been little acknowledgement that these represent "encoding strategy." Further attention specifically on this issue may reveal that a range of encoding strategies are actually used by survey respondents.

Retrieval Strategies

Considerable research has been devoted to the issue of strategy selection in the general retrieval of information from memory (Norman, 1973; Reder, 1987; Reiser, Black, & Kalamarides, 1986). Following this trend, a number of specific studies of retrieval strategies have appeared, over the past decade, in the survey research literature. Characteristic of this research is a study by Burton and Blair (1991), who list as possible retrieval strategies: episodic enumeration, rule-based estimation (recall with adjustment of the retrieved information), estimation from an availability heuristic, and automatic estimation. Burton and Blair found that even fairly simple questions sometimes elicit fairly elaborate cognitive strategies; that is, respondents do not simply retrieve the answer to a question directly.

Cognitive laboratory interviewing has also been used to investigate the extent to which strategies are used to retrieve information necessary for answering survey questions. In particular, strategic approaches to information retrieval by laboratory subjects appear to be dominant in several areas:

> *Answering knowledge questions:* Qualitative cognitive interviews reveal that respondents treat this task as problem solving, rather than as direct information retrieval. That is, respondents use a wide range of strategies, such as elimination of rejectable distractor items, use of questionnaire context, and guessing about the number of likely "correct" items in a list of presented options (Willis et al., 1991).

> *Answering questions requiring long-term recall:* Analysis of verbal protocols, using think-aloud and verbal probing techniques (Willis et al., 1991), demonstrates that survey questions about events occurring in the distant past often do not trigger attempts at retrieval, but rather result in an immediate response suggesting that the information is unlikely to be both accessible and available in memory (e.g., "There's no way that I can come up with that type of information after all this time—I would be guessing").

In sum, retrieval processes appear to be extremely rich in strategy, across several types of survey questions.

Decision/Response Strategies

The final cognitive processes that may involve use of strategies are decision and response. Here, I group these by referring specifically to processes occurring after the retrieval of information from memory has been completed. Cannell et al. (1981), Tourangeau (1984), and Willis et al. (1991) suggested that after information is retrieved, survey respondents frequently do not automatically produce a response. Instead, they may reflect on the information retrieved, in several ways:

> *Verification:* Sometimes a respondent will begin to give a response, and then pause to interject a comment such as: "No, that can't be right . . . hold on." Clearly, the respondent has invoked some form of evaluative mechanism that determines the quality and adequacy of the retrieved information, and this mechanism may then prompt further retrieval effort. It is this process that is reflected by the feedback between retrieval and decision processes in both the Cannell et al. (1981) and Willis et al. (1991) models.

> *Response modification:* The respondent may retrieve information that he or she does not want to report, because of sensitivity or due to issues related to social desirability (Sudman & Bradburn, 1989). The resultant response may therefore be based on a decision to lie outright ("No, I

have never smoked marijuana"), or to slightly modify an answer (e.g., a report of smoking one pack of cigarettes a day, when the respondent actually recalls smoking one-and-a-half packs). This is in effect the opposite of verification, which presumably results in a more accurate answer.

Satisficing: Krosnick (1991) suggested that, especially under conditions in which information retrieval is very difficult, respondents may choose to terminate the retrieval process, and instead "satisfice," or produce a response that is simply satisfactory.

Such decision strategies have begun to be studied intensively, especially in the area of responding to sensitive survey questions. Willis, Sirken, and Nathan (1994) studied the differences among laboratory subjects in their strategic approaches to survey-relevant decision making, and found that subjects differed markedly in their reliance on the protection associated with complex survey administration procedures. Furthermore, subjects were found to fall into several groups, representing disparate response strategies. For example, with respect to the randomized response procedure (Warner, 1965) that relies on the outcome of a coin flip or other randomizing device to determine the question to be answered, and where the question selected is known only to the respondent, subjects differed considerably in their understanding of the how the procedure protects responses. Those who understood procedural but not statistical aspects of the procedure often concluded, erroneously, that it was so effective that it prevented anyone (including the survey administrators) from making use of the respondent's answer. The strategy subjects sometimes reported, then, was to say "Yes" or "No" haphazardly, because they thought that it would make no difference how they responded. On the other hand, subjects who did not understand even the rudiments of the procedure concluded that it was actually a type of trick or "shell game," and suggested that they would rely on a strategy of "Just say no, in order to protect myself."

Summary: Operation of Strategic Processes

A division of the survey response process into subprocesses (encoding, retrieval, and decision/response) makes clear that different strategies may be applied by respondents for each, in the course of answering survey questions. Thus, the first condition considered, regarding respondent use of strategy, appears to be satisfied. However, this does not imply that the survey response process is universally strategic; studies of strategy use tend to focus on survey questions that elicit a rich range of strategies, rather than on questions that may be more mundane in this regard. It remains to be determined how frequently strategic processes are actually used to answer survey questions in nonexperimental situations, and whether survey designers can develop guidelines to determine whether responding will likely be strategic or nonstrategic for a particular class of question.

INSTRUCTION IN STRATEGY

The second condition that must hold, if survey designers are to profit from the study of respondent strategy use, is itself composed of three separate parts: First, it must be demonstrated that the designer can influence the strategy that respondents actually select. If respondents are either resistant or unable to comply, there is little practical value in a focus on strategy. Second, one must be able to instruct the respondent in strategy use easily and quickly. It is well documented that there are teachable strategic approaches that are effective in improving cognitive task performance (Fuson, 1986), but these may take days or weeks of training, and are therefore unusable within the context of survey administration. Finally, and perhaps most importantly, the survey designer must be able to determine an optimal strategy. In particular, it is necessary to have information indicating which specific strategy will result in accurate information, or that at least will be reliably more accurate than alternative strategies.

The practice of providing strategic instruction to survey respondents is a fairly new approach. To organize a discussion of the studies that have been done, I again divide the survey response task into the subprocesses of encoding, retrieval, and decision/response.

Instruction in Encoding Strategies

Little work has been done to instruct respondents to use particular strategies to encode survey questions, such as prompting them to adopt the strategy of trying to determine what the researcher's goals are in asking this question. Presumably this is because, as noted earlier, the nature of encoding strategies with respect to survey questions is not well understood. To some extent, interventions by researchers such as Oksenberg, Vinokur, and Cannell (1979) that induce respondents to promise effortful responding may influence encoding strategies, as well as later cognitive processes. It is also possible that the behavior of interviewers, and especially the way that they introduce the survey, will influence the degree to which respondents select a particular strategy in encoding questions. These hypotheses are admittedly speculative, because it is very difficult to define explicitly what consists of an encoding strategy and to differentiate this from strategy-free encoding. That is, simple instruction to apply more cognitive processing effort to the task of comprehension does not necessarily influence the choice of strategy. However, it may be worthwhile to consider the encoding of at least some survey questions as involving the implementation of a number of fairly sophisticated strategies, and to attempt to influence respondent selection of these. Although there is little direct evidence that encoding strategy instruction is particularly worthwhile, this may be an area worthy of further attention.

Instruction in Retrieval Strategy

With respect to information retrieval processes, several distinct strategies are possible, and this has led survey researchers to focus on the effectiveness of manipulations that affect retrieval strategy. Burton and Blair (1991) discussed the types of manipulations that might enhance recall performance, mentioning: (a) provision of retrieval cues, which may help the respondent to decide to use an enumeration (event counting) strategy; (b) control of the amount of time available to answer, which may indirectly influence the strategy that respondents use; (c) provision of information about the "average person's" answer, or about the range of answers expected; and (d) asking for effortful responding, which may induce the respondent to select an effective, but difficult, strategy. The effects of these manipulations have been studied to varying degrees. For example, Lessler et al. (1989) evaluated the effectiveness of the provision of retrieval cues for questions on 12-month dental visits, but found a weak overall positive effect, despite the fact that this practice added dramatically to the length of the question. Burton and Blair (1991) controlled the amount of time available for responding, and found inconsistent evidence that this practice improves recall performance. On the other hand, Schwarz, Hippler, Deutsch, and Strack (1985) and Schwarz and Bienias (1990) found that the provision of different response category ranges for behavioral frequency questions did affect respondent behavior. For example, modifying the response options for a question on amount of daily television watching ("up to ½ hour" to "more than 2½ hours," versus "up to 2½ hours" to "more than 4½ hours") influenced the responses given, presumably because this affected respondents' determinations of what "normal" behavior is, and therefore the degree to which they "adjusted" their own behavioral estimates. Therefore, respondent strategy, and ultimately performance, can be influenced by altering values of the response options. However, in the absence of validating information, it is unclear which values elicit "correct" responses.

Relatively more research has been conducted with respect to provision of direct recall instructions, as opposed to the study of variables that only indirectly affect strategy choice. For recall of various types of autobiographical information, such as medically related episodes, Whitten and Leonard (1981), Loftus (1984), Loftus and Fathi (1985), Jobe et al. (1990), and Loftus, Smith, Klinger, and Fiedler (1992) contrasted the use of forward, backward, or free recall. In a study of memory for cigarette smoking behavior, Means,

Swan, Jobe, Esposito, and Loftus (1989) and Means, Habina, Swan, and Jack (1992) compared four instructed strategies: additive decomposition, availability, episodic enumeration, and free strategy combined with thinking aloud. Finally, Hubbard (1992) studied recall of drug use and social behaviors, and Sudman et al. (1993) focused on recall of cancer screening tests. Both studies instructed subjects to recall through either episodic enumeration or a more general retrieval process.

In general, these studies conclude that subjects do reliably use the strategies requested. However, with respect to the effectiveness of this intervention, no clear trends have emerged to suggest that instruction in any particular strategy should be given. In fact, Jobe et al. (1990) concluded that free recall (no strategy instruction) may often be the preferred option, which is a disappointment to researchers who aim to enhance performance through strategic instruction.

Overall, the accumulated evidence indicates that respondents can be induced to use various retrieval strategies when formulating answers to survey questions. However, the more important requisite condition is that the survey designer knows which strategy to teach, and the studies reviewed earlier indicate that, if there is an optimal general strategy for survey retrieval processes, researchers are not aware of that strategy. Even with respect to specific classes of survey questions (e.g., long-term recall of medical visits), it is not clear that any particular strategy is best.

Instruction in Decision/Response Strategy Use

Manipulation of decision and response strategy selection is implicitly involved whenever the survey designer attempts to influence the respondent's decision of whether to respond in a truthful manner, especially with respect to survey questions that are sensitive. In other words, it is generally known what the optimum strategy is, from the data collector's point of view ("tell the truth"), but it is not always clear that we can induce respondents to adopt this strategy. In a sense, the problem encountered is the opposite of that existing with respect to retrieval, where respondent strategy selection can be influenced, but where it is unclear whether such instruction is particularly advantageous.

It appears evident that the basic strategy that many respondents use when presented sensitive questions is simply to protect themselves by answering with whatever response will minimize perceived undesirable consequences (Nathan & Sirken, 1988). Much work on inducing respondents to alter their response strategies, then, involves maximizing protection (anonymity or confidentiality) to lead respondents to answer as truthfully as possible. However, the value of such manipulation is open to debate, as the various procedures used have produced mixed results, and it is not possible to predict which forms of administration will be effective (Nathan, Sirken, Willis, & Esposito, 1990; Sudman & Bradburn, 1974). A limitation of some previous studies, however, is that they have tended to emphasize response protection only from the point of view of the survey administrator (the "objective" level of risk), whereas it is the perceptions of the survey respondent that are primary in determining the strategy that he or she adopts (Willis et al., 1994). This reinforces a point made earlier: Assessment of strategic selection must be made with respect to what the respondent actually does, and not with respect to the instructions given by the administrator. Recognizing this point may be critical, especially in cases where survey designers go to great lengths to develop elaborate schemes that protect response security, but that are unlikely to be understood by many survey respondents. It may therefore be vital not only that survey administration procedures be explained to respondents, but that prior testing of the explanations be conducted, to determine both the comprehension of these explanations and the ways in which different levels of understanding translate into strategy selection.

DISCUSSION

To reiterate, there is value in focusing on strategy use in survey responding, but only if certain conditions hold: strategies are in fact used to answer survey questions; we have some influence over which strategy the respondent uses; we can teach respondents to use a particular strategy quickly and effectively; and we know which strategy to teach. The discussion presented in this chapter suggests several conclusions. First, it appears that fundamentally different types of strategies are used by respondents at different points in the survey response process, and it may be profitable to conceptually differentiate these strategies. In particular, encoding, retrieval, and decision/response subprocesses give rise to very different forms of strategies, and these strategies must be addressed separately to the extent that the associated subprocesses are independent of one another.

Second, despite the attention it has received, the effectiveness of instruction in retrieval strategy is generally undemonstrated. The failure of studies to improve performance in retrieval tasks may be due to the fact that this is, in practical terms, an extremely difficult task for the survey designer. For retrieval strategy instruction to be effective, it must be the case that the respondent is willing and able to effectively use the correct strategy with literally no practice, but is not willing and able enough to have selected that strategy in the first place. This leaves only a very narrow window of respondent ability, or motivation, that is likely to be amenable to instructional intervention.

These conclusions point to several ramifications for both questionnaire design and further methodological research. First, it is important to determine which classes of survey questions elicit strategy-intensive processes, because this has direct ramifications as to the means we select to minimize response error for those questions. Development of "rules" concerning which types of questions or survey contexts elicit respondent strategic processes is essential. Second, further study should be devoted to the topic of instruction in retrieval strategy. It is possible that researchers will discover that a "free strategy" is often superior to any specific strategic instruction, or that an indirect instruction to "try to recall the best that you are able" may induce the respondent to select whatever strategy will produce the best performance. Finally, instruction in strategy use with respect to decision processes is an extremely important area of survey methodology, and must take into account the strategies that respondents use when answering sensitive survey questions, as well as the way that the introduction of the task affects the decision and response strategies that respondents select. It is likely that these efforts will result in the successful application of principles of cognitive psychology, in order to produce the best possible survey data.

REFERENCES

Burton, S., & Blair, E. (1991). Task conditions, response formulation processes, and response accuracy for behavioral frequency questions in surveys. *Public Opinion Quarterly, 55,* 50–79.

Campione, J. C., Brown, A. L., & Bryant, N. R. (1985). Individual differences in learning and memory. In R. J. Sternberg (Ed.), *Human abilities: An information-processing approach* (pp. 103–126). New York: Freeman.

Cannell, C. F., Miller, P. V., & Oksenberg, L. (1981). Research on interviewing techniques. In S. Leinhardt, (Ed.), *Sociological methodology* (pp. 389–437). San Francisco, CA: Jossey-Bass.

Fuson, K. C. (1986). Teaching children to subtract by counting up. *Journal of Research in Mathematics Education, 17,* 172–189.

Hippler, H. J., Schwarz, N., & Sudman, S. (Eds.). (1987). *Social information processing and survey methodology.* New York: Springer-Verlag.

Hubbard, M. L. (1992). Laboratory experiments testing new questioning strategies. In C. F. Turner, J. T. Lessler, & J. C. Gfroerer (Eds.), *Survey measurement of drug use: Methodological studies* (pp. 53–81) (DHHS Publication No. ADM 92-1929). Washington, DC: U.S. Government Printing Office.

Jabine, T. B., Straf, M. L., Tanur, J. M., & Tourangeau, R. (Eds.). (1984). *Cognitive aspects of survey methodology: Building a bridge between disciplines.* Washington, DC: National Academy Press.

Jobe, J. B., & Mingay, D. J. (1991). Cognition and survey measurement: History and overview. *Applied Cognitive Psychology, 5,* 175–192.

Jobe, J. B., Tourangeau, R., & Smith A. F. (1993). Contributions of survey research to the understanding of memory. *Applied Cognitive Psychology, 7,* 567–584.

Jobe, J. B., White, A. A., Kelley, C. L., Mingay, D. J., Sanchez, M. J., & Loftus, E. F. (1990). Recall strategies and memory for health care visits. *The Milbank Quarterly, 68,* 171–189.

Krosnick, J. A. (1991). Response strategies for coping with the cognitive demands of attitude measures in surveys. *Applied Cognitive Psychology, 5,* 213–236.

Lessler, J., Tourangeau, R., & Salter, W. (1989). Questionnaire design in the cognitive research laboratory. *Vital and Health Statistics,* Series 6, No. 1 (DHHS Publication No. PHS 89-1076). Washington, DC: U.S. Government Printing Office.

Loftus, E. F. (1984). Protocol analysis of responses to survey recall questions. In T. B. Jabine, M. L. Straf, J. M. Tanur, & R. Tourangeau (Eds.), *Cognitive aspects of survey methodology: Building a bridge between disciplines* (pp. 61–64). Washington, DC: National Academy Press.

Loftus, E. F., & Fathi D. C. (1985). Retrieving multiple autobiographical memories. *Social Cognition, 3,* 280–295.

Loftus, E. F., Smith, K. D., Klinger, M. R., & Fiedler, J. (1992). Memory and mismemory for health events. In J. M. Tanur (Ed.), *Questions about questions: Inquiries into the cognitive bases of surveys* (pp. 102–137). New York: Russell Sage.

Means, B., Habina, K., Swan, G. E., & Jack, L. (1992). Cognitive research on response error in survey questions on smoking. *Vital and Health Statistics,* Series 6, No. 5 (DHHS Publication No. PHS 92-1080). Washington, DC: U.S. Government Printing Office.

Means, B., Swan, G. E., Jobe, J. B., Esposito, J. L., & Loftus, E. F. (1989). Recall strategies for estimation of smoking levels in health surveys. *Proceedings of the Section on Survey Research Methods, American Statistical Association,* pp. 421–424.

Morris, P. (1978). Encoding and retrieval. In M. Gruneberg & P. Morris (Eds.), *Aspects of memory* (pp. 61–83). London: Methuen.

Moss, L., & Goldstein, H. (Eds.). (1979). *The recall method in social surveys.* London: NFER.

Nathan, G., & Sirken, M. G. (1988). Cognitive aspects of randomized response. *Proceedings of the Section on Survey Research Methods, American Statistical Association,* pp. 173–178.

Nathan, G., Sirken, M. G., Willis, G. B., & Esposito, J. L. (1990, November). *Laboratory experiments on the cognitive aspects of sensitive questions.* Paper presented at the International Conference on Measurement Error in Surveys, Tucson, AZ.

Norman, D. A. (1973). Memory, knowledge, and the answering of questions. In R. L. Solso (Ed.), *Contemporary issues in cognitive psychology: The Loyola symposium* (pp. 135–165). Washington, DC: Winston.

Oksenberg, L., Vinokur, A., & Cannell, C. F. (1979). Effects of commitment to being a good respondent on interview performance. In C. F. Cannell, L. Oksenberg, & J. M. Converse (Eds.), *Experiments in interviewing techniques.* Ann Arbor: Survey Research Center, University of Michigan.

Payne, S. L. (1951). *The art of asking questions.* Princeton, NJ: Princeton University Press.

Reder, L. M. (1987). Strategy selection in question answering. *Cognitive Psychology, 19,* 90–138.

Reiser, B. J., Black, J. B., & Kalamarides, P. (1986). Strategic memory search processes. In D. C. Rubin (Ed.), *Autobiographical memory* (pp. 100–121). Cambridge, England: Cambridge University Press.

Royston, P. N. (1989). Using intensive interviews to evaluate questions. In F. J. Fowler, Jr. (Ed.), *Health survey research methods* (pp. 3–7) (DHHS Publication No. PHS 89-3447). Washington, DC: U.S. Government Printing Office.

Schwarz, N., & Bienias, J. (1990). What mediates the impact of response alternatives on frequency reports of mundane behaviors? *Applied Cognitive Psychology, 4,* 61–72.

Schwarz, N., Hippler, H. J., Deutsch, B., & Strack, F. (1985). Response scales: Effects of category range on reported behavior and comparative judgments. *Public Opinion Quarterly, 49,* 388–395.

Sudman, S. S., & Bradburn, N. M. (1974). *Response effects in surveys.* Chicago: Aldine.

Sudman, S. S., & Bradburn, N. M. (1989). *Asking questions.* San Francisco, CA: Jossey-Bass.

Sudman, S. S., Warnecke, R., Johnson, T., O'Rourke, D., Jobe, J. B., & Davis, A. M. (1993, August). *Cognitive aspects of reporting cancer prevention examinations and tests.* Paper presented at the meeting of the American Statistical Association, San Francisco, CA.

Tourangeau, R. (1984). Cognitive sciences and survey methods. In T. B. Jabine, M. L. Straf, J. M. Tanur, & R. Tourangeau (Eds.), *Cognitive aspects of survey methodology: Building a bridge between disciplines* (pp. 73–100). Washington, DC: National Academy Press.

Warner, S. L. (1965). Randomized response: A survey technique for eliminating evasive answer bias. *Journal of the American Statistical Association, 60,* 63–69.

Whitten, W. B. II, & Leonard, J. M. (1981). Directed search through autobiographical memory. *Memory & Cognition, 9,* 566–579.

Willis, G. B., Royston, P., & Bercini, D. (1991). The use of verbal report methods in the development and testing of survey questionnaires. *Applied Cognitive Psychology, 5,* 251–267.

Willis, G. B., Sirken, M. G., & Nathan, G. (1994). *The cognitive aspects of responses to sensitive survey questions* (Working Paper Series, No. 9). Hyattsville, MD: National Center for Health Statistics, Cognitive Methods Staff.

CHAPTER TWELVE

Estimating Frequency:
A Multiple-Strategy Perspective

Frederick G. Conrad
Bureau of Labor Statistics

Norman R. Brown
University of Alberta

People are often required to judge the frequency of everyday events. For example, we are likely to consider the frequency of particular disasters when deciding whether to purchase insurance, or the number of phone calls we typically make in order to select appropriate telephone service. In addition, policymakers and market researchers rely on survey data based on people's responses to behavioral frequency questions, for example, "During the last month how many times did you receive treatment from a medical doctor?" Because frequency judgments are a part of everyday life, they have recently been explored by applied researchers. In particular, studies of how survey respondents answer behavioral frequency questions have identified several distinct strategies, and some of the conditions under which these strategies are used (e.g., Blair & Burton, 1987; Burton & Blair, 1991; Conrad, Brown, & Cashman, 1993; Menon, 1993). Based on this research, it is evident that people rely on multiple strategies in order to perform a particular estimation task.

Basic researchers in psychology have also studied the processes by which people estimate frequency. Laboratory research has identified a wide variety of strategies, but each study has tended to examine a single strategy. For example, Barsalou and Ross (1986) provided evidence that subjects retrieve and count category instances when reporting category frequency—an "enumeration" strategy; Hintzman (1988) modeled frequency judgments as a comparison of a target item's similarity to exemplars in memory—a similarity principle; and Tversky and Kahneman (1973) demonstrated that people use the ease of retrieving instances as a key to frequency—the availability heuristic. In this chapter, we argue that people judge the frequency of everyday occurrences by using whatever information their memories make available to them. Such a multiple strategy approach is plain to see when estimation is observed in its natural context; however, subjects in most laboratory studies exhibit relatively uniform behavior that varies with the experimental task. In this respect, everyday memory researchers—in particular, those studying behavioral frequency judgments—have led the way in developing a coherent picture of a fundamental human behavior.

In the following pages, we attempt to characterize frequency estimation from the multiple strategy perspective. This view is based on real-world memory research, yet it is testable in the laboratory, generalizes across tasks and situations, and provides theoretical insights that have eluded laboratory researchers. As such, it illustrates the value of moving from natural contexts to the laboratory in developing psychological theory, and serves as a response to those who have assailed the everyday memory approach (cf. Banaji & Crowder, 1989).

THE MULTIPLE STRATEGY PERSPECTIVE

The primary feature of the multiple strategy perspective is that people can estimate event frequency on the basis of several different types of remembered information. The particular types of information available for a given estimate depend largely on the characteristics of the target event. The estimation strategies associated with the various types of relevant information can have a strong effect on the size and accuracy of the resulting frequency judgments. We have constructed a taxonomy of the various strategies used by people to estimate frequencies in both laboratory and survey contexts. This taxonomy is presented in Fig. 12.1.

In Fig. 12.1, the major branch separates numerical from nonnumerical strategies. In general, studies of answering behavioral frequency questions have identified two fundamentally different strategies that rely on numerical information: episode enumeration and rate strategies. These appear in the left branch of the figure. When respondents use enumeration strategies, they simply count retrieved episodes; when they use rate-based strategies, they retrieve specific numerical facts about the regularity with which events occur, for example, "I go grocery shopping once a week so in the last month I must have gone four times." Enumeration strategies are inherently numerical because they involve counting retrieved instances or episodes of the target category. Rate strategies are numerical in that they are based on quantitative facts about regularity of occurrence.

When episodes cannot be readily retrieved and rates cannot be inferred, one is unlikely to have quantitative information available for estimating

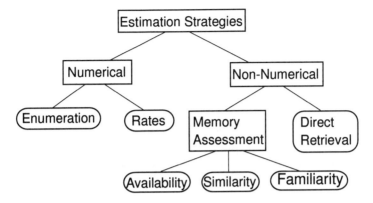

FIG. 12.1. Taxonomy of strategies implied by multiple strategy perspective.

frequency. Under these circumstances, the only available information is non-numerical, so one must deploy strategies from the right side of the figure. By our view, all of these strategies involve converting a qualitative or relative sense of frequency into a numerical form; what differs is the source of the nonnumerical information. Under certain circumstances, one might store such information, for example, that a particular event has occurred "many times" or "more than" some other event, and then recall it (direct retrieval). In contrast, one might infer qualitative frequency information by evaluating the state of ones memory for the event in question (memory assessment). For example, if one can easily recall instances of the event (availability), or if the target seems familiar (familiarity), one might conclude that its frequency is high.

Because each of these estimation techniques operates on a different type of remembered information, the circumstances under which each is used is constrained by the contents of memory. In the next section we discuss characteristics of events that affect what people remember about events and, consequently, which strategies they are most likely to use in estimating frequency for particular events.

EVENT CHARACTERISTICS
AND ESTIMATION STRATEGIES

The likelihood that one will enumerate remembered episodes depends on the ease of retrieving those episodes in the first place. One factor that might affect ease of retrieval is the distinctiveness of individual episodes. A number of autobiographical memory studies (e.g., Barclay & Wellman, 1986; Brewer, 1988; Linton, 1982; Neisser, 1986; Wagenaar, 1986) have demonstrated that events judged to be similar to one another are hard to recall and recognize. Highly similar episodes lead people to represent common features of similar episodes, but not features that distinguish one from the next (Neisser, 1981; Strube, 1987). Therefore, enumeration should be rare when instances of a target activity closely resemble one another, and should be used more often as the episodes become more distinctive and hence are easier to retrieve. A related factor is the regularity with which episodes are experienced. If one engages in a particular activity on a regular schedule, its temporal characteristics will be similar from one occurrence to the next, reducing the likelihood that each occurrence is remembered distinctly. What's more, if one is aware of those regular temporal characteristics, it becomes possible to estimate frequency on the basis of rate information.

The evidence in the behavioral frequency literature supports this view. Means and Loftus (1991) found that respondents were more likely to recall distinguishable episodes (serious medical conditions) than episodes that were similar to one another (minor medical conditions) in answering frequency questions. Menon (1993) found that everyday events such as snacking or bathing were more likely to be enumerated when they had received low similarity ratings than when similarity was judged to be high. In addition, both sets of studies provide evidence that event regularity affects people's response strategies. Means and Loftus found that when people reported frequencies of irregularly occurring doctor visits, such as those due to an injury, they were more likely to recall individual visits than when reporting frequency of visits which occur in fixed intervals, such as visits to an allergist. Menon found an increase in reported use of rate knowledge when regularity ratings were relatively high.

To explore this idea for both numerical and nonnumerical strategies, we (Conrad et al., 1993) asked a national random sample of survey respondents to answer 10 behavioral frequency questions (e.g., "During the last month, how many times did you purchase gas for your car?" "During the last month, how many times did you pay to have your car repaired?"). They were asked to think quietly as they arrived at a frequency and to report the frequency as soon as they had it in mind. After they answered each question, the respondents were asked to describe their thinking while they were determining the frequency of the target event—an immediate, retrospective, verbal protocol (Ericsson & Simon, 1993). The estimation and protocol tasks were tape recorded, enabling us to measure response times (discussed in a later section) and to analyze the protocols for evidence of particular estimation strategies. Following the frequency estimation and protocol tasks, each respondent rated the event categories in the stimulus questions on two dimensions: the similarity of individual episodes to one another and their regularity of occurrence. Respondents registered their ratings using a four point scale: Very Similar/Regular (4) to Very Different/Irregular (1).

The most common strategies evident in the protocols were episode enumeration, rate retrieval, rate estimation, rate and adjustment, and general impression. The first four of these are numerical strategies: Enumeration and the three rate-based strategies involved counts or stored numbers. We distinguished rate retrieval from rate estimation because for the former class, respondents mentioned using remembered rate information while for the latter they reported constructing a rate for a portion of the reference period by enumerating for that period—a hybrid strategy. Protocols were assigned to rate and adjustment when respondents modified a rate-based estimate because of an exception to the usual rate. General impression statements, in contrast, are nonnumerical. Protocols were assigned to this class when they included "vague quantifiers" (O'Muircheartaigh & Gaskell, 1994) such as "a lot" or "not too often," or relative frequency statements such as "I use an ATM more than I use an actual teller in the bank."

The use of these strategies varied with similarity, $F(4, 423) = 4.39$, MSE = 3.043 and regularity, $F(4, 424) = 17.41$, MSE = 12.853. (Note that all statistical test reported in this chapter are significant beyond the $p < .01$ level.) Mean ratings for each strategy are presented in Table 12.1. Episode enumeration was used when events were judged least similar (i.e., most distinctive) and least regular. Rate retrieval was used under opposite circumstances. The difference between these ratings is significant by a planned comparison for both similarity, $F(1, 423) = 12.54$, MSE = 8.696 and regularity $F(1, 424) = 54.85$, MSE = 40.493. This is consistent with the idea that one must be able to retrieve episodes in order to enumerate them; nondistinct events are probably remembered as generic or schematic event categories, making enumeration difficult, if not impossible. Rate estimation was used for activities that people rated moderately similar and regular, as one might expect for a hybrid strategy. General impression responses are also associated with events that received moderate ratings. One interpretation of the general impression responses is that people used nonnumerical information when individual episodes were not distinctive enough to be recalled and then counted, and not regular enough for people to have encoded rate information.

TABLE 12.1
Mean Regularity and Similarity Ratings and Reported Frequency
for the Major Response Strategies

Response Strategy	Similarity[a]	Regularity[b]	Frequency
(Non-zero Responses)			
1. Episode enumeration	2.86	2.39	2.3
2. Rate retrieval	3.54	3.66	7.8
3. Rate estimation	3.31	3.43	11.1
4. Rate and adjustment	3.43	3.65	11.9
5. General impression	3.11	2.91	12.3

[a]1 = very different, 4 = very similar
[b]1 = very irregular, 4 = very regular

A final characteristic of the target events that seems related to response strategy is their frequency. Blair and Burton (1987) found that respondents were more likely to enumerate low than high frequency events. Our results are also consistent with these: Strategy use varied with estimated frequency, $F(4, 425) = 10.99$, MSE = 1153.089. Mean estimated frequencies appear in the third column of Table 12.1. When our respondents enumerated, their estimates were smaller than when they retrieved rate knowledge, $F(1, 425) = 16.27$, MSE = 1707.399, by a planned comparison. In fact, episode enumeration led to smaller estimates than those produced by any other strategies, $F(1, 425) = 41.18$, MSE = 4321.430, by a Sheffé test. The largest frequency estimates were based on general impression statements, consistent with a finding by Bruce and Read (1988). Presumably the frequent occurrence of these events reduces what is remembered about the contexts of individual episodes, further discouraging enumeration. If an event is experienced frequently, there are more opportunities to directly encode this fact than if the event has a lower frequency. However, what is encoded is unlikely to be precise numerical information but rather a sense that frequency is large.

One implication of these results is that under certain circumstances, people cannot rely on the content of their memories to estimate frequency, in particular when episodes are hard to distinguish, occur irregularly, and are rare. Enumeration requires that episodes be distinguishable, rate strategies depend on regularly occurring episodes, and general impressions are most likely to be used when episodes occur frequently. By our analysis, when people cannot judge frequency based on the content of memory, they must rely on memory assessment strategies. Using this approach people can generate information regarding ease of retrieval, familiarity of the target event, or similarity of the event to what is remembered regardless of the target's characteristics. Therefore, one might consider memory assessment strategies to be available by default.

ACCURACY OF ESTIMATION STRATEGIES

Of primary concern to survey practitioners is the accuracy of respondents' estimates based on particular strategies. Unfortunately, the factors that seem to influence accuracy in the literature vary among studies, so it is hard to evaluate their effect. For example, it has been suggested that the length of the reference period—one week, one month, and so on—affects the accuracy of enumeration-based estimates (Sudman & Bradburn, 1974), and this usually varies among studies. Whether it is due to this variable or others, the accuracy of enumeration-based estimates varies widely. For example, instructions to enumerate can both increase (Means, Swan, Jobe, & Esposito, 1994) and decrease (Burton & Blair, 1991) accuracy. In addition, conditions that foster enumeration have led to lower accuracy than those which promote the use of rate strategies. Menon (1993) found highest absolute error for activities rated Dissimilar (i.e., distinctive) and Irregular, and smallest absolute error for activities rated Similar and Regular. It seems, then, that in general one needs to know more than the strategy in use to predict its accuracy; one needs to identify and measure the relevant variables. This is most easily accomplished in the laboratory, where it is straightforward to control the relevant variables including actual frequency.

To examine the accuracy of enumeration versus nonnumerical strategies, one of us (Brown, 1995) conducted a laboratory study. Instead of being asked about categories of autobiographical events, the subjects in this experiment were presented with category names, such as CITY and MAMMAL, and were questioned about their presentation frequency. Each category name was presented at one of six frequencies (0, 2, 4, 8, 12, 16), and each time a category name was presented it was paired with an instance of that category, for example, CITY—Boston. The subjects were instructed to study the presentations for a later memory test, but they were not told this would consist of frequency judgments.

The distinctiveness of the presentations was manipulated between groups. In the different-context condition, a unique category exemplar was presented each time a category name appeared (e.g., CITY—Boston, CITY—Chicago, CITY—London, etc.). In the same-context condition, a single exemplar was presented each time a particular category name appeared (e.g., CITY—London, CITY—London, CITY—London). The different-context condition created relatively distinctive presentation contexts for each category name; the same-context condition led to virtually identical presentation circumstances. After the presentation phase, the subjects were shown each category name and asked to estimate its presentation frequency. They were instructed to think aloud while producing a frequency response, that is, to provide a concurrent verbal protocol (Ericsson & Simon, 1993). If distinct episodes are needed in order to enumerate them, then the different-context condition should promote the use of enumeration strategies. On the other hand, if we are correct that people rely on nonnumerical information when they can neither retrieve episodes nor apply rate strategies, then the same-context condition should lead them to use such information in their estimation strategies.

The context manipulations seemed to affect strategy use in the expected ways. In the different-context condition, subjects enumerated on 57% of the trials and used general impressions in 20% of their protocols; in the same-context condition, they did not enumerate at all, referred to general impressions in 24% of their protocols and produced uninformative reports on the remaining 66% of the trials. Uninformative protocols would be the likely result—although not a guarantee—of using memory assessment strategies, because such strategies do not necessarily engage working memory, which is a requirement for coherent verbal reports (Ericsson & Simon, 1993).

When accuracy in the two conditions was measured in absolute terms, there was little difference between groups. However, the different-context subjects underestimated and the same-context subjects overestimated: When estimated frequency was regressed onto presentation frequency, the slope of the regression line was .73 for the different-context subjects and 1.30 for the same-context subjects, $t(38) = 3.0$; perfect accuracy would have produced a slope of 1.0. If subjects primarily enumerated in the different-context condition, this would have produced the observed underestimation: If one makes any error in this situation, it will be an error of omission; one is unlikely to report an episode that was not presented in the study phase. Overestimation is a sensible result for the use of nonnumerical strategies because in the absence of numerical guidelines, estimates can range either above or below true values, but to differing degrees: Estimates cannot fall below zero at the low end, but are essentially unbounded at the high end, and so can be quite large.

CONVERGING EVIDENCE: RESPONSE TIMES AND DIFFERENTIAL BOUNDARY EFFECTS

Verbal protocols provide a direct report on subjects' strategies, but our analysis of the protocols can be strengthened by converging evidence based on more objective measures. It is possible to derive differential response time predictions for the different strategies. If enumeration involves a series of retrieval operations, and the number of these operations is related to the number of episodes that are ultimately reported, then response time should increase with reported frequency. In contrast, using rate information should require the same amount of mental activity, regardless of the size of the retrieved rate, so response times should be unrelated to reported frequency. Similarly, response times should not vary with frequency when estimates are based on nonnumerical information: It should take no longer to retrieve "a lot" than "hardly ever," nor to compute such impressions via some memory assessment process.

We tested this in our telephone study (Conrad et al., 1993) by measuring response times from the end of the interviewer's question until the respondent uttered a number, and then regressing response times onto estimated frequency for the major strategies evident in the protocols. The regression lines for three of the strategies are presented in Fig. 12.2. It is important to notice is that for enumeration, response times increase sharply with frequency (slope = .84), but there is no relationship between response time and frequency for rate retrieval (slope = .02) and general impression (slope = .01) strategies. These effects, which were predicted on theoretical grounds, were observed in a naturalistic, noisy environment.

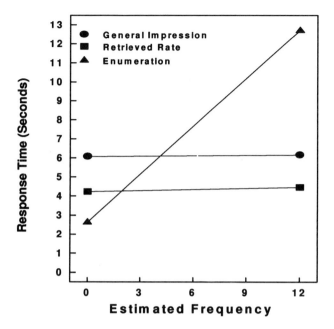

FIG. 12.2. Regression lines for three most prevalent strategies.

A comparable pattern was observed in a second lab study (Brown, 1995). Here, response times were measured from the onset of a category name until the subject began to enter a frequency at the keyboard. Fig 12.3 presents response times plotted against presentation frequency for the different-context and same-context subjects. Response time clearly increases with frequency in the different-context condition, where the conditions required to enumerate are present; the response time curve is flat in the same-context condition where enumeration is not possible. The Context × Presentation Frequency interaction was significant, $F(5, 240) = 14.62$, MSE = 6.244.

Another way to substantiate the protocol analyses is to monitor changes in accuracy while manipulating the available information. We have suggested that the process underlying nonnumerical strategies involves converting a qualitative sense of frequency into a number. If that is so, then the conversion process should be sensitive to whatever numerical referents are available. This can be explored by providing different types of response range information. Recall that subjects overestimated in the same-context condition described earlier. In a third laboratory study (Brown, 1995), these estimates were reduced by providing range information; however, range information had no effect for different-context subjects.

In both conditions, one group of subjects was told that no frequencies were greater than 16 (boundary-16), another group was told that no frequencies were greater than 24 (boundary-24), and a final (control) group was given no

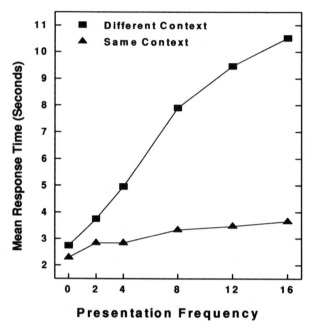

FIG. 12.3. Response times as a function of presentation frequency for same- and different-context subjects.

boundary information. Estimated frequency was regressed onto actual frequency for the three groups in each condition. In the same-context condition, where presumably subjects were relying on nonnumerical strategies, control subjects overestimated (slope = 1.65), boundary-24 subjects were relatively accurate (slope = 1.09), and boundary-16 subjects underestimated (slope = .70). In the different-context condition, where presumably subjects induced range information by enumerating episodes, all three groups underestimated and did so to the same degree (slopes were .70, .68, and .65 for control, boundary-24, and boundary-16 subjects, respectively).

NATURALISTIC AND LABORATORY RESEARCH

A multiple strategy perspective on frequency estimation emerges when one considers the range of results in the behavioral and experimental frequency literature. The principal components of this perspective are that (a) people use multiple strategies to estimate event frequency (see Fig. 12.1), (b) nonnumerical estimation strategies differ from numerical ones because they convert qualitative impressions of frequency into numerical responses, and (c) strategy use is related to event properties, in particular, distinctiveness, regularity, and frequency. It appears that distinct events promote enumeration, that regularity fosters the use of rate-based strategies, and that people are most likely to retrieve qualitative impressions when event frequency is high.

This view has emerged by studying survey respondents in their natural context. By controlling event characteristics in the laboratory it was possible to corroborate our observations and explore the implications more deeply. For example, it was possible to examine accuracy and to manipulate the numerical information that was available when subjects were likely to use nonnumerical strategies. In this case, at least, the complementary relationship of naturalistic and laboratory research has shed more light on a phenomenon than would have either approach by itself.

Banaji and Crowder (1989) complained that naturalistic research is bankrupt because, among other reasons, it does not generalize beyond the particular situation in which it is carried out. That is certainly not the case here. Our ideas grew out of performance in a natural setting but were replicable, and extendible, in the laboratory. In addition, certain aspects of what we observed about estimating frequencies apply to other forms of quantitative estimation (cf. Brown & Siegler, 1993). Moreover, this approach unifies a number of phenomena identified in disparate laboratory studies that apparently do not generalize themselves. For example, Tversky and Kahneman (1973) observed evidence of availability, not enumeration; Barsalou and Ross (1986) found that their subjects enumerated but found no evidence that they used the familiarity of the stimulus as a key to frequency; and so on. It appears that this is a case in which theoretical insight has emerged from naturalistic study; the implications of those insights were then explored in detail using the precision of the laboratory.

REFERENCES

Banaji, M. R., & Crowder, R. G. (1989). The bankruptcy of everyday memory. *American Psychologist, 44,* 1185–1193.

Barclay, C., & Wellman, H. (1986). Accuracies and inaccuracies in autobiographical memories. *Journal of Memory and Language, 25,* 93–103.

Barsalou, L., & Ross, B. (1986). The roles of automatic and strategic processing in sensitivity to superordinate and property frequency. *Journal of Experimental Psychology: Learning, Memory and Cognition, 12,* 116–134.

Blair, E., & Burton, S. (1987). Cognitive processes used by survey respondents to answer behavioral frequency questions. *Journal of Consumer Research, 14,* 280–288.

Brewer, W. F. (1988). Qualitative analysis of the recalls of randomly sampled autobiographical events. In M. M. Gruneberg, P. E. Morris, & R. N. Sykes (Eds.), *Practical aspects of memory: Current research and issues* (pp. 263–268). New York: Wiley.

Brown, N. R. (1995). Estimation strategies and the judgment of event frequency. *Journal of Experimental Psychology: Learning, Memory and Cognition, 21,* 1539–1553.

Brown, N. R., & Siegler, R. S. (1993). Metrics and mappings: A framework for understanding real world quantitative estimation. *Psychological Review, 100,* 511–534.

Bruce, D., & Read, J. D. (1988). The how and why of memory for frequency. In M. M. Gruneberg, P. E. Morris, & R. N. Sykes (Eds.), *Practical aspects of memory: Current research and issues* (pp. 317–322). New York: Wiley.

Burton, S., & Blair, E. (1991). Task conditions, response formulation processes, and response accuracy for behavioral frequency questions in surveys. *Public Opinion Quarterly, 55,* 50–79.

Conrad, F., Brown, N., & Cashman, E. (1993). How the memorability of events affects frequency judgments. *Proceedings of the American Statistical Association, Section on Survey Research Methods,* Volume 2, 1058–1063.

Ericsson, K. A., & Simon, H. A. (1993). *Protocol analysis: Verbal reports as data* (rev. ed.). Cambridge, MA: MIT Press.

Hintzman, D. L. (1988). Judgments of frequency and recognition memory in a multiple-trace memory model. *Psychological Review, 95,* 528–551.

Linton, M. (1982). Transformations of memory in everyday life. In U. Neisser (Ed.), *Memory observed: Remembering in natural context* (pp. 77–91). San Francisco, CA: Freeman.

Means, B., & Loftus, E. (1991). When personal history repeats itself: Decomposing memories for recurring events. *Applied Cognitive Psychology, 5,* 297–318.

Means, B., Swan, G., Jobe, J., & Esposito, J. (1994). The effects of estimation strategies on the accuracy of respondents' reports of cigarette smoking. In N. Schwarz & S. Sudman (Eds.), *Autobiographical memory and the validity of retrospective reports* (pp. 107–119). New York: Springer-Verlag.

Menon, G. (1993). The effects of accessibility of information in memory on judgments of behavioral frequencies. *Journal of Consumer Research, 20,* 431–440.

Neisser, U. (1981). John Dean's memory: A case study. *Cognition, 9,* 1–22.

Neisser, U. (1986). Nested structure in autobiographical memory. In D. C. Rubin (Ed.), *Autobiographical memory* (pp. 71–81). New York: Cambridge University Press.

O'Muircheartaigh, C., & Gaskell, G. (1994, May). *Vague quantifiers: Universal or segmented norms.* Paper presented at the 49th Annual Conference of the American Association for Public Opinion Research, Danvers, MA.

Strube, G. (1987). Answering survey questions: The role of memory. In H. Hippler, N. Schwarz, & S. Sudman (Eds.), *Social information processing and survey methodology* (pp. 86–101). New York: Springer-Verlag.

Sudman, S., & Bradburn, N. (1974). *Response effects in surveys: A review and synthesis.* Chicago: Aldine.

Tversky, A., & Kahneman, D. (1973). Availability: A heuristic for judging frequency and probability. *Cognitive Psychology, 5,* 207–232.

Wagenaar, W. (1986). My memory: A study of autobiographical memory over six years. *Cognitive Psychology, 24,* 666–678.

CHAPTER THIRTEEN

Answering Question Sequences: Attention Switching and Memory Organization

Paul A. Mullin
Erin R. Cashman
Bureau of Labor Statistics, Washington, DC

Holly R. Straub
University of South Dakota, Vermillion, SD

Survey respondents are sometimes asked to report about various events in the past involving different activities, persons, and time periods. For example, in the Bureau of Labor Statistics' Consumer Expenditure Interview Survey, respondents report the various types of expenditures that have been made by different members of their household over the past three months. Respondents often do not employ a systematic approach to such recall tasks on their own, and confusion or incomplete reports result (Lessler, 1989). To reduce problems of this nature, a survey designer might choose to organize the recall task hierarchically so that certain event features (time, person, activity) are nested within other event features. For example, the questions might focus on one person at a time and ask about his or her participation in various activities before switching to another person and asking about that person's participation in those activities. Alternatively, they might focus on a particular activity and ask about each person of concern before switching to another activity. An important question is whether the choice of the question sequence organization affects the recall performance of the respondents.

Virtually all memory theories hold that retrieval access is an associative process, and that activated information in short-term memory renders related information more accessible (e.g., Anderson, 1983; Gillund & Shiffrin, 1984; Ratcliff & McKoon, 1988). With respect to successive question answering, this principle of associative priming implies that the information needed to answer a question will be accessed more quickly if it is closely integrated with the information used to answer the previous question. One may reasonably argue, then, that the organizational structure of survey questions should correspond to the organization of the requested information in memory because switching attention within organizational structures in memory at recall should be more efficient than switching attention between organizational structures. For example, in designing a survey about expenditures for items within various categories, such as clothing and appliances, it should be preferable to ask about the expenditure categories successively rather than to mix questions about items in different categories. To our knowledge, however, no research has examined whether the time to respond and/or the accuracy of recall performance is affected by the correspondence between the organization of a sequence of questions and the organization of the requested information in memory. Furthermore, surveys are seldom specifically designed with the principle of correspondence in mind.

If the correspondence between memory organization and question sequence organization affects recall performance, then the issue of how autobiographical memories are organized is of great importance for the practical task of survey design. Research has shown that autobiographical memory is highly structured, although theories differ on the basis of that organization. Some researchers have argued the primary organizational feature for event memories is the type of activity (Reiser, Black, & Abelson, 1985), whereas others have proposed that event memories are organized chronologically in their relation to extended life events (Barsalou, 1988). Recent thinking has emphasized the role of temporal information and themes that are personally distinctive to the individual (Conway & Rubin, 1993).

Research results concerning the relative importance of different event features (e.g., activity, participant, time, location) are also varied, and relatively limited in number. Reiser et al. (1985) contrasted several different activity/action type organizations, but did not investigate other features such as character, time, and location. Wagenaar (1986) found that time cues, which in his study were specific dates, did not elicit memories as well as location and character cues. Barsalou (1988) reported several experiments in which the time required to retrieve autobiographical memories was approximately equal for cues involving the various event features. In a recent study, Taylor and Tversky (1992) examined organizational preferences for event descriptions presented in a story format, and found that characters were preferred over times. Their use of event descriptions provided controls that are not available in autobiographical memory studies, but it is unclear what differences might exist between genuine autobiographical experiences and events presented through discourse (Larsen, 1988). Overall, these studies provide some insights, but the question of whether certain features are more dominant than others in the organization of event information in memory appears to be far from resolved.

The lack of resolution in the issue of autobiographical memory organization makes the task of investigating whether or not the correspondence between memory and question sequence organization affects autobiographical recall performance somewhat difficult to test. Specifically, the failure to find an effect of question sequence organization on performance might be attributed either to the lack of preferred features in autobiographical memory organization, or to the possibility that the manipulation of question sequence organization is not sensitive to differences in memory organization. For this reason, we decided to investigate correspondence effects under controlled conditions where the to-be-remembered events were related though discourse in the laboratory (as in Taylor & Tversky, 1992). This permitted us to obtain accuracy measures for recall performance with greater ease than would have been the case if the recall of autobiographical memories had been requested. In addition, it allowed us to take steps to reduce the likelihood that there would be no preferred organizations by presenting well-organized information to subjects. The event information was highly complex, and presumably this helped to reduce the likelihood that subjects would attempt to reorganize the material in memory. We assumed that subjects would organize the information in memory in the manner that the information was presented to them. However, the organization of the information was manipulated with the understanding that subjects might be better able to make use of certain organizations than others.

Subjects in the study read four stories and, after each one, were asked a series of yes/no questions about the events in the story. The study was designed so that the event features of character, activity, and time were investigated in pairs. Thus, there were three experiments, each of which involved questions that concerned the conjunction of two event features in the stories, and the manipulation of story and question organization around the two relevant event features. A different group of subjects was used for each comparison. Character and activity were the features investigated in Experiment 1, activity and time were examined in Experiment 2, and character and time were studied in Experiment 3.

There were four conditions in each experiment. In two conditions, story and question organization corresponded, and in the other two, they did not. Based on the inference that subjects would organize the information in memory in the same manner as the story was presented, it was expected that response accuracy would be higher and response times lower when story and question organization corresponded than when they did not. In addition, we hypothesized that if certain organizations were preferred over others, there would be greater or more reliable correspondence effects for those organizations. For example, if a story was organized around a non-preferred feature, then subjects might not make use of this organization.

METHOD

Subjects

Ninety undergraduates at the University of South Dakota participated as subjects in exchange for extra credit in their introductory psychology courses. Four subjects were dropped from the analysis because they failed to read one or more of the stories for at least 45 seconds. These subjects were replaced so that the number of subjects participating in each of the three experiments was 30.

Design

The stories and the questions were organized by character and activity in Experiment 1, by activity and time in Experiment 2, and by character and time in Experiment 3. In each experiment, story organization and question organization were crossed, creating a 2 × 2 design. All four conditions in a experiment were administered to each subject. The conditions were presented to each subject in a random order, and one of four stories was randomly assigned to each condition for each subject.

Story Materials

The experimenters wrote four stories for use in the study (see the Appendix for a sample story). Each story had a different general plot encompassing eight events involving four characters, four activities, and four time periods. Each character in a story performed two activities, and two characters performed each activity. Similarly, each activity was performed at two times, and two activities were performed at each time. Finally, each character was active at two times, and two characters were active at each time. The general pattern of feature conjunctions for the stories is shown in Table 13.1. The pattern was developed so that no two characters performed the same two activities or were active at the same two times, and no two activities were performed at the same two times.

Each story contained a one-paragraph introduction, a four-paragraph main body, and a brief one-paragraph conclusion. Each paragraph in the main body was six sentences long and described two events. The first of the three sentences describing an event summarized the event according to the general formula: "Character did activity at location in time period." The two other sentences provided a second reference to the time period and the activity using other terms, mentioned the character's name again, and provided some personality-related information. The locations, which were irrelevant to the task, were different for every event.

TABLE 13.1
The Conjunctions of Event Features in the Stories

	Activity 1	Activity 2	Activity 3	Activity 4
Time 1	Person 1			Person 4
Time 2	Person 2	Person 3		
Time 3		Person 2	Person 4	
Time 4			Person 3	Person 1

In stories organized by character, each paragraph described two events involving the same character. In stories organized by activity, each paragraph described two events involving the same activity. And, in stories organized by time, each paragraph described two events involving the same time period. The last sentence of the introductory paragraph varied between conditions because it described (in the context of the story) the organization by which the events were presented.

Question Materials

After each story, respondents were asked a set of questions that covered all possible conjunctions of the two event features under investigation in that experiment. Because each story contained four characters, activities, and times, the conjunction of all elements of two of these features resulted in 16 questions. An equal number of the questions had correct answers of "yes" and "no."

There were three question forms used in the study:

"In the story, did [character] [activity] sometime?"
"In the story, did someone [activity] [time period]?"
"In the story, did [character] do something [time period]?"

Based on the story features about which they ask, the first question form is referred to as a character/activity question, the second as an activity/time question, and the third as a character/time question.

In a given experiment, the questions were identical across conditions. However, the organization of those questions differed. The character/activity questions in Experiment 1 were organized by either character or activity. Questions organized by character asked whether or not a particular character performed each of the four activities in the story before they asked about the next character. Questions organized by activity asked whether or not each of the four characters performed an activity before they asked about the next activity. The activity/time questions in Experiment 2 were organized either by activity or time. Questions organized by activity asked whether or not a particular activity was performed at each of the four times before asking about the next activity. Questions organized by time asked whether or not each of the four activities was performed at a particular time before asking about the next time. The character/time questions in Experiment 3 were organized either by character or time. Questions organized by character asked whether or not a character was active at each of the four times before asking about the next character. Questions organized by time asked whether or not each of the four characters was active at a time before asking about the next time. Within the constraint of these organizations, the order of the questions was randomized.

Because only two of the three features (character, activity, and time) were relevant in each experiment, subjects might learn to improve their performance by restricting their focus to the relevant story features. To limit this possibility, 4 additional questions were asked after the primary 16 question sequence. The questions involved the irrelevant feature in the experiment and the feature by which the story was organized in that condition. The four questions were selected randomly and presented in a random order. As a result of this random selection, the number of "yes" and "no" answers to these questions, and the total sequence of questions, varied.

Procedure

Task instructions were presented verbally by a research assistant, and the experiments were conducted using a DOS-based 286 personal computer. The experimental program was written with and controlled by the Micro Experimental Laboratory (MEL) software (Schneider, 1988). The program recorded reading times for the stories and response accuracy and times for the questions. The "/?" and "z" keys in the lower right and left of the keyboard were labeled "Y" and "N" and were used for "yes" and "no" responses, respectively. Subjects first practiced mapping "yes" and "no" responses to the appropriate keys on the keyboard. Subjects pressed the space bar to begin, and 20 displays containing either the word *yes* or the word *no* was presented in random order. A 200-millisecond tone provided feedback on incorrect responses. Accuracy for the 20 trial warm-up response mapping practice data averaged 97% in all three experiments.

After the response mapping practice, subjects pressed the space bar to begin reading a story. The story was presented in three displays containing the introduction, the main body, and the conclusion. Subjects pressed the space bar to proceed from one display to the next, but were not allowed to return to an earlier part of a story. Subjects were encouraged to read each section thoroughly before moving on, but to pay closest attention to the main body of the story. After reading the conclusion of a story, subjects saw a "ready?" screen for the questions that reminded them to respond "yes" or "no" and asked them to place their index fingers on the appropriate keys. One second after a subject pressed the space bar, a fixation line consisting of three plus signs 20 spaces apart from each other and centered on the screen was displayed for 500 milliseconds. A second later the first question was displayed, and after each response to a question, there was another one-second delay before the next question appeared. Subjects were instructed to respond quickly, but as accurately as possible. After all 20 questions, a "ready?" screen for the next story appeared, and the procedure was repeated for the next story.

RESULTS

Analyses were conducted to determine the effects on recall performance of the correspondence between question and story organization. In the analyses, responses to the first question after each story were excluded because performance for these questions could not have been affected by the question sequence organization. Correspondence effects were first examined in an overall analysis of data from all three experiments. Significance levels for this and all other analyses were set at $p < .05$. The accuracy of each subject's responses was calculated for the two conditions where the stories and questions were organized by the same event feature ("same conditions") and for the two conditions in which story and question organization did not match (the "different" conditions). A repeated measures ANOVA showed that the difference in the mean accuracy of the same and different conditions, 67.9% and 62.7%, respectively, was significant, $F(1, 89) = 10.28$. A similar analysis was run for the "yes" and "no" response times. The mean "yes" and "no" times for each subject in each condition were calculated by averaging the $\log_{10}$ RTs and then transforming the means back to scale. This transformation was used to reduce the influence of infrequent lengthy times (i.e., 10 to 20 seconds) on means that were based on very few question responses. The mean transformed response times (TRTs) for the "yes" responses in the same (2.19 seconds) and different (2.44 seconds) conditions were significantly different, $F(1, 89) = 17.58$, as were the mean TRTs for the "no" responses in the same (2.51 seconds) and different (2.78 seconds) conditions, $F(1, 89) = 8.41$. Mean RTs (not transformed) were 2.56 and 2.80 for "yes" responses and 2.91 and 3.25 for "no" responses in the same and different conditions. (Additional analyses on these means showed the same results.)

Separate analyses were also conducted on each of the three experiments. In addition to examining response accuracy and the TRTs, we examined the reading times for the stories. The presentation of each story's three sections on successive displays provided separate reading times for the main body of the stories. For each subject, the main body reading times for the two stories organized by a given feature and the two stories organized by the other feature were averaged. Story organization did not significantly affect reading time in any of the three experiments, but there was a trend in favor of fast reading times for stories organized by character over stories organized by activity in Experiment 1. In general, it appears that subjects did not spend additional time reorganizing the information from certain stories whose organization was not preferred (cf. Taylor & Tversky, 1992).

The results of the individual analyses for the three experiments, although relatively consistent, varied by experiment. These results are presented later in the chapter. In the accuracy analyses, the percentage of correctly answered questions in each of the four conditions was calculated for each subject and was submitted in a two-factor repeated measures ANOVA to examine the effects of story organization, question organization, and their interaction. A similar analysis was conducted on the TRT data. As in the overall TRT analysis, the "yes" responses were analyzed separately from the "no" responses, and the means for each subject in each condition were calculated by averaging the $\log_{10}$ response times, and transforming these means back to scale. In the discussion, the conditions are identified by the two features around which the story and question organizations were based, respectively. Thus, a "character–activity" condition is one in which the stories were organized by character and the questions by activity.

EXPERIMENT 1

In Experiment 1, where character and activity were the features investigated, stories organized by character tended to be read more quickly than stories organized by activity (124 versus 138 seconds), but the difference was not significant, $F(1, 29) = 3.63$, $p = .07$. It is possible, however, that some subjects may have found the stories organized by character easier to read, or may have attempted to reorganize the stories organized by activity.

The means for accuracy and the "yes" and "no" TRTs in Experiment 1 are shown in Table 13.2. The ANOVA showed that neither of the main effects of story or question organization were significant. However, their interaction was significant, $F(1, 29) = 7.30$, reflecting the fact that response accuracy was higher for conditions where story and question organization corresponded. The simple main effect of question organization for stories organized by character was significant, $F(1, 57) = 8.06$, and mean performance was best in the character–character condition and worst in the character–activity condition. The simple main effect of question organization for stories organized by activity was not significant, but mean performance was higher in the activity–activity condition than in the activity–character condition. The pattern of results suggest that subjects made use of the character

TABLE 13.2
Response Accuracy and Transformed Response Times (TRTs)

Condition	% Correct	"Yes" TRTs	"No" TRTs
Experiment 1			
Character–character	74.0	1.94	2.33
Character–activity	61.1	2.21	2.81
Activity–activity	68.4	2.00	2.31
Activity–character	63.6	1.90	2.28
Experiment 2			
Activity–activity	64.7	2.22	2.53
Activity–time	64.2	2.69	2.92
Time–time	69.1	2.59	2.93
Time–activity	62.9	2.51	2.92
Experiment 3			
Time–time	68.7	2.39	2.85
Time–character	60.0	2.65	3.08
Character–character	63.0	2.27	2.50
Character–time	62.7	2.84	3.49

organization of the stories, and it may have either helped or hurt their performance depending on how the questions were organized.

The TRT results lend themselves to a similar interpretation. The interaction of story and question organization was not significant for either the "yes" or "no" responses. However, the main effect of question organization was significant for the both the "yes" responses, $F(1, 29) = 4.07$, and the "no" responses $F(1, 29) = 4.90$. In both cases, these effects appear to result from poor performance in the character–activity condition where responses were somewhat slower compared to the character–character condition. The simple main effects of question organization for stories organized by character were significant for the "yes" TRTs, $F(1, 55) = 5.33$, and for the "no" TRTs, $F(1, 57) = 8.27$. In contrast, question organization did not significantly affect "yes" or "no" responses when the stories were organized by activity.

EXPERIMENT 2

In Experiment 2, where activity and time were the features investigated, the mean reading times for stories organized by the two event features were the same (128 and 127 seconds). The means for accuracy and the "yes" and "no" TRTs in Experiment 2 are shown in Table 13.2. The ANOVA on the response accuracy data showed that neither of the main effects or the interaction were significant. Mean performance was somewhat higher in the time–time condition than in the time–activity condition, but the simple main effect of question organization was not significant for stories organized by time, $F(1, 58) = 3.36$, $p = .08$.

The effects of story and question organization correspondence can be seen in the TRTs. The ANOVA on the "yes" TRTs revealed that the main effect of question organization was significant, $F(1, 29) = 4.83$, but the main effect of story organization was not. The interaction also failed to reached significance, $F(1, 29)=3.22$, $p = .08$. The overall main effect of question organization appears to be due to lower TRTs in the activity–activity condition than in the activity–time condition. A test of the simple main effect of question organization for stories organized by activity was significant, $F(1, 57) = 8.03$, but for stories organized by time was not. The overall analysis of the "no" TRTs showed no significant effects. However, the simple main effect of question organization for stories organized by activity was significant, $F(1, 55) = 4.06$, and mean performance was better in the activity–activity condition than in the activity–time condition. Thus, both the results of the "yes" and "no" TRTs suggests that subjects made use of the activity organization of the stories, and were affected by the correspondence of the questions to that organization.

EXPERIMENT 3

In Experiment 3, where time and character were the features investigated, the mean reading times for stories organized by the two event features were the same (122 seconds). The means for accuracy and the "yes" and "no" TRTs in Experiment 3 are shown in Table 13.2. The ANOVA on the accuracy data showed that the main effects of story organization and question organization were not significant, and neither was their interaction, $F(1, 29) = 3.44$, $p = .07$. However, the simple main effect of question organization performance for stories organized by time was significant $F(1, 57) = 5.62$, reflecting the fact that performance was higher in the time–time condition than in the time–activity condition.

The ANOVAs of the "yes" and "no" TRTs showed that the main effects of story and question organization were not significant. However, the interaction was significant for the "yes" RTs, $F(1, 29) = 16.10$, and the "no" RTs, $F(1, 29) = 4.74$. Mean TRTs for "yes" and "no" responses were lowest in the conditions where story and question organization corresponded. The simple main effect of question organization for stories organized by character was significant for "yes" TRTs, $F(1, 55) = 11.54$, and for "no" TRTs, $F(1, 56) = 7.40$, but for stories organized by time these effects were not significant.

DISCUSSION

As expected, the correspondence between story and question organization affected response accuracy and response times in the memory task. These effects were obtained under circumstances where the form of the question did not change across conditions and the order in which the different events were presented in the questions was randomized so that it did not match the order of the events in a story. The question organization manipulation produced overall effects across the three experiments on the order of five percentage points in response accuracy, one fourth of a second for "yes" responses, and one third of a second for "no" responses. In each of the three experiments, evidence of correspondence effects for one or both of the story organizations was found. In Experiment 1, the correspondence effects were seen for stories organized by character in all dependent measures, and trends existed in the accuracy data for stories organized by activity. In Experiment 2, correspondence effects were found in the TRT data for stories organized by activity, and trends were observed in the accuracy data for stories organized by time. Finally, in Experiment 3, correspondence effects were seen in the accuracy for stories organized by time and in the TRTs for stories organized by character. These results provide support for the hypothesis that attention switching within organizational structures in memory at recall is less time-consuming and more reliable than switching attention between organizational structures.

These results suggest the importance of designing questionnaires so that the sequence of questions is organized in a way that is compatible with the organizational structure of information in memory. Yet, there are a number of differences between memory task in the present study and in the survey situation. The memory task in the present study was difficult, as evidenced by accuracy levels averaging between 60% and 75% with chance performance at 50%; and although there are many survey contexts, such as proxy reporting in the Consumer Expenditure Survey, where the memory task may be as difficult as the present one, this is certainly not necessarily the case for all surveys. Indeed, it is possible that correspondence effects may vary depending on how well the relevant information is learned. For example, correspondence effects may be smaller for well-learned information because access to that information may be highly flexible, with no preferred forms of organization. In contrast, correspondence effects may be larger for well-learned information because greater structure may be imposed on such information.

Another difference between the present memory task and the survey situation is that the present study involved the retention of information over a relatively short time. It is possible that correspondence effects may be more pronounced for long term memories because access is generally slower and less reliable. Furthermore, the event information in the present study was presented in a single episode. In everyday life, it is unlikely that different events, whether experienced or learned through discourse on separate occasions, would have such a high degree of association. The high relatedness of event information acquired in a single episode may facilitate attention switching and yield smaller correspondence effects than if the information were acquired over time.

Finally, it is important to consider the general context of the survey situation, as compared to the present study. In accounting for other types of question order effects in the survey situation, researchers suggest that time pressures and less than optimal motivation lead respondents to rely heavily on information that most readily comes to mind, such as information primed from the preceding question (Schwarz & Bless, 1992). Thus, we might expect that in the survey context, where respondents often engage in incomplete memory searches (e.g., Krosnick, 1991), any slowing of memory access due to the lack of correspondence between memory and question organization could greatly accentuate the recall accuracy effects.

In addition to the implications for survey design, the results of the present study may also have implications for the design of academic examinations. For example, it is common practice to mix questions concerning different subject areas on a test with the intention to make the test more difficult. The present results indicate that this is indeed the effect. However, correspondence effects may differ based on the how well the information is learned, as discussed earlier. Depending on the nature of this interaction, the effect of mixing questions might be either to make the test more sensitive to differences in knowledge, or less sensitive.

It is interesting to note that in general the response times in Experiment 1 appear to be somewhat faster than in the other experiments. This suggests that answering the question of whether a character performed an activity may be easier than answering the question of whether an activity was performed at a certain time or whether a character was active at a certain time. The former question type may, in fact, be more common. More importantly, perhaps, the other two question forms seem to require mention of the third feature (i.e., a character and an activity, respectively) more than does the first. Further research might explore correspondence effects for questions in which all three features are specified.

The present study did not provide insights into the issue of preferences for organizing information around certain event features. Correspondence effects were observed for all three event features, and there was little to suggest that these effects are greater for certain organizations than others. In addition, the subjects did not appear to reorganize the stories as Taylor and Tversky (1992) reported their subject did, but this may be attributed to the complexity of the stories in the present study and their strong organizational format. Regardless, the method was sensitive to the effects of the correspondence between memory and question organization, and thus may be useful in future investigations of the organization of autobiographical memory.

APPENDIX
EXAMPLE OF A STORY ORGANIZED BY CHARACTER

The Memory Study

Dr. Jones needed a few more subjects to complete his memory study. There weren't many available around campus during the summer, and his list was getting short. Four students named Ann, Jim, Kate, and Mick remained. When they arrived, he gave them each 2 news events from the last 4 months, March through June. He asked them to recall what they had been doing when they heard about a news event and in what month they thought the event had occurred. Dr. Jones wasn't surprised that more than one subject reported doing the same thing because the subjects reported engaging in very common activities: daydreaming, eating, watching TV, and studying. For the purpose of making comparisons for his study, he organized the reports by person.

Ann reported daydreaming at her apartment in March. The news brought her out of her reverie. It was just as well because she was almost late for her acrobatics performance in the St. Patrick's Day parade. Ann reported eating at a campground in June. The day was one of the longest of the year, and she was happy to have several more hours of light after dinner to be active. She put down her fork to listen attentively to the news.

Jim reported daydreaming at the student union in April. He was so pre-occupied with his thoughts, his friend called him 3 times before he got his attention. When Jim heard the news he thought it was a late April's Fools joke. Jim reported watching TV in the lounge in May. He just felt like zoning-out after working hard at a May Day celebration. Jim was so en-grossed in the show, he became upset at the interruption by the news of the event.

Kate reported watching TV at a friend's house in April. She stayed late because it was pouring outside, as it often does that time of year. It was only because Kate had forgotten her novel that she heard the news on TV that night. Kate reported studying at a bus station in June. She had decided to go home for the summer solstice, and she took her summer school work with her. Kate barely looked up from her books when she heard the news.

Mick reported eating at the mall in March. He was self-conscious about having his kite with him after flying it in the early spring wind. He was starving, and paused only to gulp some cola when he heard the news. Mick reported studying by the river in May. He had trouble concentrating on his school work because the spring flowers aggravated his allergies. When he heard the news, he overcame his shyness and blurted it out to someone nearby.

Dr. Jones took their reports and analyzed them with the rest of the data he had collected. He was relieved that he'd finally finished running the study. It looked like he might have a publishable paper. At least, he could present it at the upcoming memory conference. He would see what his colleagues thought of the results. Maybe there would be a follow-up study in the works.

REFERENCES

Anderson, J. R. (1983). *The architecture of cognition.* Cambridge, MA: Harvard University Press.

Barsalou, L. W. (1988). The content and organization of autobiographical memories. In U. Neisser & E. Winograd (Eds.), *Remembering reconsidered: Ecological and traditional approaches to the study of memory* (pp. 193–243). Cambridge, England: Cambridge University Press.

Conway, M. A., & Rubin, D. C. (1993). The structure of autobiographical memory. In A. F. Collins, S. E. Gathercole, M. A. Conway, & P. E. Morris (Eds.), *Theories of memory* (pp. 103–137). Hillsdale, NJ: Lawrence Erlbaum Associates.

Gillund, G., & Shiffrin, R. (1984). A retrieval model for both recognition and recall. *Psychological Review, 91,* 1–65.

Krosnick, J. A. (1991). Response strategies for coping with the cognitive demands of attitude measures in surveys. *Applied Cognitive Psychology, 5,* 213–236.

Larsen, S. F. (1988). Remembering without experiencing: Memory for reported events. In U. Neisser & E. Winograd (Eds.), *Remembering reconsidered: Ecological and traditional approaches to the study of memory* (pp. 326–355). Cambridge, England: Cambridge University Press.

Lessler, J. T. (1989, January). *Recall strategies for question from the Consumer Expenditure Survey.* Paper presented at the annual meeting of the American Association for the Advancement of Science, New York.

Ratcliff, R., & McKoon, G. (1988). A retrieval theory of priming in memory. *Psychological Review, 95,* 385–408.

Reiser, B. J., Black, J. B., & Abelson, R. P. (1985). Knowledge structures in the organization and retrieval of autobiographical memories. *Cognitive Psychology, 17,* 89–137.

Schneider, W. (1988). Micro Experimental Laboratory: An integrated system for IBM PC compatibles. *Behavior Research Methods, Instruments, & Computers, 20,* 206–217.

Schwarz, N., & Bless, H. (1992). Constructing reality and its alternatives: An inclusion/exclusion model of assimilation and contrast effects in social judgment. In L. L. Martin & A. Tesser (Eds.), *The construction of social judgment* (pp. 217–245). Hillsdale, NJ: Lawrence Erlbaum Associates.

Taylor, H. A., & Tversky, B. (1992, November). *Who, what, when, and where: Memory organization for event descriptions.* Paper presented at the meeting of the Psychonomic Society, St. Louis, MO.

Wagenaar, W. A. (1986). My memory: A study of autobiographical memory over six years. *Cognitive Psychology, 18,* 225–252.

CHAPTER FOURTEEN

Implications of Models of Survey Cognition for Memory Theory

Jared B. Jobe
Douglas J. Herrmann
National Center for Health Statistics

Many survey questions ask about how often events occurred within a specific time period, such as "How many times did you eat green vegetables in the last month?" and "What things have you done to find work during the last four weeks?" Thus, survey interviews present challenging demands on the respondent's cognitive processes, particularly on autobiographical memory (Hippler, Schwarz, & Sudman, 1987; Jabine, Straf, Tanur, & Tourangeau, 1984; Turner & Martin, 1984). In slightly over a decade, we have learned much about the cognitive processes respondents use to answer questions, how an interviewer's behavior affects respondents' answers, and how the respondent's behavior affects the interviewer's behavior (Converse & Presser, 1986; Groves, 1989; Jobe & Mingay, 1989, 1991; Jobe, Tourangeau, & Smith, 1993; Schwarz & Sudman, 1994). During this period, several models have been proposed that explain how respondents process information to derive answers to survey questions about topics involving autobiographical memory and attitudes.

The fields of memory and survey methods research have in common the goal of understanding how to elicit accurate recall of information. Although survey methodologists have utilized techniques and findings from cognitive psychology to develop better surveys, cognitive psychologists have not been aware of survey research that can inform the study of cognition until just recently (Jobe et al., 1993). The goal of this chapter is to examine the implications of survey models for memory theory. We review extant models of survey responding, and then identify the theoretical constructs of these models that have received little or no mention by memory researchers. Finally, based on this review, we propose how these constructs might be useful to theories of autobiographical memory.

COGNITIVE MODELS OF SURVEY RESPONDING

In the past 15 years, seven models have been proposed to account for how respondents answer questions about autobiographical events. In this chapter we demonstrate that these models possess similar characteristics, but also that each has its own emphasis. These models are all information processing models. The early models are similar to stage theory, in that the time between the stimulus (question) and response (answer) is occupied by a series of mental processes arranged so that each stage does not begin until the preceding stage is completed (cf. Sternberg, 1969). Only one model assumes parallel processing of information; none use connectionist architecture. First, we describe these models. Following the descriptions of the models, we compare them for the number of stages, the kinds of stages, and some global attributes of information processing. In those instances where the authors have not named their models, we have provided names consistent with the purpose of the model.

Respondent's Question-Answering Model

The first cognitive model of survey responding was proposed by Marquis; this model has undergone several revisions (e.g., Cannell, Marquis, & Laurent, 1977; Cannell, Miller, & Oksenberg, 1981). The Respondent's Question-Answering Model, shown in Fig. 14.1, assumes that responses to survey questions are based on five major stages: (a) comprehension of the question; (b) cognitive processing of information including decisions about frames of reference or cues, retrieval, organizing information retrieved, and formulating a tentative answer; (c) evaluating whether the tentative answer fulfills the objectives of the question; (d) evaluating psychological meaning of the tentative answer in terms of personal goals of the respondent; and (e) stating the response. The defining feature of this model is that the stages executed depend on the goals of the respondent. If the respondent chooses to be careful in generating an answer, all five stages are executed. Alternatively, if the respondent does not understand the question, wants to produce an answer without expending considerable cognitive effort, or does not want to answer accurately for other social reasons, the respondent can short-circuit the process at any stage and answer based on stages 6 and 7, as shown in Fig. 14.1. This is hypothesized to affect the validity of the answer.

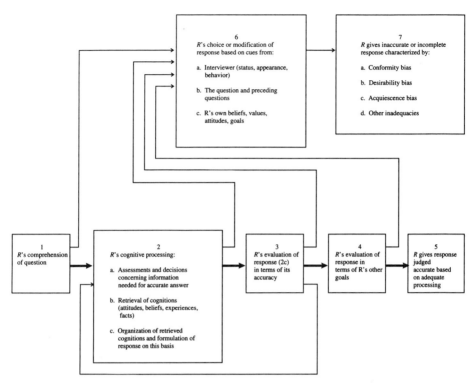

FIG. 14.1. Diagram of Respondent's Question-Answering Model (Cannell, Miller, & Oksenberg, 1981; Cannell, Marquis, & Laurent, 1977; reproduced with permission of Jossey-Bass, Inc.).

Four-Stage Model

The model proposed by Tourangeau (1984) is simpler and proposes a minimum of four discrete cognitive processing stages—comprehension, retrieval, decision/judgment, and response—and discusses the stages in terms of the psychological literature. According to what we refer to as the Four-Stage Model, the respondent typically goes through the stages in the prescribed order, but not invariably so. Sometimes the respondent must formulate an answer to an open-ended question or may short-circuit the process by selecting an answer before the question is completely read. An important feature of the Four-Stage Model is that response editing, such as those that occur based on social desirability, occurs during the response stage. Tourangeau and Rasinski (1988) extended the Four-Stage Model to address context effects. According to the extension of the model, answering a current question is assumed to be affected by prior questions, and different questions can prime or affect different stages currently used to process a question. Tourangeau's model is the one most widely referenced in the survey field.

Autobiographical Question Answering Model

The Autobiographical Question Answering Model (Schwarz, 1990) adds a fifth stage to Tourangeau's Four-Stage Model, separating the decision/judgment stage into two distinct stages. In the third stage, respondents decide whether their recalled answer occurred within the specified reference period; if the question asks about usual behavior, they decide whether their answer is representative. In the fourth stage, respondents may use general knowledge or other information (decomposition, heuristics) to infer an answer.

Forms Appraisal Model

Forsyth and Hubbard (1992) also added a fifth stage to Tourangeau's Four-Stage Model, and proposed a general model to guide forms appraisal—the technical review of questionnaire content. The Forms Appraisal Model includes an interpretive stage after the comprehension stage. Forsyth and Hubbard specified the processes used to construct a general representation of the task demands of the question as a distinct second stage; these processes guide subsequent processes by specifying what is to be retrieved from memory or specifying goals of judgment processes. In contrast, in Tourangeau's model, interpretation is performed during the comprehension stage.

Flexible Processing Model

The Flexible Processing Model (Willis, Royston, & Bercini, 1991), shown in Fig. 14.2, differs from the other models in two ways. First, the Flexible Processing Model specifies and describes decision processes that may occur before and after information is retrieved from memory. Decision processes

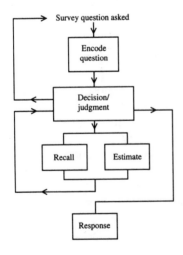

FIG. 14.2. Diagram of Flexible Processing Model (Willis, Royston, & Bercini, 1991; reproduced by permission of John Wiley & Sons, Ltd.).

occurring prior to retrieval include whether it is feasible to search memory for information, and whether is it worth the effort to search memory. Post-retrieval strategies include judged accuracy, whether additional retrieval is necessary, and whether to alter the tentative answer. The Flexible Processing Model's before-retrieval process is somewhat similar to Forsyth and Hubbard's (1992) interpretive stage. Another feature of the Flexible Processing Model is that it describes how processing may occur without going through the stages in a strict sequence.

Information Exchange Theory

Information Exchange Theory (e.g., Mullin, Conrad, Sander, & Herrmann, 1994; Sander, Conrad, Mullin, & Herrmann, 1992) makes the key assumption that respondents' reporting cannot be explained by modeling the respondents' cognitive processes alone. The Respondent Model (Fig. 14.3), is supplemented by two other models: The Interviewer Model accounts for how interviewers formulate and express survey questions, and the Interviewer Respondent Interaction Model accounts for any ensuing interaction between the interviewer and respondent. Like the model by Schwarz (1990), the Interviewer Respondent Interaction Model assumes that the information a respondent provides to the interviewer is affected by rules of etiquette in speech communication.

   A unique feature of Information Exchange Theory is that the three models assume more stages than any other model proposed thus far. As a result, the theory also makes more assumptions about the sequentiality of those stages. It also hypothesizes that information processing may be parallel, overlapping, and mutually interactive. The notion that processes may be simultaneous applies both to the different cognitive tasks the respondent performs as well as to the different strategies adopted to achieve each of the goals. Moreover, Information Exchange Theory predicts that answering strategy is affected by factors such as the time since the events in question occurred (Mullin et al., 1994). Increasing the length of the reference period is hypothesized to increase the use of self-schema in answering as opposed to direct retrieval, and because self-schema are typically biased in favor of the respondent, greater social desirability biases should occur. According to Mullin et al., such findings cannot be accounted for by models that purport that social desirability effects result only from response editing (e.g., Tourangeau, 1984).

Survey Interaction Model

The Survey Interaction Model (Esposito & Jobe, 1991) is similar to Information Exchange Theory in being a comprehensive model of the entire survey interaction process: In addition to accounting for the respondent's processes,

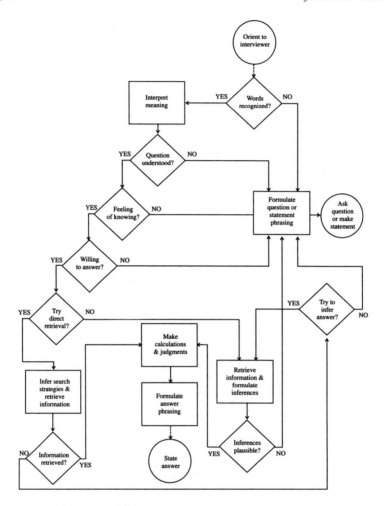

FIG. 14.3. Diagram of Respondent Model of Information Exchange Theory (Sander, Conrad, Mullin, & Herrmann, 1992; in the public domain).

it accounts for the interviewer's processes, as well as the interactions between them. The Survey Interaction Model primarily adapts the respondent's cognitive processes from Marquis' Respondent Question Answering Model, but extends that model's processes by including the effects of the respondents' biological systems (e.g., fatigue), psychophysiological processes (e.g., sensory deficits), and motivation on information processing. The influence of respondent motivation is consistent with the findings of Krosnick (1991). Krosnick presented a theory of respondent effort on attitude formation in surveys. When motivation is low, respondents engage in a behavior called *satisficing*; they either recall information incompletely or in a biased fashion, or they may not retrieve and integrate information at all (see also Tourangeau, 1984). The Survey Interaction Model also addresses a wide array of survey situations.

Other Question Answering Models

It should be noted that not all survey models are concerned with autobiographical events. Several models are related to assessing attitudes. Strack and Martin (1987) proposed a four-stage model (interpret the question, generate an opinion, format the response, edit the response) to account for cognitive processing to respond to attitude questions. Tourangeau and Rasinski's (1988) extension of Tourangeau's Four-Stage Model, mentioned earlier, applies mainly to attitude questions. In addition to the attitude-generating models, Graesser and his colleagues (e.g., Graesser & Franklin, 1990) proposed a model, called QUEST, concerned with answering questions about knowledge. These models are not be reviewed here because the focus of this chapter is on autobiographical memory.

COMPARISON OF THE MODELS

Across these models, several theoretical constructs are assumed. Table 14.1 presents the constructs used in one or more of the models reviewed previously. Inspection of these constructs reveals that the developers of these

TABLE 14.1
Cognitive Processing Components of Survey Models

General Stages	
Comprehension	Understanding a question's meaning and the meaning of the words in the question.
Interpretation	Constructing a representation of the task demands of the question.
Memory retrieval	Accessing information from long-term storage.
Feeling of knowing	Perceiving that information is available to be recalled with sufficient effort.
Reconstruction	Piecing together bits of information from memory to form an answer to a question.
Estimation	Generating a numerical answer about how often an event occurs or the time between events on the basis of knowledge and logic.
Goal evaluation	Assessing the psychological meaning of a tentative response in relation to personal goals extraneous to the question (Cannell, Miller, & Oksenberg, 1981).
Judgment	Determining the appropriateness of a tentative response.
Decision	Choosing an action from a set of alternatives.
Response	Providing an answer to a question or editing a tentative response and providing an answer.

models have given considerable thought to the kinds of processes underlying answers to questions about autobiographical memory.

With the constructs in Table 14.1, it becomes possible to compare these models for their similarities and differences. The upper section of Table 14.2 makes such comparisons possible. Examination of this section reveals that there is much agreement among the models regarding the stages they consider essential. The lower section of Table 14.2 indicates whether or not these models make additional assumptions beyond the nature of component stages. These assumptions pertain to feedback loops, whether processing is influenced by other factors such as the respondent's physical functioning, and respondent effort at processing (satisficing). Some models conceptualize the cognitive stages as a sequential process (Four-Stage Model, Forms Appraisal Model), whereas others conceptualize the stages as a continuous flow process, whereby respondents return to previous stages as necessary (e.g., Flexible Processing Model). Another way in which the models differ is how the response stage is conceptualized. In some models, the response stage merely consists of verbalizing the answer (e.g., Respondent Question-Answering Model, Flexible Processing Model), whereas in other models it

TABLE 14.2
Stage Constructs of Models of Survey Cognition

General Stages	Respond[a] Ques Ans	Four[b] Stage	Autobio[c] Ques Ans	Forms[d] Apprs	Flexible[e] Process	Inform[f] Exch	Survey[g] Interact
Comprehension	X	X	X	X	X	X	X
Interpretation				X		X	
Memory retrieval	X	X	X	X	X	X	X
Feeling of knowing						X	
Reconstruction			X			X	
Estimation					X	X	
Goal evaluation	X						X
Judgment	X	X	X	X	X	X	X
Decision				X	X	X	
Response	X	X	X	X	X	X	X
General Attributes							
Feedback loop	X				X	X	X
Flexible sequence					X		
Satisficing		X					X
Biological influence							X

[a]Respondent Question-Answering Model (e.g., Cannell, Marquis, & Laurent, 1977)
[b]Four-Stage Model (e.g., Tourangeau, 1984)
[c]Autobiographical Question Answering Model (Schwarz, 1990)
[d]Forms Appraisal Model (Forsyth & Hubbard, 1992)
[e]Flexible Processing Model (Willis, Royston, & Bercini, 1991)
[f]Information Exchange Theory (e.g., Sander, Conrad, Mullin, & Herrmann, 1992)
[g]Survey Interaction Model (Esposito & Jobe, 1991)

includes decision processes in evaluating a tentative answer and possibly changing it for reasons such as social desirability (e.g., Autobiographical Question Answering Model, Four-Stage Model).

Comparison of the models is limited here for yet another important reason. Little or no research has been attempted to determine whether the processing stages and attributes of these models occur as described. (Indeed, the models themselves offer no predictions.) Until different models are compared for each of several different survey situations (e.g., verbatim vs. nonverbatim presentation; brief surveys vs. long ones), it will not be possible to determine which model yields the best predictions overall, or which models are best for different situations.

IMPLICATIONS FOR COGNITIVE THEORY

Basic memory research attributes autobiographical recall to: (a) the state of the memory (strength, accessibility) that is the object of retrieval operations; (b) the presence, number, and type of retrieval cues; and (c) the strategy used to stimulate a memory to become available in consciousness (Conway, 1990). The primary model of autobiographical recall emphasizes three stages in retrieval: find a context, search, and verify (Williams & Hollan, 1981). Moreover, basic memory models assume that all responses reflect the truth or at least a subject's earnest attempt at truthful responding. These models do not account for the fact that people often choose to edit their answers or to make minimal cognitive effort to process information.

Survey models, conversely, assume that autobiographical recall is affected by social factors. Across these models, they assume that respondents evaluate whether their privately held answer meets the goals of the questioner, re-phrase or even change their answer in order to be polite, and choose answers that will shorten the interview. In addition, the survey models put a heavier emphasis on intelligent guessing and on what is the expected answer. Survey researchers recognize that, in the survey interview, respondents often choose to edit their answers, to make minimal cognitive effort to process information, or even to deliberately provide a false answer.

This review implies that basic memory models should incorporate stages for social editing and for intelligent guessing. Such assumptions will be necessary as the basic models are extended beyond the laboratory to the real world. In addition, social and guessing factors may be, to a degree, applicable in the laboratory because basic research involves people and interactions and tasks that allow some guesswork.

The reader may ask which of the memory and survey models provides the best account of memory phenomena? It is not a simple matter to make such a choice. Memory models may provide a good account of the memory task performed in the laboratory; survey models may provide a good account of the survey interview. As discussed here, virtually all memory models have been designed to account for a person's performance on laboratory memory tasks. In almost all cases, laboratory memory tasks are performed with minimal interaction with other people, often on machines or computers. Usually, the only social interaction a subject has in a memory task is with the experimenter or a research assistant, so that, in essence, laboratory memory tasks are asocial. Thus, memory models probably are indeed sufficient to account for the findings of most laboratory memory experiments. In assuming stages for social processes, survey models may be overly complex when applied to the laboratory environment.

Nevertheless, it may also be argued that many laboratory experiments involve a fair amount of social interaction between the subject and experimenter. In such situations, social pressure may arise and dispose subjects to attempt to impress the experimenter. The subject's desire to appear "socially desirable" could lead the subject to alter his or her behavior, for example, to adopt a conservative response and to avoid guessing in order to avoid appearing unintelligent, or to guess more than usual in the hope of appearing intelligent. The possibility also exists that a subject who finds an experimenter obnoxious may deliberately generate false memory performance. In instances where social factors lead subjects to distort their responses, the memory model will be inadequate and the survey model much more appropriate to account for laboratory findings (Gentry & Herrmann, 1990; Mullin, Herrmann, & Searleman, 1993).

It is, of course, an empirical question whether typical laboratory procedures induce subjects to manifest false memory performance. Although there is a rich literature demonstrating that subjects engage in contrivances in social psychology laboratory experiments (see, e.g., Goffman, 1969; Schlenker, 1980), little research has systematically investigated whether people contrive in a similar fashion in memory experiments. Such research is needed to determine whether survey models are superior in accounting for laboratory findings where social pressure is present, as well as to determine whether laboratory memory methodology needs to be altered to either eliminate or control social influences on memory data.

Thus, we believe that different kinds of models have been proposed by memory and survey researchers because of the *context* in which recall is attempted: the laboratory or a survey interview. We propose the following experiment to test this context hypothesis: Subjects would be asked to learn a prose passage in the laboratory and recall it later in the laboratory. They would also be asked to witness a political debate in the community and later be interviewed about it in their homes. (This design could also cross location of learning with to-be-recalled material; however, it is beyond the scope of our proposed investigation.) In the laboratory, they would be asked to recall the heroes/heroines and villains in the story and what these characters did; in the interview, they would be asked to recall who participated in the debate and what was said there. Subjects would be assessed for their beliefs relative to the actions of the story characters and relative to the positions of the debate participants.

We predict that the subjects would recall more details verbatim in the laboratory memory task than in the survey memory task, because the material to be recalled in the laboratory is more recent than the material to be recalled in the survey interview, and because in the laboratory an implicit demand exists to recall verbatim that does not exist in the survey interview. We also predict that the subjects' recall would covary with their personal values more for the survey memory task than for the laboratory memory task. That is, we believe that people will invest their values more in an event of everyday life that will be influential in their future than they will invest in a laboratory memory task.

CONCLUSIONS

As discussed previously, we conclude that the differences between memory and survey approaches are attributable to the differences in the approach of basic and applied research. But we would argue that these differences reflect a difference in philosophy of what processes should be modeled. Basic research focuses on processes that are intrinsic to memory (e.g., encoding, retrieval), whereas applied survey research focuses on both intrinsic and extrinsic processes (e.g., motivation, physical state) (Mullin et al., 1993). Thus, we conclude that memory and survey models are special cases of a general model, yet to be developed, that may be adapted to the laboratory or interview contexts. Failing the development of a general model, basic researchers could assist applied researchers if they produced a model that is as close as possible to that needed for a particular application. To develop such a model, we recommend that our basic research colleagues give greater consideration to extrinsic processes, such as social editing, in the development of future memory models.

ACKNOWLEDGMENTS

The authors gratefully acknowledge the helpful comments of Roger Tourangeau and Gordon B. Willis on an earlier version of this chapter. Jared B. Jobe is at the National Institute on Aging, National Institutes of Health. Douglas J. Herrmann is at the Department of Psychology, Indiana State University.

REFERENCES

Cannell, C. F., Marquis, K. H., & Laurent, A. (1977). A summary of studies of interviewing methodology. *Vital and Health Statistics*, Series 2, No. 69 (DHEW Publication No. HRA 77-1343). Washington, DC: U.S. Government Printing Office.

Cannell, C. F., Miller, P. V., & Oksenberg, L. (1981). Research on interviewing techniques. In S. Leinhardt (Ed.), *Sociological methodology* (pp. 389–437). San Francisco, CA: Jossey-Bass.

Converse, J. M., & Presser, S. (1989). *Survey questions: Handcrafting the standardized questionnaire.* Newberry Park, CA: Sage.

Conway, M. A. (1990). *Autobiographical memory: An introduction.* Milton Keynes, England: Open University Press.

Esposito, J. L., & Jobe, J. B. (1991). A general model of the survey interaction process. In *Bureau of the Census Annual Research Conference and CASIC Technologies Interchange* (pp. 537–560). Washington, DC: Bureau of the Census.

Forsyth, B. H., & Hubbard, M. L. (1992). A method for identifying cognitive properties of survey items. In *American Statistical Association, Proceedings of the Section on Survey Methods Research* (pp. 470–475). Alexandria, VA: American Statistical Association.

Gentry, M., & Herrmann, D. J. (1990). Memory contrivances in everyday life. *Personality and Social Psychology Bulletin, 16*, 241–253.

Goffman, E. (1969). *The presentation of self in everyday life.* London: Allen Lane.

Graesser, A. C., & Franklin, S. P. (1990). QUEST: A cognitive model of question answering. *Discourse Processes, 13*, 279–303.

Groves, R. M. (1989). *Survey errors and survey costs.* New York: Wiley.

Hippler, H. J., Schwarz, N., & Sudman, S. (Eds.). (1987). *Social information processing and survey methodology.* New York: Springer-Verlag.

Jabine, T. B., Straf, M. L., Tanur, J. M., & Tourangeau, R. (1984). *Cognitive aspects of survey methodology: Building a bridge between disciplines.* Washington, DC: National Academy Press.

Jobe, J. B., & Mingay, D. J. (1989). Cognitive research improves questionnaires. *American Journal of Public Health, 79*, 1053–1055.

Jobe, J. B., & Mingay, D. J. (1991). Cognition and survey measurement: History and overview. *Applied Cognitive Psychology, 5*, 175–192.

Jobe, J. B., Tourangeau, R., & Smith, A. F. (1993). Contributions of survey research to the understanding of memory. *Applied Cognitive Psychology, 7*, 567–584.

Krosnick, J. A. (1991). Response strategies for coping with the cognitive demands of attitude measures in surveys. *Applied Cognitive Psychology, 5*, 213–236.

Mullin, P. A., Conrad, F. G., Sander, J. E., & Herrmann, D. (1994, July). A cognitive theory of respondent behavior in the survey interview. In D. J. Herrmann (Chair), *Contributions of cognitive and social psychology to survey research.* Symposium conducted at the meeting of the American Psychological Society, Washington, DC.

Mullin, P. A., Herrmann, D. J., & Searleman, A. (1993). Forgotten variables in memory theory and research. *Memory, 1*, 43–64

Sander, J. E., Conrad, F., Mullin, P., & Herrmann, D. (1992). Cognitive modeling of the survey interview. *Proceedings of the Section on Survey Methods Research, American Statistical Association* (pp. 818–823).

Schlenker, B. R. (1980). *Impression management: The self-concept, social identity, and interpersonal relations.* Pacific Grove, CA: Brooks/Cole.

Schwarz, N. (1990). Assessing frequency reports of mundane behaviors: Contributions of cognitive psychology to questionnaire construction. In C. Hendrick, & M. Clark (Eds.), *Review of personality and social psychology* (Vol. 11, pp. 98–119). Beverly Hills, CA: Sage.

Schwarz, N., & Sudman, S. (Eds.). (1994). *Autobiographical memory and the validity of retrospective reports*. New York: Springer-Verlag.

Sternberg, S. (1969). Memory-scanning: Mental processes revealed by reaction-time experiments. *American Scientist, 57*, 421–457.

Strack, F., & Martin, L. L. (1987). Thinking, judging, and communicating: A process of context effects in attitude surveys. In H. J. Hippler, N. Schwarz, & S. Sudman (Eds.), *Social information processing and survey methodology* (pp. 123–148). New York: Springer-Verlag.

Tourangeau, R. (1984). Cognitive sciences and survey methods. In T. B. Jabine, M. L. Straf, J. M. Tanur, & R. Tourangeau (Eds.), *Cognitive aspects of survey methodology: Building a bridge between disciplines* (pp. 73–101). Washington, DC: National Academy Press.

Tourangeau, R., & Rasinski, K. A. (1988). Cognitive processes underlying context effects in attitude measurement. *Psychological Bulletin, 103*, 299–314.

Turner, C., & Martin, E. A. (Eds.). (1984). *Surveying subjective phenomena*. New York: Sage.

Williams, M. D., & Hollan, J. D. (1981). The process of retrieval from very-long-term memory. *Cognitive Science, 5*, 87–119.

Willis, G. B., Royston, P., & Bercini, D. (1991). The use of verbal report methods in the development and the testing of survey questionnaires. *Applied Cognitive Psychology, 5*, 251–267.

PART SIX

BELIEFS ABOUT MEMORY

CHAPTER FIFTEEN

Individual Differences in Memory Style and Autobiographical Memory

Jerome R. Sehulster
University of Connecticut, Stamford

The study of metacognitive phenomena has occupied cognitive psychologists for well over a decade. Metamemory phenomena include various aspects of feeling of knowing (Costermans, Lories, & Ansay, 1992; Eysenck, 1979), ease and degree of learning (Leonesio & Nelson, 1990), and the experience of recall right on the tip of the tongue (Wellman, 1977). Other metacognitive phenomena studied include aspects of reading (Byrd & Gholson, 1985), mathematical reasoning, and problem solving (e.g., Metcalfe, 1986), in both laboratory and everyday settings. Flavell (1979) and others (e.g., Paris & Winograd, 1990) demonstrated that effective learning depends as much on metacognitive skills, such as a learning strategy, as it does on a more nuts-and-bolts aspect of memory, such as memory capacity.

In addition to widening perspectives on memory performance in the laboratory, the focus on metamemory has allowed the expansion of the study of memory from the laboratory into the realm of everyday life (e.g., Herrmann, 1982; Park, Smith, & Cavanaugh, 1990; Sehulster, 1981b). Individuals hold beliefs about their ability to perform in everyday situations involving memory. Beliefs about memory ability and the relationship of these beliefs to other phenomena from autobiographical memory form the body of this chapter on metamemory.

The composite of memory beliefs has been called a self-theory of memory (Sehulster, 1981b) or, more generally, a "memory self-concept" (Searleman & Herrmann, 1994). Individuals perceive themselves as performing better in some memory situations than they do in others. One person may perceive herself to be better at remembering the details of research data than she is at remembering the names of students; another person might be able to remember the weather of every summer vacation he went on with his family, but every summer forget to pack half the necessary stuff.

When one responds to questions on a memory questionnaire that ask about memory abilities in various domains of everyday life, one is really expressing summary statements or summary beliefs about memory abilities. These summary statements are supported by the many, many moments in day-to-day life when one's abilities to remember are tested. Some memory moments will be salient enough to be remembered and incorporated intact into a cognitive representation. They may be available, subsequently, as evidence of memory ability ("I remember the time I forgot to mail the mortgage one month"). Some memory moments are repeated so frequently that they become schematized (e.g., Barclay, 1986; Brewer, 1986), summarized, and perhaps even evaluated ("I usually remember the names of film and television personalities very well"). A hierarchical arrangement, with specific memories represented at the base, schematized memories higher up, and metamemories (summaries and evaluations) at the top, seems a logical way to conceptualize the structure of this cognitive representation.

It is tempting to understand the process by which subjects respond to a memory questionnaire as one in which they arrive at a summary statement or self-rating of memory ability on the spot by accessing, scanning, reviewing, and evaluating past moments of successful remembering or forgetting (call these moments instances, exemplars, or evidence). There are good reasons, however, why this is probably not the way it works: The Memory Scale (Sehulster, 1981b), which has 60 rating questions, takes the average subject about 10 minutes to complete. These 10 minutes include reading the brief instructions, the words to the three rating scales, and the 60 questions, which range in length from 4 words to 29 words (the mean length is 10.22 words). There is not a lot of time for a subject to scan, review, weigh, and evaluate past moments of successful and failed remembering to come up with a summary statement for each question! Moreover, recent work by Klein and Loftus (1993) suggested that summary statements about traits of the self, the source of self-ratings, may actually have a separate representation apart from the cognitive representation of the relevant exemplars (the evidence from experience supporting the summary). Thus, it is more likely the case that a subject is merely accessing and reporting summary statements previously formed about memory in response to a memory questionnaire.

A memory questionnaire is not the first time we are asked to summarize or describe our memory abilities. We communicate our day-to-day experience to others through summary statements, sometimes as a way of apologizing ("I'm sorry, I'm terrible with names"), bragging ("I'm very good at Trivial Pursuit"), or self-flagellating ("I always forget to pack the suntan lotions"). Our summary statements are also formed through external sources: The interpretations of our remembering may come from others ("You have a terrible memory for names") or through social comparisons ("I remember names better than my husband does"). Summary statements about memory may have input from very early on. A child remembers a Thanksgiving dinner from when she was three. Her parents comment, "You have a great memory, dear!" Summary statements may also reflect delusion, distortion, contrivance, self-abasement, or self-aggrandizement (Gentry & Herrmann, 1990).

From a more social psychological perspective, we may consider summary statements about self, be they about one's memory or one's overall health status (Sehulster, 1994), as attitudes about the self that are formed well before the subject is asked to rate oneself on a questionnaire. As with most attitudes, self-attributions, or self-rated personality traits, the predictive relationship between self-rating and behavior across situations is often weak (Mischel, 1968; Ross & Nisbett, 1991). The relationship between self-ratings of memory on memory questionnaires and memory performance is equally variable (e.g., Herrmann, 1984; Schneider, 1985), but understandably so: A self-rating of memory on a questionnaire, a summary statement about memory ability, is best considered as a sort of "batting average" for remembering (Sehulster, 1982) over an aggregation of situations (Epstein, 1984), and, as such, cannot be perfectly predictive of behavior in any single experimental assessment of memory performance. Someone who rates his memory for names as excellent will still draw an occasional, perhaps even an embarrassing blank on a name; no global self-rating question about one's memory can cover all instances and conditions in which one may have to recall. Furthermore, regardless of one's self-rating of ability, memory performance will vary due to other temporary states, such as fatigue, health, anxiety, or stress. Researchers are at last beginning to consider the effects of these forgotten (or ignored) state variables on memory performance (Mullin, Herrmann, & Searleman, 1993).

Despite their drawbacks, metamemory questionnaires have proven useful in the description of individual differences. A person's self-perception of memory ability in various domains of everyday life, as measured by The Memory Scale, has been shown to cluster into three meaningful factors (Sehulster, 1981b): (a) memory for verbal and factual material (i.e., remembering trivia, facts, names, plots of books or films), (b) memory for autobiographical material (i.e., remembering personal events, especially emotional events), and (c) memory for prospective material (i.e., remembering to observe someone's birthday, meeting an appointment, and remembering the whereabouts of personal items). By combining high or low settings of the three factors, one can suggest qualitatively different styles of remembering that relate not only to memory performance, but also to self-perceptions of other nonmemory abilities, such as enjoying computers and mathematics, being effective in arguments, being sensitive to the moods of others, enjoying music, and so on (Sehulster, 1988, 1995). Implicit in the analysis of memory styles is the notion that differences in composites of self-ratings may in fact represent real underlying individual differences in processing, organization, retention, and retrieval from memory.

It is always possible, however, that differences in composites of self-ratings do not in fact represent real processing or retention differences. At minimum, the self-rating of memory ability is an attitude about one's memory, a statement of how an individual wishes her memory ability to be perceived by others. The analysis of memory styles at least suggests that individuals are different in the ways in which they present themselves to others in their social worlds (Sehulster, 1995).

STUDY 1

Through their self-perceptions of memory abilities, people appear to be different in the ways in which they remember their world and in the ways in which they present themselves to the world. A next question is: Do these differences in self-report relate in systematic ways to other cognitive abilities, self-perceptions, and self-presentations? Specifically, do subjects differ in the ways in which they organize memories of events and experiences from their pasts? How is autobiographical memory structured?

Neisser (1986) and Barsalou (1988) argued that the structure of autobiographical memory must mirror the structure of the events themselves in the real world. Neisser suggested that a hierarchical organization describes autobiographical memory, where the smaller, more molecular actions, images, emotions, and so on are nested within larger, more molar chunks or events.

But is the "event" structured from without or from within? Gregory Bateson (1972) suggested that individuals "punctuate" or place meaningful boundaries on the continuous stream of their conscious experience so as to create meaningful contexts (events) in which to understand stimuli and to respond accordingly. Two individuals may bound the same "event" differently and may differ in their perceptions of what antecedent events are related. Often a sequence of interchanges (e.g., an argument) is bounded or punctuated so as to preserve a belief about self ("You *started* this argument. I don't start arguments. I am reasonable and fair and only get angry when provoked").

To a large extent, of course, consensus and culture define our reality (Berger & Luckmann, 1967), and the meanings of things will tend to be conventionalized (Schachtel, 1959). We can expect that boundaries for events in autobiographical memory will also be more often conventional, stereotypical, and consensus driven. Time and immediate location are obvious markers we employ to punctuate day-to-day experience; we also punctuate larger month-to-month, year-to-year units of experience, again using time (the calendar) and location. Robinson (1986) referred to these time contexts as *temporal reference systems*, and showed that temporal boundaries do indeed affect a subject's ability to recall autobiographical memories. Conway and Bekerian (1987) observed other organization systems: Subjects seemed to organize their pasts with such boundaries as relationships, schools, jobs, pets, friends, and so on. These organizations provided effective cues in the retrieval of autobiographical memories.

The choice of boundaries is not arbitrary. The boundaries used by subjects to mark off lifetime periods often were events that represented global themes in the individual's life, such as career, education, or family (Conway & Bekerian, 1987); the organization also may represent implicit beliefs about one's own personal stability and change (Ross, 1989). The work of Csikszentmihalyi and Beattie (1979) and McAdams (1985) is relevant here.

Gender differences have been observed in the uses of themes to organize recall. Gergen and Gergen (1993), in an analysis of popular autobiographies, reported that: "Whereas men's stories concentrate on the pursuit of single goals, most often career oriented, women's are more complex. Women's stories usually weave together themes of achievement, along with themes of family obligations, personal development, love lives, children's welfare, and friendship. Whereas men's stories are rarely revealing about emotional experiences, traumas, self-deprecation, self-doubt, and self-destructiveness, women's stories often express these aspects" (Gergen & Gergen, 1993, p. 196). On a broader level, research by Luborsky (1993) suggested that cultural themes, organized around the perceived cultural expectations of the audience, will give structure to personal narratives, such that what one selects or remembers from one's life is what one's audience will wish to hear. It follows that there may be profound differences in the ways the genders or cultures represent and structure experience into events.

Study 1 explored differences in the structuring of autobiographical memory, as reflected in a lifeline division task, and related these differences to gender and to differences in memory style, as reflected in the self-report of memory abilities. Sixty-two undergraduates from two introductory psychology classes participated in Study 1. Each had completed The Memory Scale some weeks prior to data collection. The mean age was 21.26 years; 24 were males and 38 were females. Small groups of subjects were told that they were about to participate in an event-dating task in which they would be asked to give as much temporal information as they could about public, landmark events in recent, experienced history. Examples of events were given: The explosion of the Space Shuttle *Discovery*, the fall of the Berlin Wall, and so on. In preparation for the event-dating task, subjects were asked to construct a lifeline by drawing a 27.9 cm line (11 inches) on an 8½ × 11 piece of blank paper. The left end of the line was to be labeled "my birth" and the right end of the line was to be labeled "today." Then subjects were asked to divide the line into as many meaningful (but useful) sections as would be necessary to do the event dating task (which, incidently, never followed). Subjects asking for clarification or examples were told to think of landmarks in their lives or public events that might be useful for figuring out the date of an event. "Choose landmarks so that you can say to yourself it happened before _____, or after _____, or while I was _____, or during _____."

Nineteen types of boundaries were noted and counted. A boundary was counted twice if it had two labels on it (such as "1987" and "living in New Jersey"). Nine types of boundaries accounted for 90% of the 983 boundaries created. These were, in descending order (with percentage of total in parentheses): schools/grades attended (29%), years (23%), homes (9%), other (8%), ages (7%), relationships (6%), jobs (3%), deaths (3%), and places (2%). Less frequently observed were weddings (self), weddings (other), births (other), public events, vacations, injuries (self), injuries (other), birthdays, and pets. "Unlabeled" was the final type of boundary. Public events comprised only 1.7% of the total number of boundaries.

Subjects used a mean of 15.85 boundaries (SD = 8.11, range of 3 to 35) to divide the lifeline. Because a boundary could be counted two or three times depending on the number of labels it received, an equally important variable is the number of divisions of the lifeline bounded by the boundaries. The mean number of divisions was 10.31 (SD = 5.29, range of 2 to 26).

Individual differences in the construction of the lifelines were manifest in a variety of ways. Men in the sample tended to have more divisions than women, and, consequently, the mean length of their divisions and the mean standard deviation of the lengths of their divisions were less. Within the types of boundaries employed to divide the lifeline, men and women differed significantly in the number of job-related boundaries and public event boundaries. Men used more of each, as if they were saying, "My jobs define me, so I'll show you that they are important steps in my life by making the job changes conspicuous divisions of my lifeline." Women tended to use weddings (of self and others) and births (of siblings and relatives) as meaningful boundaries more frequently than men, though not significantly so. All relationships listed as significant were so at the $p < .05$ level.

Does an individual's memory style, as represented by the three factors of self-perception of memory ability, relate to characteristics of the construction of the lifeline? The answer here is also yes. There are four memory styles (Sehulster, 1988), four bipolar compositions that can be constructed from high and low values of the three factors: The style that has high values for all three factors, high verbal memory, high autobiographical memory, and high prospective memory (VhAhPh), will have an opposite style of VlAlPl. The other three bipolar composites are VlAhPh/VhAlPl, VhAlPh/VlAhPl, and VhAhPl/VlAlPh. Four combination formulae are used to create the four bipolar dimensions.

As in previous studies (e.g., Sehulster, 1988, 1995), persons of the VlAhPh style tend to be women, whereas those of the opposite style (VhAlPl) tend to be men. This is the only significant gender difference in memory style in Study 1.

There were significant relationships between the styles and the kinds of divisions of lifelines. Persons of styles that had high settings for verbal memory and prospective memory (VhAhPh and VhAlPh) tended to use years as boundaries. Interestingly, the style VhAlPh was the style that tended to use public events more often as boundaries as well as years. Thus, although the combination of Vh and Ph tended toward more impersonal organization systems, the setting of a low autobiographical component drew public events into the fray.

It follows that the contrasting style (VlAhPl) tended to eschew the abstract (Vl) and concentrate on more personal and idiosyncratic (Ah) divisions of their lifelines. Persons of the VlAhPh style, who, in previous work, agreed with statements that reflected a more emotional responsivity to the social world (Sehulster, 1981a), tended to use relationships, weddings, and births as boundaries. When these three boundary types were combined into a composite variable of "emotional" boundaries, the relationship between style and boundary type composite was significant. This result is consistent with the results of earlier research on styles (Sehulster, 1981a): Given the more private, internal focus of persons who are high on the autobiographical memory factor, it is not surprising that more personal, emotional events take the fore whereas public events or abstract organizations play a lesser role.

If these results can be interpreted as representing real differences in the perception of, storage of, and organizing of events in autobiographical memory, then we may conclude that persons of the high verbal/high prospective styles tend, over time, to attach more abstract, impersonal schemes to their memories, such as the year or the actual date. If they are also low in autobiographical memory, they tend to place personal memories in context of public events. Perhaps a preference for an orientation in the abstract structures of time (years) characterizes these people whereas their counterparts, VlAhPl, prefer more emotional, more personal, more idiosyncratic organizations.

Of course, the segments of a lifeline on a piece of paper in a psychology experiment may not reflect the same structures that rule and organize autobiographical memory. Is it likely that in completing the lifeline task a subject is really reporting (metacognitively) the organizational scheme of autobiographical memory? I think it unlikely.

Certainly subjects are presenting a lifeline divided according to a system of events they feel would be useful in an event dating task. But they are also dividing a lifeline with boundaries they feel are important in presenting or identifying themselves in public. For instance, persons who perceive themselves to have a strong verbal memory, which includes memory for facts, trivia, names, and so on, are choosing to present themselves in a way that is consistent with a strong verbal memory by arranging their lifelines according to some more abstract, factual scheme such as dates or by public events; persons who pride themselves at their ability to remember family and emotional affairs choose to demonstrate this once more by organizing their lifelines according to family and events of emotional impact. Abstract temporal schemes, such as actual years or regularly spaced divisions, are of secondary importance to these persons.

STUDY 2

Study 2 was an extension of the first in that it asked for specific autobiographical memories in addition to The Memory Scale and the lifeline task. In one-to-one interviews, conducted as part of a research seminar by senior undergraduate psychology majors, the autobiographical memories of 15 older subjects (ages 27 to 65) were probed with 10 queries. The queries were constructed to sample a wide range of autobiographical situations and age periods.

In the first stage of the interview, The Memory Scale was administered to each subject; in the second stage, a lifeline was constructed by each subject following the same general instructions as used in Study 1. The third stage of the interview consisted of the 10 queries. The 10 queries were designed to explore a number of different facets of a subject's remembrance of things past. They were: (a) a fairly long trip, but not necessarily a vacation (ages 5–12); (b) when you lost, misplaced, or broke something important or valuable (present time); (c) seeing a film that you feel was special and really captures the essence of you (any time); (d) a joke you found to be funny (any time); (e) an experience with bad weather threatening or interfering with a special event (ages 20–25); (f) an experience that you feel had a great impact on the course of your life (any time); (g) a romantic date in which one of your favorite pieces of music was playing (any time); (h) the presidents and vice presidents of the United States since you've been alive; (i) an experience in which you felt very proud of an accomplishment (ages 7–12); and, finally (j) an experience involving a delicious meal (any time). Subjects' responses were taped and transcribed for the following qualitative analysis.

For contrasting examples, take the cases of Ellen and Kurt, both interviewed by the same senior. Ellen's memory style, defined by her three factor scores from The Memory Scale, is VhAhPh, but the actual values of the scores show her to be very high in Verbal Memory, high, but less so, in Autobiographical Memory, and positive but very near zero in Prospective Memory. Kurt's three negative factor scores suggest the opposite style (VlAlPl), but the actual values of the scores show him to be very low in Verbal and Prospective Memory, and still negative but near zero in Autobiographical Memory.

Ellen, age 29, produced a lifeline with 19 sections. Her boundaries, which showed considerable overlap and complexity, included relationships (both romantic and friendly), cars she has owned, jobs, club membership (Gaelic Club), favorite activities (Irish Dancing), homes lived in, schools attended, and lifestyle commitments (e.g., her vegetarianism). In contrast, Kurt, age 35, gave a lifeline that was more simple: He had 8 sections, with towns lived in, one current relationship, bands he played in, and lifestyles (e.g., "the hermit days").

The memory style and the degrees of complexity of the lifeline are mirrored by the details and complexity of Ellen's and Kurt's responses to the first query, in which they were asked to recall a long trip or vacation that occurred between the ages of 5 and 12. Ellen quickly plunged into her memory in response to the query. The high Verbal Memory factor suggests that her recall will be wordy and contextualized, perhaps abstractly so with specific dates; the high Autobiographical Memory factor suggests that her recall will be immediate, detailed, and chocked with images and sensations. Indeed, Ellen generated over 2,600 words in response to the first query as she recalled the first time she visited her father's family in Ireland in 1972. Much of it was recall of immediate experience, but also much of it was comment about the recall or contextualizations: the explanation of relationships, evaluation of experiences, drawing of conclusions, and, ultimately, the relating of this autobiographical experience to general life themes. She contextualized mainly through ages, birthdays, deaths, and family relationships, but there were exact dates as well. Structurally, Ellen's recall was not a time-linear narrative, but followed rather a recursive structure (Luborsky, 1993): She took a detail of the experience and followed it through to some form of completion and then, often associatively, as if "reminded" of some other facet of the experience, took another detail, followed it through, and so on. Ellen's recalled incidents that support her current identity as an Irish-American, but she also recalled incidents that support her identity as a vegetarian: Her narrative contained vivid images of and strong reactions to slaughtered animals for food, specifically freshly killed chickens for dinner one night in Ireland.

Kurt took considerable time getting started, as if he either could not use the query to narrow his search or he could not remember the time period clearly enough to find an appropriate memory. He finally recalled a vacation to Nova Scotia with his father when Kurt was in his late teens. It was a short recall (about 200 words), with little detail and little actual recall in the sense of images or descriptions. Much of what he said contained reconstructions, asides, and claims that he just did not remember ("I don't remember flying, but I know we flew there"). This vacation was (apparently) a disconnected event in his life, whereas Ellen's memories of her trip to Ireland remain an important part of her identity.

DISCUSSION

The results of Study 2, partially offered here, support the notion that there is consistency in the metamemory (self-report and lifeline task) and memory domains (recall from autobiographical memory). The results may be interpreted from two different but perhaps overlapping perspectives. A nuts-and-bolts cognitive processing perspective would posit that Ellen and Kurt have observed metacognitively the workings of their memory performance over the years and, by this time, have formed some summary evaluations of their memory abilities such that, when tapped by The Memory Scale, they are able to rate themselves quickly. Their memory styles, assessed from these ratings, thus reflect real differences in processing. Highly verbal, attentive to detail, and effective in her ability to scan autobiographical memory, Ellen is able to construct a detailed and complicated lifeline; Kurt, whose remembering in comparison is more effortful, is less able to perform this task. Because her memory ability really is as she reported it to be, Ellen's recall to the first query is extensive, detailed, and factual, yet laden with image and emotion. Kurt's recall, in contrast, is scant and sketchy, as his self-report suggested it would be.

A presentation-of-self perspective would posit that although Ellen and Kurt may or may not be reporting their memory abilities accurately, they are accurately making a statement about whom they perceive themselves to be, with respect to memory abilities, and how they wish to be perceived by others. Ellen wishes to be perceived as a person who, through her memory, maintains an efficient, organized, yet sensitive and emotionally rich world. Kurt, in contrast, almost seems to be wishing to avoid responsibility for remembering anything. The construction of their lifelines shows Ellen's care and attention to detail, whereas Kurt struggles to find a system. Finally, Ellen strives to live up to her self-perceptions by generating a rich flood of recall with little prompting from the interviewer. Kurt's recall, on the other hand, is effortful and slow and requires much cajoling and encouragement. (Hostility or resistance on Kurt's part can be ruled out by the friendly relationship between him and the interviewer.)

It is possible that both the processing perspective and the presentation-of-self perspective can peacefully coexist, because, we assume, one's presentation of self will be reasonably consistent with the reality of one's cognitive processing. The results of Study 2 do not distinguish between perspectives. I prefer to pursue the perspective that has individuals presenting, through self-report, a somewhat consistent self that may be based on actual memory ability, but it also may not. Glimpses of organizations of autobiographical memory may actually be revealed in tasks like the lifeline, but it is possible that here, too, subjects are merely presenting themselves to the experimenter. To the claim that because narratives from autobiographical memory often bear a relationship to identity and to life themes it follows that autobiographical memory must be organized according to these themes, I would suggest that we first investigate more external constraints on the organization of narratives.

We should first explore the frequency with which one's autobiographical narratives are queried within one's social world. We should also evaluate narratives as social currency. Remembering a great performance, such as Maria Callas in *Tosca* at the Met in 1965 (Holland, 1993; Sehulster, 1989) has enormous value in discussions about opera, just as remembering Woodstock (1969) has great value in discussions about music and culture in the 1960s. From Study 2, Ellen's extensive recall of a trip to Ireland when she was 8 contains a wealth of material that must have been recalled repeatedly over the ensuing 20 years. Ellen is a member of an Irish-American family, a member of the Gaelic Club, takes Irish dancing lessons, and so on. Thus, her remembrances of certain sections of the Ireland trip are quite valuable in terms of social currency and are frequently queried. Most likely she has often narrated the section about the meeting of her father's family in response to queries by other family members ("Whom did you meet over there?"), most likely she described other features of Ireland to anyone else interested: She may have discussed the trains in Ireland versus the United States in conversations about transportation differences; she may have discussed the profound impact of the immediacy of the slaughtering of animals in Ireland whenever her vegetarianism comes up. In a circular way, each recounting of a section of the trip to Ireland solidifies the narrative, sharpens its focus around identity, and makes it easier to recall.

Thus, if autobiographical memory appears to be organized according to themes of self-identity (Csikszentmihalyi & Beattie, 1979; McAdams, 1985), it may be because most conversations are: The most frequently required information in recall is that which relates to identity issues. Other recall that is not central to identity or to themes often discussed within one's culture (Luborsky, 1993) is either soon forgotten or, if retained, may remain as an isolated, private, unspoken remembrance. This suggests that the proper analysis of individual differences in the organization of autobiographical memory must include some description, perhaps normative, of the differences in the frequency of queries asked within one's social context and differences in the value of personal narratives as social currency.

REFERENCES

Barclay, C. (1986). Schematization of autobiographical memory. In D. Rubin (Ed.), *Autobiographical memory* (pp. 82–99). New York: Cambridge University Press.

Barsalou, L. (1988). The content and organization of autobiographical memories. In U. Neisser & E. Winograd (Eds.), *Remembering reconsidered* (pp. 193–243). New York: Cambridge University Press.

Bateson, G. (1972). The logical categories of learning and communication. In G. Bateson (Ed.), *Steps to an ecology of mind* (pp. 279–308). New York: Ballantine Books.

Berger, P., & Luckmann, T. (1967). *The social construction of reality.* New York: Anchor Books.

Brewer, W. (1986). What is autobiographical memory. In D. Rubin (Ed.), *Autobiographical memory* (pp. 25–49). New York: Cambridge University Press.

Byrd, D., & Gholson, B. (1985). Reading, memory, and metacognition. *Journal of Educational Psychology, 77,* 428–436.

Conway, M., & Bekerian, D. (1987). Organization in autobiographical memory. *Memory & Cognition, 15,* 119–132.

Costermans, J., Lories, G., & Ansay, C. (1992). Confidence level and feeling of knowing in question answering: The weight of inferential processes. *Journal of Experimental Psychology: Learning, Memory and Cognition, 18,* 142–150.

Csikszentmihalyi, M., & Beattie, O. (1979). Life themes: a theoretical and empirical exploration of their origins and effects. *Journal of Humanistic Psychology, 19,* 46–63.

Epstein, S. (1984). The stability of behavior across time and situations. In R. A. Zucker, J. Aronoff, & A. I. Rabin (Eds.), *Personality and the prediction of behavior* (pp. 209–268). New York: Academic Press.

Eysenck, M. (1979). The feeling of knowing a word's meaning. *British Journal of Psychology, 70,* 243–251.

Flavell, J. (1979). Metacognition and cognitive monitoring: A new area of cognitive-developmental inquiry. *American Psychologist, 34,* 906–911.

Gentry, M., & Herrmann, D. (1990). Memory contrivances in everyday life. *Personality and Social Psychology Bulletin, 16,* 241–253.

Gergen, M., & Gergen, K. (1993). Narratives of the gendered body in popular autobiography. In R. Josselson & A. Lieblich (Eds.), *The narrative study of lives* (Vol. 1, pp. 191–218). Newbury Park, CA: Sage.

Herrmann, D. (1982). Know thy memory: the use of memory questionnaires to assess and study memory. *Psychological Bulletin, 92,* 434–452.

Herrmann, D. (1984). Questionnaires about memory. In J. Harris & P. Morris (Eds.), *Everyday memory, actions, and absent-mindedness* (pp. 133–151). London: Academic Press.

Holland, B. (1993, November 14). I'll trade you two Callases for a Mel Ott. *The Sunday New York Times,* Section Two, Arts & Leisure, p. 29.

Klein, S., & Loftus, J. (1993). The mental representation of trait and autobiographical knowledge about the self. In T. Srull & R. Wyer (Eds.), *The mental representation of trait and autobiographical knowledge about the self* (pp. 1–49). Hillsdale, NJ: Lawrence Erlbaum Associates.

Leonesio, R. J., & Nelson, T. (1990). Do different metamemory judgments tap the same underlying aspects of memory? *Journal of Experimental Psychology: Learning, Memory, and Cognition, 16,* 464–470.

Luborsky, M. (1993). The romance with personal meaning in gerontology: cultural aspects of life themes. *The Gerontologist. 33,* 445–452.

McAdams, D. (1985). *Power, intimacy, and the life story: Personological inquiries into identity.* Homewood, IL: Dorsey.

Metcalfe, J. (1986). Feeling of knowing in memory and problem solving. *Journal of Experimental Psychology: Learning, Memory, and Cognition, 12,* 288–294.

Mischel, W. (1968). *Personality and assessment.* New York: Wiley.

Mullin, P., Herrmann, D., & Searleman, A. (1993). Forgotten variables in memory research. *Memory, 1,* 43–64.

Neisser, U. (1986). Nested structure in autobiographical memory. In D. C. Rubin (Ed.), *Autobiographical memory* (pp. 71–81). New York: Cambridge University Press.

Paris, S., & Winograd, P. (1990). How metacognition can promote academic learning and instruction. In B. F. Jones & L. Idol (Eds.), *Dimensions of thinking and cognitive instruction* (pp. 15–51). Hillsdale, NJ: Lawrence Erlbaum Associates.

Park, D., Smith, A., & Cavanaugh, J. (1990). Metamemories of memory researchers. *Memory & Cognition, 18*, 321–327.

Robinson, J. A. (1986). Autobiographical memory: A historical prologue. In D. C. Rubin (Ed.), *Autobiographical memory* (pp. 19–24). New York: Cambridge University Press.

Ross, L., & Nisbett, R. (1991). *The person and the situation: Perspectives of social psychology.* New York: McGraw-Hill.

Ross, M. (1989). Relation of implicit theories to the construction of personal histories. *Psychological Review, 96*, 341–357.

Schachtel, E. (1959). *Metamorphosis.* New York: Basic Books.

Schneider, W. (1985). Developmental trends in the metamemory–memory behavior relationship: An integrative view. In D. Forrest-Pressley, G. MacKinnon, & T. Waller (Eds.), *Metacognition, cognition, and human performance* (pp. 57–105). San Diego, CA: Academic Press.

Searleman, A., & Herrmann, D. (1994). *Memory from a broader perspective.* New York: McGraw-Hill.

Sehulster, J. (1981a). Phenomenological correlates of a self theory of memory. *American Journal of Psychology, 94*, 527–537.

Sehulster, J. (1981b). Structure and pragmatics of a self theory of memory. *Memory & Cognition, 9*, 263–279.

Sehulster, J. (1982, August). *Phenomenological and behavioral correlates of a self theory of memory: A global picture.* Paper presented at the meeting of the American Psychological Association, Washington, DC.

Sehulster, J. (1988). Broader perspectives on everyday memory. In M. Gruneberg, P. Morris, & R. Sykes (Eds.), *Practical aspects of memory: Current research and issues* (Vol. 1, pp. 323–328). New York: Wiley.

Sehulster, J. (1989). Content and temporal structure of autobiographical knowledge: Remembering twenty-five seasons at the Metropolitan Opera. *Memory & Cognition, 17*, 590–606.

Sehulster, J. (1994). Health and self: Paths for exploring cognitive aspects underlying the self-report of health status. In *Proceedings of the 1993 NCHS Conference on the Cognitive Aspects of Self-Reported Health Status*, Office of Research and Methodology, National Center for Health Statistics, Working Paper Series, No. 10, pp. 89–105.

Sehulster, J. (1995). Memory styles and related abilities in presentation of self. *American Journal of Psychology, 108*, 67–88.

Wellman, H. (1977). Tip of the tongue and feeling of knowing experiences: A developmental study of memory monitoring. *Child Development, 48*, 13–21.

CHAPTER SIXTEEN

Relations Among Basic Processes, Beliefs, and Performance: A Lifespan Perspective

John C. Cavanaugh
University of Delaware

David Baskind
Delta University

Trying to understand how memory works is an ancient and noble enterprise. Since the time of the ancient Greek philosophers (and probably earlier), theorists and researchers alike have sought to unlock the secrets of why people seem to be good at remembering some things and not others, and why some people seem to be better at remembering in general than others. To be sure, important advances have been made over the past 2,500 years; indeed, we suspect that Aristotle himself would be impressed at the recent advances in neuroscience and cognitive science. The researchers whose new findings are described in this chapter may not impress Aristotle as much, but they do provide significant insights into some heretofore vexing problems in applied memory research. This chapter describes work presented during a session on Memory Across the Life Span at the Third Practical Aspects of Memory Conference.

Despite our many advances over the millennia, many fundamental questions about memory in applied contexts remain. One of the most important modern questions concerns how people's self-assessments relate to their performance, and how such belief systems fit into the overall memory system. Although the research presented in this session may not produce the memory theory or research equivalent of the Holy Grail, it does incorporate observations and insights that make important advances toward understanding memory development and functioning in applied contexts across the lifespan.

In general, the research in this session addresses two aspects of memory in applied contexts across the lifespan: How should memory beliefs be assessed and related to memory performance; and what underlying memory processes appear to be most important in understanding memory development, and how do they differ with age? The common theme in all of this research is the importance of testable theory and good measurement in assessing the variables of choice. We have more to say about this later.

Four research teams address the first issue. Borkowski and Muthukrishna (1992) applied principles of metacognitive development and children's beliefs in their ability to the domain of mathematics problems and discovery learning. They pointed out that there are important linkages between cognitive strategies and personal beliefs and goals. Cavanaugh and Baskind (1994) focused on the importance of good measurement of beliefs as a prerequisite for investigating linkages between beliefs and performance in adults, and report results from a psychometric study on the issue. Bachrach and Best (1994) discussed how memory performance in older adults can be understood by taking their causal attributions into account. Berry, Acosta, Baldi, Burrell, and Rotondi (1994) took these linkages one step further (and provided a bridge to the second question listed earlier) by focusing on a topic in which good measures exist—self-efficacy—and examining how age differences in memory processing, outcome, and appraisal can be understood in self-efficacy terms.

Other researchers dealt specifically with the underlying abilities issue. Kail (1994) searched for evidence pointing to a global mechanism to account for processing speed differences across the lifespan, and for connections between processing speed and memory. Such speed differences are sometimes taken into account by older adults in their self-evaluations; thus, understanding the nature of processing speed differences may help us understand the origin of these beliefs. McGuire (1994) examined memory performance in the real-world situation of remembering medical information. Because physician visits are an especially salient aspect of older adults' lives, knowing how well they remember this type of information is important to understanding how they view themselves.

Given the diversity of topics, we think it is important to have a sense of the theoretical frameworks that provide hypotheses about the connections between basic processes and beliefs. These frameworks can be used to generate research questions addressing both of the issues identified previously, and especially about how people experience memory in everyday life; we consider two. Next, we briefly consider an example of research aimed at addressing a common aspect of these frameworks, namely, establishing good measures of beliefs. Finally, we briefly consider implications for application.

MEMORY IN EVERYDAY LIFE:
LIFESPAN THEORETICAL FRAMEWORKS

Trying to describe the linkages between basic memory processes and belief systems requires that theorists address issues outside the boundaries of most mainstream theories of cognition. Moreover, developmentalists have the additional requirement of building processes for change into their models. Although no single theory yet exists that accounts for development across the entire lifespan, it is possible to juxtapose two frameworks and gain significant insights into much of child and adult development. Each of these theories originates in different traditions: the instructional approach and everyday cognitive aging (for a more thorough discussion of these issues, see Cavanaugh, 1996; Cavanaugh, Feldman, & Hertzog, 1994).

The Instructional Approach

Based on two decades of research, Borkowski (Borkowski, Carr, & Pressley, 1987; Borkowski, Carr, Rellinger, & Pressley, 1990; Borkowski & Cavanaugh, 1979; Borkowski & Muthukrishna, 1992) developed a model of cognitive, motivational, and self-system components of metacognition. Borkowski's model integrates the instructional technology literature and research on getting individuals to reflect on their own learning processes (i.e., engage in metacognition).

Borkowski and colleagues (e.g., Borkowski et al., 1990; Borkowski & Muthukrishna, 1992) provided a detailed analysis of what happens to people when they receive high quality instruction. In brief, individuals begin by learning and practicing a new skill, such as a new memory strategy, thereby gaining strategy-specific knowledge about its utility and limitations. As additional strategies are learned, additional knowledge is acquired, increasing the available repertoire of memory knowledge. As increased ability in applying strategies appropriately is acquired, higher-order executive and monitoring skills are gained to assist in planning for effective learning and remembering. At this point, general strategy knowledge and beliefs about self-efficacy emerge, and people begin to make attributions about their performance. Self-efficacy is reinforced and the motivation to learn is enhanced. A feedback loop emerges linking successful performance to specific causes, which energizes the personal–motivational states for future strategy selection and implementation. General and domain-specific memory knowledge continue to increase, and may in some cases be sufficient to solve problems without additional strategies (i.e., a kind of specific-knowledge bypass of strategies). Finally, after much practice the person begins to acquire a sense of self in this particular domain (e.g., "competent memorizer") that, in turn, influences subsequent memory behavior.

Several aspects of Borkowski's model are especially relevant to the papers in this session. One key aspect is the development of self-evaluative beliefs (e.g., self-efficacious beliefs, personal–motivational states, attributions, a sense of self-as-competent-memorizer, etc.). Borkowski and colleagues emphasized that these beliefs help provide motivation for continued efficient processing and good performance; indeed, instantiating such beliefs is an important part of the instructional approach. A second aspect is less obvious. In order for good strategies to develop, it must be the case that underlying memory processing skills are sound. Although Borkowski's model was developed in the context of improving instruction in classrooms of children, its potential for posing testable hypotheses about many other aspects of memory should not be overlooked.

Everyday Memory Aging

Beginning with a different premise, Cavanaugh and colleagues independently developed a very similar model (Cavanaugh, 1989; Cavanaugh & Green, 1990; Cavanaugh & Morton, 1989; Cavanaugh, Morton, & Tilse, 1989). Rather than attempting to understand cognitive training, they were attempting to explain normative cognitive aging in everyday life. In brief, Cavanaugh described a complex network of reciprocal, dynamic interrelationships that denote the influence of underlying cognitive developmental level, personality, situational factors, knowledge, self-efficacy, and various feedback and evaluation processes.

One important aspect of the model is that self-evaluations (self-efficacy, outcome expectations, and performance evaluation) are not conducted on the basis of direct input from content knowledge about memory processes and functions (labeled "knowledge base"). Rather, the influence of content knowledge is mediated through memory beliefs. The importance of this mediation should not be overlooked. The framework implies that evaluations of ability are not made by simply retrieving and applying objective "memory facts." Rather, evaluations of ability in a given context are constructed by using previously stored information in addition to ongoing processing. It also means that considerable attention must be paid to developing sensitive measures of these processes in order to tease apart the various components.

To a greater extent than did Borkowski and colleagues, Cavanaugh and associates explicitly emphasized the importance of basic information processing skills. For example, the latter model argues that underlying cognitive abilities in general provide the foundation on which the belief system is built. Thus, understanding how beliefs influence performance must be done in the context of understanding the connection between basic processes and performance, much in the way that Kail addressed it in this session.

An Integrated Framework

A careful comparison of Borkowski and colleagues' and Cavanaugh and associates' models shows many similarities. Although the specific labels may vary, both emphasize the roles of basic information processing skills, situational/task, personal background, memory knowledge, and personal (i.e., memory) beliefs as key influences on strategy selection and subsequent performance. Given that the original goals of the frameworks were quite different (developing good instructional programs vs. describing everyday cognitive aging), their overlap indicates the power and importance of the variables in question. Differences between the models are also apparent; Borkowski and colleagues emphasized motivational, implicit theory, and attributional components more, whereas Cavanaugh and associates focused more on basic skills, personal background, knowledge, and belief systems in interaction with situational factors.

Focusing on the commonalities of both approaches provides a more complete explanation of developmental changes. Most important, both frameworks make it clear that an exclusive focus on only content knowledge, strategies, and performance provides an incomplete picture at best of memory processing, irrespective of the target age group. Rather, we must also focus the basic processing skills that underlie these other components.

Finally, both models make it clear that theoretical frameworks that focus on applied situations (instruction and everyday life) can serve to build important bridges between research on basic processes and beliefs about those processes. Of course, for research in either area to be useful, it must be based on sound measures. In this regard, recent work on assessing beliefs has done much to advance research on the linkages proposed by the frameworks described here. In the next section, we use our own work as an example.

IN SEARCH OF GOOD MEASURES: THE CASE OF MEMORY CONTROL BELIEFS

As noted earlier, one of the linkages between beliefs and performance concerns attributions about performance. One of the most important kinds of attributions is control beliefs. Growing out of the attribution literature, the notion of control beliefs in the context of memory concerns people's judgments of the causes of their memory performance. As noted previously, attributions are thought to be important in both children's and adults' performance.

Lachman, Weaver, Bandura, Elliott, and Lewkowicz (1992) developed the Memory Controllability Inventory (MCI) to assess beliefs about memory ability, memory control, and memory changes in adults. The MCI as originally conceived had four subscales with three items each (possibility of improvement, role of effort, belief in inevitable decrement, need for assistance in remembering from others) and two subscales with four items each (current level of competence and concern about eventual Alzheimer's disease). However, no psychometric evidence was reported to support the claim that the scale indeed reflected these dimensions. Additional information concerning scale development (e.g., item–total correlations) was also lacking in the original report. These gaps pose important limitations in understanding not only what the scale measures, but also how scores may relate to performance.

Establishing whether specific scales are adequate measures of particular components of memory self-evaluations is extremely important. One of the problems encountered in the 1970s in metamemory research with children was the lack of psychometrically sound scales due to the proliferation of measures that were published prior to the requisite scale development work (Cavanaugh & Perlmutter, 1982). We hoped to avoid similar problems in the self-evaluation area by addressing the issue relatively early in the process. Identifying good measures will help focus researchers' attention on issues of additional validation efforts; identifying poor measures will point the way to additional scale development research.

Measuring Memory Control Beliefs

One current area in need of such attention is the assessment of memory control beliefs. Several scales purportedly assess memory control beliefs; some, such as the Metamemory in Adulthood instrument (MIA; Dixon, Hultsch, & Hertzog, 1988) include control beliefs as a subscale, whereas others, such as the Memory Controllability Inventory (MCI; Lachman et al., 1992) are specific to control beliefs. Establishing whether topic-specific scales and subscales of larger inventories tap the same construct is important, as it may not always be feasible (or necessary) to administer long, inclusive questionnaires. In addition, it is important to demonstrate that scales aimed at assessing control beliefs can be discriminated from scales tapping conceptually related topics, such as self-efficacy (Bandura, 1986).

In an effort to begin examining the measurement properties of memory control beliefs scales, we administered three memory self-evaluation scales to 234 undergraduates: the MIA, MCI, and the Memory Self-Efficacy Questionnaire (MSEQ; Berry, West, & Dennehey, 1989). Previous research had demonstrated good psychometric properties of the MIA and MSEQ in several disparate groups. However, Lachman et al. (1992) did not provide comparable data; thus, the primary focus of the study was on the measurement properties of the MCI, and secondarily on its relation to the other two scales.

A total of 209 respondents provided complete data. Initial analyses of the MCI were computed on the original 20-item scale. Internal consistency analyses were mixed ($\alpha = .44$ for the total scale, with a range between .51 and

.77 for the subscales). Additional analyses were then performed to identify poor items and to improve the scale's psychometric properties. Item–total correlation analyses revealed that 12 items exceeded a .33 criterion. The remaining items from the original scale were dropped from subsequent analyses. Internal consistency was recomputed on the 12-item version and was acceptable for the total scale (α = .76). Item–total correlations on the reduced scale all exceeded the cutoff. (The revised 12-item scale is available from the senior author on request.)

The revised 12-item MCI was then subjected to a principal components analysis with a varimax rotation. Results revealed three eigenvalues greater than 1.0, as indicated in Table 16.1. This three-factor solution, accounting for a total of 54.4% of the variance, was adopted. Loadings on the rotated factor matrix are also reported in Table 16.1. Six items (2, 3, 8, 12, 16, and 18) had loadings above the .50 criterion on Factor 1, and three items had similar loadings on each of Factors 2 (7, 10, and 17) and 3 (9, 14, and 15). Due to the types of items loading on each factor, the factors were labeled as follows: Factor 1, Memory Failure; Factor 2, Effort; Factor 3, Memory Usage. Internal consistency for the three subscales were as follows: .72 for Memory Failure; .77 for Effort; and .54 for Memory Usage. Scores for the three subscales were computed for subsequent analyses by summing across the items in each respective subscale.

To address the second focus of the study concerning redundancy across scales, scores on the three measures were intercorrelated. Separate scores

TABLE 16.1
Final Statistics and Factor Loadings for the MCI Analysis

Factor	Eigenvalue	Cumulative Percentage of Variance
1	3.43	28.6
2	1.78	43.4
3	1.32	54.4

Item	Factor 1: Memory Failure	Factor 2: Effort	Factor 3: Memory Usage
2	−.51		
3	.61		
8	.75		
12	.70		
16	−.58		
18	.56		
7		.69	
10		.82	
17		.71	
9			.80
14			.68
15			.60

were computed for each of the subscales of the MIA, two scores [Self-Efficacy Level (SEL) and Self-Efficacy Strength (SEST)] were computed for the MSEQ, and three separate scores were computed for the MCI based on the factor analysis reported above. Results of this analysis are presented in Table 16.2. Several aspects of the correlational data should be noted. None of the MCI subscales correlated significantly with the MIA Task or MIA Strategy. In general, moderate correlations were found among the MCI subscales and remaining MIA subscales. Only the MCI Memory Failures subscale correlated significantly with MSEQ measures.

Because the present investigation marks one of the first efforts to examine interrelationships among several memory self-rating scales, the correlation results add new information to the literature. Most important, the lack of high intercorrelations indicates that the three scales examined here may not measure the same underlying construct, and should not be viewed as interchangeable. These correlational results highlight the need for additional psychometric research. For example, none of the subscales from the MCI correlated highly with the MIA Locus subscale, despite the fact that both are supposed to be indexes of memory locus of control. The lack of clear convergence points out the need for investigations of the construct, discriminant, and convergent validity of these scales.

The patterns and magnitude of the intercorrelations provide support for the theoretical models of the role of memory beliefs and attributions in memory performance reviewed earlier (e.g., Borkowski & Muthukrishna, 1992; Cavanaugh & Green, 1990). These frameworks make clear distinctions among self-efficacy, memory beliefs, and attributions, and argue that these concepts operate at different points during memory processing. The current data support this view; the relatively low correlations, as noted earlier, indicate a lack of overlap among the constructs measured by the scales.

The Need for Continued Refinement

Perhaps the most important conclusion from this investigation is the continuing need for further clarification concerning memory self-evaluation scales. It is obvious that the scales examined here should be the focus of additional psychometric explorations. The first step must involve distinguishing self-evaluation of ability, self-efficacy, and controllability. At a theoretical level such distinctions are routinely made both in frameworks of children's (Borkowski & Muthukrishna, 1992) and adults' (Cavanaugh & Green, 1990) memory development. However, empirical measures making such distinctions have lagged.

Second, careful consideration must be given to scale development. Continued examination of validity issues is essential. Understanding why scores from apparently similar scales do not correlate strongly will be key to future

TABLE 16.2
Intercorrelations of the MCI with the MIA and MSEQ

	MIA Strategy	MIA Task	MIA Capacity	MIA Change	MIA Anxiety	MIA Achieve	MIA Locus	MSEQ SEL	MSEQ SEST
MCI MemFail	-.083	.031	.375^c	.440^c	-.385^c	.130	.246^c	.255^c	.143^a
MCI Effort	.031	.117	.087	.259^c	-.202^b	.200^b	.374^c	.060	-.034
MCI MemUse	.094	.120	.069	.256^c	-.034	.221^b	.476^c	-.034	.023

Note: [a]$p \leq .05$; [b]$p \leq .01$; [c]$p \leq .001$; MCI MemFail = MCI Memory Failure; MCI MemUse = MCI Memory Usage.

measurement refinement. It is possible that the issue may relate to differences
in either instructional sets (e.g., akin to state vs. trait anxiety scales) or in
response rating anchors. Understanding these issues is potentially possible,
but will present challenging problems.

We are optimistic about finding the solutions. Certainly, the social cognition arena faced similar difficulties, and managed to deal with them effectively (Cavanaugh et al., 1994). To the extent that memory self-ratings of
any type represent a form of social cognition, it may be possible to apply
some of the approaches used there to the memory self-rating measurement
dilemma. Moreover, as we discuss next, better measurement and mapping
of the components of the theoretical models outlined earlier will be essential
for understanding memory in applied contexts.

FROM THEORY TO MEASUREMENT TO APPLICATION: WHERE DO WE GO FROM HERE?

We have argued throughout this chapter that understanding how memory
operates in real-world settings depends critically on having sound theoretical
models that link basic information processing skills with self-evaluation,
strategies, and performance, as well as psychometrically sound measures of
these theoretical constructs. In this final section, we build the case that only
by linking theory-driven research with methodological improvements will
progress toward this understanding be made (see also Wohlwill, 1991).

On the theory side, there is a pressing need for research aimed at testing
specific predictions made by the models described earlier. To date, neither
model has had all of its components tested simultaneously. However, of the
two, Borkowski's framework has been examined more systematically, perhaps because it is grounded in a more experimental, intervention-oriented
approach. Much of the research emphasis has been on determining effective
ways to get children to learn, rather than on developing specific measures
for particular aspects of the model. Indeed, Borkowski and Muthukrishna's
research presents data demonstrating the effectiveness of the model in accounting for performance in discovery learning. In contrast, most of the
focus in the applied cognitive aging area, such as with Cavanaugh's model,
has been on establishing the linkages among beliefs, self-efficacy, and performance, with less emphasis on testing specific predictions. Clearly, research
in each area could be better informed of work in the other. The result would
be more attention to differentiating the concepts at the measurement level
in the instructional area, and more focus on experimental work examining
specific hypotheses in the applied cognitive aging area.

On the measurement side, much more emphasis needs to be paid to
establishing sound psychometric assessment instruments. To date, the tend-

ency has been for investigators to develop their own scales or interviews to suit the needs of a particular study, rather than to spend the time to develop programmatic efforts aimed at refining extant measures. This problem is not unique to applied memory research, of course. It is more critical, however, for applied memory researchers to have sound measures, because these investigators often wish to use them in situations where responses may be used to differentiate depression from dementia, or normal from abnormal. Only when researchers have reliable and valid measures will they be in a position to address the requisite theoretical research outlined previously.

The Need for Integration

One of the most important accomplishments of this research is apparent from the title of this chapter. It marks one of the first times that researchers examining basic processes, beliefs, and performance across the lifespan have come together. The research presented, and the topics it addresses, are important for two reasons. First, they point to a conspicuous and extensive gap in the literature, and second, they point to similar issues being important irrespective of the age of the target population being studied.

In terms of the first point, there has been little research examining the extent to which intra- and interindividual differences in people's beliefs about their cognitive abilities in general and memory in particular may reflect similar differences in basic processing skills. For example, are people who are demonstrably faster processors aware of this, and does it somehow get incorporated into their belief system? Could part of the explanation of why the relation between beliefs and performance is moderate at best be due to large individual differences in how well this incorporation of knowledge about one's basic skills occurs? Could part of the problem also be individual differences in how basic processes come into play in providing a person with quick access to key information needed to make on-line judgments about such things as task difficulty, and in the efficiency with which such information is integrated with previously stored knowledge and judgments about one's abilities? Although these questions are implied by current theoretical accounts of memory beliefs (Cavanaugh et al., 1994), they have not been well articulated. However, it seems to us that such questions must be addressed in order to more fully understand the relations among basic processes, beliefs, and performance.

As regards the second point, the issues addressed in the research could be examined at virtually any point in the lifespan. Earlier we pointed out several similarities in two theoretical frameworks that had their origins in two different literatures. The questions raised in the previous paragraph concerning connections involving basic processes are excellent ones for pursuing developmental differences; indeed, documenting the nature of such links at various ages would add a great deal to our understanding of memory development. Our point is that there is much that researchers focusing on one aspect of the lifespan can learn from research on a different aspect. For example, cognitive aging research has much to learn from Borkowski and Muthukrishna's work in learning, which could be used as a basis for examining how older adults learn new information and concepts. Likewise, child researchers could glean important ideas from the psychometric work being conducted with older adults in how to construct better, age-appropriate measures of beliefs.

In sum, we see the need for a symbiotic relation between theory-driven and methodological research, and between child and adult developmental research. Much remains to be done: Existing frameworks need to be refined, better measures need to be developed, more integrative questions need to be asked. The research presented points us in the right direction. It will be up to the rest of us to continue the journey.

REFERENCES

Bachrach, P. S., & Best, D. L. (1994, August). *Casual attribution and memory performance in the elderly*. Paper presented at the Third Practical Aspects of Memory Conference, College Park, MD.

Bandura, A. (1986). *Social foundations of thought and action: A social cognitive theory*. Englewood Cliffs, NJ: Prentice-Hall.

Berry, J., Acosta, M., Baldi, R., Burrell, C., & Rotondi, J. (1994, August). *Age differences in memory processing, outcome, and appraisal: A Self-efficacy analysis*. Paper presented at the Third Practical Apsects of Memory Conference, College Park, MD.

Berry, J. M., West, R. L., & Dennehey, D. M. (1989). Reliability and validity of the Memory Self-Efficacy Questionnaire. *Developmental Psychology, 25*, 701–713.

Borkowski, J. G. (1994, August). *Discovery learning and metacognition development*. Paper presented at the Third Practical Aspects of Memory Conference, College Park, MD.

Borkowski, J. G., Carr, M., & Pressley, M. (1987). "Spontaneous" strategy use: Perspectives from metacognitive theory. *Intelligence, 11*, 61–75.

Borkowski, J. G., Carr, M., Rellinger, L., & Pressley, M. (1990). Self-regulated cognition: Interdependence of metacognition, attributions and self-esteem. In B. Jones & L. Idol (Eds.), *Dimensions of thinking and cognitive instruction* (Vol. 1, pp. 53–92). Hillsdale, NJ: Lawrence Erlbaum Associates.

Borkowski, J. G., & Cavanaugh, J. C. (1979). Maintenance and generalization of skills and strategies by the retarded. In N. R. Ellis (Ed.), *Handbook of mental deficiency: Psychological theory and research* (2nd ed., pp. 569–617). Hillsdale, NJ: Lawrence Erlbaum Associates.

Borkowski, J. G., & Muthukrishna, N. (1992). Moving metacognition into the classroom: "Working models" and effective strategy teaching. In M. Pressley, K. R. Harris, & J. T. Guthrie (Eds.), *Promoting academic competence and literacy in school* (pp. 477–501). San Diego, CA: Academic Press.

Cavanaugh, J. C. (1989). The importance of awareness in memory aging. In L. W. Poon, D. Rubin, & B. Wilson (Eds.), *Everyday cognition in adulthood and late life* (pp. 416–436). New York: Cambridge University Press.

Cavanaugh, J. C. (1996). Memory self-efficacy as a key to understanding cognitive aging. In T. M. Hess & F. Blanchard-Fields (Eds.), *Perspectives on cognitive changes in adulthood and aging* (pp. 488–507). New York: McGraw-Hill.

Cavanaugh, J. C., & Baskind, D. (1994, August). *Relationships among memory self-evaluation scales.* Paper presented at the Third Practical Aspects of Memory Conference, College Park, MD.

Cavanaugh, J. C., Feldman, J., & Hertzog, C. (1994). *Memory beliefs as social cognition: A reconceptualization of what memory questionnaires assess.* Unpublished manuscript, University of Delaware.

Cavanaugh, J. C., & Green, E. E. (1990). I believe, therefore I can: Personal beliefs and memory aging. In E. A. Lovelace (Ed.), *Aging and cognition: Mental processes, self-awareness, and interventions* (pp. 189–230). Amsterdam: North-Holland.

Cavanaugh, J. C., & Morton, K. R. (1989). Contextualism, naturalistic inquiry, and the need for new science: A rethinking of childhood sexual abuse and everyday memory aging. In D. A. Kramer & M. Bopp (Eds.), *Transformation in clinical and developmental psychology* (pp. 89–114). New York: Springer-Verlag.

Cavanaugh, J. C., Morton, K. R., & Tilse, C. S. (1989). A self-evaluation framework for understanding everyday memory aging. In J. D. Sinnott (Ed.), *Everyday problem solving: Theory and application* (pp. 266–284). New York: Praeger.

Cavanaugh, J. C., & Perlmutter, M. (1982). Metamemory: A critical examination. *Child Development, 53,* 11–28.

Dixon, R. A., Hultsch, D. F., & Hertzog, C. (1988). The Metamemory in Adulthood (MIA) questionnaire. *Psychopharmacology Bulletin, 24,* 671–688.

Kail, R. (1994, August). *Memory and speed of processing throughout the lifespan.* Paper presented at the Third Practical Apsects of Memory Conference, College Park, MD.

Lachman, M. E., Weaver, S. L., Bandura, M., Elliott, E., & Lewkowicz, C. J. (1992). Improving memory and control beliefs through cognitive restructuring and self-generated strategies. *Journal of Gerontology: Psychological Sciences, 47,* P293–P299.

McGuire, L. C. (1994, August). *What did the doctor say? Adult age differences in retention of physician feedback.* Paper presented at the Third Practical Aspects of Memory Conference, College Park, MD.

Wohlwill, J. F. (1991). Relations between method and theory in developmental research: A partial-isomorphism view. In P. Van Geert & L. P. Mos (Eds.), *Annals of theoretical psychology* (Vol. 7, pp. 91–138). New York: Plenum.

CHAPTER SEVENTEEN

Mnemonics and Metacognition

Cesare Cornoldi
Rossana De Beni
University of Padua, Italy

The study of mnemonics represents one of the most rooted areas of human reflection on memory. As Yates (1966) and several other authors documented, many of the greatest thinkers in the history of the study of the mind have shown their interest in the art of memory. A particular but significant example is the Italian Renaissance, which saw the publication of a large number of mnemonic handbooks. As we pointed out elsewhere (Cornoldi, 1988), this interest cannot be attributed only to the positive but somewhat restricted benefits mnemonics can give. A better understanding of how memory works has long been the focus of research, whether by examining memory in exceptional contexts, when it fails—as happens in psychopathological research—or when it is particularly successful—as in the present case.

Some recent research can be both seen in this light and considered for its practical implications. For example, by studying the first letter strategy, Gruneberg and Owen (1994) were able to examine the nature of retrieval blocking and suggest ways to contrast it. Similarly, Groninger and Groninger (1994), while studying face–name mnemonics, gave a remarkable contribution on the mediation problems implicit in a context requiring the self-generation of mediators; De Beni, Moe, and Cornoldi (1994), by studying the loci mnemonics, were able to find modality-specific interference effects between visual imagery and reading. In this presentation the focus is on the practical aspects of mnemonics and their possible theoretical implications. As Gruneberg recently (1993) suggested (see also Higbee, 1988), the application range of mnemonics can be misinterpreted and thus create an unmotivated diffidence toward mnemonics. In particular, although mnemonics cannot be considered a panacea useful in every context, its usefulness appears demonstrated, even if it is applied in very particular situations. Some supporters of this line of thinking maintain that these situations must be identified and that mnemonic trainings must be adapted to them. We agree with them in principle, but we think that research has not yet explored all the implications of traditional training programs involving the presentation of basic mnemonics, without focusing on particular application contexts. In fact, correctly administered programs can not only teach the use of specific mnemonics, but also enhance metacognition (i.e., increase knowledge about memory) and develop a more positive attitude toward the study of memory and the search for its most appropriate uses. Evidence in support of this hyphothesis comes from some recent research (e.g., Noice & Noice, 1994) showing that good memorizers do not use standard mnemonics but, presumably starting from mnemonic knowledge, develop flexible strategies that are specific to the different memory contexts.

The concept of metacognition has been widely studied in memory and cognitive psychology since Flavell and Wellman (1977) furnished a general presentation of the topic. In recent years, metamemory has been referred to as a pool of knowledge and abilities based on memory beliefs, motivations, and strategies that may affect subjects' ability to control their overall memory processes. It is argued that if subjects' metamemory is satisfactory, they will better analyze the nature of the task, choose suitable strategies in a flexible way, spend the necessary amount of resources, allocate them productively, and so on. Metacognition and mnemonics are related because they both refer to the knowledge and processes that control cognitive activity. In particular, metamemory knowledge of strategies, which can be increased through mnemonic training, affects the use of those strategies. Further, a metacognitive attitude strongly believing in the effectiveness of memory strategies and mnemonics may stimulate the subject towards a more active use of mnemonics.

These aspects of the relation between metamemory and mnemonics are particularly interesting when elderly people's memory is involved, both because they appear especially influenced by their metamemory and because they present memory failures that could be compensated by a mnemonic training. The decrease of memory abilities as age increases has been widely studied and the many given explanations have underlined both neuropsychological and psychological aspects. The aim of this chapter is to demonstrate that metamemory plays an important role in elderly memory failure and that modification, through training, of subjects' metamemory has practical implications.

Metamemory in elderly people has been the object of much research (e.g., Dixon & Hertzog, 1988; Lachman, Lachman, & Thronesbery, 1979).

More in particular, Cornoldi and De Beni (1989), by means of a metamemory questionnaire, found that—compared with subjects of other ages—the elderly tend to underestimate their own memory and have a poor idea of memory functioning. Cavanaugh and Morton (1988) also tried to specify the attributional aspects of memory beliefs. Referring to Weiner's (1985) attributional analysis, which explores the factors considered by subjects as responsible for memory success or failure, they argued that older adults' memory attributions provide a great deal of insight into both normal functioning and clinical problems. In particular, it is possible to verify whether subjects attribute their results to personal effort exerted during the task or to factors independent of the deliberate allocation of cognitive resources, such as personal ability, task difficulty, help received, and luck.

Also Hultsch, Hertzog, Dixon, and Davidson (1988) stressed that metamemory and its implications for memory behavior change with age. Differently from other age groups, which are mainly influenced by knowledge about memory tasks, strategies, and individual differences, elderly people are largely affected by task knowledge and by the achievement motivation related to situations requiring memory problem solving and confidence in one's own memory. Underestimation of own memory and of the role of own efforts appears to be related to the clinical characteristics of some elderly people (low self-esteem, depression) and may explain why their responses to metamemory questionnaires and their memory complaints are sometimes pessimistic with respect to their real memory deficits and why they do not make sufficient attempts to exploit their abilities to the full. These considerations suggest that the memory questionnaires widely used to obtain ecological measures of elderly subjects' memory ability in fact give measures of subjects' beliefs rather than of their memory ability (Cavanaugh & Morton, 1988). The present research, aiming at exploring the role of metamemory in elderly people and the implications of their mnemonic training, made use of a selection of items from a memory questionnaire—Sunderland, Harris, and Baddeley's (1983) Everyday Memory Questionnaire (EMQ). The EMQ includes descriptions of 35 everyday life situations referring to five areas of ability (language, reading and writing, memory for faces and places, memory for actions, and learning new things). In our Italian adaptation, subjects were asked to rate on a five-point scale how frequently they have problems related to the mentioned situations. We wanted to see to what extent the questionnaire described real memory abilities for the five areas considered and whether scores also reflected the degree of confidence subjects had in their own cognitive functioning.

For a measure of subjects' metamemory, we included items from two other questionnaires. First, we took some critical questions from the QM questionnaire used by Cornoldi and De Beni (1989) on estimation of memory abilities at different ages and the explanations given for success or failure with memory. Second, we adapted a questionnaire prepared by Reid and

Borkowski (1987) aimed at exploring the attributions given by subjects to memory success or failure. In this case, we were particularly concerned with the number of successes subjects attributed to their own efforts and the number of failures explained by lack of the same construct.

Elderly people's insufficient metamemory could be a partial explanation of their poorer perfomance. This hypothesis seems supported by the literature (Dixon, 1989), which actually shows that elderly people see themselves as having poor and progressively worsening memory as well as being convinced that this deficit cannot be improved on. Thus, one explanation of elderly people's memory inadequacies based on metamemory constructs is related to their poor use of controlled processes and of memory strategies (Roberts, 1983). In connection with metamemory, the role of mnemonic strategies in the elderly and the possibility of training them in these strategies seemed therefore well worth exploring. A mnemonic training could have two interconnected effects on elderly people's metamemory: improve their knowledge of memory functioning and make them aware that it can be controlled, and increase confidence in their own memory efficacy.

Research on elderly people's use of mnemonics has shown that, although they are less skilled in memory strategies (Perlmutter & Mitchell, 1982), especially as regards internal mnemonics (Lovelace & Twohig, 1990), they can be trained to improve on it (Roberts, 1983). In the literature on elderly people, memory training does appear to be successful with some type of mnemonics like the simple creation of interactive images (e.g., Yesavage, Sheikh, Friedman, & Tanke, 1983) and loci (Yesavage & Rose, 1984). However, the literature does not consider many other well-known mnemonic techniques, for example, chaining (link) and story-memonics that also could be appropriate for the elderly, because they do not require too much effort.

A potential limitation of mnemonics based on organization and association of visual images is that older people find it difficult to produce and remember visual images and visual imagery associations (Poon, Walsh-Sweeney, & Fozard, 1980). This has led to suggestions that memory training based on visual image associations may be less effective than verbal techniques in the aged (Cermak, 1980). Therefore, it appeared particularly interesting to compare the relative effectiveness of different types of mnemonics, irrespective of whether they required visual imagery.

EXPERIMENT 1

The first experiment studied whether metacognition affects performance and whether performance may be improved by special treatment (e.g., training in memory strategies). In particular, as concerns memory training based on the use of chaining (link) and interactive imagery mnemonics, it was our purpose to check whether elderly people of different ages could benefit from their use and maintain the strategies learned, whether age played a role in this, and whether these two types of mnemonics had different effects on learning and long-term recall of items.

Method

To carry out this experiment we needed elderly volunteers willing to take part in several training sessions. In selecting them we divided them in two groups according to their age, so as to have one group of younger elderly (aged between 60 and 70) and one group of older elderly subjects (over 70). The subjects were 60 noninstitutionalized volunteers, 28 men and 32 women, of similar schooling (school attended for a period of between 3 and 7 years) and in good general health, living in a small town in northeastern Italy. They were divided into four groups of 15 subjects each, matched for gender and schooling: (a) younger elderly experimental group (YEEG, mean age 64.06); (b) younger elderly control group (YECG, mean age 66.2); (c) older experimental group (OEG, mean age 79.13); and (d) older control group (OCG, mean age 81.13). The subjects were administered a short metacognitive questionnaire composed of three items from the Cornoldi and De Beni (1989) QM. Question 1 dealt with estimated memory ability at various ages (6, 12, 36, 72). Questions 2 and 3 asked the subjects to indicate the order of importance of different factors contributing to forgetting (Question 2) and good memory abilities (Question 3). The memory material was 90 concrete high-imagery value and medium-high frequency nouns divided into three 20-item and three 10-item lists. The 20-item lists were used for a paired-associates learning task, to form 10 pairs of unrelated items.

The subjects were individually tested in their own homes over six sessions. In Session 1, the experimental groups filled in the metacognitive questionnaire and were tested on a single-trial paired-associates task used as baseline. In each pair, the second noun was presented 2 seconds after the first and was followed by a 10-second interval. After a 1-minute interpolated phase used to obtain biographic information, the subjects were asked to predict the number of items they thought they would be able to recall. Then the experimenter read out the first item of each pair and waited for the subjects' answers.

In Session 2, a serial recall baseline task for a 10-item list was administered. The nouns were presented at 10-second intervals and followed by a 1-minute interpolated conversation, a prediction requirement, and the serial recall test. In Session 3, the experimenter trained subjects to use the interactive imagery strategy and then asked them to do a paired-associates task following the same procedure used in session 1. Sessions 1, 2, and 3 were separated by intervals of 2 or 3 days, whereas Session 4 followed exactly 1 week after Session 3. The following day the subjects were involved in another paired-associates task (maintenance PA test) without prompting, and began chaining mnemonic training. In Session 5 they were trained in the use of the strategy and did a serial recall task as in the baseline. In Session 6, 1 week later, they were tested for maintenance. At the end of Session 6 the subjects filled in the questionnaire for the second time.

The control groups also took part in six sessions in which they filled in the questionnaire (Sessions 1 and 6). They were also involved in the same memory tasks but, rather than receiving specific training, they talked with the experimenter and tried to remember remote events.

Results

Throughout the study we used a significance level of 0.05. Our first analysis aimed at evaluating the effects of training. Table 17.1 shows the mean scores of the four groups in the three paired-associates tests. A $2 \times 2 \times 3$ ANOVA for complete mixed design (treatment $\times$ age $\times$ trials) revealed the following significant main effects: treatment: $F(1, 56) = 33.08$, $MS = 92.45$, due to the efficacy of training; age: $F(1, 56) = 13.27$, due to the better performance of the young elderly groups; trials: $F(2, 112) = 54.69$, $MS = 39.22$.

Moreover, all interactions were significant. The treatment $\times$ age interaction [$F(1, 56) = 6.92$, $MS = 19.34$] was due to the fact that the younger elderly group benefited more from training than the older elderly group. The age $\times$ trials interaction [$F(2, 112) = 6.28$, $MS = 4.51$] was due to the fact that improvements on the baseline were greater in the younger subjects. The treatment $\times$ trials interaction [$F(2, 112) = 47.44$, $MS = 34.02$] was also due to the fact that the improvement was more evident in the trained groups. These two double-grade interactions are made clearer by the third-grade interaction [$F(2, 112) = 4.33$, $MS = 3.11$]. As Table 17.1 shows, there was a slight improvement in the control groups, whereas both experimental groups benefited from the training. However, improvement on the maintenance task was more evident in the young elderly group.

TABLE 17.1
Mean Number of Pairs Correctly Remembered in Paired-Associates Trials

Trial	1		2		3		Total
Control groups:							
Younger elderly	0.60	(0.63)	0.80	(0.78)	1.00	(1.13)	0.80
Older elderly	0.47	(0.74)	0.53	(0.64)	0.60	(0.74)	0.53
Experimental groups:							
Younger elderly	0.88	(1.55)	4.93	(1.19)	2.87	(1.85)	2.89
Older elderly	0.40	(0.51)	2.53	(1.51)	1.00	(1.07)	1.31

Note: Standard deviations in parentheses.

TABLE 17.2
Mean Number of Words Correctly Recalled in Order on Serial Recall Trials

Trial	1	2	3
Control groups:			
Young elderly	1.73	1.87	2.13
Old elderly	1.20	1.33	1.47
Experimental groups:			
Young elderly	1.80	3.60	3.07
Old elderly	.67	2.40	1.47

A similar ANOVA involving the mean scores on the three serial recall tests (Table 17.2) showed that—as before—all three main effects were significant: groups: $F(1, 56) = 13.34$, $MS = 3.76$; age: $F(1, 56) = 40.14$, $MS = 11.31$; trials: $F(2, 112) = 14.58$, $MS = 14.41$. Only one interaction was significant, that is, groups and trials: $F(2, 112) = 10.19$, $MS = 10.09$. As Table 17.2 shows, this interaction was due to the fact that training improved the performance of the experimental groups more than that of the control groups.

We now examine the changes produced by the training in metacognitive beliefs. Although the training did not involve a general discussion with the subjects on memory functioning, we had hypothesized that the subjects' involvement in memory activities would give rise to spontaneous reflections on and awareness of memory. An example of this effect is presented in Table 17.3, which shows the typical memory performance attributed to different ages (the given example mentioned a free recall test after slow presentation of 30 unrelated words). A $2 \times 2 \times 4$ ANOVA for complete mixed design (groups × test–retest × performance expected at different ages) showed significant main effects due to attribution to different life-span ages and to test–retest, showing that all the subjects recognized that performance varies with age and that the retest produced a generally more cautious

TABLE 17.3
Mean Recall Scores Attributed to Different Ages Before
and After Mnemonic Training

	Children— 6 years		Adolescent— 12 years		Adult— 36 years		Elderly— 72 years	
Pretest:								
Control groups	8.3	(4.7)	14.8	(6.1)	21.4	(6.4)	7.9	(4.8)
Experimental groups	10.7	(5.8)	19.1	(6.2)	25.7	(5.9)	7.2	(4.8)
Posttest:								
Control groups	6.6	(3.8)	10.4	(4.5)	16.8	(5.3)	6.9	(5.7)
Experimental groups	6.1	(3.2)	11.2	(3.7)	15.9	(5.6)	6.4	(4.3)

Note: Standard deviations in parentheses.

attitude [test–retest effect: $F(1, 58) = 54.77$, $MS = 2283.77$]. All the interactions were significant. In particular, the third-grade interaction [$F(3, 174) = 3.45$, $MS = 38.75$] was due to the fact that a decrease in estimated memory abilities specifically concerned the experimental groups and all the other ages except their own. In other words, elderly people, especially those in the experimental group, recognized that they had previously' overestimated human memory abilities and therefore gave lower ratings to themselves.

The explanations given for forgetting and the factors indicated as producers of memory improvement were analyzed on the basis of Cornoldi and De Beni's (1989) procedure that gives correctness scores by comparing the indicated order of factor importance with the order established on the basis of psychological research on memory and includes the possibility of a strategic control of memory. The significant interaction found between groups and retest was due to the fact that at the retest only the trained groups improved their metacognition level. In the retest the mean scores were, respectively, 2.38 and 1.89 for the overall experimental and control groups.

One of our hypotheses was that metacognitive improvement could also affect the accuracy of the prediction of correct performance and, therefore, for each trial we compared predicted performances on both the paired-associates and serial recall tasks with actual performance. To this aim we used a rigorous criterion represented by the number of correct answers given in the right order. We took predicted and actual values as two levels of a memory performance within-subjects variable. Prediction values were always significantly higher than actual performance. Also, because of their higher performance, the subjects generally tended to be more accurate in later trials (although this was not so evident in control and older subjects), as highlighted by the significant interactions of the expected-actual variable with groups and trials shown in Fig. 17.1.

Fig. 17.1 shows the expected–actual gap. For each group a final E means a reference to the expected performance and a final R a reference to the real performance [e.g., Expected performance by the Young Elderly Experimental Group (YEEGE)]. The gap decreases in the second and third trials, mainly for the experimental goups. However, the older experimental group was influenced by success in the second trial and predicted better-than-actual performance in Trial 3 (maintenance). Similar results were also observed for serial recall.

The results of Experiment 1 confirm that elderly people can improve their inappropriate memory beliefs and can, at least partially, maintain trained mnemonics, but these benefits are shown to be greater in younger elderly people. Given the similarity (and functional interdependence) between the two types of mnemonics used, we were not able to evaluate which was the more appropriate. Also, given the fact that each type of mnemonic was

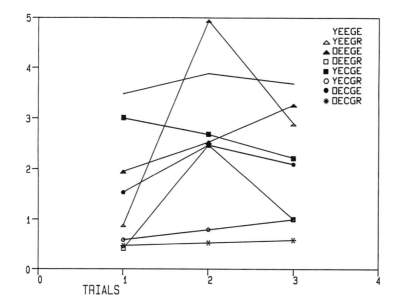

FIG. 17.1. Expected and real performance as a function of age and treatment group.

learned only for a limited number of sessions, we could not evaluate whether perfectly learned mnemonics would cause greater improvement and guarantee long-term maintenance of learned items. These aspects were considered in a further training experiment.

EXPERIMENT 2

The second experiment aimed at comparing two different types of mnemonics—stories and loci. They were chosen because, albeit partially, they represent two different processes. Imagining semantically unrelated representations is envisaged in the case of loci and organizing semantic information is envisaged in the case of stories. It could be expected that both would be useful to the elderly, but that they would give rise to different effects. In general, the loci mnemonic could produce minor benefits for elderly people, who are generally better at learning semantically structured materials than unrelated items and can have problems in the use of images. From this viewpoint, one could expect that only a few subjects would prefer loci, the others performing better at and preferring story mnemonics. However, although these two difficulties occur in principle in the loci mnemonics, they may be overcome with practice by avoiding both the use of uncommon images and nonfamiliar pathways (elderly people seem to have good memory for very familiar pathways).

In order to contrast these two types of mnemonics we needed a group of volunteers who had been well trained. This made it impossible to have subgroups of subjects who could be analyzed with respect to other population variables and in particular to age. We only checked that the overall sample had characteristics similar to the sample of Experiment 1.

By proposing both types of mnemonics, we also intended to explore metacognitive attitude in selecting strategies at the end of training. We wished to see on what basis selection was made and its effects on immediate recall as well as on a delayed test.

Last, to get a better measure of the variations caused by training on the subjects' attributional characteristics, self-perception, and metacognition, we decided to administer at both test and retest an Attributional Questionnaire, an Everyday Memory Questionnaire, and the metacognitive questions used in Experiment 2.

Method

Sixty-five noninstitutionalized elderly volunteers, aged between 60 and 83 (mean age 67), 51 women and 14 men, with various levels of schooling, living in a medium-sized town in northeastern Italy, were divided into two subgroups matched for age, gender, and schooling.

We administered 8 attributional questions, 10 of the EMQ questions, the 3 metacognitive questions already presented in Experiment 1, and a fourth question in which subjects were asked to estimate their free recall abilities on a 16-item list. One hundred and twenty concrete high-imagery words of medium-high frequency in Italian were divided into 12 10-item lists, 2 practice lists, and 10 experimental lists.

The subjects were divided into two subgroups, according to the order of mnemonic training administration. They were tested collectively about 10 at a time, in a quiet room made available by the town authorities, over seven sessions (one every other two days, except for the last session, which took place two weeks after Session 6). For Subgroup 1 (trained first in the loci technique and then in the story one), the order of sessions was the following:

- *Session 1:* Presentation of questions, baseline with a serial recall test (items presented at 10-second intervals, interpolated with a 1-minute task consisting of filling in a form, written serial recall test), and first phase of loci mnemonic training. During this phase the subjects learned the use of interactive imagery and, as homework, were asked to identify a familar pathway with 10 loci on it (examples were given).

- *Session 2:* The subjects reported their personally memorized pathways and were trained to use them to learn sets of words. The images they had created were examined during a discussion. The subjects were then tested on the use of the loci mnemonic with the first experimental list (Trial 1—loci), following the same procedure as the baseline.

- *Session 3:* To allow the subjects to evaluate whether the mnemonic had a long-term effect, they were tested on the list memorized three days before, and then received training in the story mnemonic. They were told that even unrelated items can be better memorized by constructing a story that includes them. They discussed examples given by the experimenter and prepared by themselves, and were asked to make up a story from a practice list. Last, they were tested in the use of the story mnemonic with one of the new experimental lists (Trial 1—story).

- *Session 4:* The subjects underwent a three-day delayed test on the list learned using the story mnemonic. They were also trained again in both tecniques, first with the loci on the final test (Trial 2—loci) and then with the story (Trial 2—story).

- *Sessions 5 and 6:* Training was further developed, instructions were repeated, and new examples given. In both sessions the subjects were tested in both types of mnemonics (Trials 3— and 4—loci; Trials 3— and 4—story). At the end of Session 6 the subjects were asked to memorize a final list using the mnemonic technique they preferred and were then tested in it.

- *Session 7 (two weeks later):* The subjects were asked to recall the final list they had been given and also to fill in again the questionnaires presented in Session 1. They were instructed to disregard what they had answered before, and only to express their present point of view. No time limit was set on the serial recall tests. The subjects were asked to state which type of mnemonic they had used.

The presentation order of the type of mnemonic was reversed for Subgroup 2 (trained first in the story mnemonic and then in the loci one). The only difference was that, because the story mnemonic did not require prior knowledge of a list of items, as is the case with the loci technique, Session 1 was devoted to questions and baseline only (without final mention of any mnemonic). At the end of Session 2, the subjects were asked, as homework, to learn a pathway and were given some information on interactive imagery.

Results

Table 17.4 shows the mean numbers of items recalled in the correct order in the four loci-mnemonic and four story-mnemonic trials, together with the baseline performance given in Session 1. In the absence of a control group, we could not be sure that the mnemonics used had been useful, but, very likely, the improvements from the baseline to the later sessions clearly shown

TABLE 17.4
Mean Number of Words Recalled in Order in Four Training Sessions

	Baseline	Trials			
		1	2	3	4
Loci mnemonic	3.85	6.12	5.26	6.12	7.00
Story mnemonic	3.85	5.91	6.14	5.71	7.26

by the data could not have been due only to practice. However, our aim was to compare the two types of mnemonics and to examine their relationship with metacognition. The ANOVA revealed a significant main effect due to trials [$F(3, 192) = 19.64$, $MS = 53.35$]. As Table 17.4 also shows, in both types of mnemonics, Trial 4 sees the best performance. In Trials 2 and 3 the subjects were probably at a disavantage due to the introduction of the second type of mnemonic and were not in a position to show any improvement on Trial 1, presented in a session that did not include a test for the first type of mnemonic. By Session 6, although it included both tests, the subjects had improved their mnemonic ability. In other words, prolonged training is useful in improving expertise in mnemonics.

We also found a significant interaction between groups and trials, due to the different fluctuations in performance on Trials 2 and 3 with the two types of mnemonic: in particular, the loci-learned list is negatively affected by the first appearance of the story mnemonic, whereas the opposite occurs with the story-learned list. The 3-day delayed test was aimed at examining which type of mnemonic in the first phases of training guarantees better maintenance of the material. An ANOVA on the number of items remembered in the correct order (Trial 1) for the two types of mnemonics in the immediate and delayed tests revealed the expected significant main effect due to interval and a significant interaction [$F(1, 64) = 4.51$, $MS = 10.40$], due to the fact that, in the delayed test, the loci mnemonics showed a greater decline in recall (from 6.12 to 4.57) than did the story mnemonic (from 5.91 to 5.15). Story mnemonic appeared to be more effective in maintaining information than loci mnemonic. However, the picture changes if we consider the delayed recall of the final list, when the subjects had practised more and had been allowed to choose their preferred strategy: In fact, at the end of Session 6, the subjects were asked to memorize a final 10-item list using the strategy they liked better. To our surprise, the great majority of subjects chose the loci rather than the story mnemonic (44 and 21, respectively).

To verify whether the subjects had developed sufficient knowledge of their specific abilities, we further investigated whether those who selected the loci mnemonic had been particularly successful with it in the preceding trial, and vice versa. To this aim, we considered two groups of subjects: Group 1, who had selected the loci mnemonic, and Group 2, who had selected the story mnemonic. A baseline comparison of these two groups did not yield significant differences. Instead, the groups did differ in mean performance in the training trials. A 2×2 ANOVA revealed a significant main effect due to groups [$F(1, 63) = 4.91$, $MS = 44.31$]. Group 1 generally performed better, and a significant interaction [$F(1, 63) = 12.21$, $MS = 24.71$] was found. The interaction underlined that the subjects' choice corresponded to the effective abilities shown in the last tests in which they were examined. In fact, the loci group's mean recall was 7.71 words with the loci mnemonics and 7.36 words with the story mnemonics, whereas the story group's mean recall was 5.52 words and 7.05 words with the loci and story mnemonics, respectively. The fact that Group 1 (loci mnemonic) had performed better in the previous trial—in other words, was more expert in mnemonics—may explain its better performance over Group 2 (story mnemonic) in recalling the items of the final list presented 15 days later, when the difference between the two groups was particularly relevant (7.75 vs. 5.10 words recalled). Thus, the general pattern of the last set of data indicates that well-trained subjects prefer the loci mnemonic, which gives excellent long-term maintenance of items despite the fact that the same loci are used to memorize other lists of items.

As to the role of effort attribution, first we examined whether it affected performance. Because the numbers of answers that attributed success to effort and failure to lack of effort were significantly correlated on both test (Pearson's $r = .352$) and retest ($r = .354$), we decided to assign a single effort-attribution score to each subject (EAS = number of cases out of eight that were explained on the basis of an effort attribution) to determine the overall number of effort answers. With reference to the median EAS value on the test, we divided the subjects into high-EAS (EAS greater than 3) and low-EAS groups (EAS lower than or equal to 3). At this point, we checked whether a high EAS (i.e., a prior greater attribution of the effects of performance to effort) was related to recall and we found a significant main effect of attribution [$F(1, 63) = 5.73$, $MS = 153.17$]. In fact, the mean performance of the high-EAS subjects was constantly higher over the eight trials (mean recall = 6.70 vs. 5.60 of the low-EAS group). Prior effort attribution affected performance. Conversely, did training modify subjects' effort attribution? To examine this point, we contrasted the EAS before and after training (mean EAS 1.76 on test and 1.99 on retest, respectively), and the difference approached significance ($p = .06$). On the 10 items drawn from the EMQ, training also led to a significant variation related to improved self-rating (Table 17.5). The fact that this variation was not specific to memory abilities, which could be related to specific training, but concerned many different aspects (e.g., Item 8 concerns the ability of following a conversation) suggests that the subjects' rating was influenced both by greater self-confidence and effective improvements in performance. We also observed a general improvement in metacognition. For example, as regards

TABLE 17.5
Mean Scores and Student's t Before and After Mnemonic Training

Item	Before Training		After Training		t (df = 64)	p
Language (Item 4)	3.26	(1.16)	3.61	(1.07)	2.64	.005
Language (Item 5)	3.37	(0.99)	3.57	(0.88)	2.03	.023
Language (Item 6)	3.61	(1.04)	3.92	(0.78)	2.81	.004
Language (Item 8)	3.40	(1.04)	3.68	(0.85)	2.01	.025
Reading and writing (Item 14)	3.45	(0.90)	3.51	(1.02)	0.43	.333
Reading and writing (Item 15)	3.29	(1.07)	3.57	(1.09)	2.12	.019
Faces and places (Item 18)	3.05	(1.02)	3.41	(0.92)	2.91	.002
Actions (Item 27)	3.66	(0.99)	3.83	(0.86)	1.26	.106
Learning new things (Item 30)	3.05	(1.04)	3.21	(1.01)	1.21	.115
Learning new things (Item 31)	3.55	(1.20)	3.41	(1.06)	0.94	.175

Note: Standard deviation in parentheses. High scores correspond to less difficult problems.

typical performance attributed to different ages, the data replicated the results of Experiment 1, showing significant effects due to performance, as expected for different ages, training, and the interaction between the two factors. For example, in this case, too, after the training the subjects reduced their overestimation of expected performance at various ages for all ages but their own.

CONCLUSIONS

As some other research works have also shown, old people may have inadequate knowledge of memory. Several reasons may concur to produce underestimation of one's own memory as well as estimation of memory at other ages: personal experience, generalization of observations of own or other people's memory problems, and few life events involving memory and attention. These factors may also contribute to a drop in the level of general knowledge or to a tendency to reflect on memory functioning, and cast doubts on the usefulness of self-rating questionnaires. Some authors are skeptical about the reliability and validity of memory questionnaires (see Herrmann, 1984). Their skepticism seems well motivated and can be extended to the largely used EMQ proposed by Sunderland et al. (1983). Its Italian adaptation appeared to give memory measures uncorrelated with other objective measures of memory abilities (Cavallarin, Perin, Pavan, De Bani, & Cornoldi, 1990). We would like to stress the fact that memory questionnaires are to be considered useful measures of subjects' confidence in their own memory. In Experiment 2, devoted to modifying both subjects' specific memory ability and general self-confidence, we were able to find significant variations in many items of the EMQ. Given the high specificity of the training, we can explain some of these variations on the basis of modifications in attitudes rather than in the specific cognitive abilities examined by the questionnaire. These changes appear to be related to improvements in memory knowledge, as shown by the higher number of correct answers given to the metamemory questions after the training. We believe that these developments are also related to an increased effort attribution. In fact, if subjects attribute their success or failure to factors independent of effort, such as good or bad luck, help, or unmodifiable ability, they will be less able to recognize that controlled processes, strategies, and so on may help memory.

It is interesting to observe that such beliefs are not only widespread in elderly people, but also related to their memory performance. The subjects with low effort attribution scores gave a consistently poorer performance over the whole training of Experiment 2. Although low effort attribution scores may simply have been the consequence of experiencing failure, we are tempted to consider them also as a possible cause of poor performance. It is logical to think that subjects, who, for many reasons (including repeated failure), ascribe little importance to effort will be less likely to devote effort and attention not only to memory tasks but also to many other activities demanding the use of high attentional resources. From this point of view, mnemonic training may have the effect of improving specific abilities, awareness, self-confidence, and effort attribution. In other words, the implementation of memory courses for elderly people may have positive consequences in many respects. Our elderly subjects participated in the experiments with great interest and enthusiasm, found opportunities for new interests, and also met new people (Experiment 2). As the experiments were presented as part of research devoted to verifying the effectiveness of memory training in the preparation of master's theses, special empathy may have been created between experimenter and subjects—a situation that cannot be easily replicated. However, some further research has shown that elderly people take great interest and pleasure in participating in these training programs.

We observed that, both at the end of training and in a maintenance test, mnemonic training may be effective even for elderly people, but that the advantages are more evident in high-functioning subjects (as in Experiment 2 and, in Experiment 1, those aged between 60 and 70). The fact that mnemonic training improves performance shows that the memory deficit also concerns a production aspect, which is not irreversible. By contrasting two different types of mnemonics (Experiment 2) we were able to verify that imaginal strategies are equally useful for elderly people, but that specific differences and preferences may be found between subjects. Nevertheless, an imaginal and effortful type of mnemonic like the loci method also can produce positive effects. Furthermore, our elderly subjects were able to maintain long-term recall of items learned through mnemonics. In our opinion, the particularly satisfactory results obtained in Experiment 2 (as compared to results quoted in the literature) are due to the sufficient length of training.

ACKNOWLEDGMENTS

The research was partially supported by a national CNR grant (*progetto finalizzato invecchiamento*) to the Unit directed by M. Cesa Bianchi, University of Milano. The authors are deeply indebted to F. Capitanio, A. Cavallarin, G. Pavan, and I. Perin for their help in data collecting.

REFERENCES

Cavallarin, A., Perin, I., Pavan, G., De Beni, R., & Cornoldi, C. (1990). L'uso di questionari di autovalutazione nello studio della memoria degli anziani ed il ruolo degli aspetti metacognitivi [The use of self-assessment questionnaire in the study of aged memory and the role of metacognition]. In D. Salmaso e P. Caffarra (Eds.), *Le funzioni cognitive nell'invecchiamento* (pp. 93–99). Milano: F. Angeli.

Cavanaugh, J. C., & Morton K. R. (1988). Older adults' attribution about everyday memory. In M. M. Gruneberg, P. E. Morris, & R. N. Sykes (Eds.), *Practical aspects of memory: Current research and issues* (vol. 1, pp. 209–214). London: Wiley.

Cermak, L. S. (1980). Comments on imagery as therapeutic mnemonics. In L. W. Poon, J. L. Fozard, L. S. Cermak, D. Aremberg, & L. W. Thompson (Eds.), *New directions in memory and aging* (pp. 507–510). Hillsdale, NJ: Lawrence Erlbaum Associates.

Cornoldi, C. (1988). Why study mnemonics? In M. M. Gruneberg, P. E. Morris, & R. N. Sykes (Eds.), *Practical aspects of memory* (vol. 2, pp. 397–402). Chichester, England: Wiley.

Cornoldi, C., & De Beni, R. (1989). Ciò che gli anziani pensano della loro memoria [What elderly people think about their memory]. In A. Dellantonio (Ed.), *Ricerche psicologiche sull'invecchiamento* (pp. 20–36). Milano: F. Angeli.

De Beni, R., Moe, A., & Cornoldi, C. (1994, August). *The oral effect of loci mnemonics.* Paper presented at the Third Practical Aspects of Memory Conference, College Park, MD.

Dixon, R. A. (1989). Questionnaire research on metamemory and aging: Issues of structure and function. In L. W. Poon, D. C. Rubin, & B. Wilson (Eds.), *Everyday cognition in adulthood and late life.* New York: Cambridge University Press.

Dixon, R. A., & Hertzog, C. (1988). A functional approach to memory and metamemory development in adulthood. In F. E. Weinert & M. Perlmutter (Eds.), *Memory development across the life-span: Universal changes and individual differences.* Hillsdale, NJ: Lawrence Erlbaum Associates.

Flavell, J. H., & Wellman, H. M. (1977). Metamemory. In R. V. Kail & J. W. Hagen (Eds.), *Perspective on the development of memory and cognition* (pp. 3–33). Hillsdale, NJ: Lawrence Erlbaum Associates.

Groninger, L. D., & Groninger, D. H. (1994, August). *Assessing mnemonic effectiveness in face–name learning and retention.* Paper presented at the Third Practical Aspects of Memory Conference, College Park, MD.

Gruneberg, M. M. (1993). The practical application of memory aids. In M. M. Gruneberg & P. Morris (Eds.), *Aspects of memory* (2nd ed.) (vol. 2, pp. 168–195). London: Routledge.

Gruneberg, M. M., & Owen, D. (1994, August). *The value of the first letter retrieval strategy in facilitating recall of previously unrecalled items.* Paper presented at the Third Practical Aspects of Memory Conference, College Park, MD.

Herrmann, D. J. (1984). Questionnaires about memory. In J. E. Harris & P. E. Morris (Eds.), *Everyday memory, actions and absent-mindedness* (pp. 133–151). London: Academic Press.

Higbee, K. L. (1988). *Your memory: How it works and how to improve it* (2nd ed.). New Jersey: Prentice-Hall.

Hultsch, D. F., Hertzog, C., Dixon, R. A., & Davidson H. (1988). Memory self-knowledge and self-efficacy in the aged. In M. L. Howe & T. J. Brainerd (Eds.), *Cognitive development in adulthood* (pp. 65–92). New York: Springer-Verlag.

Lachman, J. L., Lachman, R., & Thronesbery, C. (1979). Metamemory through the adult lifespan. *Developmental Psychology, 15,* 543–551.

Lovelace, E. A., & Twohig, P. T. (1990). Healthy older adults' perceptions of their memory functioning and use of mnemonics. *Bulletin of the Psychonomic Society, 28,* 115–118.

Noice, H., & Noice, T. (1994, August). *A mnemonist's approach to learning a theatrical script.* Paper presented at the Third Practical Aspects of Memory Conference, College Park, MD.

Perlmutter, M., & Mitchell, D. B. (1982). The appearance and disappearance of age differences in adult memory. In F. I. M. Craik & S. Threhub (Eds.), *Aging and cognitive processes* (pp. 127–144). New York: Plenum.

Poon, L. W., Walsh-Sweeney, L., & Fozard, J. L. (1980). Memory skill training in the elderly: Salient issues on the use of imagery mnemonics. In L. W. Poon, J. L. Fozard, L. S. Cermak, D. Arenberg, & L. W. Thompson (Eds.), *New directions in memory and aging* (pp. 461–484). Hillsdale, NJ: Lawrence Erlbaum Associates.

Reid, M. K., & Borkowski, J. G. (1987). Causal attribution of hyperactive children: Implications for teaching strategies and self-control. *Journal of Educational Psychology, 79,* 296–307.

Roberts, P. (1983). Memory strategy instruction with the elderly: What should memory training be the training of? In M. Pressley & J. R. Levin (Eds.), *Cognitive strategy research.* New York: Springer-Verlag.

Sunderland, A., Harris, J. H., & Baddeley, A. D. (1983). Do laboratory tests predict everyday memory? A neuropsychological study. *Journal of Verbal Learning and Verbal Behavior, 22,* 341–357.

Weiner, B. (1985). An attributional theory of achievement motivation and emotion. *Psychological Review, 92,* 548–573.

Yates, F. A. (1966). *The art of memory.* London: Routledge & Kegan.

Yesavage, J. A., & Rose, T. L. (1984). Semantic elaboration and the method of loci: A new trip for older learners. *Experimental Aging Research, 10,* 155–159.

Yesavage, J. A., Sheikh, J. I., Friedman, L., & Tanke, E. (1983). Interactive imagery and affective judgments improve face–name learning in the elderly. *Journal of Gerontology, 38,* 197–203.

PART SEVEN

SOCIAL AND EMOTIONAL
ASPECTS OF MEMORY

CHAPTER EIGHTEEN

Biases in Children's Memory for Collaborative Exchanges

Mary Ann Foley
Skidmore College

Hilary Horn Ratner
Wayne State University

Misattributions about the origins of information occur in a variety of contexts (e.g., Belli, Lindsay, Gales, & McCarthy, 1994; Foley, Durso, Wilder, & Friedman, 1991; Gerrig & Prentice, 1991). For example, individuals sometimes confuse who said what in conversations (Foley, Johnson, & Raye, 1983), particularly when speakers physically resemble each other or when they talk about similar topics (Lindsay, Johnson, & Kwon, 1991). Similarly, cryptomnesia, or inadvertent plagiarism, occurs when individuals generate responses they believe are original to them but that were expressed by someone else (Brown & Murphy, 1989; Marsh & Bower, 1993). These sorts of misattribution biases may occur for a number of reasons. For instance, if individuals attend more to what they are going to say than to what another person is currently saying, they may fail to encode who said what and believe they are responsible for the other person's statements (e.g., Brown & Murphy, 1989). Or if individuals covertly anticipate what another person is likely to say, they may later take credit for the utterance, forgetting their own ideas occurred only in thought (Johnson, Hashtroudi, & Lindsay, 1993).

Misattribution biases also occur within the context of collaboration. Describing the consequences of collaborative activities, Rogoff (1990) suggested that children appropriate the actions of another person in the context of shared exchanges, making these actions their own, and then adopt the other's actions as self-regulatory routines. For example, when interacting with an adult or peer to solve a problem, children come to appropriate the actions of the other person, assimilating through the other person's actions that other person's knowledge (e.g., knowledge of solutions, knowledge of problem-solving strategies), and then execute these actions in new and varied situations. Although the mechanisms underlying appropriation have not been specified (Foley, Ratner, & Passalacqua, 1993; Ratner & Foley, 1994), if children make another person's actions their own they should claim undue responsibility for the outcomes of shared goal-directed activities and misattribute who did what. According to Rogoff (1990), "Individuals are constantly involved in exchanges that blend internal and external . . . (making) it impossible to say whose an object of joint focus or whose a collaborative idea is" (p. 195).

We have initiated a program of research to assess misattributions and to characterize appropriation by studying children's memory for who contributes what to the outcomes of collaborative exchanges. Our goal is to understand the cognitive processes contributing to the construction of a representation for collaborative exchanges, and, in the long run, to identify the mechanisms facilitating learning in social contexts. The reality-monitoring model provides us with a framework for raising questions about children's memory for collaboration by way of its description of the processes individuals use to make decisions about the origin of their memories (e.g., self vs. other; Johnson et al., 1993; Johnson & Raye, 1981), and the resulting misattributions that often occur.

According to the reality-monitoring framework, the self is conceptualized as an "internal" agent, regulating the anticipation, initiation and execution of actions. In contrast, other individuals are conceptualized as "external" agents, providing perceptual sources of information. Although a number of factors contribute to agent identification (Foley et al., 1993; Johnson et al., 1993), our primary interest is in what has been called *cognitive operations information.* This information results from the anticipation, initiation, and production of one's own actions, real or imagined (Foley et al., 1983; Raye, Johnson, & Taylor, 1980). The reality-monitoring model proposes that these operations are represented in memory and later serve to facilitate agent discrimination (e.g., self vs. other performed actions) (Johnson et al., 1993; Johnson & Raye, 1981). According to this view, agent discriminations are more accurate when individuals regulate their own actions, because the cognitive operations mediating the regulations later serve as cues facilitating memory, and, indeed, they do (Foley et al., 1991; Johnson, Raye, Foley, & Foley, 1981). For example, in nonsocial tasks such as word searches or anagram solving, people are better able to discriminate their responses (internal) from those of the experimenter (external) when the cognitive operations involved are more effortful (Johnson et al., 1981). In contrast, when the cognitive operations mediating one's responses are more automatic and less attention deploying, discrimination ability decreases (e.g., Foley et al., 1991).

In the context of shared collaborative exchanges, cognitive operations may involve the anticipation of one's own actions as well as the actions of another person. For example, these operations may involve an individual's anticipation of the way she would perform an action, anticipations of the consequences of her actions or reflections on the effort required by the enactment. Similarly, an individual may anticipate the actions of another, thinking about how the person with whom he is collaborating will perform an action, how that person's actions will contribute to the goal, or how he would perform the actions if it was his "turn." Subsequent activation of these thoughts (e.g., anticipations, re-creations of other's actions), which are instances of cognitive operations information, could lead an individual to misattribute the actions of another person, claiming them as his or her own. For example, when asked to identify who contributed what to a shared collaborative exchange, a person may be confused about these contributions if his or her anticipations were reactivated during testing.

In a recent series of studies involving collage making, we have shown that preschoolers are more likely than older children to misattribute the agents of actions, claiming undue responsibility for the outcomes of collaborative exchanges (Foley et al., 1993). After making identifiable collages (e.g., rabbits, teddy bears) with adults, young children mistakenly claim they contributed pieces actually placed by the adult ("I did it" errors) more often than they mistakenly claim that their pieces were placed by the adult ("You did it" errors). We interpret this asymmetric bias as an indication that young children appropriate the actions of others, making these actions their own. Furthermore, we have evidence that these misattributions involve cognitive operations information. Preschoolers' overall tendency to make reality-monitoring errors depends on the nature of their involvement in the collaborative exchange. When they have little control over the unfolding of the joint activity, the overall level of errors increases, suggesting that their judgments are affected by information about the cognitive operations involved (Foley et al., 1993, Experiment 3).

We know that preschoolers' tendency to claim undue responsibility for the outcome of a shared collaborative activity is not a general response bias. For instance, the tendency to claim responsibility for the outcomes of the adult's actions was not observed when preschoolers completed collages partially begun by an adult who was identified as the agent of the work but whom the child did not see placing the pieces (Foley et al., 1993, Experiment 4).

This finding is also important for two other reasons. First, it emphasizes the importance of the shared component of the activity for the emergence of the bias (Foley et al., 1993). Second, it speaks against the simple notion that the misattributions were caused by failures to encode or access source information during the making of the collages. It is possible that when alternating turns with an experimenter, children may have encoded information about their own actions but not about the actions of the adult. If this were the case, children would be certain about their own actions, rarely claiming "You did it!" when asked to judge who contributed a piece to the collage. At the same time, they would experience uncertainty about the other person's actions, possibly claiming "I did it!" more often than was the case simply because there were no other possible responses. Children's response options were limited because they were always tested in context. That is, the experimenter pointed to the puzzle pieces embedded in the completed collages and asked whether the child or adult had placed the pieces. Thus, children were never given the opportunity to reject a puzzle piece that was actually used, nor were they given the opportunity to make judgments about pieces that were not used to make the collages. Nevertheless, the bias only emerged in the collaborative condition suggesting that neither encoding failures nor response limitations led to our findings.

Still, it is possible that when working in the presence of another person, young children were less likely to encode (or access) the others' actions and that the response constraints masked this poor memory. Children may have been attending only to their own actions, making decisions about what pieces to place, and then later guessed about who positioned the adult's pieces. To test this possibility, response options were increased in the present studies. During testing, children were shown two types of puzzle pieces, old pieces used to create the collages and new pieces the child had never seen. These materials allowed three kinds of responses. Children could report they placed a puzzle piece, the experimenter placed a puzzle piece, or a puzzle piece was new. If children were less likely to encode information about the other person's actions than their own, they should miss the pieces placed by the adult, mistakenly claiming the pieces were not part of the puzzle. This would lead to a difference in children's ability to recognize original puzzle pieces as a function of who placed them. Furthermore, if the limitation in responses contributed in earlier studies to observing the bias for pieces actually used, the bias should disappear when response options are expanded.

Providing children with three response options also allowed us to examine potential biases in false positives, incorrect responses to distractor pieces. False positive biases are often interpreted as indices of the kinds of information activated during encoding. For example, when words are presented during encoding, implicit associative responses may be activated or related words may become more accessible (e.g. Glanzer & Bowles, 1976; Johnson et al., 1981; Underwood, 1965). Subsequently, if the implicit associative responses "reappear" as distractor items during testing, individuals may mistakenly identify them as words presented during encoding.

A similar logic has been applied to the interpretation of false positive responses occurring as part of reality-monitoring tests (Foley et al., 1983; Foley, Ratner, & McLean, 1994; Johnson et al., 1981). If information presented during encoding evokes cognitive operations information, and this information is reactivated at retrieval in response to a distractor, then distractors falsely recognized as old should be identified as self-generated (Johnson et al., 1993). On the other hand, if cognitive operations information is reactivated at test only in response to items the individual generated during encoding, there should be little evidence for misattributing distractors as self-generated items. Instead, if a distractor seems only vaguely familiar, the individual should be more likely to claim it was an item presented by the experimenter rather than one they generated, and this is indeed the case for both adults and older children. Individuals are more likely to claim "You did it!" than "I did it!" if misclassifying a distractor as old (Foley et al., 1983; Johnson et al., 1981).

If our characterization of reality-monitoring decisions following shared, collaborative exchanges is accurate, similar patterns in preschoolers' false positive biases may occur. If children's tendency to claim "I did it!" more often than they did is an expression of their anticipation of the actions of the person with whom they are making collages, this bias may be observed for false positive responses, when distractors are mistakenly classified as old. For instance, if the distractor pieces bear some resemblance to the target pieces, then anticipations created during encoding might be reactivated during test. If so, children might be more likely to misattribute the placement of a distractor item to themselves than the other person. On the other hand, if the distractor pieces do not resemble target items, then there would be no reason to expect a reactivation of anticipatory responses during encoding and no "I did it" bias. Finally, if a general response bias to say "I did it" occurs independent of test materials, it would suggest that children's anticipatory processes are not specifically tied to components of the shared activity.

These possibilities were explored in the present studies. In each case, children made collages with an adult and were later asked to identify whether each of several pieces was one they used to make the collage, one the adult used, or a new piece. In the first study, the shapes of the target and distractor pieces resembled each other; many were curved in shape. Presumably, this resemblance among the pieces would increase the likelihood that the distractor items reactivate cognitive operations information associated with anticipations and would lead to a misattribution bias for target items and distractors misclassified as old (i.e., false positive). In the second study, the shapes of the target and distractor pieces were less similar, with the distractors angular in shape. Here we predicted no bias for false positive responses.

EXPERIMENT 1

Method

Subjects. The subjects ($N = 32$) were 4-year-olds attending the nursery school program at Skidmore College. Their mean age was 4.5 years (range 4.1–4.9).

Materials and Procedures.   Each child was given a poster board 14″ × 11″ in size. A model collage of a bunny (or bear), centered on a second poster board, was in view as the child worked with a female adult to make a collage which looked like the model. The adult placed the first piece, illustrating how the gluestick worked, and then handed a second piece to the child. They continued alternating the placement of pieces, with the adult distributing the pieces, until the collage was completed. The collage was then removed from view ("so the pieces could dry better") and the child engaged in conversation with the experimenter for a 2-minute retention interval. For the surprise memory test, the experimenter showed the child a stack of 24 cards, each containing a different shape, 12 of which were the pieces (same size and same orientation) used to make the collages. The 12 distractor pieces resembled the shapes of the targets, both sets including rounded pieces. In fact, the pieces used to create the rabbit collages served as the distractors for children who made bears and vice versa. For the surprise reality-monitoring test, the child was asked "Is this one of the shapes we used to make the collage?" If the child responded "yes," the experimenter then said "Who put this piece on the collage?" The order in which the target pieces were presented was different from the order in which they were placed when making the collage.

Results

There were three kinds of dependent variables of interest to us: misattribution errors on pieces used to create the collages, misses or calling puzzle pieces "new," and false positives or calling distractor pieces "old." Within each type, two kinds of errors could occur. For the misattribution errors, given that the pieces were recognized as those that were part of the collage, the child could mistakenly claim he or she placed a piece actually placed by the experimenter, responding "I did it!" *or* the child could mistakenly claim the experimenter placed a piece actually placed by the child, responding "You did it." An analysis of variance indicated that preschoolers were more likely to claim "I did it" when a piece was actually placed by an adult (M = 2.12) than the reverse (M = 1.19), $F(1, 15) = 6.04$, replicating our previous findings (Foley et al., 1993). Thus, even when response options were increased, the bias was still observed.

Recognition for the parts of the puzzle was assessed by analyzing the misses and false positives. For misses, the child could claim a piece that he or she placed was "new," *or* that a piece placed by the experimenter was "new." The number of times a child mistakenly called a puzzle piece "new" that he or she placed did not differ from the number of times the child mistakenly called a puzzle piece "new" that was placed by the adult, $F(1, 15) = .92$. The means were .94 and 1.25, respectively. The absence of a difference in the misses as a function of agent refutes the notion that the misattribution bias just reported, or in our previous work, was a reflection of young children's failure to encode the other person's puzzle pieces. If children had not adequately encoded the adults' pieces during the making of the collage, then they should have missed more of the adults' pieces than their own.

Finally, when responding to distractors, the child could commit two kinds of errors. When incorrectly calling a new piece one that was part of the collage, the child could mistakenly claim "I did it" or "You did it." Preschoolers were more likely to claim "I did it!" ($M = 3.12$) than the reverse ($M = 1.62$) if they misidentified a distractor item as one that was used to create the puzzle, $F(1, 15) = 6.28$. This indicates that when children thought an item was a target the misattribution bias occurred just as it did for items that were actual targets.

Discussion

Preschoolers' bias to claim they contributed more than they actually did to the outcome of a shared exchange replicates our previous work and shows that our previous findings are not confined to retrieval situations in which the product of the shared collaborative exchange is present during testing, providing contextual support for reality monitoring decisions. Furthermore, the bias does not seem to reflect an encoding failure of source information during the making of the collage. When children did not recognize an actual piece, they were no more likely to make mistakes on the adult's pieces than on their own. Finally, the false positive data provide additional evidence that the bias occurs because of cognitive operations information. If children thought that a piece had been used, even when it wasn't, the bias was observed. This suggests that at least some of the distractor pieces reactivated cognitive operations like those occurring during the collage-making activity. Our preferred interpretation of these cognitive operations is that they involved anticipations about how the adult would place the piece or how the child would do it himself or herself if it were his or her turn.

This interpretation would be more convincing if we found that the bias in the false positives was not evident when the resemblance between the target and puzzle pieces was reduced, minimizing the likelihood that the distractor pieces would evoke operations like those occurring when children were making the puzzles. This possibility was considered in Experiment 2 by creating distractor pieces that were distinctly different from the collage pieces. Here, the distractors were angular and jagged in shape.

EXPERIMENT 2

Method

Subjects.   The subjects were 4-year-olds ($N = 12$) attending the nursery school programs at Skidmore College and the Beagle School in Saratoga Springs, NY. Their mean age was 4.6 years, with range 4.1–4.9.

Materials and Procedure. The materials and procedure used in Experiment 1 were identical to those used here. The only procedural change was in the nature of the distractor pieces. For the surprise memory test, the experimenter showed the child a stack of cards containing 24 puzzle shapes, 12 of which were the pieces used to make the collage and 12 of which were distractors. The child was asked "Is this one of the shapes we used to make the collage?" If the child responded "yes," the experimenter then said "Who put this piece on the collage?"

Results

As in the first experiment, three dependent variables were of interest: misattributions, misses, and false positives. An analysis of variance on the misattribution errors showed that preschoolers were more likely to claim "I did it!" when a piece was actually placed by the adult ($M = 2.25$) than the reverse ($M = .83$), $F(1, 11) = 14. 00$, replicating Experiment 1. Again, the average number of times preschoolers mistakenly classified one of their pieces as new ($M = 1.00$) did not differ from the number of times they misclassified one of the adult's pieces as new ($M = 1.25$). Finally, in contrast to Experiment 1, when responding to distractors, the tendency to claim a new item was one "I did" ($M = .08$) did not differ from the tendency to claim it was one "You did" ($M = .25$).

Discussion

As in the first study, young children took more credit than they should have for the completion of the collages by claiming they placed pieces actually positioned by the adult. Unlike the first study, however, this bias was not evident in the false positive data. To be sure that children's judgments were not a reflection of a guessing strategy (i.e., guessing correctly the pieces that could be used to make the collages even though they never saw the pieces embedded in the collage), a separate group of preschoolers ($N = 10$) were asked to decide whether each test piece (12 target and 12 distractors, randomly presented) looked like it could be part of a bunny (or bear) collage. These judgments were made without showing the children the completed collages.

Overall, the incidence of saying yes was quite low. On average 22.6 of the 24 pieces were rejected by the children. Of the ones not rejected, two children each said "yes" to a different one of the smaller distractor pieces, saying "It looks like a nose . . . it looks like teeth." (The actual pieces were not shaped as a nose or teeth.) These same children along with four others said "yes" to a few of the smaller pieces used in the target puzzle, but their labels did not necessarily match the "function" the piece served. For example, one child said "It could be an eye," but the piece actually served as a nose in that particular target puzzle. Thus, the absence of the bias in the false positive data from Experiment 2 was not a reflection of children's ability to guess accurately which pieces were in the puzzle.

GENERAL DISCUSSION

The results of these studies clearly show that preschoolers claim they contributed more to an outcome of a collaborative exchange than was the case. Children, like adults, may anticipate another person's actions, making them their own, and subsequently take credit for those actions. This bias extends to instruments of action (puzzle pieces) that were not part of the actual exchange but might have been. We interpret this bias in response to both target and distractor pieces as evidence for the reactivation of cognitive operations information when making source monitoring decisions. Evidently these operations can be evoked by action results really involved in the shared activity or by those resembling the original context (Experiment 1).

We have proposed that anticipations of another person's actions may provide an understanding of the mechanisms of appropriation as the basis of learning in social contexts and help to predict if learning is successful (Foley et al., 1993). Children who perform best on their own after participation in a similar joint activity may actually display misattribution biases to a greater extent than those who perform poorly. If the bias is a reflection of children's more frequent anticipations or subsequent re-creations of the actions of another person, increasing confusion between self and other, actions themselves may be better understood and better remembered. This suggests the intriguing possibility that cryptomnesia in the young promotes or reflects better learning of the actions (e.g., deeds, strategies) of another. Our finding that anticipations are activated in response to similar but new contexts also suggests anticipations may support generalizations to new situations.

The fact that the bias was not evident for false positives when distractor pieces were unlike those used to create the collages suggests the bias is not simply a general response bias to say "me!" More important, this finding indicates that when the results of actions are not identified as part of an event, cognitive operations associated with the encoding of that event are not reactivated. This point extends as well to children's misses. Even though these pieces were actual targets, if they were not identified as such, the bias did not emerge, indicating again that cognitive operations information was not activated and did not influence the memory judgments.

The asymmetric bias in the false positive data of Experiment 1 also emphasizes the sensitivity of reality-monitoring decisions to the goal-directed nature of actions. In previous studies of children's and adults' memory for the agent of actions, biases that have occurred have been expressed as the tendency to claim "You did it!" rather than "I did it!" when a new item was incorrectly classified as old (Foley et al., 1983; Johnson et al., 1981). In these cases, responses were unrelated to each other and were not performed for any purpose other than to meet the experimenter's requests to perform individual speech acts (e.g., repeating words, generating associates).

Our previous work seemed to refute the "encoding failure" interpretation of the misattribution bias because no bias occurred when the experimenter was not present to position her pieces. Nevertheless, it was still plausible that the other person's pieces were not encoded at all, or as well, in the context of an exchange because the child was "caught up" in her own thoughts or actions. The fact that children were equally good at recognizing pieces placed by themselves and those placed by the adult provides further refutation that encoding failures can explain the misattribution bias. In conclusion, our findings converge to suggest that the bias we have observed is mediated by cognitive operations information. In future studies we will need to determine whether these operations reflect anticipations of the others' actions as we have suggested and when anticipations occur. Indeed, the boundary conditions for defining events as collaborative in nature warrants further attention and will help determine when anticipations are likely to occur. What makes an event a collaborative one? Do these boundary conditions vary with development? For an event to be collaborative in nature, a younger child may require the physical presence of another, directly witnessing that person's contributions, in order for this person to be a resource, activating mechanisms of appropriation (e.g., anticipations, re-creations of actions). In contrast an older child or adult may not require the physical presence of another to perceive an activity as a collaborative one. Nonetheless, for all age groups, the incidence of cryptomnesia may be tied to the physical presence of another, regardless of age, because it may be in these circumstances that the individual is most susceptible to confusion between memories for responses he or she anticipated making and responses actually produced by the collaborator.

ACKNOWLEDGMENTS

We would like to express our thanks to the staff members of the Skidmore Nursery School Program and the Beagle School as well as to the children attending these programs for their continued help.

REFERENCES

Belli, R. F., Lindsay, D. S., Gales, M. S., & McCarthy, T. (1994). Memory impairment and sourcemisattribution in postevent misinformation experiments with short retention intervals. *Memory & Cognition, 22,* 40–54.

Brown, A. S., & Murphy, D. R. (1989). Cryptomnesia: Delineating inadvertent plagiarism. *Journal of Experimental Psychology: Learning, Memory and Cognition, 15,* 432–442.

Foley, M. A., Durso, F. T., Wilder, A., & Friedman, R. (1991). Developmental comparisons of explicit versus implicit imagery and reality monitoring. *Journal of Experimental Child Psychology, 51,* 1–13.

Foley, M. A., Johnson, M. K., & Raye, C. L. (1983). Age-related changes in confusions between memories for thoughts and memories for speech. *Child Development, 54,* 51–60.

Foley, M. A., Ratner, H. H., & McLean, M. (1994, April). *Developmental differences in source monitoring judgments about actual and imagined actions.* Paper presented at the Eastern Psychological Association Meetings, Providence, RI.

Foley, M. A., Ratner, H. H., & Passalacqua, C. (1993). Appropriating the actions of another: Implications for children's memory and learning. *Cognitive Development, 8,* 373–401.

Gerrig, R. J., & Prentice, D. A. (1991). The representation of fictional information. *Psychological Science, 2,* 336–340.

Glanzer, M., & Bowles, N. (1976). Analysis of the word frequency effect in recognition memory. *Journal of Experimental Psychology: Human Learning and Memory, 2,* 21–31.

Johnson, M. K., Hashtroudi, S., & Lindsay, D. S. (1993). Source monitoring. *Psychological Bulletin, 114,* 3–28.

Johnson, M. K., & Raye, C. L. (1981). Reality monitoring. *Psychological Review, 88,* 67–85.

Johnson, M. K., Raye, C. L., Foley, H. J., & Foley, M. A., (1981). Cognitive operations and decision bias in reality monitoring. *American Journal of Psychology, 94,* 37–64.

Lindsay, D. S., Johnson, M. K., & Kwon, P. (1991). Developmental changes in memory source monitoring. *Journal of Experimental Child Psychology, 52,* 297–318.

Marsh, R. L., & Bower, G. H. (1993). Eliciting cryptomnesia: Unconscious plagiarism in a puzzle task. *Journal of Experimental Psychology: Learning, Memory and Cognition, 19,* 673–688.

Ratner, H. H., & Foley, M. A. (1994). A unifying framework for the development of children's memory for activity. In H. W. Reese (Ed.), *Advances in child development and behavior* (Vol. 25, pp. 33–105). New York: Academic Press.

Raye, C. L., Johnson, M. K., & Taylor, T. T. (1980). Is there something special about memory for internally generated information? *Memory & Cognition, 8,* 141–148.

Rogoff, B. (1990). *Apprenticeship in thinking: Cognitive development in social context.* New York: Oxford University Press.

Underwood, B. J. (1965). False recognition produced by implicit verbal responses. *Journal of Experimental Psychology, 70,* 122–129.

CHAPTER NINETEEN

Conversational Remembering

David Manier
Elizabeth Pinner
William Hirst
New School for Social Research

Surprisingly, although remembering frequently occurs in spontaneous conversations (Miller, Potts, Fung, Hoogstra, & Mintz, 1990), conversational remembering has only recently become the focus of intensive psychological investigation. Fivush, Haden, and Reese (1994) studied how the conversational strategies of parents facilitate the development of their children's narrative skills. Middleton (1994) explored how conversational devices push any act of remembering in specific directions, leaving some past events unrecalled while increasing the availability of others. We have concentrated on two distinct, but related aspects of conversational remembering: (a) the way in which the social dynamics of a conversation structure remembering within a conversation, and (b) the effect of an act of conversational remembering on subsequent acts of remembering.

SOCIAL DYNAMICS AND CONVERSATIONAL REMEMBERING: FAMILY REMEMBERING AS A CASE STUDY

One group in which discussions about the past figure prominently is the family. Families gather together around dinner tables at the end of the day and converse about the day's events; they converge on holidays and jointly assess the year gone by; at funeral ceremonies, they share their recollections of departed relatives. As a reasonable approximation to such everyday joint

269

recollections, we located a family who allowed us into their home and agreed to participate in a study of conversational remembering. We were interested in exploring how the social dynamics of the family structured their conversational remembering. The family members were paid for their participation; they responded readily and without apparent difficulties to our requests for their participation. Our observation, like that of others who have undertaken conversational analysis (e.g., Tannen, 1989), was that except for a few moments of awkwardness the family members spoke quite naturally and animatedly, and that in their joint conversations they seemed at times to forget the presence of the experimenter. Overall, we were satisfied that the data we collected were sufficiently "ecologically valid" (Neisser, 1978) to merit detailed analysis (see also Hirst & Manier, 1996).

The four-member family we studied, which we will call the Patels, immigrated to New York from India two years prior to our study (we chose an immigrant family because of an interest of one of the authors in the effect of culture on memory). The father, 44 years old, was working toward a doctorate in engineering; the 36-year-old mother was an administrative assistant. There was a 17-year-old son, who had just graduated from a Catholic high school and was planning to start college soon, and a 15-year-old daughter, who had just finished her sophomore year in high school. Everyone in the family was thoroughly bilingual, with both Telegu and English spoken at home.

A week prior to bringing the family together to record their joint rememberings, we went to the family's home and videotaped each family member separately as they recollected eight different family events (through a questionnaire given to all family members we had previously established that all four family members had participated in these events). An experimenter unknown to the family gave each family member simple instructions, for example, "Tell me everything you can remember about the family outing to Coney Island." The experimenter did not interrupt the family member's narrative. After the story had ended, the experimenter requested more information—"Can you tell me anything else about what happened?"—until the family member reported that there was nothing more to say. The experimenter then probed for the next event.

The group recounting followed the same format and was also videotaped. This time the entire family was assembled in a single room and allowed to sit anywhere they wanted. A new experimenter, again unknown to the family, asked the same questions raised in the individual (pregroup) recall and again followed up the recollections with a query for more information. The experimenter addressed her instructions to the entire family and advised that all family members should feel free to join in the discussion (an almost superfluous instruction given the volubility of this family). The videotapes we collected were subsequently transcribed and formed the basis for our analysis.

The Importance of Conversational Roles
in This Family's Group Recountings

As scholars have noted for at least the last 40 years (e.g., Benne & Sheats, 1948), participants in a group effort can assume identifiable roles in the course of this effort. There is, however, no a priori reason why one might expect to be able to discern conversational roles in an act of recounting. Thus, we decided to begin our analysis of the family recountings we collected by first determining if we could identify the conversational roles in our family recountings and then examining how the conversational roles adopted by the family members structured the recountings of the family. Conversational roles, which can be thought of in part as a kind of "division of labor" in the conversation, seemed to be present in the joint recollections we studied, and we set out to analyze with some precision their characteristics and consequences. In this analysis, we looked on conversational roles as patterns of speech taken on by participants in a conversation, either for the entire conversation or for some fragment of it; they provide for each participant in the conversation a function and "place" vis-à-vis other participants. Conversational roles are defined in terms of the manner in which they aid (or hinder) the goals of the conversation—this, in turn, will be determined by what kinds of things each person says. Although the goals of the conversation may shift quite rapidly (cf. Tracy, 1991), and so may the roles adopted, we believe that some conversations do have an overarching goal, and in these instances, it may be possible to discern similarly "overarching" roles held by different conversational participants.

In order to study more carefully what kinds of things were said by each family member, we developed a coding scheme that broke the transcript into narrative and nonnarrative units, and each of these categories into structural units (see Hirst & Manier, 1996; Manier & Hirst, 1996, for details). A narrative unit consists of a subject (perhaps implicit) and predicate and describes a single "state," "action," or "event." It could include temporal tags and other descriptive phrases, but these phrases may not describe an additional state, action, or event. The sentences "I enjoyed the amusement rides" and "We saw the polar bear," which describe respectively a state and an event, are narrative units. The sentence "We went to Coney Island the year we came to the United States" also constitutes a single narrative unit, whereas the sentence "We went to the amusement park and to the beach" contains two narrative units because it describes two actions. Nonnarrative units comprise discrete utterances (composed in most cases of a subject and a predicate) that express a thought that does not contribute directly to the story or narrative being told. Examples are metamemory statements ("I remember that") and overt requests for assistance ("Who went with us?") (cf. Middleton & Edwards, 1990).

We divided narrative and nonnarrative units more narrowly into carefully defined structural units. Certain structural units in our coding scheme predominated in our family's narratives and figured prominently in our analyses. Our discussion focuses on relatively more predominant structural units:

> *Narrative tellings* describe states or events that are linked together (causally, temporally, or spatially) and that relate to a central topic or theme. Examples include: "We went to all these other places and then we went to Coney Island, and we went to the aquarium. We went to th—um, amusement park and we went to the beach."
>
> *Facilitating remarks* attempt to spur someone else to further the narrative, provide more details, or "search their memory." Also, they may evaluate someone else's narrative with (implicit or explicit) reference to standards of narrative structure. Examples include: "What did we eat there?" "What did you, what else do you remember?" "Keep to the point," "That's irrelevant."
>
> *Assessing statements* are statements that agree, disagree, or in some other way judge the validity of a previous statement that is not an overt request for assistance. They may include the confirmatory repetition of a phrase just spoken by someone else. Examples include: "Yeah, that's right," "No, you're wrong," "Sure," "Certainly," "No way."

One other type of structural unit frequently occurred in the speech particularly of one family member (the mother):

> *Affective–evaluative remarks* provide editorial judgments or express overall emotional reactions from a current perspective to narrative tellings about past events, or report the general attitude or summarize the pervasive mood of participants in a past event. (They are not recountings of someone's specific past affective reactions—these would be coded as narrative tellings.) Examples include: "A very boring Christmas," "It was a lot of fun," "They enjoyed themselves."

We defined a *conversation* as the story jointly told in response to a single probe (e.g., everything said about the trip to Coney Island). We initially confined our analysis to two conversations: one about a family outing to Coney Island, another about the preceding Christmas the family spent together. We focused on three conversational roles—Narrator, Mentor, and Monitor—defined as follows:

> *Narrators:* Assume the main burden of telling the story. Most of their utterances are intended to "further the narrative." Generally speaking, a

Narrator's utterances will preserve "narrative continuity." That is, any given narrative telling will be interlinked (either causally, spatially, temporally, or thematically) with narrative tellings that precede or follow it. By definition, a family member is identified as a Narrator in a conversation when both of the following are true:

1. Narrative tellings are the preponderant structural unit in his or her contributions to the conversation.
2. Her or his share of all narrative tellings uttered in the conversation is greater than would be expected from chance (e.g., for a family of four, the Narrator contributes more than 25% of the narrative tellings in the conversation).

Mentors: Assume the function of prompting Narrators to further their narratives and provide more details. They encourage Narrators to adhere to standards of narrative form and content, spurring Narrators on by providing criticisms, directions, helpful remarks, substantial queries, and memory probes. Rather than furthering the narrative directly through their own utterances, Mentors guide the narrative telling, often by providing retrieval cues to Narrators in order to elicit further recollections from them. By definition, a family member is identified as a Mentor when both of the following are true:

1. Facilitating remarks are among the two most frequent structural categories in her or his contributions to the conversation.
2. He or she contributes a greater share of the total number of the facilitating remarks uttered in the conversation than would be expected from chance.

Monitors: Assume the function of explicitly agreeing or disagreeing with the utterances of the Narrator, without taking personal responsibility for constructing the narrative. They evaluate whether the narrative, as told by the Narrator, correctly and completely describes the episode, as remembered by the Monitor. They assume a relatively passive role within the collective remembering. By definition, a family member is identified as a Monitor when both of the following are true:

1. Assessing statements are among the two most frequent structural categories in her or his contribution to the conversation.
2. He or she contributes a greater share of the total number of assessing statements uttered in the conversation than would be expected from chance.

Others: Conversational participants who do not meet the criteria for any of the three conversational roles defined here will be classified as "Other."

Conversational roles, then, are specified by two defining criteria. The defining criteria for the role of Narrator differ somewhat from those of Mentor and Monitor. For a Narrator narrative tellings must be the preponderant structural unit, but for a Mentor and Monitor the critical structural units need be only the second most frequent unit. We impose a weaker standard for Mentors and Monitors because we expect narrative tellings could preponderate in the utterances of all members of the conversation, including Mentors and Monitors. After all, our instructions were for the family members to tell narratives.

According to our definitions, in both conversations (the one about Christmas and the one about Coney Island) the daughter served as the Narrator and the father as the Mentor. The son and mother both served as Monitors in the Coney Island conversation, and both had an undefined "Other" role in the Christmas conversation (see Manier & Hirst, 1996, for details). The daughter produced substantially more narrative tellings in her contributions to both conversations than any other structural unit, uttered more narrative tellings than did anyone else in both conversations, and contributed a majority of the words spoken in both cases. Facilitating remarks were one of the two most frequent structural units in the father's contributions to both conversations. Moreover, he contributed a greater share of facilitating remarks to the conversations than would be expected from chance. Finally, for both the mother and son, assessing statements were one of the two most frequent structural units in their contribution to the Coney Island conversation. Additionally, they each contributed more assessing statements to this conversation than would be expected from chance. In the Christmas conversation, the mother and son each contributed fewer than 100 words, and failed to occupy any definite conversational role. Therefore, under our scheme they are classified as "Other."

It should be noted that the mother appeared to have an additional role. She offered more affective–evaluative remarks than did anyone else, in both the Christmas and the Coney Island conversations. The mother may have been inclined to put an emotional cast on the events, providing editorial judgments that imbued a general affective tone into the recollections. For example, she stated regarding the previous Christmas: "But it was very new to us, I mean we were trying to copy something, which . . . people did here, but we, I, I literally did not enjoy it."

How Do the Different Conversational Roles Shape Conversational Remembering?

The roles participants adopted while conversationally remembering had an effect on what was remembered. We compared the narrative units produced in the pregroup recountings across individuals. We called *shared pregroup narrative units* those narrative units the meaning of which (in the opinion of two judges) was expressed in the utterances of more than one participant in the pregroup recountings (i.e., those narrative units the meaning of which was "shared" by more than one participant). We called *unshared pregroup narrative units* those narrative units the meaning of which appeared in the utterances of one and only one participant in the pregroup recounting. For instance, in their pregroup recountings, family members gave different versions of the time of day they attended Christmas service. The son said: "Uh, it's like just we went to a Christmas mass, like th—the night mass." The daughter stated: "We went, I think, at 11:30 or something to church" (later she clarified that she intended 11:30 P.M.). The mother recalled: "So we wanted to experience the night mass, in, uh, the church. So we went, um, all decked up in Indian clothes?" The father's account was quite different from those of the other family members: "Uh, the only thing I can remember is we all went together to church in the, m—, morning, I don't know, it is 9:00 or 10:00." In these differing versions, there is only one shared narrative unit, which we might express as: "We went to night mass." This narrative unit was "shared" because it was expressed (albeit in somewhat different words) by the son, the daughter, and the mother. The daughter expressed an unshared pregroup narrative unit specifying the time as 11:30; the mother, two unshared pregroup narrative units relating to what the family wore to church and what they "wanted to experience"; and the father offered only unshared pregroup narrative units, because his recollection was that the family had gone to a morning mass.

The narratives that the family members produced in their pregroup recountings differed greatly from each other. The four family members recalled in their pregroup recountings a total of 288 narrative units, of which 129 (45%) occurred in the pregroup recounting of only one family member. Only four narrative units (2%) were recounted by all four family members. In other words, each family member told a rather different story, although a few basic facts (such as "We went to the amusement park, the aquarium, and the beach") were expressed by all four.

What determines what gets into the group recollection? Can we predict what will appear in the group narrative by considering what was said in the pregroup recollections and the conversational roles of the participants? At least in the present instances of conversational remembering, almost half of the narrative units in the group recall did not appear in *any* of the pregroup recollections. This interesting fact means that the story told in the group differed substantially from that told by the separate individuals, presumably because the group recollection was influenced in some manner by interpersonal dynamics. But what of the other half, that is, what of those narrative units in the group recall that captured the meaning of a narrative unit expressed in at least one of the pregroup recollections? Specifically, how effective were family members at introducing unshared narrative units from their pregroup recall (i.e., their "unique recollections"), into the group recollection? Conversational role plays an important part in the answer to this question.

One might expect that the daughter, functioning as Narrator, would have an advantage in introducing her unshared pregroup narrative units into the group recollection. This was the case. The daughter introduced into the group recollection 33% of her unshared pregroup recollections, whereas the father inserted 25% of his unshared narrative units into the group recollection. The son and the mother both contributed to the group recounting less than 10% of their unshared pregroup narrative units.

To further explore this issue, following the scheme applied to pregroup narratives, we may divide the narrative units of the group conversations into three categories: (1) new units, which are narrative units that did not appear in any family member's pregroup recollection; (2) unshared group narrative units, which are narrative units in the group recall that captured the gist of an unshared narrative unit (i.e., one appearing in the recollections of only one family member) in the pregroup recall; and (3) shared group narrative units, which are narrative units in the group recall that captured the gist of a shared narrative unit (i.e., one appearing in the recollections of more than one family member) in the pregroup recall. We were interested in discovering whether the contributions of family members were distributed evenly over these three categories or whether the conversational role of a member could skew the distribution. If the distribution were even, then we would expect that the frequency with which a family member introduced a new, shared, or unshared narrative unit into the group recounting should reflect the overall predominance of that family member in the conversation.

We did not find an even distribution (see Table 19.1). A striking difference appeared when comparing the overall predominance of family members in the group conversations and their predominance in uttering unshared group narrative units (i.e., narrative units that reproduce a detail contained in only one pregroup narrative, namely, a narrative unit appearing in their own pregroup recollection). The daughter predominated overall in the conver-

TABLE 19.1
Narrative Unit Distribution Among Family Members

	Types of Narrative Units			
	New	*Unshared*	*Shared*	*All*
Daughter	51%	76%	51%	58%
Father	25%	8%	24%	20%
Mother	11%	8%	14%	11%
Son	13%	8%	11%	11%

Note. Table includes both group recountings.

sation, contributing 58% of all narrative units. But her predominance in unshared group narrative units was even more pronounced: She uttered 76% of such utterances in the group recollection. This predominance is not part of the definition of a narrator: The definition does not differentiate between shared and unshared narrative units, but the data clearly suggest that this Narrator not only contributed a preponderant number of narrative tellings, but contributed in particular a specific kind of narrative telling— unshared narrative units from her own pregroup recall. For other family members, the difference between their overall share in the conversation and their proportion of unshared group narrative units went in the opposite direction, that is, they contributed fewer unshared group narrative units than predicted by their overall predominance within the conversation (for details, see Manier & Hirst, 1996). The daughter's ability to interject unshared group narrative units (i.e., her own unique recollections) into the group conversation reflects (but is not defined by) her role as Narrator. As Narrator, she got to tell the story she had told in her pregroup recollection to an extent that other family members did not. In other words, the group recounting reflected the daughter's unique view of the past events to a degree that substantially exceeded her overall predominance in the conversation.

Remembering as Communicating

In our analysis of the recountings of the Patels, we were able to discern three conversational roles—Narrator, Monitor, and Mentor—and chart how these roles shaped the recountings. The Narrator provided the recounting with a voice as well as much of its content. Although all four family members were capable of telling a story in the pregroup recountings, the Narrator did most of the storytelling in the group recounting. The resulting tale reflected her perspectives on the past. Thus, the daughter's unshared pregroup narrative units were more likely to appear in the group recounting than were the unshared pregroup narrative units of the other family members, even if we take into account her proclivity to talk more than anyone else.

The Narrator is not the only character to play a role in the Patel's recountings, however. Monitors impose their perspectives by providing assurance and confirmation to the Narrator (or another family member), or by questioning certain statements in the recounting. When contradicted, the person telling the story can revise his or her account. The subsequent recollection becomes an interplay between the perspective of the Monitor, who simply questions a statement, and the perspective of the person telling the story, who articulates the revised narrative.

A similar interaction arises when the Mentor offers facilitating remarks. The perspective or internalized schema of the Mentor no doubt partially motivates his or her facilitating remarks, but the perspective of the Narrator (or other family member currently telling the story) shapes the narrative response to these probes. Finally, some family members (in this case, primarily the mother) provide to the account an affective tone that summarizes emotional reactions to the described events.

Conversational roles, we are arguing, play an important part in determining what is recollected when families talk about the past. Some might argue that conversational roles affect only what is said, and not what is actually remembered. These skeptics would maintain that there is much that is remembered that is left unsaid. For example, in another story we solicited from the Patels, both son and daughter reported in their individual recollections an incident related to their mischievous play with firecrackers. They may well have "recalled" these incidents to themselves even during the family recounting, but they did not recount them. They were perhaps remembered, but left unspoken. Our current analysis leaves such "recollections" unexamined.

We leave these "recollections" unexamined in part because we have grave doubts about the psychological claim that autobiographical memories consist of mental representations that are stored in the head waiting to "reappear" in an act of remembering (cf. Neisser, 1967). Although we do not doubt that there are cognitive "traces" of the past that have a neurophysiological basis to them, we question whether one can discover with any degree of accuracy and precision just what these representations are, or how they are stored (e.g., whether as neuronal nets, propositions, schemata, or sets of procedures). As is so often the case in cognitive psychology (Newell, 1973), the debate about the nature of "representation" has remained inconclusive, without a hint that a resolution is in sight.

We suspect that it is difficult, if not impossible, to detect a "putative" memory beneath the surface of an act of remembering. It may simply be improper to speak of the reappearance of a trace prior to its articulation. What we remember is inevitably affected by the situation in which we choose to communicate our memories. Memories emerge out of particular social contexts, including those that mold a conversation. Suppose that John tries to remember what he did at Christmastime last year. He will tell himself a story. This story leaves out much that happened, and may well include things that did not happen, yet this story, call it Story 1, is the story he tells at the moment. If he were then to meet Jan, with whom he spent last Christmas, simply seeing her might remind him of some further details and shift his focus away from others. If he got into a conversation with her, they would jointly construct a rather different account of the previous Christmas—call it Story 2. Suppose that Story 2 is, in the final analysis, better and more complete than Story 1. Where was Story 2 when John told Story 1? Presumably somewhere "in his head," but he could not access it. No amount of prodding or probing on John's part would have worked—John needed

Jan to help him remember. Sometime after meeting Jan, John might collect his thoughts in solitude and compose Story 3. Will Story 3 be more complete than Story 1? Than Story 2? There is no sure answer to this. John might reflect deeply and remember even more details about his Christmas with Jan, or he might decide that Jan was mistaken, that he had spent the previous Christmas alone, and been with Jan two Christmases ago. Which is his "true memory"—Story 1, 2, or 3? There is no correct answer to this question. Documents might help to determine the "facts," but they cannot provide evidence about the memory "in John's head." Even John cannot know what that memory is except insofar as he tells a story about it, either to himself or to someone else. The circumstances of that storytelling will radically influence the story he tells, including any conversational partners he might have, as well as the role he takes in the conversation. If he is alone, he may imagine himself speaking to Jan, or to someone else, and that will also influence the story he tells. As cliché has it, "You don't know what you think until you say it."

It is wrong to treat this complex of social interactions as merely a set of retrieval cues provided by Jan and John in different contexts. The act of communicating about the past involves more than just providing retrieval cues and retrieving memories. One must take into account the audience, conversational conventions that shape the conversation, and, of current interest, the roles participants adopt while conversing. As our research with the Patels makes clear, we cannot fully understand what they remembered without considering the roles they adopted.

Conversational Remembering's Effect on Subsequent Acts of Remembering

There is another saying, "You can't learn anything while you're talking." We want to argue just the opposite—that what we remember or learn depends on how we talked about it in the past, with ourselves and with others. In our work on family remembering, we showed that the social dynamics of the family—specifically, the conversational roles family members adopt—shape the memories the family constructs as a group. Although our family research so far has focused on how the conversational roles family members hold within a conversation structure what is remembered within that conversation, we expect that the influence of conversational roles reaches beyond the confines of the immediate conversation. Conversational roles also might shape how the family remembers in subsequent conversations, among themselves and with others. The social dynamics of a family may not only mold memories constructed in a particular family conversation; they may also have a determining effect on how family members talk about their past outside the family as well as on what families come to remember within the family in future conversations.

There is only scant evidence for these speculations, but what does exist provides some hope that subsequent research will be able to offer firmer support. By and large, extant research has not looked at conversational roles. It has mainly tried to establish the more general point that how people talk about an event or object affects how they remember it in the future.

Wilkes-Gibbs (1994) provided some support for such a subsequent memory effect. In her experiment, pairs of subjects described to each other ambiguous figures. They were permitted to ask each other questions, and the resulting conversations were often detailed and elaborate. Subjects either shared the same "perspective" toward the figure or held different perspectives. After the conversational phase of the study ended, subjects were asked to recall the figures by drawing them. Wilkes-Gibbs found that the conversations the subject pairs had about the figures differed depending on whether the members of the pairs shared the same perspective or held different perspectives. Moreover, subject pairs who shared a perspective recalled the figures in a manner that was consistent with their shared perspective, whereas subjects who held different perspectives recalled the figures as a composite of the two perspectives. The conversations subjects had about the figures clearly affected their memory for the figures.

We also pursued the issue of the effect of conversation on subsequent memory, but in a different context than that employed by Wilkes-Gibbs. Although we eventually hope to link up this research with our work on family remembering and explore the relation between conversational roles and subsequent acts of remembering, we believed that, for logistical reasons, we should begin our project by examining groups of unrelated subjects and concentrate on merely establishing that a relation between conversation and subsequent memory exists. This limited goal might seem preliminary, but we deemed it to be indispensible groundwork for our future research.

The 16 unrelated subjects participating in the experimental condition of our study were divided into four four-person groups. Another 16 unrelated subjects served as controls. All subjects read a 264-word article designed to resemble an actual newspaper article. They were asked to "read the article once carefully" without regard to time constraints. Immediately after this reading, subjects individually wrote "as detailed recollection as possible" of the article (the pretest phase). After 10 minutes, subjects in the experimental condition were assembled into groups of four and asked to "recall the article as a group" (the test phase). They did not have to produce a "consensus" recollection. Subjects in the control condition orally recalled the article to the experimenter, one subject at a time. Again, the experimenter imposed no time constraints. Following the group recall session and another 20-minute distraction task, both experimental and control subjects once again recalled the article individually, on paper (the posttest phase).

Two coders divided the original article following the scheme used in our family research, as discussed previously. They disagreed 10% of the time, and these discrepancies were resolved to produce 54 idea units. The two coders then compared this final list of idea units to the pretest and posttest texts as well as to the transcriptions of the recall protocols produced in the test phase. They tabulated the number of idea units from the original article in each of the test phases. The coders again disagreed 10% of the time, and again these discrepancies were resolved.

The literature on "group recall" clearly establishes that a "consensus" memory produced by a group contains more details or idea units than any of the individual memories of the group, but also contains less information than the sum total of all the information contained in the individual recollections (Clark & Stephenson, 1989). Results from the present study offer further support for this claim. Our interest, however, was not so much in replicating previous findings in another experimental context, but in investigating the effect the groups' conversations had on members' memory in the posttest.

Thus, we examined the mean number of idea units experimental and control subjects recalled, contrasting the performance in the pretest and posttest. We found a significant main effect for test (i.e., pretest compared to posttest) and a significant interaction between test and group (i.e., experimental versus control). As Fig. 19.1 illustrates, the experimental and control subjects' memory in the pretest were comparable: The difference between the mean number of idea units recalled by these two groups of subjects was not significant. Moreover, the performance of the control subjects did not differ in the pretest and posttest. However, the experimental

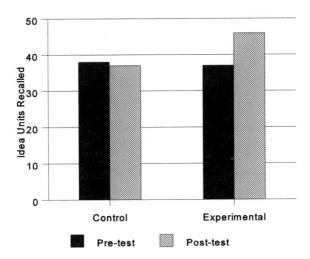

FIG. 19.1. Percentage of idea units recalled by experimental and control subjects in the pretest and posttest phases.

subjects recalled significantly more idea units in the posttest than in the pretest. The conversations of the groups facilitated subsequent memory more than did the second individual recall of the control subjects.

What about the conversations led to this facilitation? Here we begin our discussion where we ended our consideration of family remembering: with the idea that autobiographical remembering can be treated as an act of communication. As an act of communication, remembering is not limited to what goes on in an individual's head, but also involves the interaction between speaker and listener, between the person making an utterance about the personal past and people listening to the utterance. The speaker's utterance can evoke fresh memories from the listener. An item absent from a group member's pretest recall could surface in her posttest recall, "jogged" by its introduction by another group member in the test phase.

We are interested in a refinement of this hypothesis. We do not doubt that the mere mention of new information during the test can affect posttest memory, either by facilitating or interfering with subsequent remembering. Nevertheless, there may be conditions that make it more likely that the introduction of new information in the test phase will facilitate subsequent remembering. We can rephrase the familiar levels-of-processing maxim into: The more effectively something is communicated, the better it is remembered. All things being equal, new information introduced in the test phase should, therefore, be more likely to find its way into the posttest recall the more effectively it is communicated. Although most discussions of "communicative effectiveness" concentrate on the effectiveness of the "speaker," recent treatments of conversations have treated communicative effectiveness in terms of the interaction between speaker and listener. For instance, Schober and Clark (1989) documented that "participation" is an important factor for imparting meaning to a conversation. They found that partners in a conversation showed a greater understanding of the content of the conversation if they actively participated in the conversation than if they merely listened to others conversing. Thus, an idea is communicated effectively not only because the speaker has said it well, but also because the listener has participated in the speech act.

The implication for the effect of conversation on subsequent remembering is clear: If memory improves with increased communicative effectiveness, new information introduced in a conversation should be more likely to find its way into subsequent recollection if partners in the conversation adopt a more active role and participate in the construction of the information than if they hold a passive role and merely listen. For Clark and his colleagues (Clark & Schaefer, 1989; Shober & Clark, 1989), a "participation" refers to either the initiation or the continuation of that idea unit or a verbal acknowledgment of or disagreement with the idea unit being presented, for example, a person saying "yeah," "right," or "no way." Or to use our terminology, a person "participates" in the construction of an idea unit if they either Narrate it or Monitor it.

We focused our analyses on those idea units that were not recalled in the pretest of a given Subject A, but emerged in the test phase, our *baseline* set. We were interested in determining whether Subject A's participation in the construction of a new idea unit in the test phase influenced the likelihood of the idea unit appearing in the posttest of Subject A. There are many ways one could frame this comparison. We chose two and found that those items in the baseline set that Subject A participated in constructing during the test phase had a probability of appearing in the posttest phase that was greater than both (a) the probability of any item in the baseline appearing in the posttest of Subject A and (b) the probability of an idea unit appearing in the posttest phase when Subject A did not participate in its construction during the test phase. No matter what measure we used, we found that participation in the construction of an idea unit improved the subsequent recollection of a new unit.

Thus, when individuals recount an article in a group, the group as a whole shows an enhancement when compared to the individual recollections of a group member. This enhancement has a lasting mnemonic effect on the members of the group. Not only is memory improved within a conversation, but subsequent memory also improves. This effect on subsequent memory is more effective when listeners adopt an active role in the construction of the idea unit. That is, a broad measure of social dynamics, the active participation of members of the group, predicts in part what is subsequently remembered. We have not analyzed the data in the detail with which we approached the work on family remembering, detecting the roles of the participants in this study during the group recounting phase and then specifically exploring the relation between these roles and subsequent recall. Nor have we looked at groups for which the social dynamics are to some extent preestablished and relatively more complex, as they are for families. Nevertheless, the finding that idea units that emerge for the first time in a group recounting are more likely to find their way into a subsequent act of remembering of an individual if that individual actively participated in their construction provides some insight into what we might expect to find as we undertake more thorough analyses. Specifically, some roles, such as Narrator and Monitor, are more likely to participate actively in the construction of the narrative than are others, such as Mentor. As such, one might expect subsequent recountings of Monitors and Narrators to be more influenced by acts of conversational remembering than would the subsequent recountings of Mentors.

GENERAL DISCUSSION

What have we learned by studying remembering in the context of a conversation? In some sense, every act of remembering is conversational. Although it is rarely acknowledged, even putatively controlled laboratory experiments involve a conversation—in most cases, between the experimenter and a single subject. Did we learn something about remembering by studying it in a complex conversational context that we would not learn by ignoring the conversational aspects of remembering?

The answer would appear to be "Yes." In the research on family remembering, we could only appreciate the family's struggle to reconstruct their past by considering the conversational roles that they adopted. What was remembered was not a consequence of the individual recollections of family members summed together, but a reflection of the family social dynamics—with some members taking a more active role of Narrating while others assumed roles of Monitoring and Mentoring. The resulting "family memory" was a complex interaction between the potential each family member had to tell his or her story and the roles they adopted while telling the story. This interaction could only be understood by focusing on the fact that the remembering was occurring within a conversation among family members. We would not have considered the contribution of conversational roles if we had concentrated on what was "remembered."

But our study of family remembering pushed us beyond the consideration of family dynamics and conversational roles to a reconsideration of the act of remembering itself. Remembering is often thought of in structural terms, as an internal process occurring within an individual. We want to stress functional aspects of remembering. Within a conversation, remembering serves as a device for communicating the past to others. From this perspective, remembering is an act of communication, or more specifically in the present context, a conversational act of communicating. In viewing remembering as an act of communication, we are turning away from the consideration of internal processes within an individual, or the representation of the past within the individual, and are heading toward a socially based theory of memory. In doing so, we must consider the large and growing literature on discourse and conversation, exploring the effect of speaker on listener and listener on speaker, the importance of conversational participation, the functions or roles of conversational participants, and the consequences of violations of conversational maxims.

In the present research, we focused on the functions or roles of conversational participants. The importance of "role" in group dynamics has long been acknowledged (Benne & Sheats, 1948), but its import for remembering has not been fully recognized. The work on family remembering demonstrates that conversational roles are a necessary component in any model of the communicative act of remembering. The roles people adopt within a conversation shape what is remembered within the conversation. Narrators provide the memory with a voice, whereas Monitors and Mentors shape the Narrator's recollection.

But the ability of roles to shape remembering is not confined to what happens in the conversation itself. Some roles require active participation in the construction of a memory whereas others do not, and active participation appears to influence the degree to which a previously neglected detail introduced in the conversation surfaces in subsequent individual recollections. We have not examined the contribution of conversational role here in as much detail as we did in our work on family remembering, although we intend to do so in future research. Nevertheless, the results suggest that not only do conversational roles shape conversational remembering, they also impact on subsequent recollections of participants in the conversation.

Our viewpoint that autobiographical remembering is an act of communication has led us to treat it as more than a confluence of internal processing and internal representations. Rather, we were driven to look at factors outside of those traditionally discussed as important for encoding, storage and retrieval, focusing on the importance of conversational roles. These roles exist not "in the head," but in the social dynamics of the group. Remembering, as an act of communication, is a social phenomenon, and we will never really understand it by focusing on isolated individuals.

ACKNOWLEDGMENTS

We would like to acknowledge the support of NIMH grants #42064 and #50131 and a grant from the McDonnell Foundation.

REFERENCES

Benne, K., & Sheats, P. (1948). Functional roles of group members. *Journal of Social Issues, 4*, 41–49.

Clark, H. H., & Schaefer, E. F. (1989). Referring as a collaborative process. *Cognition, 22*, 1–39.

Clark, N. K., & Stephenson, G. M. (1989). Group remembering. In P. B. Paulus (Ed.), *Psychology of group influence* (pp. 357–391). Hillsdale, NJ: Lawrence Erlbaum Associates.

Fivush, R., Haden, C., & Reese, E. (1994). *The development of autobiographical memory in social context.* Paper presented at the Third Practical Aspects of Memory Conference, College Park, MD.

Hirst, W., & Manier, D. (1996). Remembering as communication: A family recounts its past. In D. Rubin (Ed.), *Constructing our past: An overview of autobiographical memory.* New York: Cambridge University Press.

Manier, D., & Hirst, W. (1996). The brain doesn't tell the whole story. In E. Manier (Ed.), *Neurobiology and narrative.* Notre Dame, IN: University of Notre Dame Press.

Middleton, D. (1994). *Collective remembering: Some socio-cultural issues.* Paper presented at the Third Practical Aspects of Memory Conference, College Park, MD.

Middleton, D., & Edwards, D. (1990). Conversational remembering: A social psychological approach. In D. Middleton & D. Edwards (Eds.), *Collective remembering* (pp. 23–45). London: Sage Publications.

Miller, P. J., Potts, R., Fung, H., Hoogstra, L., & Mintz, J. (1990). Narrative practices and the social construction of self in childhood. *American Ethnologist, 17,* 292–311.

Neisser, U. (1967). *Cognitive psychology.* New York: Appleton-Century-Crofts.

Neisser, U. (1978). Memory: What are the important questions? In M. M. Gruneberg, P. E. Morris, & R. N. Sykes (Eds.), *Practical aspects of memory* (pp. 3–24). London: Academic Press.

Newell, A. (1973). You can't play twenty questions with nature and win. In W. Chase (Ed.), *Visual information processing* (pp. 283–308). New York: Academic Press.

Schober, M. F., & Clark, H. H. (1989). Understanding by addressees and overhearers. *Cognitive Psychology, 21,* 211–232.

Tannen, D. (1989). *Talking voices: Repetition, dialogue, and imagery in conversational discourse.* New York: Cambridge University Press.

Tracy, K. (Ed.). (1991). *Understanding face-to-face interaction: Issues linking goals and discourse.* Hillsdale, NJ: Lawrence Erlbaum Associates.

Wilkes-Gibbs, D. (1994). *Conversation, collaboration, and remembering.* Paper presented at the Third Practical Aspects of Memory Conference, College Park, MD.

CHAPTER TWENTY

Selective Encoding of Emotional Information

Andrew Mathews

MRC Applied Psychology Unit, Cambridge, England

The relationship between memory and emotion has been studied within several distinct domains, with research and theory in each area proceeding with little or no reference to the others. My intention here is to review current developments in these domains, drawing out connections that may be useful but seem to have been ignored: These links suggest relatively general hypotheses about the interaction between emotion and memory. The three topics to be discussed are: memory deficits associated with emotion, memory for emotional events, and memory for mood-congruent information in normal and abnormal populations. After a brief and necessarily selective review of each, I summarize common themes, and suggest unifying hypotheses. To anticipate, I argue that the main theme emerging from the data in each domain is that emotional information is given priority for processing over competing neutral information, and is thus preferentially encoded.

MEMORY DEFICITS AND EMOTION

Negative mood states have commonly been found to be associated with general deficits in memory, and converse advantages may accompany positive mood. For example, depression is associated with relative deficits in memory when the to-be-remembered material requires intentional organization to maximize performance (such as mixed word lists that can, with effort, be organized into categories for retrieval purposes). Depressed subjects perform adequately when only automatic processing is required, so that these deficits can be attributed to reduced availability of capacity-limited cognitive resources, or to a failure to adopt strategies requiring cognitive initiative (Ellis & Ashbrook, 1988; Hertel & Hardin, 1990). Note that these explanations make no reference to the emotional nature of the to-be-remembered material: Rather, they assume that the emotional state itself leads to a general failure to use cognitive resources effectively. This may well be true, but it is also possible that emotional states like depression do not lead to an absolute deficit in the resources available, or in the ability to deploy them, but rather to a reallocation of processing priorities to emotional information. That is, depression may lead people to assign high priority to processing negative self-referent information, in preference to the task-performance priorities imposed by the experimenter.

Similar suggestions have been made in the case of anxiety (Eysenck & Calvo, 1992). In their cognitive model of anxiety, working memory capacity is preempted by worry (repetitive processing of information relevant to potential threats), so that correspondingly more effort is required to perform other tasks. For present purposes, the relevant point is that for both anxiety and depression, the evidence of cognitive performance deficits can be interpreted as being due either to a general lack of capacity-limited resources, or to the deployment of these resources to processing self-generated emotional concerns, in preference to other priorities imposed by task instructions. The two remaining research domains discussed here address this issue more directly: the study of memory for emotional events in normal-mood subjects; and the impact of emotional states on the memory for congruent information. Both suggest that there is something special about memory for emotionally relevant information, and support the general idea that this arises because emotional information is given priority for processing, at the expense of other competing input or ongoing tasks.

MEMORY FOR EMOTIONAL EVENTS

In a typical eyewitness study, unselected subjects in normal mood are exposed to pictures (usually sequences of slides) depicting simulated traumatic events, such as crimes or accidents, or to matched control scenes that are affectively neutral. The accuracy of memory for these events is then tested, either immediately or after an interval, often using recognition tests in which subjects make forced choices among sets of scenes that include one of the preexposed slides, mixed with matched foils. Conclusions from these studies are converging on the hypothesis that certain central aspects of emotional information are better retained, whereas other aspects may be retained poorly or not at all. Thus, subjects remember that they saw an upsetting traffic accident very well (and may even suffer from intrusive images of it later on), but despite this, have less accurate memory for other, more peripheral details.

One of the difficulties with this conclusion is that of defining what are the "central" aspects of emotional information. Are we to understand central in the sense of being within a spatial focus of attention, or in the sense of the semantic attributes that cause the event to be perceived as emotional? In many cases these may be confounded, as in the memory that the pedestrian was injured and covered in blood, whereas other people walking by in the background were forgotten. In this case the person's injuries and blood are both spatially and semantically central to the event. It is possible, however, to separate the two senses by considering detailed information that is central in the spatial sense, but not in the emotional meaning sense, such as the color of the clothes worn by the injured person. These spatially but not emotionally central details are consistently recalled better than are equivalent details that are far from the spatial focus, or than are the same details in nonemotional scenes (Burke, Heuer, & Reisberg, 1992; Christianson & Loftus, 1991). In sum, what is better recalled includes emotional gist (that the event happened), and details, emotional or otherwise, that were very close to the spatial focus of the emotional event. Other details that do not have special emotional meaning and are not within this spatial focus tend to be forgotten.

This conclusion leaves unspecified the nature of the processes leading to selective memory for emotional events. Two main candidates have been proposed: a narrowed attentional focus centered on the location of the most emotional aspect of the event, and subsequent elaboration on the meaning and implications of that event (Christianson, 1992). It has been further suggested that attentional capture is brought about automatically, after a preattentive analysis of emotional significance. Work by Ohman and others (e.g., Ohman & Soares, 1993), for example, indicates that certain types of stimuli such as snakes and angry faces are biologically prepared to capture attention and evoke fear. Autonomic responses are persistently evoked by such stimuli even under "subliminal" presentation conditions, such that subjects cannot report the presence of the evoking stimuli. Similarly, it is possible that components of some traumatic scenes studied in eyewitness research, such as blood and injuries, have the capacity to attract attention automatically.

Such attention-focusing effects seem sufficient to account for the better recall of details that are located close to the most emotional part of the event, such as the clothing worn by the injured victim. The corresponding neglect of spatially distant aspects should similarly lead to poorer memory for background details. However, there is another puzzling aspect of the data not easily explained by attentional capture alone: that the relative advantage in memory for emotional gist grows if anything stronger over time (e.g., Burke et al., 1992). One plausible hypothesis is that these aspects are the subject of selective elaborative processing, both at the time of initial exposure and subsequently. For an event to be emotional implies that it is directly relevant to the desires, concerns, or fears of the observer, and is thus more likely to be encoded in relation to these preexisting goals, and to prompt later spontaneous intrusions or ruminative thoughts. As a result we might expect the elaborated aspects to be more accessible for immediate recall, and to be forgotten more slowly than nonelaborated aspects.

However, there is a strong alternative hypothesis that has been proposed. The persistence of so-called "flashbulb" memories for dramatic emotional events has been commonly attributed to a biological mechanism, associated with arousal, that produces particularly indelible memories. Indeed, there is good evidence from the animal learning literature that moderate elevations in adrenaline secretion are associated with better retention, although this advantage is lost again at very high levels of arousal (McGaugh, 1992).

Clearly, this evidence indicates that arousal has important effects on memory, but it is argued here that not all of the characteristics of memory for emotional events can be explained in this way. First, any such general biological mechanism would presumably be nonselective in the sense that all events occurring at times of high arousal should be better retained. In fact, there is quite good evidence that information present during an emotionally arousing event but not connected with it (in meaning or in location) is poorly retained (Burke et al., 1992; Christianson & Loftus, 1991). If arousal enhances memory via a quite general mechanism, it is not obvious why these unconnected aspects are lost, so that it becomes necessary to add other selective cognitive mechanisms to account for this loss. Second, it is by no means clear that all emotional events that are selectively encoded are associated with peripheral sympathetic arousal: Under some circumstances of emotional "arousal," heart rate may actually decline (e.g. Heurer & Reisberg, 1990). Finally "flashbulb" memories do not appear to be any more accurate for details than are memories for neutral events that subjects are simply told they should remember; rather, the former tend to be associated only with higher confidence ratings (Weaver, 1993). Thus, although physiological arousal undoubtedly does have effects on memory, it is unlikely that selection and slowed forgetting of central aspects of an emotional event, or the failure to encode peripheral details, can be completely explained in this way.

The alternative hypothesis is that elaborative encoding and rehearsal of emotional events leads to delayed forgetting of central aspects of meaning, due to creation of links with personal concerns. Heuer and Reisberg (1990) found more errors concerning the "plot" of neutral events, but more intrusion errors about the motives or emotions of the characters involved in emotional events. Presumably this reflects the nature of the elaborative encoding prompted by the emotional event, which is later confused with what actually happened. This account is also consistent with the finding of an increased advantage over time for the recall of "gist" and "plot" of emotional (relative to neutral) events, because these should be supported by such elaboration (Burke et al., 1992). On the other hand, we would not expect "central" details, that just happened to be within the attended focus but were not otherwise emotional, to be elaborated in the same way. Again consistent with this expectation, the Burke et al. (1992) study failed to find any gain over time in the relative advantage for these spatially central details.

If the selective nature of memory for emotional events arises because of a combination of attentional capture and elaboration, it could be argued that there is nothing unique about memory for emotional events. Perhaps any unusual event having these properties would be recalled in the same way. Christianson and Loftus (1991) examined this issue and claimed that their findings could not be explained in terms of distinctiveness, on the grounds that a control condition in which subjects saw an "unusual" event (a woman carrying her bicycle on her shoulder) did not produce the same results. More subjects noted the absence of an injured woman from a test slide (95%) than noted the absence of a woman carrying a bicycle in the "unusual" slide (70%) or riding a bicycle in the neutral control slide (60%). Nonetheless, the unusual slide did produce some effects, both in making the central event more memorable, and making peripheral details less memorable.

It is, therefore, possible that an even more distinctive or unusual event could have produced results approaching or even identical to those for the emotional slide. However, it seems unlikely that distinctiveness alone is sufficient to account for all the effects of emotionally traumatic events, in part because the latter invoke already established concerns or fears, as argued earlier. Indeed, if a distinctive event could be made to do so by virtue of being extremely surprising or incongruent, it could then be argued to have emotional effects itself. For both this reason, and because it is argued later that the emotional reaction and interpretation of the individual concerned is critical in determining how an event is encoded, it does not seem likely that the "distinctiveness" hypothesis will prove productive.

A remaining problem is to account for the (admittedly rare) instances when victims claim not to recall real-life traumatic events, despite remembering other peripheral details (Christianson, 1992). In such instances, victims might say they remember little of the assault itself, but are able to report visual impressions of the place where the attack took place, or a smell associated with the attacker. Only after some time has passed, or strong recall cues are present, does the central event itself become retrievable. If the memory loss is veridical, it may be that some biological process associated with extreme emotion interferes with the encoding process, such as high levels of adrenergic stimulation to the amygdala (McGaugh, 1992). Alternatively, it is possible that loss of ability to recall could reflect effortful avoidance of processing extremely distressing material: the converse of elaborative rehearsal as postulated previously. Such a possibility is suggested by results of research in the third domain to be considered here: the effect of mood on memory for congruent versus incongruent information.

MEMORY FOR MOOD-CONGRUENT INFORMATION

In studies of mood-congruent memory, subjects may have a negative or positive mood induced, or be selected as having a preexisting mood disorder, and are then exposed to stimuli (usually words) that are either congruent or incongruent with their mood state. Results have been mixed (see the later discussion), but the usual finding is that congruent material is better retained than is incongruent or emotionally neutral information. In depressed patients, for example, negative descriptors (e.g., stupid, disliked) are recalled as well or better than are equivalent positive words (e.g., clever, likable), whereas normal mood controls consistently recall more positive words. The relative advantage for negative descriptors in depressives depends on self-encoding, however: If required to encode words in relation to others, they then show the same positive bias as normal controls (Bradley & Mathews, 1983).

This dependence of mood-congruent recall on encoding method has been taken as an indication that mood-congruent recall depends on the to-be-remembered word being associated with other self-related information in memory. Preferential recall thus results from the advantage gained by linking the new item with already elaborated structures, which can be used during later retrieval. Such a view is consistent in some respects with Bower's modified model of mood and memory (Bower & Mayer, 1989), in which items are linked into an emotional network, but only if they are encoded as causing, or causally belonging to, that emotion. However, both these views suggest that mood-congruent recall is *not* strongly automatic, but depends on encoding and retrieval processes that are at least partly under intentional control. This conclusion is strongly reinforced by the failure to show that depression is associated with mood-congruent bias in so-called implicit tests, such as word completion, in which no reference is made to memory and subjects are asked to complete stems or fragments with the first word that comes into their mind (Watkins, Mathews, Williamson, & Fuller, 1992). MacLeod (1994) demonstrated that, irrespective of the perceptual or conceptual nature of the task, depressed subjects show mood-congruent effects when explicitly trying to recall positive or negative words, but do not do so when responding with the first word that occurs to them as required in implicit tests. Explicit tests, such as cued recall, are known to be sensitive to elaborative encoding manipulations, whereas implicit tests such as word completion are not, so that these findings are consistent with the hypothesis that mood-congruent bias depends on differential elaboration of negative self-related information by depressed subjects.

Similar conclusions apply to studies in which normal subjects have a sad mood induced, either by being required to think about depressing things or by being exposed to events having incidental depressing effects, such as listening to sad music. Several notable findings from this research are that: (a) normal subjects instructed to self-induce a sad mood show recall biases similar to those seen in depression, particularly in those with high "neuroticism" or trait negative-emotionality scores (Bradley, Mogg, Galbraith, & Perrett, 1993); (b) normal mood subjects instructed to act "as if" they were depressed show similar effects (Perrig & Perrig, 1988); and (c) subjects who have had a negative mood induced incidentally, but without instructions to create or maintain it, sometimes show mood-*incongruent* memory; that is, they recall more positive events than subjects in positive mood (Parrott & Sabini, 1990). Furthermore, the occurrence of incongruence of this kind is related to self-reports that these subjects typically try to control their mood (Parrott, 1994). The implication is that the tendency for sad subjects to recall negative information is at least partly under intentional control, and that some subjects use this as a means of regulating their own mood.

Thus, just as has been suggested in the case of unselected subjects exposed to traumatic events, emotional effects on memory in sad or depressed subjects seem to depend on elaborative rehearsal. Support for this hypothesis in depression has been obtained using encoding manipulations and implicit tests of memory, so that similar techniques could perhaps be applied in related fields to test the same hypothesis. That is, we expect that neither negative recall bias in induced-mood experiments, nor the increase in memory for simulated traumatic events over time, should be reflected in equivalent changes when implicit memory tests are used, because the latter are relatively insensitive to elaborative encoding processes.

The second process thought to be involved in memory for central aspects of traumatic events is attentional capture, perhaps elicited by automatic preattentive encoding of certain perceptual features. Again, a remarkable similarity exists between this theorizing and the findings of an attentional bias in anxious individuals. Initial experiments with anxious patients showed that words associated with threat (e.g., death, failure) capture attentional resources in preference to other competing neutral stimuli (for a review, see Mathews & MacLeod, 1994). These data were obtained not using memory tasks, but using latency to detect neutral targets in the location of threatening words to directly assess attentional deployment. Similar findings emerged from studies of high trait-anxious normals, particularly when these subjects were currently under stress or reported feeling currently anxious. Even more recent data shows that these effects are not confined to words, but occur in complex visual environments: for example, angry faces "pop out" more readily for high-anxious subjects. The tentative hypothesis emerging from this work is that anxiety is associated with the allocation of high attentional priority to potentially threatening stimuli in the environment (vigilance), even when such stimuli are only very distantly related to any real danger. The issue of cause, and causal direction is, of course, a difficult one: It may be that anxiety leads to attentional vigilance, or it may be that vigilance causes anxiety, or (the hypothesis that we favor) it may be that both directions operate in a circular manner.

In addition to evidence on attentional capture, there are also clear indications that threatening distracters interfere with the performance of anxious subjects on other ongoing tasks, such as attentional search for neutral targets, or color-naming emotional words. This effect remains even when the threatening distracters are presented very briefly and then masked, so that subjects claim not to be able to see them (Mogg, Bradley, Williams, & Mathews, 1993). This apparently nonconscious process thus resembles the automatic encoding effect claimed to explain the focus on central emotional aspects of some traumatic events. It should be noted, however, that the attentional and interference effects documented in anxious subjects do not typically apply to low-anxious controls. If anything, low-anxious subjects shift attention away from threatening words, and typically fail to show interference from threatening distracters. How, then, can it be claimed that these effects arise from the same processes that explain memory for emotional events in eyewitness studies using normal subjects?

The explanation advanced here is that unselected normal subjects do indeed resemble anxious individuals when encoding threatening stimuli, but only in the case of unambiguously emotional events. Recall that the stimuli used in most of the research described with anxious subjects were single words, designated as threatening or nonthreatening, but hardly equivalent to a highly emotion-provoking series of scenes. It is, therefore, proposed that anxiety-prone subjects react to stimuli that are relatively trivial and distant from danger, in the way that normal subjects reserve for events that are more intense and more directly related to threat. Put another way, normal (nonanxious) subjects simply have a higher threshold for encoding a stimulus event as a threat than do anxiety-prone individuals. Stimuli that are not very intense, or are not very closely related to danger, are actively ignored by most subjects, thus avoiding unnecessary distraction. When faced with a more severely emotional event, however, they respond adaptively by giving that event priority, using the same mode that anxious subjects adopt habitually.

Returning to the second process that has been postulated to explain memory for emotional events, the line of argument might suggest that anxious subjects should be more likely to elaborate on the meaning of threatening words, and thus recall them better. Unfortunately for this prediction, no consistent pattern has emerged from the research on memory for threat in anxiety-prone subjects. Several studies have found evidence for better recall for threatening words, but many do not, and some even find poorer memory for threat in highly anxious subjects (Eysenck & Mogg, 1992). However, in the light of the research on mood-incongruent memory in normals, an obvious explanation suggests itself. Some subjects choose to avoid elaborative processing as a means of mood regulation. Thus, extremely anxious subjects who find themselves distressed by thinking about even such a trivial stimulus as the word *death* may be motivated to avoid it. In this case, two opposed tendencies determine the encoding of threatening stimuli in very anxious individuals: The first process is the capture of attentional resources by any threat-related cue, and the second is the intentional avoidance of elaborative rehearsal. Although the same two basic factors are invoked as in the earlier discussion of memory for emotional events, the second process may operate in the reverse direction, leading to paradoxically poorer recall.

This account is speculative, but receives some support from a few studies using implicit memory tests. Even when failing to show a recall advantage for threatening words, anxious subjects are more likely to use them again when completing word stems, and to identify them when they are presented tachistoscopically (Mathews & MacLeod, 1994). This implies that the emotional word had indeed been encoded, but not necessarily in a semantically elaborated form. Such a relatively inaccessible form of representation might possibly account for instances when victims of assault have difficulties in recalling the traumatic events that they experienced. In any event, the data continue to support the idea that emotional information is selectively encoded, but add another important variable: individual differences. Variations in trait emotionality, and any habitual control strategies associated with them, are probably critical in determining both the type of emotional stimuli necessary to evoke selective encoding, and the extent to which the selectively encoded information is elaboratively rehearsed and becomes more retrievable. The eventual form of memory for emotional events is, therefore, the product of an interaction between the nature of the event and the attributes of the individual experiencing it.

GENERALIZING ACROSS RESEARCH DOMAINS

To some extent, the independence of the three research domains illustrated here is understandable. They address different questions, often draw on different populations, and use different experimental methods. Despite these apparent differences, it still seems surprising that so little theoretical contact has been made between them, when obvious parallels could be drawn. For example, events that are relatively neutral for nonemotional individuals might be quite distressing for a more reactive person, such as an anxious patient. If so, then memory for emotional events might depend on an interaction between the characteristics of the person involved and the type or intensity of the event themselves.

One way of investigating this idea is to look for individual differences between normal subjects showing more or less of an advantage in memory for emotional information. An example of this is provided by Andrews (1990, cited by Reisberg & Heuer, 1992). Recognition questions about recently shown movies (e.g., *Fatal Attraction*) revealed that, overall, the details of emotional scenes were more accurately reported than were details of matched neutral scenes. Of more interest from the present perspective was the finding that subjects with low scores on a measure of emotional arous-ability did not differ in this respect: The advantage for emotional detail in memory was present only for subjects with moderate or high scores. As Reisberg and Heuer pointed out, this "implies that emotionality is indeed the key factor in distinguishing the neutral and emotional scenes" (p. 174). Without this finding one might be concerned that the scenes were not matched in some other important way, such as relevance to the plot. How-ever, any such difference should apply to all subjects, rather than only those with relatively high levels of emotional arousability.

We (Mathews & Milroy) recently found another example in our own research on the phenomenon described by Christianson (1994) as "tunnel memory." Normal subjects were briefly shown 16 news photographs that varied in emotionality, ranging from starving children in Biafra to cheering crowds, and were required to rate them for pleasantness or unpleasantness on a 1 through 5 scale. After a short interval, they were given a forced recognition choice between two versions of each picture, one that showed a more close-up view of the central focus, and one that showed a slightly more wide-angle view, so as to include more of the surrounding detail. Although neither was identical with the original, subjects were simply asked to pick the version that they thought was the one that they had seen earlier. Following the perceptual-schema hypothesis (Intraub, Bender, & Mangels, 1992), we expected subjects to show an overall bias favoring the wide-angle version, as indeed they did: by 72% to 28%. However, if subjects showed attentional focusing effects with emotional pictures, they might be more likely to pick the close-up version. This proved not to be the case, with a near-zero positive correlation between affective rating and the probability of picking the wide-angle version ($r = .06$). Similarly, there was no difference between the mean pleasantness ratings of pictures chosen in their close-up versus their wide-angle versions (3.41 vs. 3.39).

A different picture emerged, however, when we took individual differences into account, using the trait version of the Positive and Negative Affectivity

Scales (PANAS; Watson, Clark, & Tellegen, 1988). For pictures rated as "very unpleasant," for example, negative affectivity was strongly correlated with the probability of picking the close-up version ($r = .54$, $p < .01$), but positive affectivity was not ($r = -.29$). Similarly, the difference between pleasantness ratings for close-up versus wide-angle versions was strongly correlated with negative affectivity ($r = .58$), but not with positive affectivity ($r = -.04$). In sum, there was evidence for attentional focusing with emotional pictures, but only in subjects with high negative affectivity scores.

To conclude, it is possible to offer some tentative generalizations in the hope that they will encourage experimental collaboration and theoretical synthesis. These conclusions are cast in a more definite form than is warranted by present evidence, but they are intended to serve a heuristic purpose, and are offered in this spirit.

1. People selectively encode emotional features of events, at the expense of other competing aspects occurring simultaneously, which may be ignored or forgotten.

2. There is some evidence that emotional encoding begins at an early, nonconscious stage. Brief presentations of angry faces and threatening words, masked so that subjects are unable to report their presence, still cause physiological and interference responses.

3. Detection of an emotional event leads to attention being centered at the location associated with greatest emotional significance. This attentional effect is associated with faster detection, and better perceptual memory, for information at that location.

4. It is typically easier to recall the gist of an emotional event than to recall a similar neutral event, and this advantage tends to strengthen over time. When it occurs, this memory advantage is due (at least in part) to more extensive elaborative rehearsal. However, some subjects may choose to avoid elaborative as a mood control strategy.

5. Individual differences powerfully influence both the ease with which emotional cues attract attention, and the extent that subjects engage in elaborative rehearsal. Thus, selective emotional encoding depends on an interaction between type of event and the individual concerned.

As argued earlier, these tentative conclusions may not be unique to threatening or upsetting events, and further research may allow us to make similar generalizations about how other significant events are encoded, including very unexpected or positive stimuli. It seems likely, for example, that events involving an intensely loved person would also lead to attentional capture, and subsequent elaboration. However, the way in which threatening events are processed has particular relevance to several important applied questions, including the accuracy of eyewitness reports, and cognitive factors contributing to anxiety states. Because both of these research areas have been well developed (albeit independently), the time seems ripe to look for ways to integrate them. Such integration might throw light on a number of otherwise puzzling questions, such as why traumatic events are sometimes recalled too well, to the extent of causing intrusive thoughts and flashback images, but are sometimes poorly recalled or may even be inaccessible. Real-life traumas involve highly emotional events, but also individuals who vary in their emotional reaction to those events, and in their habitual encoding styles. The answer to such puzzling questions may require us to consider all of these factors together.

ACKNOWLEDGMENTS

I am grateful to Dan Reisberg and Friderike Heuer for their helpful comments on an earlier version of this chapter.

REFERENCES

Bower, G. H., & Mayer, J. D. (1989). In search of mood-dependent retrieval. *Journal of Social Behaviour and Personality, 4*, 121–156.

Bradley, B. P., & Mathews, A. (1983). Negative self-schemata in clinical depression. *British Journal of Clinical Psychology, 22*, 173–181.

Bradley, B., Mogg, K., Galbraith, M., & Perrett, A. (1993). Negative recall bias and neuroticism: State vs. trait effects. *Behavioural Research and Therapy, 31*, 125–127.

Burke, A., Heuer, F., & Reisberg, D. (1992). Remembering emotional events. *Memory & Cognition, 20*, 277–290.

Christianson, S.-A. (1992). Emotional stress and eyewitness memory: A critical review. *Psychological Bulletin, 112*, 284–309.

Christianson, S.-A. (1994, August). *Emotional stress and memory: Critical factors.* Paper presented at the Third Practical Aspects of Memory Conference, College Park, MD.

Christianson, S.-A., & Loftus, E. F. (1991). Remembering emotional events: The fate of detailed information. *Cognition and Emotion, 5*, 81–108.

Ellis, H. C., & Ashbrook, P. W. (1988). Resource-allocation model of the effects of depressed mood states on memory. In K. Fiedler & J. Forgas (Eds.), *Affect, cognition & social behavior* (pp. 25–43). Gottingen, Germany: Hogrefe.

Eysenck, M. W., & Calvo, M. G. (1992). Anxiety and performance: The processing efficiency theory. *Cognition and Emotion, 6*, 409–434.

Eysenck, M. W., & Mogg, K. (1992). Clinical anxiety, trait anxiety, and memory bias. In S.-A. Christianson (Ed.), *The handbook of emotion and memory: Research and theory* (pp. 429–450). Hillsdale, NJ: Lawrence Erlbaum Associates.

Hertel, P. T., & Hardin, T. S. (1990). Remembering with and without awareness in a depressed mood: Evidence for deficits in initiative. *Journal of Experimental Psychology: General, 119*, 45–59.

Heuer, F., & Reisberg, D. (1990). Vivid memories of emotional events: The accuracy of remembered minutiae. *Memory & Cognition, 18,* 496–506.

Intraub, H., Bender, R. S., & Mangels, J. A. (1992). Looking at pictures, but remembering scenes. *Journal of Experimental Psychology: Learning, Memory and Cognition, 18,* 180–191.

MacLeod, C. (1994, August). *Locus of the implicit–explicit dissociation in mood-congruent memory.* Paper presented at the Third Practical Aspects of Memory Conference, College Park, MD.

Mathews, A., & MacLeod, C. (1994). Cognitive approaches to emotion and emotional disorders. *Annual Review of Psychology, 45,* 25–50.

McGaugh, J. M. (1992). Affect, neuromodulatory systems and memory storage. In S.-A. Christianson (Ed.), *The handbook of emotion and memory: Research and theory* (pp. 245–268). Hillsdale, NJ: Lawrence Erlbaum Associates.

Mogg, K., Bradley, B. P., Williams, R., & Mathews, A. M. (1993). Subliminal processing of emotional information in anxiety and depression. *Journal of Abnormal Psychology, 102,* 304–311.

Ohman, A., & Soares, J. J. F. (1993). On the automatic nature of phobic fear: Conditioned electrodermal responses to masked fear-relevant stimuli. *Journal of Abnormal Psychology, 102,* 121–132.

Parrott, W. G. (1994, August). *Mood-incongruent recall and emotional self-control.* Paper presented at the Third Practical Aspects of Memory Conference, College Park, MD.

Parrott, W. G., & Sabini, J. (1990). Mood and memory under natural conditions: Evidence for mood incongruent recall. *Journal of Personality and Social Psychology, 59,* 321–336.

Perrig, W. J., & Perrig, P. (1988). Mood and memory: Mood-congruity effects in the absence of mood. *Memory & Cognition, 16,* 102–109.

Reisberg, D., & Heuer, F. (1992). Remembering the details of emotional events. In E. Winograd & U. Neisser (Eds.), *Affect and accuracy in recall: Studies of "flashbulb" memory.* New York: Cambridge University Press.

Watkins, P., Mathews, A. M., Williamson, D. A., & Fuller, R. (1992). Mood congruent memory in depression: Emotional priming or elaboration? *Journal of Abnormal Psychology, 101,* 581–586.

Watson, D., Clark, L. A., & Tellegen, A. (1988). Development and validation of brief measures of positive and negative affect: The PANAS Scales. *Journal of Personality and Social Psychology, 54,* 1063–1070.

Weaver, C. A., III. (1993). Do you need a "flash" to form a flashbulb memory? *Journal of Experimental Psychology: General, 122,* 39–46.

CHAPTER TWENTY-ONE

Cursing: A Damned Persistent Lexicon

Timothy B. Jay
North Adams State College

The purpose of this chapter is to convince cognitive psychologists that cursing language is a subject that merits attention. Episodes of cursing using taboo, vulgar, offensive, or obscene words to express emotions occur frequently in spoken English. Unfortunately, psychologists interested in language and memory have virtually ignored the subject of cursing. As a result of inattention, the research, theory, and concept of "normal" language remain incomplete for descriptions of anger expression, humor, personality, sexuality, and other major areas of psychological study. Psychologists have treated the cursing lexicon as an epiphenomenon rather than an integral part of a speaker's emotional expression. The ignorance of cursing and a focus on polite speech produces models and theories of language that are inadequate. As a result, social and legal problems involving offensive language (e.g., sexual harassment) remain unsolved. Perhaps psychologists need more compelling evidence that cursing is a necessary component of normal language usage.

Americans use curse words to express a wide range of negative (hatred or racism) and positive thoughts (humor or sex talk). In this respect, offensive language serves several pragmatic functions, like joking, regardless of a speaker's age. Consider one positive usage, a joke told to a bus driver at an Elderhostel outing: "How many New Yorkers does it take to screw in a lightbulb?" Answer: "None of your fucking business." Psycholinguists and memory researchers must explain how and why these words and joke frames persist into old age, as well as the persistence of sex talk, hate speech, and verbal aggression. These offensive frames are not epiphenomena; they are fundamental verbal-linguistic expressions of deep emotional feelings. If emotional expression is a necessary component of a theory of language, then cognitive psychologists *must* include cursing in models of language.

Evidence from elderly Americans is sought here to support the contention that the topic of cursing is important because it may be frequent in usage, and persist through old age. It is the frequency and persistence of this phenomenon that could convince language and memory researchers. It already has been reported that children use obscenities as soon as they can speak and that gender-related trends emerge, regarding the frequency and offensiveness of words used, as soon as children go off to school (Jay, 1992). But what about the elderly? Are the patterns of cursing similar to youthful speakers? What contextual variables influence cursing and what words do elderly speakers use? Could an obscene lexicon persist in the face of Alzheimer's disease, senile dementia, and devastating psychological and cognitive decline? If cursing occurs frequently in the elderly population and if it persists until death, then it is a phenomenon important enough to incorporate in language and memory research. One simple goal here is to describe how elders use curse words and to determine if cursing is a damned persistent lexicon.

Older Americans have experienced wide changes in language standards and media content. What needs to be documented is how they use curse words and what curse words have meant to them. Thus, two concerns emerge. One concern is to assess the degree to which elderly speakers use the cursing lexicon in public along with their attitudes about such language. They may have more conservative attitudes about using offensive speech relative to young speakers, that is, the frequency issue. A second concern is to assess the degree to which cursing language persists through a decline in normal cognitive and linguistic functioning, that is, the persistence issue. The remainder of this chapter addresses these two issues. First, a sample of elders' cursing in public is examined along with a survey using word scaling techniques. Second, cursing in two different nursing home populations is examined to establish the persistence of the cursing lexicon before death.

CURSING BY HEALTHY ELDERLY AMERICANS

Consider what is already known about how older Americans curse. The author has published an extensive literature review (Jay, 1980) and a book on the topic of cursing in America (Jay, 1992). Table 21.1 summarizes data from a large field study of cursing language used in public (Jay, 1992). It shows the use of curse words by speakers estimated to be over the age of 45 years. This set of 245 words represents 11% of the original 2,171-word corpus. These data indicate that older males outcurse females on the order of 4 to 1 (195 to 50), and that most of the cursing is accounted for by a

TABLE 21.1
Word Frequency and Speaker Gender (from Jay, 1992)

Word	Female Speaker	Male Speaker	Total
Ass	3	16	19
Asshole	4	2	6
Balls	0	2	2
Bastard	2	10	12
Bitch	1	13	14
Blows	0	1	1
Blowjob	0	1	1
Bullshit	0	4	4
Damn	6	16	22
Dildo	0	1	1
Fuck	3	21	24
God(damn)	3	30	33
Hell	15	30	45
(Jesus)(Christ)	5	23	28
Jew	0	1	1
Motherfucker	0	1	1
Prick	0	3	3
Shit	8	25	33
Total	50	195	245

small set of words that are repeated often. This public production lexicon totaled only 18 unique words. Males used all of these words but females used only 10 of them. The four most frequently used words, *hell, god(damn), shit*, and *Jesus(Christ)* alone account for 57% of the data. Notice that these words are mainly milder profanities, and more offensive sexual and obscene words are used less frequently (with the exception of *fuck*).

There is nothing surprising in these data; they confirm swearing patterns established in childhood. Males swear more than females, and they use stronger words than females. However, for elders the production lexicon is small and includes mainly mild profanities. The unique and valuable addition to cognitive research is to have documented these behaviors with elder speakers. In order to further extend these field data with a different procedure, the second study was designed to assess elders' use of offensive language with a survey method.

FREQUENCY AND OFFENSIVENESS RATINGS

Although the field method gives an accurate picture of what people say in public settings, it does not reveal what other words people use privately or how frequently they use them. It does not reveal what words are understood but not spoken, or how speakers feel about the language they use and hear. Using a survey requiring subjects to provide scale ratings for frequency of usage and degree of offensiveness is one way to overcome these shortcomings and thus provides the rationale for the second study.

Method

Procedure. In the summer and fall of 1993 surveys were administered anonymously in two phases to an elderly population in western Massachusetts. The first phase was designed to be a pilot study, because the laboratory staff had no prior experience surveying subjects over 60 years of age and were uncertain how elders would react to offensive language. The pilot survey contained 30 taboo words derived from previous research in this laboratory, printed in large, easy-to-read type. Age, gender, birthplace, and use of foreign languages were recorded on a cover page. Subjects were asked to rate the taboo words simultaneously on two 1-to-9 scales for degree of offensiveness and frequency of use, based on their own use and reactions. The offensiveness anchors were 1 "not offensive" and 9 "very offensive," and the frequency anchors were 1 (*never*) and 9 (*very often*). After administering the pilot survey to 30 elderly subjects, the responses were examined and problem areas were revised, producing a second format. These pilot data were not further analyzed.

The final survey contained 26 taboo words. Words that were deemed too offensive, such as *motherfucker*, and words that were unfamiliar, such as *dink*, were eliminated. Four control words—*flower, table, dirty*, and *danger*—were added. The randomized word list was repeated for each separate scale judgment. The first set of judgments was to rate the words on the 1-to-9 offensiveness scale described previously. The second set of judgments was to rate the list on the frequency scale described previously. The survey was printed in large, easy-to-read type, and age, gender, birthplace, and use of foreign languages were recorded on a cover page.

Subjects. Participants, all 60 years or older, included 53 volunteers recruited from the Elderhostel program at North Adams State College and 48 people associated with western Massachusetts councils on aging (one council refused to participate and wrote letters to the administrators of the college in order to stop the research project). The average age was 72, and 18.8% had knowledge of a foreign language. A total of 101 surveys were completed, 71 by females and 30 by males. Seven surveys were deleted because they had more than 12 missing answers, leaving 94 usable surveys, 65 by females and 29 by males.

Word ratings and ratings as a function of rater gender were calculated using SPSS programs for both frequency of use and degree of offensiveness. Zeros were substituted for missing answers and entered into the data analysis.

Results and Discussion

Mean ratings for frequency and offensiveness are reported in Table 21.2. Frequency ratings range from a high of 5.83 (*damn*) to a low of 2.17 (*spic*) for males and a high of 4.98 (*hell*) to a low of 1.38 (*spic*) for females. Mean ratings of frequency are higher for males than for females, 3.63 and 2.58, respectively. Combined (over gender) means for frequency of use range

TABLE 21.2
Frequency and Offensiveness Ratings

Word	Frequency			Offensiveness		
	Both	Male	Female	Both	Male	Female
Hell	5.12	5.41	4.98	2.64	2.31	2.78
Damn	5.11	5.83	4.78	2.32	2.17	2.38
Goddamn	4.13	5.31	3.60	4.29	3.59	4.60
Shit	3.86	4.93	3.38	4.63	4.34	4.75
Bullshit	3.72	5.14	3.09	3.92	3.55	4.08
Son of a bitch	3.52	4.79	2.95	5.59	5.03	5.83
Ass	3.51	4.34	3.14	4.07	3.59	4.29
Jesus Christ	3.45	4.31	3.06	5.10	4.31	5.45
Bitch	3.33	4.34	2.88	5.00	4.86	5.06
Pig	3.30	3.31	3.29	3.86	4.07	3.77
Bastard	3.28	4.14	2.89	5.00	4.86	5.06
Fart	2.95	3.41	2.74	4.13	3.90	4.23
Asshole	2.82	3.66	2.45	6.03	5.21	6.40
Piss	2.76	3.90	2.25	5.51	4.41	6.00
Whore	2.45	2.83	2.28	5.59	5.41	5.66
Tits	2.33	3.79	1.68	5.52	4.55	5.95
Slut	2.32	2.62	2.18	5.56	5.14	5.75
Queer	2.28	2.24	2.29	5.38	5.24	5.45
Prick	2.23	3.00	1.89	6.50	6.14	6.66
Fuck	2.05	2.93	1.66	7.37	7.21	7.45
Nigger	1.98	2.38	1.80	7.50	6.90	7.77
Cock	1.95	2.86	1.54	6.39	5.86	6.63
Dipshit	1.93	2.31	1.75	5.12	4.38	5.45
Fag	1.86	2.24	1.69	6.16	5.34	6.52
Peckerhead	1.73	2.21	1.52	6.09	4.86	6.63
Spic	1.63	2.17	1.38	5.11	5.07	5.12
Mean	2.91	3.63	2.58	5.17	4.70	5.37
Danger	4.45	3.86	4.72	1.05	1.21	.98
Dirty	4.44	4.66	4.34	1.90	1.72	1.98
Table	4.21	3.76	4.42	1.22	1.55	1.08
Flower	4.17	3.83	4.32	1.27	1.59	1.12

Note. For frequency, 1 meant (*never*) and 9 meant (*very often*). For offensiveness, 1 meant (*not offensive*) and 9 meant (*very offensive*).

from a high of 5.12 (*hell*) to a low of 1.63 (*spic*), with a mean of 2.91. Notice that the control words were rated higher in frequency in general than curse words. The correlation between these frequency ratings and the field count (Table 21.1) is $r(12) = .59$, which is pretty solid agreement between frequency estimation and actual recordings in public.

Degree of offensiveness ratings range from a high of 7.21 (*fuck*) to a low of 2.17 (*damn*) for males and a high of 7.77 (*nigger*) to a low of 2.38 (*damn*) for females. Mean ratings of offensiveness are lower for males than for females, 4.70 and 5.37, respectively. Combined means range from a high of 7.50 (*nigger*) to a low of 2.32 (*damn*), with a mean of 5.17. Notice that the control words were rated less offensive than the curse words.

In summary, the data from the surveys indicate that the elderly population know a larger lexicon of curse words than they used in public in the initial field study. Males indicated that they used these words more frequently than did females, further validating the field study. Females rated curse words as more offensive than did males, also in line with previous research. It was also found that these words vary in degrees of offensiveness and that curse words used most frequently are those that have relatively low offensiveness ratings, such as *damn* or *hell*. Conversely, words with higher offensiveness ratings, *fuck* or *nigger*, are used less frequently. One reason why curse words are heard infrequently from elderly speakers in public may be because they are more offensive to the elderly than to younger speakers (Richard, Clermont, & Jay, 1994). There is some support for this contention. The correlation between frequency and offensiveness ratings for combined means in this experiment is $r(26) = -.82$.

The purpose of the first two studies was to document the usage of offensive language in a population of healthy elderly Americans. The two different methods in general show a pattern of gender-related influences found with younger speakers, but it was also found that elders have a smaller and less extensive production vocabulary than do younger speakers, probably due to a more restrictive language environment in the elders' past.

The second part of this research was designed to determine if these curse words persist in the lexicons of the elderly during the final months of life, often accompanied by dramatic decline in cognitive and linguistic abilities. One might wonder, for example, when much of autobiographical memory becomes inaccessible, if cursing abilities still remain? At any rate, the lifetime persistence of cursing was to be further established in the next two studies of cursing in nursing homes.

CURSING IN THE NURSING HOME

In recent years, awareness of problems of the elderly and syndromes of aging, such as Alzheimer's dementia, have drawn attention to the thought and behavior patterns of nursing home residents. Reports have documented changes in residents' memory, language, and emotions. Recently, several reports have focused on the anger and agitation expressed by both nonimpaired and dementia patients in nursing home settings (Alessi, 1991; Cohen-Mansfield, Marx, & Rosenthal, 1989, 1990; Meddaugh, 1992; Sloane & Mathew, 1991). In particular, these reports indicate that many residents are verbally aggressive and frequently use cursing, swearing, and insulting language to vent their frustrations on staff and residents. Many first-time family visitors of newly admitted nursing home residents are puzzled by the language and behavior they witness there. Several question arise. Why are family members surprised by cursing; was cursing previously unheard? What does the cursing represent? What can be done about cursing? In response to these questions, some nursing homes and health care staff have prepared brochures to inform families of Alzheimer's patients (and those with other syndromes) about what to expect; however, the specifics and root causes are not yet known.

One major problem in all the previous work stems from a lack of specificity. To date, no detailed analysis has shown the types of words and phrases that these dementia patients and healthier residents are using. What are the residents saying that is interpreted as an act of anger, cursing, or verbal aggression? An observational study of cursing episodes in nursing home residents would alleviate the shortcoming.

A second area of concern is elucidating the variables and conditions that give rise to episodes of verbal aggression and cursing in the nursing home population. Loss of control, lack of freedom and privacy, intrusions on personal space, physical or verbal attacks by fellow residents, lack of intimacy, and disorientation have been listed as probable causes in previous studies. It would be helpful for the purposes here if these prevailing conditions could be linked to specific episodes of cursing. It may be the case that certain factors inhibit cursing, whereas others give rise to it. Simply put, why are residents cursing?

In the studies discussed in the next sections, the interest is in the pragmatic variables behind cursing language as well as the nature of the cursing lexicon. The goals were to determine the important speaker characteristics, pragmatic uses (anger, joking, or conversations), and types of curse words used by nursing home residents. Two samples were recorded.

NURSING HOME 1

Method

The research assistant was an employee of a nursing home. She worked 40 hours per week during the summer months of 1990. She was instructed to record any and all patient episodes of the use of taboo, vulgar, obscene, or insulting speech, as broadly defined in previous studies in our laboratory.

The gender and age of both the speaker and target of abuse were recorded, as were the perceived loudness (from soft to loud) and the pragmatic use of the speech (frustration-anger, conversation, joking, or sarcasm). Data were recorded on preprinted 3″ × 5″ field cards used in previous research (see Jay, 1992, for an example). The assistant met with the supervisor (TJ) when questions about recording methods or language samples would arise.

Subjects. Residents, 16 males and 84 females, of the nursing home were from middle-class (according to the nursing home), White families in western Massachusetts and received assistance from Medicare or Medicaid. The research assistant cared for a group of seven males and eight females, who were over 70 years of age, classified as Level 2 or Level 3 patients, requiring minimal help. Most of the smaller group were there due to health problems and exhibited little confusion, according the assistant. Unfortunately, patients' physical and mental health records were not available.

Setting. Data were collected from a nonprofit nursing home located in western Massachusetts. The single-floor home houses 100 residents. Data were collected on the 3:00 P.M. to 11:00 P.M. shift.

Results and Discussion

A total of 139 episodes were recorded. A lexicon of 11 unique word-types appears in Table 21.3, along with the frequency of usage and pragmatic usage data. Most of these data, 110 episodes, were recorded from female speakers and less were from male speakers, 29 of 139. Because the amount of language monitored as a function of speaker gender was not controlled, a detailed analysis by speaker gender is not possible.

TABLE 21.3
Word Frequency and Pragmatic Use

Word	Frequency	Anger	Joke	Conversation
Ass	9	4	4	1
Bastard	1	1	0	0
Bitch	4	3	0	1
Bullshit	2	2	0	0
Jesus(Christ)	3	2	0	1
Damn	27	23	0	4
Goddamn	15	12	0	3
Hell	60	36	6	18
Piss	1	0	0	1
Shit	15	7	1	7
Son of a bitch	2	2	0	0
Total	139	92	11	36

Lexicon. Most of the cursing recorded by these residents consisted of profanity, insults, and scatology. As in previous studies, most of the cursing episodes involved a small number of words that were used frequently. Here, two words, *damn* and *hell* accounted for 62% of the data, 43% and 19% respectively. Five words, *hell, damn, shit, goddamn,* and *ass,* accounted for 90% of the data. Notice that these words are mildly offensive and are not the type of words that teenagers and college students use in public.

Pragmatic Use. Most of the episodes of cursing were related to the expression of anger or frustration, 66%. Cursing language was used to intensify conversations some 26% of the time and to a lesser degree, 8%, in a joking manner. What is the importance of these pragmatics data? By documenting the nature of these correlated factors, nursing home workers could develop strategies for controlling and reducing frustration and anger, making residents' lives more peaceful and less troublesome. Some of these factors may be patient-centered, such as dementia, and others may be environmental, such as being coerced by a co-patient. It is important to document what patients say, as well as the cause of cursing.

This first sample produced data indicating how cursing language is used in the context of a nursing home. In this sample, the lexicon was limited to a small set of mildly offensive profanities, insults, and scatological references, as opposed to more offensive language used by younger speakers. But why is the sample so small, smaller than the field study? One reason for the small sample was our definition of cursing words, that is, the research assistant relied mainly on the offensiveness of a single word and not the overall offensiveness of a phrase or a sentence. For example, referring to someone as *old* or *stupid* or telling them to "shut up" is also offensive and insulting, but these examples would not have been included here because the recording focused on offensive words not phrases or sentences. What is needed is a more inclusive sample and a more liberal criterion for cursing.

As for pragmatic use, the main purpose of cursing appeared to be the expression of anger, as has been found in previous research. However, because these words were only sampled in one time period by a female recorder, and because gender of speaker was not controlled, many broader generalizations cannot be made from this limited sample about causative forces. Thus, it was decided that a second sample was needed to overcome some of the shortcomings of the first sample.

NURSING HOME 2

Method

The research assistant was an employee of a nursing home. She worked approximately 20 hours per week on weekends during the academic year and full-time during the summer from February 1992 until March 1993, as an activities supervisor. Her total time in the nursing home setting was 1,054 hours. She was instructed to record any and all patient episodes of the use of taboo, vulgar, obscene, name calling, or insulting speech. The types of episodes were expanded to be more inclusive than the previous sample. Speaker gender and age, as well as age and gender of the target of abuse, were recorded. Speech volume and the pragmatic use (anger-frustration, conversation, sarcasm, or joking) were noted. Data were recorded on field cards described earlier. The assistant met with the supervisor (TJ) on a weekly basis to discuss the procedure and resolve any difficulties.

Subjects. The home had a total of 55 female and 6 male residents. The sample of cursers was a subset of 29 female and 6 male residents who used abusive language. They ranged in age from 70 to 95 years with the median age of 79 (females) and 83 (males). Speakers exhibited a variety of psychiatric and medical diagnoses, with dementia being most prevalent (38%).

Setting. The facility was a single-floor, intermediate care nursing home in western New England. It is a for-profit, corporation-owned home.

Results and Discussion

A total of 755 curse words were recorded as used in 718 separate episodes of cursing. Some of these episodes included more than one curse word, for example, *goddamn son of a bitch.* Because the criteria for cursing were liberalized to include insulting phrases and name calling, the lexicon is both larger and more diverse than any previous research.

Lexicon. For the 755 words, there were 313 unique utterance tokens. These separate tokens were condensed into curse word-types; for example, *hell* and *what the hell* are different tokens of the root word-type, *hell.* Looking only at the root word-types and collapsing over tokens, there is a root lexicon of 56 curse word-types. The root lexicon appears in Table 21.4 and rank order appears in parentheses for the 10 most frequent words. The 10 most frequent words (*damn, hell, goddamn, shit, Jesus(Christ), shut up, son of a bitch, bitch, bullshit,* and *stupid*) accounted for 77% of the data. In fact, the first four words alone accounted for over 50% of the sample. Thus, the lexicon of cursing in the nursing home is limited and revolves around a small number of words and phrases that are repeated often, a result in line with previous research.

Pragmatic Use. The use of cursing here, as in the previous sample, was predominantly to express anger or frustration, as 73% of the episodes were classified as such. Conversational use and joking forms accounted for 19% of

TABLE 21.4
Lexicon of Word Types and Frequency of Occurrence

Ass	20	Godsakes	9
Asshole	2	Hell (2)	94
Baldheaded	2	Hillbillies	1
Bastard	10	Horseshit	1
Bitch (8)	27	Jackass	10
Brownnoser	2	Jerk	4
Bullshit (9)	25	Kook	3
Jesus (Christ) (5)	45	Nigger	1
Cocksucker	2	Nut	1
Cow	2	Old	9
Crab	2	Pig	3
Crackpot	1	Piss	8
Crap	11	Pollock	3
Crazy	5	Prick	1
Cripesake	1	Rat	1
Crying out loud	1	Rotten	1
Cunt	1	Shit (4)	51
Damn (1)	166	Shut up (6)	40
Dick	1	Sissy	1
Dirty	2	Sit on it	1
Drunk	1	Snot	1
Dumb (dummy)	10	Son of a bitch (7)	35
Fart	1	Stink	7
Fat	2	Stupid (10)	23
Fool	6	Wacko	1
Fuck	18	Whore	1
Goat	1	Worthless	1
Goddamn (3)	74	You make me sick	2

Note. Rank orderings of the top 10 words are in parentheses.

the data, and seemed to be used more by some residents than by others. The pragmatic form sarcasm accounted for the remaining 8% of the data.

In sum, it has been confirmed that nursing home residents frequently use abusive language to express anger or frustration at those around them. These episodes involve a lexicon of words and phrases that mainly rely on insults, blasphemy, and profanity, rather than stronger obscenities of youthful speakers. Psychologists still need to know more about the nursing home environment, however, to discover why patients get angry and swear. Additional male patient data are needed to make comparisons based on gender; however, it is noteworthy that most of the residents are females and most of the cursing in the nursing home setting is from female speakers. It would also prove informative to examine each resident's history of cursing prior to admission and how a resident's cursing changes after admission. It must also be determined if patients swear differently around male staff members, as these studies used female research assistants.

GENERAL DISCUSSION

In general, this research has accomplished a simple goal of describing elderly Americans' cursing lexicons in four different public and private settings. What has been found? The frequencies of elders' relatively mild curse words have shown that cursing is not infrequent in this population, and the nature of words selected depends on speaker gender. Furthermore, it has been shown that cursing persists throughout one's lifetime and, for some, through the course of cognitive decline. Elders' attitudes about the offensiveness of curse words has been recorded, noting that elders use less offensive words than do younger speakers. It was also found that elders' knowledge of curse words is greater than their use of them in public, a common finding in psycholinguistic research, where lexical comprehension overshadows production. Finally, the types of words that are used in nursing homes have been specified, and anger and frustration were major causes of their use. These curse words are persistent. Although convincing cognitive psychologists to study cursing may take some time, here is evidence that cursing is a frequent and persistent aspect of American elders' language and thought. What are some applications of this research?

The immediate applicability and worth of these data are in the nursing home setting. Families and staff must be educated about residents' use of cursing and its relationship to anger. Health care practitioners may begin to explore the reasons why residents are cursing and compare different types of nursing home facilities on the basis of anger episodes. One might ask whether cursing is a sign of staff or resident abuse or if it is a function of a resident's socioeconomic status or coping skills. One might wonder what the relationship is between quality of care and frequency of cursing in a facility. However important, these applications to nursing homes may be minor compared to a wider application of cursing research.

Whatever the reasons for psychologists' failure to study Americans' use of and reaction to cursing, the exclusion of offensive words from psycholinguistic theory is a serious omission with several practical ramifications. One obvious effect of ignoring cursing is to exacerbate legal and social problems that could be alleviated through a better understanding by applied psycholinguists. What are these social problems? Psychologists have offered wholly incomplete explanations in legal discussions involving verbal sexual harassment, hate speech, racial discrimination, child abuse, spouse abuse, elder abuse, media language standards, censorship, schoolchildren's verbal aggression, and gang violence caused by verbal insults and graffiti. This negligence must be addressed. These are all language-related problems that require psychologists' insights not indifference. Applied psychologists should take some responsibility and initiative for solutions here.

Previously, a cursing episode was viewed as a loss of control or lack of a "proper" lexicon by academic psychologists. However, for most under-educated Americans cursing is a fact of everyday life. Problems involving ordinary language may someday force psychologists to offer explanations and recommendations for solutions. Both the practical aspects and the theoretical importance of studying cursing should be clear. By studying cursing and colloquial speech, cognitive psychologists will have more complete models of language and solutions to the language problems mentioned previously. In the effort to increase the validity and applicability of memory research, this research has established the persistence of a cursing lexicon through old age, and it is believed that this persistence is not less important than the persistence of any knowledge that cognitive psychologists have previously studied. The fact that psychologists have found the subject taboo, humorous, odd, lower class, or irrelevant does not solve the practical problems, and this type of exclusive attitude about cursing must change. These descriptive studies are one step toward the goal of building more accurate models of language usage.

ACKNOWLEDGMENTS

The author would like to thank research assistants from North Adams State College, Department of Psychology, Karla Hull, Rebecca Olson, and Adam Clermont for their data collection, data analysis, and other contributions to the project. I thank Jim May for his comments on this chapter. An earlier version of this chapter was presented at the Eastern Psychological Association Meeting in 1993.

REFERENCES

Alessi, C. A. (1991). Managing the behavioral problems of dementia in the home. *Clinics in Geriatric Medicine, 7,* 787–799.

Cohen-Mansfield, J., Marx, M., & Rosenthal, A. (1989). A description of agitation in a nursing home. *Journal of Gerontology, 44,* 77–84.

Cohen-Mansfield, J., Marx, M., & Rosenthal, A. (1990). Dementia and agitation in nursing home residents: How are they related. *Psychology and Aging, 5,* 3–8.

Jay, T. B. (1980). Sex roles and dirty word usage: A review of the literature and reply to Haas. *Psychological Bulletin, 88,* 614–621.

Jay, T. B. (1992). *Cursing in America.* Philadelphia: John Benjamins.

Meddaugh, D. L. (1992, July). Lack of privacy, control may trigger aggressive behaviors. *Provider,* p. 39.

Richard, D., Clermont, A., & Jay, T. B. (1994, April). *Cursing: Elderly and college student attitudes.* Paper presented at Greater Boston Undergraduate Psychological Research Conference, Framingham, MA.

Sloane, P. D., & Mathew, L. J. (1991). An assessment and care planning strategy for nursing home residents with dementia. *The Gerontologist, 31,* 128–131.

PART EIGHT

MEMORY AIDS—FROM STRATEGIES TO AUTOMATION

CHAPTER TWENTY-TWO

Memory Aids

Margaret Jean Intons-Peterson
Indiana University

The central purpose of this chapter is to compare three markedly different and complex ways to aid retrieval from memory. From time to time, we all fail to retrieve information from memory—a frustrating situation we would like to correct. To counteract forgetting, we often rely on memory aids (e.g., Harris, 1980; Intons-Peterson & Fournier, 1986; Intons-Peterson & Newsome, 1992). Most memory aids and strategies have been rather simple or have been targeted at reminding specific kinds of memories; examples include writing a note on a calendar to help us remember an appointment or using a timer to remind us to turn off an oven. This chapter is focused on three more demanding, complicated, or explanatory memory strategies than those typically studied in the past. The approaches chosen are diverse and thereby extend previous work. Indeed, one of the strategies failed, a result that may signal important boundary considerations.

In the first approach, "postcuing," one tries to reduce the age-old problem of having recent information interfere with older memories by telling subjects after they have learned the second list some information that might make it easier for them to suppress this list. Postcuing involves the conscious application of a cue as an internal memory aid or strategy. The second approach deals not with an individual's own memory, but rather with the kind of collective or societal memory represented in large resource compendia. For example, suppose we try to search for specific information in a library, such as facts about memory retrieval. What key words will we use: *remembering, retrieval, recollection, recall, reconstruction,* or *recogni-*

tion? Chances are that the responses delivered by the system for the various key words will not be identical. Is there a way to program automated retrieval systems to capture the human mind's use of synonyms and near-synonyms to increase the effectiveness of these devices as memory retrieval systems? Specifically, the approach asks whether useful retrieval cues can function as effective memory aids when people use different key words to label the same concept or the same key words to refer to different concepts, as is characteristic of a flexible language like English. The third type of memory aid is the use of a cue (a museum) to retrieve memories of the past (recollections of visits to the museum) when the participants did not know at the time of the original visit that they would be asked for recall. What kinds of memories will be retrieved when a relatively nonspecific cue is used? Will this kind of autobiographical memory cue enrich our understanding of memory by divulging social, emotional, and situational components of memory?

The purpose of addressing these three, highly disparate types of memory aids is to gain some insight into their effectiveness and the boundary conditions that might govern the use of memory aids. I begin with a brief introduction to memory aids, and then examine the evidence for the three types of memory aids, before discussing the implications of these experiments for our knowledge of memory aids.

BACKGROUND

The defining characteristic of a memory aid strategy is that it constitutes a means to the end of retrieving a target memory or memories. Memory aid strategies are often divided into two types: internal and external. Internal strategies involve processes that occur in the mind, such as repetition, imagery, or rehearsal. External memory aids are devices such as notes, libraries, maps, and timers to assist memory retrieval. The postcuing technique examined in the first example is an internal aid; the electronic retrieval system and the museum visit are external aids.

Historically, psychologists have emphasized internal memory aid strategies, perhaps because of their portability: Our heads are always with us. Notes, timers, and electronic address books can be left behind. Some psychologists have assumed that the use of these latter aids does not really influence the access and retrieval of target memories. This attitude apparently arises from the view that external memory aids function like crutches, that they are little more than external storage devices and therefore do not qualify as "true" memory. Note, however, that although crutches themselves do not heal a broken leg, they facilitate healing. By analogy, external memory aids may not be core or target memories (defined as critical information encoded in mental representations), but they may facilitate retrieval of such memories.

We now know that a simple act such as writing reminder notes improves the chances of remembering the recorded items even when the notes are left behind (Intons-Peterson & Fournier, 1986). Furthermore, memory aids facilitate retention more through their use as retrieval cues than through rehearsal (Vortac, Edwards, & Manning, 1995). Thus, the role of external memory aids is important to the understanding and management of memory. Perhaps the most persuasive argument for external memory aids is the frequency of their use. In some survey studies (e.g., Harris, 1980; Intons-Peterson & Fournier, 1986) virtually all adult subjects claimed to use memory aids of one kind or another. This is not surprising when we think of how often we rely on reminder notes, both those we carry along with us and the calendar notes we may leave in our offices or homes. We rely on maps to guide our travels, photographs or other pictures to remind us of past journeys, calculators to supplement mental mathematical skills, and so forth. External memory aids are our constant companions.

More generally, memory aids and strategies function as context cues (Intons-Peterson, 1993; Intons-Peterson & Newsome, 1992). These cues may be part of the context associated with a target memory at the time of its original encoding, just as the images of a restaurant and of the meal may be stored as concomitants of a conversation at the restaurant. These associated cues enrich the target's stored representation. They also constitute cues for accessing the target discussion. This view of memory aids has the marked advantages of applying to both external and internal memory aids and bringing all memory aids into the fold of traditional memory research, with its extensive set of explanatory models, literature, and phenomena. Potential disadvantages are those of overlooking unique characteristics of memory aids that might distinguish among different types of memory aids or that might set memory aids apart from other memorial cues more centrally associated with target representations.

Memory aids may be classified in other ways. Some are noncommercial (e.g., notes, tying a string on one's finger); others are commercial (e.g., electronic address books, pill reminders). Memory aids vary in the generality of their use. Some are situationally specific (timers), whereas others have more widespread utility (writing reminder notes). Memory aids also vary in terms of flexibility, adaptability, and rated usefulness, with external aids typically viewed as more reliable and easier to use than internal ones. Some aids are relatively simple (e.g., maps, timers); others are more complex (e.g., strategies, computer databases, museums, musical scores). These more complex forms of memory aids are the focus of this chapter; studies of simpler forms have been reported previously (e.g., Harris, 1980; Intons-Peterson & Fournier, 1986; Intons-Peterson & Newsome, 1992).

In traditional memory models (e.g., Raaijmakers & Shiffrin, 1981), stimulus representations typically are assumed to contain information about characteristics of the stimulus, such as its name, contextual information, and conceptual associations. The memory for this multiassociational or networked representation is hypothesized to be accessed by retrieval cues. Retrieval of the memory for the stimulus is assumed to increase with the overlap between the representation of the original stimulus and the retrieval cue, a kind of encoding specificity (Tulving & Thomson, 1973). Thus, the greater the similarity of the retrieval cue to the original stimulus, the better recall will be. This view easily handles such internal memory aids as rehearsal, repetition, and imagery, because these aids may redintegrate part or all of the original stimulus. The view has difficulty with external memory aids, for many of these aids overlap only minimally with the original stimulus.

One purpose of this chapter is to examine three different, complex types of memory aids to ascertain the effectiveness of these three memory aid strategies. If they aid memory, how do they do so? What are the underlying mechanisms? Do these mechanisms relate to extant memory models?

POSTCUING AS A MEMORY AID

Suppose I introduce you to four strangers, one after the other. The first one turns to leave, and you want to use the person's name to acknowledge the introduction. What are the chances that you will remember the name? They are considerably lower than if you had chatted only with the first person. Introduction to the other people interferes with retention of the first name.

In this situation, new experiences interfere with retention of older information, the classical *retroactive interference* situation. Retroactive interference is pervasive. It plagues us constantly; hence, it would be beneficial to find a way to preserve older memories Obtaining an answer is not easy, because at least two problems hamper efforts to solve the dilemma. The first is that as time moves on, we constantly experience new situations and thereby place earlier memories in jeopardy. In the real world, learning does not exist in a vacuum. The second is that, once we are exposed to new knowledge, it is difficult, if not impossible, to "unlearn" it as a means of freeing older memories. These considerations suggest that we need to find a way either to eliminate new knowledge (which we may not want to do) or to isolate it (which seems difficult, but more promising). Extant memory models do not provide for a *re*coding of interpolated material. Obviously, we need a mechanism that can be applied, retroactively, to separate and distinguish recent from older material, such that the recent memories are isolated from the older ones.

Currently, models of memory search explain retroactive interference in terms of the greater availability of more recent items. They do not accommodate ex post facto recoding of new information. Is it possible for such recoding to occur? Bower and Mann (1992) answered affirmatively. They told subjects who had learned a second list about some distinctive, organizing characteristic of the second list (e.g., that the letters formed a word, that the city names also named American presidents). This "postcued" group recalled more items from the first list than did subjects who learned both lists but did not hear the postcue. Control subjects who did not learn a second list showed the best recall of the first list.

What underlies this retroactive cuing (postcuing) of the interpolated list? Presumably, the ex post facto information enables the subject to partition memory search such that candidate words retrieved from List 2 are rejected and retrieval of List 1 items is thereby facilitated. This partitioning might be achieved by a reorganization or restructuring of List 2, by editing retrieved items and suppressing those judged to come from List 2 (the time saved by rapid suppression of List 2 items could be allocated to additional memory search, an editing-plus-suppression hypothesis), or by consolidation (integration, increased cohesion) of List 2.

In the first experiment, we focused on restructuring and the editing-plus-suppression hypotheses. Although Bower and Mann (1992) posited restructuring, they did not present any evidence to support the conjecture. The restructuring hypothesis predicts a change in the organization of original List 2 recall after postcuing. The editing-plus-suppression notion holds that postcued subjects would edit and suppress more List 2 items than uninformed subjects would, so that the postcued subjects would show fewer List 2 intrusions on List 1 recall than uninformed subjects. Furthermore, if some List 1 items share characteristics of the List 2 items, the editing-plus-suppression hypothesis predicts that these special List 1 items will be more likely to be misassigned to List 2 on final free recall than will List 1 items that do not share the characteristics.

These predictions were tested with two lists of names of U.S. cities. The first list contained 16 names that were not names of U.S. presidents and 4 names of cities that also were names of U.S. presidents. The second list contained 20 city names that also were names of U.S. presidents. The names comprising each list were presented in a random order, for 5 seconds each. Then the names for the list were presented a second time, followed by a recall test, in which the subjects were asked to recall as many names as they could from List 2. After a delay filled with rating of cartoons for humor, the subjects were asked to try to recall all previously seen city names, placing those seen in the first list under the *List 1* heading, those seen in the second list under the *List 2* heading, and those names for which they could not remember the original list under the *Not Sure* heading. This procedure was used for a "postcued" group and for an "uninformed" group. The only difference in the treatment of these two groups was that just before final free recall, only the postcued group was told that the names of cities in List

2 also were names of presidents of the United States. Presumably, if postcuing facilitates retention of List 1, the postcued group would remember more List 1 names correctly than would the uninformed group, and List 1 final recall should be best for a control group that learned and was tested on List 1 only. The interval separating initial from final testing of List 1 was held constant for the three groups by having the experimental groups rate cartoons for humor for 6 minutes before the final test and having the control group do humor ratings for 11 minutes. The control group's performance on final List 1 recall provides a standard for judging the effects of List 2 on final List 1 retention.

The restructuring hypothesis predicts that, compared to the uninformed group, the postcued group would show a greater change in the organization of List 2 from initial to final recall. The editing-plus-suppression hypothesis predicts that, compared to the uninformed group, the postcued group would show fewer List 2 assignments to List 1 and more assignments of List 1 president-name cities to List 2.

After final free recall, all subjects who received both lists were asked if they had noticed anything "interesting" about List 2 during its first presentation and, if so, to write what they had found interesting on the back of their test paper. This procedure was followed because Bower and Mann (1992) found that some uninformed subjects detected that List 2 cities also were presidents' names. They did not report comparable information for the postcued group, so there is some possibility that their postcued group had detected the list differentiating principle during initial exposure to List 2. If so, this detection would invalidate the notion of a postcue.

Subsequent examination of the postexperimental responses of our postcued group indicated that 21 subjects realized that the names of List 2 were also those of U.S. presidents. These 21 subjects were called a "pre-post" group because they might have cued themselves during initial exposure to List 2, and they heard the postcue. The remaining 9 subjects constituted the true "postcue" group. Of the 48 subjects in the uninformed group, 35 detected the presence of presidents' names during initial exposure to List 2. These subjects were reassigned to a "self-cued" group, and the remaining 13 subjects were assigned to a "naive" group and treated as uninformed for purposes of prediction assessment. Subsequent analyses were conducted on five groups: postcued, pre-post, self-cued, naive, and control.

What did we find? The first question is whether List 1 recall would manifest retroactive interference by being significantly higher for the control group (List 1 only) than for the four other groups (List 1 plus List 2). The answer was yes. The mean final recall for List 1, adjusted for differences in initial List 1 recall, was significantly higher for the control group (10.20) than for the postcued (8.22), the self-cued (8.19), or the pre-post (7.40) groups, with the naive group (6.52) showing the poorest performance. Subsequent Tukey

HSD analyses showed that the pre-post and naive groups recalled significantly fewer List 1 items than did the control group, thus showing retroactive interference. However, List 1 final recall for the postcued and self-cued groups did not differ from that of the control, a situation Bower and Mann considered a reduction in retroactive interference.

These results could not be attributed to the control group's initial superior recall of List 1 because, although the differences among groups did not quite reach statistical significance, initial List 1 performance was used as a covariate for the analysis presented earlier. Moreover, the poorer performance of the naive group on final List 1 recall did not result from this group's greater attention to List 2, compared to the other groups, because the naive, postcued, self-cued, and pre-post groups had about the same mean initial List 2 recall (postcued = 11.00, self-cued = 13.23, pre-post = 12.90, and naive = 12.15). Similarly, final List 2 recall did not differ for these four groups when adjusted for initial List 2 recall (to be consistent with the List 1 analyses). The means for adjusted final List 2 recall for the four groups (in the same order) were 11.48, 11.77, 11.62, and 10.82.

So, having demonstrated retroactive interference, we probed the reasons for it. The restructuring hypothesis implied that the serial order of initial and final List 2 recall would change more for the postcued and self-cued groups than for the pre-post and naive groups. To examine this prediction, we first calculated the mean serial position of recall of each item recalled on the initial test and on the final test separately for the postcued, self-cued, pre-post, and naive groups. The associations between initial and final derived serial position means were analyzed for each of the four groups by calculating Spearman rank order correlations. The correlations were all nonsignificant, in contradiction to the restructuring hypothesis.

To further assess the restructuring hypothesis, we examined categorization shown by the four groups in original and final List 2 recall, when categorization of the president's names was defined in terms in serial order of input, of recall, alphabetically, or in chronological order of their service as president. The same analysis was applied to List 1 recall. In both cases, we were unable to find evidence that the postcued and self-cued groups had restructured List 2 (or List 1) representations more than had the pre-post and naive groups. These measures did not support a restructuring view.

Next, we considered an editing-plus-suppression retrieval search strategy. Suppose the postcued and self-cued groups were more likely than the pre-post and naive groups to adopt the strategy that when a retrieval search yielded a president's name, the city name should be assigned to List 2. Then postcued or self-cued subjects should be more likely than pre-post and naive subjects to assign president-name cities from List 1 to List 2. Furthermore, they should correctly recall and assign fewer presidents' names to List 1 than should the pre-post and naive groups. Neither prediction was supported, in part because erroneous list attributions were generally rare. Overall, most items recalled on final recall were assigned to the correct lists (95% of List 1 and 98% of List 2).

One interpretation of the results is that the negative impact of interpolated material can be attenuated by providing ex post facto cues about the interpolated material. We are skeptical. Our skepticism derives partly from the transparency of the presidents' name design. This very transparency may render the results artifactual in the sense that any intimation of the factor distinguishing List 2 from List 1 that occurs during initial exposure to the lists invalidates the concept of postcuing. The fact that 67% of the subjects exposed to List 2 detected the presence of presidents' name in List 2 makes us worry that the subjects who failed to detect the presidents' names were tired, daydreaming, inattentive, or somewhat history-deficient.

Consequently, we conducted another experiment in which all city names in List 1 had initial letters coming from the first half of the alphabet and all the new city names in List 2 had initial letters coming from the second half of the alphabet (or vice versa). This alphabetical distinction was camouflaged by including in the 20 cities of List 1, 4 cities that named animals and 4 that named natural features, and dividing the 20 cities of List 2 between animal names and natural feature names. When asked, postexperimentally, about unusual aspects of List 2, all subjects noticed the animal name and natural feature name aspects. It seemed, therefore, that we were successful in concealing the alphabetical split until it was mentioned just prior to final recall to the postcued group.

A fourth, "restructure," group was added to the postcued, uninformed, and control groups in Experiment 2. The restructure group was given 2 minutes to think about how they could keep items from the two lists apart.

The results showed that neither postcuing nor restructure instructions inhibited retroactive interference. Thus, neither strategy aided retention of the targeted memories. None of the groups exposed to List 2 showed a reduction in retroactive interference compared to the naive group. Adding to the negative evidence, Professor G. Bower told us that he has been unable to replicate his earlier findings. We must conclude that, at least with the current design and materials, postcuing is not an effective memory aid strategy. This conclusion is not surprising, given the lengthy history of unsuccessful attempts to combat retroactive interference, but it is disappointing.

What does the failure portend for memory aid strategies? We may glean hints, at most, from the failure of a single paradigm. Those hints are that, as noted in the brief history, internal memory strategies tend to be less effective than external ones, perhaps because they are more demanding. With an internal strategy, such as postcuing, the subject must understand the strategy, how to apply it, and then execute the strategy. To effectively reduce retroactive interference from List 2, the subjects had to recode, restructure, isolate, or in some way prevent the List 2 items from suppressing retrieval of List 1 items. Such recoding would have been both theoretically and practically significant. It was not to be. I turn next to a highly complex external memory aid, a computerized database.

STATISTICALLY DISCOVERED ASSOCIATIVE INFORMATION AS A MEMORY AID

Consider the problem of trying to retrieve information from large reference sources such as libraries, the yellow pages of a telephone book, or a medical encyclopedia. We may try to use an index, including electronic versions. If we are lucky enough to select a critical word we may find many references, some that are appropriate to our search, and some that are inappropriate. Inappropriate items presumably are delivered when the cue word references some relatively obscure connotation. More often than not, we will miss identifying some important items.

One reason the retrieval of information from external sources has been slighted is that the searcher's language may not match key words used to access the target information. Searchers may have only a vague notion of the most appropriate cue words. They may discover that the words they are considering differ from those in an index. In these cases, the information may be in the source, but the searcher can't access it. These retrieval difficulties, or "vocabulary mismatches," occur when an information seeker's words for finding an object or item of information differ from the words used by authors or indexers to describe the object or item. This problem is common; Dumais and her colleagues found that, for a wide array of domains, two people (a researcher and an indexer) generated the same descriptor for objects only 10% to 20% of the time (Furnas, Landauer, Gomez, & Dumais, 1987).

Vocabulary mismatches are barriers to the effective use of external databases because most of them are word-based. Two problems exist: synonymy and polysemy. With synonymy, different words may be used to describe essentially the same idea or concept, so the likelihood of a match is low. Blair and Maron (1985) found that up to 80% of known relevant materials were missed even by trained searchers familiar with their legal database. With polysemy, the same word may refer to different things or concepts. In a search, polysemy frequently yields irrelevant items. The problems of synonymy and polysemy must be overcome if electronic databases are to function as effective memory aids.

One way of thinking about the retrieval failures of word-based systems is that synonymous words and concepts may be uncorrelated. That is, a query about "cars" may be no more likely to retrieve information about "automobiles" than about "cats." Retrieval of "automobiles" is based on conceptual and semantic similarity, whereas retrieval of "cats" reflects superficial physical and syntactic similarity. This is clearly untrue of human memory, except when searching for alliterative words, and seems undesirable—even maladaptive—in computer systems. Dumais and her colleagues developed an automatic statistical method (Latent Semantic Indexing, or LSI) that can be used to discover important patterns in the use of words across different document contexts. The resulting "semantic space" can be used to improve people's ability to retrieve information from computer databases.

The LSI model uses a computerized analysis of the associations among words to identify vectors in "semantic space" that represent the location of each term in each document. The similarity of objects is measured by using the cosine or angle between vectors. In this model, the similarity of terms and documents is determined by the overall pattern of word usage in the entire collection, so documents can be similar to each other regardless of the precise words they contain. From a user's perspective, this means that documents can be similar to a query even if they share no common terms.

Dumais and her colleagues applied the LSI analysis of associative structure to several standard information-science text collections for which user queries and relevance assessments are available. LSI was an average of 20% better (and as much as 30% better) than other comparable word-based retrieval methods in discriminating relevant from irrelevant documents for these text queries (Deerwester, Dumais, Landauer, Furnas, & Harshman, 1990; Dumais & Schmitt, 1991). LSI has been equally successful for a variety of other related applications (e.g., information filtering, assigning manuscripts to reviewers, retrieving noisy pen input, cross language retrieval, and word sense disambiguation).

Finally, as Landauer and Dumais noted in their chapter (Vol. 1, chap. 7), LSI does not always identify synonyms. For example, the best matching *in*correct item for "nurse" was "doctor." "Doctor" was closer to "nurse" (.50) than to the correct synonym, "physician" (.43). Interestingly, although LSD delivered an incorrect synonym for "doctor," it identified an item, "nurse," that shares many associations with the target word of "doctor." Moreover, LSI performance improved as the size of the sample increased and when the sample represented the first 2,000 characters or approximately 350 words rather than full articles. Apparently, the most relevant information is contained in the early portions of texts.

Obviously, an electronic retrieval system aids identification of underlying networks of associations not necessarily immediately explicit to the searcher. The computer may know more about what the searcher wants to find than the searcher articulates easily! These systems are not perfect, however, and much work remains to be done, including extensions to units of analysis other than words. More needs to be learned about the correlations between LSI scores and human errors.

This research is designed to facilitate effective information retrieval from external electronic retrieval systems. It is clear that this form of external memory aid is reasonably successful and holds promise for increased effectiveness. Its utility stems from systematizing in a many-vectored space some of the associational relations among words. In brief, this systematizing and externalization of what is typically internal to human memory may be the key to its effectiveness. This is not to say that making the associations themselves explicit would enable subjects to consciously compute closeness or similarity functions in a large matrix. Instead, the intriguing result is that formalization of word association, correlational matrices exploits these relations to improve retrieval over the rate achieved by expert searchers of databases in their expertise.

MUSEUMS AS EXTERNAL MEMORY AIDS

Visits to museums serve a number of functions. They entertain, they introduce new concepts, and they may help to consolidate or amplify existing knowledge. Each of these functions may serve, individually or collectively, as aids to remembering knowledge or experience gained at a museum. Museum visits typically engage the visitor personally and often socially with the museum's physical objects, thereby further enhancing the utility of museums as memory aids. The importance of each of the latter components led Falk and Dierking (1992) to propose an "interactive experience" model to explain the impact of a museum visit on various facets of memory.

According to Falk and Dierking (1992), a participant's personal context (i.e., the knowledge, interests, and motivations) partly determines the influence of a visit. Similarly, a viewer's social context (coming alone, coming with peers, coming with families, etc.) also colors the visit, just as the physical context (the objects on display) affects what is retained. All three contexts appear in retrospective reports of people's memories of museum visits.

For example, the following summary emerged from more than 200 interviews of museumgoers conducted by Falk and Dierking (1992), Fivush, Hudson, and Nelson (1984), and Wolins (1991). According to Falk and Dierking (1992):

1. All had personalized the museum visit. Most details recalled directly to an interest or concern that existed *before* the museum visit.
2. All could explain whom they were with and why.
3. All could place the museum visit within a general geographical context. Nearly all referred to some aspect of the museum's physical context.
4. Most could recall at least a few exhibits and some specific details about them, although none could recall everything seen.

5. Nearly everyone remembered roughly the length of time in the museum and their mental state at the time, such as being bored or "hassled" (Falk & Dierking, p. 119).

Falk and Dierking considered these recollections to be best explained by their interactive experience model, and this seems to be a reasonable surmise. Moreover, the apparent significance of personal, social, and situational factors points to aspects of memory aids not usually considered.

The recollections tell us about museumgoers' general memories of the visit. This information may be sufficient for some purposes. The recollections do not tell us, however, about the extent to which the museum experience facilitated learning, aided organization of diverse experiences about a concept, or assisted memory in specific ways that could be tied directly to the museum experience.

These questions require controls to hold relatively constant previous exposure to the materials, knowledge of the concepts being tested, and the like. After these potential influences are controlled, some learners would have to be introduced to specific museum displays and explanations, whereas others would be deprived of this opportunity. Finally, the two groups would be tested to ascertain any increase in knowledge gained by the museum-exposed group. Needless to say, this rigorous approach to assessing the role of the museum as an external aid is difficult to engineer and probably would encounter parental and teacher resistance. It would be interesting to assess the degree of dependency on such knowledge on simultaneous retrieval of personal, social, and situational memories associated with the visit. Similarly, we could ask whether different kinds of museums vary in the kinds of memory matrices they deliver.

Overall, the use of an external cue (such as the name of a real-life experience) to investigate the contents of memory is clearly effective and may inform us about components of memory and their interactions not yet exploited. Thus, an external memory aid of this type is useful in exploring autobiographical memory.

COMMENTS AND CONCLUSIONS

Some central and enduring questions arise about memory aids (e.g., Herrmann & Searleman, 1990, 1992; Hertel, 1993; Intons-Peterson, 1993; Intons-Peterson & Newsome, 1992; Norman, 1988). Two theoretically important issues have to do with the degree to which the memory aids overlap with memory representations (a kind of encoding specificity; Tulving & Thomson, 1973). As external storage devices or reminder cues, external memory aids nicely demonstrate encoding specificity. They also tend to be relatively easy to use.

The most effective aids are those that closely capture the central information—a stipulation that may be difficult to achieve in retrieval from large reference sources due to vocabulary mismatches between original coders of information and subsequent information seekers, as shown by Dumais and her colleagues. Their use of computer databases to extract basic but at least partially implicit similarities suggests not only that encoding specificity is important but also that codifying surface characteristics of the language may not be particularly effective for individuals other than the original coders; this is a significant boundary condition.

The use of an electronic system also illustrates the difficulty of application. Some techniques are judged to be less reliable and more difficult to use than others (e.g., Intons-Peterson & Fournier, 1986). Unreliability may stem from vagaries in application (some people are more adept than others) or be inherent in the aids. Difficulty may reflect the use of a particularly complicated or multifaceted strategy or even an incompatibility with brain mechanisms.

Falk and Dierking's explorations of recall of museum visits suggest that less specific explicit memory aids elicit more varied, less predictable recollections. This unpredictability may be an asset if the purpose is to examine the diversity of associations to a previous experience. This approach, often used in studies of autobiographical memory, may enrich our conceptions of memory by demonstrating the influence of personal, social, and situational factors often overlooked by memory researchers.

At the internal aid end of the spectrum, the memory aid strategy of postcuing was not effective. Why? Encoding specificity was minimal. The postcue itself overlapped with the characteristics of List 2 only to the level of matching a vague categorization of the concepts of List 2 with the description given by the postcue. In other words, the learner had to conceptualize the items in List 2 as cities that also named presidents or that began with certain letters to utilize the postcue information. The postcue itself did not overlap specific List 2 items. Furthermore, internal aids do not seem to be as effective as external aids (as noted earlier). It was clear that subjects in the postcuing experiments were unable to use the postcuing information in a reliable, effective manner. If these healthy young adults had trouble, there is little reason to hope that the technique will assist the memory of impaired or elderly individuals. Indeed, some memory aid strategies may be too difficult or cumbersome to use efficiently. Alternatively, they may be incompatible with memorial mental machinery.

Encoding specificity is intertwined with the concept of context specificity that I assume underlies the context-sensitivity of memory aid strategies. It follows that to have an understanding of the conditions under which memory aids function effectively and to develop an appropriate model we must investigate the utility of more complex memory aid strategies, such as the three discussed in this chapter.

In summary, the current research extends previous efforts with simpler memory aids to more complex ones. The resulting data are compatible with a previous construal of memory aids as context-sensitive cues currently incorporated into models of memory retrieval (e.g., Search of Associative Memory; Raaijmakers & Shiffrin, 1981) or models with even broader scopes (e.g., Herrmann & Searleman, 1990, 1992; Johnson, 1983). This perspective of memory aids as context-sensitive disputes the notion that memory aids are unimportant to the study of memory. It has the attractive feature of bringing a substantial array of these cues into the memory framework, of melding memory aids with more traditional memory research, and of providing a more comprehensive understanding of the totality of memory.

REFERENCES

Blair, D. C., & Maron, M. E. (1985). An evaluation of retrieval effectiveness for a full-text document-retrieval system. *Communications of the ACM, 28*(3), 289–299.

Bower, G. H., & Mann, T. (1992). Improving recall by recoding interfering material at the time of retrieval. *Journal of Experimental Psychology: Learning, Memory, & Cognition, 18*, 1310–1320.

Deerwester, S., Dumais, S. T., Landauer, T. K., Furnas, G. W., & Harshman, R. A. (1990). Indexing by latent semantic analysis. *Journal of the Society for Information Science, 41*, 391–407.

Dumais, S. T., & Schmitt, D. G. (1991). Iterative searching in an online database. *Proceedings of Human Factors, Annual Meeting*, 398–402.

Falk, J. H., & Dierking, L. D. (1992). *The museum experience*. Washington, DC: Whalesback Books.

Fivush, R., Hudson, J., & Nelson, K. (1984). Children's long-term memory for a novel event: An exploratory study. *Merrill-Palmer Quarterly, 30*, 303–317.

Furnas, G. W., Landauer, T. K., Gomez, L. M., & Dumais, S. T. (1987). The vocabulary problem in human system communication. *Communication of the ACM, 30*, 964–971.

Harris, J. E. (1980). Memory aids people use: Two interview studies. *Memory & Cognition, 8*, 31–38.

Herrmann, D. J., & Searleman, A. (1990). The new multi-modal approach to memory improvement. In G. Bower (Ed.), *The psychology of learning and motivation* (pp. 175–205). New York: Academic Press.

Herrmann, D. J., & Searleman, A. (1992). Memory improvement and memory theory in historical perspective. In D. J. Herrmann, H. Weingartner, A. Searleman, & C. McEvoy (Eds.), *Memory improvement: Implications for memory theory* (pp. 8–20). New York: Springer-Verlag.

Hertel, P. T. (1993). Implications of external memory for investigations of mind. *Applied Cognitive Psychology, 7*, 665–674.

Intons-Peterson, M. J. (1993). External memory aids and their relation to memory. In C. Izawa (Ed.), *Cognitive Psychology Applied* (pp. 135–158). Hillsdale, NJ: Lawrence Erlbaum Associates.

Intons-Peterson, M. J., & Fournier, J. (1986). External and internal memory aids: When and how often do we use them? *Journal of Experimental Psychology: General, 115*, 267–280.

Intons-Peterson, M. J., & Newsome, G. L., III. (1992). External memory aids: Effects and effectiveness. In D. J. Herrmann, H. Weingartner, A. Searleman, & C. McEvoy (Eds.), *Memory improvement: Implications for memory theory* (pp. 101–121). New York: Springer-Verlag.

Johnson, M. K. (1983). A multiple-entry, modular memory system. In G. H. Bower (Ed.), *The psychology of learning and motivation* (Vol. 17, pp. 81–123). New York: Academic Press.

Norman, D. A. (1988). *The psychology of everyday things.* New York: Basic Books.

Raaijmakers, J. G. W., & Shiffrin, R. M. (1981). Search of associative memory. *Psychological Review, 88,* 93–134.

Tulving, E., & Thomson, D. M. (1973). Encoding specificity and retrieval processes in episodic memory. *Psychological Review, 80,* 352–373.

Vortec, O. U., Edwards, M. B., & Manning, C. (1995). Functions of external cues in prospective memory. *Memory, 3,* 201–219.

Wolins, I. S. (1991, May). *Children's memories for museum field trips: A qualitative study.* Paper presented at the 86th Annual Meeting of the American Association of Museums, Denver, CO.

CHAPTER TWENTY-THREE

The Promise of Compact Disc-interactive Technology for Memory Training With the Elderly

Dana J. Plude
Lisa K. Schwartz
University of Maryland

The memory training literature shows that older adults benefit from strategy training conducted by an instructor (or therapist) in either individualized or classroom settings (West, 1989; Yesavage, 1985). However, despite their demonstrated effectiveness among elderly trainees, mnemonic techniques are often abandoned within a relatively short span of time (Anschutz, Camp, Markley, & Kramer, 1985, 1987). Recently, Neely and Backman (1993) found that six months after mnemonic training elderly participants could effectively use learned strategies to facilitate word recall; however, fewer than 40% of the subjects reported actually using the strategies in their everyday life. Failure to generalize strategy usage outside the laboratory setting may reflect a deficiency in standard memory training procedures in that they typically do not involve real-life situations. In addition, the failure to generalize training outside of the laboratory may reflect the lack of sustained exposure to mnemonic training (Finkel & Yesavage, 1990; Riley, 1992). In order to be retained and effectively integrated into the older adult's strategic arsenal, mnemonic strategies must be continued and reinforced within the individual's everyday environment (Yesavage, 1985). Rarely, however, are memory training interventions available to the elderly on a daily basis, and this lack of availability doubtless undermines the sustained use of such skills. Clearly, additional means of training and education are necessary.

One alternate mode of training involves videotape. Videotape is desirable because it provides both visual and auditory information to aid remembering, thus providing a realistic analogue of everyday life. In fact, West and Crook

(1992) demonstrated that videotaped mnemonic training is effective in improving memory performance in middle-aged and older adults. Using a wait-list control design, they showed that both age groups learned and benefited from a variety of imagery-based mnemonic strategies. The authors concluded that videotape training has advantages over standard training methodologies in that it offers a cost-effective, self-paced intervention that can be enacted in the user's own home. Although it is clear that videotape incorporates these advantages, it is limited by its lack of interactivity. Viewing videotapes (or other standard television programming) is essentially a passive process, and there is evidence to suggest that interactive learning yields greater benefits, particularly in the acquisition of new skills (Barker & Tucker, 1990; Cunningham & Hubbold, 1992).

Another alternate mode of training, and one that is interactive in nature, involves computer-aided instruction (CAI), which has proven to be as effective in mnemonic training and memory assessment with the elderly as in vivo training with an instructor (e.g., Finkel & Yesavage, 1990; Larrabee & Crook, 1989). However, there is evidence to suggest that elderly individuals may be reluctant to work with computer systems (e.g., Temple & Gavillet, 1990), and even those who are positively inclined to do so (Thompson, 1992) are unlikely to have access to such systems in their homes (Hoot & Hayslip, 1983). Thus, although CAI has proven useful in mnemonic training with the elderly (Larrabee & Crook, 1992), because it is not a technology that many older adults have available within their households its suitability for maintaining trained skills is not evident.

Participants in a pilot study conducted in our laboratory expressed this very sentiment when asked about the prospect of using computer-based programs for memory training. Of the 48 subjects (community-residing adults between 59 and 81 years of age) who participated, none owned a computer and only three indicated that they had ever worked with a computer system. Moreover, none of the subjects indicated an interest in receiving memory training via a computer system. Thus, based on the evidence gathered to date, it appears that the best training alternative would combine the most desirable features of videotape training and CAI. Such an alternative is embodied in Compact Disc-interactive (CD-i) technology.

COMPACT DISC-INTERACTIVE TECHNOLOGY

Compact discs are no longer just for music. CD-i multimedia technology was introduced in Europe by NV Philips of Holland at the beginning of 1990 for industrial training. Currently, Philips, Magnavox, Sony, Goldstar, and others are marketing CD-i compatible players for residential use. CD-i technology offers consumers an easy-to-use interactive multimedia format that combines the power of computers with the ease of television. This new generation of compact disc player adds sophisticated graphics, video, and software to the hi-fidelity audio of CDs. CD-i represents as dramatic an improvement in video quality as compact discs do with stereo music and, in fact, CD-i players also play standard music CDs. The consumer needs only to connect the CD-i player to a television for use in the home. True interaction by the viewer with the disc program is accomplished through a simple hand-held remote control unit (similar to a TV remote control). CD-i technology and the remote control unit turn passive television viewing into an interactive experience.

The elderly constitute an especially important end-user group for CD-i technology for several reasons. First, CD-i technology minimizes complexity by interfacing directly with the user's own television set, a familiar medium that provides important scaffolding for CD-i programming. Second, CD-i technology bypasses potential "computer phobia" by making the system's on-board microprocessor invisible to the user. The availability of an interactive system that does not involve a microcomputer interface, but which provides the user with the equivalent power and flexibility of computer-based systems, is particularly desirable for the elderly population. And, third, CD-i technology provides a unique and revolutionary information/training medium that is well suited to elderly adults, especially in light of the cognitive (and other) changes that characterize normal aging.

In addition to the accessibility of the technology, CD-i programs are necessarily interactive and hold great promise for increasing home-based education. CD-i programs are particularly well suited for applications within educational gerontology because they: individualize the learning experience, enable the learner to set learning goals, provide feedback to the learner, provide positive reinforcement, and facilitate the practice of necessary skills. These are particularly desirable features of CD-i in light of the widely documented benefit derived by elderly adults from self-paced as compared with alternative procedures (Craik, 1977; Kausler, 1990), and especially so with respect to mnemonic training (Kotler-Cope & Camp, 1990). There is increasing evidence that self-control over training materials and options plays a key role in the efficacy of mnemonic training among the elderly (Elliot & Lachman, 1989), further enhancing the suitability of CD-i for this population. Moreover, instantaneous feedback is highly desirable and, as in commercially available video games, the CD-i system can be programmed to "remember" progression levels and provide individualized feedback to aid in self-pacing. The fact that CD-i programs comprise different channels of communication, such as visual (pictures and text), auditory (music and voice), and tactile (operating the remote control to select options), further enhances the learning experience. Because CD-i can be programmed to include all these factors in a learning experience, the technology represents a great improvement over videotapes for education and training. Moreover, as with audio CD players, the cost of CD-i systems has steadily declined as more manufacturers compete for market share. CD-i technology is, therefore, more affordable than CAI technology.

Their increasing affordability positions CD-i systems for replacing audio-only CD players and, with the recent development of full-motion video capability, videotape players for in-home use. Furthermore, our pilot research shows that older adults are likely to use such technology when it is available in the home. Indeed, the same pilot subjects (described previously) who rejected computer-based memory training expressed overwhelming interest in CD-i as a vehicle for skill development. After interacting individually with a CD-i program entitled "Treasures of the Smithsonian," all but 4 of the 48 subjects rated the CD-i system as either extremely enjoyable or considerably enjoyable (scores of 5 or 4 on a 5-point Likert scale). The availability of such programming within the comfort and convenience of one's own home provides opportunity for CD-i programs to be consulted frequently in order to solidify learning. As noted earlier, everyday availability is an important adjunct to successful mnemonic training programs for the elderly but one that is often absent (Anschutz et al., 1985, 1987).

CD-i BASED MEMORY TRAINING

Given the receptivity to CD-i technology expressed within our initial pilot study, we embarked on developing a CD-i based memory training program called "The Memory Works." The program is motivated by an approach to memory training that emphasizes the necessity of tailoring particular strategies to meet individual needs and task demands (Herrmann, 1991; Herrmann & Searleman, 1990). Thus, the program comprises a multidimensional approach to training that explicitly recognizes the increased range of individual differences among older adult learners (Riley, 1992). Many studies have shown that compared to younger adults who use both internal and external memory strategies, the elderly rely disproportionately on external aids (Jackson, Bogers, & Kerstholt, 1988; West, 1988), and it is not clear that their usage is optimal (West, 1989). Whether the elderly's overreliance on external aids represents a compensatory adjustment in later life or acquiescence to a negative stereotype of aging remains an unresolved issue (Backman, 1989; Rebok & Offerman, 1983). Nevertheless, numerous studies have demonstrated unequivocal benefits of mnemonic training among the elderly (Yesavage, Lapp, & Sheikh, 1989), and The Memory Works program capitalizes on the multimedia environment of CD-i for mnemonic skill development.

The memory improvement literature shows that training on tasks that simulate everyday activities yields effective gains among elderly adults and generalizes to the real-world activities being simulated (West, 1992; West & Crook, 1990). In addition, Poon (1980) identified five critical ingredients for a successful cognitive intervention program: (a) it should inculcate the attitude that the learner is capable of carrying out the desired changes in behavior and will be successful in undertaking efforts to do so, (b) it should provide some measure of progress to demonstrate the efficacy of the skill for the learner, (c) it should provide salient intrinsic and extrinsic reinforcers to maintain the skill, (d) it should encourage the learner to practice the skills periodically, and (e) it should be sensitive to individual differences. Not only does The Memory Works program incorporate each of these objectives, but it also provides for a sixth ingredient suggested by Poon as being perhaps the most pivotal: The program should provide appropriate feedback that the newly acquired skills are helping the learner in daily life. Such positive feedback provides convincing evidence that the acquired skills are of constructive use, and thereby strengthens the learner's resolve to continue using the skills to advantage.

The initial development of the program focused on name–face memory; however, the ultimate goal of the project is to address a wide variety of everyday memory situations and the strategies best suited for their successful navigation (Herrmann, 1991). In addition, to aid in solidifying the techniques that are trained, the program will provide information about different conceptualizations of memory (e.g., short-term and long-term storage, visual and verbal memory, etc.). The intent is to provide the user with an integrative training medium and explicit rationale for such training, both of which are crucial components of effective mnemonic training programs for the elderly (Yesavage, 1985). In addition, gamelike simulations of everyday memory situations (e.g., the market, a dinner party) will be used in assessing the user's ability to implement such newly acquired techniques.

A review of the literature identifies several domains of memory as excellent candidates for inclusion in the prototype; however, by far the most commonly cited domain centers on name–face memory (Plude & Murphy, 1992; Smith & Winograd, 1978; Yesavage, Rose, & Bower, 1983). In addition to the empirical and theoretical bases for developing this particular component as established in the cognitive aging literature, there was also a practical rationale for its development. The practical rationale centered on our interest in utilizing the full potential of the multimedia environment of CD-i. Among the various strategies proven effective for remembering names and faces are several that rely on visual imagery. In light of the fact that visual imagery appears to pose a particular difficulty for older subjects (Poon, Walsh-Sweeny, & Fozard, 1980; Winograd & Simon, 1980), the name–face memory component provided opportunity to exploit the full potential of the CD-i format. Thus, the domain of name–face memory was targeted for full-scale development in the prototype, with other domains, such as remembering misplaced objects, lists, and important facts, to be included in the final version of the program.

Further support for the focus on name–face memory in the prototype was obtained from a sample of 74 older adults (58–81 years of age) who provided feedback about the memory-training domains targeted in the long-term project. We developed a questionnaire containing five general domains of memory intervention: (a) General Information About Memory (e.g., common memory problems, effects of disease, etc.), (b) Knowledge (e.g., facts, phone numbers, etc.), (c) Events (e.g., personal introductions, misplaced items, etc.), (d) Intentions (e.g., routine tasks, errands, etc.), and (e) Actions (e.g., interrupted activity, conversational slips, etc.). Subjects indicated their interest in each topic by checking the appropriate response (Yes/No). The survey responses confirmed this sample of older adults' interest in memory training generally, and remembering names and faces in particular. For example, fully 100% of the sample responded in the affirmative to "Ways to improve your memory" and 91% responded likewise to "Common memory problems." Importantly, 93% of the sample indicated an interest in improving memory for "Names of people introduced to you" and 88% indicated an interest in remembering "Names of old acquaintances." Thus, the survey results supported the full-scale development of the name–face memory component.

The name–face memory module of the prototype assists the user in making memory strategy choices in everyday situations, such as meeting new acquaintances at a community center or super market. The module incorporates two strategies proven effective in enhancing memory for names and faces. One strategy is based on the "double transposition" mnemonic (Cermak, 1975; McCarty, 1980), which combines verbal mediation and visual imagery of names and faces. In brief, the procedure involves creating bizarre, interacting images that combine a distinctive feature of the person's face and an image based on the person's name. Older persons have been shown to benefit from this technique (cf. Kotler-Cope & Camp, 1990). The second strategy is based on the "SALT" method (Herrmann, 1991), in which the label serves as an acronym for enacting the strategy: *S*ay the person's name; *a*sk the person a question, using the name; (at) *l*east one time during the interaction use the person's name again; and *t*erminate the interaction by using the person's name a last time. Recent evidence suggests that individuals who are adverse (for whatever reason) to using imagery-based strategies (such as the double transposition mnemonic) benefit by employing the SALT method (Herrmann, 1991). Thus, in order to accommodate individual differences in strategy preference, the SALT method was included as an option in the prototype. It should be noted that despite the proven effectiveness of both techniques for enhancing name–face memory few attempts have made to implement them on computer-based systems due to the considerable graphics-memory demands of name–face stimulus materials (Finkel & Yesavage, 1990). CD-i offers the perfect solution to this limitation by providing sufficient memory capacity and flexibility to provide quality graphics, text, and auditory presentation.

CD-i MEMORY TRAINING PILOT STUDY

The prototype CD-i program was tested for interest and use by another sample of 24 older adults (63–82 years of age) who were community-residing participants in a senior citizen fitness and activity program at a local community college. The pilot test materials included The Memory Works prototype disc, which was played in a Phillips CDi-6102 player interfaced to a color television monitor, and two questionnaires, one of which was completed upon entering the test session (i.e., the intake interview) and the other of which was completed after the CD-i training session (i.e., posttraining interview). The intake interview included questions regarding demographic background, such as years of education and experience with video and computer-based systems. The posttraining interview included questions specifically tailored to the contents of The Memory Works prototype and to CDi-based training more generally. The training session engaged the subject in working directly with The Memory Works prototype program, which includes background information (the introduction), a name–face memory pretest, strategy training, a name–face memory posttest, and a simulation within which to practice remembering names. Within the pre- and posttests, a grid of eight photographs was displayed, and the subject was prompted to query each photograph for the person's name. After all eight cells were queried, the photographs were rearranged in the grid and the subject was required to remember each name. For the purpose of collecting recall data, the subject was provided with a data sheet containing eight cells spatially arrayed as on the screen with instructions to write each person's name within the cells of the data sheet. Upon completing as many names as possible, the subject was provided feedback about recall accuracy.

Data were evaluated for both the pre-/posttests as well as the questionnaire responses. Name–face memory scores increased reliably from the pretest ($M = 1.9$, $SD = 1.9$) to the posttest ($M = 3.25$, $SD = 2.1$). However, this difference must be taken with a note of caution insofar as there was no control group against which to evaluate the efficacy of training. Because we were interested primarily in the subject's evaluation of the names and faces module, all subjects were exposed to the training content. (A full-scale controlled experiment is underway.)

The intake interview yielded several noteworthy findings. First, the intake data confirmed our earlier pilot research by revealing that the majority of subjects (79%) reported experiencing memory problems generally defined and that one half of them (50%) reported experiencing problems with attention. Second, the pilot data indicate that although 75% of the subjects own a VCR, only 25% of them own or have used a computer. Third, when asked whether they prefer an interactive (question-and-answer) or noninteractive (lecture-style) learning format, 74% favored the former. And, fourth, when asked to indicate a preference for one of five training formats (i.e., textbook, audiotape, video, lecture, or specialist), the most popular choice was "video," with 39% of the subjects favoring this format. Based on these latter two findings, it appears that an interactive video format is most attractive.

The posttraining interview also yielded several noteworthy results that support further development of CD-i memory training programs. In brief, subjects expressed that they enjoyed working with the program, that learning with it was easy, that it took little time to feel comfortable with the program, and that they would like to use the program again. The subjects also indicated that the information was presented clearly and that sufficient information was presented to learn the strategy. In fact, a follow-up phone survey in which 22 of the 24 subjects were contacted between 3 and 4 weeks after pilot testing revealed that 20 of the subjects (91%) were able to reiterate the basic components of the name–face mnemonic strategy.

In summary, the work we have completed to date supports the viability of CD-i technology as an effective, enjoyable, and interactive mode of memory training. Thus, it holds great promise as an alternative medium for skill development not only for elderly adults but for other age groups as well.

ACKNOWLEDGMENTS

We thank Jacqueline Levasseur, Mark Mann, and Patricia Staughton for assisting in data collection, and Paula Hertel for providing feedback on an earlier draft of this chapter. We also thank Bob Rager of Compact Disc Inc. for use of the CD-i program entitled, "THE MEMORY WORKS," and one of the CD-i players used in our research. We also wish to express our gratitude to Dr. Richard Manse and the participants in the Senior Adult Program at Prince George's Community College, Largo, MD. The research reported here was supported in part by the Graduate Research Board of the University of Maryland, College Park.

REFERENCES

Anschutz, L., Camp, D. J., Markley, R. P., & Kramer, J. J. (1985). Maintenance and generalization of mnemonics for grocery shopping by older adults. *Experimental Aging Research, 11*, 157–160.

Anschutz, L., Camp, D. J., Markley, R. P., & Kramer, J. J. (1987). Remembering mnemonics: A 3-year follow-up on the effects of mnemonics training in elderly adults. *Experimental Aging Research, 13*, 141–143.

Backman, L. (1989). Varieties of memory compensation by older adults in episodic remembering. In L. W. Poon, D. C. Rubin, & B. A. Wilson (Eds.), *Everyday cognition in adulthood and late life* (pp. 509–544). New York: Cambridge University Press.

Barker, J., & Tucker, R. N. (1990). *The interactive learning revolution: Multimedia in education and training.* New York: Nichols.

Cermak, L. S. (1975). *Improving your memory.* New York: McGraw-Hill.

Craik, F. I. M. (1977). Age differences in human memory. In J. E. Birren & K. W. Schaie (Eds.), *Handbook of the psychology of aging* (pp. 384–420). New York: Van Nostrand Reinhold.

Cunningham, S., & Hubbold, R. J. (1992). *Interactive learning through visualization: The impact of computer graphics in education.* New York: Springer-Verlag.

Elliot, E., & Lachman, M. E. (1989). Enhancing memory by modifying control beliefs, attributions, and performance goals in the elderly. In P. S. Fry (Ed.), *Psychological perspectives of helplessness and control in the elderly* (pp. 339–367). Amsterdam: Elsevier.

Finkel, S. I., & Yesavage, J. A. (1990). Learning mnemonics: A preliminary evaluation of a computer-aided instruction package for the elderly. *Experimental Aging Research, 15,* 199–201.

Herrmann, D. (1991). *Supermemory.* New York: Random House.

Herrmann, D., & Searleman, A. (1990). The new multimodal approach to memory improvement. In G. H. Bower (Ed.), *The psychology of learning and motivation* (Vol. 26, pp. 175–205). New York: Academic Press.

Hoot, J. L., & Hayslip, B., Jr. (1983). Microcomputers and the elderly: New directions for self-sufficiency and life-long learning. *Educational Gerontology, 9,* 493–499.

Jackson, J. L., Bogers, H., & Kerstholt, J. (1988). Do memory aids aid the elderly in their day to day remembering? In M. M. Gruneberg, P. E. Morris, & R. N. Sykes (Eds.), *Practical aspects of memory: Current research and issues* (Vol. 2, pp. 137–142). Chichester, England: Wiley.

Kausler, D. H. (1990). *Experimental psychology and human aging* (2nd ed.). New York: Wiley.

Kotler-Cope, S., & Camp, C. C. (1990). Memory interventions in aging populations. In E. A. Lovelace (Ed.), *Aging and cognition: Mental processes, self-awareness, and interventions* (pp. 231–261). Amsterdam: Elsevier.

Larrabee, G. J., & Crook, T. H. (1989). Dimensions of everyday memory in age-associated memory impairment. *Psychological Assessment: A Journal of Consulting and Clinical Psychology, 1,* 92–97.

Larrabee, G. J., & Crook, T. H. (1992). A computerized battery for assessment of memory. In R. L. West & J. D. Sinnott (Eds.), *Everyday memory and aging: Current research and methodology* (pp. 54–65). New York: Springer-Verlag.

McCarty, D. L. (1980). Investigation of a visual imagery mnemonic device for acquiring face–name associations. *Journal of Experimental Psychology: Human Learning and Memory, 6,* 145–155.

Neely, A. S., & Backman, L. (1993). Maintenance of gains following multi-factorial and uni-factorial memory training in late adulthood. *Educational Gerontology, 19,* 105–117.

Plude, D. J., & Murphy, L. J. (1992). Aging, selective attention, and everyday memory. In R. L. West & J. D. Sinnott (Eds.), *Everyday memory and aging: Current research and methodology* (pp. 235–245). New York: Springer-Verlag.

Poon, L. W. (1980). A systems approach for the assessment and treatment of memory problems. In J. M. Ferguson & C. B. Taylor (Eds.), *The comprehensive handbook of behavioral medicine* (Vol. 1, pp. 191–212). New York: Spectrum.

Poon, L. W., Walsh-Sweeney, L., & Fozard, J. L. (1980). Memory skill training for the elderly: Salient issues on the use of imagery mnemonics. In L. W. Poon, J. L. Fozard, L. S. Cermak, D. Arenberg, & L. W. Thompson (Eds.), *New directions in memory and aging: Proceedings of the George A. Talland Memorial Conference* (pp. 461–484). Hillsdale, NJ: Lawrence Erlbaum Associates.

Rebok, G. W., & Offerman, L. R. (1983). Behavioral competencies of older college students: A self-efficacy approach. *The Gerontologist, 23,* 428–432.

Riley, K. P. (1992). Bridging the gap between researchers and clinicians: Methodological perspectives and choices. In R. L. West & J. D. Sinnott (Eds.), *Everyday memory and aging: Current research and methodology* (pp. 182–189). New York: Springer-Verlag.

Smith, A. D., & Winograd, E. (1978). Adult age differences in remembering faces. *Developmental Psychology, 14,* 443–444.

Temple, L. L., & Gavillet, M. (1990). The development of computer confidence in seniors: An assessment of changes in computer anxiety and computer literacy. *Activities, Adaptation & Aging, 14,* 63–76.

Thompson, D. (1992). Applications of psychological research for the instruction of elderly adults. In R. L. West & J. D. Sinnott (Eds.), *Everyday memory and aging: Current research and methodology* (pp. 173–181). New York: Springer-Verlag.

West, R. L. (1988). Prospective memory and aging. In M. M. Gruneberg, P. E. Morris, & R. N. Sykes (Eds.), *Practical aspects of memory: Current research and issues* (Vol. 2, pp. 119–125). Chichester, England: Wiley.

West, R. L. (1989). Planning and practical memory training for the aged. In L. W. Poon, D. C. Rubin, & B. A. Wilson (Eds.), *Everyday cognition in adulthood and late life* (pp. 573–597). New York: Cambridge University Press.

West, R. L. (1992). Everyday memory and aging: A diversity of tests, tasks, and paradigms. In R. L. West & J. D. Sinnott (Eds.), *Everyday memory and aging: Current research and methodology* (pp. 3–22). New York: Springer-Verlag.

West, R. L., & Crook, T. H. (1990). Age differences in everyday memory: Laboratory analogues of telephone number recall. *Psychology and Aging, 5,* 520–529.

West, R. L., & Crook, T. H. (1992). Video training of imagery for mature adults. *Applied Cognitive Psychology, 6,* 307–320.

Winograd, E., & Simon, E. W. (1980). Visual memory and imagery in the aged. In L. W. Poon, J. L. Fozard, L. S. Cermak, D. Arenberg, & L. W. Thompson (Eds.), *New directions in memory and aging: Proceedings of the George A. Talland Memorial Conference* (pp. 485–506). Hillsdale, NJ: Lawrence Erlbaum Associates.

Yesavage, J. A. (1985). Nonpharmacologic treatments for memory losses with normal aging. *American Journal of Psychiatry, 142,* 600–605.

Yesavage, J. A., Lapp, D., & Sheikh, J. I. (1989). Mnemonics as modified for use by the elderly. In L. W. Poon, D. C. Rubin, & B. A. Wilson (Eds.), *Everyday cognition in adulthood and late life* (pp. 598–611). New York: Cambridge University Press.

Yesavage, J. A., Rose, T. L., & Bower, G. H. (1983). Interactive imagery and affective judgments improve face–name learning in the elderly. *Journal of Gerontology, 38,* 197–203.

Automated Voice Messages for Health Care

Von O. Leirer
Elizabeth Decker Tanke
Daniel G. Morrow
Decision Systems, Los Altos, CA

> *Could we know what men [people] are most apt to remember, we might know what they are most apt to do.*
>
> —Halifax

This chapter summarizes our efforts toward developing and commercializing automated voice message reminders for increasing adherence to health care instructions. Most automated voice messaging in health care is concerned with improving patients' performance of some future behavior. Our research focuses on improving recall and performance of such future behaviors as taking medication and attending appointments because of their prevalence in health care and because of the potential cost savings from improved adherence (Barron, 1980; Cooper, Love, & Raffoul, 1982; Ulmer, 1987). This report marks the beginning of automated message design research. Because of its importance in a variety of technology applications (i.e, more and more machines are talking to us) we believe that automated voice messaging research should be a rapidly growing area of applied cognitive psychology.

Nonadherence to health care instructions results in unnecessary illness and reduced health care provider efficiency (Carasanos, Stewart, & Cluff, 1974; Cooper et al., 1982; Snyder & Hutton, 1989; Ulmer, 1987) and, therefore, increases health care costs for patients and society. The potential health care cost savings from reducing nonadherence is great. For example, an estimated 3% of all hospitalizations in the United States are due to medication nonadherence (Cooper et al., 1982). Appointment nonadherence is also a significant problem (Barron, 1980). In our own public health research, we conservatively estimated[1] the cost savings from using automated voice messages to increase appointment adherence in tuberculosis care to total $62,670.50 per year in one local clinic. If this is typical of the 1,700 tuberculosis clinics across the United States, then using automated reminders would save taxpayers $106,539,850 each year in tuberculosis treatment and at the same time improve patient care (Tanke, 1992). Later in this chapter, we overview much larger savings potential in hospital, HMO, and group practices.

The research discussed here was completed in the context of developing and validating an automated, microcomputer-based voice messaging system we have named TeleMinder® (Leirer, Morrow, Pariante, & Doksum, 1989; Leirer, Tanke, & Morrow, 1993). TeleMinder® is designed to telephone patients or receive calls from patients and, speaking in prerecorded human voice, give individualized and interactive health care instructions. These instructions are typically such things as reminders to take medications (Leirer, Morrow, Tanke, & Pariante, 1991), preappointment health care procedure instructions (Leirer et al., 1989), or reminders for upcoming appointments (Tanke & Leirer, 1994). The instructions are individualized: Messages automatically include information specific to individual patients. The instructions are interactive: Patients can request additional information or respond to questions by pressing numbers on their phone's number pad. For example, an appointment reminder might include the appointment time, date, location, health care giver's name, clinic or room number, and any preappointment procedures that must be followed. TeleMinder® may interact by asking the patient to press numbers on the telephone's keypad to have information repeated or to verbally confirm that the patient will be attending the appointment. Individualized and interactive voice messaging provides a much more precise and effective communication medium than simple tape-recorded messages or postcard reminders.

In the following sections, we review our research related to effective message design and, in the process, discuss both our successes and failures in increasing patients' adherence through automated instructions. Both the successes and failures emphasize the importance of validating message protocols before releasing them for general use by the health care industry.

THE IMPORTANCE OF TESTING
AND VALIDATING AUTOMATED MESSAGES

Prior to TeleMinder®, a number of unsuccessful attempts were made at developing an effective automated voice messaging system. A principal suspect in these failures was faulty message design that confused and/or

---

[1]This estimate does not include the resulting cost savings from the more difficult to measure, increased prevention of active cases of tuberculosis, more rapid identification and treatment of active cases, and fewer instances of drug resistant tuberculosis brought on by nonadherence.

alienated patients. Thus, like all other health care procedures, the success of automated voice messaging depends on designing and validating specialized message protocols so they can, in turn, be used with good effect by health care providers.

Our research in automated voice message design and validation involves three areas of cognitive psychology: prospective memory, discourse processing, and social cognition. To be an effective prospective memory aid, automated voice message instruction must be intelligible, rememberable, and provide all of the necessary information to successfully perform the specified actions. As such, automated reminders are a specialized form of spoken, instructional discourse and are therefore subject to all of the factors affecting discourse processing and comprehension. Finally, there is a social-cognitive component to the automated voice message. Automated messages should address such aspects of the listeners as: preferred language, culturally specific communication protocol, health care beliefs and attitudes, and interpersonal perceptions of health care providers.

As suggested earlier, generic messages may not effectively address the needs of different patient populations. For example, an automated message designed and validated for improving appointment adherence of well-educated, middle socioeconomic class, English-speaking patients to hypertension clinics may have little impact on adherence of poorly educated, low socioeconomic class, non-English-speaking patients to tuberculosis clinics. Likewise, speech rates and sentence structures easily understood and remembered by young patients may be poorly comprehended and remembered by older patients (Marics & Williges, 1988; Stine, Wingfield, & Poon, 1986). Thus, designing and then validating specialized messages for use in automated voice message systems is an essential part of successfully using this technology.

Prospective Memory and Automated Reminders

When we first began research on improving health care adherence, there was a growing opinion in the adherence literature that prospective memory failure was not part of the adherence problem, particularly among older patients. Researchers argued that social-cognitive aspects such as patients' attitudes and beliefs were the principal reasons for nonadherence (e.g., Carasanos et al., 1974).

Our initial experiments provided evidence that there is, in fact, a substantial component of prospective memory failure involved in nonadherence. In two separate studies we used a simulated medication adherence task, so that neither adverse side effects nor cost factors could contribute to intentional nonadherence. We found nonadherence levels in the control conditions as high as those found in previously published literature where intentional nonadherence was presumably the cause (Leirer, Morrow, Pariante, & Sheikh, 1988; Leirer et al., 1991). By using automated voice message reminders to reduce prospective memory demands, we were able to virtually eliminate nonadherence in simulated medication adherence (Leirer et al., 1991).

Instructional Discourse Processing and Automated Reminders

Our initial studies in medication adherence used automated reminder messages with explicit instructions about what medications to take and were sent by telephone at the exact times the medications were to be taken (Leirer et al., 1988, 1991). This began our ongoing series of basic research studies investigating: what information should be included in medication instructions (e.g., Morrow, Leirer, & Sheikh, 1988), and how people's preexisting cognitive representations or schemes for medication and appointment instructions affects preferred organization, comprehension, and recall (Morrow, Leirer, Altieri, & Tanke, 1991; Morrow, Leirer, Andrassy, & Tanke, 1993).

To date, we have found intersubject consistency when people are asked to arrange individual sentences (i.e., information units) of an instruction set in their preferred ordering. We found intersubject consistency when we asked people to group individual sentences of an instruction set according to subjective categories of information that go together. We found independent groups of subjects most preferred these sentence orderings and grouping formats to other formats. Finally, we found that free recall of instruction sets is highest when presented in a way that is consistent with the preferred ordering and grouping of sentences (Morrow et al., 1991, 1993; Morrow, Leirer, & Altieri, 1995). These findings suggest that patients have a preferred ordering for information about how to take medication and how to attend appointments and that automated instructions organized according to these preferred orderings should optimize patients' comprehension and recall of the instructions.

Social/Cognitive Factors and Automated Reminders

In this area of message design we have made significant advances but have also encountered significant failures. Our greatest success has been in developing and implementing in the TeleMinder® software an automated multilanguage capability. Although it is relatively easy to create static messages in different languages, it is difficult to create dynamic messages that automatically speak such things as appointment times, dates, and quantitative information. This is because of differences in speech rules across languages and because of irregularities within languages when speaking times, dates, and numbers. For example, in English, the numbers 11 through 19 are spoken irregularly and do not follow the conventions used for speaking other numbers. Solving this problem has made it possible for us to automate messages in virtually any language no matter how obscure or unique its syntax (Tanke, 1993). Having this multilanguage capability makes it possible to provide automated instructions to all patients in their primary language. To date we have conducted field studies of automated instruction protocols using 14 different languages.

When we have attempted to increase instruction adherence by adding persuasive content, we have been less successful. For example, authority endorsement (Hass, 1981; Hovland, Janis, & Kelley, 1953) and importance statements (Janz & Becker, 1984; Larson, Bergman, Heidrich, Alvin, & Schneeweiss, 1982) should either independently or in combination improve adherence. However, to date, we have found no evidence of such an effect (Tanke & Leirer, 1994).

Speaking patients' names and asking them to confirm their intention to adhere as part of the reminder should increase adherence (Werner, 1978; Wurtele, Galanos, & Roberts, 1980). Again, we have found no impact of these alone or in combination (Tanke, 1993).

Our own patient surveys suggest that many public health care patients have difficulty arranging either time away from work or transportation to get to appointments. Thus, a reminder call 3 or 5 days before an appointment should give patients more time to arrange to go to appointments and therefore increase adherence over a reminder call the evening before the appointment. We have not found that the 3- and 5-day preappointment reminder improved adherence over the 1-day reminder. However, we did find that two reminders (one the evening before and one five days before the appointment) reduced nonadherence more than either one alone (Tanke, 1993). It may be that the 5-day ahead reminder gave patients an opportunity to arrange to go to the appointment and the 1-day ahead reminder helped them to remember to actually go to their appointment. Or, it may be that two calls simply increased the probability of accurate prospective recall. Similarly, we found that giving both preappointment reminders and one or two follow-up calls (when the patient failed to keep the original appointment) increases eventual adherence (Tanke, 1993). This suggests that for some patient populations, two automated reminder calls may significantly improve appointment adherence.

Within the context of automated reminders, we have failed to support a number of social-cognitive theory-driven guidelines for message design. Although such failures are important for theory development, they are also important for applied automated message design. For example, although it is intuitively appealing, we have found no evidence to support the need to include the patient's name in many types of reminder messages. This means that simpler (e.g., nameless) messages can be used with as much effectiveness as more complex ones in some types of reminder calls. Finding opportunities to shorten and simplify messages without sacrificing effectiveness translates into time and money savings for the users of automated voice message technology.

In the next section we overview some of the success we have had by employing this integrated, empirical approach to designing automated voice messages.

INCREASED APPOINTMENT ADHERENCE THROUGH AUTOMATED REMINDERS

Our initial investigation of automated voice messaging to increase appointment adherence was in the area of influenza vaccination clinic and tuberculosis medication clinic appointments among older adult populations. In the influenza study we were able to increase adherence by several hundred percent (Leirer et al., 1989). In the tuberculosis medication clinic adherence study we decreased elders' appointment nonadherence by 21% across a number of different ethnic groups (Tanke & Leirer, 1993).

Since then we have designed and investigated the effectiveness of automated appointment reminders in a number of different types of health care settings and clinics. A general pattern of findings is emerging and it is summarized in Fig. 24.1. First, nonadherence can be reduced across a broad range of clinical settings and applications by using specialized messages that are well designed and validated. Reduction of nonadherence is typically 20% or greater and this applies across all ethnic groups studied, as long as preferred languages are used in the messages (Tanke & Leirer, 1994). Using well-designed reminders can mean an average reduction in immediate lost opportunity cost of 20% or more. Less immediate and more difficult to measure lost opportunity costs include increased and/or prolonged patient illness because of missed opportunities for earlier treatment. Reducing missed appointments also reduces attendance variance, which means health care providers can more effectively use such techniques as overbooking to increase clinic or office efficiency.

INCREASED MEDICATION ADHERENCE THROUGH AUTOMATED REMINDERS

Medication nonadherence has long been recognized as one of the most dangerous, costly, and widespread problems in health care. For example, between 4% and 35% of nonadhering elders endanger their lives (Carasanos et al., 1974), and 90% of this nonadherence is underadherence (Stewart &

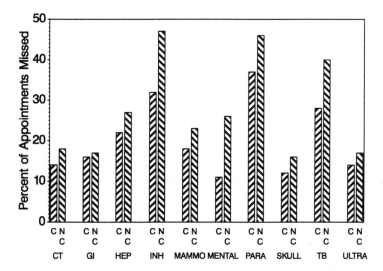

FIG. 24.1. Appointment nonadherence with and without TeleMinder® reminder calls. C = TeleMinder® call, NC = No TeleMinder® call. CT, GI, MAMMO, SKULL, and ULTRA are University Medical Center Radiology Clinics. HEP, INH, PARA, and TB are County Health Department Clinics. MENTAL is a VA–Medical Center Clinic.

Cluff, 1972). We have designed and investigated the effectiveness of automated medication reminders in simulated adherence studies and are now conducting validation studies in actual clinical settings. In a simulated medication adherence study, we found that even complicated, 10-dose-per-day schedules are adhered to at a constant rate of 98% by older adults who received well-designed automated voice message reminders. When no reminders were given, average performance dropped below 70% by the end of a 2-week period (Leirer et al., 1991).

We are currently conducting clinical trials at two separate tuberculosis treatment clinics to assess the impact of a specialized automated voice message protocol for a standard 6-month prevention therapy. This treatment requires patients to take one pill per day for 6 months. During this time, patients come to the clinic once per month to get medication refills and checkups. Patients in the Automated Message Reminder condition receive one phone call per day at a time of their choosing and a reminder message in their preferred language is automatically spoken. Using a special pill cap containing electronic circuitry, we are monitoring the dates and times patients open their pill bottles to take medication. We are already finding a statistically significant and ecologically meaningful 36% decrease in nonadherence in the Automated Message Reminder condition compared to the No Call condition (Tanke, 1995). This finding offers a significant improvement in tuberculosis prevention in the United States.

CONCLUSIONS FROM OUR RESEARCH

Automated voice message design is only now being recognized as a critical and emerging area of applied cognitive psychology. Empirically validated message protocols are an essential part of technology employing automated voice messaging. Effective design and validation of message protocols requires an integration of different areas of cognitive research. Developing automated health care instructions has required an integration of prospective memory, discourse processing, and social-cognitive psychology. Although expertise, intuition, and theories may make explicit claims about what content and organization should be used, it is only through empirical validation in controlled experiments that we have been able to establish the effectiveness of messages for specific health care applications. With the systematic design and validation of automated voice message protocols, applied cognitive psychology is able to make a significant contribution to a cost-effective technology for improving health care and reducing treatment costs for patients and society as a whole.

ACKNOWLEDGMENTS

Dr. Leirer's research was supported by SBIR Grant # R44 AG10659-02 from the National Institute on Aging, NIH. Dr. Tanke's research was supported by SBIR Grant # R44 AI31750-02 from the National Institute on Allergies and Infectious Diseases, NIH. Dr. Morrow's research was supported by Grant # R01 AG09254-01 from the National Institute on Aging, NIH.

REFERENCES

Barron, W. M. (1980). Failed appointments: Who misses then, why they are missed, and what can be done. *Primary Care, 7,* 563–574.

Carasanos, G. J., Stewart, R. B., & Cluff, L. E. (1974). Drug-induced illness leading to hospitalization. *Journal of the American Medical Association, 228,* 713–717.

Cooper, J. K., Love, D. W., & Raffoul, P. R. (1982). Intentional prescription nonadherence (noncompliance) by the elderly. *Journal of the American Geriatrics Society, 30,* 329–334.

Hass, R. G. (1981). Effects of source characteristics on cognitive responses and persuasion. In R. E. Petty, T. M. Ostrom, & T. C. Brock (Eds.), *Cognitive responses in persuasion. II* (pp. 141–172). Hillsdale, NJ: Lawrence Erlbaum Associates.

Hovland, C., Janis, I., & Kelley, H. (1953). *Communication and persuasion.* New Haven, CT: Yale University Press.

Janz, N. K., & Becker, M. H. (1984). The health belief model: A decade later. *Health Education Quarterly, 11,* 1–47.

Larson, E. B., Bergman, J., Heidrich, F., Alvin, B. L., & Schneeweiss, R. (1982). Do postcard reminders improve influenza vaccination compliance? A prospective trial of different postcard "cues." *Medical Care, 20,* 639–648.

Leirer, V. O., Morrow, D. G., Pariante, G., & Doksum, T. (1989). Increasing influenza vaccination adherence through voice mail. *Journal of the American Geriatrics Society, 37*, 1147–1150.

Leirer, V. O., Morrow, D. G., Pariante, G., & Sheikh, J. (1988). Elders' nonadherence, its assessment, and computer assisted instruction for medication recall training. *Journal of the American Geriatrics Society, 36*, 877–884.

Leirer, V. O., Morrow, D. G., Tanke, E. D., & Pariante, G. (1991). Elders' nonadherence: Its assessment and medication reminding by voice mail. *The Gerontologist, 31*, 514–520.

Leirer, V. O., Tanke, E. D., & Morrow, D. G. (1993). Commercial cognitive/memory systems: A case study. *Applied Cognitive Psychology, 7*, 675–689.

Marics, M., & Williges, B. (1988). The intelligibility of synthesized speech in data inquiry systems. *Human Factors, 30*, 719–732.

Morrow, D. G., Leirer, V. O., & Altieri, P. (1995). Explicit formats help older adults understand medication instructions. *Educational Gerontology, 21*, 151–167.

Morrow, D. G., Leirer, V. O., Altieri, P., & Tanke, E. D. (1991). Elders' schema for taking medication: Implications for instruction design. *Journal of Gerontology, 46*, 378–385.

Morrow, D. G., Leirer, V. O., Andrassy, J. M., & Tanke, E. D. (1993, November). *Designing reminder messages for older adults.* Paper presented at the Forty-Sixth Annual Meeting of the Gerontology Society of America, New Orleans.

Morrow, D. G., Leirer, V. O., & Sheikh, J. (1988). Adherence and medication instructions: Review and recommendations. *Journal of the American Geriatrics Society, 36*, 1147–1160.

Snyder, J. D. E., & Hutton, M. D. (1989). *Improving patient compliance in tuberculosis treatment programs.* Atlanta: Centers for Disease Control.

Stewart, R. B., & Cluff, L. E. (1972). A review of medication errors and compliance in ambulant patients. *Clinical Pharmacological Therapy, 13*, 463–468.

Stine, E., Wingfield, A., & Poon, L. (1986). How much and how fast: Rapid processing of spoken language in later adulthood. *Psychology and Aging, 1*, 303–311.

Tanke, E. D. (1992). *TeleMinder®-TBC: Automated reminder to reduce health care costs in public health tuberculosis clinics* (Technical Report No. T-1992-01). Los Altos, CA: Decision Systems.

Tanke, E. D. (1993). *TeleMinder®-TBC: Automated reminders to improve tuberculosis care adherence in public health.* (Technical Report No. T-1993-01). Los Altos, CA: Decision Systems.

Tanke, E. D. (1994). *TeleMinder®-TBC: Preliminary report on INH medication adherence using TeleMinder® automated reminder telephone calls* (Technical Report No. T-1995-01). Los Altos, CA: Decision Systems.

Tanke, E. D., & Leirer, V. O. (1993). Use of automated telephone reminders to increase elderly patients' adherence to tuberculosis medication appointments. *Proceedings of the Human Factors and Ergonomic Society, 37th Annual Meeting* (pp. 193–196). Santa Monica, CA: Human Factors and Ergonomics Society.

Tanke, E. D., & Leirer, V. O. (1994). Automated telephone reminders in tuberculosis care. *Medical Care, 32*, 380–389.

Ulmer, R. A. (1987). Editorial: Patient noncompliance and health care costs. *Journal of Compliance in Health Care, 2*, 3–4.

Werner, C. (1978). Intrusiveness and persuasive impact of three communication media. *Journal of Applied Social Psychology, 8*, 145–162.

Wurtele, S. K., Galanos, A. N., & Roberts, M. C. (1980). Increasing return compliance in a tuberculosis detection drive. *Journal of Behavioral Medicine, 3*, 311–318.

CHAPTER TWENTY-FIVE

Automation of Flight Data
in Air Traffic Control

O. U. Vortac
Ami L. Barile
Chris A. Albright
Todd R. Truitt
University of Oklahoma

Carol A. Manning
Federal Aviation Administration Civil Aeromedical Institute

Dana Bain
Federal Aviation Administration Academy

Every day, the airspace of the United States accommodates hundreds of thousands of aircraft movements. Some 70% of all flights occur under instrument flight rules and are thus handled by the nation's air traffic control (ATC) system. Currently, a major ATC center may handle as many as 7,000 flights a day, the majority of them jetliners traveling at airspeeds in excess of 450 knots. The responsibility for the separation of these flights rests with individuals or small teams of controllers, each assigned a volume of airspace, a sector. The controller manages the sector using technologies that, given the traffic loads and the rapid evolution of in-flight avionics, appear anachronistic. For example, some important data pertaining to a flight are currently recorded on small strips of paper, known as flight progress strips (FPSs), whose format and function have changed little since they were introduced in the 1930s and 1940s.

The FPS augments the primary flight information displayed on the computer-enhanced radar: The radar screen shows the position of each aircraft in the sector together with a representation of sector boundaries and other landmarks. Each aircraft is shown together with its call sign, altitude, and a limited choice of other information. Additional flight data, such as planned route, time of arrival, assigned altitude, type of aircraft, and so on, are printed on the FPS that is associated with each flight and that is posted in a "bay"

353

next to the radar display. The FPSs are printed prior to departure of an aircraft and are thus primarily based on projected altitudes and times.

Several minutes prior to entering the sector, forthcoming flights are posted in a "suspense" bay, and once a flight becomes active by entering the sector, its FPS is moved by the controller to the "active" bay. While a flight is active, the controller frequently interacts with the corresponding FPS, noting activities entered into the computer, recording instructions to the pilot, and indicating the controller's plans for that flight. Estimated times are updated and turned into actual times, reroutings are noted, changes in altitude are recorded, and so on. All these changes are recorded on the strip by crossing out the previous data and writing the new information in its place. In addition, controllers often "offset" (move horizontally beyond the edge of the bay) an FPS to remind themselves that an aircraft requires some activity (e.g., clearance to descend) in the near future. In short, the FPS contains a record of the flight's progress through the sector, and, in fact, using the FPS to retain a legal record of the flight (at the time of this writing) is required by Federal Aviation Administration (FAA) procedures (U.S. Department of Transportation, 1989).

It should be clear, even from this brief description, that the FPS appears to form an integral component of the ATC task with potentially important and unique cognitive functionality. For example, the seemingly simple act of moving the strip of an incoming flight from the suspense to the active bay entails scanning other FPSs in order to find the appropriate place for the new flight, perhaps consolidating the controller's memory for the traffic pattern (Hopkin, 1988; see also Slamecka & Graf, 1978). Similarly, the fact that an FPS maintains the history of a flight, because previous information remains visible even when crossed through, has been listed as a unique and important advantage of paper strips (e.g., Hopkin, 1991; Weston, 1983). Finally, the frequent use of FPSs as memory aids (e.g., their offsetting when a flight requires some future control action) may reveal another important cognitive role of this seemingly simple strip of paper.

The gap between advanced in-flight technology and the more traditional ATC equipment is expected to close during the next decade. Because the most dramatic change in en route[1] control is likely to be the replacement of the paper FPSs with electronic versions, there has been some concern that the cognitive functionality provided by the current paper strip may be lost: Incoming flights will (by default) appear automatically in the active portion of the electronic display, the previous history of a flight will not be readily available, and highlighting an electronic entry to serve as a reminder cue will require keystrokes as opposed to a simple manual offset (see Ammerman & Jones, 1988, for more details). It follows that the introduction of

---

[1]En route control handles flights outside the immediate perimeter of major airports; this chapter specifically addresses issues in en route control.

automation, as feared by Hopkin (e.g., 1988), may entail diverse negative consequences for controller performance because the cognitively beneficial interaction with FPSs is eliminated. We call this the *interaction hypothesis*.

On the other hand, it is possible that removal of the FPSs will merely relieve the controllers of tedious, but required, record keeping that has little to do with the primary task of separating aircraft. That reduction in workload may improve performance, because the controller has more cognitive resources available for resolving traffic conflicts. We refer to this as the *workload hypothesis*.

The available data tentatively support the workload hypothesis. Consider a relevant study by Vortac, Edwards, Fuller, and Manning (1993), in which the availability of FPSs was manipulated between groups of controllers. In one condition, air traffic controllers controlled traffic normally, using paper FPSs as they would in the field. A second group of controllers controlled the same scenarios, but received skeleton FPSs that contained only a subset of the typically available information. In addition, as an extreme analog of automation, controllers in that condition were prohibited from writing, touching, or manipulating the skeleton strips. The study included a set of cognitive measures (attention, visual search, spatial recall, flight data recall, prospective memory, planning) as well as a battery of possible performance indices (over-the-shoulder evaluation by a subject-matter expert, completeness of relief briefings, overall efficiency of traffic management).

Contrary to the interaction hypothesis, Vortac et al. (1993) found few differences between the two conditions. Even when controllers were prevented from interacting with (restricted) flight data, they controlled traffic as efficiently and safely as their counterparts in the control condition. Similarly, and to our surprise, the only cognitive effects favored the group that had less interaction; of relevance here was the result that controllers granted more requests and granted them sooner when they did not interact with the FPSs.

Specifically, the study included several requests by pilots that the controller could not grant without some delay, because the aircraft was still outside the sector. In those cases, the controller must rely on prospective memory, memory for activities to be performed in the future (e.g., Einstein & McDaniel, 1990; Meacham & Singer, 1977). Given that FPSs function as external memory aids, for example by "offsetting" when future actions are required, a prospective memory advantage (Meacham & Leiman, 1982) constitutes the a priori most likely prediction of the interaction hypothesis (cf. Lansdale, Simpson, & Stroud, 1990). The fact that the opposite result was obtained by Vortac et al. (1993) suggests that workload is considerably reduced when FPS updating tasks are eliminated.

However, any conclusions based on that study must remain tentative because the experimental manipulation was not a complete analog to automation. Any automation of a data display likely entails two major consequences: greater operator passivity and enhanced display dynamics. Vortac et al. (1993) captured the former by restricting access to the strips, but they ignored the latter by presenting a single static set of FPSs that remained unchanged throughout the experiment.

The present study, then, was designed to provide a further contrast between the interaction and workload hypotheses using a more sophisticated experimental instantiation of automation. Each controller managed traffic under three different conditions: With the current paper FPSs (normal), with a completely automated electronic display (full), and with a partially automated display (partial). Under full automation, the electronic strips were automatically moved between bays, updated as necessary, and removed once a flight was handed off to the next controller. Under partial automation, updating of the electronic strips was automated, but it remained the controller's responsibility to move strips from the suspense to the active bay, to remove them when no longer needed, and to resequence and highlight them if so desired. Both instantiations of automation used a one-line electronic strip, modeled after the current plans for ISSS.

Turning to the predictions for this experiment, the interaction hypothesis would expect poorest performance under full automation, owing to the absence of controller interaction with flight data. Even under partial automation, performance should be impaired because interaction with the flight data is indirect, via some input device, rather than through direct physical manipulation. Conversely, the workload hypothesis would predict best performance under full automation, and a simple version of this hypothesis would also expect partial automation to be superior to the normal condition.

A second purpose of the current experiment was to investigate the extent to which flight-strip or board management responsibilities can be divided between the controller and the automation. Inclusion of the partial condition allowed assessment of the likely ease with which board management duties can be relegated to automation. We argued that partitioning of subtasks across distributed intelligences may be an important aspect of ATC automation (see Vortac, Edwards, & Manning, 1994, for details).

METHOD

Subjects

A total of 12 full-performance level controllers participated. All were instructors at the FAA Academy, had been controllers for an average of 6.4 years, and last served in the field 26 months prior to the study. All subjects participated in all conditions (normal, full, and partial) during a single 3-hour session.

Materials

Facility and Apparatus. The experiment was conducted at the Radar Training Facility (RTF) at the FAA's Mike Monroney Aeronautical Center in Oklahoma City. The RTF provides high-fidelity air traffic simulation using the fictitious Aero Center airspace. Subjects were familiar with the airspace and with the standard en route equipment. Automation was provided by a laptop computer with an external 17-inch color monitor and a trackball. The monitor was mounted at eye level at a comfortable viewing distance from the subject, and the trackball was used by the subject to move and sequence the electronic "strips" in the partial condition (see Fig. 25.1). Input not provided by the subject (e.g., updating of altitudes, etc.) was entered on the keyboard of the laptop by an experimenter who had received extensive training on that particular scenario. Thus, the experimenter was able to automate the flight data display because he or she could anticipate probable commands, knew likely flight paths, and was familiar with all relevant call signs and flight data.

In the automated conditions, flight data were displayed in the form of one-line entries (see Fig. 25.2). The top two thirds of the display corresponded to the active bay, the bottom one third to the suspense bay. Each strip contained the aircraft call sign and aircraft type, assigned altitude, route of flight, and the flight's computer identification number.

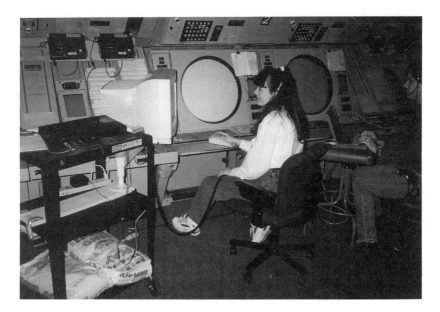

FIG. 25.1. Subject in the partial automation condition seated in front of the radar display, manipulating electronic strips through the trackball. The experimenter is using a laptop to control the automated aspects of the display.

○ N405GA	C421/A	130	OKC SNL090004 MLC U6 HOT	010
○ N47332	C182/A	080	MIO BLOCK MLC U9 DAL	011
○ N913AX	LR55/A	220	MIO J101 ICT	019
○ N858TC	BE99/A	180	MLC J106 OKC	017
○ N743PA	G4/R	220	MLC DFW	016
○ N47516	SW4/A	110	ICT ICT144085 MAPLE U9 MIO U2 FYV	012

○ AAL54	MD80/A	220	STL SGF050015 SGF SPRIN1 TUL	001
○ TWA186	B727/A	200	FYV FSM070015 FSM FORTS1 TUL	031
○ N672AL	AC56/R	120	LIT FSM110015 FSM U8 GCK	014
○ N6755C	PA46/R	090	OKC OKC090011 BOLEY U6 HOT	015
○ G63416	C130/A	160	LRF FSM120035 OKC	004
○ N8835	E120/A	180	MKC J107 DAL	018
○ DAL310	B737/A	210	TUL BOLDE1 SGF STL	003
○ SWA46	B737/A	230	DAL J107 TUL	020

FIG. 25.2. The electronic display of flight data used in the automated conditions. Each strip had a control point, the call sign, the aircraft type and transponder, altitude, route, and computer identification number.

Scenarios. Three scenarios were constructed, each approximately 25 minutes in length and consisting of an average of 21 planes (8.7 departures, 3.7 arrivals, and 8.7 overflights). They were judged by a subject-matter expert to represent a traffic density that an individual controller could handle in the field. None of the subjects were familiar with the scenarios. Assignment of scenario to condition was counterbalanced such that each scenario appeared four times in each condition. All subjects first controlled traffic normally; then half of the subjects were exposed to partial automation, and the remaining half to full automation.

Prospective Memory Events. Each scenario contained three prospective requests spaced on average 7.5 minutes apart. These were pilot requests for an altitude change or rerouting made prior to entering the controller's airspace, when the controller cannot issue commands without permission from the adjacent facility.[2] Hence, we could be certain that the controller had to remember to grant these requests at some time in the future. We measured whether or not the request was granted once the aircraft entered the sector, as well as the latency to grant the request.

---

[2]Unlike in the field, any attempts to achieve control were denied by the (simulated) adjacent facility. Only one subject commented on the inability to obtain control of out-of-sector flights as unrealistic. Analyses were conducted excluding this subject, but did not alter any of the patterns reported in this chapter.

Conditions

Normal. In the normal condition subjects received their flight data on paper FPSs, just as they do in the field. Subjects were instructed to interact with the FPSs as they normally did. This included a certain amount of legally required strip marking, as well as movement of the strips from the suspense to the active bay, offsetting the strips when desired, and removing a strip after a flight was handed off to the next controller.

Full Automation. The experimenter was responsible for updating altitude and route changes on the electronic strips. By retyping what the controller entered on the en route keyboard, the experimenter provided the necessary information to update the electronic strips on the monitor. Subjects were told that the electronic strips would automatically appear in the suspense bay. The strips were then automatically moved to the active bay when a hand-off was taken; they would turn yellow for 10 seconds before reverting to the background green. The strips were sequenced in ascending order by time of arrival. The automation also removed strips from the active bay 1 minute after the aircraft had been handed off to the next sector. Similarly, updates for route and altitude replaced the existing route and altitude.

Partial Automation. The partial automation was similar to full automation with the following exceptions. Subjects were required to use the trackball to click a strip in the suspense bay to move it into the active bay. A method analogous to offsetting a strip was provided by allowing the controller to click a strip in the active bay, whereupon it was highlighted in red. Subjects were also told how to resequence and remove strips from the active bay by using drag and drop operations with the trackball. Finally, subjects were told that they had to keep their electronic strip "bay" managed in order to ensure that new flight data would become available at appropriate times. However, offsetting and resequencing were optional, as they are in the field.

Procedure

Subjects first completed a background questionnaire and were then familiarized with the particulars of controlling traffic in Aero Center (letters of agreement, hand-off procedures, radio frequencies, etc.). The paper strips for the initial normal condition were prepared and the controllers were given several minutes to adjust the FPSs to their preferences. Subjects were given minimal instructions ("control traffic as you normally would in the field") for the normal condition.

At a predetermined stopping point, the scenario was frozen and the controller was dismissed for a 15-minute break. The subject-matter expert then conducted a postscenario performance analysis (Vortac et al., 1993): For each aircraft remaining in the airspace, the subject-matter expert decided how many speed, route, altitude changes, and so on remained to get the aircraft out of the controller's airspace safely. Because the scenario was stopped at the same point and had the same starting conditions for all subjects, we reasoned that a more efficient controller should have fewer control actions remaining at the end of the scenario than would a less efficient controller. A postscenario analysis was conducted after each scenario.

Subjects next participated in the automated conditions, in an order determined by counterbalancing. For familiarization, subjects first viewed electronic versions of the FPSs from the immediately preceding normal scenario. In the case of partial automation, subjects also practiced the allowable trackball operations using electronic versions of the strips from the preceding scenario. Subjects were given another 15-minute break between the automated scenarios. After completion of the third scenario, subjects were given a questionnaire assessing their views on the scenarios, the automation, and the format of the electronic strips. Subjects also indicated whether or not they controlled traffic any differently than they would in the field.

RESULTS

Postscenario Analysis

The mean number of control actions remaining at the stopping point of the scenarios is shown in Table 25.1. The results provide no support for the contention that automation impairs efficient management of traffic. If anything, full automation appears superior to normal, although this difference did not reach significance [$t(11) = 1.69, p < .12$]. Moreover, although decomposing the total number of remaining actions into different classes of actions further increased variability, the table indicates a general superiority of the full

TABLE 25.1
Mean Number of Control Actions

	Normal	Partial	Full
Total remaining actions	27.0	25.6	23.3
Communications/hand-offs	24.1	22.8	20.8
Altitude changes	1.6	1.9	1.3
Speed changes	.7	.6	.8
Point-outs	.4	.1	.3
Route amendments	.2	.2	.2

automation condition. These aspects of the data cast doubt on the interaction hypothesis stated at the outset. Finally, note that partial automation yields performance between the normal and full automation conditions.

Controller Opinion

Mean Likert judgments were used to help quantify controllers' opinions. Table 25.2 compares the three conditions, with lower scores indicating more favorable opinions. There was no apparent difference between partial and full on these scales. However, there seemed to be some interesting differences between the paper FPSs (normal) and the electronic conditions. Electronic strips were rated as slightly less useful than FPSs; however, electronic strips were rated as slightly easier to use and were liked slightly more than were the paper FPSs. For ease of use, six controllers preferred electronic strips, two preferred FPSs, and three did not indicate a preference. For satisfaction, five preferred the electronic strips, two preferred paper, and five did not indicate a preference. These leanings toward electronic strips were reversed, however, when usefulness was judged: Seven controllers thought the traditional paper strip more useful, two preferred the electronic strips, and three thought the two formats equally useful.

Protocols helped illuminate the Likert values. The most mentioned likable feature of the electronic strip was the automatic update ($n = 5$) of altitude and route information. The ability to highlight a strip ($n = 4$) in partial automation was also well liked. Subjects thought the electronic strip required less physical manipulation due to the ease with which they could be moved, the ease of their removal, and the automatic update. Overall, controllers felt as if they spent less time on board management.

The electronic strips were apparently judged less useful than the FPSs because they lacked information. Subjects recommended the addition of a beacon code ($n = 10$) as the single most agreed-on addition. Others suggested a space for writing on the strip or a small notepad ($n = 8$), that both interim and final requested altitudes should be visible along with filed true airspeed ($n = 4$), and that more than one active bay would be helpful ($n = 3$). It is interesting that despite the feeling that more information was needed on the electronic strips, the controllers were at least as efficient (postscenario

TABLE 25.2
Mean Likert Judgments

	Normal	Partial	Full
Usefulness	2.1	2.4	2.5
Ease of use	2.5	1.9	1.8
Satisfaction	2.6	2.0	2.2

TABLE 25.3
Prospective Memory Measures

	Normal	Partial	Full
Time from boundary to request granted (seconds)	77.4	79.4	70.4
Proportion of requests correctly granted	.83	.78	.90

analysis) in the full automation condition as they were when controlling traffic normally.

Prospective Memory

We looked at both the proportion of times the controller remembered to grant a request, and how long the controller waited to grant the request once he or she had control of the aircraft. As shown in Table 25.3, under full automation, controllers granted slightly more requests and granted them sooner than in the normal condition. This replicates our earlier finding (Vortac et al., 1993), although here the trends were not significant. Despite this null effect, it is important to note that again the pattern is opposite to that predicted by the interaction hypothesis. It is also worth noting that any advantage over normal conditions gained with full automation is completely lost under partial automation.

Other features of the data were interesting, although they do not distinguish among types of automation. Only one request was granted incorrectly: A controller cleared an aircraft direct to Wichita rather than to Kansas City. There were eight additional occurrences in which the controller remembered that he or she had received a request but did not remember the content of the request. The frequency with which this partial failure occurred supports Einstein and McDaniel's (1990) componential analysis of prospective memory: The component that triggers an action was intact, but the content of the required action was lost. In these cases, the controller contacted the aircraft and asked the pilot to repeat the request.

DISCUSSION

Notwithstanding meager statistical support, integrating across performance, opinion, and cognitive variables suggests that full automation has an advantage over the way traffic is controlled currently: Subjects were slightly more efficient, having fewer actions left to perform at an arbitrary stopping point; they liked the ease of use of the automation and were more satisfied with full automation than the standard system; finally, delayed pilot requests were granted 7% more often and a few seconds earlier under full automation. By contrast, there is no evidence supporting the competing interaction hypothesis, namely that automation will inhibit performance or cognition.

On the other hand, it is more difficult to marshal a similar argument for partial automation. First, partial automation was not always superior to the normal condition (e.g., prospective measures), and even when it was, the size of the difference did not invite lack-of-power excuses. Because partial and full automation used the same one-line electronic strips, it is unlikely that this particular display format explains the patterns of results. However, partial automation and normal operations both involved the controller engaging in board management. Apparently, when the controller must take time and resources to keep the flight data bay organized, we cannot expect automation of other functions, such as updating altitude and route, to yield an advantage. Thus, the current data suggest that it may be difficult to divide responsibility for board management between the computer and controller. In our simulation of partitioned board management between computer and controller (partial condition), the advantage of automation was completely (prospective memory) or partially (performance) lost.

We have argued elsewhere that board management is a behavioral module to experienced controllers, and that if automation replaces part of, rather than the entire, module, then no advantage (possibly even an inhibition) can be caused by the automation. This modular automation hypothesis (Vortac, 1993; Vortac et al., 1994) is based on the argument (Hayes-Roth, 1977) that cognitive processes that frequently occur together will eventually become unitized. When a unitized assembly of processes exists for the task at hand, cognitive processing should be most efficient. If, instead, processes must be combined to deal with the task, then additional time and resources would be needed. Or, if a unitized module must be disassembled or fractionated in Hayes-Roth's terms, then again additional time and resources would be needed.

Modularity may prove to be an important part of the success of automation attempts and should be considered in the design of automated systems. Fractionation could occur if uninformed attempts to automate a complex dynamic system places part of an existing cognitive or behavioral module under automation. This argument, we believe, is especially applicable to a situation like that of the current ATC system where expert, highly skilled individuals will be placed in a similar environment with automated aids designed to replace existing skilled behaviors. In such a situation, existing modules will be brought to bear; the new situation will force their fractionation; performance will be comparable to, or in extreme cases worse than, no automation. Whether a particular module should be automated or left under manual control depends on other factors (Vortac et al., 1994), but the module in its entirety should either be automated or preserved as a manual subtask.

In a related laboratory experiment using undergraduate volunteers (Vortac & Manning, 1994), we found support for the disruptive impact of automation that fractionates existing modules. Subjects learned to enter sequences of commands to control various aspects of a fictional complex process. Each task required that the subject enter eight keystrokes. By requiring subjects to make the same four-stroke entries frequently and in various situations we forced the subjects to create modules. Thus, the training ensured that the eight keystroke tasks comprised two four-keystroke modules, and it also ensured that the experimenters knew which sequences of keystrokes were unitized and which were not. We then automated some of the functions. In the modular automation condition, entire modules were automated: The computer performed one four-keystroke module and left the subject to perform the other module. In the fractionated condition, the same number of keystrokes were automated, but they fractionated the preexisting modules: The computer would perform two keystrokes from each of the two modules constituting the task. Fractionation caused a disruption in performance that required many subsequent retraining sessions to reduce.

Thus, we have some reason to believe that the fractionation tenet of modular automation holds. In addition, earlier work with air traffic controllers working singly and in teams supplied data that bear on the modules that exist in experienced air traffic controllers. Using the Pathfinder scaling algorithm (Vortac, Edwards, Jones, Manning, & Rotter, 1993; Vortac et al., 1994) and time-series analysis (Edwards, Fuller, Vortac, & Manning, in press) we investigated the structural characteristics of transition frequencies between various behaviors emitted by controllers in different traffic situations. Of relevance here is the finding that manipulating strips and writing on strips appeared to represent a module to controllers. We referred to this complex of writing and manipulating FPSs as the *board management module*. Board management meets several criteria suggestive of a module. Writing and manipulating strips co-occur frequently and in a variety of situations and were strongly linked in the Pathfinder network. When the task of ATC was divided between two controllers, all of board management becomes the responsibility of one controller, whereas the events that trigger board management are the actions of the other controller. Thus, teams of controllers do not fractionate the board management module.

Given that board management appears to be a module in ATC, it is likely that the partial automation used in the current experiment fractionated that module. Thus, we should not be surprised that there was no real benefit to partial automation, and in some cases a slight inhibition. We mention this because it may be the case that other partial automation configurations can be developed that would not fractionate board management, although it is difficult to imagine a more natural partition of responsibilities than the one implemented here.

Overall, we suspect that full automation will surpass the normal ATC configuration because it should relieve the controller of all board management responsibilities, allowing him or her to focus on the control of active traffic. We believe that to the extent that automation allows controllers to be relieved of all board management responsibilities it will prove to be a successful system. We warn, however, of the problems associated with automating only part of the board management module.

ACKNOWLEDGMENTS

O. U. Vortac was the collaborative research effort of Francis T. Durso, Scott D. Gronlund, and Stephan Lewandowsky. Lewandowsky is now at the University of Western Australia. This work was supported by contract #DTFA-02-91-C-91089 from the FAA. We are grateful to the instructors and management of the FAA Academy at Mike Monroney Aeronautical Center.

REFERENCES

Ammerman, H. L., & Jones, G. W. (1988). *ISSS impact on ATC procedures and training* (FAA Report No. DTF-A01-85-Y-0101304). Washington, DC: Federal Aviation Administration.

Edwards, M. B., Fuller, D. K., Vortac, O. U., & Manning, C. A. (in press). The role of flight progress strips in en route air traffic control: A time series analysis. *International Journal of Human-Computer Studies.*

Einstein, G. O., & McDaniel, M. A. (1990). Normal aging and prospective memory. *Journal of Experimental Psychology: Learning, Memory, and Cognition, 16,* 717–726.

Hayes-Roth, B. (1977). Evolution of cognitive structures and processes. *Psychological Review, 84,* 260–278.

Hopkin, V. D. (1988). *Human factors aspects of the AERA 2 program.* Farnborough, Hampshire, UK: Royal Air Force Institute of Aviation Medicine.

Hopkin, V. D. (1991). The impact of automation on air traffic control systems. In J. A. Wise, V. D. Hopkin, & M L. Smith (Eds.), *Automation and systems issues in air traffic control* (pp. 3–19). Berlin: Springer-Verlag.

Lansdale, M. W., Simpson, M., & Stroud, R. M. (1990). A comparison of words and icons as external memory aids in an information retrieval task. *Behavior and Information Technology, 9,* 111–131.

Meacham, J. A., & Leiman, B. (1982). Remembering to perform future actions. In U. Neisser (Ed.), *Memory observed: Remembering in natural context* (pp. 327–336). San Francisco, CA: Freeman.

Meacham, J. A., & Singer, J. (1977). Incentive effects in prospective remembering. *The Journal of Psychology, 97,* 191–197.

Slamecka, N. J., & Graf, P. (1978). The generation effect: Delineation of a phenomenon. *Journal of Experimental Psychology: Human Learning and Memory, 4,* 592–604.

U. S. Department of Transportation, Federal Aviation Adminstration. (1989). *Air traffic control* (Publication No. 7110.65). Washington, DC: Author.

Vortac, O. U. (1993). Should Hal open the pod bay doors? An argument for modular automation. In D. J. Garland & J. A. Wise (Eds.), *Human factors and advanced aviation technologies* (pp. 159–163). Daytona Beach, FL: Embry-Riddle Aeronautical University Press.

Vortac, O. U., Edwards, M. B., Fuller, D. K., & Manning, C. A. (1993). Automation and cognition in air traffic control: An empirical investigation. *Applied Cognitive Psychology, 7,* 631–651.

Vortac, O. U., Edwards, M. B., Jones, J. P., Manning, C. A., & Rotter, A. J. (1993). En route air traffic controllers' use of flight progress strips: A graph-theoretic analysis. *The International Journal of Aviation Psychology, 3,* 327–343.

Vortac, O. U., Edwards, M. B., & Manning, C. A. (1994). Sequences of actions for individual and teams of air traffic controllers. *Human Computer Interaction, 9,* 319–343.

Vortac, O. U., & Manning, C. A. (1994, April). *Modular automation: Automating sub-tasks without disrupting task flow.* Paper presented at the First Automation Technology and Human Performance Conference, Washington, DC.

Weston, R. C. W. (1983). Human factors in air traffic control. *Journal of Aviation Safety, 1,* 94–104.

CHAPTER TWENTY-SIX

Automated Instructional Systems and Ecological Notions of Memory

Theodore M. Shlechter
U.S. Army Research Institute
Fort Knox, KY

Over 15 years ago, Ulric Neisser (1978) challenged cognitive psychologists to find out more about the practical uses of memory. This challenge has led to the ecological movement in memory research with the objective of exploring human cognition vis-à-vis naturalistic reference situations (Herrmann & Gruneberg, 1993; Hoffmann & Deffenbacher, 1993). The ecological memory movement has also been concerned with testing the usefulness of basic theories on memory processes, which were derived from laboratory research, for naturalistic settings (Herrmann & Gruneberg, 1993).

Instructional technologists have also become interested in similar issues. This literature has recently burgeoned with works on the relationships among emerging instructional technologies and memory phenomena for real-life events (e.g., Hooper & Hannafin, 1991; Kozma, 1991). Hooper and Hannafin, for example, suggested that theoretical concepts regarding cognitive processes can help guide the development of an emerging generation of instructional systems.

This chapter thus explores the relationships among the theoretical notions of ecologically oriented cognitive scientists and automated instructional systems (AIS). AIS are defined as any instructional system that uses computer technology to either deliver or manage the instructional program. Also discussed is the usefulness of basic research findings on cognitive processes for helping instructional technologists to develop AIS.

AN UNDERSTANDING OF ECOLOGICAL NOTIONS
ON MEMORY PHENOMENA

Ecologically oriented cognitive scientists view memory phenomena as resulting from a dynamic interaction between the individual and his or her
environment (Shlechter & Robinson, 1987). Shlechter and Robinson suggested
a marriage metaphor to describe this interaction with each partner "coming to
terms with each other." The primary function of memory, for example, is to
help human beings adapt to the outside world that is removed from them in
time and space (Jarvik, 1966). Each partner also brings properties of its own
into this marriage.

Affordances are the environment's major contribution to this marriage
(Gibson, 1966, as cited by Shaw & Hazelett, 1986). Gibson defined affordances as the invariant perceptual information made available by objects and
events that can be picked up by an active organism. As stated by Shaw and
Hazelett (1986): affordances, by Gibson's own usage, refers to just those
properties of objects or events that possess ecological significance for some
organisms (p. 49).

Bransford, Franks, Morris, and Stein (1979) modified this fundamental
ecological belief by suggesting that environmental contexts can help set the
stage (or can "attune" subjects) for later remembering. They also argued that
subjects are more aware of environmental events that relate to their knowledge base. Their arguments were based on findings from laboratory studies
showing that college subjects' comprehension and remembrance of linguistic
information depend on their environmental knowledge (e.g., Bransford, Barclay, & Franks, 1972).

An ecological view also holds that memory is a function of one's learning
process. Learning is a function of a constant interaction among materials within
the organism and the many different events in the environment (Jarvik, 1966).
Perhaps, then, environmental affordances attune one's learning process and
consequently memory to the student's internal cognitive materials.

Support for this hypothesis comes from research on developmental processes and intellectual expertise (e.g., Huston & Wright, 1994; Schoenfield &
Herrmann, 1982). Huston and Wright showed that young children's attentional processes while watching television are controlled by the program's
surface features (e.g., the visuals). More developmentally mature children's
attentional processes are less likely to be controlled by such features. Schoenfield and Herrmann (1982) found that novice mathematicians perceived the
task based on its surface features—the words in the problem statement. The
more competent students perceived the word problem on the basis of underlying mathematical principles. Surface environmental cues should have
the most ecological significance for the remembering activities of younger
or less intellectually competent subjects, whereas task demands seemingly
have more significance for older and more advanced students.

Summary of the Ecological Notions on Memory. Ecological psychologists believe that learning processes and memory phenomena are closely linked. Each occurs vis-à-vis a dynamic interaction between environmental affordances and the organism. Ecological variables are thus any environmental event that attunes the organism's learning processes to the information contained in the environmental situation.

AIS AS ECOLOGICAL VARIABLES

AIS are seemingly well suited for attuning students' learning to the instructional situation. This hypothesis is based on the belief that such systems inherently contain instructional design features for facilitating students' learning and retention capabilities (Kozma; 1991; Rieber, 1990).

Rieber (1990) argued that the computer's graphic display capabilities can facilitate students' retention capabilities by allowing them to visually and graphically code the information. This argument has been based on Paivio's (1986) dual-coding theory of information processing, which postulates that human cognition consists of both a visual and auditory (verbal) coding system. Information presented both verbally and visually is then the most resistant to forgetting, because it inherently corresponds to the students' cognitive materials. Salomon (1979) discovered that audiovisual materials are easier for children to code than textual materials. However, as previously discussed, such perceptual cues may only be an ecological variable for the less advanced students.

Hypermedia Systems as Ecological Variables

Hypermedia systems represent another example of the possible inherent correspondence between AIS and students' cognitive materials. These systems, whose development has been technologically driven, use the power of the computer to arrange the instructional materials vis-à-vis hierarchically organized stacks (sets) of nodes (instructional content) and links (Park, 1992). The stacks are designed to convey the *structure* of the particular subject matter to students, whereas the links allow the students to access the subject matter in any given sequence. For example, a hypermedia program on e.e. cummings would start with overview stacks of nodes on his poems, which would then be linked to textual and graphic information on his style, philosophy, and themes (Scheidler, 1993).

Hypermedia's inherent instructional scheme relates to Collins and Qullian's (1969) concept of semantic memory. They argued that people organize semantic information in long-term memory vis-à-vis a series of hierarchically organized nodes and links. Collins and Quillan noted, for example, that people link the statement "A canary can fly" with their nodes for birds and canaries. Hypermedia systems should thus afford organization and retention of semantic memories, because their instructional scheme corresponds to one's semantic memory scheme.

Several writers have noted that the less advanced student may not benefit from using hypermedia (Kozma, 1991; Marchionini, 1988). Kozma suggested that such students may have problems with building semantic sequences because they lack the relevant domain-based selection criteria. Marchionini correspondingly suggested that the hypertext system's complexity may lead the less advanced learner to become disoriented in "hyperspace."

Hypermedia systems must then be embedded with additional instructional cues (supports) in order for the less advanced students to receive any learning benefits. Tripp and Roby (1990) found evidence for this hypothesis. Their study consisted of 80 college students completing a hypertext program for a Japanese–English lexicon. These subjects had little experience with reading Japanese and using a hypertext system. Two interesting findings emerged from this study. One, adding pictures to the hypertext increased the students' retention of the Japanese words. More evidence has thus been provided for the argument that visual cues have ecological significance for less advanced learners. Two, verbal information that was cognitively congruent to the visual metaphors led to greater learning. Thus, hypertext systems embedded with the cited orienting devices should have educational benefits for students of all educational levels.

Hypermedia systems, geared to all educational levels, are being developed vis-à-vis a constructivist approach to instructional design. A primary tenet of this approach, rooted in Wittrock's (1986) generative theory of learning and cognition, is that learning systems must provide authentic learning-by-doing activities. Solving math word problems relevant to one's daily experience is an example of an authentic learning-by-doing activity. As previously discussed, learning activities that relate to the students' knowledge base should help students attune their retention processes to the instructional materials.

One such constructivist hypermedia system is Knowledge Acquisition by Nonlinear Exploration (KANE; Spiro & Jehng, 1990). This system, which is still being refined, consists of a 30-minute videodisc presentation of different thematic segments of the movie *Citizen Kane*. The students can choose to access the different thematic segments in a linear (from the movie's beginning to its end) or "nonlinear" order, or they can even search for scenes that portray several different themes.

Simulation Systems as Ecological Variables

The military has made extensive use of simulation systems to provide students with learning environments that replicate working conditions. The Army has developed the SIMulation NETworking (SIMNET) system to give armor soldiers a safe and realistic environment to practice their tactical skills. SIMNET is a simulated battlefield environment consisting of combat vehicle simulators and combat support equipment, which operates under constraints similar to those affecting actual battlefield conditions. SIMNET is thus a simulation system with relatively high fidelity (Shlechter, Bessemer, & Kolosh, 1991).

The Navy has developed a relatively low-fidelity simulation system, STEAMER, to train steam propulsion operators. This system's design was based on a functional context approach to instructional design (Hollan, Hutchins, & Weitzman, 1984). That is, STEAMER replicates the working environment of a steam propulsion system by having small computers create a graphical interface of a simulation (mathematical model) of a 1,200 psi propulsion system (Montague, 1988). STEAMER thus allows students to have large amounts of time-compressed practice with using the complex cognitive skills needed to run a steam propulsion system. Consequently, then, STEAMER is expected to help students develop the mind of an expert steam propulsion operator.

The ecological perspective warns instructional designers to create simulation systems with perceptual cues appropriate to the students' level of understanding. This point has also been made in the instructional technology literature (e.g., Alessi, 1988; Thurman, 1993). Thurman suggested that the perceptual cues associated with a simulation system must allow students to form a mental image congruent with their level of understanding and task conditions; otherwise they would develop a deficient mental model for performing the task.

Alessi (1988) correspondingly noted that designers must ascertain the correct level of fidelity for a simulation system based on the student's current instructional level. High-fidelity systems, for example, would inhibit initial learning. It must be noted that SIMNET has been mainly used as a supplement to the classroom training given to the less advanced armor officers or as refresher training for experienced units. Also, Bessemer (1991) indicated that SIMNET's effectiveness for training the less advanced armor officers relates to the feedback provided by their instructors.

Computer-Based Tutoring Systems as Ecological Variables

Tutoring systems are being developed that use the power of the computer to provide students with instructional guidance. The Strategic Instruction for Vocabulary Learning (SILV) System illustrates the use of such a tutoring system for facilitating student's acquisition and retention of a foreign language (Rabinowitz & Sabnani, in press). The functions of this tutor include providing students with KEYWORD mnemonics to facilitate initial language acquisition, but gradually removing this contextual support from them. This design feature has been based on numerous findings from the cognitive literature, which show that the KEYWORD method can facilitate learning of a foreign language by linking the new words by contextual supports found in one's native language (e.g., Atkinson & Raugh, 1975). For example, the Spanish word for "letter" is *carta*, which is linked with the following sentence: "The post office puts letters into mailing carts."

This system's tutor is also designed to provide students with immediate feedback regarding their speed and accuracy in completing the task, and to provide hints about the amount of cognitive load that the students have to assume. These features are expected to help students reduce their working memory load when learning and memorizing the words.

This system is also a gaming task with the tutor becoming a game once the students have completed the acquisition trial. The tutor randomly presents the words to the students who receive points for their speed and accuracy in recalling them. And, recalling words without the KEYWORD context is worth more points than recalling them with this context. This game has been based on motivational theories (e.g., Ames, 1984) that encourage quick and accurate retrieval of the foreign words without the use of mnemonics. Rabinowitz and Sabnani (in press) thus used basic psychological research findings to create a tutoring system that attunes students' learning to the instructional situation by providing them with appropriate contextual supports.

Intelligent Tutoring Systems (ITS) as Ecological Variables

Other forms of AIS have also been embedded with algorithms based on findings from basic memory research for attuning students' learning processes to the instructional materials. ITS are examples of such systems. The development of ITS has been based on the idea that computer technology can easily individualize instruction by making "intelligent decisions" regarding each student's knowledge structure (Derry & Murphy, 1986; Jonassen, 1988; Regian & Shute, 1992). By making such decisions, the systems then have the capability to map the subject matter directly onto the student's knowledge structure (Jonassen, 1988). The subject matter will correspond to the student's cognitive materials. Regian and Shute thus found automatically tailored instruction to be more instructionally effective than nontailored instruction.

Many of these systems have also been designed to provide the appropriate instructional supports for helping students to achieve higher levels of intellectual expertise. Most ITS contain, for example, instructional supports for helping the less advanced students to reduce their working memory load (Glaser & Bassock, 1989). Studies have shown that the less advanced students have problems with fully utilizing their working memory system, which is a crucial component of learning (e.g., Swanson, 1993).

ITS development has thus involved the efforts of the artificial intelligence, educational, and instructional design communities (Frasson & Gauthier, 1990). From the artificial intelligence community came findings from basic research on knowledge acquisition and expert models. The educational community has provided the framework for applying these findings to classroom settings. Additionally, the instructional design community has provided the courseware know-how.

The products of these efforts are illustrated by the ITS that are dealt with in the following discussions. Other examples of ITS include systems for teaching avionics skills (SHERLOCK: Lesgold, Lajoie, Bunzo, & Eggan, 1992), scientific inquiry skills (Smithtown: Shute & Glaser, 1990), and business skills (ASK: Schank, 1990).

The LISP System. LISP is one of the best-known ITS (Frasson & Gauthier, 1990). This system, created as an intelligent tutoring system for LISP programming, was based on Anderson's (1983) ACT* theory of cognitive learning. The ACT* theory maintains that a cognitive skill like LISP can be represented as if-then goals (production rules), which are acquired by employing the declarative knowledge associated with the task in the context of an authentic problem-solving activity. Declarative knowledge information enters the cognitive system by observations and direct instruction. This theory also holds that students need immediate and explanatory feedback regarding their wrong responses to the practical exercises. Such feedback is expected to reduce the students' working memory load while learning a new ACT production (Anderson, Conrad, & Corbett, 1989).

The LISP tutoring system has been embedded with 500 production rules that represent the cognitive skills for LISP programming. Special testing and branching routines have been devised to provide students with appropriate practice opportunities. Students have also been provided with immediate and explanatory feedback about their errors (Anderson et al., 1989; Anderson, Corbett, Koedinger, & Pelletier, 1995).

Anderson et al.'s (in press) experience with LISP and other programs for ITS in educational settings has led to changes in their views regarding such systems. A tutoring system is no longer seen as a human emulation but rather as a learning environment in which helpful information is provided and useful problems can be selected. Also, a tutoring system does not have to provide immediate feedback to students regarding their errors.

The ACT* theory has correspondingly become the ACT*R(evised) theory (Anderson, 1993). The revised theory holds that students learn from problem-solving products rather than from records of problem-solving traces. Also, the learner's production rules are now theorized to be built by examining the resulting solutions rather than by just using the declarative knowledge information. It does not then matter whether all the critical steps in cognitive skill learning occur temporally together or not (Anderson et al., in press). The ACT*R theory thus indicates that cognitive skill learning involves fewer demands on the students' working memory than does the ACT* theory. Other aspects of the ACT* theory have remained intact. Production rules, for example, are still theorized to be learned independently from other units of knowledge (Anderson et al., 1989).

Minnesota Adaptive Instructional System (MAIS). MAIS was designed vis-à-vis a basic research program conducted by Tennyson and his associates (Tennyson & Christiansen, 1988; Tennyson & Park, 1987). This research program examined the connections among learning factors dealing with individual differences, cognition, and instructional technology. MAIS thus consists of interacting components dealing with learning processes (macrocomponents) and instructional conditions (microcomponents). For example, the tutor is continuously assessing the students' memory structures, a macrocomponent function, and then makes moment-to-moment adjustments in the instructional sequence to meet these assessments (Tennyson & Park, 1987).

Based on his experience with MAIS, Tennyson developed an educational learning theory for instructional design (Tennyson, 1992). This theory holds that there is a cognitive system of learning with affective, long-term memory, working memory, and executive control (e.g., attentional processes) components. Information enters this cognitive system either externally or internally. The latter mode is the result of either the exchange between the various system components or the construction of new knowledge. This instructional paradigm is expected to provide a foundation for the varied conditions of instructional design and development.

REFLECTIONS

As discussed, AIS seemingly contain instructional features for attuning students' learning processes to the instructional situation. These features are either inherent components of AIS or the result of algorithms based on basic memory research findings. AIS are thus ecological variables. This review has correspondingly illustrated the interaction described by Brunswik's (1957) famous E(nvironment)-O(rganism)-E(nvironment) arc. As indicated previously, one's environmental perceptions are guided by environmental affordances that correspond to the individual's cognitive materials. These perceptions then cause changes to occur within the individual and, subsequently, with the affordances needed to elicit the individual's future perceptions of that environmental situation. ITS, for example, have been designed to continually adapt the content and form of their instructional materials to changes in the student's level of learning.

This review has also indicated the ecological relevance of basic cognitive research findings. Such findings have led to the development of an emerging generation of AIS, which promise to revolutionize education. These practical applications have conversely demonstrated the usefulness and limitations of cognitive theories. As discussed, Anderson's (1983) hypotheses regarding cognitive phenomena have been revised because of his experience with the LISP system.

This review, however, has not fully established the utility of memory theories for naturally occurring phenomena. That is, the gap between extrapolations from basic laboratory findings in memory and the performance of students for AIS remains embarrassingly large (Davies, 1993). Also, this author had trouble finding information about the effectiveness of AIS for facilitating students' cognitive processes. Information was not found, for example, about STEAMER's effectiveness for helping students to develop the mind of an expert steam propulsion operator. Until more research findings on this topic are readily available, one can only speculate about the ecological significance of AIS and of basic cognitive research findings.

In closing, ecological notions of memory have relevance for both cognitive scientists and instructional technologists. Questions, however, remain about the validity of these notions vis-à-vis students' performance in computerized learning environments. By answering these questions, cognitive scientists will move closer toward meeting Neisser's (1978) challenge of understanding the natural consequences of memory phenomena. They will also move closer toward a convergence of basic and applied memory research.

ACKNOWLEDGMENTS

The opinions expressed in this chapter are those of the author and do not necessarily reflect the opinions of the U.S. Army Research Institute, the U.S. Army, or the U.S. Department of Defense.

REFERENCES

Alessi, S. M. (1988). Fidelity in the design of instructional simulations. *Journal of Computer-Based Instruction, 15,* 40–47.

Ames, C. (1984). Competitive, cooperative, and individualistic goal structures: A motivational analysis. In R. Ames & C. Ames (Eds.), *Research on motivation in education: Student motivation* (Vol. 1, pp. 177–207). New York: Academic Press.

Anderson, J. R. (1983). *The architecture of cognition.* Cambridge, MA: Harvard University Press.

Anderson, J. R. (1993). *Rules of the mind.* Hillsdale, NJ: Lawrence Erlbaum Associates.

Anderson, J. R., Conrad, F. G., & Corbett, A. T. (1989). Skill acquisition and the LISP tutor. *Cognitive Science, 13,* 467–505.

Anderson, J. R., Corbett, A. T., Koedinger, K. R., & Pelletier, R. (1995). Cognitive tutors: Lessons learned. *Journal of the Learning Sciences, 4*(2), 167–207.

Atkinson, R. C., & Raugh, M. R. (1975). An application of the mnemonic keyword method to the acquisition of a Russian vocabulary. *Journal of Experimental Psychology: Human Learning and Memory, 104,* 126–133.

Bessemer, D. W. (1991). *Transfer of SIMNET training in the Armor Officer Basic Course* (ARI Tech Rep. 920). Alexandria, VA: U.S. Army Research Institute for the Behavioral and Social Sciences.

Bransford, J. D., Barclay, J. R., & Franks, J. J. (1972). Sentence memory: A constructive versus interpretive view. *Cognitive Psychology, 3,* 193–209.

Bransford, J. D., Franks, J. J., Morris, C. D., & Stein, B. S. (1979). Some general constraints on learning and memory research. In L. S. Cermak & F. I. M. Craik (Eds.), *Levels of processing in human memory* (pp. 162–181). San Francisco, CA: Freeman.

Brunswik, E. (1957). Scope and aspect of the cognitive problem. In R. Jessor & K. Hammond (Eds.), *Cognition: The Colorado Symposium* (pp. 1–27). Chicago: University of Chicago Press.

Collins, A. M., & Quillian, M. R. (1969). Retrieval time from semantic memory. *Journal of Verbal Learning and Verbal Behavior, 8,* 240–247.

Davies, G. (1993). Afterword. *Applied Cognitive Psychology, 7,* 691–693.

Derry, S. J., & Murphy, D. A. (1986). Designing systems that train learning ability: From theory to practice. *Review of Educational Research, 56,* 1–39.

Frasson, C., & Gauthier, G. (1990). Introduction. In C. Frasson & G. Gauthier (Eds.), *Intelligent tutoring systems: At the classroom of artificial intelligence and education* (pp. 1–5). Norwood, NJ: Ablex.

Gibson, J. J. (1966). *The senses considered as perceptual systems.* Boston: Houghton Mifflin.

Glaser, R., & Bassock, M. (1989). Learning theory and the study of instruction. *Annual Review of Psychology, 40,* 609–625.

Herrmann, D. J., & Gruneberg, M. M. (1993). The need to expand the horizons of the "practical aspects of memory" movement. *Applied Cognitive Psychology, 7,* 553–565.

Hoffmann, R. R., & Deffenbacher, K. A. (1993). An analysis of the relations between basic and applied psychology. *Ecological Psychology, 5,* 315–352.

Hollan, J. D., Hutchins, E. L., & Weitzman, L. (1984). Steamer: An interactive inspectable simulation-based training system. *AI Magazine, 5,* 15–27.

Hooper, S., & Hannafin, M. J. (1991). Psychological perspectives on emerging instructional technologies: A critical analysis. *Educational Psychologist, 26,* 69–95.

Huston, A. C., & Wright, J. C. (1994). Educating children with television: The forms of the medium. In D. Zillmann, J. Bryant, & A. C. Huston (Eds.), *Media, children, and the family: Social scientific, psychodynamic, and clinical perspective* (pp. 73–84). Hillsdale, NJ: Lawrence Erlbaum Associates.

Jarvik, M. E. (1966). A functional view of memory. In K. R. Hammond (Ed.), *The psychology of Egon Brunswik* (pp. 237–257). New York: Holt, Rinehart & Winston.

Jonassen, D. H. (1988). Integrating learning strategies into courseware to facilitate deeper processing. In D. H. Jonassen (Ed.), *Instructional designs for microcomputer courseware* (pp. 151–181). Hillsdale, NJ: Lawrence Erlbaum Associates.

Kozma, R. B. (1991). Learning with media. *Review of Educational Research, 61,* 179–211.

Lesgold, A., Lajoie, S. P., Bunzo, M., & Eggan, G. (1992). A coached practice environment for an electronics troubleshooting job. In J. Larkin, R. Chabey, & C. Cheftic (Eds.), *Computer assisted instruction and intelligent tutoring systems: Shared goals and complementary approaches* (pp. 201–238). Hillsdale, NJ: Lawrence Erlbaum Associates.

Marchionini, G. (1988, November). Hypermedia and learning: Freedom and chaos. *Educational Technology,* pp. 8–13.

Montague, W. E. (1988). Promoting cognitive processes and learning by designing the learning environment. In D. H. Jonassen (Ed.), *Instructional designs for microcomputer courseware* (pp. 125–150). Hillsdale, NJ: Lawrence Erlbaum Associates.

Neisser, U. (1978). Memory: What are the important questions. In M. M. Gruneberg, P. E. Morris, & R. N. Sykes (Eds.), *Practical aspects of memory* (pp. 3–24). London: Academic Press.

Paivio, A. (1986). *Mental representations: A dual coding approach.* New York: Oxford University Press.

Park, O. (1992). Instructional applications of hypermedia: Functional features, limitations, and research issues. *Computers in Human Behavior, 8,* 259–272.

Rabinowitz, M., & Steinfeld, R. (1995). SIVL: The instructional design underlying a foreign language vocabulary tutor. In C. Hedly, P. Antonucci, & M. Rabinowitz (Eds.), *Thinking and literacy: The mind at work* (pp. 141–152). Hillsdale, NJ: Lawrence Erlbaum Associates.

Regian, J. W., & Shute, V. J. (1992). Automated instruction as an approach to individualization. In J. W. Regian & V. J Shute (Eds.), *Cognitive approaches to automated instruction* (pp. 1–13). Hillsdale, NJ: Lawrence Erlbaum Associates.

Rieber, L. P. (1990). Animation in computer-based instruction. *Educational Technology Research & Development, 38,* 77–86.

Salomon, G. (1979). *Interaction of media, cognition, and learning.* San Francisco, CA: Jossey-Bass.

Schank, R. C. (1990). *Teaching architectures* (Technical Rep. 3). Evanston, IL: Northwestern University, The Institute for Learning Science.

Scheidler, K. (1993, February). Students cross discipline boundaries with hypermedia. *The Computing Teacher,* pp. 16–21.

Schoenfield, A. H., & Herrmann, D. J. (1982). Problem presentation and knowledge structure in expert and novice mathematical problem solvers. *Journal of Experimental Psychology: Learning, Memory, and Cognition, 8,* 484–494.

Shaw, R. E., & Hazelett, W. M. (1986). Schemas in cognition. In V. McCabe & G. J. Balzano (Eds.), *Event cognition: An ecological perspective* (pp. 45–58). Hillsdale, NJ: Lawrence Erlbaum Associates.

Shlechter, T. M., Bessemer, D. W., & Kolosh, K. P. (1991). *The effects of simnet role-playing on the training of prospective platoon leaders* (Tech. Report 938). Alexandria, VA: U.S. Army Research Institute for the Behavioral and Social Sciences.

Shlechter, T. M., & Robinson, J. A. (1987). Ecological perspectives on memory and Brunswik's E-O-E arc. In M. M. Gruneberg, P. E. Morris, & R. N. Sykes (Eds.), *Practical aspects of memory: Current research and issues* (pp. 309–316). Chicester, England: Wiley.

Shute, V. J., & Glaser, R. (1990). Large-scale evaluation of an intelligent discovery world: Smithtown. *Interactive Learning Environments, 1,* 51–77.

Spiro, R. J., & Jehng, J-C. (1990). Cognitive flexibility and hypertext: Theory and technology for the nonlinear and multidimensional traversal for complex subject matter. In D. Nix & R. J. Spiro (Eds.), *Cognition, education, and multimedia: Exploring ideas in high technology* (pp. 163–205). Hillsdale, NJ: Lawrence Erlbaum Associates.

Swanson, H. L. (1993). Individual differences in working memory: A model testing and subgroup analysis of learning disabled and skilled readers. *Intelligence, 17,* 285–332.

Tennyson, R. D. (1992, January). An educational learning theory for instructional design. *Educational Technology,* pp. 31–41.

Tennyson, R. D., & Christiansen, D. L. (1988). MAIS: An intelligent learning system. In D. H. Jonassen (Ed.), *Instructional designs for microcomputer courseware* (pp. 247–274). Hillsdale, NJ: Lawrence Erlbaum Associates.

Tennyson, R. D., & Park, O. C. (1987). Artificial intelligence and computer-based learning. In R. M. Gagne (Ed.), *Instructional technology: Foundations* (pp. 319–342). Hillsdale, NJ: Lawrence Erlbaum Associates.

Thurman, R. A. (1993). Instructional simulation from a cognitive psychology viewpoint. *Educational Technology Research and Development, 14,* 75–89.

Tripp, S. D., & Roby, W. B. (1990). Orientation and disorientation in a hypertext lesson. *Journal of Computer-Based Instruction, 17,* 120–124.

Wittrock, M. C. (1986). Students' thought processes. In M. C. Wittrock (Ed.), *Handbook of research on teaching* (pp. 297–314). New York: Macmillan.

PART NINE

CLINICAL ASPECTS
OF MEMORY

CHAPTER TWENTY-SEVEN

Correlated Testing to Detect Cognitive Change

Herman Buschke
Martin Sliwinski
Gail Kuslansky
Albert Einstein College of Medicine

Cognitive *change* must be detected to infer acquired cognitive *impairment* in previously normal individuals. Cognitive change is detected by comparing individual test scores with some estimate of expected performance. The usual estimate of expected performance for all individuals is the mean of the distribution of normal scores. Although the mean and standard deviation are appropriate for describing the distribution of scores, for detecting group differences, and for characterizing individual performance relative to others, deviation from the mean is not appropriate for detecting cognitive change in individuals. A more sensitive and accurate estimate of expected performance can be obtained for each individual by correlated testing.

IMPAIRMENT AS DEVIATION FROM THE MEAN

Unless previous test scores or cutting scores are available, cognitive impairment is usually inferred by deviation from the mean. Individual test scores that are significantly different from (usually below) the mean of unimpaired normal subjects are taken to indicate acquired impairment (change) in previously normal individuals. Instead of estimating the expected performance for each individual, the mean is used to estimate expected performance for all individuals.

Using the mean score of unimpaired normal subjects as the single common estimate of expected performance by all individuals is self-contradictory. The mean is obtained by averaging scores that range from high to low, which is why the standard deviation is needed to describe the distribution of normal scores. The contradiction is most apparent when the standard deviation of the normal test scores is used to obtain z-scores. It is not reasonable to expect the same performance from all individuals, because the normal distribution shows that there is a range of normal performance (ability) that should be taken into account when expected performance is estimated. The range of normal scores above and below the mean shows real individual differences in ability that are not just due to measurement error. If the range of normal scores were due to random measurement error, then individual scores on repeated tests would not be correlated. However, it is well known that individual scores on repeated tests are correlated (and such correlation is used to demonstrate test reliability), indicating that the range of normal individual test scores is due to individual differences in ability. Detection of impairment by deviation from the mean does not take into account individual differences in ability.

Using the mean as the only reference point for detecting change (impairment) in all individuals has undesirable consequences. If impairment (change) cannot be detected until performance is significantly below the mean, then:

1. Impairment will not be detected until late when performance is so impaired that testing is hardly necessary.

2. Impaired performance by high-ability individuals who previously would have scored well above the mean will not be detected until late when impairment is great.

3. Performance by low-ability individuals who always would have scored well below the mean will be misclassified as impaired even though their performance has not changed. Using deviation from the mean to detect impairment delays detection of early impairment needed for early treatment; those with mild impairment who may benefit most from treatment will be not identified until it may be too late for effective treatment.

Figure 27.1 (top) illustrates how using the normal mean to estimate expected performance (EP = Mean) will not detect impairment in high-ability individuals when performance (P_1) has decreased but still is normal, and will misclassify low-ability individuals as impaired when performance (P_2) has not changed.

IMPAIRMENT AS DEVIATION FROM EXPECTED PERFORMANCE

A more accurate estimate of expected performance can be obtained for each individual by testing each individual on correlated control and experimental tests, so that their expected performance on the experimental test can be

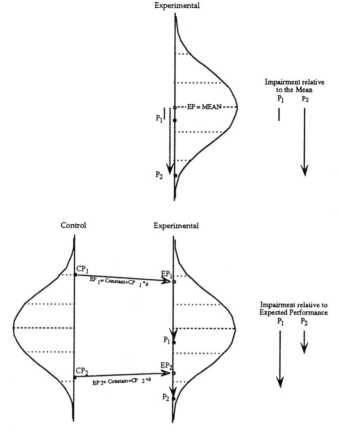

FIG. 27.1. Predicting expected performance using the normal mean (top of figure) or using correlated cognitive testing (bottom of figure).

predicted more accurately from their control performance. Then impairment can be detected by a significantly large difference (residual) between their actual performance and their expected performance. Detecting impairment by deviation from expected performance takes individual differences in ability into account by adjusting expected performance for ability shown by performance on the control test.

As in any cognitive experiment, correlated control and experimental conditions (tests) should be identical except for specific, theoretically based experimental differences. Performance on control and experimental tests will be correlated when the cognitive abilities measured by the control test also are needed for the experimental test.

When control and experimental tests are well correlated, the regression of experimental performance on control performance obtained from unimpaired normal subjects can be used to predict expected performance on the experimental test from performance on the control test. This regression describes the normal relationship between experimental and control performance. Experimental performance that is significantly less than the expected performance shows that change (impairment) has occurred, because such performance no longer conforms to the normal relationship between experimental performance and control performance.

Figure 27.1 (bottom) illustrates how correlated cognitive testing can detect impaired performance (P_1) by a previously high-ability individual, without misclassifying as impaired the performance (P_2) of a low-ability individual whose performance has not changed. Instead of using the mean to estimate expected performance, expected performance (EP_1 or EP_2) for each individual is predicted from their own control performance (CP_1 or CP_2), using the regression ($EP = Constant + CP*b$) obtained from normal unimpaired subjects. EP_1 is predicted from CP_1; the difference (residual) between EP_1 and P_1 is large, detecting impairment when performance (P_1) by a high-ability individual on the experimental test still is normal. EP_2 is predicted from CP_2; the difference (residual) between EP_2 and P_2 is small, so that low performance (P_2) by a low-ability individual will not be misclassified as impaired. The same experimental test scores (P_1 and P_2) are shown at the top and bottom of Fig. 27.1, but the relative impairment is quite different. Deviation from the mean (Fig. 27.1, top) indicates that P_1 is not impaired and P_2 is impaired. Deviation from expected performance predicted by correlated testing (Fig. 27.1, bottom) indicates that P_1 is impaired and P_2 is not impaired.

CORRELATED TESTING VERSUS DEVIATION
FROM THE MEAN

The insensitivity of deviation from the mean to early change is impressive. The normal distribution specifies that 2% of the scores are 2 or more *SD* below the mean, and only 16% are 1 or more *SD* below the mean. If the score of every individual in the distribution declined 1 *SD* from his or her previous level, only 16% of the scores then would be 2 or more *SD* below the previous normative mean; 84% of the scores still would be less than 2 *SD* below the mean and would not be identified as impaired. Even if the score of every individual declined 2 *SD* from his or her previous level, only 50% of the scores would be 2 or more *SD* below the normative mean. The other 50% of such impaired individuals would not be identified as impaired even though their scores had declined 2 *SD*. Many individuals whose performance has declined substantially will not be identified by significant deviation from the mean. Deviation from the mean is especially insensitive to early impairment in individuals with high premorbid ability. To be identified by scoring 2 *SD* below the mean, high-ability individuals with pre-morbid scores 2 *SD* above the mean must decline 4 times as much as low-ability individuals with premorbid scores 1 *SD* below the mean.

The following example was designed to illustrate deviation from expected performance can identify early impairment not identified by deviation from the mean, without false detection of impairment when change has not occurred. Assume that the control test mean = 17 (*SD* = 6.0), the experimental test mean = 36 (*SD* = 6.0), the normal regression of experimental on control scores is: expected score = .35 * control score + 30 and the standard error = 5.5.

For a high-ability individual with a control score of 29 (2 *SD* above the mean of the control test), the regression predicts an expected score of 40.2 on the experimental test. If the actual score obtained by that individual on the experimental test is 29, then the difference (residual) between the expected score and the actual score on the experimental test is −11.2. Because the standard error of the residuals is 5.5, the residual of −11.2 is 11.2/5.5 = 2 standard errors below the mean of the residuals (which is always 0.0). This shows that the experimental score of 29 is significantly different from the expected score of 40.2 when the expected score is adjusted for high ability shown by the control test, and indicates that change (impairment) has occurred.

On the other hand, because the normal mean score on the experimental test by unimpaired normal subjects is 36 with *SD* = 6.0, the experimental score of 29 is only 1.16 *SD* below the mean on the experimental test, which does not indicate impairment. This shows that deviation from the mean is not sensitive to early impairment in high-ability individuals that is detected by deviation from expected performance on correlated testing.

For a low-ability individual with a control score of 5 (2 *SD* below the mean of the control test), the regression predicts an expected score of 31.75 on the experimental test. If the actual score obtained by that individual on the experimental test is 24, then the difference (residual) between the expected score and the actual score on the experimental test is −7.75. Because the standard error of the residuals is 5.5, the residual of −7.75 is only −7.75/5.5 = 1.41 standard errors below the mean of the residuals. This shows that the experimental score of 24 is not significantly different from the expected score of 31.75 when the expected score is adjusted for low ability shown by the control score, and does not indicate impairment when change has not occurred.

On the other hand, because the normal mean score on the experimental test by unimpaired normal subjects is 36 with *SD* = 6.0, the experimental score of 24 is 12/6 = 2.0 *SD* below the mean on the experimental test, which is supposed to indicate acquired impairment. This shows that deviation from the mean will result in false detection of acquired impairment in low-ability individuals when change has not occurred.

LIMITATIONS OF CORRELATED COGNITIVE TESTING

Expected Performance Is Not an Estimate
of Premorbid Performance

The expected performance predicted by correlated cognitive testing is an estimate of *current* expected performance, not previous performance prior to the onset of impairment. Premorbid performance can be estimated only if the predictor test correlated with premorbid performance is a "hold" test of unchanged abilities, such as the New Adult Reading Test (Nelson & O'Connell, 1978), which estimates premorbid verbal IQ from unchanged ability to read irregular words aloud. The control test in correlated testing is not a "hold" test, and expected performance can change because control performance can change.

Control Performance Must Change
Less Than Experimental Performance

If performance on the control test changes at the same rate as performance on the experimental test, then the relationship between expected and actual performance on the experimental test will appear unchanged and the difference (residual) between expected and actual performance will not increase. Impairment will not be detected by correlated testing when control performance is as impaired as experimental performance. Correlated testing can detect impairment only when experimental performance is more impaired than control performance.

Test Scores Must Fall in the Range
of the Normative Regression

The normative regression can be used to predict expected performance from control performance only if control and experimental scores are in the range of scores used to obtain the regression. The regression does not apply to higher or lower test scores than those on which the regression is based.

Specific Cognitive Deficits Can Be Inferred Only
if the Experimental Test Is Not More Difficult
Than the Control Test

If the experimental test is more difficult than the control test (as shown by poorer average performance on the experimental test), then significantly large differences (residuals) between expected and actual performance may be due only to the greater difficulty of the experimental test (Chapman & Chapman, 1973). If the experimental test is an easier test that shows improvement, then significantly large differences (residuals) between expected and actual performance indicate impairment of the cognitive abilities needed to benefit from the conditions that result in better performance on the experimental test. This limitation applies to any cognitive test, not just to correlated testing. To show that impaired performance on any more difficult test is not due just to greater difficulty it is necessary to show that performance on other difficult tests is not impaired.

The Residual Does Not Preserve Information About Performance on the Control Test

The residual reflects performance on the experimental test, adjusted for ability shown by performance on the control test; the residual is highly correlated with performance on the experimental test. The residual does not retain information about performance on the control test; the residual is not correlated with performance on the control test. It is possible that adding information about performance on the control test may enhance the detection of impairment.

ADVANTAGES OF CORRELATED COGNITIVE TESTING

Change and Impairment Can Be Detected by Testing at Only One Time

A single test can only show that current performance is low relative to performance by others in the normative distribution, but cannot show that low performance is the result of change, and therefore cannot detect impairment. Correlated testing can show that low performance is the result of change, and therefore can detect impairment. Experimental performance that deviates significantly from expected performance shows that performance has changed and is impaired, because such performance no longer conforms to the normal relationship between experimental and control performance.

Impairment of Specific Cognitive Processes Can Be Identified

Impairment on a single test shows only that performance on that test as a whole is impaired, but does not identify impairment of any specific cognitive processes involved in that test. Impairment on correlated testing shows impairment of the specific cognitive processes that are involved in the experimental test but not in the control test. Impairment of specific cognitive processes can only be detected by testing under control conditions as well as under experimental conditions. Identification of the specific cognitive processes that are impaired is needed to analyze and understand the mechanisms of cognitive impairment.

Impairment Can Be Detected Earlier, With Greater Sensitivity

Detection of impairment by deviation from expected performance is more appropriate and sensitive than detection of impairment by deviation from the mean. Impairment cannot be detected by deviation from the mean until performance has fallen significantly below the mean. Deviation from the mean cannot detect impairment when performance has declined but still is in the normal range. Deviation from expected performance can detect impairment when performance has declined but still is in the normal range. Deviation from expected performance shown by correlated testing allows earlier detection of milder impairment that may be more responsive to treatment.

The Relationship of Correlated Test Scores May Be Affected Less by Cohort Effects

Age differences on a single cognitive test may be confounded by cohort effects. However, if cohort effects influence control and experimental tests to the same degree, then the *relationship* between control and experimental tests should be relatively free of cohort effects. Because the control and experimental tests are very similar and are correlated, it is plausible that both may be affected by the same cohort effects to approximately the same extent. When that is the case, cohort effects on the relationship between control and experimental tests may be less than cohort effects on either test alone. Attenuation of cohort effects would not be expected when two correlated tests are not similar. When correlated tests are as similar as control and experimental tests, cohort effects on the relationship between control and experimental tests may be less than cohort effects on either test alone.

CONCLUSIONS

Acquired cognitive impairment can only be detected by detecting cognitive change. A single test cannot show change, but correlated testing under correlated control and experimental conditions can detect cognitive change (impairment). The regression of experimental performance on control performance by unimpaired subjects can predict expected performance on the experimental test from performance on the control test. Experimental performance that deviates significantly from expected performance shows change (impairment), because such performance no longer conforms to the normal relationship between experimental and control performance. Deviation from expected performance is a more appropriate and sensitive measure of individual impairment than deviation from the mean.

ACKNOWLEDGMENTS

This work was supported by National Institute on Aging Grant AGO3949 (Project 2) and National Institute of Child Health and Human Development Grant HD-01799. We thank Robert Golden, Richard Lipton, John Kessler, Steven Mattis, and Walter Mischel for valuable discussion.

REFERENCES

Chapman, L. J., & Chapman, J. P. (1973). Problems in the measurement of cognitive deficit. *Psychological Bulletin, 79,* 380–385.

Nelson, H. E., & O'Connell, A. (1978). Dementia: the estimation of premorbid intelligence levels using the New Adult Reading Test. *Cortex, 14,* 234–244.

CHAPTER TWENTY-EIGHT

The Functional Deficits That Underlie Amnesia: Evidence From Amnesic Forgetting Rate and Item-Specific Implicit Memory

Andrew R. Mayes
University of Sheffield
Sheffield, England

Organic amnesia is a syndrome with four major features. First, patients show anterograde amnesia in which there is impaired recall and recognition of postmorbidly experienced facts and personal episodes. Second, they show retrograde amnesia in which there is impaired recall and recognition for premorbidly experienced facts and personal episodes. Third, they may show preservation of intelligence. Fourth, they may show preservation of short-term or immediate memory as assessed by the digit span or Corsi blocks tests. These features can be found following lesions to any one of several interconnected brain regions including the medial temporal lobes, the midline diencephalon, and the basal forebrain. It remains unresolved whether the deficits characteristic of amnesia are dissociable and, therefore, whether one or more kind of functional deficit underlies the syndrome. The characteristics of this or these functional deficits also remain unresolved. Relevant to the resolution of these issues is the neuroanatomy of amnesia, because the precise location of the lesions within the medial temporal lobes, midline diencephalon, and basal forebrain will help determine whether one or more deficits underlie amnesia, and perhaps even what their characteristics are likely to be.

The detailed characterization of the anatomy of amnesia is still controversial. Although it is believed that amnesia is caused by lesions to the medial temporal lobes, the midline diencephalon, or the basal forebrain, it is uncertain to which structures within these regions the damage occurs. Within the medial temporal lobes, it was argued by Squire (1992) that amnesia can be caused by hippocampal, but not by amygdala, lesions. In addition, he argued that parahippocampal and perirhinal cortex lesions cause severe amnesia. There has been insufficient exploration of these claims in humans, although Zola-Morgan, Squire, and Amaral (1986) described a patient who suffered bilateral damage to the CA1 field of the hippocampus following an ischaemic episode that caused an anterograde amnesia of moderate severity, but no measurable retrograde amnesia. Postencephalitic amnesics with damage to hippocampus, amygdala, parahippocampal, and perirhinal cortices, which may also extend to other cortical structures, show a far more severe anterograde amnesia and often a devastatingly severe retrograde amnesia. Finally, although evidence from monkeys shows that selective amygdala damage does not contribute to an impairment on delayed nonmatching-to-sample performance, the few extant case studies of humans with selective amygdala damage suggest that damage to this structure causes recall and recognition deficits for nonverbal material (e.g., see Tranel & Hyman, 1990). Amygdala damage and damage to its downstream diencephalic connections might, therefore, exacerbate at least the nonverbal amnesia shown by patients with medial temporal lobe lesions.

The parahippocampal and perirhinal polysensory association cortices provide about two thirds of the input to the hippocampus, which itself sends projections back to them as well as to other polysensory cortices that feed it with processed sensory information. Amnesia might, therefore, result from damage to any part of this system. This is most unlikely to be a complete account of amnesia, however, because it not only ignores the role of the diencephalic and basal forebrain structures believed to be implicated in amnesia as well as the possible contributory role of the amygdala in nonverbal amnesia, but also ignores the strong evidence that suggests that damage to the parahippocampal and perirhinal cortices produces a far more severe amnesia than does hippocampal damage. Damage to these cortices may cause a more severe amnesia than hippocampal lesions for one or both of two reasons. First, as they also send back projections to earlier stages of sensory processing, a lesion to them is likely to cause a much more severe disruption of the back projected information than would a lesion further downstream in the hippocampus. Provided the back projected information is involved in memory processing as seems likely, then a more severe amnesia should result from parahippocampal and perirhinal cortex lesions than from hippocampal lesions. Second, these cortices may project to midline thalamic nuclei, involved in memory processing, that do not form part of the hippocampal circuit.

If the amnesic syndrome can be caused by lesions to a polysensory cortex-hippocampal loop and separately by lesions to a polysensory cortex-nonhippocampal-midline diencephalic loop, the older view that it can also be caused by damage to a downstream hippocampal circuit should not be ignored. This third circuit, damage to which may cause amnesia, is the downstream projection path from the hippocampus to the midline diencephalon. It runs from the hippocampus via the fornix to the mammillary bodies and the anterior thalamus (which also receives an indirect projection via the mammillothalamic tract). There is evidence that links damage to each of these structures with memory disturbances that have at least some of the features of organic amnesia. Thus, Hodges and Carpenter (1991) found that fornix damage following removal of a third ventricle colloid cyst was associated with an anterograde amnesia primarily comprising a recall deficit. Gaffan (1992) argued, however, that fornix lesions in monkeys and humans disrupt recognition for previously encountered complex scenes, a form of recognition that centrally involves spatial memory. Dusoir, Kapur, Byrnes, McKinstry, and Hoare (1990) studied a patient with a penetrating paranasal injury, which magnetic resonance imaging (MRI) showed had primarily damaged the mammillary bodies, and found similar effects to those that have been described following fornix lesions. Their patient was impaired on tests of free recall, but relatively normal on recognition tests, and gave no indication of having a severe retrograde amnesia. Some evidence also links lesions of the anterior thalamic nucleus to amnesia, although it is unlikely that any lesion is completely specific to this structure. Daum and Ackerman (1994) formally assessed a woman with bilateral ischemic damage affecting the blood supply of the paramedian thalamic artery. The damage was shown by MRI to have primarily affected the anterior thalamic region of the patient who showed recognition as well as recall deficits.

One of the issues that requires much more detailed study is the extent to which hippocampal, fornix, mammillary body and anterior thalamic lesions cause recognition as well as recall deficits. Midline thalamic lesions to structures that do not form part of the hippocampal circuit may also cause memory deficits (e.g., see Mennemeier, Fennell, Valenstein, & Valenstein, 1992), although it remains to be shown whether or not these deficits are amnesic in kind. If they are, it would be of interest to determine whether the lesions responsible are to structures that receive projections from the parahippocampal and/or perirhinal cortices.

It remains uncertain how the downstream hippocampal and nonhippocampal circuits through the midline diencephalon are routed back to the medial temporal lobe (if indeed they are). The midline thalamic nuclei do, of course, have projections to the prefrontal association cortex, and the anterior thalamus is known to project back to the medial temporal lobe area. It has reciprocal connections to the posterior cingulate and retrosplenial cortices, both of which are densely interconnected with the hippocampus. A case study has shown that retrosplenial cortex lesions may cause a mild memory deficit that has some of the features of the full amnesia syndrome, although the fornix may also have been damaged in the patient described (Valenstein et al., 1987), and Cramon and Schuri (1992) argued that retrosplenial lesions may not cause a permanent amnesia.

There has also been very little research on the effects on memory of basal forebrain lesions in humans. Some evidence exists that implicates septal lesions in the production of an amnesiclike memory deficit. Thus, Berti, Arienta, and Papagno (1990) described a patient who suffered a lesion that damaged the upper part of the septum, but may have spared the diagonal band of Broca following the removal of a tumor. This patient displayed a moderate degree of anterograde amnesia that persisted for at least four months after surgery. Rupture and repair of anterior communicating artery aneurysms can also damage the septum as well as other structures within the basal forebrain, and is known to cause amnesia. For example, Phillips, Sangalang, and Sterns (1987) reported anterograde amnesia in a case who, at postmortem, was shown to have suffered damage to the septum, diagonal band of Broca, and the nucleus accumbens, but not the nucleus basalis of Meynert. Cramon and Schuri (1992) argued that lesions to basal forebrain structures such as the septum may cause an amnesiclike disturbance because they disrupt the modulation of the hippocampus that these structures normally perform.

The current picture of the neuroanatomy of amnesia is, therefore, unclear. It needs to be determined by systematic study whether lesions to the structures discussed previously really cause a complete amnesic syndrome, a partial amnesic syndrome, or a different kind of memory deficit. Only when this has been decided will be it be possible to say whether amnesia is caused by damage to one or more circuits, and hence whether it is likely to be underlain by more than one kind of functional deficit. At present, it remains an open possibility that separate damage to a polysensory cortex-hippocampal circuit, to the hippocampal-fornix-midline diencephalic circuit, and to a polysensory cortex-nonhippocampal midline diencephalic circuit could each cause distinct memory deficits, some or all of which are found in most amnesics.

THEORIES OF THE FUNCTIONAL DEFICIT(S) AND WHAT THEY PREDICT

It remains uncertain, therefore, whether the amnesic syndrome comprises one or more functional deficits. Functional deficit theories have nearly all assumed that there is only one underlying deficit so if it turns out that the symptoms of the syndrome can be dissociated, these theories will have to be modified. At the most general level, all hypotheses about the functional deficit that underlies amnesia must postulate a disruption of the encoding, storage, and/or retrieval of some or all components of information about facts and personally experienced episodes. Although encoding deficits may contribute to the memory deficits of amnesics with additional cognitive impairments (such as Alzheimer's disease patients), there is little reason to believe that encoding deficits are a feature of amnesia per se. Not only is poor encoding hard to reconcile with patients' preserved intelligence, but their memory also improves to the same degree as does that of normal subjects when they are encouraged to process information semantically (see Mayes, 1988). When amnesics are asked unpredictable questions about briefly displayed complex pictures immediately after the pictures are removed, it has been shown that they are able to answer questions about the pictures' meaning and about items' spatial location, color, and size as well as their control subjects (Mayes, Downes, Shoqeirat, Hall, & Sagar, 1993). Normal performance was found in amnesic patients with probable lesions in the medial temporal lobes, the midline diencephalon, and the basal forebrain. It, therefore, seems likely that amnesics encode information at the same rate as and in qualitatively the same manner as normal people unless they have additional brain damage that affects the ability to represent incoming sensory information in a rich manner. Amnesia must then be caused either by a failure to store or a failure to retrieve some or all aspects of fact and event information.

At present, storage deficit accounts of amnesia seem to be dominant (e.g., see Squire, 1992). Such accounts can differ from each other in several ways (see Mayes, 1988). One way relates to the nature of the storage deficit. Damage to some or all of the structures implicated in amnesia is postulated on one account to disrupt the modulation of storage processes that take place in the association neocortex. The effect of this disruption is that storage is very deficient. An alternative and more widely held view is that key aspects of fact and event information are held initially in the hippocampus, but that, with the passage of time, these memories are transferred to the association neocortex (e.g., see Squire, 1992). The work of Zola-Morgan and Squire (1990) suggested that, in monkeys, medial temporal cortex lesions only disrupt memories that were acquired up to around four weeks before the lesions. This work requires replication but, if correct, it would be consistent with transfer of storage to neocortex in a fairly short period of time. Unless the temporal characteristics of transfer are different in humans, there would be a severe problem in explaining retrograde amnesias that extend back 20 or 30 years before the occurrence of brain damage as has been reported about many human amnesics.

Another way in which storage deficit hypotheses about amnesia differ is with respect to what aspects of fact and event information they postulate are not stored properly. Many accounts are not at all clear on this issue, so it is plausible to suppose that the accounts intend to claim that all aspects of fact and event information are inadequately stored. To deny this would be to claim that these accounts postulate that some aspects of fact and event information are stored normally. One hypothesis that does make exactly this assumption is the context-memory deficit hypothesis (CMDH) of amnesia (see Mayes, Meudell, & Pickering, 1985). This hypothesis makes a distinction between target information that lies at the focus of attention during a learning experience and the background context of this target information that typically receives far less attention. Exactly what kinds of information constitute context has never been clearly worked out, but it is usual to distinguish between spatiotemporal features that do not affect the meaningful interpretation of targets (independent context) and features that do influence the meaningful interpretation of targets (interactive context). Some versions of the CMDH postulate a selective storage deficit in some or all aspects of independent context (e.g., see Gaffan, 1992), others concentrate more on interactive context (Warrington & Weiskrantz, 1982), whereas yet others postulate that storage of both kinds of context is impaired in amnesics. The CMDH postulates that amnesics are impaired at storing some or all aspects of a target item's context or the associations between the target and those contextual features, and as a result are impaired at recalling or recognising the target, which has been stored normally.

Recently, Eichenbaum, Otto, and Cohen (1994) formulated another hypothesis that has many of the features of a storage deficit account that applies to specific components of fact and event information. They proposed that hippocampal lesions disrupt the ability to store particular kinds of flexible relational information that presumably incorporates certain complex contextual-target associations. Hippocampal-neocortical interactions are deemed necessary to establish lasting memories for these relationships. They also postulated that parahippocampal and perirhinal cortex lesions disrupt the workings of an intermediate memory store for specific items (presumably targets in the terminology of the CMDH). Such lesions would also prevent the ability of an intact hippocampus to store relational information because, of course, these polysensory cortices not only provide the major input of processed sensory information to the hippocampus but also intermediate memory is necessary to help form many complex relational memories.

Although retrieval deficit accounts of amnesia used to be widely held (see, e.g., Mayes, 1988; Warrington & Weiskrantz, 1982, for discussions), they are currently far less influential than are storage deficit hypotheses. Nevertheless, there has been little discussion of the evidence that is relevant for discriminating between these broad groups of hypotheses. Any hypothesis about the functional deficit underlying amnesia must be able to explain the pattern of memory performance shown by patients with the amnesic syndrome. Two aspects of memory performance found in patients offer a powerful means of discriminating between storage and retrieval deficit hypotheses. The first concerns areas of preserved memory in amnesia and the second concerns forgetting rate patterns in amnesia.

It is well known that amnesics show preservation of certain forms of implicit memory such as skill learning (see Mayes, 1988). It is probable, however, that all this reveals is that skill memory is radically different from recall and recognition of facts and events and is mediated by brain regions, such as the basal ganglia and cerebellum, that are organized in a very different way from the regions implicated in amnesia. Skill does not involve implicit memory for specific items, but it has been claimed that amnesics also show preservation of what might be referred to as *item-specific implicit memory*. This is a form of memory revealed by a change in the way that the rememberer processes repeated items or components of repeated items. This item-specific processing change does not involve the kind of awareness of pastness that is the central feature of recall and recognition (collectively referred to as *explicit memory*) and, unlike recall and recognition that involve effortful retrieval processes, implicit memory retrieval is believed to be automatic. But the key point is that implicit and explicit memory can be of apparently the *same* information. If amnesics show preservation of item-specific implicit memory for information that was novel prior to learning, then it becomes plausible to argue that they must have stored this information normally, even though they show very impaired explicit memory for it. In other words, to the extent that amnesics show preserved item-specific implicit memory for novel information, they cannot be said to have a storage deficit, and, therefore, they must have a kind of retrieval deficit that prevents normal explicit memory being shown.

The only way to avoid this conclusion is to argue that the same information is held in different stores, one for implicit and one for explicit memory, with amnesics having a storage deficit that is selective for explicit memory. No one seems to hold this view. Of course, apparently comparable explicit and implicit item-specific memory tests may tap slightly different information. Nevertheless, it is difficult to avoid the conclusion that preservation of item-specific implicit memory for previously novel information in amnesics shows that they can store fact and event information normally. If their item-specific implicit memory is normal for all fact/event information, then all storage accounts of amnesia would be refuted, but if they show impaired implicit memory only for novel contextual associations or complex relations, then the CMDH and Eichenbaum's hippocampal hypothesis would be respectively supported. It is, therefore, critical to determine whether amnesics show preservation of item-specific implicit memory for some or all aspects of novel fact and event information.

Amnesics seem to encode facts and events normally and hold the encoded information normally in immediate memory, but, following distraction, an impairment in the ability to recall and recognize the same information becomes apparent. If this impairment is caused by a deficit in an explicit memory retrieval process, there is no clear reason to expect it to worsen as the learning-test delay is increased (i.e., to expect amnesics to show accelerated forgetting). This would only be expected if amnesics show increased susceptibility to interference during the delay. For example, retroactive interference might build up in the delay to cause forgetting, the degree of which would depend on how much interference there was and how susceptible to it one was. It has been claimed that amnesics are more susceptible to interference. The claim rests on the use of a paradigm that depends on the learning of related paired associate words like *soldier–rifle*. Subjects first learn an A–B list comprising items like *soldier–rifle*, and then learn an A–C list comprising items like *soldier–army*. When tested on the A–B list using the first word as a cue for the second, it has been claimed that amnesics perform normally. But when tested on the A–C list, it has been claimed that they are abnormally sensitive to interference because they are grossly impaired and make many intrusion errors from the A–B list.

We examined this effect further under two conditions (Mayes, Pickering, & Fairbairn, 1987). In the first condition, at test subjects were shown the first words from the pairs one at a time and asked to do their best to recall which word had been presented with it in the earlier learning phase. In the second condition, at test subjects were again shown the first words from the pairs one at a time and asked to produce the first related associate word that came to mind. In the first condition, the amnesics showed worse cued recall of the A–C list and made more intrusion errors than did their control subjects, just as had previously been reported. But, unlike in some of the earlier work, their memory was also worse for the A–B list. In the second condition there was no difference between the two groups, and they both performed on the A–C list like the amnesics had in the first condition. We interpreted this as showing that the amnesics had worse explicit memory on the A–B list and that their sensitivity to proactive interference arose because their performance depended on item-specific implicit memory, which does not use contextual information, and so is very susceptible to proactive interference. When normal people also rely on item-specific implicit memory, they show a similar level of sensitivity to interference. There is, therefore, no direct evidence that amnesic explicit memory is any more sensitive to proactive and retroactive interference than is normal people's explicit memory. Given this, it is highly probable that a retrieval deficit account of amnesia should predict a normal rate of forgetting in patients following the initial distraction that reveals their explicit memory deficit.

If amnesia is caused by a deficit in the storage processes that lead to long-term memory, then it is plausible to argue that their explicit memory deficit should become more severe as consolidation into long-term memory progresses in normal people in the period after learning (i.e., they should show accelerated forgetting). This would be the case whether amnesics fail to modulate consolidation processes in an optimal manner or whether their fact and event memories are initially maintained in a structure damaged in patients so as to impair the development of their long-term memories. The time scale over which forgetting might be expected to be accelerated is uncertain, because this depends on the time course of the affected consolidation processes. This prediction leaves a major problem that has been inadequately addressed in the literature. The problem concerns what supports memory while consolidation into long-term memory is occurring. However, although this problem is unsolved, its solution should not undermine the validity of the prediction of accelerated amnesic forgetting by storage deficit accounts. Which kinds of explicit memory should be lost at an accelerated rate should be a function of the storage deficit account. For example, if all aspects of fact and event information are deficiently stored, then forgetting should be accelerated for recall and recognition of any aspect of this information. If, on the other hand, the CMDH is correct, then forgetting should only be accelerated when it depends on explicitly retrieving contextual associations.

ITEM-SPECIFIC IMPLICIT MEMORY

It is widely agreed that amnesics, regardless of probable lesion location, show preserved item-specific implicit memory for verbal, nonverbal, and contextual information that was familiar prior to learning (see Mayes, 1988; Priestley & Mayes, 1992). One popular way of explaining this pattern of results is to postulate that the learning experience activates an extant long-term memory, that the memory remains active for some time or is modified in some relatively long-lasting manner, so as to influence how items whose memories have been activated are processed at test. This does not require one to postulate that amnesics have stored new fact/event memories normally. Other accounts of item-specific implicit memory for items familiar prior to learning are possible, but there is currently no agreed-on theoretical position so it is unwise to view preservation of this kind of item-specific implicit memory as support for preservation of storage of fact and event information in amnesics.

The same cannot be said for item-specific implicit memory for information that was novel prior to learning, because memory for such information must depend on the creation of new memories. There is, however, no agreed-on position as to whether amnesics show preserved implicit memory for all kinds of novel items, although some workers now believe that amnesics show impaired implicit memory for novel associations, particularly if these are semantic in nature (see Graf & Masson, 1993). For example, we and others have failed to find normal (indeed any) enhanced word-stem completion priming in amnesics (Mayes & Gooding, 1989). Performance on this test is likely to depend on memory for semantic associations between previously unassociated or weakly associated words, so it might be argued that amnesics fail to store such associations whereas normal people do.

There is, however, a major interpretative problem that relates to how item-specific implicit and explicit memory are measured. Implicit memory is supposed to be tapped by indirect memory tasks in which no reference is made to memory or the learning experience and subjects' memories are revealed by how they process repeated items or components/associates of repeated items. In contrast, explicit memory is supposed to be tapped by direct memory tasks in which reference is made to the learning experience and subjects are overtly asked to remember information encoded during that experience. It has been argued, however, that performance on both direct and indirect memory tasks may often depend on both explicit and implicit memory to varying degrees, and explicit memory could be used to either enhance or inhibit performance on indirect memory tasks (Jacoby & Kelley, 1992). For example, amnesics have been reported to show a normal tendency to complete dot templates with previously shown patterns (Gabrieli, Milberg, Keane, & Corkin, 1990). Although we have replicated this result at least with some measures of pattern completion (Gooding, van Eijk, Mayes, & Meudell, 1993), we have also found strong evidence that normal subjects' performance on this task seems to rely almost entirely on explicit memory. We are left with an unexplained puzzle about why amnesics' performance on this indirect memory task seems to be preserved.

If the impurity of item-specific indirect memory tests is to be taken seriously, then much current work on amnesia is hard to interpret. If amnesics' performance is normal, this could either be because they have preservation of item-specific implicit memory or because their controls are inhibiting their performance by using their superior explicit memory. Conversely, if patients' performance is impaired, this could be either because their item-specific implicit memory is deficient or because normal subjects are enhancing their performance by using their superior explicit memory.

To resolve the question of whether amnesic novel item-specific implicit memory is preserved, it will be necessary to adopt a convergent operations approach in which results must be obtained using several procedures designed to minimize or control for the contribution of explicit memory to memory performance. These procedures could include: (a) tasks in which implicit memory is indicated by a reduction in reaction time to repeated items so as to reduce the chances of explicit memory contributing to performance, (b) tasks in which implicit memory is indicated by changed autonomic responses to repeated items, (c) tasks in which attention is divided at test so as to prevent a significant contribution from explicit memory, and (d) the use of a modified form of Jacoby's procedure (see Jacoby & Kelley, 1992) to estimate the strengths of both explicit and implicit memory from task performance. All these procedures make different assumptions, so one can only be confident about conclusions reached by using them when these conclusions are reasonably congruent.

Using a modification of Jacoby's procedure, which employs multidimensional signal detection theory with the famous names task (Jacoby, Woloshyn, & Kelley, 1989), we (Mayes, van Eijk, & Isaac, 1995) found that an amnesic group with patients of several etiologies showed impaired recollection for the names, but completely preserved familiarity, which Jacoby believed to be based on an automatic attribution dependent on increased fluency of processing, a form of implicit memory. This effect applied equally regardless of whether the names were likely to have had some degree of preexperimental familiarity or to have been completely familiar. Before one can be confident about this conclusion, however, it would be desirable to assess implicit memory for the novel names using procedures that rely on different assumptions from Jacoby's modified procedure. Only when this method is followed can we be confident about whether amnesics show preserved item-specific implicit memory for all fact/event information, none of it, or only some parts of it so as to discriminate between different storage deficit and retrieval deficit accounts of amnesia.

FORGETTING RATE IN AMNESIA

Nearly all work on amnesic forgetting rates has investigated rate of loss of recognition at delays beyond 10 minutes with the intention of determining whether patients with medial temporal lobe lesions show a different pattern of memory breakdown than do patients with midline diencephalic lesions. In order to make the comparison of amnesic and normal forgetting rates, it was necessary to avoid floor and ceiling effects and possible scaling effects by matching patient and control recognition at the shortest delay used. This was achieved by allowing amnesics longer to learn the target material. Thus, for example, amnesics might receive 8-second exposures to each of 120 targets whereas their controls would be given only 1-second exposures. A 10-minute delay would then typically be given before testing recognition for a proportion of the items. This procedure gives rise to an artifact in which amnesic forgetting rates tend to be underestimated because the initial mean item presentation-to-test delay is actually longer for them than it is for their controls (see Mayes, 1988). Thus, results of studies using the procedure are difficult to interpret with confidence. Nevertheless, it has to be said that there is currently little good evidence suggesting that patients with medial temporal lobe lesions lose the ability to show recognition of recently perceived items over delays between 10 minutes and 1 week faster than do patients with midline diencephalic lesions. Indeed, there is little evidence to suggest that any amnesics lose the ability to recognize pictures and simple verbal material over these delays faster than do normal people.

There has been hardly any research that has looked at forgetting over shorter delays in amnesics and examined their rate of loss of free and cued recall as well as recognition. Recently, we did this using short story material similar to that found in the Logical Memory subtest of the Wechsler Memory

Scale (Isaac & Mayes, submitted). A large number of these stories were matched for difficulty in a pilot study with student subjects. Recognition tests were constructed with a subset of the stories. These tests comprised 12 recognition test items that tapped memory for specific components of the stories. Amnesic free recall of the stories was matched to that of their controls after a filled delay of 15 seconds by giving the patients up to five presentations of each story, compared to the controls' single presentation. Free recall of equivalent stories was tested after the same exposures at delays of 1 minute, 2 minutes, 5 minutes, and 10 minutes. Recognition was tested in the same way except that the delays used were 15 seconds, 10 minutes, and 1 hour because recognition was lost more slowly. During all of the longer delays for both recall and recognition tests, subjects were occupied with other tasks to minimize rehearsal. At the shortest delay, amnesics and their controls were matched on free recall and recognition performance, which suggests that these forms of explicit memory are equally impaired at this delay. After 10 minutes, however, the amnesics had lost free recall, but not recognition, pathologically fast, so that at this delay they were more impaired on free recall of the stories than they were at recognizing them.

Further experiments eliminated several explanations of these results. First, we showed that they were not caused by the normal subjects engaging in surreptitious rehearsal during the longer delays. Second, we showed that the results were not caused by the matching procedure itself artifactually accelerating the loss of free recall ability in subjects. Third, we showed that even at the 15-second delay, short-term memory was making a minimal contribution to performance because severe amnesics with normal short-term memory recalled little or nothing at this delay following five learning trials. This eliminated the possibility that long-term memory free recall was lost at a normal rate in the amnesics, but seemed to be lost pathologically fast because short-term memory contributed to performance after a 15-second delay, but not after a 10-minute delay.

We confirmed the main results in a second experiment in which we matched at a short filled delay of 20 seconds and tested free recall, cued recall, and recognition at 10 minutes. When the cues provided some of the information that needed to be recalled, we found that cued recall, like recognition, was lost at a normal rate by the amnesics, although free recall was lost pathologically fast. In a third experiment, we examined the effects of proactive interference on free recall at 15-second and 1-minute delays, and of retroactive interference on recognition at delays of 10 minutes and 1 hour. In all cases, interference was produced by presentation of three stories that were very similar to the target story. Both amnesic and control memory was disrupted to a similar, small degree by the interference, which makes it hard to argue that the amnesic accelerated loss of free recall resulted from increased sensitivity to interference. The effects, found in the three experiments, occurred in amnesics of several etiologies, who probably had lesions respectively in the medial temporal lobes, the midline diencephalon, and the basal forebrain. Lesion location, therefore, did not seem to influence the degree to which loss of free recall was accelerated.

We postulated that whereas free recall depends primarily on recollection of items in association with the encoding context in which they occurred, recognition depends on this process, but also on a familiarity process in which familiarity is attributed to items that are processed more fluently as a result of their recent exposure (see Jacoby & Kelley, 1992). If amnesics have a storage deficit that affects target-context associations as the CMDH states, then they should lose free recall ability pathologically fast as we found. Recognition, on the other hand, depends partially on familiarity that our other work suggests may not be impaired in amnesics, and a second study using our modification of the Jacoby procedure indicates that familiarity and recollection may decline at the same rate in normal people (Isaac, Mayes, & van Eijk, in preparation). Thus, it may be much harder to find evidence of accelerated forgetting of recognition in amnesics. If this account is correct, then amnesics should show accelerated loss of free recall for all fact and event information. In order to test this possibility, Isaac repeated the forgetting rate procedure with three kinds of word list: unrelated word lists, lists of related words that are randomly arranged, and lists of related words that are arranged so as to facilitate the organization of their semantic encoding. The results with the two kinds of related word list were similar to those that we had already obtained with the stories, but with the unrelated word lists we found no evidence of accelerated loss of free or cued recall, or of recognition, in the amnesics. This result agrees with that of Haist, Shimamura, and Squire (1992), who found that amnesic recall and recognition of unrelated word lists decays at a normal rate between delays of 15 seconds and up to 2 weeks.

Free recall of related word lists (and stories), but not of unrelated word lists, probably depends on forming complex associations between semantically related words and their encoding context, whereas recognition of individual words does not depend on retrieving these complex associations. The most likely explanation of our results is that amnesics, regardless of lesion location, have a storage deficit for complex target-contextual associations that involve two or more targets. If this is correct, then recognition that depends on retrieving such complex associations should also decline at an accelerated rate in amnesics in the first 10 minutes after learning. For example, if the pairs *horse–chisel* and *train–mountain* appeared in a list, amnesics should show accelerated loss of the ability to decide whether *horse–chisel, horse–mountain,* or *horse–train* appeared in the list. This prediction remains to be tested. It also needs to be determined why amnesics show impaired explicit memory for all fact and event material after filled delays of 15 or fewer seconds. Is this caused by a different functional deficit or can it be explained as a more extreme manifestation of the basic storage deficit? In general, however, our results support the view that all amnesics, regardless of lesion location, fail to store complex target-context associations normally.

REFERENCES

Berti, A., Arienta, C. & Papagno, C. (1990). A case of amnesia after excision of the septum pellucidum. *Journal of Neurology, Neurosurgery and Psychiatry, 53*, 922–924.

Cramon, D. Y. von, & Schuri, U. (1992). The septo-hippocampal pathways and their relevance to human memory: A case report. *Cortex, 28*, 411–422.

Daum, I., & Ackerman, H. (1994). Dissociation of declarative and nondeclarative memory after bilateral thalamic lesions: A case study. *International Journal of Neuroscience, 75*, 153–165.

Dusoir, H., Kapur, N., Byrnes, D., McKinstry, S., & Hoare, R. D. (1990). The role of diencephalic pathology in human memory disorder: Evidence from a penetrating paranasal brain injury. *Brain, 113*, 1695–1706.

Eichenbaum, H., Otto, T., & Cohen, N. J. (1994). Two functional components of the hippocampal system. *Behavioral and Brain Sciences, 17*, 449–518.

Gabrieli, J. D. E., Milberg, W., Keane, M. M., & Corkin, S. (1990). Intact priming of patterns despite impaired memory. *Neuropsychologia, 28*, 417–427.

Gaffan, D. (1992). The role of the hippocampal-fornix-mammillary system in episodic memory. In L. R. Squire & N. Butters, (Eds.), *Neuropsychology of memory* (2nd ed., pp. 336–346). New York: Guilford.

Gooding, P. A., van Eijk, R., Mayes, A. R., & Meudell, P. R. (1993). Preserved pattern completion priming for novel abstract geometric shapes in amnesics of several aetiologies. *Neuropsychologia, 31*, 789–810.

Graf, P., & Masson, M. E. J. (1993). *Implicit memory.* Hove, England: Lawrence Erlbaum Associates.

Haist, F., Shimamura, A. P., & Squire, L. R. (1992). On the relationship between recall and recognition memory. *Journal of Experimental Psychology: Learning, Memory and Cognition, 18*, 691–702.

Hodges, J. R., & Carpenter, K. (1991). Anterograde amnesia with fornix damage following removal of a third ventricle colloid cyst. *Journal of Neurology, Neurosurgery and Psychiatry, 54*, 633–638.

Isaac, C., & Mayes, A. R. (submitted). *Forgetting rate in amnesics of several aetiologies.*

Jacoby, L. L., & Kelley, C. (1992). Unconscious influences of memory: Dissociations and automaticity. In A. D. Milner & M. D. Rugg (Eds.), *The neuropsychology of consciousness* (pp. 201–233). London: Academic Press.

Jacoby, L. L., Woloshyn, V., & Kelley, C. (1989). Becoming famous without being recognised: Unconscious influences of memory produced by dividing attention. *Journal of Experimental Psychology: General, 118*, 115–125.

Mayes, A. R. (1988). *Human organic memory disorders.* Cambridge, England: Cambridge University Press.

Mayes, A. R., Downes, J. J., Shoqeirat, M., Hall, C., & Sagar, H. J. (1993). Encoding ability is preserved in amnesia: Evidence from a direct test of encoding. *Neuropsychologia, 31*, 745–759.

Mayes, A. R., van Eijk, R., & Isaac, C. L. (1995). Assessment of familiarity and recollection in the false fame paradigm using a modified process dissociation procedure. *Journal of the International Neuropsychology Society, 1*, 469–482.

Mayes, A. R., & Gooding, P. (1989). Enhancement of word completion priming in amnesics by cueing with previously novel associates. *Neuropsychologia, 27*, 1057–1072.

Mayes, A. R., Meudell, P. R., & Pickering, A. (1985). Is organic amnesia caused by a selective deficit in remembering contextual information? *Cortex, 21*, 167–202.

Mayes, A. R., Pickering, A., & Fairbairn, A. (1987). Amnesic sensitivity to proactive interference: Its relationship to priming and the causes of amnesia. *Neuropsychologia, 25*, 211–220.

Mennemeier, M., Fennell, E., Valenstein, E., & Valenstein, K. M. (1992). Contributions of the left intralaminar and medial thalamic nuclei to memory: comparisons and report of a case. *Archives of Neurology, 49*, 1050–1058.

Phillips, S., Sangalang, V., & Sterns, G. (1987). Basal forebrain infarction. *Archives of Neurology, 44*, 1134–1138.

Priestley, N. M., & Mayes, A. R. (1992). Preservation of priming for interactive context. *Cortex, 28*, 555–574.

Squire, L. R. (1992). Memory and the hippocampus: A synthesis from findings with rats, monkeys, and humans. *Psychological Review, 99*, 195–231.

Tranel, D., & Hyman, B. T. (1990). Neuropsychological correlates of bilateral amygdala damage. *Archives of Neurology, 47*, 349–355.

Valenstein, E., Bowers, D., Verfaellie, M., Heilman, K. M., Day, A., & Watson, R. T. (1987). Retrosplenial amnesia. *Brain, 110*, 1631–1646.

Warrington, E. K., & Weiskrantz, L. (1982). A disconnection syndrome? *Neuropsychologia, 20*, 233–248.

Zola-Morgan, S., & Squire, L. R. (1990). The primate hippocampal formation: Evidence for a time-limited role in memory storage. *Science, 250*, 288–290.

Zola-Morgan, S., Squire, L. R., & Amaral, D. G. (1986). Human amnesia and the medial temporal region: Enduring memory impairment following a bilateral lesion limited to field CA1 of the hippocampus. *Journal of Neuroscience, 10*, 2950–2967.

CHAPTER TWENTY-NINE

A Taxonomy of Priming: Implications for Aging

John M. Rybash
Hamilton College

OVERVIEW

A multitude of developmental and neuropsychological investigations have revealed that aging is accompanied by decrements in explicit memory. Empirical studies that have examined the relationship between age and implicit memory, however, have yielded an array of equivocal findings. The research evidence suggesting variability in the pattern of implicit memory performance in older adults raises several important issues. What types of implicit memory are spared (or impaired) during the course of normal aging? What are the psychological and neurological mechanisms underlying the age-related stability (or decline) of different categories of implicit memory? What is the relationship between the changes in implicit memory associated with normal aging vis-à-vis neuropathological aging (e.g., Alzheimer's disease) and neurological disorder (e.g., amnesia)? What insights about memory training and remediation can be gained from an understanding of age-related changes in implicit memory? The aim of this chapter is to provide some preliminary answers to these questions.

Implicit and Explicit Memory

Explicit memory, which is measured by tasks such as recognition and recall, involves the intentional conscious recollection of past experience. Implicit memory, on the other hand, is assessed by priming tasks in which subjects are

407

asked to make judgments about stimuli, some of which were previously presented and some of which were not. Priming is demonstrated if exposure to items during a study phase results in enhanced performance (e.g., reduced latency of response, or increased accuracy of response) relative to control items during a test phase. Consequently, implicit memory does not depend on the deliberate conscious awareness of previous events (Graf & Komatsu, 1994).

Squire (1994) suggested that explicit and implicit memory tasks are performed by the *declarative* and *nondeclarative (procedural)* memory systems, respectively. He proposed that structures in medial temporal region, hippocampus, and diencephalon provide the neurological foundation for declarative memory. Alternatively, he speculated that nondeclarative memory has its basis in posterior cortical loci that influence performance on different priming tasks, and subcortical zones that regulate the retention of perceptual-motor skills.

Roediger (Roediger, 1990; Roediger & Challis, 1992) argued for the existence of a single memory system with two different modes of operation. He suggested that performance on tasks of explicit memory is usually supported by conceptually driven processes, whereas implicit memory is enhanced by data-driven processes. He also maintained that performance on any type of memory task depends on the degree to which the processing operations used at study match those at test, and that it is possible to construct implicit as well explicit memory tasks that benefit from different blends of conceptually driven and data-driven processing.

Currently, there is little agreement about whether implicit memory refers to a neuroanatomically distinct memory system, a data-driven processing strategy, or simply to a particular type of memory task that yields findings that are different from standard explicit measures. It has been suggested that the terms *indirect* and *direct* be substituted for *implicit* and *explicit* memory, respectively. The use of these neutral terms was viewed as a way of avoiding a number of unresolved (and potentially unresolvable) theoretical issues. I suggest that some of the confusion surrounding the construct of implicit memory can be alleviated by the use of a taxonomic system that distinguishes among various categories of priming.

A Taxonomy of Priming Tasks

There are a number of important dimensions on which priming tasks differ. First, priming tasks vary with regard to their retrieval demands. On some tasks, such as perceptual identification, a subject is required to make a simple response to a stimulus that contains all of the perceptual information that was available during a study period—a subject sees the word *motel* at study and is simply required to read the word *motel* at test. Other tasks, such as word stem completion, impose far greater retrieval demands. Now, the subject is presented with portions of previously presented items (*mot__*) and is instructed to complete the stems with the first letters that "pop into their mind" that spell valid words. Even though the subject is not instructed to compete the word stem with a study item, the task is such that the subject must retrieve words (*motel, motor, motion*, etc.) in order to perform the task.

Second, priming tasks may be associative or nonassociative in nature (Howard, 1991; Light & LaVoie, 1993). The stimuli in associative tasks consist of semantically unrelated pairs of words (*motel–truck*) or pictures, or novel sequences of body movements. Nonassociative tasks, on the other hand, contain individual study items (*motel*).

Third, different mental representations have been found to underlie performance on different types of priming tasks. Some types of priming depend on the activation of presemantic representations of words and/or objects (Petersen, Fox, Snyder, & Raichle, 1990; Posner, Petersen, Fox, & Raichle, 1988; Schacter, 1994). Other forms of priming have their basis in motoric representations of specific sequences of body movements (Petri & Mishkin, 1994).

Fourth, priming tasks vary to the degree to which conceptually driven versus data-driven factors affect task performance (Challis & Brodbeck, 1992; Weldon, 1993). For example, a blend of conceptually driven and data-driven processes facilitates performance on a word fragment completion task, whereas data-driven processes, by themselves, enhance performance on tasks of perceptual identification.

Fifth, performance on different priming tasks may depend on the participation of different neural systems or subcomponents. Tasks that involve the activation of semantic and presemantic representations of word forms draw on the resources of anterior and posterior cortical areas, respectively (Schacter, 1994). Furthermore, tasks that generate strong retrieval demands, at least for verbal material, are more likely to depend on anterior (i.e., prefrontal) cortical loci (Monsch et al., 1994; Moscovitch & Winocur, 1992; Randolph, Braun, Goldberg, & Chase, 1993). Alternatively, tasks that measure the priming of specific motor sequences depend on subcortical-striatal components (Knopman & Nissen, 1991; Petri & Mishkin, 1994).

I suggest that priming tasks may be placed in four categories as follows: retrieval-free priming, retrieval-dependent priming, retrieval-dependent-associative priming, and motoric priming (see Table 29.1). The primary consideration in developing these categories, and in assigning tasks to categories, was the presumed retrieval demands generated by different priming tasks. The decision to emphasize retrieval requirements had its roots in two interrelated sources. First, Tulving offered a number of convincing arguments about the dominant role played by retrieval processes in explicating human memory phenomena. To quote: "*The key process of memory is retrieval.*

TABLE 29.1
Examples of Priming Tasks Within Each Category
of the Proposed Taxonomy

Categories			
Retrieval-Free Tasks	Retrieval-Dependent Tasks	Retrieval-Dependent-Associative Tasks	Motoric Tasks
Word naming	Word stem completion	Priming of new associations	Nissen
Lexical decision	Word fragment	word stem completion	Serial RT
Sentence reading	completion	format	Task
Compound word reading	Homophone spelling	Priming of new associations	
Picture naming	Exemplar generation	word fragment completion	
Object decision		format	

Note. A fuller version of this table, including examples of study and test items, descriptions of subjects' tasks, and specification of dependent measures, is available from the author upon request.

The storage or engram alone, in the absence of retrieval, is no better than no storage and no engram at all. . . . An engram does *not exist independently of retrieval.* . . ." (Tulving, cited in Gazzaniga, 1991, p. 91; italics in original).

Second, a large body of evidence suggests that deficient retrieval processes underlie age differences in memory (Bäckman, 1992; Burke & Light, 1981; Light, 1991). For example, Craik and his colleagues (Craik, 1992; Craik & Jennings, 1992) showed that environmental support at retrieval either attenuates or exacerbates age-related memory loss. I suggest that retrieval requirements play a central role in determining age differences in implicit memory as well as the basic nature of different implicit memory tasks. Priming tasks that offer the greatest amount of environmental support at retrieval are the least likely to be negatively affected by age or neurological disease, whereas tasks that offer the least amount of support at retrieval are the most likely to show the opposite age- and disease-related trajectories.

Retrieval-Free Priming. Tasks of retrieval-free priming are those in which a subject must make a simple response to a test stimulus that is presented in its entirety. At test, a subject may be shown the visual word *spoon* or a picture of a spoon, and may be instructed to read the stimulus, name the stimulus, or decide if the stimulus represents a valid word or picture. Priming is typically measured by comparing the subject's reaction times to items that appeared at study relative to those that did not. These tasks are retrieval-free in that the environment supplies the subject with all of the information (e.g., the visual word *spoon*) that is necessary to make the required judgment, even if the test stimulus is presented at threshold and/or is perceptually degraded.

The priming tasks within this category are retrieval-free in a relative sense rather than an absolute sense. For example, asking a subject to name a word or picture necessitates the retrieval or activation of a phonological code. There are several factors that could prevent a subject (especially one who is neurologically impaired) from accessing this phonological code, which, in turn, could impair the subject's performance on a priming task—even if the priming task was, by the current definition, retrieval-free. Put somewhat differently, if a priming task were completely free of any sort of retrieval demand in an absolute sense, there would be no task for the subject to perform.

Performance on retrieval-free priming tasks is extremely sensitive to data-driven factors (Challis & Brodbeck, 1992; Jacoby & Dallas, 1981), and depends on presemantic representations of words and/or objects as well as the participation of posterior cortical areas (Schacter, 1994). Furthermore, performance on tasks within this category is unaffected by whether task items are associative or nonassociative in nature. Given all of the previously mentioned characteristics, performance on tasks of retrieval-free priming should be very robust in the face of age and/or neurological insult.

Retrieval-Dependent Priming. Tasks of retrieval-dependent priming are those in which a subject must use a portion of a single stimulus, or an ambiguous version of a single stimulus, as a retrieval cue in order to recreate the holistic form of that specific stimulus. For example, a subject must retrieve items from semantic memory (*motel*, *motor*, *motion*, etc.) in order to complete a word stem (*mot__*). Consistent with this line of reasoning, Moscovitch and Winocur (1992) theorized that "a hypothesis worth pursuing is that the frontal lobes contribute to those implicit tests that require organizational skills or have a strategic, lexical, or semantic search component" (p. 337). Other researchers (Frith, Friston, Liddle, & Frackowiak, 1991; Monsch et al., 1994; Randolph et al., 1993) emphasized the role played by frontal cortex in the initiation and maintenance of retrieval processes.

Performance on tasks within this category, unlike performance on tasks of retrieval-free priming, may be facilitated by conceptually driven processes such as semantic elaboration during study (Challis & Brodbeck, 1992; Chiarello & Hoyer, 1988). Furthermore, retrieval-dependent priming is measured by the accuracy, not the speed, of response. Tasks of retrieval-dependent priming should be more likely to yield an age deficit than tasks of retrieval-free priming, because they provide less support at retrieval, are more computationally complex, and are more likely to draw upon anterior cortical functions.

Retrieval-Dependent-Associative Priming. The term *retrieval-dependent-associative priming* has its basis in what Graf and Schacter (1985) termed the "priming of new associations." In tasks within this category, a subject must form an association between two semantically unrelated words (*piano–truck, radio–motel*). There are six reasons why retrieval-dependent-associative priming represents the most demanding and cognitively complex category of priming. First, tasks within this category possess significant retrieval demands. Second, retrieval-dependent-associative priming occurs only if subjects engage in some type of elaborative, or interpretative, processing of word pairs during a study period. Elaborative processing (Schacter & Graf, 1989) entails reading or generating sentences that contain both items of a word pair (The *piano* was loaded into the *truck*). Interpretative processing (Micco & Masson, 1991) involves establishing a conceptual link between the items of a word pair (e.g., a subject is asked to think of a piano as a big, clumsy, and difficult-to-move object rather than as an instrument that produces beautiful music). Other categories of priming do not depend on elaborative or interpretative encoding.

Third, only those subjects who display test awareness (i.e., the realization that the items on a priming task previously appeared on a study list) demonstrate retrieval-dependent-associative priming (Bowers & Schacter, 1990; Rybash, 1994). Test awareness is not necessary for the manifestation of retrieval-free or retrieval-dependent priming.

Fourth, the effectiveness of a retrieval cue (e.g., a word stem) is constrained by the context within which it appears during a test phase. A word stem may appear in the same context (*radio–mot_*) or a different context (*piano–mot_*) relative to the word it was paired with during a study phase. Thus, retrieval-dependent-associative priming may depend on an individual's ability to distinguish, albeit implicitly, relevant (i.e., same context) from irrelevant (i.e., different context) information. Because of age-related deficits in attentional mechanisms (Hasher & Zacks, 1988; Sugar & McDowd, 1992) it may be very difficult for older adults to make the distinction between relevant versus irrelevant contextual cues.

Fifth, the criteria for demonstrating retrieval-dependent-associative priming is more strict than the criteria for retrieval-dependent and retrieval-free priming. In order to display retrieval-dependent-associative priming using the word-stem completion format, subjects need to complete more stems for items in the same context than the different context condition. For other tasks, priming is demonstrated if subjects complete more target items than control items. Furthermore, it has been shown that retrieval-dependent priming is a necessary, but not a sufficient, precondition for retrieval-dependent-associative priming (Rybash, 1994).

Sixth, retrieval-dependent-associative priming, more so than any other category of priming, seems to depend on frontal cortex. Several different lines of research suggest that normal aging may be associated with impaired frontal function (e.g., Daigneault, Braun, & Whitaker, 1992; Libon et al., 1994; Moscovitch & Winocur, 1992; Parkin & Walter, 1992). All of these mentioned factors point to the conclusion that age affects are very likely to be observed on tasks within this category.

Motoric Priming. Tasks of motoric priming such as the Nissen Serial Reaction Time Task (Nissen & Bullemer, 1987) place minimal retrieval demands and response requirements on a subject. However, unlike other categories of priming, measures of motoric priming do not employ lexical or pictorial materials as stimuli. Tasks within this category are designed to measure whether performing a specific psychomotor activity on one occasion facilitates performance of the same activity on another occasion. Furthermore, subjects' performance on tasks within this category seems to be dependent upon a motoric representation as well as the participation of subcortical structures such as basal ganglia (Mishkin, Malamut, & Bachevalier, 1984; Petri & Mishkin, 1994).

Relationship to Previous Taxonomies

Gabrieli and Keane (Gabrieli, 1991; Keane, Gabrieli, Fennema, Growdon, & Corkin, 1991) distinguished between *perceptual* and *conceptual* priming. Perceptual and conceptual priming, from their perspective, are similar to what I have termed *retrieval-free* and *retrieval-dependent priming*, respectively. The taxonomy proposed by Gabrieli and Keane, however, did not address the phenomenon of retrieval-dependent-associative priming or motoric priming.

Tulving and Schacter (1990) also made a distinction between *perceptual* and *conceptual* priming. However, they used perceptual priming as a catch-all category that included, from the perspective of the current taxonomy, tasks of retrieval-free and retrieval-dependent priming. Their notion of conceptual priming mapped onto the current category of retrieval-dependent-associative priming. Furthermore, Tulving and Schacter (1990) neglected motoric priming.

Howard (1988, 1991) as well as Light and LaVoie (1993) developed the categories of *associative* and *item* priming. Associative priming entails the retention of novel associations that could be semantic (i.e., combinations of semantically unrelated words or pictures), or motoric (e.g., motor sequences on the Nissen Serial Reaction Time Task). These tasks vary widely with regard to retrieval demands. For example, sentence and compound word reading tasks of associative priming possess minimal retrieval demands. Amnesics, older adults, and demented individuals have been found to perform very well on these measures (Light, LaVoie, Valencia-Laver, Owens, & Mead, 1992; Musen & Squire, 1993). In comparison, tasks of associative priming that use the word stem or fragment completion formats make more pronounced retrieval demand, and are likely to be impaired by age or neurological insult (Rybash, 1994). Item priming tasks contain individual study and test items that possess preexisting knowledge representations. These tasks include perceptual identification, lexical decision, picture naming, word stem completion, word fragment completion, homophone spelling, and so on. From the point of view of the current taxonomy, tasks of associative priming could fall into the categories of retrieval-dependent-associative priming, retrieval-free priming, or motoric priming, whereas tasks of item priming could be placed into the categories of retrieval-dependent priming or retrieval-free priming.

Thus, when compared with other available taxonomies, the current taxonomy seems more comprehensive and integrative in terms of the breadth of the tasks considered as well as the degree to which the relationship between the cognitive and neurological components of the tasks within each category is articulated. And, as is shown in the next section, the present taxonomy is better able to accommodate the wealth of research findings that bear on age-related and disease-related differences in priming.

Priming, Aging, and Neurological Impairment

Examining the relationship between aging and implicit memory is important when one considers that various groups of neurological patients display contrasting patterns of preservation and impairment on different types of priming tasks. Amnesic patients display poor performance on only one type of priming task—retrieval-dependent-associative priming (Cermak, Blackford, O'Connor, & Bleich, 1988; Cermak, Bleich, & Blackford, 1988; Graf & Schacter, 1985; Shimamura & Squire, 1989; Tulving, Hayman, & McDonald, 1991). Other forms of priming are very robust in this patient group (Musen & Squire, 1993; Schacter, 1987; Schacter & Graf, 1986). Alzheimer's disease (AD) patients, in comparison, perform poorly on tasks of retrieval-dependent and retrieval-dependent-associative priming, but they do not display impaired performance on tasks of retrieval-free or motoric priming (Graf, Squire, & Mandler, 1984; Heindel, Salmon, Shutts, Walicke, & Butters, 1989; Keane et al., 1991; Knopman & Nissen, 1987; Randolph, 1991; Shimamura, Salmon, Squire, & Butters, 1987). Alternatively, Huntington's disease (HD) patients perform poorly only on tasks of motoric priming (Heindel, Butters, & Salmon, 1988; Heindel et al., 1989; Knopman & Nissen, 1991).

These findings suggest several alternatives for understanding the mechanisms that might account for the effects of normal aging on priming. First, it might be found that healthy older individuals show deficits only on tasks of retrieval-dependent-associative priming. This would suggest that the neurological changes that accompany normal aging are similar to those associated with the amnesia. Second, healthy older individuals may be impaired on tasks of retrieval-dependent and retrieval-dependent-associative priming, but not retrieval-free or motoric priming. These findings would indicate that the neural changes that accompany normal aging are similar to those associated with AD. Third, age-related deficits might only be found on tasks of motoric priming. This would lead to the inference that the neurological changes that accompany normal aging correspond to those associated with HD. Thus, comparisons across studies of age-related and dementia-related differences in priming may help us to understand the nature of the relationship between brain aging and memory aging.

Using the taxonomy described in this chapter as a guide, a literature review that examined age differences in priming was conducted. This review took into consideration the results of 42 experiments in which a total of 1,372 younger and 1,737 older adults participated. It was found that performance on tasks of retrieval-free and motoric priming was unaffected by age, whereas performance on tasks of retrieval-dependent and retrieval-dependent-associative priming was impaired by age. Furthermore, the performance of healthy older adults on various priming tasks was found to be more similar to the performance of AD patients than amnesics or HD patients. The crucial finding is that AD patients and healthy older adults display impaired performance on tasks of retrieval-dependent and retrieval-dependent-associative priming, but not on tasks of retrieval-free and motoric priming. Amnesics and HD patients display impaired performance on tasks of retrieval-dependent-associative priming and motoric priming, respectively. Other forms of priming are spared in these populations. Collectively, these findings suggest that neither amnesia or HD serves as an adequate model for understanding normative, age-related changes in human memory, and that the memory changes associated with AD and normative aging are united by a common thread. These conclusions do not necessarily mean, of course, that AD represents an acceleration of the normal aging process, or that normal aging is inherently pathological.

These conclusions would not have emerged in such a clear-cut manner if a different taxonomy of implicit memory tasks had been used. As previously mentioned, several investigators have argued for the existence of two categories of priming: item priming and associative priming. Light and LaVoie (1993) performed a meta-analysis that had its basis in this classification system. They analysed the results of 33 separate experiments, all of which employed verbal stimuli, that included 936 younger and 1,004 older subjects. Light and LaVoie (1993) found that younger adults exhibited significantly better performance on tasks of both item priming and associative priming than did older adults (see Table 29.2). More important, they reported age differences on some, but not all, of the tasks within each of these broad categories. However, they offered no analysis of why performance on particular tasks within each of these categories was either spared or impaired. When the results of their meta-analysis are viewed from the perspective of the current taxonomy a rather clear-cut picture emerges: Performance on tasks of retrieval-free priming (i.e., lexical decision, word naming, nonword naming, and word identification) is spared by age regardless of whether the tasks involve individual items or newly associated items, whereas performance on tasks of retrieval-

TABLE 29.2
Results of the Meta-Analysis Conducted by Light and LaVoie (1993)

Light and LaVoie's Classification System	Observed Age Difference?
Nonassociative Priming	Yes
Word naming	No
Word identification	No
Word stem/fragment completion*	Yes
Homophone spelling*	Yes
Associative Priming	Yes
Word stem/fragment completion*	Yes
Lexical decision	No
Naming compound words	No

Note. From the point of view of the present taxonomy, tasks with an asterisk would be classified as retrieval-dependent or retrieval-dependent-associative, whereas tasks without an asterisk would be classified as retrieval-free or motoric.

dependent and retrieval-dependent-associative priming (e.g., word stem/fragment completion, item recognition, and homophone spelling) is impaired by age regardless of whether the tasks involve individual items or newly associated items. These findings reinforce the notion that a taxonomy of priming tasks based solely on whether the stimuli in those tasks consist of single items or novels pairs of items is inadequate.

Implications for Memory Rehabilitation

Camp and his colleagues (Camp, 1989; Camp et al., 1993; Camp & McKitrick, 1992) commented that memory rehabilitation programs have relied on conscious/effortful learning strategies in combination with either external (e.g., appointment books) or internal (e.g., guided imagery) memory aids. Research has shown that this approach is most likely to boost the memory performance of those individuals who are least likely to suffer memory failures—younger adults. Healthy older adults are much less willing to use effortful internal mnemonic strategies than are younger adults. Additionally, they do not profit from these strategies as much as do younger adults. For example, Baltes and his associates (Baltes, 1993; Baltes & Kliegl, 1992) reported that older adults who displayed the best performance at the end of an extensive training program had scores similar to those of younger adults who displayed the worst performance within their age group. Furthermore, Camp et al. (1993) observed that demented older adults are unlikely to benefit from any effortful mnemonic strategy, regardless of whether it involves the use of internal of external aids.

Researchers would be well advised to design remediation programs that capitalize on the preserved implicit memory abilities of older adults and demented individuals. Along these lines, Camp (1989) developed a memory improvement technique termed the "spaced-retrieval" method that was based on Bjork's (1988) suggestion that memory is enhanced by the continued activation of retrieval mechanisms. Extensive retrieval-based practice makes the act of remembering automated and effortless (i.e., implicit). Camp (1989) taught Alzheimer's disease patients to remember the names of hospital staff on a long-term basis by the spaced-retrieval method. Interestingly, patients became capable of remembering staffers' names in a very automatized manner but had no idea of when or where they acquired this information. Camp used this source memory deficit as an indication that patients learned and remembered the names on an implicit basis.

At face value, the spaced retrieval method seems to be a type of retrieval-dependent-associative priming, because subjects were required to learn novel associations (i.e., name–face pairs) and were expected to retrieve the name from a facial cue. It is important to realize, however, that at the beginning of the training session the name–face pairs were presented concurrently and the time lag between the presentation of the face and the generation of the name was gradually increased during training. Thus, the task began in a retrieval-free format and was gradually "shaped" into a retrieval-dependent-associative mode.

Based on the taxonomy presented in this chapter, it would seem that older healthy and demented individuals would be most likely to benefit from implicit memory training programs that involved retrieval-free and motoric priming. Camp's research on the spaced retrieval method provides valuable insight into how these very robust forms of priming may be gradually transformed into more demanding tasks that provide individuals with skills that boost their level of everyday functioning.

REFERENCES

Bäckman, L. (1992, April). *Memory functioning in dementia.* Paper presented at the Cognitive Aging Conference, Atlanta, GA.

Baltes, P. B. (1993). The aging mind: Potential and limits. *The Gerontologist, 33,* 580–594.

Baltes, P. B., & Kliegl, R. (1992). Further testing of limits of cognitive plasticity: Negative age differences in a mnemonic skill are robust. *Developmental Psychology, 28,* 121–125.

Bjork, R. A. (1988). Retrieval practice and maintenance of knowledge. In M. M. Gruenberg, P. Morris, & R. Sykes (Eds.), *Practical aspects of memory* (Vol. 2, pp. 396–401). London: Academic Press.

Bowers, J. S., & Schacter, D. L. (1990). Implicit memory and test awareness. *Journal of Experimental Psychology: Learning, Memory, and Cognition, 16,* 404–416.

Burke, D. M., & Light, L. L. (1981). Memory and aging: The role of retrieval processes. *Psychological Bulletin, 90,* 513–546.

Camp, C. J. (1989). Facilitation of new learning in Alzheimer's disease. In G. Gilmore, P. Whitehouse, & M. Wykle (Eds.), *Memory and aging: Theory research and practice* (pp. 212–225). New York: Springer-Verlag.

Camp, C. J., Foss, J. W., Stevens, A. B., Reichard, C. C., McKitrick, L. A., & O'Hanlon, A. M. (1993). Memory training in normal and demented elderly Populations: The E-I-E-I-O Model. *Experimental Aging Research, 19,* 277–290.

Camp, C. J., & McKitrick, L. A. (1992). Memory interventions in Alzheimer's-type dementia populations: Methodological and theoretical issues. In R. L. West & J. D. Sinnott (Eds.), *Everyday memory and aging: Current research and methodology* (pp. 155–172). New York: Springer-Verlag.

Cermak, L. S., Blackford, S. P., O'Connor, M., & Bleich, R. P. (1988). The implicit memory ability of a patient with amnesia due to encephalitis. *Brain and Cognition, 7,* 145–156.

Cermak, L. S., Bleich, R. P., & Blackford, S. P. (1988). Deficits in the implicit retention of new associations by alcoholic Korsakoff patients. *Brain and Cognition, 7,* 312–323.

Challis, B. H., & Brodbeck, D. R. (1992). Levels of processing affects priming in word fragment completion. *Journal of Experimental Psychology: Learning, Memory, and Cognition, 18,* 595–607.

Chiarello, C., & Hoyer W. J. (1988). Adult age differences in implicit memory: Time course and encoding effects. *Psychology and Aging, 3,* 358–366.

Craik, F. I. M. (1992, May). *Environmental and schematic support in normal and abnormal aging.* Paper presented at TENNET III (Theoretical & Experimental Neuropsychology Neuropsychologie Experimentale & Theoretique), Montreal, Canada.

Craik, F. I. M., & Jennings, J. M. (1992). Human memory. In F. I. M. Craik & T. A. Salthouse (Eds.), *Handbook of cognition and aging* (pp. 52–110). Hillsdale, NJ: Lawrence Erlbaum Associates.

Daigneault, S. Braun, C. M. J., & Whitaker, H. A. (1992). Early effects of normal aging on perseverative and non-perseverative prefrontal measures. *Developmental Neuropsychology, 8,* 99–114.

Frith, C. D., Friston, K. J., Liddle, P. F., & Frackowiak, R. S. J. (1991). A PET study of word finding. *Neurophsychologia, 29,* 1137–1148.

Gabrieli, J. E. D. (1991). Differential effects of aging and age-related neurological diseases on memory subsystems of the brain. In F. Boller & J. Grafman (Eds.), *Handbook of neuropsychology* (pp. 149–166). Amsterdam: Elsevier/North Holland.

Gazzaniga, M. S. (1991). Interview with Endel Tulving. *Journal of Cognitive Neuroscience, 3,* 89–94.

Graf, P., & Komatsu, S. (1994). Process dissociation procedure: Handle with caution! *European Journal of Cognitive Psychology, 6,* 113–129.

Graf, P., & Schacter, D. L. (1985). Implicit and explicit memory for new associations in normal and amnesic subjects. *Journal of Experimental Psychology: Learning, Memory, and Cognition, 11,* 501–518.

Graf, P., Squire, L. R., & Mandler, G. (1984). The information that amnesic patients do not forget. *Journal of Experimental Psychology: Learning, Memory, and Cognition, 10,* 164–178.

Hasher, L., & Zacks, R. T. (1988). Working memory, comprehension, and aging: A review and a new view. In G. H. Bower (Ed.), *The psychology of learning and motivation* (Vol. 22, pp. 193–225). San Diego, CA: Academic Press.

Heindel, W. C., Butters, N., & Salmon, D. P. (1988). Impaired learning of a motor skill in patients with Huntington's disease. *Behavioral Neuroscience, 102,* 141–147.

Heindel, W. C., Salmon, D. P., Shults, C. W., Walicke, P. A., & Butters, N. (1989). Neuropsychological evidence for multiple memory systems: A comparison of Alzheimer's, Huntington's, and Parkinson's Disease patients. *Journal of Neuroscience, 9,* 582–587.

Howard, D. V. (1988). Implicit and explicit assessment of cognitive aging. In M. L. Howe & C. J. Brainerd (Eds.), *Cognitive development in adulthood: Progress in cognitive development research* (pp. 3–33). New York: Springer-Verlag.

Howard, D. V. (1991). Implicit memory: An expanding picture of cognitive aging. In K. W. Schaie (Ed.), *Annual review of gerontology and geriatrics* (Vol. 11, pp. 1–22). New York: Springer.

Jacoby, L. L., & Dallas, M. (1981). On the relationship between autobiographical memory and perceptual learning. *Journal of Experimental Psychology: General, 110,* 306–340.

Keane, M. M., Gabrieli, J. D. E., Fennema, A. C., Growdon, J. H., & Corkin, S. (1991). Evidence for a dissociation between perceptual and conceptual priming in Alzheimer's Disease. *Behavioral Neuroscience, 105*, 326–342.

Knopman, D. S., & Nissen, M. J. (1987). Implicit learning in patients with probable Alzheimer's Disease. *Neurology, 37*, 784–788.

Knopman, D. S., & Nissen, M. J. (1991). Procedural learning is impaired in Huntington's Disease: Evidence from the serial reaction time task. *Neuropsychologia, 29*, 245–254.

Libon, D. J., Glosser, G., Malamut, B. L., Kaplan, E., Goldberg, E., Swenson, R., & Sands, L. P. (1994). Age executive functions, and visuospatial functioning in healthy older adults. *Neuropsychology, 8*, 38–43.

Light, L. L. (1991). Memory and aging: Four hypotheses in search of data. *Annual Review of Psychology, 42*, 333–376.

Light, L. L., & LaVoie, D. (1993). Direct and indirect measures of memory in old age. In P. Graf & M. Masson (Eds.), *Implicit memory: New directions in cognition, development, and neuropsychology* (pp. 207–230). Hillsdale, NJ: Lawrence Erlbaum Associates.

Light, L. L., LaVoie, D., Valencia-Laver, D., Owens, S. A. A., & Mead, G. (1992). Direct and indirect measures of memory for modality in young and older adults. *Journal of Experimental Psychology: Learning, Memory, and Cognition, 18*, 1284–1297.

Micco, A., & Masson, M E. J. (1991). Implicit memory for new associations: An interactive process approach. *Journal of Experimental Psychology: Learning, Memory, and Cognition, 17*, 1105–1123.

Mishkin, M., Malamut, B., & Bachevalier, J. (1984). Memories and habits: Two neural systems. In J. L. McGaugh, G. Lynch, & N. M. Weinberger (Eds.), *Neurobiology of learning and memory* (pp. 69–77). New York: Guilford.

Monsch, A. U., Bondi, M. W., Butters, N., Paulsen, J. S., Salmon, D. P., Brugger, P., & Swenson, M. R. (1994). A comparison of category and letter fluency in Alzheimer's disease and Huntington's disease. *Neuropsychology, 8*, 25–30.

Moscovitch, M. M., & Winocur, G. (1992). The neuropsychology of memory and aging. In F. I. M. Craik & T. A. Salthouse (Eds.), *Handbook of aging and cognition* (pp. 315–372). Hillsdale, NJ: Lawrence Erlbaum Associates.

Musen, G., & Squire, L. R. (1993). On the implicit learning of novel associations by amnesic patients and normal subjects. *Neuropsychology, 7*, 119–135.

Nissen, M. J., & Bullemer, P. (1987). Attentional requirements of learning: Evidence from performance measures. *Cognitive Psychology, 19*, 1–32.

Parkin, A. J., & Walter, B. M. (1992). Recollective experience, normal aging, and frontal dysfunction. *Psychology and Aging, 7*, 290–298.

Petersen, S. E., Fox, P. T., Snyder, A. Z., & Raichle, M. E.(1990). Activation of extrastriate and frontal cortical areas by visual and word-like stimuli. *Science, 249*, 1014–1044.

Petri, H. L., & Mishkin, M. (1994). Behaviorism, cognitivism and the neuropsychology of mind. *American Scientist, 82*, 30–37.

Posner, M. I., Petersen, S. E., Fox, P. T., & Raichle, M. E. (1988). Localization of cognitive operations in the human brain. *Science, 240*, 1627–1631.

Randolph, C. (1991). Implicit, explicit, and semantic memory functions in Alzheimer's Disease and Huntington's Disease. *Journal of Clinical and Experimental Neuropsychology, 13*, 479–494.

Randolph, C., Braun, A. R., Goldberg, T. E., & Chase, T. N. (1993). Semantic fluency in Alzheimer's, Parkinson's, and Huntington's disease: Dissociation of storage and retrieval failures. *Neuropsychology, 7*, 82–88.

Roediger, H. L. (1990). Implicit memory: Retention without remembering. *American Psychologist, 45*, 1043–1056.

Roediger, H. L., & Challis, B. A. (1992). Effects of exact repetition and conceptual repetition on free recall and primed word fragment completion. *Journal of Experimental Psychology: Learning, Memory, and Cognition, 18*, 3–14.

Rybash, J. M. (1994). Aging, test awareness and associative priming. *Aging and Cognition, 1,* 158–173.

Schacter, D. L. (1987). Implicit memory: History and current status. *Journal of Experimental Psychology: Learning, Memory, and Cognition, 12,* 432–444.

Schacter, D. L. (1994). Priming and multiple memory systems: Perceptual mechanisms of implicit memory. In D L. Schacter & E. Tulving (Eds.), *Memory systems 1994* (pp. 233–268). Cambridge, MA: MIT Press.

Schacter, D. L., & Graf, P. (1986). Preserved learning in amnesic patients: Perspectives from research on direct priming. *Journal of Clinical and Experimental Neuropsychology, 8,* 727–743.

Schacter, D. L., & Graf, P. (1989). Modality specificity of implicit memory for new associations. *Journal of Experimental Psychology: Learning, Memory, and Cognition, 15,* 3–12.

Shimamura, A. P., Salmon, D. P., Squire, L. R., & Butters, N. (1987). Memory dysfunction unique to Alzheimer's disease: Impairment of word priming. *Journal of Clinical and Experimental Neuropsychology, 9,* 20.

Shimamura, A. P., & Squire, L. R. (1989). Impaired priming of new associations in amnesia. *Journal of Experimental Psychology: Learning, Memory, and Cognition, 15,* 721–728.

Squire, L. R. (1994). Declarative and non-declarative memory: Multiple brain systems supporting learning and memory. In D. L. Schacter & E. Tulving (Eds.), *Memory systems 1994* (pp. 203–232). Cambridge, MA: MIT Press.

Sugar, J., & McDowd, J. M. (1992). Memory and attention in aging. In J. E. Birren (Ed.), *Handbook of mental health and aging* (pp. 307–337). San Diego, CA: Academic Press.

Tulving, E., Hayman, C. A. G., & Macdonald, C. A. (1991). Long-lasting priming in amnesia: A case experiment. *Journal of Experimental Psychology: Learning, Memory, and Cognition, 17,* 595–617.

Tulving, E., & Schacter, D. L. (1990). Priming and human memory systems. *Science, 247,* 301–306.

Weldon, M. S. (1993). The time course of perceptual and conceptual contributions to word fragment completion priming. *Journal of Experimental Psychology: Learning, Memory, and Cognition, 19,* 1010–1023.

PART TEN

INTERVENTIONS FOR MEMORY-IMPAIRED POPULATIONS

CHAPTER THIRTY

The NMDA Receptor Complex: Enhancement of Memory in Aging and Dementia

Barbara L. Schwartz
Department of Veterans Affairs Medical Center
Georgetown University School of Medicine

Shahin Hashtroudi
George Washington University

Robert L. Herting
T. Daniel Fakouhi
G.D. Searle

Stephen I. Deutsch
Department of Veterans Affairs Medical Center
Georgetown University School of Medicine

Alzheimer's disease is a progressive condition that is manifested by loss in a variety of cognitive domains such as memory, object naming, and visuospatial ability that interferes with an individual's social and occupational functioning. As the number of people aged 65 and older grows in the United States, there is increasing interest in the cognitive problems associated with aging and age-related disturbances such as Alzheimer's disease. There is general agreement in the field of geropsychiatry that a component of treatment of age-associated cognitive loss will require pharmacological treatment (Bartus, 1986).

Currently, considerable efforts are directed toward developing medications to improve memory, language, and other cognitive functions that are impaired in Alzheimer patients. This chapter is concerned with pharmacological agents that interact with the glutamatergic system to make L-glutamate a more effective neurotransmitter. In particular, we are interested in the effectiveness of these agents to improve language and memory problems that are related to normal and pathological processes of aging.

MODULATION OF THE NMDA SUBTYPE
OF GLUTAMATE RECEPTOR

The N-methyl-D-aspartate (NMDA) receptor is a subtype of glutamate receptor, and it has been implicated in processes of learning and memory. L-glutamate, the naturally occurring neurotransmitter, and NMDA, a synthetic substance, can attach or bind to the NMDA receptor and regulate its activity. Specifically, glutamate and NMDA promote channel opening allowing positively charged ions to flow into the nerve cell, thereby exciting the neuron. In addition, the NMDA receptor complex possesses another distinct site, the glycine modulatory site. Glycine has no effect in the absence of glutamate, but in the presence of glutamate, glycine potentiates glutamate's ability to promote channel opening.

Two drugs that act at the glycine modulatory site can facilitate learning and memory in animals and humans. The first drug, milacemide, is a glycine derivative that crosses the blood–brain barrier and is converted to glycine in the brain (DeVarbeke, Cavalier, David-Remacle, & Youdim, 1988). The second drug, d-cycloserine, is a partial glycine agonist (Hood, Compton, & Monahan, 1989). That is, d-cycloserine behaves as an agonist to increase glycine's effects when there are low levels of glycine in the brain and as an antagonist to decrease its effects when there are high levels of glycine in the brain. The antagonist property of d-cycloserine can prevent overstimulation of the cell, which can lead to excitotoxicity and eventual cell death. Therefore, drugs that are partial glycine agonists ultimately may be more useful for elderly demented patients, who may be sensitive to excitotoxicity (Herting, 1991).

THE ROLE OF THE NMDA RECEPTOR
IN LEARNING AND MEMORY

Early studies suggested that glutamic acid improved maze learning in experimental animals (Zimmerman & Ross, 1944) and intellectual abilities in children, retarded individuals, and elderly adults (for reviews of the early literature, see Deutsch & Morihisa, 1988; Vogel, Broverman, Draguns, & Klaiber, 1966). The recent discovery that modulation of NMDA type glutamate receptors could influence memory led to a resurgence of interest in glutamate. Many of these studies seemed to suggest that NMDA receptors were predominantly involved in forms of memory dependent on the hippocampus.

Evidence From Animal Studies

One line of evidence that implicates the NMDA receptor complex in memory is its role in long-term potentiation in the hippocampus. Long-term potentiation, which occurs following brief high-frequency stimulation, is a physiological analogue of information storage in the brain. The activation of NMDA receptors with glutamate or NMDA leads to the induction of long-term potentiation in postsynaptic neurons, whereas blockade of this receptor with NMDA antagonists impedes long-term potentiation (Collingridge & Bliss, 1987; Harris, Ganong, & Cotman, 1984; Morris, Anderson, Lynch, & Baudry, 1986; Zalutsky & Nicoll, 1990). This link between NMDA receptors and long-term potentiation suggests that these receptors might underlie the neural events that lead to memory storage.

Additional evidence that this receptor complex is involved in learning is that NMDA receptor antagonists impair certain forms of learning (Butelman, 1989; Danysz, Wroblewski, & Costa, 1988; Morris et al., 1986). Morris et al. (1986) examined the effects of an NMDA receptor antagonist (2-amino-5-phosphonopentanoate, AP5) on spatial learning in the water maze. In this task, animals learn to find their way through a pool of opaque water to a platform submerged in the water. There is widespread interest in the water maze because different measures of learning on this task are sensitive to damage with hippocampal lesions, and, therefore, it may serve as an animal model of human amnesia. Morris and his colleagues found that AP5 impaired spatial learning in a dose-dependent manner: The higher the dose of the drug, the greater was the impairment in learning. Furthermore, the doses of AP5 that produced an impairment in spatial learning were those that blocked the induction of long-term potentiation in the hippocampus.

There is also a growing body of evidence indicating that drugs that potentiate the effects of glutamate at NMDA receptors enhance learning and memory. For instance, the administration of the glycine prodrug milacemide improved acquisition and retention in a passive avoidance task, reversed a drug-induced amnesia in a spontaneous alternation task, and reduced forgetting produced by a 14-day retention interval in both passive and active avoidance tasks (Handelmann, Nevins, Mueller, Arnolde, & Cordi, 1989; Quartermain, Nuygen, Sheu, & Herting, 1991). Similarly, d-cycloserine facilitated one-trial learning in a passive avoidance task and spatial learning in a variety of mazes (Monahan, Handelmann, Hood, & Cordi, 1989; Quartermain, Mower, Rafferty, Herting, & Lanthorn, in press).

Thompson, Moskal, and Disterhoft (1992) found that d-cycloserine produced a striking level of enhancement in a trace-eyeblink conditioning task, in which the conditioned stimulus (tone) and the unconditioned stimulus (puff of air to eye) are separated by a time interval. Animals treated with d-cycloserine required 43% fewer learning trials to attain an 80% criterion level on this task. Trace conditioning is also of some interest to the study of human memory disorders because it is disrupted following hippocampal damage.

An important question for the treatment of age-associated memory problems is whether or not glutamatergic drugs can alleviate a deficit in learning and memory. In fact, research has shown that d-cycloserine alleviates drug-induced amnesia. In one study, d-cycloserine attenuated a deficit of spatial working memory in a radial maze that was produced when quinolinic acid was injected bilaterally into the hippocampus (Schuster & Schmidt, 1992). Hippocampal-lesioned animals who were treated with d-cycloserine made significantly fewer errors in the radial maze than did lesioned animals treated with placebo. Further, the performance of animals treated with d-cycloserine did not differ from that of control animals who received only sham lesions, suggesting that d-cycloserine reversed the decrement in memory.

There also is real interest in whether d-cycloserine can alleviate impairments in memory produced with scopolamine (a muscarinic cholinergic receptor antagonist), because administration of this drug to healthy humans produces reversible memory impairments that mimic age-associated memory impairments (Drachman & Leavitt, 1974; Wesnes, Simpson, & Kidd, 1988). Sirvio, Ekonsalo, Riekkinen, Lahtinen, and Riekkinen (1992) reported that d-cycloserine attenuated a scopolamine-induced deficit of spatial learning in the water maze. Animals treated with both scopolamine and d-cycloserine had shorter latencies to escape onto a platform in the water maze than those treated with scopolamine alone.

The findings of other experiments suggest that d-cycloserine can ameliorate impairments in learning and memory that are found in aged animals. The drug improved spatial learning in the water maze in aged rats, reducing the magnitude of their deficit relative to younger animals (Baxter et al., 1994). In addition, d-cycloserine enhanced learning in a shock-motivated avoidance task in a senescence-accelerated mouse strain, in which changes associated with aging appear at an earlier stage in life (Flood, Morley, & Lanthorn, 1992).

Evidence From Human Studies

Although the majority of experiments examining the effects of glutamatergic agents on memory are conducted with animals, the findings of a few studies suggest that milacemide and d-cycloserine facilitate remembering in humans. These drugs appear to facilitate predominantly performance on declarative or explicit memory tests in which subjects are required to refer to prior experiences to perform the test. Early observations showed that milacemide improved short-term numerical memory, recognition performance, and vigilance in young as well as older subjects (Saletu & Grunberger, 1986; Saletu, Grunberger, & Linzmayer, 1986).

We examined the effects of an oral dose of milacemide (1,200 mg) on performance in a source memory task (Schwartz, Hashtroudi, Herting, & Deutsch, 1991). In this task, subjects watched a videotape of two people saying words and then were asked to identify which of the two speakers

TABLE 30.1
Mean Percentages (With Standard Deviations in Parentheses)
of Correct Source Memory Judgments for Young and Older
Adults as a Function of Drug Treatment Condition

	Drug Condition	
	Placebo	Milacemide
Young	74.50	79.31
	(18.32)	(12.42)
Older	74.88	84.00
	(11.87)	(13.22)

Note. From: Schwartz, B. L., Hashtroudi, S., Herting, R. L., & Deutsch, S. I. (1992). The effects of milacemide on item and source memory. *Clinical Neuropharmacology, 15,* 114–119. Reprinted by permission.

("sources") said the words. Both young (mean = 23 years) and older healthy adults (mean = 68 years) participated in the study. Their performance on the source memory task is shown in Table 30.1. Young and older adults who had received milacemide identified the source of spoken words more accurately than those who had received a placebo.

Evidence also suggests that d-cycloserine alleviated deficits in memory when scopolamine was given to humans. Healthy young and older adults' performance on tasks of vigilance and memory for recently presented items was disrupted following administration of scopolamine (Jones, Wesnes, & Kirby, 1991; Wesnes, Jones, & Kirby, 1991). However, d-cycloserine improved young subjects' deficient performance on tasks of memory scannning, recall, and recognition, and improved older subjects' performance on a task of recognition. The drug did not benefit attentional performance.

Summary

There is growing evidence to suggest that the NMDA subtype of glutamate receptor plays a key role in learning and memory phenomena, particularly in those that depend on the integrity of hippocampal and other mesial temporal lobe structures. For instance, behavioral studies with animals showed that drugs that potentiate NMDA receptor activity facilitate trace eyeblink conditioning, spatial working memory in a radial maze, and spatial learning in a water maze, all of which are hippocampal-mediated functions. In contrast, drugs that block NMDA activity can impair these types of learning. The studies of human memory reveal that milacemide and d-cycloserine have positive effects on the conscious or explicit retrieval of recently studied items in tasks of recall, recognition, and source identification.

GLUTAMATE AND FACILITATION OF SEMANTIC
AND IMPLICIT MEMORY

It is understandable why efforts to identify the role of NMDA receptors in memory have focused on hippocampal-dependent functions. There is a high density of these receptors in the hippocampus (Monaghan & Cotman, 1986), so potentiation of NMDA receptor activity with drugs is expected to affect functions subserved by this neural system. Furthermore, extensive evidence suggests that the hippocampus and its connections to limbic and diencephalic regions are essential for declarative forms of memory in animals and humans (for review, see Squire, 1992).

However, there are several reasons for exploring the effects of glutamatergic drugs on other forms of memory. One reason is that NMDA receptors are widely distributed throughout the brain, not only in the hippocampus but in the cerebral cortex and striatum (Monaghan & Cotman, 1986, 1989; Procter, Wong, Stratmann, Lowe, & Bowen, 1989). Moreover, these receptors are involved in corticocortical association projections and corticostriatal connections (Jones, 1986). Among cortical areas, NMDA receptors are found in the frontal cortex, anterior cingulate, and in the outer layers of the parietal cortex (layers I to III and layer Va). In the basal ganglia, they are found in the nucleus accumbens, caudate, and putamen. These structures and their projections subserve a variety of higher-order functions such as lexical-semantic processing, visuospatial abilities, and cognitive skill learning. Glutamatergic drugs might influence these memory functions as well as the more standard measures of recall and recognition.

Second, the primary application for drugs that enhance memory presumably will be for age-associated memory deficits. Patients with dementia and healthy older adults are impaired on certain semantic memory and implicit memory tasks. For instance, Alzheimer patients have word-finding problems in spontaneous speech and in naming common objects (for review, see Nebes, 1989), and they are impaired on several tasks that assess repetition priming (Heindel, Salmon, & Butters, 1990; Salmon, Shimamura, Butters, & Smith, 1988; Shimamura, Salmon, Squire, & Butters, 1987). Ideally, medications that treat age-associated cognitive dysfunctions will improve several memory functions, only one of which is recall.

We conducted a study to examine whether the glycine prodrug, milacemide, would improve retrieval from semantic memory in older adults (Schwartz, Hashtroudi, Herting, Handerson, & Deutsch, 1991). Problems of language occur with increasing age, and one common complaint of older adults is their difficulty in retrieving a name. Older adults are both less accurate and slower to produce the name of an object from a picture or from a verbal description of the object (Albert, Heller, & Milberg, 1988; Borod, Goodglass, & Kaplan, 1980; Bowles & Poon, 1985a; Byrd, 1984; Thomas, Fozard, & Waugh, 1977).

To test the effects of milacemide on word retrieval, we used a task in which subjects were shown a definition of a word and were asked to name the defined word (Bowles & Poon, 1985a; Brown, 1979). There were two conditions in this task. In the "neutral" condition, a row of Xs preceded the definition of a word (e.g., "XXXXX—an imaginary line around the middle of the earth") and in the "semantic" condition, a word that was meaningfully related to the target word preceded the definition (e.g., "horizon—an imaginary line around the middle of the earth"). The target word in each example is *equator.*

We observed that young (mean = 23 years) and older (mean = 68 years) adults who received milacemide (1,200 mg) retrieved a greater number of words (see Fig. 30.1A) and had shorter response latencies to retrieve these words (see Fig. 30.1B) than those who received a placebo. It should be noted that milacemide did not selectively improve older adults' ability to retrieve words. Statistical analyses yielded only main effects with drug condition, revealing that both young and older adults' retrieval of words benefited from milacemide.

The question here is what is the cognitive mechanism by which milacemide acts. It would be important to understand what cognitive processes are enhanced with milacemide. Bowles and Poon (1985b) suggested that a way to envision the components or processes of word retrieval is to conceptualize semantic memory as comprising two components (Collins & Loftus, 1975). The first component is a semantic network that contains information about word meanings and their relations. The second component is a lexical network that contains orthographic and phonetic information

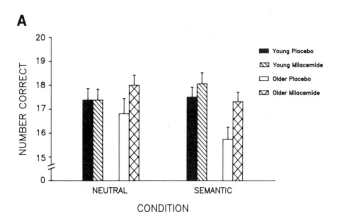

FIG. 30.1A. The number of words retrieved in the neutral and semantic conditions for young and older adults as a function of drug treatment condition. From: Schwartz, B. L., Hashtroudi, S., Herting, R. L., Henderson, H., & Deutsch, S. I. (1991). Glycine prodrug facilitates memory retrieval in humans. *Neurology, 41,* 1341–1343. Reprinted by permission.

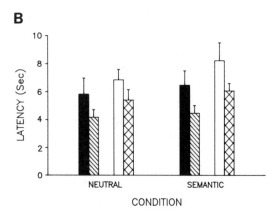

FIG. 30.1B. The latency, reported in seconds, to retrieve words in the neutral and semantic conditions for young and older adults as a function of drug treatment condition.

about words. The word retrieval task used in our study requires access to a concept in the semantic network and access to orthographic or phonetic information in the lexical network to produce the word name. We also assume that access to, and coordination of, conceptual and lexical information requires attention-demanding processes. Therefore, the cognitive processes on which milacemide might act include semantic processing, lexical processing, or attentional processes, which may increase the efficiency by which all subcomponents of the task are performed.

We recently conducted another study to examine the effects of d-cycloserine on implicit memory in Alzheimer patients (Schwartz, Hashtroudi, Herting, Schwartz, & Deutsch, in press). Implicit memory is revealed in tests that do not require subjects to deliberately recollect their past experiences. On implicit tests, memory is inferred from the effects that prior study items or practice has on performance. The issue of whether or not priming is preserved in Alzheimer patients seems to depend on the type of task used to measure priming. Alzheimer patients are impaired on several tasks of repetition priming such as word-stem completion, picture-fragment identification, and word association (Bondi & Kazniak, 1991; Heindel et al., 1990; Salmon et al., 1988; Shimamura et al, 1987). However, they show normal priming on tasks of lexical decision, object decision, and word identification (Keane, Gabrieli, Fennema, Growdon, & Corkin, 1991; Martin, 1993; Ober & Shenaut, 1988). With respect to skill learning, the evidence suggests that Alzheimer patients acquire and retain a variety of perceptual and motor skills (Bondi & Kazniak, 1991; Eslinger & Damasio, 1985; Heindel, Salmon, Shults, Walicke, & Butters, 1989). However, few studies have investigated skill learning with verbal materials in these patients (e.g., Deweer, Pillon, Michon, & Dubois, 1993; Moscovitch, Winocur, & McLachlan, 1986).

To study the effects of d-cycloserine on implicit memory, we employed a paradigm that provides a measure of both priming and skill learning in the same task. Subjects view visually degraded words in the partial-word identification task for three days, with three trials given on each day. Each trial consists of degraded words that are repeated on each trial and degraded words that are unique or new on each trial. Skill learning is demonstrated in this task by an increase in the number of new words identified across the nine trials. Priming is demonstrated when repeated (old) words are identified with greater accuracy than are new words.

Using this paradigm, we observed previously that experimental variables such as normative word frequency and aging have different effects on priming and skill learning (Hashtroudi, Chrosniak, & Schwartz, 1991; Schwartz & Hashtroudi, 1991). Such findings are consistent with those from neuropsychological studies suggesting that priming and skill learning depend on different neural systems (Butters, Heindel, & Salmon, 1990; Heindel et al., 1989). Based on evidence that priming and skill learning may represent distinct forms of learning, it is possible that d-cycloserine would have different effects on priming and skill learning in Alzheimer patients. The drug could enhance one type of implicit memory but not the other.

In our study (Schwartz et al., in press), Alzheimer patients were given the partial word identification test according to the 3-day procedure described earlier. The patients had undergone treatment with a placebo or d-cycloserine (5 mg, 15 mg, or 50 mg twice daily) for approximately 70 days when they performed the test on the first day. As can be seen in Fig. 30.2, patients who received 15 mg of d-cycloserine showed a greater increase in priming across the nine trials compared with those who received a placebo. It should be noted that patients in both the placebo and 15 mg group showed a significant amount of priming. The important point here is that patients who were treated with d-cycloserine revealed a greater benefit from viewing repeated words across the trials. They also showed no hint of a decay in performance over the 24-hour retention intervals that occurred between Trials 3 and 4 and between Trials 6 and 7. In contrast, d-cycloserine did not enhance the patients' identification of new words across trials, suggesting that the drug did not affect skill learning in this task.

We can only speculate about what aspect of priming in partial word identification was facilitated with d-cycloserine. One possibility is that the drug influenced explicit remembering for items repeated across the nine trials. However, this explanation seems unlikely because d-cycloserine did not affect performance on multiple unrelated tests of verbal and nonverbal explicit memory included in this study (G. D. Searle & Co., NC6-93-06-009). The improvement observed in this task is more likely to be related to mechanisms of priming.

It has been proposed that certain priming phenomena are mediated by a structural–perceptual memory system (Keane et al., 1991; Schacter, 1990),

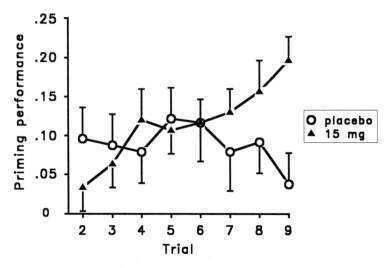

FIG. 30.2. The proportion of priming (difference in proportion of old and new words identified) observed on each trial for Alzheimer patients who received 15 mg d-cycloserine ($N = 25$) or a placebo ($N = 20$).

whereas others are mediated by a lexical–semantic system (Keane et al., 1991). There is some suggestion that priming in the partial word identification task involves both perceptual and lexical components (Hashtroudi, Ferguson, Rappold, & Chrosniak, 1988). A shift in the sensory–modality between study and test phases of an experiment reduces priming in this task, suggesting that priming is dependent on perceptual processes. However, the finding that priming was not eliminated with a change in modality suggests that priming is also somewhat dependent on lexical processes.

In our study, Alzheimer patients viewed the same visual array of dot patterns that comprised "repeated" words for 9 times over 3 days. The drug could have influenced learning by preserving familiar perceptual information over this extended period. An alternative interpretation of the results is that the drug enhanced activation of lexical representations in memory. Alzheimer patients have a relatively spared knowledge of phonological and orthographic rules of English words, as evidenced by their normal reading and normal priming performance in tasks of word naming and lexical decision (Balota & Duchek, 1991; Ober & Shenaut, 1988). It is possible that the patients utilized this knowledge to decipher individual letters or letter combinations from the degraded cues. The drug may have facilitated their ability to access word names given the impoverished perceptual information. Clearly, further studies are required to identify the language and memory components that may be enhanced with drugs that modulate NMDA receptor activity.

CONCLUSIONS

Studies of animal and human memory suggest that drugs that potentiate NMDA receptor activity enhance memory phenomena supported by the hippocampus and related structures in the mesial temporal lobe. Our recent studies with normal elderly adults and Alzheimer patients suggest that these pharmacological agents affect cognitive processes that involve predominantly neocortical regions as well. The semantic memory task involves several subcomponents such as access to conceptual knowledge, access to orthographic or phonetic information, and speech output. Studies employing brain imaging techniques have provided an opportunity to identify the cerebral areas that are involved in these higher-order cognitive processes. Such studies suggest that semantic–lexical processing and generation of words is associated with activation in the left prefrontal cortex (Frith, Friston, Liddle, & Frackowiak, 1991; Kapur et al., 1994; Petersen, Fox, Posner, Mintun, & Raichle, 1988) and in the posterior and middle temporal regions (Demonet et al., 1992). In addition, evidence from brain imaging studies and neuropsychological studies suggests that priming phenomena are supported by structures in the temporal, parietal, and occipital regions (Gabrieli et al., in press; Keane et al., 1991; Squire et al., 1992).

The emerging picture is that potentiation of the NMDA receptor complex may enhance several processes or systems of memory that involve neocortical and subcortical structures. It may prove fruitful to examine the effects of novel drugs on different forms of memory that are impaired with normal and abnormal aging. That complex language and memory functions can be enhanced with drugs that act at the glycine modulatory site on the NMDA receptor holds promise for the treatment of patients with dementia, particularly Alzheimer patients, in whom pharmacotherapy must treat multiple cognitive dysfunctions.

ACKNOWLEDGMENTS

Our research reported in this chapter was supported by G.D. Searle & Co. We thank John Mastropaolo for his valuable comments.

REFERENCES

Albert, M. S., Heller, H. S., & Milberg, W. (1988). Changes in naming ability with age. *Psychology and Aging, 3*, 173–178.

Balota, D. A., & Duchek, J. M. (1991). Semantic priming effects, lexical repetition effects, and contextual disambiguation effects in healthy aged individuals and individuals with senile dementia of the Alzheimer type. *Brain and Language, 40*, 181–201.

Bartus, R. T. (1986). Drugs to treat age-related cognitive disorders: On the threshold of a new era in the pharmaceutical industry. In T. Crook, R. T. Bartus, S. Ferris, & S. Gershon (Eds.),

Treatment development strategies for Alzheimer's disease (pp. 15–33), Madison, CT: Mark Powley Associates.

Baxter, M. G., Lanthorn, T. H., Frick, K. M., Golski, S., Wan, R., & Olton, D. S. (1994). D-cycloserine, a novel cognitive enhancer, improves spatial memory in aged rats. *Neurobiology of Aging, 15,* 207–213.

Bondi, M. W., & Kazniak, A. W. (1991). Implicit and explicit memory in Alzheimer's disease and Parkinson's disease. *Journal of Clinical and Experimental Neuropsychology, 13,* 339–358.

Borod, J., Goodglass, H., & Kaplan, E. (1980). Normative data on the Boston Diagnostic Aphasia Examination, parietal lobe battery, and Boston Naming Test. *Journal of Clinical Neuropsychology, 2,* 209–215.

Bowles, N. L., & Poon, L. W. (1985a). Aging and retrieval of words in semantic memory. *Journal of Gerontology, 48,* 71–77.

Bowles, N. L., & Poon, L. W. (1985b). Effects of priming in word retrieval. *Journal of Experimental Psychology: Learning, Memory, and Cognition, 11,* 272–283.

Brown, A. S. (1979). Priming in semantic memory retrieval processes. *Journal of Experimental Psychology:Human Learning and Memory, 5,* 65–77.

Butelman, E. R. (1989). A novel NMDA antagonist, MK-801, impairs performance in a hippocampal-dependent spatial learning task. *Pharmacology Biochemistry & Behavior, 34,* 13–16.

Butters, N., Heindel, W. C., & Salmon, D. P. (1990). Dissociation of implicit memory in dementia: Neurological implications. *Bulletin of the Psychonomic Society, 28,* 359–366.

Byrd, M. (1984). Age differences in the retrieval of information from semantic memory. *Experimental Aging Research, 10,* 29–33.

Collingridge, G. L., & Bliss, T. V. P. (1987). NMDA receptors—their role in long-term potentiation. *Trends in Neuroscience, 10,* 288–293.

Collins, A. M., & Loftus, E. F. (1975). A spreading activation theory of semantic processing. *Psychological Review, 82,* 407–428.

Danysz, W., Wroblewski, J. T., & Costa, E. (1988). Learning impairment in rats by N-methyl-D-aspartate receptor antagonists. *Neuropharmacology, 27,* 653–656.

Demonet, J. F., Chollet, F., Ramsay, S., Cardebat, D., Nespoulous, J. L., Wise, R., Rascol, A., & Frackowiak, R. (1992). The anatomy of phonological and semantic processing in normal subjects. *Brain, 115,* 1753–1768.

Deutsch, S. I., & Morihisa, J. M. (1988). Glutamatergic abnormalities in Alzheimer's disease and a rationale for clinical trials with L-Glutamate. *Clinical Neuropharmacology, 11,* 18–35.

DeVarbeke, P. J., Cavalier, R., David-Remacle, M., & Youdim, M. B. H. (1988). Formation of the neurotransmitter glycine from the anticonvulsant milacemide is mediated by brain monoamine oxidase B. *Journal of Neurochemistry, 50,* 1011–1016.

Deweer, B., Pillon, B., Michon, A., & Dubois, B. (1993). Mirror reading in Alzheimer's disease: normal skill learning and acquisition of item-specific information. *Journal of Clinical and Experimental Neuropsychology, 15,* 789–804.

Drachman, D. A., & Leavitt, J. (1974). Human memory and the cholinergic system. *Archives of Neurology, 30,* 113–121.

Eslinger, P. J., & Damasio, A. R. (1985). Preserved motor learning in Alzheimer's disease: Implications for anatomy and behavior. *The Journal of Neuroscience, 6,* 3006–3009.

Flood, J. F., Morley, J. E., Lanthorn, T. H. (1992). Effects on memory processing by D-cycloserine, an agonist of the NMDA/glycine receptor. *European Journal of Pharmacology, 221,* 249–254.

Frith, C. D., Friston, K. J., Liddle, P. F., & Frackowiak, R. S. J. (1991). A PET study of word finding. *Neuropsychologia, 29,* 1137–1148.

Gabrieli, J. D. E., Keane, M. M., Stanger, B. Z., Kjelgaard, M. M., Corkin, S., & Growdon, J. H. (1994). Dissociations among structural–perceptual, lexical–semantic, and event–fact memory systems in Alzheimer, amnesic, and normal subjects. *Cortex, 30,* 75–103.

Handelmann, G. E., Nevins, M. E., Mueller, L. L., Arnolde, S. M., & Cordi, A. A. (1989). Milacemide, a glycine prodrug, enhances performance of learning tasks in normal and amnestic rodents. *Pharmacology, Biochemistry, and Behavior, 34*, 823–828.

Harris, E. W., Ganong, A. H., & Cotman, C. W. (1984). Long-term potentiation in the hippocampus involves activation of N-methyl-D-aspartate receptors. *Brain Research, 323*, 132–137.

Hashtroudi, S., Chrosniak, L. D., & Schwartz, B. L. (1991). Effects of aging on priming and skill learning. *Psychology and Aging, 6*, 605–615.

Hashtroudi, S., Ferguson, S. A., Rappold, V. A., & Chrosniak, L. D. (1988). Data-driven and conceptually driven processes in partial word identification and recognition. *Journal of Experimental Psychology: Learning, Memory and Cognition, 14*, 749–757.

Heindel, W. C., Salmon, D. P., & Butters, N. (1990). Pictorial priming and cued recall in Alzheimer's and Huntington's disease. *Brain and Cognition, 13*, 282–295.

Heindel, W. C., Salmon, D. P., Shults, C. W., Walicke, P. A., & Butters, N. (1989). Neuropsychological evidence for multiple implicit memory systems: A comparison of Alzheimer's, Huntington's, and Parkinson's disease patients. *Journal of Neuroscience, 9*, 582–587.

Herting, R. L. (1991). Milacemide and other drugs active at glutamate NMDA receptors as potential treatment for dementia. *Annals of the New York Academy of Science, 640*, 237–240.

Hood, W. F., Compton, R. P., & Monahan, J. B. (1989). D-cycloserine: A ligand for the N-methyl-D-aspartate coupled glycine receptor has partial agonist characteristics. *Neuroscience Letters, 98*, 91–95.

Jones, E. G. (1986). Neurotransmitters in the cerebral cortex. *Journal of Neurosurgery, 65*, 135–153.

Jones, R. W., Wesnes, K. A., & Kirby, J. (1991). Effects of NMDA Modulation in scopolamine dementia. *Annals of the New York Academy of Science, 640*, 241–244.

Kapur, S., Craik, F. I. M., Tulving, E., Wilson, A. L., Houle, S., & Brown, G. M. (1994). Neuroanatomical correlates of encoding in episodic memory: Levels of processing effect. *Proceedings of the National Academy of Science, 91*, 2008–2011.

Keane, M. M., Gabrieli, J. D. E., Fennema, A. C., Growdon, J. H., & Corkin, S. (1991). Evidence for a dissociation between perceptual and conceptual priming in Alzheimer's disease. *Behavioral Neuroscience, 105*, 326–342.

Martin, A. (1993). Degraded knowledge representations in patients with Alzheimer's disease: Implications for models of semantic and repetition priming. In L. R. Squire & N. Butters (Eds.), *Neuropsychology of memory* (pp. 220–232). New York: Guilford.

Monaghan, D. T., & Cotman, C. W. (1986). Identification and properties of N-methyl-D-aspartate receptors in rat brain synaptic plasma membranes. *Proceedings of the National Academy of Science, 83*, 7532–7536.

Monaghan, D. T., & Cotman, C. W. (1989). Regional variations in NMDA receptor properties. In J. C. Watkins & G. L. Colingridge (Eds.), *The NMDA receptor* (pp. 53–64). Oxford, England: Oxford University Press.

Monahan, J. B., Handelmann, G. E., Hood, W. F., & Cordi, A. A. (1989). D-cycloserine, a positive modulator of the N-methyl-D-aspartate receptor, enhances performance of learning tasks in rats. *Pharmacology, Biochemistry, and Behavior, 34*, 649–653.

Morris, R. G. M., Anderson, E., Lynch, G. S., & Baudry, M. (1986). Selective impairment of learning and blockade of long-term potentiation by an N-methyl-D-aspartate receptor antagonist, AP5. *Nature, 319*, 774–776.

Moscovitch, M., Winocur, G., & McLachlan, D. (1986). Memory as assessed by recognition and reading time in normal and memory-impaired people with Alzheimer's disease and other neurological disorders. *Journal of Experimental Psychology: General, 115*, 331–347.

Nebes, R. D. (1989). Semantic memory in Alzheimer's disease. *Psychological Bulletin, 106*, 377–394.

Ober, B. A., & Shenaut, G. K. (1988). Lexical decision and priming in Alzheimer's disease. *Neuropsychologia, 26*, 273–286.

Petersen, S. E., Fox, P. T., Posner, M. I., Mintun, M., & Raichle, M. E. (1988). Positron emission tomographic studies of the cortical anatomy of single-word processing. *Nature, 331*, 585–589.

Procter, A. W., Wong, E. H. F., Stratmann, G. C., Lowe, S. L., & Bowen, D. M. (1989). Reduced glycine stimulation of ³[H]MK-801 binding in Alzheimer's disease. *Journal of Neurochemistry, 53*, 698–704.

Quartermain, D., Mower, J., Rafferty, M. F., Herting, R. L., & Lanthorn, T. H. (1994). Acute but not chronic activation of the NMDA coupled glycine receptor with D-cycloserine facilitates learning and retention. *European Journal of Pharmacology, 257*, 7–12.

Quartermain, D., Nuygen, T., Sheu, J., Herting, R. L. (1991). Milacemide enhances memory storage and alleviates spontaneous forgetting in mice. *Pharmacology, Biochemistry, and Behavior, 39*, 31–35.

Saletu, B., & Grunberger, J. (1986). Early clinical pharmacological trials with a new anti-epileptic, milacemide, using pharmaco-EEG and psychometry. *Methods and Findings in Experimental and Clinical Pharmacology, 6*, 317–330.

Saletu, B., Grunberger, J., & Linzmayer, L (1986). Acute and subacute CNS effects of milacemide in elderly people: Double-blind, placebo-controlled quantitative EEG and psychometric investigations. *Archives of Gerontology and Geriatrics, 5*, 165–181.

Salmon, D. P., Shimamura, A. P., Butters, N., & Smith, S. (1988). Lexical and semantic priming deficits in patients with Alzheimer's disease. *Journal of Clinical and Experimental Neuropsychology, 10*, 477–494.

Schacter, D. L. (1990). Perceptual representation systems and implicit memory. Toward a resolution of the multiple memory systems debate. In A. Diamond (Ed.), *The development and neural bases of higher cognitive functions* (pp. 543–567). New York: New York Academy of Sciences.

Schuster, G. M., & Schmidt, W. J. (1992). D-cycloserine reverses the working memory impairment of hippocampal-lesioned rats in a spatial learning task. *European Journal of Pharmacology, 224*, 97–98.

Schwartz, B. L., & Hashtroudi, S. (1991). Priming is independent of skill learning. *Journal of Experimental Psychology: Learning, Memory, and Cognition, 17*, 1177–1187.

Schwartz, B. L., Hashtroudi, S., Herting, R. L., & Deutsch, S. I. (1992). The effects of milacemide on item and source memory. *Clinical Neuropharmacology, 15*, 114–119.

Schwartz, B. L., Hashtroudi, S., Herting, R. L., Handerson, H., & Deutsch, S. I. (1991). Glycine prodrug facilitates memory retrieval in humans. *Neurology, 41*, 1341–1343.

Schwartz, B. L., Hashtroudi, S., Herting, R. L., Schwartz, P., & Deutsch, S. I. (in press). d-Cycloserine enhances implicit memory in Alzheimer patients. *Neurology*.

Shimamura, A. P., Salmon, D. P., Squire, L. R., & Butters, N. (1987). Memory dysfunction and word priming in dementia and amnesia. *Behavioral Neuroscience, 101*, 347–351.

Sirvio, J., Ekonsalo, T., Riekkinen, P., Jr., Lahtinen, H., & Riekkinen, P., Sr. (1992). D-cycloserine, a modulator of the N-methyl-D-aspartate receptor, improves spatial learning in rats treated with muscarinic antagonist. *Neuroscience Letters, 146*, 215–218.

Squire, L. R. (1992). Memory and the hippocampus: A synthesis from findings with rats, monkeys, and humans. *Psychological Review, 99*, 195–231.

Squire, L. R., Ojemann, J. G., Miezin, F. M., Petersen, S. E., Videen, T. O., & Raichle, M. E. (1992). Activation of the hippocampus in normal humans: A functional anatomical study of memory. *Proceedings of the National Academy of Science, 89*, 1837–1841.

Thomas, J. C., Fozard, J. L., & Waugh, N. C. (1977). Age-related differences in naming latency. *American Journal of Psychology, 90*, 499–509.

Thompson, L. T., Moskal, J. R., & Disterhoft, J. F. (1992). Hippocampus-dependent learning facilitated with a monoclonal antibody or D-cycloserine. *Nature, 359*, 638–641.

Vogel, W., Broverman, D. M., Draguns, J. G., & Klaiber, E. L. (1966). The role of glutamic acid in cognitive behaviors. *Psychological Bulletin, 65*, 367–382.

Wesnes, K., Jones, R. W., & Kirby, J. (1991). The effects of D-cycloserine, a glycine agonist, in a human model of the cognitive deficits associated with ageing and dementia. *British Journal of Clinical Pharmacology, 31*, 577–578.

Wesnes, K., Simpson, P., & Kidd, A. (1988). An investigation of the range of cognitive impairments induced by scopolamine 0.6 mg s.c. *Human Psychopharmacology, 3*, 27–41.

Zalutsky, R. A., & Nicoll, R. A. (1990). Comparison of two forms of long-term potentiation in single hippocampal neurons. *Science, 248*, 1619–1624.

Zimmerman, F. T., & Ross, S. (1944). Effect of glutamic acid and other amino acids on maze learning in the rat. *Archives of Neurology and Psychiatry, 51*, 446–451.

CHAPTER THIRTY-ONE

Conceptual and Practical Issues in the Development and Assessment of Drugs That Would Enhance Cognition

H. J. Weingartner
D. Hommer
*Brain Imaging and Cognitive Neurosciences Sections
of Laboratory of Clinical Studies, NIAAA*

S. Molchan
*Section on Geriatric Psychopharmacology,
Laboratory of Clinical Science, NIMH*

A. Raskin
Department of Psychiatry, University of Maryland

J. K. Robinson
*Department of Psychology,
State University of New York at Stony Brook*

T. Sunderland
*Section on Geriatric Psychopharmacology,
Laboratory of Clinical Science, NIMH*

Impairments in memory and related cognitive functions are common to a wide array of neuropsychiatric syndromes as well as the result of highly varied environmental conditions. It is therefore not surprising that the determinants of these many forms of impaired memory are also quite varied. Likewise, no single type of treatment is likely to be useful for all forms of memory impairment.

During the past several decades clinicians, as well as basic memory researchers, have developed both the tools and some of the knowledge that have allowed them to begin to develop effective remediation strategies for reversing impairments in memory. Pertinent knowledge and theory necessary for developing "memory enhancers" comes from many disciplines. For

439

example, in examining current memory remediation research we immediately note the important influences of contemporary neuroscience research (i.e., studies of simple neural systems that learn and remember), cognitive science (i.e., studies that allow us to understand in functional terms normal and impaired memory and to model what we know), neuropsychology (i.e., research that allows us to map specific cognitive functions to underlying neurobiology using both behavioral as well as brain imaging methods), neuropathology (i.e., studies of syndrome specific changes of neurophysiology, neurochemistry, and neuroanatomy of impaired cognition), and neuropharmacology (i.e., studies that can define the cognitive response to drug treatments in terms that can be directly related to normal and impaired brain function). Our challenge, as cognitivists interested in treating memory dysfunctions, is to integrate what we know from these different perspectives, as illustrated in several treatments of this theme (Gazzaniga, 1988; Lister & Weingartner, 1991; Posner, 1989; Squire & Zola-Morgan, 1988) and reflect that integration of information in programs of research to develop treatments for disordered memories.

In this chapter we consider some of the techniques and knowledge that come from each of these approaches to the study of memory. In the first section of the chapter we consider some of the logic behind the use of animal models of impaired memory such as is expressed in patients suffering from Alzheimer's disease (AD). Such a model must include cognitive effects that are specific to AD, discriminative from other disorders, and consistent with the neuropathology of AD. In the second section we consider the utility of using a pharmacological model of impaired memory as expressed in anticholinergic treatment of elderly normal volunteers. This model simulates some of the specific features of AD, in contrast to other forms of impaired memory, such as the domain specific form of memory dysfunction expressed in amnestic disorders (Lister & Weingartner, 1987; Molchan et al., 1992; Sunderland et al., 1986). This research provides a powerful tool with which to explore memory, because drugs such as anticholinergics and benzodiazepines induce graded and reversible brain dysfunction with which to explore memory mechanisms.

The determinants of drug-induced impairments or improvements in memory may be direct or indirect. This theme is considered in the third section, in which we review recent findings of simulated memory impairment through the use of benzodiazepines, and explore the question of whether this induced amnesia is mediated or modulated by sedation or the attention-impairing effects of the drug. Finally, in the fourth section we review some of the issues involved in clinical trials design and evaluation of potential memory-enhancing drugs. These issues and strategies for uncovering mechanisms important to understanding impaired and enhanced memory are outlined in Fig. 31.1.

Framework for programmatic research for drugs
that may enhance cognition (memory)

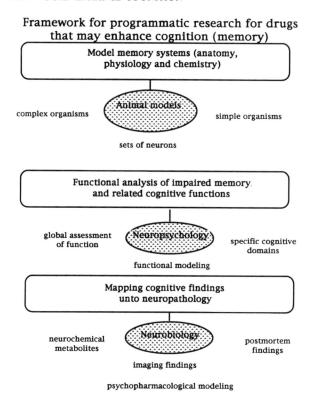

FIG. 31.1. Framework for research designed to develop memory-enhancing drugs: Domains of knowledge and methods.

RODENT MODELS OF IMPAIRED MEMORY AND COGNITION

Over this century, the animal learning field produced a number of useful behavioral paradigms (i. e., the Thorndike Puzzle Box, the Lashley Jumping Stand, the elaborate mazes of Edward Tolman and others, and B. F. Skinner's early rat and pigeon operant chambers). Today neuroscientists draw heavily on these historical influences, but employ customized versions of these paradigms. In particular, the memory paradigms most commonly used by neuroscientists include the shuttle box passive avoidance paradigm (e.g., Haroutunian, Barnes, & Davis, 1985), the Morris water maze (Morris, 1984), T-maze delayed alternation (e.g., Givens & Olton, 1990), Olton's radial arm maze (Olton, 1987), and the operant-delayed nonmatching-to-sample paradigm (e.g., Dunnett, 1985; Otto & Eichenbaum, 1992).

To neuroscientists, each of these tasks represents compromises between issues of practicality and issues of validity and reliability. All of these ostensibly measure short-term or working memory because they involve some period of time between the experience of the stimulus and the subsequent response. Each task possesses features and liabilities. Some require few training trials but many subjects. Some require a human experimenter to manually provide experimental events, but are inexpensive when compared to automated tasks. Primary concerns with all are the *reliability* of observations both within and between subjects; the *selectivity* of the dependent variable for measuring remembering and only remembering; the *sensitivity* of the task to an experimental manipulation; the *ethological validity*, that is, how well the task takes into account the unique adaptations and abilities of the organism; and *face validity*, or how well the cognitive construct as defined in the task is analogous to the human cognitive concept (see Olton, 1985, for discussion of related issues). All of these issues must be considered by the modeler in choosing a paradigm, and, unfortunately, how these factors vary across these paradigms is not well understood.

In addition to the behavioral paradigm, animal models must include a manipulation that produces some of the neurochemical and neuroanatomical aspects of the underlying neuropathology seen in the human affliction, with the understanding that any rodent model only incorporates selective aspects of the human disorder and is never more that an approximation of the complete disease state. The behavioral and cognitive deficits associated with AD are extensive and variable over the course of the disease and among patients. The initial onset is slow, and reasonably distinct stages of the disease are commonly identified, with worsening degrees of agnosia, aphasia, ataxia, and amnesia (McKann et al., 1984). However, it is the disruption of memory that has been the almost exclusive focus of the behavioral paradigms used in robust models of AD.

AD neuropathology is correspondingly widespread. Postmortem analysis of AD brains has shown several prominent cellular changes, including neuritic plaques and neurofibrillary tangles found most often in the hippocampus and neocortex. However, it has been pathological changes to the cholinergic neurotransmitter system that have most often been incorporated into rodent models of the disease. Although changes in markers for other transmitter systems have also been observed, including the biogenic amines norepinephrine, dopamine, serotonin (see Haroutunian, Santucci, & Davis, 1990), amino acids (Reisine, Yamamura, Bird, Spokes, & Enna, 1978), and peptides (Bouras, De St. Hilaire-Kafi, & Constantinidis, 1986), the cholinergic changes have remained of greatest interest. This selective interest in the cholinergic system was based on observations in the 1970s of extensive loss of the acetylcholine catalytic enzyme, choline acetyltransferase in AD (Bowen, Smith, White, & Dawson, 1976; Davies & Maloney, 1976), and the selective degeneration in the area of the nucleus basalis which is a major source of cholinergic afferents to the neocortex and amygdala (Coyle, Price & DeLong, 1982). These findings, taken together with other longstanding observations that cholinergic muscarinic receptor antagonists such as atropine and scopolamine caused temporary Alzheimer's-like confusion and amnesia (see Molchan et al., 1992), suggested that degeneration of the baso-cortical and septo-hippocampal cholinergic systems might account for the mild to moderate cognitive disruption evident in early and middle stages of AD.

One of the most often-used manipulations in rodent models involves the administration of cholinergic muscarinic receptor antagonists such as scopolamine, as well as newer subtype-selective antagonists like pirenzipine, an M_1-receptor-selective antagonist. Although specifically targeting cholinergic cells, the peripheral administration of drugs lacks anatomical specificity (see Hagan & Morris, 1988), affecting other central and peripheral cholinergic systems. Another approach involves lesioning the cholinergic cell body regions of the nucleus basalis and medial septum-diagonal band electrolytically or with excitotoxins (see Olton & Wenk, 1987). This approach targets specific cholinergic cell populations but simultaneously destroys adjoining noncholinergic populations. Attempts to develop more selective cholinergic neurotoxins are under way, and other experimental manipulations have incorporated site-specific injections of muscarinic antagonists (e.g., Dunnett, Wareham, & Torres, 1991) and simultaneous targeting of more than one neurotransmitter system (e.g., Sakurai & Wenk, 1990).

Unfortunately, numerous putative pharmacotherapies that showed initial promise in reversing behavioral deficits in rodent models have later not shown to be efficacious in treating AD in human clinical trials (see Boller & Forrette, 1989; Sarter, Hagan, & Dudchenko, 1992). Possible factors that could account for these failures include: The specific neuropathology modeled may be incorrect (in particular, the cholinergic system may be overemphasized), the behavioral paradigms used may suffer from reliability and validity problems, the emphasis on short-term memory may be misplaced, and metabolic differences between rats and humans may restrict the effective dose ranges of drugs. However, it should be considered that systematic exploration of the processes mediating these problems may in themselves provide tremendous insights into basic processes, and their utility should not be overlooked. And, despite limitations, few attractive alternatives to rodent models for conducting basic investigations exist.

PHARMACOLOGICAL MODELING
OF THE MEMORY IMPAIRMENT EXPRESSED
IN ALZHEIMER'S DISEASE PATIENTS

Two decades ago, Drachman and Leavitt (1974) showed that when young normal subjects were given scopolamine, the resulting episodic memory impairment was similar to that which occurs in normal aging. Since then the effects of the anticholinergic drug scopolamine have been proposed to model aspects of the cognitive impairment that occurs with aging and with Alzheimer's disease. Cognitive decline with age has been most consistently demonstrated on tests involving new learning and episodic memory, psychomotor speed, concept formation, visuospatial praxis, and attention (Buschke & Grober, 1986; Flicker, Ferris, Crook, Bartus, & Reisberg, 1986), whereas immediate memory, language, and retrieval from knowledge memory are generally considered to be spared with age. After scopolamine administration, immediate memory and retrieval from knowledge memory have been variably reported to be impaired with studies that have used higher doses of drug, more direct routes of administration, and/or older subjects tending to demonstrate greatest impairment in these areas (Molchan et al., 1992). Age is an important variable in evaluating scopolamine's effects, because older subjects appear to experience impairment in more cognitive arenas and to be quantitatively more impaired on measures of episodic memory (Molchan et al., 1992). The increased sensitivity to scopolamine in older people is consistent with other data showing that deficiencies in the cholinergic system occur in the aging brain and may contribute to age-associated memory impairment (see Molchan et al., 1992, for review).

The effects of scopolamine, when administered to older people, are similar to some aspects of the cognitive impairment in Alzheimer's disease (Molchan et al., 1992; Sunderland et al., 1986). These include decreased performance on tests of episodic memory, retrieval from knowledge memory, vigilance-attention, and digit span, as well as increased production of intrusions. Furthermore, older people, after scopolamine treatment, seem unable to utilize and benefit significantly from a second presentation of an item (Molchan et al., 1992), an impairment that is also observed in patients with Alzheimer's disease (Salmon, Shimamura, Butters, & Smith, 1988; Weingartner et al., 1993).

Controversy exists on how much of the cognitive effects of scopolamine are due to effects on early information processing or attention, as scopolamine can cause significant sedation (Curran & Birch, 1991). Measures such as reaction time, stimulus descrimination, and the P300 component of evoked potentials are impaired at higher scopolamine doses, and measures of sustained attention are impaired at lower doses (Brandeis, Naylor, Halliday, Callaway, & Yano, 1992; reviewed by Molchan et al., 1992). Dunne and Hartley (1986) described the effect as a decreased ability to optimally utilize attentional resources. Others suggested that scopolamine acts on more than just attentional mechanisms, and that the central executive component of working memory is impaired by the drug (Rusted, Eaton-Williams, & Warburton, 1991).

A number of studies have shown that scopolamine's effects on vigilance, attention, and sedation are distinct from its effects on memory (reviewed by Molchan et al., 1992). Other evidence comes from the demonstration that the benzodiazepine lorazepam, at doses that produce sedation comparable to that produced by scopolamine does not produce cognitive impairment (Sunderland et al., 1989). Also, attempts to attenuate scopolamine-induced memory impairment using stimulant drugs have been mostly unsuccessful, whereas cholinergic drugs consistently attenuate anticholinergic induced impairments (Molchan et al., 1992). Stimulants, such as dextroamphetamine and nicotine, that have little or no muscarinic activity at doses used, generally have been shown to attenuate scopolamine's effects on reaction time and other attentional measures, but not on measures of memory (Martinez et al., submitted; Rusted & Eaton-Williams, 1991). The peptide thyrotropin releasing hormone, which has stimulant effects, has been shown to attenuate scopolamine-induced episodic memory impairment in young normal volunteers (Molchan et al., 1990).

Besides its sedative and attentional effects, other limitations of the scopolamine model as it relates to Alzheimer's disease include a lack of effect on naming and other language functions, and on retrograde memory (see Molchan et al., 1992, for review). Effects on measures of implicit memory, which is impaired at least later in Alzheimer's disease, have been divergent. Two studies reported no significant effect on performance on skill learning tasks (Kopelman & Corn, 1988; Nissen, Knopman, & Schacter, 1987), although others found impairments using a pursuit rotor task (Curran & Birch, 1991) and a tracking task (Frith, McGinty, Gergel, & Crow, 1989). Variable results on repetition priming have been shown, and it has been suggested that there may be a continuum of effects of scopolamine on what are thought of as implicit memory processes (Molchan et al., 1992).

A number of other drugs, which have little or no muscarinic receptor activity, have been shown to attenuate scopolamine-induced cognitive impairment in humans, for example, nootropic agents like aniracetam (Wesnes, Anand, Simpson, & Christman, 1990) and cycloserine, a glycine agonist (Jones, Wesnes, & Kirby, 1991). Some of these compounds are known to interact with the cholinergic system; for others, possible mechanisms are unknown. Certainly in cases of Alzheimer's disease, deficits in a number of neurotransmitter systems are well documented, so it is probably unrealistic to think that the blockade of one type of receptor, as with scopolamine, could model all of the cognitive changes that occur (Molchan et al., 1992). However, the actions of scopolamine on cognitive processes have made it a useful tool for the study of learning, memory, and attention.

STRATEGIES FOR UNCOVERING COGNITIVE AND NONCOGNITIVE DETERMINANTS OF DRUG-INDUCED AMNESIAS

The syndrome produced by acute benzodiazepine (BZ) administration in humans appears to closely resemble the amnesic syndrome (Lister & Weingartner, 1987; Wolkowitz et al., 1987) as observed in patients with damage limited to the medial temporal lobe (Squire, 1987). There is, however, one important difference between the BZ-induced pattern of cognitive impairment and the pattern seen in the human amnesic syndrome. In the amnesic syndrome there is usually little or no sedation or impairment of attention (Squire, 1987). In contrast, following acute BZ administration normal volunteers experience a dose-dependent increase in self-rated sedation as well as a dose-dependent impairment in recent memory. These two effects are highly correlated (Hommer et al., 1986). Thus, it is possible that the cognitive effects of BZ may be secondary to sedation and decreased vigilance, and thus of minimal value in modeling memory impairment.

However, there are several reasons to suspect that BZ-induced memory impairment is not simply secondary to sedation and decreased vigilance. During chronic BZ treatment tolerance develops to the sedative effects, but not to the memory-impairing effects of the drug (File & Lister, 1982; Ghoneim, Mewaldt, Berie, & Hinrichs, 1981). Flumazenil, a specific BZ receptor antagonist, blocks sedative and other effects but not the amnesic effects of BZ in rodents (Thiebot, 1985). In humans, two studies found that both the sedative and amnestic effects of BZs were reversed by flumazenil (Dorow, Berenberg, Duka, & Sauergrey, 1987; Gentil, Tavares, Gorenstein, Bello, et al., 1990), but others have found evidence for dissociation between the sedative and amnestic effects of several different BZs (Birch & Curran, 1990; Dunton, Schwam, & Pitman, 1988; Ghoneim, Dembo, & Block, 1989; O'Boyle et al., 1983). These findings suggest further investigation of the possibility that BZ antagonist pretreatment combined with BZ agonist administration might provide a way to selectively impair episodic memory in normal human subjects without inducing sedation or attentional dysfunction.

In a recent study, we attempted to selectively impair episodic memory without increasing sedation by treating group of normal controls with flumazenil or placebo followed by increasing doses of i.v. diazepam at 20-minute intervals (Hommer, Weingartner, & Brier, 1993). When subjects were pretreated with placebo, diazepam produced a significant increase in self-rated sedation. At baseline, before placebo for flumazenil, the mean sedation score was 60, and after the cumulative dose of diazepam subjects rated their sedation as a significantly lower 15.4. Pretreatment with flumazenil prevented the diazepam-induced sedation. Before flumazenil subjects rated their sedation as 62.8, but after the highest dose of diazepam the sedation ratings had decreased nonsignificantly to only 40.9, indicating that flumazenil blocked the sedative effects of diazepam.

Subjects pretreated with placebo and then administered diazepam demonstrated dose-dependent effects on attention and working memory. During the flumazenil placebo–diazepam combination there was a significant diazepam induced impairment in attention. Baseline attention score was 5.5 (out of a possible 6 words correctly identified). Following the highest dose of diazepam the attention score decreased significantly to 3.6. Pretreatment with flumazenil blocked the ability of diazepam to impair attention. Baseline attention score was 5.4 and after diazepam administration it was nonsignificantly lower at 4.5.

In contrast to its antagonist effects on sedation and attention, flumazenil failed to block diazepam-induced impairment in verbal free recall. Baseline free recall score prior to placebo for diazepam was 8.1 (out of a possible 12). After the highest dose of diazepam following placebo free recall decreased significantly to 5.4 words. When diazepam was preceded by flumazenil the baseline free recall score was 8.4 words, and after the final dose of diazepam preceded by flumazenil the free recall score was significantly lower, at 5.1. Thus flumazenil failed to antagonize the amnestic effects of diazepam.

The results demonstrate that it is possible to pharmacologically disrupt explicit episodic memory without significantly impairing attention or producing sedation, thereby demonstrating an important dissociation of sedation and cognition in the effects of diazepam. This is of relevance not only when considering the behavioral effects of the benzodiazepines but also other drugs, such as alcohol, known to produce robust effects on cognitive functions. Although we do not know the exact mechanism by which flumazenil blocks the nonamnesic effects of diazepam while failing to antagonize diazepam-induced amnesia, clearly these drugs provide a valuable new tool for the biological study of cognition.

ISSUES IN THE CONDUCT OF CLINICAL TRIALS OF MEMORY ENHANCERS

Animal models, neurotransmitter models, and pharmacological models are all involved in identifying compounds as potentially useful memory enhancers. Once identified, these compounds must be entered in a controlled clinical trial. The pharmaceutical company then decides how to design such a trial to maximize drug–placebo differences.

Current drugs available to treat Alzheimer patients, or in the pipeline as possible treatments, are mainly viewed as palliative, hopefully slowing the progression of the disease until a definitive treatment is found. Currently the Food and Drug Administration (FDA) requires that drugs used to treat this disorder show not only efficacy, which is generally defined in statistical terms, but clinical effectiveness. Demonstrating clinical effectiveness places a heavy burden on the treatment under investigation, compounded by the fact that the patient's condition is likely to deteriorate during the course of the trial. Several important issues in designing clinical trials that demonstrate effectiveness are described in the subsections that follow.

Cognitive Screens

Clinical trials generally include a screen to measure cognitive deficit and a screen to measure depression. The cognitive screen that is currently most used is the Mini-Mental State Exam (MMSE; Folstein, Folstein, & McHugh, 1975). However, in an effort to liberalize patient entry into the study, the limits set tend to be overinclusive, for example, 10 to 26 (out of a possible 30) on the MMSE in the tacrine trial. If one converts these scale points into levels of cognitive decline on an instrument such as the Global Deterioration Scale (GDS; Reisberg, Ferris, DeLeon, & Crook, 1982), a score of 10 on the MMSE would probably translate into moderate to moderately severe cognitive decline on the GDS, whereas a score of 26 on the MMSE would probably translate into very mild to mild cognitive decline on the GDS. In this context Crook and colleagues (Crook et al., 1991) used a MMSE cutoff of 27 for their Age Associated Memory Impairment subjects, which is only one point higher than the cutoff in the tacrin trial. It is important that limits set for entry in clinical trials are high enough to eliminate patients too deteriorated to show a positive response, and low enough to allow room for improvement.

Depression Screen

These studies also include a depression screen, usually the Hamilton Rating Scale for Depression (HAM-D; Hamilton, 1960). What is unclear is the purpose of this screen. If one is looking for diagnostic purity and wishes to eliminate patients with depression diagnoses, then a structured interview designed for this purpose is the proper route and not the HAM-D. If one wishes to eliminate patients with syndromal depression, then a depression rating scale designed for use with the elderly and with more emphasis on observable signs of depression is a better choice than the HAM-D. The HAM-D also contains a number of items, such as sleep and sexual disturbances, that are negatively impacted by age and give a false impression of depression. It is not a bad idea to exclude patients from these trials with significant syndromal depression. Syndromal depression is seen in 10% to 20% of Alzheimer patients especially in the early stages of the illness (Schneider, 1993). If the drug has some antidepressant action, as seems to have been the case with Hydergine, then the lifting of depression may have general patholytic effects and improve cognitive functioning as well.

As noted, the FDA is now strongly recommending that drug trials in this area show clinical effectiveness and not just statistical efficacy. The Hydergine approval some time ago probably set the stage for this requirement. The package insert for Hydergine notes the specific items on the Sandoz Clinical Assessment Geriatric (SCAG; Shader, Harmatz, & Salzman, 1974) scale on which modest but statistically significant changes were observed. It was these changes that served as the basis for Hydergine's approval.

Effectiveness

The tactic being taken by pharmaceutical companies to meet the requirement of effectiveness is to include a clinical global change measure. The current favorite is called the Clinician's Interview Based Impression of Change (CIBIC). Ratings are made on a seven-point scale from "very much worse" to "very much improved." To add meaning to these ratings some studies include a semi-structured interview with the patient containing mental status items as well as a semi-structured interview with a caregiver tapping activities of daily living.

A major problem with global change measures is the need for the clinician to recall what the patient was like at baseline, particularly as trials extend into six months and a year. One solution to this problem is making a video-tape of the baseline interview for later comparisons. Global change measures also are not especially sensitive to treatment effects, in particular to identifying differences between two active treatments (Raskin & Crook, 1976), as was the case in the tacrin trial (Davis et al., 1992).

An option that has been used to demonstrate clinical effectiveness is to require a specified percentage drop in scores on a rating scale, for example, a 50% drop in HAM-D scores from baseline as an indication of clinically meaningful change. However, in Alzheimer trials one is not likely to see a 50% or even a 10% drop in scores in a scale such as the Alzheimer's Disease Assessment Scale (ADAS; Mohs, Rosen, & Davis, 1983). A possible remedy is to include a different type of change measure, one that has clinically meaningful change built in as anchors for the rating scale points. The GDS referred to earlier is a case in point. For example, a rating of 2, very mild cognitive decline, is defined behaviorally as "subjective complaints of memory deficit, most frequently in the following areas: (a) forgetting where one has placed familiar objects," etc. (Reisberg et al., 1982).

Enrichment Phase

A design feature that was used in the tacrin trial to enhance treatment response was the inclusion of an enrichment phase (Davis et al., 1992). Patients were assigned to two doses of tacrin or a placebo for two weeks at a time, and their response to these treatments was evaluated to determine the best dose to use for the drug trial itself. Only patients who showed a predetermined response to tacrin during this phase were subsequently entered into the study. Although there is no doubt that this approach did "enrich" or enhance drug–placebo differences in the drug trial, there are inherent problems in using this enrichment phase. Most important, it compromises generalizations about the drug's effects on a nonpreselected sample of patients. Only about a third of the patients entered into the enrichment phase showed the predetermined response to tacrin and were entered into the trial itself. When the drug is marketed, it is marketed for use with all Alzheimer patients, not just for those who showed a positive response in an enrichment phase. The second problem is the inability to truly say that one dose was better than another. There was no washout period between dosages; hence, it is conceivable that carryover effects from a 2-week period on one dose may have influenced results during the 2-week period on the second dose. An alternative is to find the best dose for use by most patients. In this model, patients are assigned to two doses of the active drug or to a placebo in a parallel drug design. However, sample size permitting, patients are overassigned to one of the two active treatments.

Recommendations

1. Narrow cognitive-screen limits for study entry to eliminate cognitive decline in normal aging and those too deteriorated to respond to any treatment (perhaps 15–23 on the MMSE).

2. Include a scale such as the GDS to stage the patient's current level of functioning in clinically meaningful terms.

3. Substitute for the HAM-D a depression screen with norms for the elderly and a greater emphasis on observable symptoms of depression and secondary symptoms of depression that are not age related. An alternative would be the NIMH Dementia Mood Assessment Scale (DMAS; Sunderland et al., 1988) that has norms for the elderly, anchor points, and observable signs of depression.

CONCLUSIONS AND FUTURE RESEARCH DIRECTIONS

At present, there is no reliable, effective pharmacotherapy available for the treatment of impaired memory in patient populations such as AD. However, the knowledge base necessary for developing such treatments is expanding rapidly. Over the last decade we have made enormous progress in developing the research milieu that allows us to systematically consider the efficacy of a whole host of candidate drugs. We are far more knowledgeable about the details of the neuropathology of some of the classic forms of impaired memory functioning (such as AD, amnesic syndromes) than we were a decade ago. We have become increasingly aware of the value of appreciating the heterogeneity of disease presentation, such as AD, and the implications of that heterogeneity for developing therapies for AD. This has resulted in detailed data about the specificity of the expressed memory impairment, which is proving useful in considering why a treatment may "work" in some patients and not others. These same approaches have been useful in defining the nature of the differentiated memory-cognitive response to candidate treatments. Consequently, we have begun to examine the mechanisms by which a drug may alter memory functions (based on both a functional analysis of an observed cognitive response as well as findings that would relate possible changes to underlying brain mechanisms, i.e., through the use of imaging methods in combination with cognitive activation techniques). The very basis on which we consider a drug to be of value in treating impaired memory has broadened and become more differentiated. For example, a drug may be considered useful if it attenuates the progression of impaired memory or the onset of a disease such as AD, even if it does not reverse memory symptoms.

Finally, an important byproduct of research on potentially memory-enhancing drugs is what such studies can teach us about the mechanisms of both impaired and normal memory. This clearly has been the case in attempts to develop animal models of memory impairments. Likewise, drug trials, when well designed, using sensitive and specific methods for characterizing subjects and response to treatments, can be enormously useful for testing our notions about the psychobiology of memory.

REFERENCES

Birch, B., & Curran, H. (1990). The differential effects of flumazenil on the psychomotor and amnesic actions of midaazolam. *Psychopharmacology, 4,* 29–34.

Boller, F., & Forrette, F. (1989). Alzheimer's disease and THA: A review of the cholinergic theory and of preliminary results. *Biomedicine and Pharmacotherapy, 43,* 487–491.

Bouras, C., De St. Hilaire-Kafi, S., & Constantinidis, J. (1986). Neuropeptides in Alzheimer's disease: A review and morphological results. *Progress in Neuro-Psychopharmacology and Biological Psychiatry, 10,* 271–286.

Bowen, D. M., Smith, C. B., White, P., & Dawson, A. N. (1976). Neurotransmitter-related enzymes and indices of hypoxia in senile dementia and other atrophies. *Brain, 99,* 459.

Brandeis, D., Naylor, H., Halliday, R., Callaway, E., & Yano, L. (1992). Scopolamine effects on visual information processing, attention, and event-related potential map latencies. *Psychophysiology, 29,* 315–336.

Buschke, H., & Grober, E. (1986). Genuine memory deficits in age-associated memory impairment. *Developmental Neuropsychology, 2,* 287–307.

Coyle, J. T., Price, D. L., & DeLong, M. R. (1982). Alzheimer's Disease: A disorder of cortical cholinergic innervation. *Science, 219,* 1184–1190.

Crook, T. H., Tinklenberg, J., Yesavage, J., Petrie, W., Nunzi, M. G., & Massari, D. C. (1991). Effects of phosphatidylserine in age-associated memory impairment. *Neurology, 41,* 644–649.

Curran, H. V., & Birch, B. (1991). Differentiating the sedative, psychomotor and amnesic effects of benzodiazepines: A study with midazolam and the benzodiazepine antagonist, flumazenil. *Psychopharmacology, 103,* 519–523.

Davies, P., & Maloney, A. J. F. (1976). Selective loss of central cholinergic neurons in Alzheimer's disease. *Lancet, 2,* 1403.

Davis, K. L., Thal, L. J., Gamzu, E. R., Davis, C. S., Woolson, R. F., Gracon, S. I., Drachman, D. A., Schneider, L. S., Whitehouse, P. J., Hoover, T. M., et al. (1992). A double-blind placebo controlled multi-center study of tacrin for Alzheimer Disease: The Tacrin Collaborative Study Group. *New England Journal of Medicine, 327,* 1253–1259.

Dorow, R., Berenberg, D., Duka, T., & Sauergrey, N. (1987). Amnestic effects of lormetazepam and their reversal by the benzodiazepine antagonist Ro 15-1788. *Psychopharmacology, 93*, 507–514.

Drachman, D. A., & Leavitt, J. (1974). Human memory and the cholinergic system. *Archives of Neurology, 30*, 113–121.

Dunne, P., & Hartley, L. R. (1986). Scopolamine and the control of attention in humans. *Psychopharmacology, 89*, 94–97.

Dunnett, S. B. (1985). Comparative effects of cholinergic drugs and lesions of the nucleus basalis and fimbria-fornix on delayed matching in rats. *Psychopharmacology, 87*, 357–363.

Dunnett, S. B., Wareham, A. T., & Torres, E. M. (1991). Cholinergic blockade in prefrontal cortex and hippocampus disrupts short term memory in rats. *Neuroreport, 1*, 61–64.

Dunton, A., Schwam, E., & Pitman, N. (1988). Flumazenil: US clinical pharmacology studies. *European Journal of Anaesthesiology, 82*, 81–95.

File, S. E., & Lister, R. G. (1982). b-CCE and chlordiazepoxide reduce exploratory head-dipping and rearing: No mutual antagonism. *Neuropharmacology, 21*, 1215–1218.

Flicker, C., Ferris, S. H., Crook, T., Bartus, R. T., & Reisberg, B. (1986). Cognitive decline in advanced age: Future directions for the psychometric differentiation of normal and pathological age changes in cognitive function. *Developmental Neuropsychology, 2*, 309–322.

Folstein, M. F., Folstein, S. E., & McHugh, P. R. (1975). A practical method for grading the cognitive state of patients for the clinician. *Journal of Psychiatric Research, 12*, 189–198.

Frith, C. D., McGinty, M. A., Gergel, I., & Crow, T. J. (1989). The effects of scopolamine and clonidine upon the performance and leaning of a motor skill. *Psychopharmacology, 98*, 120–125.

Gazzaniga, M. (1988). *Perspectives in memory research.* Cambridge, MA: MIT Press.

Gentil, V., Tavares, S., Gorenstein, C., Bello, C., et al. (1990). Acute reversal of flumitrazepam effects by Ro 15-1788 and Ro 15-3505: Inverse agonism, tolerance, and rebound. *Psychopharmacology, 100*, 54–59.

Ghoneim, M., Dembo, J., & Block, R. (1989). Time course of sedative and amnesic effects of diazepam by flumazenil. *Anasthesiology, 70*, 899–904.

Ghoneim, M. M., Mewaldt, S. P., Berie, J. L., & Hinrichs, J. V. (1981). Memory and performance effects of single and 3-week administration of diazepam. *Psychopharmacology, 73*, 147–151.

Givens, B. S., & Olton, D. S. (1990). Cholinergic and GABAergic modulation of the medial septal area: Effect on working memory. *Behavioral Neuroscience, 104*, 849–855.

Hagan, J. J., & Morris, R. G. M. (1988). The cholinergic hypothesis of memory: A review of animal experiments. In L. L. Iversen, S. D. Iversen, & S. H. Snyder (Eds.), *Handbook of psychopharmacology: Psychopharmacology of the aging nervous system* (Vol. 20, pp. 217–323). New York: Plenum Press.

Hamilton, M. (1960). A rating scale for depression. *Journal of Neurology, Neurosurgery and Psychiatry, 23*, 56–62.

Haroutunian, V., Barnes, E., & Davis, K. L. (1985). Cholinergic modulation of memory in rats. *Psychopharmacology, 87*, 266–271.

Haroutunian, V., Santucci, A. C., & Davis, K. L. (1990). Implications of multiple neurotransmitter system lesions for cholinomimetic therapy in Alzheimer's disease. In S. M. Aquilonius & P. G. Gillberg (Eds.), *Progress in brain research* (Vol. 84, pp. 333–346). New York: Elsevier.

Hommer, D. W., Matsuo, V., Wolkowitz, H., Chrousos, G., Greenblatt, D., Weingartner, H., & Paul, S. (1986). Benzodiazepine sensitivity in normal human subjects. *Archives of General Psychiatry, 43*, 542–551.

Hommer, D., Weingartner, H. J., & Brier, A. (1993). Dissociation of benzodiazepine induced amnesia from sedation. *Psychopharmacology, 112*, 455–460.

Jones, R. W., Wesnes, K. A., & Kirby, J. (1991). Effects of NMDA modulation in scopolamine dementia. *Annals of the New York Academy of Science, 640*, 241–244.

Kopelman, M. D., & Corn, T. H. (1988). Cholinergic 'blockade' as a model for cholinergic depletion. *Brain, 111*, 1079–1110.

Lister, R. G., & Weingartner, H. (1987). Neuropharmacological strategies for understanding psychobiological determinants of cognition. *Human Neurobiology, 6*, 119–127.

Lister, R., & Weingartner, H. (1991). *Perspectives on cognitive neuroscience.* New York: Oxford University Press.

Martinez, R., Molchan, S., Lawlor, B. A., Thompson, K., Martinson, H., Latham, G., Weingartner, H., & Sunderland, T. (submitted). *Minimal effects of dextroamphetamine on scopolamine induced cognitive impairments in humans.*

McKann, G., Drachman, D., Folstein, M., Katzman, R., Price, D., & Stadlan, E. M. (1984). Clinical diagnosis of Alzheimer's disease: Report on the NINCDS-ADRDA work group under the auspices of the Department of Health and Human Services task force on Alzheimer's disease. *Neurology, 34*, 939–944.

Mohs, R. C., Rosen, W. G., & Davis, K. L. (1983). The Alzheimer's Disease Assessment Scale: An instrument for assessing treatment efficacy. *Psychopharmacological Bulletin, 19*, 448–450.

Molchan, S. E., Hill, A., Weingartner, H. J., Mellow, J. L., Vitello, B., Martinez, R., & Sunderland, T. (1992). Increased cognitive sensitivity to scopolamine with age and a perspective on the scopolamine model. *Brain Research Review, 17*, 215–226.

Molchan, S. E., Mellow, A. M., Lawlor, B. A., Weingartner, H. J., Cohen, R. M., Cohen, M. R., & Sunderland, T. (1990). TRH attenuates scopolamine-induced memory impairment in humans. *Psychopharmacology, 100*, 84–89.

Morris, R. G. M. (1984). Development of water maze procedure for studying spatial learning in the rat. *Journal of Neuroscience Methods, 11*, 47–60

Nissen, M. J., Knopman, D. S., & Schacter, D. L. (1987). Neurochemical dissociation of memory systems. *Neurology, 37*, 789–794.

O'Boyle, C., Lambe, R., Darragh, A., Taffe, W., Brick, I., & Kenny, M. (1983). Ro17-1788 antagonises the effects of diazepam in man without affecting its bioavailability. *British Journal of Anaestheology, 55*, 349–355.

Olton, D. S. (1985). Criteria for establishing and evaluating animal models. In D. S. Olton, E. Gamzu, & S. Corkin (Eds.), *Memory disfunction: An integration of animal and human research from preclinical and clinical perspectives* (p. 121). New York: New York Academy of Sciences.

Olton, D. S. (1987). The radial arm maze as a tool in neuropharmacology. *Physiology & Behavior, 40*, 793–797.

Olton, D. S., & Wenk, G. L. (1987). Dementia: animal models of the cognitive impairments produced by degeneration of the basal forebrain cholinergic system. In H. Y. Meltzer (Ed.), *Psychopharmacology: The third generation of progress* (pp. 941–953). New York: Raven Press.

Otto, T., & Eichenbaum, H. (1992). Complementary roles of the orbital prefrontal cortex and the perirhinal-entorhinal cortices in an odor guided delayed non-matching-to-sample task. *Behavioral Neuroscience, 106*, 762–775

Posner, M. (1989). *The foundations of cognitive neuroscience.* Cambridge, MA: MIT Press.

Raskin, A., & Crook, T. H. (1976). Sensitivity of rating scales completed by psychiatrist, nurses, and patients to antidepressant drug effects. *Journal of Psychiatric Research, 13*, 31–41.

Reisberg, B., Ferris, S. H., DeLeon, M. J., & Crook, T. (1982). The Global Deterioration Scale for assessment of primary degenerative dementia. *American Journal of Psychiatry, 139*, 1136–1139.

Reisine, T. D., Yamamura, H. I., Bird, E. D., Spokes, E., & Enna, S. J. (1978). Pre- and post-synaptic neurochemical alterations in Alzheimer's disease. *Brain Research, 159*, 477–482.

Rusted, J. M., & Eaton-Williams, P. (1991). Distinguishing between attentional and anmestic effects in information processing: The separate and combined effects of scopolamine and nicotine on verbal free recall. *Psychopharmacology, 104*, 363–366.

Rusted, J. M., Eaton-Williams, P., & Warburton, D. M. (1991). A comparison of the effects of scopolamine and diazepam on working memory. *Psychopharmacology, 105*, 442–445.

Sakarai, Y., & Wenk, G. L. (1990). The interaction of acetylcholinergic and serotonergic neural systems on performance in a continuous non-matching to sample task. *Brain Research, 519*, 118–121.

Salmon, D. P., Shimamura, A. P., Butters, N., & Smith, S. (1988). Lexical and semantic priming deficits in patients with Alzheimer's disease. *Journal of Clinical and Experimental Neuropsychology, 10*, 477–494.

Sarter, M., Hagan, J. J., & Dudchenko, P. (1992). Behavioral screening for cognition enhancers: From indiscriminate to valid testing.: Part II. *Psychopharmacology, 107*, 461–473.

Schneider, L. S. (1993). Efficacy of treatment for geropsychiatric patients with severe mental illness. *Psychopharmacology Bulletin, 29*, 501–524.

Shader, R. I., Harmatz, J. S., & Salzman, C. (1974). A new scale for assessment in geriatric populations: Sandoz Clinical Assessment-Geriatric (SCAG). *Journal of the American Geriatric Society, 22*, 107–113.

Squire, L. R. (1987). *Memory and brain.* New York: Oxford University Press.

Squire, L. R., & Zola-Morgan, S. (1988). Memory: Brain systems and behavior. Special Issue: Learning and memory. *Trends in Neurosciences, 11*, 170–175.

Sunderland, T., Alterman, I., Young, D., Hill, J. L., Tariot, P. N., Newhouse, P. A., Murphy, D. L., & Cohen, R. M. (1988). A new scale for the assessment of depressed mood in dementia subjects. *American Journal of Psychiatry, 145*, 955–959.

Sunderland, T., Tariot, P. N., Weingartner, H., Murphy, D. L., Newhouse, P. A., & Cohen, R. M. (1986). Pharmacologic modelling of Alzheimer's disease. *Progress in Neuro-Psychopharmacology and Biological Psychiatry, 10*, 599–610.

Sunderland, T., Weingartner, H., Cohen, R. M., Tariot, P. N., Newhouse, P. A., Thompson, K. E., Lawlor, B. A., & Mueller, E. A. (1989). Low-dose oral lorazepam administration in Alzheimer subjects and age-matched controls. *Psychopharmacology, 99*, 129–133.

Thiebot, M. H. (1985). Some evidence for amnesic-like effects of benzodiazepines in animals. *Neuroscience and Biobehavioral Reviews, 9*, 95–100.

Weingartner, H. J., Eckardt, M., Grafman, J., Molchan, S., Putnam, K., Rawlings, R., & Sunderland, T. (1993). The effects of repetition on memory performance in cognitively impaired patients. *Neuropsychology, 7*, 385–395.

Wesnes, K., Anand, R., Simpson, P., & Christman, L. (1990). The use of a scopolamine model to study the potential nontropic effects of aniracetam and piracetam in healthy volunteers. *Journal of Psychopharmacology, 4*, 219–232.

Wolkowitz, O. M., Weingartner, H., Thompson, B. S., Pickar, D., Paul, S. M., & Hommer, D. W. (1987). Diazepam-induced amnesia: A neuropharmacological model of an "organic amnestic syndrome." *American Journal of Psychiatry, 144*, 25–29.

CHAPTER THIRTY-TWO

Curious Memory Phenomena: Implications for Treatment After Traumatic Brain Injury

Rick Parenté
Amie Elliott
Towson State University

Maxwell Twum
Dalhausie University

Curious memory phenomena are research results that are inconsistent with previous research findings, are counterintuitive or contraindicate existing theory, or are simply unexpected. The authors' work with traumatically brain injured patients over the years has produced many curious memory phenomena. These observations have provided dramatic insights into the nature of memory failure after head injury and a wealth of practical recommendations for improving treatment of memory deficits.

Although several of these curious memory phenomena have emerged, only three are discussed here. The first involves the transfer of learning that occurs between overlapping tasks. We show that results that would normally occur in studies of college students who learn overlapping lists of words are actually reversed with brain injured patients. The results of two overlapping list experiments discussed later in the chapter lead to predictions about how to improve cognitive skills after head injury via the transfer of organization.

The second curious memory phenomenon involves our attempts to train cognitions that were previously described as "preconscious" or "preverbal." This type of experiment shows that persons with brain injury can improve their ability to scan the visual iconic memory. Moreover, the training also provides positive transfer to a real world task such as reading.

The third curious memory phenomenon involves the effect of incentive on memory after head injury. This type of experiment shows that when a significant incentive is provided, amnesic patients' memories can improve markedly and immediately, often to near average levels.

THE TRANSFER OF COGNITIVE SKILL
AFTER HEAD INJURY

The transfer of organization has been studied extensively since the mid-1960s. Tulving (1966) demonstrated how subjective organization of word lists could produce negative transfer when college students learned two lists of words and the second list of words contained the first. Tulving explained that subjects in the experimental group developed an organization for learning the part-list items that became inappropriate for learning the whole-list items. He further suggested that the negative transfer the students experienced when they learned the second list resulted because the subjects in the experimental group had to merge their organization of part-list words into the organization formed when they learned the whole-list words. Because the part-list and whole-list organizations were unique for the two lists, the two organizations were incompatible, which produced negative transfer.

College students typically do not have neurological deficits and are therefore able to use organizational strategies when learning verbal information (Raaijmakers & Shiffrin, 1981). The organization occurs spontaneously, seemingly without any conscious effort. This type of mental activity proceeds by clustering words into chunks organized hierarchically as learning proceeds (Buschke, 1976), and it has been shown to make materials more memorable (Chase & Simon, 1973) and easier to learn (Brown & Siegler, 1991).

After a traumatic brain injury, many individuals lose their ability to spontaneously organize. For example, persons with frontal lobe brain lesions have difficulties with tasks that require organization, prioritization, and sequential ordering (Cicerone, Lazar, & Shapiro, 1983; Lhermitte, Derouesne, & Signoret, 1972; Luria & Tsvetkova, 1964; Milner, 1971, 1982; Petrides & Milner, 1982; Rochetta della, 1986). Patients with left and right frontal lobe lesions also lose the ability to organize and to categorize pictures (Halstead, 1940; Milner, 1971, 1982). Immediate and delayed recall deficits involving semantic clustering of verbal materials have been shown in patients with right hemispheric damage (Villardita, 1987). Patients with right brain damage also have difficulty with the semantic clustering of concrete and highly imaginable nouns (Villardita, Grioli, & Quatropanni, 1988). Other studies show that whereas subjects without neurological deficits spontaneously organize words to facilitate recall, head injury survivors do not spontaneously organize words. This effect has been interpreted as evidence that head injury disrupts the person's ability to actively and spontaneously organize (Brooks, 1975; Levin & Goldstein, 1986).

If head injury robs the person of the ability to organize, then it is reasonable to suggest that survivors of traumatic head injury should not experience the negative transfer that is commonly reported in part-to-whole learning studies performed with college students. This is because subjects with head injury will not organize part-list words and thus there will be no part-list organization to interfere with the learning of whole-list words. It follows that brain injured patients who learn one half of the whole list may show better whole-list learning relative to a control group who initially learns an unrelated list. This curious memory phenomenon would be exactly the opposite of what is typically reported in studies of part–whole learning with college students.

Twum (1994) investigated how head injury would effect part-to-whole learning with a group of 40 head injury survivors. The subjects ranged in age from 17 to 45 years, with most the subjects having high school education. One half of the subjects learned a list of 12 unrelated nouns. The other group learned a different list of unrelated nouns. Each group was given several trials to learn the words to a criterion of two perfect recalls of the entire list. Afterwards, both groups learned the same second list of nouns that was twice as long as the first. In the experimental condition, the two lists overlapped and the second list literally contained the first. In the control condition, the second list did not contain the first. The part–whole negative transfer of learning phenomena is the fact that the control condition usually learns the second list faster than the experimental group. This is counterintuitive, because the experimental group has already learned half of the second list.

It was hypothesized that brain damaged patients did not spontaneously organize verbal materials to facilitate recall. Therefore, because they were asked to memorize materials to which no ready organization could be formed, head injury survivors, unlike college students, would not impose a subjective organization onto the first list items that would transfer to the second list task. However, because the experimental group would have learned part of the whole-list words during part-list learning, they would still benefit from prior frequency of exposure to one half the words without any organizational interference when they learned the whole-list words. It is, therefore, reasonable to suggest that the experimental group would experience positive transfer from part- to whole-list learning, just the opposite of what one would expect from college students.

The results of Twum's (in press) study are shown in Fig. 32.1. Twum's statistical analysis confirmed the prediction that with head injury survivors, the experimental group recalled more of the whole-list words. There were no differences in the performance of the groups during part-list learning. The part and whole lists had no obvious internal organization that could be used to facilitate recall. There was, however, a transfer of the specific words learned in the part list to the whole list. Twum's interpretation of these facts was that participants in the experimental group, because of their head injuries, could not organize part-list materials. Therefore, these subjects did not experience negative transfer when learning the whole list.

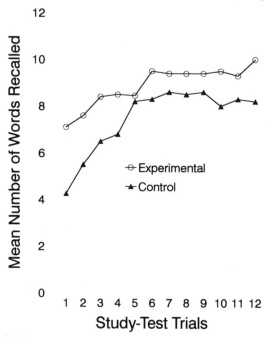

FIG. 32.1. Mean recall of words by head injury survivors in whole-list learning. Adapted with permission from Twum (1994).

Twum carried out a second experiment to find out how the transfer of organization would influence learning with head injury survivors under conditions where there was an obvious organization to the part lists, and the presentation order encouraged the subjects to use it to improve their recall. Eighty brain injured persons learned words organized into semantic categories: directions, colors, furniture, human beings, animals, planets, and so on. Once again, two lists of words were used with each subject. In each condition, the part list contained six words and the whole list contained 12 words. The whole list for each condition was identical. The part-list items were read aloud to patients according to a serial order of presentation. The same order of initial presentation of words was maintained for all subjects in the same condition. The conditions differed, however, because the word order was designed to create a specific organization for the patient before that person learned the whole list.

The subjects were consecutively but randomly assigned to four learning conditions. The groups were defined in terms of their part list learning. In the Same Words/Same Grouping condition, participants learned a part list composed of one half of the whole list. Moreover, the words were semantically organized exactly as they would appear on the whole list. This condition preserved both the words and the organization from part to whole. In the Different Words/Same Grouping condition, subjects learned a part list made of different words but from the same categories of words that were used in the whole list. The list was semantically organized and the presentation order encouraged the subject to learn the organization. This condition maintained the list organization but not the list elements. Participants in the Same Words/Different Grouping condition learned a part list made up of the same words but the task required subjects to organize the words differently than they would during whole-list learning. The words were not semantically grouped and the presentation order encouraged the subject to adopt a serial organization. This condition preserved the words but not the organization across tasks. Subjects in the Different Words/Different Grouping condition learned a part list made of words and categories that were different from any of the items in the whole list. This was a control condition where neither the words nor the structure was maintained across the tasks.

A statistical analysis showed that patients who learned part lists from the same categories of words as the whole list learned the words faster and showed generally better performance when compared to the other conditions. These relationships are shown in Fig. 32.2.

In general, these results indicated that those patients who initially learned word lists that maintained the organization from part to whole learned more of the whole-list words and learned them faster than did those patients in the other conditions. Apparently, preexposure to the semantic organization facilitated the acquisition of the whole-list items. Because the whole-list items from the same categories were not grouped together at presentation, the subjects had to see the organization and to apply it during part-list training. Therefore, one value of the part-list training was that the subjects were shown an organizational strategy that would transfer. Prior exposure to the organization allowed more efficient encoding of the whole-list items (Tulving & Thomson, 1973).

Figure 32.2 also shows that the Different Organization condition experienced negative transfer relative to the control group (Rundus, 1978). The most likely explanation of this finding is that the subjects in this condition were forced to reorganize the items from a serial into a semantic structure. The two sets of findings are consistent with Bruce (1933) and Wylie (1919), who summarized transfer phenomena with a simple principle: Similarity of elements from training and transfer ensures that some amount of transfer will occur. Similarity of organization determines the direction of the transfer. These principles can explain the present findings. Positive transfer occurred in those conditions where the organization was maintained from part to whole. Negative transfer occurred in those conditions where the organization differed from part to whole. These results are also consistent with Singley and Anderson (1989), who said that positive transfer of learning will occur when the same information is used in the same way from training to transfer. However, these principles may only apply in situations where the first task

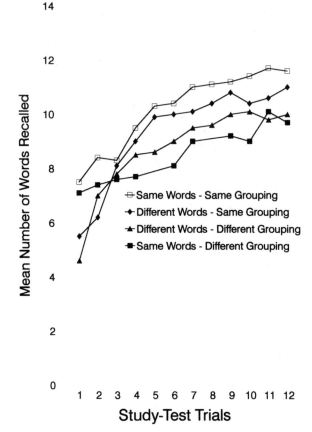

FIG. 32.2. Mean recall of whole-list words by participants in the different conditions. Adapted with permission from Twum (1994).

organization is obvious or is predetermined. For example, it is not clear how these rules would explain the results of Twum's first experiment.

ICONIC MEMORY TRAINING

Parenté, Anderson-Parenté, and Shaw (1989) reported two experiments that investigated changes in the iconic memory after traumatic brain injury. These experiments measured iconic memory using a method initially developed by Sperling (1969). There were several curious memory phenomena that emerged from this investigation. First, the results showed that trauma to the brain resulted in serious impairment of information processing in the visual iconic system. This result was later replicated by McClur, Browing, Vantrease, and Bittle (in press). Second, the iconic memory improved to near average levels over time. Indeed, in one study, persons with head injury who were at least one year postinjury actually outperformed controls.

The third finding was completely unexpected. The results showed that visual iconic memory improved significantly with practice and that the training was sufficient to improve performance on a transfer task that measured reading comprehension and word recognition. This effect was replicated in a recent study by Garner (1994). A portion of Parenté et al.'s (1989) results are presented in Fig. 32.3.

Although the design was complex, a brief discussion is presented here. Nine persons with head injury were each subjected to three tasks. The first involved either an iconic training procedure (ITP) or a letter span task (LST). The ITP procedure was described in detail by Sperling (1969) and Dick (1974). The patient was asked to fixate on a computer screen and was subsequently exposed to a 3 × 4 array of consonants for 100 milliseconds. A tone sounded immediately after the array was erased from the screen, which signaled the person to report either the top row (high tone), middle row (middle tone), or bottom row (low tone) of the array. The training went on for 360 trials and the computer measured performance across the entire session.

Each subject also participated in a LST that involved recalling consonant strings presented by the computer for an equal number of trials. These tasks

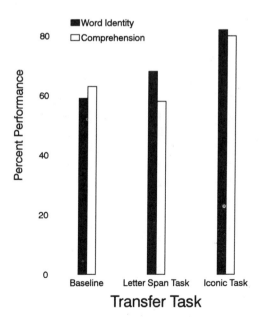

FIG. 32.3. Transfer effects for iconic versus letter span training conditions. Adapted with permission from Parenté, Anderson, and Shaw (1989).

were counterbalanced across subjects so that half received the ITP first and the LST second. The remaining subjects received the LST followed by the ITP.

After each task, the patient went through a computer-administered reading program that measured word recognition, reading rate, and reading comprehension. Word recognition testing involved recognizing words flashed on the screen. Reading rate and comprehension were measured by the computer as the patient read a 1,000-word story and later answered questions about its content. The reading tasks were the transfer portions of the experimental design. Specifically, this test occurred twice for each subject with two different sets of words and paragraphs counterbalanced across the sample and the training (iconic and letter span) conditions.

Statistical analysis of the data in Fig. 32.3 revealed that reading comprehension and reading rate were significantly enhanced by iconic memory training when compared to the letter span condition and compared to baseline. Word recognition was enhanced in both the letter span and iconic pretraining conditions; however, the iconic training produced significantly better word recognition.

These findings are curious because the iconic memory has been described by most authors as a "preconscious" or "preverbal" information processing stage (Dick, 1974; Ellis & Hunt 1993; Sperling, 1969). It is, therefore, unclear how it would be possible to train the iconic memory, and why this type of training would transfer positively to tasks that involve reading comprehension or other verbal skills. There is, however, little doubt that these effects occur and they are not simply an artifact of improved visual scanning (McClur et al., in press). In addition, Garner (1994) showed that different types of iconic training produced different transfer effects. Specifically, prolonged training using the Sperling (1969) paradigm produced significant improvement in reading rate, whereas similar training that involved flashing phrases and short sentences for 50-millisecond durations improved reading comprehension, but not reading rate, on subsequent transfer tasks.

THE EFFECT OF MONETARY INCENTIVES ON PERFORMANCE AFTER TRAUMATIC BRAIN INJURY

What motivates a person with head injury to comply with treatment suggestions from therapists? Parenté (in press) suggested that thinking and memory skills could improve markedly if a significant monetary incentive was provided. He proposed an incentive-based model of cognitive rehabilitation. This model assumed that there were two types of learning that occur during the rehabilitation process, *strategy learning* and *incentive learning*. These two types of learning can occur independently; they can also coexist. Strategy learning occurs when the person learns behaviors or skills that compensate for poor memory. Incentive learning occurs when the client realizes that when he or she uses the strategy, a reward is achieved. Incentive learning only occurs with real-world experience, and it will never occur if the client does not apply the newly learned skills in a real-world context or does so and is not rewarded for it.

Two experiments investigated this phenomena in various situations that measured the subjects' ability to attend and concentrate. One group of 10 subjects participated in a letter span task. Briefly, each subject was asked to recall consonant strings that increased in size until the subject could no longer recall the string correctly. The largest string that he or she could recall correctly was that person's letter span. A second group of 10 subjects participated in a digit span task. The procedures were generally the same as described for the letter span task. The largest number string recalled correctly was the person's digit span.

The results of these experiments are presented in Fig. 32.4. In each experiment, when the subjects were initially tested without any incentive, their performance fell within a range that one would expect from clients with head injury (letter spans of 3 to 4 and digit spans of 5 to 6). However, when a $100 reward was provided, the clients' performance improved to levels comparable

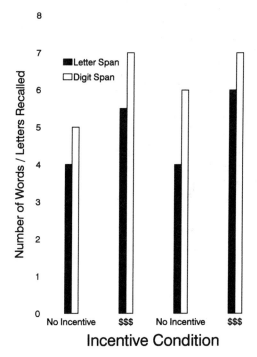

FIG. 32.4. Changes in letter and digit span performance as a function of monetary incentive. Adapted with permission from Parenté (1994).

to college students (letter spans of 5 to 7 and digit spans of 7 to 9). When the reward was removed, performance fell dramatically. When the reward was reinstated, performance again increased to within the college student range.

DISCUSSION

These experiments create more questions than they answer. This is why they are described as curious memory phenomena. They also, however, provide direction for the development of cognitive rehabilitation therapy and for improving memory with "normals."

The first curious phenomenon is the fact that persons with traumatic brain injury do not show the typical part–whole negative transfer effect. This result is consistent with Tulving's original organizational theory because these subjects had, presumably, lost their ability to organize and would therefore not have experienced the negative transfer that resulted from subjective organization during the first list learning. The more important phenomena occurred in the second experiment that showed that teaching a compatible organization facilitated memory with these subjects. Teaching an incompatible organization created negative transfer. Along with earlier findings, these data show that despite their limited ability to learn semantically related materials, head injured subjects can probably use semantic organization (Levin & Goldstein, 1986) so long as it is obvious and they are encouraged to use it.

These results lead to several suggestions for the development of cognitive rehabilitation therapies. Therapists must ensure that they teach perceptual sets and strategies that transfer and apply in a variety of contexts. This is perhaps the only way to create generalization. Reiterating Bruce (1933) and Wylie (1919), similarity of the elements of the training task ensures only that there will be transfer. However, similarity of the organization that the person takes from treatment into the real world determines whether the training creates positive or negative transfer. Therapists must also make certain that the patient is not forced to reorganize. For example, the authors are reminded of several situations where patients were taught schematics of their bedrooms with the hope that the training will facilitate eventual reentry into the home. However, these patients were sometimes confused on returning home after a well-meaning family member reorganized their rooms.

The iconic memory results also have theoretical and practical significance. From a theoretical perspective, the results indicate that the iconic memory store, which was previously thought to be a preconscious and preverbal information processing store, can be trained. It is exactly why the training of a preverbal process would transfer to a primarily verbal task such as reading. It is, therefore, reasonable to suggest that what was once thought to be a preverbal process may actually be subject to verbal manipulations.

The results also illustrate that cognitive deficits occur much earlier in the system than was previously thought. These types of deficits could restrict information processing in the entire system. As McClur et al. (in press) and Parenté and Anderson-Parenté (1989, 1991) pointed out, this type of training should precede conventional cognitive rehabilitation therapy designed to improve working memory strategies and organization skills. At a minimum, subjects should be routinely tested to determine if there is an impairment of iconic memory. Moreover, the results point to a need for tests to measure other types of sensory memory deficits, for example, echoic memory loss, tactile, and so forth.

The results of the incentive studies show that persons with documented serious amnesic syndromes can muster their memory skills to the point where they can perform as well as college students, so long as there is a relevant incentive. This result does not mean that the subjects are malingerers. It does suggest that the actual mechanism of memory may not be as impaired after a head injury as has been previously thought. Perhaps the primary damage is to a cognitive mechanism that controls or allocates memory resources. Hertel (in press) provided an especially cogent exploration of this deficit process. Alternatively, the person with head injury may be able to muster attentional energy for brief periods but not without considerably more fatigue than would normally occur.

Regardless of the explanation, therapists are well advised to spend a considerable amount of their effort identifying appropriate incentives and including these in the treatment program to insure a consistent effort. As Parenté (in press) pointed out, money can be a powerful incentive. Social companionship or the opportunity for employment can also serve as a powerful incentive. Moreover, the results illustrate that strategy learning may not lead to any noticeable real world improvement if there is no corresponding incentive learning. Therapists must teach strategies that apply in the real world and the patient must experience a successful application. Unless the client is rewarded for using a strategy, incentive learning will not occur and there will be little chance that the client will, after that, use the strategy spontaneously.

REFERENCES

Brooks, D. N. (1975). Long and short term memory in head injured patients. *Cortex, 11,* 329–240.

Brown, N. R., & Siegler, R. S. (1991). Subjective organization of U.S. Presidents. *American Journal of Psychology, 104,* 1–33.

Bruce, R. W. (1933). Conditions of transfer of training. *Journal of Experimental Psychology, 16,* 333–361.

Buschke, H. (1976). Learning is organized by chunking. *Journal of Verbal Learning and Verbal Behavior, 15,* 313–324.

Chase, W. G., & Simon, H. A. (1973). The mind's eye in chess. In W. G. Chase (Ed.), *Visual information processing* (pp. 242–312). New York: Academic Press.

Cicerone, K. D., Lazar, R. M., & Shapiro, W. R. (1983). Effects of frontal lobe lesions on hypothesis sampling during concept formation. *Neuropsychologia, 21*, 513–521.

Dick, A. O. (1974). Iconic memory and its relation to perceptual processing and other memory mechanisms. *Perception and Psychophysics, 16*, 575–596.

Ellis, H. C., & Hunt, R. R. (1993). *Fundamentals of cognitive psychology.* Dubuque, IA: Brown & Benchmark.

Garner, R. (1994). *Training iconic memory: Effects on reading rate and comprehension.* Unpublished master's thesis, Towson State University, Towson, MD.

Halstead, W. C. (1940). Preliminary analysis of group behavior in patients with cerebral injury by the method of equivalent and nonequivalent stimuli. *American Journal of Psychiatry, 96*, 1263–1294.

Hertel, P. (1994). Depressive deficits in memory: Implications for memory improvement following traumatic brain injury. *Neurorehabilitation, 4*(3), 143–150.

Levin, H. S., & Golstein, F. C. (1986). Organization of verbal memory after severe closed head injury. *Journal of Clinical and Experimental Neuropsychology, 8*, 643–656.

Lhermitte, F., Derouesne, J., & Signoret, J. L. (1972). Analyses neurologique aux syndrome frontal [Analysis of the frontal lobe syndrome]. *Revue Neurologique, 127*, 415–440.

Luria, A. R., & Tsvetkova, L. S. (1964). The programming of constructive activity in focal brain injuries. *Neuropsychologia, 2*, 95–104.

McClur, J. T., Browing, R. T., Vantrease, C. M., & Bittle, S. T. (1994). The iconic memory skills of brain injury survivors and non-brain injured controls after visual scanning training. *Neurorehabilitation, 4*(3), 151–156.

Milner, B. (1971). Interhemispheric differences in the localization of psychological processes in man. *British Medical Bulletin, 27*, 272–277.

Milner, B. (1982). Some cognitive effects of frontal lobe lesion in man. *Philosophical Transactions of the Royal Society of London, B298*, 211–226.

Parenté, R. (1994). An incentive based model of cognitive rehabilitation. *Neurorehabilitation, 4*(3), 198–203.

Parenté, R. (in press). Effects of monetary incentives on performance after traumatic brain injury. *Neurorehabilitation.*

Parenté, F. J., & Anderson-Parenté, J. K. (1989). Retraining memory: Theory and application. *Journal of Head Trauma Rehabilitation, 4*, 55–65.

Parenté, F. J., & Anderson-Parenté, J. K. (1991). *Retraining memory: Techniques and applications.* Houston: CSY Publishers.

Parenté, F. J., Anderson-Parenté, J. K., & Shaw, B. (1989). Retraining the mind's eye. *Journal of Head Trauma Rehabilitation, 4*(2), 53–65.

Petrides, M., & Milner, B. (1982). Deficits on subject-ordered tasks after frontal and temporal lobe lesions in man. *Neuropsychologia, 20*, 249–262.

Raaijmakers, J. G. W., & Shiffrin, R. M. (1981). Search of associative memory. *Psychological Review, 88*, 93–131.

Rocchetta della, A. I. (1986). Classification and recall of pictures after unilateral frontal or temporal lobectomy. *Cortex, 22*, 189–211.

Rundus, D. (1978). Organization and part-to-whole transfer. *Journal of Verbal Learning and Verbal Behavior, 17*, 91–101.

Singley, M. K., & Anderson, J. R. (1989). *The transfer of cognitive skill.* Cambridge, MA: Harvard University Press.

Sperling, G. A. (1969). A model for visual memory tasks. In R. N. Haber (Ed.), *Information processing approaches to visual perception.* New York: Holt, Rinehart & Winston.

Tulving, E. (1966). Subjective organization and effects of repetition in multi-trial free recall learning. *Journal of Verbal Learning and Verbal Behavior, 5*, 193–197.

Tulving, E., & Thomson, D. M. (1973). Encoding specificity and retrieval processes in episodic memory. *Psychological Review, 80*, 352–373.

Twum, M. (1994). Maximizing generalization of cognitions and memories after traumatic brain injury. *Neurorehabilitation, 4*(3), 157–167.

Villardita, C. (1987). Verbal memory and semantic clustering in right brain damaged patients. *Neuropsychologia, 25,* 277–280.

Villardita, C., Grioli, S., & Quatropanni, M. C. (1988). Concreteness, abstractness of stimulus words and semantic clustering in right brain damaged patients. *Cortex, 24,* 563–571.

Wylie, H. H. (1919). An experimental study of transfer of response in the white rat. *Behavioural Monographs, 3,* 16–36.

CHAPTER THIRTY-THREE

Multimodal Memory Rehabilitation for the Toxic Solvent Injured Population

Miriam Schooler Bendiksen
Ivan Bendiksen
Sandefjord, Norway

Although there is increasing recognition within the scientific community that exposure to toxic organic solvents causes chronic neuropsychological impairment, there has been little focus on the cognitive rehabilitation of the toxic solvent injured population, referred to as TE. The clinical picture presented by TE is diffuse, but it most often includes memory problems, loss of concentration, irritability, anxiety, depression, sleep and appetite problems, as well as disturbances in olfaction, skin problems, hyper/hypotension, and respiratory ailments.

The TE population, often industrial workers who have spent many years on the job, experience malfunctioning on such a level that their quality of life is substantially reduced. It should be a challenge for clinical practitioners and researchers to find a rehabilitation strategy that meets the needs of this TE population and enhances their psychosocial well being and cognitive functioning. In an intervention study for TE workers, Bendiksen and Bendiksen (1992), utilized a multimodal approach that showed promising results. With a focus on the memory impairment found in the TE population, this chapter reviews the multimodal approach for memory improvement. Theoretical considerations are discussed and intervention strategies are reviewed.

COGNITIVE IMPAIRMENT
FROM ORGANIC SOLVENT EXPOSURE

High acute exposure to organic solvents has long been known to give short-term euphoric effects. The effects of long-term, lower-level exposure to a variety of substances, especially in the workplace, have been slower to reach the attention of clinicians and researchers. The psychological effects, however, were already noted as far back as 1902. Hartman (1988) referred to a book *Dangerous Trades* (Oliver, 1901), where the author described "the extremely violent maniacal condition" of carbon disulfide workers. The solution at the time was far from setting safety standards for the factory or rehabilitation for the workers, but rather putting bars on the windows to prevent the workers from "precipitating" themselves (Oliver, 1901, cited in Hartman, 1988, p. 138).

Early studies linking chronic solvent exposure to a range of psychological impairments were found mostly in Scandinavia, for example, Arlien-Soberg, Bruhn, Gyldensted, and Melgaard (1979). Studies eventually began to appear outside Scandinavia and there is now a substantial body of evidence linking exposure to organic toxic solvents with neuropsychological impairment. Complete references can be found in Hartman (1988).

Hartman (1988) and Miller (1993) described the effects of exposure to organic solvents. Memory impairment is reported for the following solvents:

Toluene is found in paint solvents, varnish, and rubber adhesive. It is also the most widely abused solvent because it is the active ingredient in glue sniffing. Miller (1993) referred to Eskenazi and Maizlish (1988), who reported decrements in short-term memory, impaired vigilance, and impaired nerve conduction.

Styrene is a widely used industrial solvent found in plastic production, boat building, and at home in floor waxes, varnishes, and paints. Hartman (1988) referred to Seppalainen, Husman, and Mattenson (1978) and Rosen, Haeger-Aronsen, Rehnstrom, and Welinder (1978), who reported memory complaints. They also reported initial irritation of the mucous membranes, nausea and dizziness, fatigue, giddiness, and headaches. Miller (1993) referred to Eskenazi and Maizlish (1988), who added concentration problems, abnormal EEGs, and impaired visuomotor and psychomotor performance.

Trichloroethylene (TCE) has previously been used in the dry cleaning industry, as a metal degreaser, and as an ingredient in home cleaners, lubricants, and adhesives. Hartman (1988) referred to a report by Baker and Woodrow (1984) that TCE is also being used in the electronics industry for cleaning, stripping and degreasing.

Miller (1993) referred to Eskenazi and Maizlish's study (1988) in which they reported that TCE produces impaired memory as well as impairments in manual dexterity, cognitive flexibility, spatial perception, and reaction time. They also reported fatigue, dizziness, alcohol intolerance, excessive perspiration, and various tremors and palpitations. Hartman referred to a study reported by Lindstrøm (1982) in which a group of 50 workers exposed to TCE from one month to 15 years were examined. Nine of these workers showed symptoms of what Lindstrøm (1982) called the "organic psychosyndrome" of "memory disturbances, difficulties in understanding, and changes in affective states" (cited in Hartman, 1988, p. 156).

Perchloraethylene (PCE) is now the most widely used dry-cleaning agent. Hartman (1988) referred to Gold (1969), who reported changes in recent memory and personality.

Although memory impairment has not been specifically mentioned as an effect of other organic solvents, studies have referred to a host of symptoms that could easily effect memory functioning as well. Carbon disulfide, for example, produces impairment in general intelligence, visuospatial reasoning, depressed mood, and introversion, according to Eskenazi and Maizlish (1988; referred to by Miller, 1993). Hartman (1988) referred to Hanninen, Eskeline, Husman, and Nurminen (1976), who also reported depression, irritability, and insomnia as effects of exposure. Miller (1993) reported that methyl chloride has been shown to produce headaches, drowsiness, giddiness, depression, and irritability according to Eskenazi and Maislish (1988). Repko et al. (1976) reported chronic personality changes as well as visual disturbances and euphoria from methyl chloride.

TE workers often complain about changes in olfaction. Whereas some report a loss of smell, others are hypersensitive to particular odors, often those associated with organic solvents. Miller (1993) referred to a study linking olfaction and memory. Ryan, Morrow, and Hodgson (1988) tested solvent exposed workers on a wide range of cognitive skills. The authors reported that subjects who told of experiencing nausea after contact with certain odors performed particularly poorly on tests of verbal learning or visual memory. Ryan et. al. (1988) presented the hypothesis that chronic solvent exposure may affect the limbic and medial temporal lobe structures that are known to be involved in both olfaction and memory. Morrow, Callender, et al. (1990) used PET scan data on a patient with acute toxic solvent exposure, and their findings have led them to suggest that memory impairment is related to left temporal lobe and hippocampal dysfunction. Miller (1993) referred to Morrow, Ryan, Hodgson, and Robin (1990), who stated that without the PET scan data, the cognitive deficits revealed could easily be misdiagnosed as a result of affective or psychiatric disorders.

Morrow, Ryan, Hodgson, and Robin (1991) used MMPI assessment as well as neuropsychological testing on a group of solvent-exposed workers with a matched group of nonexposed controls. Miller (1993) reported their findings that the exposed subjects showed evidence of learning and memory impairment, as well as impairment on other neuropsychological measures. At the same time, the workers showed significant MMPI scale elevations indicating anxiety, depression, disturbed thinking, and somatization. Miller (1993) summarized that the effects of brain injury due to solvent exposure, as with any other brain injury, cannot be confined to the cognitive sphere alone. Personality and psychological functioning are affected.

The Assessment of Memory Functioning

Clinical evaluations and studies generally find that the neuropsychological functioning of TE workers who have had low to moderate exposure fall within the normal or mildly impaired ranges and rarely score within the "brain-damaged" range on standard psychometric tests (Hartman, 1988). Miller (1993) questioned the accuracy of these standard tests in determining the kinds of neurological impairment found in TE patients. As yet there is no effective test battery that is sensitive enough to the effects of exposure to toxic solvents and for which there is normative data based on a large enough sample (Ryan, Morrow, Bromet, & Parkinson, 1987).

Miller (1993) referred to Ryan et al. (1987), who report that performance on the WAIS Digit Span and WMS Logical Memory and Associate Learning subtests appears to be affected following solvent exposure. Lindgren (1992) reported that verbal learning and verbal memory function are affected by exposure, and Stollery and Flindt (1988) reported that the effects of exposure can be registered in paired associates and immediate free recall tasks.

Although researchers continue to develop better tests for pinpointing the effects of exposure to toxic solvents, practitioners have to find tests that address the clinical issues involved in rehabilitation. The Rivermead Behavioral Memory Test (Wilson, Cockburn, & Baddeley, 1985) is a memory test that addresses practical issues in memory rehabilitation. Although the Rivermead (RBMT) was originally designed for use in a severely brain-injured population, it can be used for the TE population as well. The RBMT correlates positively with a battery of standard memory tests and it has normative scores based on a noninjured sample (Wilson et al., 1985).

Bendiksen and Bendiksen (1992) used the RBMT in their study for assessment of memory impairment and to identify target areas for rehabilitation. Subjects were independently diagnosed for TE before entering the study. On the baseline RBMT assessment, memory performance scores were well below the normative score on six of the subtests. Bendiksen and Bendiksen were then able to target the intervention on types of memory skills that were linked to subtests measured by the RBMT.

Self-Perception and Beliefs About Memory

Bendiksen and Bendiksen (1992) stipulated that the most frequently reported concerns prior to the intervention were memory problems and changes in emotional functioning. Miller (1993) referred to Morrow, Ryan, Goldstein, and Hodgson (1989), and Morrow, Ryan, et al. (1990), who reported that the likely reason why TE patients seek medical treatment in the first place is because they experience emotional symptoms, memory problems, dizziness, fatigue, concentration difficulties, and other disturbances. These changes in functioning, including memory impairment, are experienced by the TE worker before testing on a psychoneurological battery.

Memory researchers have become increasingly aware of the role of self-perception in memory functioning. Memory self-perceptions affect both memory performance and memory strategy selection (Herrmann, 1982). Self-report memory questionnaires have low to moderate correlation with actual memory performance (Herrmann, 1982, 1984). A study done by Herrmann, Grubs, Sigmundi, and Grueneich (1986) concluded that the moderate validity is a function of the inaccurate beliefs people have about their memory performance. Herrmann (1982) stated that inaccuracy of self-perception leads to less than optimal or even inappropriate memory strategies. Clinical experience with amnesiacs shows that patients who have accurate self-perceptions about their poor memory ability will not attempt memory tasks they know they cannot perform. Amnesiacs who do not have accurate self-perception get into difficulties because they do not recognize their impairment (Herrmann, 1990).

An important strategy in a memory rehabilitation program should be to focus on the memory self-perceptions of the target group. This is especially pertinent to the TE population, because as a group they appear to demonstrate much concern about their changed perceptions of memory performance. Memory rehabilitation for the TE population should address memory performance, perceptions about memory functioning, and psychosocial concerns. The multimodal approach to memory improvement is discussed from this perspective.

THE MULTIMODAL APPROACH
TO MEMORY REHABILITATION

Until recently, memory theorists viewed memory phenomena as the manifestations of a singular memory system. Strategies for memory improvement, based on this memory mode theory, have not produced adequate results. Even memory researchers seldom use strategies, such as the method of loci or the peg-word, outside the memory training setting (Herrmann & Searleman, 1992). Neither are these memory improvement methods applicable to all types of memory tasks and situations (Herrmann & Searleman, 1990).

The call for a new approach to memory improvement came in the 1970s, largely from memory practitioners and researchers who, in their work with memory-impaired individuals, became increasingly aware of the shortcomings of the classical memory improvement methods (Herrmann & Searleman,

1992). New methods for memory improvement were introduced by, among others, Backman (1989), Herrmann, Rea, and Andrzejewski (1988), Herrmann and Searleman (1990), Khan (1986), McEvoy and Moon (1987), Poon (1980), Wilson and Moffat (1984), and Yesavage, Lapp, & Sheikh (1989).

The multimodal approach places memory in the framework of other psychological processes (Herrmann & Searleman, 1990). Psychological processing modes, which are outside the memory system, influence memory functioning, either directly or indirectly. Consequently, memory improvement strategies should train for better means of thought processing, and provide interventions that enhance these other relevant psychological modes. Multiple modes of psychological functioning are involved; therefore, it is called a *multimodal approach* (Herrmann, 1993).

Herrmann (1993) identified three active and five passive psychological modes. Active modes involve conscious and continuous thought processes, and passive modes occur without conscious control. The primary active mode is (a) the conscious use of mental strategies in order to register, learn, remember, and solve problems. Optimal thought processes are involved and mental manipulations such as mnenmonics, heuristics, and logical rules are employed. Two other psychological modes are actively involved in supporting thought processing and they are (b) perceiving important cues in the environment (such as always putting one's glasses in the same place), and (c) recognizing signals in the social setting that are necessary in acquiring relevant information to be remembered and to communicate this information effectively.

The passive modes can be referred to as states and they change continuously. Two of these states, (d) the person's physical condition and health and (e) the person's chemical state (including use of medication, alcohol and drugs, caffeine, and exposure to toxins), are crucial in providing the energy needed to engage in active thought processing. The multiple health problems found in TE workers presents a case in point as to how these states influence active thought processing.

The other passive modes include (f) self-perceptions and attitudes about memory, (g) the emotional state, and (h) motivation. These modes influence the selection of stimuli or information attended to and the person's inclination to engage in active thought processing.

The multimodal approach is based on the concept that the individual can gain control over these psychological processes and thereby optimize thought processing, which ultimately leads to memory improvement. Nutrition, drug intake, sleep habits, and stress management all become a part of the memory improvement process. The concept of self-efficacy (Bandura, 1977) is most relevant. Harrel, Parenté, Bellingrath, and Lisicia (1992) also referred to empowerment as a crucial ingredient in the cognitive rehabilitation process.

Considering the multiple problems found in the TE population, the multimodal approach provides a means for addressing memory impairment in the context of a total situation. Gaining control (empowerment) over a difficult life situation becomes the ultimate focus of the intervention. The empowerment model (Harrel et al., 1992) involves setting specific task goals and then meeting these goals by teaching and practicing appropriate strategies. Although Harrel et al. worked with a more severely head-injured population, the strategy is relevant for the TE population.

The new approach to memory improvement recognizes that each memory task requires specific strategies (Herrmann & Searleman, 1990). Herrmann (1991) discussed four categories of memory tasks: knowledge tasks, events, intention, and actions. Self-report questionnaires are used to assess memory functioning in each of these task areas. An overview of task/content specific manipulations is presented that can be tailored to individual needs.

The multimodal approach to memory improvement combines a general strategy with specific manipulations. Gaining control over the indirect psychological processes (e.g., physical, chemical, and emotional states) provides the conditions for activating optimal thought processes. Mental manipulations for specific memory tasks can then be employed successfully.

In the Bendiksen and Bendiksen intervention study (1992), the subjects were given four questionnaires similiar to those found in Super Memory (Herrmann, 1991). These questionnaires were an integral part of the intervention. The subjects were asked to fill out these questionnaires as "homework," and results were reviewed at the following group session. Memory tasks involving events and intentions were perceived as most difficult by the subjects, and these results matched the RBMT subtests on which they had showed the poorest performance. Intention tasks and event tasks were targeted in the intervention and in this general manner approached the type of tasks found on several subtests on the RBMT. The subjects did not train specifically for these subtests, because each chose his or her own goal tasks. Specific manipulations were discussed in the group, and each subject practiced the chosen tasks both in the group setting and later at home. Feedback was given on a continuous basis. Memory improvement was seen as both a group and individual task.

One of the most striking results of this strategy was that memory attitudes and beliefs changed during the intervention. The subjects came to the intervention with concerns about not being able to remember "anything," and gradually these beliefs began to change as they became aware of the specificity of memory tasks. For example, although it was difficult to remember appointments and shopping lists (intention), or remember what happened at last night's soccer match (events), one subject became aware that his ability to learn and remember a new sea map system (information) and navigate (actions) his boat through the fjords was not impaired. Awareness of the differentiation between types of memory tasks supported the development of more realistic self-perceptions, both in terms of memory weaknesses and, not least, memory strengths. This enhanced self-esteem, which influenced the motivational and emotional state and created better conditions for active thought processing. Interest in the use of mental manipulations and memory supports increased.

Many of the subjects showed initial resistance to the use of well-known memory supports such as shopping lists and alarm clocks. The inaccuracy of their self-perceptions played an important role. Several of the subjects felt that they ought to be able to remember what to buy in the supermarket and it was regarded as a defeat to write down a shopping list. The strategies used were inappropriate for the task and ultimately led to a further confirmation of their poor memory performance. As memory self-perception changed, the use of memory supports became more acceptable. Some subjects had actually been using quite intricate mnemonics without being aware that this was relevant or even productive. On the contrary, they had the impression that memory aids were just tricks that had to be used to cover up deficiencies. The subjects were encouraged to further develop their own strategies, which had a clearly positive effect on their sense of control.

Intervention Studies With Toxic Solvent Injured Workers

The Bendiksen and Bendiksen study (1992) is one of the two studies found in the research literature that deals specifically with the rehabilitation of TE workers. Twenty factory workers, 18 men and 2 women, who worked in a paint factory in Norway, participated in the intervention. They all had paint solvent exposure ranging from 7 to 40 years. Only those workers who had had their insurance claims settled were included in the program. The subjects were randomly assigned to one of four work groups, each group comprised of four to seven participants. The intervention used a combination of cognitive, psychodynamic, and interpersonal strategies presented in a group dynamic and psychoeducational framework. Coping skills, knowledge, and insight were developed through instruction and discussion. All the sessions were led by two leaders (the authors). Each memory session included at least one memory task as well as a homework assignment. The psychosocial support sessions were less task oriented, giving the subjects time to air their concerns regarding the particular topic of the day. In one session the subjects were joined by their spouses. This session, which was 4 hours long, included an informative talk on various aspects of toxic solvent injuries, given by the Director of Health Services at the paint factory. Part of this session included a discussion for the spouses alone, led by one of the group leaders, while the men prepared lunch. The lunch preparation provided a natural opportunity for a variety of memory tasks, as well as a pleasant social context that was apparently appreciated by all the participants. The intervention lasted 9 weeks, with two sessions per week.

The other intervention study was conducted in Sweden as part of a doctoral dissertation by Lindgren (1992). These two intervention programs are similar in several ways. Both used a group approach and both conducted one memory training session per week and one group therapy session per week. Whereas Bendiksen and Bendiksen used 9 weeks, Lindgren's intervention was 10 weeks for the memory intervention. Lindgren continued the psychosocial intervention until the 6-month follow-up evaluation.

Memory performance tests were used in both studies. Lindgren (1992) used a standard test battery, and Bendiksen and Bendiksen (1992) used the Rivermead (Wilson et al., 1985). Both studies employed self-report questionnaires in order to target complaints, and both registered the number and category of complaints. The Bendiksen and Bendiksen study also measured the perceived intensity of complaints.

Lindgren (1992) found a small improvement in verbal and visuospatial memory, with long-term effects only for the verbal memory. Bendiksen and Bendiksen (1992) found a performance improvement for all targeted memory subtests on the RBMT, and the improvement remained at the 6-month follow-up. The increase was significant for two of the subtests. The difference in results on memory performance can be attributed to the use of different memory improvement strategies, but it can also be attributed to the memory assessment. Bendiksen and Bendiksen were able to measure changes in targeted subtests on the RBMT, whereas Lindgren used a standard test battery assessment.

On the self-report questionnaires, Lindgren (1992) reported no changes in perceived cognitive complaints after the intervention but a reduction of other symptoms. Bendiksen and Bendiksen (1992) reported a significant reduction of both cognitive and emotional concerns 6 months after the intervention ceased. An interesting result found in the Bendiksen and Bendiksen study is the shift in the nature of the subjects perceived complaints. A decrease in reported emotional and cognitive concerns was recorded after the intervention, but there was an increase in reported social/economic concerns. Somatic concerns remained stable. The clinical interpretation of this shift is that as the subjects became more efficient in coping both with their emotions and with their memory problems, they shifted focus and began to view themselves in a larger context. The shift was from internal concerns, that is, how they feel about themselves, to issues in their social environment, such as family, job, finances, and social relations.

Issues for Further Studies

Because these are the only two studies available, there is much research to be done in this field. Issues for further studies would be to separate the memory intervention from psychosocial intervention, the role of specific versus general memory training, and the role of self-perception and self-efficacy in memory improvement. An interesting study would be to correlate the Super Memory (Herrmann, 1991) self-report questionnaires with Rivermead subtests. Comparisons with populations who have had memory impairment due to other environmental and workplace toxins would be of interest.

CONCLUSION

There has been little work done on the rehabilitation of the TE population. The symptoms found in this group include memory impairment as well as a host of emotional and somatic complaints. A multimodal approach to memory improvement that views memory processing as being interrelated with other psychological processing modes provides a highly relevant approach to rehabilitation. Intervention studies are needed in order to provide an adequate rehabilitation for the TE population, which can alleviate symptoms and enhance quality of life.

REFERENCES

Arlein-Soberg, P., Bruhn, P., Gyldensted, C., & Melgaard, B. (1979). Chronic painters' syndrome: Toxic encephalopathy in house painters. *Acta Neurologica Scandinavica, 60,* 149–156.

Backman, L. (1989). Varieties of memory compensation of older adults in episodic remembering. In L. Poon, D. Rubin, & B. Wilson (Eds.), *Everyday cognition in adulthood and late life* (pp. 509–544). New York: Cambridge University Press.

Baker, R., & Woodrow, S. (1984). The clean light image of the electronics industry: Miracle or mirage? In W. Chavkin (Ed.), *Double exposure: Women's health hazards on the job and at home* (pp. 21–36). New York: Monthly Review Press.

Bandura, A. (1977). Self-efficacy: Towards a unifying theory of behavioral change. *Psychological Review, 84,* 191–125.

Bendiksen, M. S., & Bendiksen, I. (1992). A multi-dimensional intervention for a toxic solvent injured population. *Journal of Cognitive Rehabilitation, 10,* 20–27.

Eskenazi, B., & Maizlish, N. A. (1988). Effects of occupational exposure to chemicals on neurobehavioral functioning. In R. E. Tarter, D. H. Van Thiel, & K. L. Edwards (Eds.), *Medical neuro-psychology: The impact of disease on behavior* (pp. 223–264). New York: Plenum.

Gold, J. H. (1969). Chronic percloroethylene poisoning. *Canadian Psychiatric Association Journal, 14,* 627–630.

Hanninen, H., Eskeline, L., Husman, K., & Nurminen, M. (1976). Behavioral effects of long-term exposure to a mixture of organic solvents. *Scandinavian Journal of Work Environment and Health, 4,* 240–255.

Harrel, M., Parenté, F., Bellingrath, E. G., & Lisicia, K. A. (1992). *Cognitive rehabilitation of memory.* Gaithersburg, MD: Aspen.

Hartman, D. E. (1988). *Neuropsychological toxicology, identification and assessment of human neurotoxic syndromes.* New York: Pergamon Press.

Herrmann, D. J. (1982). Know thy memory: The use of questionnaires to assess and study memory. *Psychological Bulletin, 92,* 434–452.

Herrmann, D. J. (1984). Questionnaires about memory. In J. Harris & P. Morris (Eds.), *Everyday memory* (pp. 133–151). London: Academic Press.

Herrmann, D. J. (1990). Self-perceptions of memory performance. In J. Rodin, C. Schooler, & K. W. Schaie (Eds.), *Self-directedness: Cause and effects throughout the life course* (pp. 199–211). Hillsdale, NJ: Lawrence Erlbaum Associates.

Herrmann, D. J. (1991). *Super memory.* Emmaus, PA: Rodale Press.

Herrmann, D. J. (1993, September). *Multi-modal approach to improving cognition: Imagery and self care.* Presented at Cognitive Rehabilitation Meeting, Tysons Corner, VA.

Herrmann, D. J., Grubs, L., Sigmundi, R. A., & Grueneich, R. (1986). Awareness of memory ability before and after relevant memory experience. *Human Learning, 5,* 91–107.

Herrmann, D. J., Rea, A., & Andrzejewski, S. (1988). The need for a new approach to memory training. In M. M. Gruneberg, P. E. Morris, & R. N. Sykes (Eds.), *Practical aspects of memory* (Vol. 2, pp. 415–420). Chichester, England: Wiley.

Herrmann, D. J., & Searleman, A. (1990). The new multimodal approach to memory improvement. *The Psychology of Learning and Motivation, 26,* 175–205.

Herrmann, D. J., & Searleman, A. (1992). Memory improvement and memory theory in historical perspective. In D. J. Herrmann, H. Weingartner, A. Searleman, & C. McEvoy (Eds.), *Memory improvement: Implications for memory theory* (pp. 8–20). New York: Springer.

Khan, A. R. (1986). *Clinical disorders of memory.* New York: Plenum.

Lindgren, M. (1992). *Neurological studies of patients with organic solvent induced chronic toxic encephalopathy: Prognosis, personality characteristics, and rehabilitation.* Unpublished thesis, Department of occupational and environmental medicine, University of Lund, Sweden.

Lindstrøm, K. (1982). Behavioral effects of long-term exposure to solvents. *Acta Neurologica Scandinavica,* Suppl. *92*(66), 131–141.

McEvoy, C. L., & Moon, J. R. (1987). Assessment and treatment of everyday memory problems in the elderly. In M. M. Gruneberg, P. E. Morris, & R. N. Sykes (Eds.), *Practical aspects of memory* (Vol. 2, pp. 153–160). Chicester, England: Wiley.

Miller, L. (1993, January/February). Toxic torts: Clinical, neuropsychological, and forensic aspects of chemical and electrical injuries. *The Journal of Cognitive Rehabilitation,* pp. 6–18.

Morrow, L. A., Callender, T., Lottenberg, S., Buchsbaum, M. S., Hodgson, M. J., & Robin, N. (1990). PET and neurobehavioral evidence of tetrabromoethane encephalopathy. *Journal of Neuropsychiatry, 2,* 431–435.

Morrow, L. A., Ryan, C. M., Goldstein, G., & Hodgson, M. J. (1989). A distinct pattern of personality disturbance following exposure to mixtures of organic solvents. *Journal of Occupational Medicine, 31,* 743–746.

Morrow, L. A., Ryan, C. M., Hodgson, M. J., & Robin, N. (1990). Alterations in cognitive and psychological functioning after organic solvent exposure. *Journal of Occupational Medicine, 32,* 444–450.

Morrow, L. A., Ryan, C. M., Hodgson, M. J., & Robin, N. (1991). Risk factors associated with persistance of neurosychological deficits in persons with organic solvent exposure. *Journal of Nervous and Mental Disease, 179,* 540–545.

Oliver, T. (1901). *Dangerous trades.* London: Murray.

Poon, L. W. (1980). A systems approach for the assessment and treatment of memory problems. In J. M. Fergusen & C. B. Taylor (Eds.), *The comprehensive handbook of behavior medicine* (Vol. 1, pp. 191–212). New York: Spectrum.

Repko, J. D., Jones, P. D., Garcia, L. S., Schieder, E. J., Roseman, E., & Corum, C. R. (1976). *Final report of the behavioral and neurological evaluation of workers exposed to solvents: Methyl chloride.* [DHEW Publication N. (NIOSH) 77-125]. Washington, DC: U.S. Government Printing Office.

Rosen, I., Haeger-Aronsen, B., Rehnstrom, S., & Welinder, H. (1978). Neurophysiological observations after chronic styrene exposure. *Scandinavian Journal of Work Environment and Health,* Suppl. *2*(4), 184–194.

Ryan, C. M., Morrow, L. A., Bromet, E. J., & Parkinson, D. K. (1987). An assessment of neuro-psychological dysfunction in the workplace: Normative data from the Pittsburgh Occupational Exposures Test Battery. *Journal of Clinical and Experimental Neuropsychology, 9,* 665–697.

Ryan, C. M., Morrow, L. A., & Hodgson, M. J. (1988). Cacosmia and neurobehavioral dysfunction associated with occupational exposure to mixtures of organic solvents. *American Journal of Psychiatry, 145,* 1442–1445.

Seppalainenn, A. M., Husman, K., & Mattenson, G. (1978). Neurophysiological effects of long-term exposure to a mixture of organic solvents. *Scandinavian Journal of Work, Environment and Health, 4,* 304–314.

Stollery, B. T., & Flindt, M. L. (1988). Memory sequelae of solvent intoxication. *Scandinavian Journal of Work, Environment and Health, 14,* 45–48.

Wilson, B., Cockburn, J., & Baddeley, A. (1985). *The Rivermead Behavioral Memory Test* (Second supplement). Titchfield, Hants, England: Thames Valley Test Company.

Wilson, B., & Moffat, N. (1984). *Clinical management of memory problems.* Rockville, MD: Aspen Systems.

Yesavage, J. A., Lapp, D., & Sheikh, J. I. (1989). Mnemonics as modified for use by the elderly. In L. W. Poon, D. C. Rubin, & B. A. Wilson (Eds.), *Everyday cognition in adulthood and late life* (pp. 598–611). New York: Cambridge University Press.

Author Index

T

U

V

Z

Subject Index